The Encyclopedia of Technical Market Indicators

Robert W. Colby

and

Thomas A. Meyers

IRWIN
Professional Publishing
Burr Ridge, Illinois
New York, New York

To the members of and subscribers to the Market Technicians Association, whose constitutional purpose is to:

"Educate the public and the investment community to the uses and limitations of technically oriented research and its value in the formulation of investment decisions."

Acquisitions editor: *Richard A. Luecke*
Production manager: *Stephen K. Emry*
Designer: *Ray Machura*
Compositor: *Publication Services*
Typeface: *11/13 Times Roman*
Printer: *Arcata Graphics/Kingsport*

ISBN 1-55623-049-4

Library of Congress Catalog Card No. 87-73023

Printed in the United States of America
11 K 5

PREFACE

It has been shown that the single most important determinant of price performance for any individual stock is the trend of the overall market as represented by the Dow Jones Industrial Average and other indexes. If the stock market moves up, the vast majority of stocks move up. Likewise, if the stock market moves down, most stocks move in sympathy to the downside.

Over the years, investors have devised literally hundreds of technical market indicators in their effort to forecast the trend of the overall market. Some of these indicators consistently signal the best time to buy and sell, while others work poorly.

Although the pages of this book represent thousands of hours of research our goal is simple—to present objective, quantifiable guidance to investors regarding how to calculate and interpret scores of widely-followed technical market indicators, as well as some lesser known indicators. Our disclosures separate Wall Street myth from reality and show you the true forecasting value of these indicators.

This book can serve as both an introduction to technical market indicators and an ongoing reference source. Part I presents several of the methods and techniques that noted technicians use to determine the forecasting value of various indicators, while Part II examines over 100 indicators one by one. For quick reference, indicators are arranged in alphabetical order.

Original research results are presented for the majority of indicators. For others, we have drawn upon the wealth of research conducted by other technicians.

We strongly believe in the merits of the technical approach to investing. We recommend that you study the indicators presented in this book and use them to increase your chances of making money on Wall Street.

Robert W. Colby and Thomas A. Meyers

ACKNOWLEDGMENTS

We wish to thank the following people for their valuable assistance in preparing this book: Anthony Tabell for his generous supply of computing power, data, and encouragement; Steven L. Kille for the use of his Back Trak software; Tim Slater for the use of Compu Trac software; David R. Aronson of Raden Research Group for his contribution of very advanced research concepts; Ted C. Earle of *Market Timing Report* for ideas, encouragement, and research contribution; Louis B. Mendelsohn of Investment Growth Corporation for his research and suggestions on the manuscript; Alan R. Shaw of Smith Barney for infinite help and inspiration; Ronald F. Daino of Smith Barney for data assistance and ideas; Susan Stern of Smith Barney for research assistance; Lori Willi of Smith Barney and Lois Cleveland for manuscript preparation assistance; J. Rodman Wright for his valuable help with numerous research studies; Dr. Martin Zweig for his research; J. Welles Wilder, Jr. for his new concepts; Ned Davis, Ed Mendel, and Joe Kalish of Ned Davis Research, Inc. for their generous contributions of charts and research; Arthur Merrill and John McGinley of Merrill Analysis, Inc. for their research; Norman G. Fosback of The Institute for Econometric Research for his research; Yale Hirsch of the Hirsch Organization, Inc. for his research; Mark Leibovit for thoughts on the Volume Reversal Technique; Robert Nurock of *The Astute Investor* for his input on The Wall $treet Week Technical Market Index; Deirdre Colby for her encouragement; and Marianne Meyers for invaluable research assistance and support.

CONTENTS

PART 1

METHODS OF EVALUATING TECHNICAL MARKET INDICATORS

CHAPTER 1

INTRODUCTION TO THE ENCYCLOPEDIA OF TECHNICAL MARKET INDICATORS: A CONSTRUCTIVE APPROACH

During the decade of the 1970s, when the stock market was erratic and trendless, there was a popular theory that it was fruitless to attempt to predict the market. Assuming that the market was perfectly efficient, this theory continued, one should give up analysis and merely adopt a passive buy-and-hold strategy. The conclusions in this book refute such negative thinking.

Investment strategy can be approached in a systematic, scientific way. Historical data can be collected and tested to establish specific rules for buying and selling securities with the objective of maximizing profit and minimizing risk of loss. Relatively inexpensive computers and software make this task easier than in the past. Moreover, there are useful books, articles, and newsletters to provide ideas for hypothesis testing.

Unfortunately for the unwary, however, there is much information (some of it from respectable sources) that is misleading, untested, overstated, ill-conceived, or just plain wrong. Valuable knowledge and information have never been efficiently or evenly distributed on Wall Street. You can assume that the market knows more than you do and knows it earlier. Not only does much of the information available prove to be incomplete or incorrect, but the market often reacts in ways contrary to ordinary logic. (But not contrary to its own logic!) Finally, the investor's own emotional biases all too often interfere with the desired goal of maximizing investment returns. Disciplined management skills are as important as accurate knowledge in actually making money.

For clues to a successful approach one might look to the methods of successful investors or traders. According to a February 16, 1986 article in *Barron's*, Richard Dennis of Chicago ran $1600 into a couple of hundred million in 16 years in the futures market. (Futures "speculation" is about the same as stock market "investing" except for high leverage, which greatly magnifies gains and losses.) Dennis is a technician who studies the behavior of the market itself and views the underlying fundamental economic data as largely outdated, already anticipated, or fully discounted by current prices. He carefully follows underlying trends in the empirical trading data and looks for subtle clues of trend change such as market excesses and failures to respond. Several years ago, with the help of a mathematician, a computer expert, and two DEC VAX-750 computers, Dennis began to test all known trading methods. Many methods had to be discarded as obsolete and statistically insignificant. What survived formed the basis of a proprietary set of trading rules that jumps on price breakouts, rides trends, and cuts losses quickly.

So, one does not have to observe the market every day for many years to gain useful knowledge of its behavior. Optimization of trading rules through back testing data is an easier and quicker way to evaluate historical experience.

Optimization has proved useful in actual practice because the market's behavior patterns do not change much over time, particularly the longer-term trends. While future events can indeed be very different from any past events, the market's way of responding to brand-new uncertainties is usually similar to the way it handled them in the past. The market's response typically unfolds over time as people perceive the implications of new developments at different rates. Thus, directional price trends unfold and persist.

Our research has revealed that in order to achieve consistently good performance, an effective discipline is needed that goes with major trends, avoids significant losses, and allows for prudent diversification. The investor should develop and test a precise set of trading rules to deal with all kinds of market behavior—rules that leave no room for uncertainty or confusion. Of course, you should modify your rules if your research uncovers better ones. But never break the rules because undisciplined trading has produced disastrous losses, even for seasoned investors. Keep detailed records of your research and investment results. Be totally objective, organized, consistent, and disciplined.

Relevant investment information may be distributed fairly efficiently, but it is not distributed perfectly, nor will it ever be. Even if it were, some investors, through superior analysis and insight, would always have an edge over the majority of investors and would act first. Therefore, valuable information can be deduced by studying transaction activity. Much historical data is available, so stock market analysis can be made to be totally objective and precisely quantifiable. We can find decision rules that maximize the potential for profit and minimize the risk of significant loss.

Perhaps the greatest advantage of historical research is the development of methods of effective risk control that allow greater consistency of profitable results. Whenever one invests capital, there are only five possible outcomes: no change, small profit, small loss, large profit, and large loss. In the long run, the first three don't matter. In the short run, however, a series of small losses can severely test the character of the technical investor in a nontrending whipsaw market. The fourth outcome, the large profit, comes along every now and again to make it all worthwhile. The fifth outcome, the large loss, is to be avoided at all costs, and it can be effectively eliminated by tested decision rules. This is the most conservative and prudent argument in favor of our research approach.

As in other disciplines, early technicians and other market analysts observed and catalogued all kinds of transaction data. In time, some repetitive patterns were identified, and some general theories emerged. Historically, the dominant statistical tool of the technician is the chart, which effectively displays price (and usually volume) data in simple time series that are relatively easily grasped. There are many books that illustrate the implications of a wide variety of chart patterns. At considerable risk of oversimplification, the purpose of chart interpretation is to determine the direction of the significant trend and to gain a sense of the probability of any change in trend. What is "significant" may depend on the individual's own goals, whether they be short-term trading, long-term investing, or something in between. In our experience, the longer-term trends offer a more reliable and profitable focus for most investors.

The *momentum* or, more accurately, *price velocity* concept is central to technical analysis. The rate of change of price movement is a leading indicator of a change in trend direction. Momentum precedes price. In a typical major market cycle, price begins a new uptrend with very high and rising momentum. This positive velocity gradually diminishes as the slope of the price advance lessens. Almost invariably, momentum hits its peak well before the price hits its ultimate high. Then velocity gradually tapers off as price begins to make little further upward progress on rally attempts. Momentum decreases as price rallies begin to fall short of previous peaks on minor rally attempts. This is bullish exhaustion. Suddenly momentum breaks sharply into negative territory as price drops below previous minor lows, thus beginning the downward part of the cycle. Finally, after a long decline, price velocity bottoms out before actual price hits its ultimate low. Gradually, price velocity becomes less and less negative on minor price declines. As this negative momentum diminishes, the stage is being set for a new upward cycle.

Basic chart reading, pattern interpretation, and trendlines frequently are supplemented by a variety of statistical calculations such as various kinds of moving averages, least squares fits, rates of change, and other formulas.

Calculations employing price and volume, breadth (advances and declines), new highs and lows, and various stock groups are all widely used. The purpose of these calculations is to reveal and quantify the market's velocity or momentum. These are sometimes referred to as *tape indicators*, recalling old-fashioned market interpretation based on the observation of stock prices as they appeared on the ticker tape report of all transactions.

Sentiment and monetary indicators are also widely followed. For example, sentiment indicators based on the theory of contrary opinion (such as short sales or investment advisory service opinion polls) are used to highlight junctures of potential bullish or bearish excesses, which are useful leading indicators of trend exhaustion. Also, monetary and interest rate indicators have proven valuable as leading or coincident indicators of stock prices. Most of these important concepts are tested and discussed in this book.

CHAPTER 2

COMPUTER SOFTWARE AND DATA USED FOR THIS BOOK

For most of the breadth (advance-decline and high-low) studies and most sentiment (short sales, advisory service opinion, put/call ratios) studies, we used the software, Digital Equipment hardware, and data (daily from January 1928) generously provided to us by Anthony Tabell of Delafield, Harvey, Tabell Inc., Member New York Stock Exchange, Inc. and National Association of Securities Dealers, Inc., 600 Alexander Road, Princeton, NJ 08540. Tabell's broker-dealer firm offers its research services and facilities to institutional clients. Tabell's powerful hardware and software can handle more than 60 years of daily data in a single pass.

For most of the price momentum studies, we used IBM PC software provided by Compu Trac, Inc., P.O. Box 15951, 1021 Ninth Street, New Orleans, LA 70175. This flexible software can load 510 periods into memory at a time. This translates into approximately 42 years of monthly data, 9.75 years of weekly data, or 2 years of daily data.

For chart pattern recognition studies and certain price and volume velocity studies, we used Back Trak IBM PC software by Steven L. Kille of MicroVest, P.O. Box 272, Macomb, IL 61455. This is a powerful program that runs relatively quickly. Its memory is unlimited: one can run data in batches up to the size limitations of the computer hardware. In our studies, we loaded and tested more than 1800 periods at a time. This would translate into more than 150 years of monthly data, 34 years of weekly data, and 7 years of daily data.

Several charts were prepared using The Technician IBM PC software from Computer Asset Management, P.O. Box 26743, Salt Lake City, UT 84126. This fast and easy-to-use package includes more than 9 years of historical data and tracks 50 of the indicators in this book.

For certain spread sheet analysis, we used Lotus 1-2-3, 161 First Street, Cambridge, MA 02142.

Most of our price momentum studies used 19 years of weekly data starting from January 1968 for the broad-based New York Stock Exchange Composite

Common Stock Price Index (which includes all NYSE listed common stocks and is capitalization weighted) from Commodity Systems, Inc., 200 West Palmetto Park Road, Boca Raton, FL 33432.

Data for the month-end closing price of Standard & Poor's Composite Index of 500 Stocks, Standard & Poor's U.S. Government yields for short-term maturities of 3 to 4 years, Standard & Poor's 500 monthly average dividend yields, and Standard & Poor's 500 trailing 12-months earnings per share were gathered from *Standard & Poor's Statistical Service, Security Price Index Record, 1986 Edition*, Standard & Poor's Corporation, 25 Broadway, New York, NY 10004. Net free reserves, the discount rate, and the prime rate data were gathered from the *Board of Governors of The Federal Reserve System, Banking and Monetary Statistics 1941–1970* and *Annual Statistical Digest*, Publications Services, Division of Administrative Services, Board of Governors of the Federal Reserve System, Washington, D.C. 20551. These data were entered into our computers by hand.

Ted C. Earle contributed a long-term moving average study he conducted on software and data which he offers for sale through *Market Timing Report*, P.O. Box 225, Tucson, AZ 85702 (see Chapter 9).

David R. Aronson, President of Raden Research Group, Inc., P.O. Box 1809, Madison Square Station, New York, NY 10159, contributed a study conducted on state-of-the-art mainframe computers and high-powered statistical analysis software developed by his company (see Chapter 15).

Louis B. Mendelsohn of Investment Growth Corporation, 50 Meadow Lane, Zephyrhills, Florida 34249-9748, contributed his thoughts on short-term trading with daily data and a model he developed with his ProfitTaker software (see Chapter 11).

We wish to acknowledge our gratitude to these hardware, software, and data providers who made this book possible.

CHAPTER 3

GENERAL INTRODUCTION TO MODEL BUILDING

Investment management is subject to similar considerations and methods as business management. In both areas, quantitative analysis has gained increasing influence as an effective tool for decision making.

The typical alternative to a quantitative decision model is to allow the entire decision-making process to flow from the mind of the decision maker in an informal, subjective, unstructured, and possibly biased manner. This approach can lead to inconsistent, unsatisfactory results, as exemplified by the statistics showing most investment managers underperforming the general market indexes most of the time. Moreover, because of the absence of structure in this kind of decision making, it is often difficult or impossible to analyze exactly what went wrong, thus impeding learning and improvement of the decision-making process.

The following introduction to quantitative decision making and model building has been adapted from *Quantitative Analysis For Business Decisions, 7th Edition* by Bierman, Bonini, and Hausman, Richard D. Irwin, Inc., Homewood, IL 60430, 1986, pages 4–19.*

Managerial decision making is a process whereby management, when confronted by a problem, selects a specific course of action, or "solution," from a set of possible courses of action. Since there is generally some uncertainty about the future, we cannot be sure of the consequences of our decision, and we cannot be sure that our decision will produce the best results. Furthermore, the problem may be quite complex because there are either a large number of alternatives to consider or many factors to take into account.

The following general process of solution is common to all types of decision situations:

1. Establish the criterion to be used. For example, in a simple situation the criterion may be to choose the act that maximizes profit.

---

* Reprinted with permission.

2. Select a set of alternatives for consideration.
3. Determine the model to be used and the values of the parameters of the process.
4. Determine which alternative optimizes (i.e., produces the best value for the criterion established in step 1).

The critical factors, or variables, from the empirical situation are then combined in some logical manner to form a counterpart or model of the actual problem. A model is a simplified representation of an empirical situation. Ideally, it strips a natural phenomenon of its bewildering complexity and duplicates the essential behavior of the natural phenomenon with a few variables, simply related. The simpler the model, the better for the decision maker, if the model serves as a reasonably reliable counterpart of the empirical problem. A simple model is:

1. Economical of time and thought.
2. Readily understood by the decision maker.
3. Capable of being modified quickly and effectively, when necessary.

The object of the decision maker is not to construct a model that is as close as possible to reality in every respect. Such a model would require an excessive length of time to construct, and then it might be beyond human comprehension. Rather, the decision maker wants the simplest model that predicts outcomes reasonably well and is consistent with effective action.

The appropriate technique for describing and relating selected variables depends to a large extent on the nature of the variables. If the variables are subject to measurement of some form, and particularly if they can be given a quantitative representation, then there are strong reasons for selecting a mathematical representation of the model. First, there is a rigorous inherent discipline in mathematics that ensures a certain orderly procedure on the part of the investigator: You must be specific about what variables you have selected and what relationships you are assuming to exist among them. Second, mathematics is a powerful technique for relating variables and for deriving logical conclusions from given premises. Mathematics combined with modern computers makes it possible to handle problems of great complexity, and it facilitates the decision-making process.

So, a decision model is an abstraction and simplification of a real problem, incorporating the essential elements and relationships. Solving a model means obtaining the logical conclusions that follow, and these conclusions should be an effective guide to decision making if the model is designed and solved properly.

CHAPTER 4

TED C. EARLE ON INVESTMENT TIMING MODELS PATTERN RECOGNITION DECISION RULES

Ted C. Earle, editor of *Market Timing Report* (P.O. Box 225, Tucson, AZ 85702), holds advanced degrees in engineering and finance. He approaches investment decision making with a highly disciplined, scientific perspective that has been gaining in popularity in recent years. This approach seems to be working for Earle, who in 1986 was named most accurate market analyst in the United States by *Timer Digest* (Fort Lauderdale, FL). The following material has been adapted by Mr. Earle from his article "Modeling with Pattern Recognition Decision Rules," *Technical Analysis of Stocks & Commodities* (P.O. Box 46518, Seattle, WA 98146), April 1986, p. 30–39.

The scientific tradition of empirical modeling should be considered for wider utilization in the areas of finance and economics. Empirical models may be of value when the more formal theoretical models are deemed inadequate due to high uncertainties or an inability to adequately express the complexities. Empirical models are developed by analyzing experimental data or, in the case of finance and economics, historical data.

These models provide little insight or understanding of the cause and effect relationships of the process being studied, but they do recognize identifiable events that can then predict other events in the process with various degrees of accuracy. The methodology of theoretical modeling relies on the statistical relevance of quantitative results derived from mathematical functions used to test hypothetical causal relationships. Empirical modeling simply tests the statistical relevance of qualitative correspondence between observed events. To the extent that the model is accurate, an empirical model may be all that is required by its users.

Modeling with pattern recognition decision rules is an application of the empirical modeling methodology. Patterns may be usefully defined as any repetitive events in a time series. Patterns may be seasonal, cyclical, or other recurring variations in the data field series. Pattern recognition decision rules utilize the identification of patterns in a set of indicator series to predict the occurrence of patterns in the forecast series. Through research, the decision maker knows that the occurrence of a pattern in the indicator series has foreshadowed the occurrence of a pattern in the forecast series with a known degree of historical correlation.

Researchers can identify indicator patterns by analyzing historical time series. Pattern recognition indicators are discovered by observing changes in the data series that have occurred at about the same time as the events that the researcher is trying to predict. The series studies can be anything that the researcher believes to be relevant or useful in identifying the events predicted. By statistically testing the patterns as indicators of events, the researcher can confirm or reject the existence of a useful qualitative correspondence between the indicator patterns and the predicted events. The acceptance criteria are based on the degree of reliability of the indicators.

Pattern recognition decision rules contain some common characteristics and some significant differences from another research approach—technical analysis. Technical analysis assumes that there are patterns in market price action that will recur in the future and, thus, these patterns can be used for predictive purposes. To this extent, technical analysis is a type of empirical modeling. However, some technical analysis rules are not well defined. Without a clear definition, technical analysis procedures cannot be utilized unambiguously by different people. This is especially true when the medium of analysis used consists of charts instead of numerical systems. Thus, identical technical analysis procedures are subject to different interpretations and applications by different users. Also, some adherents of technical analysis tend to test their systems over a very short period of recent history. With so little testing, the statistical validity of the system can rarely be ascertained. Pattern recognition decision rule modeling emphasizes precise definitions and adequate historical testing, as well as pattern recognition.

The very nature of empirical modeling results in certain advantages and disadvantages. If a pattern recognition decision rule simply works consistently, it can be extremely useful, particularly if it either outperforms existing theoretical models or if no theoretical model exists. Empirical models are not subjective; they can be explicitly duplicated and tested by someone else. When tested on the same historical time series data, they will always yield identical results. If the model is tested over a sufficiently long period of time to give statistically significant results, it should acquire a certain degree of confidence from its users.

In conducting a pattern recognition research study, there are six phases that are generally common to all types of mathematical modeling:

1. Formulating the problem.
2. Collecting or mathematically creating the data series to be used in identifying and indicating the patterns to be studied.
3. Developing decision rules that will identify the initiation of patterns from the indicator series.
4. Testing the decision rules and evaluating the predictive results in the forecast series.
5. Establishing control over the use of the decision rule.
6. Proceeding to implement the actual use of the decision rules.

Each of these phases generally consists of several steps that are subject to frequent reevaluation and reworking as a study progresses. Moreover, there are an infinite number of relationships from which to choose in using this approach. Selecting the relationships to be tested and having the ability to modify the tests (after reviewing the preliminary results) determines how efficiently the study effort is conducted. Experience in utilizing the empirical approach, familiarity with the market to be studied, and the ability to spot unexpected quirks in the data greatly help in conducting a study.

Establishing controls over the use of the rules is necessary because, no matter how well the rules work on the historical data, they will not always work in the future. Thus, guidelines must be established as to what to do when the rules don't work. For instance, guidelines might be established for protective sales whenever a specified percent loss (i.e., 10% or 20%) is exceeded. Similarly, if there were two consecutive losing trades, use of the rules might be suspended until the rules were revised to work successfully with both the original data and the new data.

While a historically successful model has no guarantee of working in the future, any model that does not work historically (when based on the same information and assumptions) is certainly a questionable model for use in the future. Similarly, if a theoretically based model cannot pass muster on historical data, then something is wrong with the theory or the expression of the underlying assumptions. These pitfalls can be sidestepped by supplementing research with historical testing procedures. By utilizing statistical standards for validation, empirical models that meet or exceed the same standards as the theoretically based models can be developed. Pattern recognition decision rules and other empirical modeling approaches can be used effectively for financial and economic applications.

CHAPTER 5

NED DAVIS ON INVESTMENT
TIMING MODELS

One of the most advanced researchers today is Ned Davis (Ned Davis Research, Inc., P.O. Box 2089, Venice, FL 34284). Davis believes that timing the purchase and sale of investments can yield substantially better returns than a simple buy-and-hold strategy. Davis has developed a computer program that builds investment timing models by mathematically blending the best and most reliable timing indicators from both technical (tape action) and fundamental (economic, monetary, valuation, etc.) research. These models provide clear-cut signals and strategies. As the timing models are computer derived, no emotional judgment is involved and past results can be documented over significantly long time periods.

Just as there is no limit to the number of "systems" that can be invented to trade the market, there is no limit to the variety of data that can be used as source information in modeling. Indeed, investment timing models are simply another type of system, and their degree of success depends on the quality of source information and rules used in their building.

One basic set of source information is the price action of the investment itself. Trend models and momentum models are derived from "the tape" and have proved quite useful in calling major moves both up and down. Also, external fundamental data—such as the Consumer Price Index, Money Supply, and Interest Rates—can be used in timing models.

Good source information that is well correlated to market cycles has the potential of making a good timing model, but good information alone does not guarantee success. The other key ingredient in a model is the set of rules applied to the source information to yield a value for the model. Rules, like data, are as numerous and diverse as one's imagination and creativity allow. However, there are several common ways of transforming source information into a model. These rules can be applied to any type of data and are fairly simple to use.

One elementary way of deciding when to buy and sell a market is the moving average crossover rule. It goes like this: First, calculate a moving average of the raw price data of the investment. Then, buy whenever the price climbs above its moving average and sell when it drops below. A moving average provides a means of determining the general direction or trend of a market by examining its recent history. A six-period moving average is computed by adding together the six most recent periods of data, then dividing by 6. This average is recalculated each period by dropping the oldest data and adding the most recent, so the average "moves" with its data but does not fluctuate as much. A 12-period moving average is "smoother" than a six-period moving average and measures a longer-term trend. Generally, a long-term moving average will make a model with a relatively high gain per trade and a relatively low gain per annum. A short-term moving average yields lower gains per trade (because there are more trades) and higher gains per annum (because the investment is compounded more frequently). Variations in the method of calculating moving averages can give heavier weight to more recent data than to old data or can double-smooth the data. The crossover rule is applied the same, regardless of the nature of the moving average. Whenever an investment makes a big move up or down, the price is certain to lead its moving average. Therefore, the moving average crossover rule is guaranteed to put an investor on the right side of the move.

There has been a tendency among market technicians to use the same time frames in a variety of models, that is, to use a 200-day moving average or a 13-week momentum for every stock in the portfolio. This consistency ignores the fact that different markets have different cyclical characteristics. With the assistance of a computer, a wide range of time frames can be tested to determine which moving average or momentum formula has the "best" historical record in calling turns. Models can then be constructed with short- and long-term attributes that match the cycles of the market. In addition, the moving average crossover rule can, at times, give signals of very short duration. One method of reducing this undesirable feature is to apply a filter to the rule, stating that the price must cross its moving average by 1% or 2%.

Many types of source information will tend to oscillate within a narrow range. Annual rates of growth for a particular stock might vary from +50% to −30%. Inflation normally runs from +15% to 1%. The Slope Rule builds models based upon whether the source information for the latest period is higher or lower than it was for the previous period.

Some source information has extremes in high and low values that possess good predictive capacity. These extremes can be identified as high and low cut-off points, partitioning the information into one of three brackets: bullish, neutral, and bearish. Overbought/oversold models frequently utilize this bracket rule. Often, such indicators give signals in advance of an actual top or bottom. This characteristic can allow the model to be used as a "screen," permitting another model's buy signals to be acted upon only when both are in a bullish mode. Another refinement is shifting or "dynamic" bracket levels which change according to the readings of a separate filter model.

Davis says his investment timing models have produced above-average returns if followed blindly—and we don't doubt it. The clearly defined, workable discipline of a well-conceived model can effectively remove the all too human emotional biases that impede performance. We believe that an objective, disciplined, and properly tested trading plan is the necessary foundation for consistent investment success. And that is what an investment timing model can provide.

CHAPTER 6

CRITERIA FOR JUDGING INVESTMENT TIMING MODELS

A model should provide a complete, tested strategy. It should leave no room for doubt. Instead, it should offer a precise set of instructions that tightly control investment risks while allowing maximum profits to accumulate. Moreover, it must effectively handle reward and risk considerations in all kinds of market environments, making effective trade-offs along the way. Trading frequency must be moderate enough to leave good profits net of transactions costs, commissions, and slippage.

This is, of course, a tall order. The very complexity of the model-building effort discourages many investors from the attempt to construct and test a model. Instead, most investors choose to go with their instincts and the "conventional wisdom" made readily available in the popular press. Unfortunately, that course most often leads to below-average results.

Naturally, total profits are an important yardstick for judging a model. If transaction costs are high, profit per trade becomes vital. Percentage accuracy (or profitable trades to total trades) is interesting to many traders but is probably overrated. That is because some highly effective models are wrong more often than they are right, while some marginally effective models are right more often than they are wrong. Maximum equity drawdown or loss string is a vital risk measurement of the workability of a strategy. A model that sustains very large losses simply is not practical, even if total profits are high in the end. Note that maximum equity drawdown should be regarded as the largest overall downtrend in capital and not simply as the largest cumulative loss of consecutive losing trades, as some have suggested. A bad performance period could be interrupted by an insignificant profit only to resume the equity downtrend to still a lower low. A key performance measure is the ratio of total profit to maximum equity drawdown, also known as the *reward/risk ratio*. There are many other performance measures, some involving complex statistical manipulations, but the simple measurements discussed here should suffice for most purposes.

CHAPTER 7

OPTIMIZATION OF INVESTMENT TIMING MODELS: CONSISTENTLY GOOD PROFITS THROUGH TIME?

According to Steven L. Kille (P.O. Box 272, Macomb, IL 61455), the developer of the Back Trak modeling software that we used extensively to produce this book, the time has come to optimize timing models. Although even with good computers, software, and data, the development of an investment timing model is a complicated and time-consuming process, optimization of timing models is one of the most powerful analytical techniques yet devised. It is increasingly considered to be a necessary, even crucial, step to find effective market strategies. If we can isolate those models that have proved most consistently profitable historically, then we might quite realistically expect better actual results than if we used some untested rule of thumb or seat-of-the-pants decision-making process. Identifying poor decision rules to avoid is equally important.

Optimization is the systematic search for the best indicator formula—best in the sense that the formula produces the highest and/or the most consistent profit over a long historical database. The optimization effort is controversial. Critics are quick to point out that future market behavior and price patterns may not match those of the past. Proponents reply that there is enough similarity to make the optimization search worthwhile.

We set up a simple test to see if a widely followed technical decision rule actually does produce consistently good profits when optimized over past data, then projected forward through time. The correct way to test technical decision rules is *blind simulation* or *ex-ante cross validation*. According to David R. Aronson of Raden Research, optimized rules should be precisely defined on old historical data, then tested on more recent data not included in the prior optimization search. In this way we can gain a realistic perspective on how it would be to project past-optimized rules forward through time, just like in real time. This testing process imposes the rigor of the scientific method on technical analysis theories. If our optimization methods produce consistently good results when projected forward into future periods, then perhaps we can use them with greater confidence now. Even if the testing effort fails, we still may be rewarded with more realistic insights into unsuccessful (and perhaps successful) trading approaches.

To test for consistency when moving ahead through time, we started with the longest database that Compu Trac IBM PC technical analysis software could handle, the Standard & Poor's 500 Composite Stock Price Index (S&P) from 1910 through 1986, with monthly average prices prior to 1930 and month-end closing prices thereafter. We arbitrarily broke this database into seven pieces, the first one 17 years long (from January 1910 through December 1926) and the rest 10 years long (December 1926 through December 1936, 1936 through 1946, 1946 through 1956, 1956 through 1966, 1966 through 1976, and 1976 through 1986). We began at year-end 1926, then optimized backward and projected forward in six iterations, six decades into the future. Thus, we rigorously tested our decision rules over 60 years of unseen data in a realistic blind simulation. At the end of each 10-year forward test, we reoptimized over the past years, up to 42 past years at one time (a limit imposed by Compu Trac software, which can load a maximum of 42 years of monthly data at a time). This simulation allowed our optimized decision rule to adapt gradually through time to any possible long-term evolutionary change in the market's cyclic rhythms. Moreover, by designing our simulation around the software limitations and breaking our test periods into logically arbitrary decades, we hoped that this test might be above the usual criticisms of biased design based on time period selection.

For our optimization study, we tested one of the simplest, oldest, and most popular technical indicators: the simple moving average crossover rule. In order not to take advantage of the hindsight fact that the stock market has had a strong bullish (upward) bias over the past 60 years, we chose a totally unbiased, two-sided, bullish and bearish, long and short rule: Buy long when the S&P month-end closing price crosses from below to above its own trailing simple moving average; sell and sell short when the S&P crosses from above to below its moving average. We cover shorts and buy long when price moves back above its simple moving average again. Note that a random long-and-short strategy would have the opportunity to lose significant sums on the short side and should substantially underperform a passive buy-and-hold strategy in an uptrending market. Indeed, most studies have shown that it is very difficult to outperform buy-and-hold in uptrending markets.

With such a simple, unbiased approach, there is only one parameter (or variable) to optimize: the number of months included in the simple moving average. The fewer the number of months and the more sensitive the decision rule, then the greater the number of buy and sell signals and the closer the moving average will fit the raw data. The greater the number of months included in the moving average, on the other hand, the less sensitive, the fewer the number of buy and sell signals, and the looser the fit to the raw data. The greater the length of the moving average, the greater the tolerance will be for random movement without triggering a trade or change in long or short positions. Moving average smoothing is the basis of many trend-following approaches and systems, and our rule is its simplest form.

For this presentation we offer the profit and loss result of all six decades of forward blind simulations. Simple moving averages, varying in length from 2 to 20 months were tested. They varied in upwardly progressive incremental steps of 1 month. There is no need to test a one-period simple moving average, since that is the month-end close itself and it will never signal a trade. Also, additional tests (not shown here) indicate that profitability gradually tapers off after 16 to 20 months simple moving average length. For simplicity, dividends, interest costs, and transaction costs were not included in our testing. The latter in particular can vary widely from insignificant to substantial, depending upon the trading vehicle selected and the nature of the trading. So we leave it to the reader to plug his own trading cost allowance into the trading data. Dividends and interest were assumed to be largely offsetting.

The first optimization was conducted with data from January 1910 through December 1926. This 17-year start-up period provided us our first idea of which length of simple moving average resulted in maximum profit. All periods, 2 through 20 months, produced positive returns. The maximum equity peak occurred with the 2-month simple moving average crossover rule.

Now the key question is: How well might this hindsight optimized decision rule perform in the future? For the answer, we performed a blind simulation. First, we loaded the next 10 years, from December 1926 to December 1936, into the computer's memory, then we applied the 2-month simple moving average crossover rule to this unseen data. Results were positive with a gain in cumulative net equity of 30.61 points or 226.91% of the beginning S&P Index level of 13.49 on December 31, 1926. This beat the passive buy-and-hold strategy, which produced 3.69 points or 27.35% gain.

After we tested the 1927–1936 decade in a blind simulation, we added that decade to our old 17-year optimization database, then reoptimized to see if the new decade's data caused the best time length parameter to change over the entire 27-year new optimization period. The 2-month moving average again produced maximum total cumulative net equity in those past 27 years, from January 1910 through December 1936.

For our next blind simulation, we applied our 2-month simple moving average crossover rule to the next decade's unseen data, for 1936 through 1946. This time, the gain in net equity came to only 1.82 points or 10.59% of the beginning S&P Index level of 17.18 on December 31, 1936. Still, this outperformed a passive buy-and-hold strategy, which lost 1.88 points or 10.94%.

Next, we added our just simulated data for 1936–1946 into the optimization base, now 37 years long. This time, we were rewarded with a parameter shift, as the new maximum profit simple moving average using hindsight stretched out to 6 months.

Testing the new optimal 6-month moving average crossover rule for 1946–1956, we found a cumulative net equity gain of 16.97 points or 110.92%. This, however, fell short of the 31.37 points or 205.03% gain of the passive buy-and-hold strategy, thus confirming common knowledge that it is more difficult to beat the buy-and-hold approach in very strong bull market uptrends.

We added the latest tested decade's data from 1946 through 1956 to our optimization database and reoptimized over the 42-year Compu Trac software memory loading limit. Once again we found the 6-month simple moving average was the best.

Applying the 6-month rule consistently for the next 10 years (1956 through 1966) produced a profit of 50.24 points or 107.65% of the beginning S&P Index level of 46.67 on December 31, 1956. This actually beat a buy-and-hold strategy, which produced a gain of 33.66 points or 72.12%.

With the addition of the 1956–1966 data to our optimization database, the optimal parameter remained stable at the 6-month simple moving average crossover rule. Applied in a forward simulation for unseen data from 1966 through 1976, total profit was 38.85 points or 48.36% of the beginning index level of 80.33 as of December 31, 1966. In contrast, the buy-and-hold strategy accumulated 27.13 points or 33.77% appreciation over the same decade.

We added to our 42-year moving optimization study the 10 years from 1966 through 1976, and we found that the new optimal moving average period lengthened to 11 months.

Applying an 11-month simple moving average crossover rule forward in time to the 120 months from December 1976 through December 1986 yielded a profit of 93.13 points or 86.66% of the beginning S&P Index value of 107.46 on December 31, 1976. In this decade, a buy-and-hold strategy would have been better, as the S&P Index jumped 134.71 points or 125.36% from 107.46 to 242.17. As in the 1950s, when the market was strongly bullish with no substantial and sustained downward trends, it becomes more difficult to beat a passive, fully-invested strategy. Moreover, unbiased long-and-short timing strategies, such as our simple moving average crossover rule, are vulnerable to losses on the short side in strong bull trends. In 1976–1986, for example, short sales lost a total of 20.79 points in our test. Even without short selling, however, a "long or neutral" simple moving average crossover strategy couldn't keep pace, resulting in a profit of 113.92 points or 106.01%.

Exhibit 1 summarizes the results of our blind simulation. For the six decades from 1926 through 1986, the most basic and simplistic (many would argue *too* simplistic) optimized technical trend-following decision rule, based on the crossing of a simple moving average, applied blindly forward on unseen month-end only data, outperformed a buy-and-hold strategy. Moreover, it did so in four of the six periods. Given the fact that the overall market trend was strongly biased upward over the six decades, it is perhaps remarkable that the timing strategy's results were not penalized noticeably by short selling. Although profitability did fall behind somewhat in the strongest market trend periods, this disadvantage was overcome in markets that experienced both up and down price movements of significance. This leads one to wonder how the two strategies might stack up in a prolonged bear market. Obviously, a buy-and-hold strategy would lose, while a long and short simple moving average crossover strategy would offer the possibility of significant short side profits.

In conclusion, this and other studies suggest that optimized timing decision rules can demonstrate reasonably worthwhile results when projected ahead through real-time simulation. Of course, the most accepted and rational general approach to forecasting the future has always involved a careful study of past data. Because the future is always somewhat different from the past, however, it would be unwise to expect future results to be as perfect as past optimized performance. Nevertheless, we believe that optimization profitability testing offers a reasonable approach to selecting effective decision rules and practical investment strategies.

We would caution investors to test substantial quantities of data covering all kinds of market environments and to guard against excessive curve fitting involving too many conditions or rules. The wisdom of the ages, "Keep It Simple," is confirmed by our work. Finally, we have concluded that decision rules based on more sensitive weekly data can outperform relatively insensitive and inflexible decision rules based solely on monthly data. (Refer to Chapter 9, Fine Tuning with Weekly Data.)

EXHIBIT 1:
Summary of Blind Simulation Results from 1926 to 1986

10-Year Periods From 12/31 Through 12/31	Prior Optimal S.M.A. Period Length (in months)	Applying an Optimized Simple Moving Average Crossover Rule, Forward Blind Simulation, Ex Ante Cross Validation for 1926 Through 1986, in 10-Year Steps					Applying a Passive Buy-and-Hold Strategy	
		Total S&P Points Gained	Total S&P Percentage Gained	Number of Trades	Number of Trades Profitable	Percentage of Trades Profitable	Total S&P Points Gain	Total S&P Percent Gain
1926 – 1936	2	30.61	226.91	45	21	46.67	3.69	27.35
1936 – 1946	2	1.82	10.59	57	24	42.11	-1.88	-10.94
1946 – 1956	6	16.97	110.92	25	8	32.00	31.37	205.03
1956 – 1966	6	50.24	107.65	20	7	35.00	33.66	72.12
1966 – 1976	6	38.85	48.36	22	11	50.00	27.13	33.77
1976 – 1986	11	93.13	86.66	16	7	43.75	134.71	125.36
Totals		231.62	591.09	185	78	249.53	228.68	452.69
Simple Annual Averages (Totals ÷ 60)		3.86	9.85	3.08	1.30	41.59	3.81	7.54

CHAPTER 8

UPDATE ON THE MONTHLY SIMPLE MOVING AVERAGE CROSSOVER RULE STRATEGY

In view of the foregoing testing, we can have some confidence in reasonably profitable results with the approach going forward in time from the end of our test period on December 31, 1986. Adding the latest decade's data (for 1976–1986) to the previously optimized decades and reoptimizing over the most recent 42 years from 1944 through 1986 revealed a new optimal simple moving average of 12 months.

Exhibit 2 shows the total equity (defined as the total number of points gained) for each simple moving average from a 1-month simple moving average (the month-end closing price itself) through a 24-month simple moving average (shown at the extreme right of the chart). Note the relatively smooth "bell-shaped curve." Such a curve implies a nonrandom distribution and gives us confidence in the reliability of the indicator. In contrast, Exhibit 3 is an example of a random distribution, which implies no reliability for the optimized parameter.

Exhibit 4 (page 26) shows the total profit and loss results for each of the 24 passes (n = 1 to 24 months). The total equity is plotted in Exhibit 2. Other columns are explained at the bottom of the table. Note that short sales (short equity) lost money for every simple moving average period except the 12-month simple moving average, and even there it contributed only 1.22 points of profit.

Exhibit 5 (page 27) shows the Standard & Poor's (S&P) 500 Index month-end close (the more erratic line) with its 12-month simple moving average (the smoother line). Note that the simple moving average closely follows but lags after the trend of the raw data (the S&P month-end close).

Exhibit 6 (page 27) is a monthly plot of the total equity of the 12-month simple moving average crossover strategy, going long on a closing price cross above the 12-month simple moving average and selling long and going short on a price cross below the 12-month simple moving average. Note that there has not been a loss of 30 points in the post-World War II period in contrast to

EXHIBIT 2:

Profitability Chart for Standard & Poor's 500 Index Month-End Data (Simple Moving Average Period Lengths of 1 to 24 from 1944 to 1986)

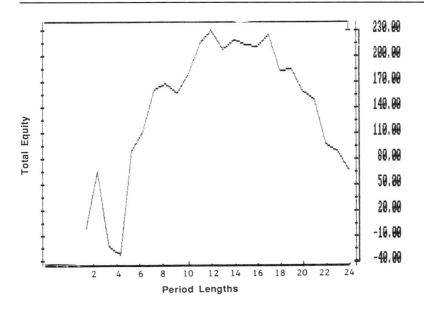

EXHIBIT 3:

Profitability Chart for High/Low Volatility Ratio Rate of Change (Period Lengths of 1 to 100 weeks from 1977 to 1986)

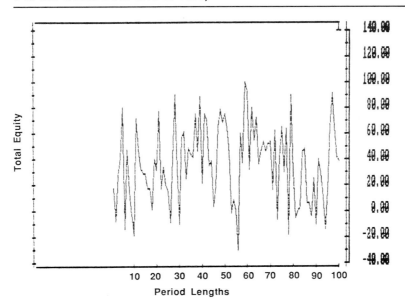

EXHIBIT 4:

Profit Table for Standard & Poor's 500 Index Month-End Data Simple Moving Average Period Lengths of 1 to 24 from 1944 to 1986

Pass	Total Equity	Short Equity	Long Equity	Max. Equity	Min. Equity	P/L	Best Trade	Worst Trade	Max. Open P/L	Min. Open P/L
1	0.00	0.00	0.00	0.00	0.00	0.00	N/A	N/A	0.00	0.00
2	64.21	-82.59	146.80	143.54	-6.74	64.21	45.70	-21.61	49.08	0.00
3	-23.81	-126.60	102.79	43.76	-42.36	-23.81	46.30	-21.61	60.98	-4.20
4	-33.10	-131.22	98.12	44.88	-36.31	-31.29	46.30	-21.61	60.98	-4.34
5	88.65	-70.12	158.77	156.22	-1.64	88.65	46.30	-21.61	60.98	-4.20
6	111.52	-58.59	170.11	179.09	0.00	111.52	46.30	-21.61	60.98	-4.20
7	160.11	-33.88	193.99	196.19	-0.66	160.11	44.04	-12.66	63.11	-4.20
8	168.41	-30.06	198.47	204.49	0.00	168.41	43.90	-12.66	63.11	-4.20
9	157.53	-34.90	192.43	193.61	-0.18	157.53	43.90	-12.66	63.11	-4.20
10	179.88	-23.64	203.52	215.96	-2.79	179.88	43.90	-12.66	63.11	-4.20
11	215.19	-6.01	221.20	251.27	-0.30	217.00	64.64	-12.66	86.25	-4.20
12	229.95	1.22	228.73	240.71	-0.64	154.46	37.55	-9.62	86.25	-4.20
13	207.70	-9.48	217.18	218.46	-1.49	132.21	37.55	-9.62	86.25	-3.56
14	218.19	-3.91	222.10	228.95	-1.72	142.70	37.55	-9.62	86.25	-3.56
15	213.84	-5.84	219.68	224.60	-1.69	138.35	37.55	-9.62	86.25	-3.56
16	211.14	-6.92	218.06	221.90	-3.03	135.65	36.64	-9.62	86.25	-3.56
17	223.85	-0.48	224.33	234.61	-1.52	148.36	30.13	-16.13	86.25	-3.56
18	182.86	-20.37	203.23	193.62	-1.92	107.37	19.93	-16.13	86.25	-3.56
19	185.71	-19.59	205.30	196.47	-3.60	110.22	19.93	-16.13	86.25	-3.56
20	157.91	-33.09	191.00	168.67	-5.20	82.42	19.67	-16.13	86.25	-3.47
21	149.63	-36.89	186.52	160.39	-5.88	74.14	19.96	-16.13	86.25	-3.47
22	96.35	-63.32	159.67	107.11	-6.30	20.86	19.56	-16.13	86.25	-5.71
23	89.18	-67.28	156.46	99.94	-5.55	13.69	19.56	-16.13	86.25	-5.71
24	67.03	-78.59	145.62	77.79	-11.56	-8.46	19.56	-16.02	86.25	-5.71

Pass indicates period length.
Equity indicates the total number of points gained or lost.
Short equity indicates the number of points gained or lost on short positions.
Long equity indicates the number of points gained or lost on long positions.
Max. equity indicates the highest total profit recorded over the tested period.
Min. equity indicates the lowest total profit recorded over the tested period.
P/L indicates total number of points gained or lost in closed positions.
Best trade indicates the highest number of points gained in any closed trade.
Worst trade indicates the highest number of points lost in any closed trade.
Max. open P/L indicates the highest gain in a position which remains open at the end of the test run.
Min. open P/L indicates the highest loss in a position which remains open at the end of the test run.

the passive buy-and-hold strategy, which lost nearly 60 points from January 1973 to October 1974. This seems like a meaningful reduction in risk.

Exhibit 7 (page 29) shows detailed profit summary results of the 12-month simple moving average crossover strategy from 1944 through 1986. Note that the best trade/worst trade ratio (in the upper right corner of the table) was 37.55 to 9.62, or 3.9 to 1. Ratios in excess of 3 to 1 are generally

EXHIBIT 5:

Standard & Poor's 500 Index Month-End Data with 12-Month Simple Moving Average from 1944 to 1986

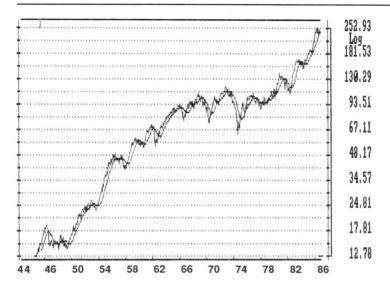

EXHIBIT 6:

Total Equity for 12-Month Simple Moving Average Crossover Rule Applied to Standard & Poor's 500 Index Month-End Data from 1944 to 1986

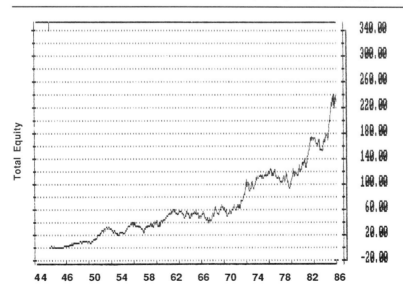

considered good. Also note that there were 52 trades in 509 months, about one every 10 months, and that 44.23% of these trades produced a profit. Although there was a 55.77% majority of losing trades, losses were obviously much smaller than profits, so the crossover rule was effective. We have found this to be true for many investment timing models, and we have concluded that reward/risk ratios are much more meaningful than percentage of profitable signals.

Exhibits 8, 9, and 10 (pages 30–31) show similar results for the pre-World War II period from 1910 through 1945. Note in Exhibit 9 that the total equity appeared more erratic than in the postwar period. The final result was favorable, however, since total equity ended at 31.47 points of profit versus only about five points of positive price change for the S&P, which would represent the capital appreciation of a passive buy-and-hold strategy.

With one eye steadily fixed on the rear view mirror, most investors avoid the short side. This is quite understandable in view of the market's general uptrend over the years. Short sellers had to be plenty smart and flexible to profit against that broad upsweep. Exhibits 11 and 12 (pages 32–33) were prepared assuming no short selling: Either we were 100% invested in the S&P or we held our money idle, collecting no return. We did, however, reinvest our profits each time (as shown in Exhibit 12) in contrast to the way both Compu Trac and Back Trac software programs did not reinvest any profits but merely accumulated points (or dollars) of price change as gains or losses. This reinvestment of profits does wonders for total portfolio value, which jumped from $1 to $75.01. This means we would have made 75 times our original investment following this 12-month simple moving average crossover rule from February 28, 1911 through May 29, 1987.

Also, note on Exhibit 11 that the closing price of the S&P can be divided by its own 12-month simple moving average to create an oscillator. This is simply another way to view the data, and it offers additional insights into momentum, trend acceleration or deceleration, and momentum divergences.

In conclusion, the historical record of trading using the 12-month simple moving average crossover rule would have been quite profitable. Interestingly, short selling added relatively little to total equity gains over the past 76 years, no doubt due to the strongly bullish secular bias of the market since 1910. Thus, the number of transactions could have been cut in half without much cost to profits by ignoring the aggressively bearish short side. But, of course, there can be no guarantee that the secular uptrend will continue into years ahead. Instead, short selling could conceivably be the path to investment success in the future.

EXHIBIT 7:

Profit Summary for 12-Month Simple Moving Average Crossover Rule, 1944 to 1986

Item		Long	Short	Net
		--- Per Trade Ranges ---		
Per Trade Ranges				
Best Trade	(Closed position yielding maximum P/L)	37.55	29.93	37.55
.. Date		840229	750228	840229
Worst Trade	(Closed position yielding minimum P/L)	-4.93	-9.62	-9.62
.. Date		660531	840831	840831
Max Open P/L	(Maximum P/L occurring in an open position)	86.25	47.98	86.25
.. Date		860831	740930	860831
Min Open P/L	(Minimum P/L occurring in an open position)	-3.10	-4.20	-4.20
.. Date		841130	800430	800430
		--- Overall Ranges ---		
Overall Ranges				
Max P/L	(Maximum P/L from all closed positions during the run)	164.08	154.46	164.08
.. Date		840229	840831	840229
Min P/L	(Minimum P/L from all closed positions during the run)	-0.17	-0.64	-0.64
.. Date		481130	490831	490831
Max Equity	(Maximum P/L from all closed and open positions)	240.71	170.59	240.71
.. Date		860831	840531	860831
Min Equity	(Minimum P/L from all closed and open positions)	-0.64	-0.64	-0.64
.. Date		490831	490131	490131
		--- Statistics ---		
Statistics				
Periods	(The number of periods in each position and entire run)	348	161	509
Trades	(The number of trades in each position and entire run)	26	26	52
# Profitable	(The number of profitable trades...)	16	7	23
# Losing	(The number of unprofitable trades...)	10	19	29
% Profitable	(The percent of profitable trades to total trades)	61.54	26.92	44.23
% Losing	(The percent of unprofitable trades to total trades)	38.46	73.08	55.77
		--- Results ---		
Results				
Commission	(Total commission deducted from closed trades)	0.00	0.00	0.00
Slippage	(Total slippage deducted from closed trades)	0.00	0.00	0.00
Gross P/L	(Total points gained in closed positions)	153.24	1.22	154.46
Open P/L	(P/L in a position which remains open at the end)	75.49	0.00	75.49
P/L	(Net P/L: Gross P/L less Commission and Slippage)	153.24	1.22	154.46
Equity	(Net P/L plus Open P/L at the end of the run)	228.73	1.22	229.95

There are columns for Long trades, Short trades and Net. In the Long column, results are reported only for Long positions. In the Short column, results are reported for Short positions only. In the Net column for the "Per Trade Ranges" and "Overall Ranges," entries will be the extreme from either the Long or Short column. Net column entries for the "Statistics" and "Results" categories are the combined results of entries in the Long and Short columns.

29

EXHIBIT 8:
Standard & Poor's 500 Index Month-End Data with 12-Month Simple Moving Average from 1910 to 1945

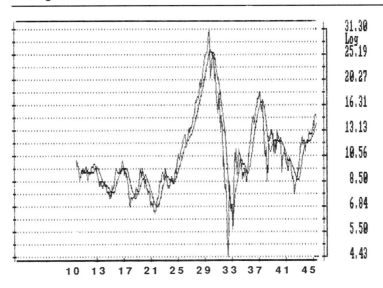

EXHIBIT 9:
Total Equity for 12-Month Simple Moving Average Crossover Rule Applied to Standard & Poor's 500 Index Month-End Data from 1910 to 1945

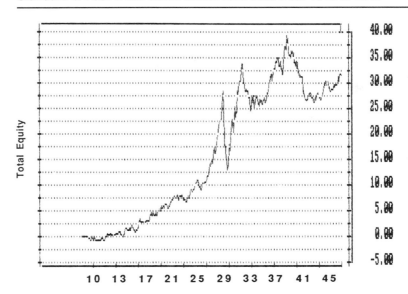

EXHIBIT 10:

Profit Summary for 12-Month Simple Moving Average Crossover Rule, 1910 to 1945

Item		Long	Short	Net
		--- Per Trade Ranges ---		
Per Trade Ranges				
Best Trade	(Closed position yielding maximum P/L)	8.47	12.19	12.19
..Date		291130	320831	320831
Worst Trade	(Closed position yielding minimum P/L)	-3.75	-2.66	-3.75
..Date		400531	330430	400531
Max Open P/L	(Maximum P/L occurring in an open position)	19.19	16.15	19.19
..Date		290930	320630	290930
Min Open P/L	(Minimum P/L occurring in an open position)	-0.97	-4.56	-4.56
..Date		400131	300331	300331
		--- Overall Ranges ---		
Overall Ranges				
Max P/L	(Maximum P/L from all closed positions during the run)	34.11	35.53	35.53
..Date		390331	380731	380731
Min P/L	(Minimum P/L from all closed positions during the run)	-0.69	-0.77	-0.77
..Date		121231	120331	120331
Max Equity	(Maximum P/L from all closed and open positions)	36.34	39.43	39.43
...Date		381231	380331	380331
Min Equity	(Minimum P/L from all closed and open positions)	-0.77	-0.77	-0.77
..Date		120331	120331	120331
		--- Statistics ---		
Statistics				
Periods	(The number of periods in each position and entire run)	248	179	427
Trades	(The number of trades in each position and entire run)	17	18	35
# Profitable	(The number of profitable trades...)	9	9	18
# Losing	(The number of unprofitable trades...)	8	9	17
% Profitable	(The percent of profitable trades to total trades)	52.94	50.00	51.43
% Losing	(The percent of unprofitable trades to total trades)	47.06	50.00	48.57
		--- Results ---		
Results				
Commission	(Total commission deducted from closed trades)	0.00	0.00	0.00
Slippage	(Total slippage deducted from closed trades)	0.00	0.00	0.00
Gross P/L	(Total points gained in closed positions)	15.55	12.93	28.48
Open P/L	(P/L in a position which remains open at the end)	2.99	0.00	2.99
P/L	(Net P/L: Gross P/L less Commission and Slippage)	15.55	12.93	28.48
Equity	(Net P/L plus Open P/L at the end of the run)	18.54	12.93	31.47

There are columns for Long trades, Short trades and Net. In the Long column, results are reported only for Long positions. In the Short column, results are reported for Short positions only. In the Net column for the "Per Trade Ranges" and "Overall Ranges," entries will be the extreme from either the Long or Short column. Net column entries for the "Statistics" and "Results" categories are the combined results of entries in the Long and Short columns.

EXHIBIT 11:
12-Month Simple Moving Average Crossover Strategy

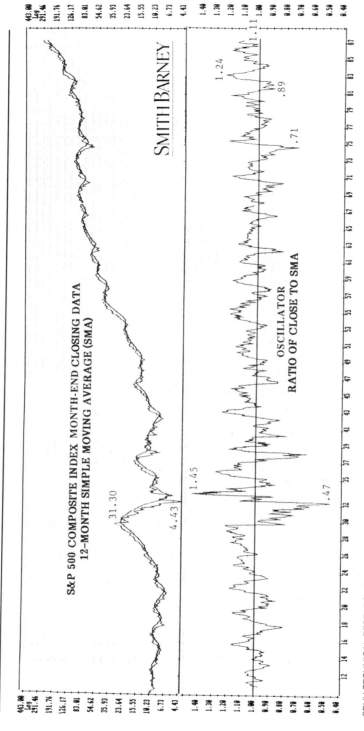

S&P 500 COMPOSITE INDEX MONTH-END CLOSING DATA
12-MONTH SIMPLE MOVING AVERAGE (SMA)

SMITH BARNEY

OSCILLATOR
RATIO OF CLOSE TO SMA

SBHU TECHNICAL RESEARCH'S 12-MONTH SMA CROSSOVER STRATEGY—This simplified system buys when the S&P 500 moves above its own trailing 12-month SMA at month end. It sells when the S&P closes under the 12-month SMA. Using this system, portfolio value rose 75.01 fold since 1911, while a buy-and-hold strategy portfolio rose 31.01 fold. Thus, the SMA crossover rule performed 2.42 times or 142% better. Profitable signals were 26 to total signals of 44, or 59.09%. Measuring in points, the best *closed* transaction profit to worst *closed* transaction loss was 7.62 to 1 (Reward/Risk). In percentage terms, the worst peak to low loss string (maximum equity drawdown) was suffered from 2/28/37 to 9/30/42 when equity fell 47.87% of the S&P index value of 18.09 on 2/27/37. In contrast, buy-and-hold lost 85.85% (or 79.34% worse than the timing strategy) from 9/30/29 to 6/30/32. Finally, the oscillator gave good divergence early warnings of trend change.

EXHIBIT 12:

Profit Summary for 12-Month Simple Moving Average Crossover Strategy

TRADE NUMBER	BUY DATE	SELL DATE	BUY PRICE	SELL PRICE	POINT CHANGE	% CHANGE	TOTAL %	$ GAIN	PORTFOLIO VALUE	NUMBER RIGHT	NUMBER WRONG
								$1.00	$1.00		
1	2 28 11	8 31 11	9.43	9.17	-0.26	-2.76%	-2.76%	($0.03)	$0.97		1
2	3 31 12	12 31 12	9.30	9.38	0.08	0.86%	-1.90%	$0.01	$0.98	1	1
3	2 28 14	3 31 14	8.48	8.32	-0.16	-1.89%	-3.79%	($0.02)	$0.96	1	2
4	4 30 15	2 28 17	8.14	9.03	0.89	10.93%	7.15%	$0.11	$1.07	2	2
5	7 31 18	1 31 20	7.51	8.83	1.32	17.58%	24.72%	$0.19	$1.26	3	2
6	11 30 21	5 31 23	7.06	8.67	1.61	22.80%	47.53%	$0.29	$1.54	4	2
7	1 31 24	1 31 24	8.83	11.48	2.65	30.01%	77.54%	$0.46	$2.00	5	2
8	6 30 26	11 30 29	12.11	20.58	8.47	69.94%	147.48%	$1.40	$3.41	6	2
9	8 31 32	10 31 32	8.39	6.96	-1.43	-17.04%	130.44%	($0.58)	$2.83	6	3
10	12 31 32	2 28 33	6.89	5.66	-1.23	-17.85%	112.59%	($0.50)	$2.32	6	4
11	12 31 32	5 31 34	8.32	9.61	1.29	15.50%	128.09%	$0.36	$2.68	7	4
12	4 30 35	4 30 37	9.28	16.43	7.15	77.05%	205.14%	$2.07	$4.75	8	4
13	7 31 37	8 31 37	16.98	16.04	-0.94	-5.54%	199.60%	($0.26)	$4.48	8	5
14	7 31 38	3 31 39	12.40	10.98	-1.42	-11.45%	188.15%	($0.51)	$3.97	8	6
15	9 30 39	5 31 40	13.02	9.27	-3.75	-28.80%	159.35%	($1.14)	$2.83	8	7
16	7 31 41	10 31 41	10.39	9.50	-0.89	-8.57%	150.78%	($0.24)	$2.58	8	8
17	9 30 42	11 30 43	8.85	11.02	2.17	24.52%	175.30%	$0.63	$3.22	9	8
18	12 31 43	8 31 46	11.67	16.65	4.98	42.67%	217.98%	$1.37	$4.59	10	8
19	7 31 47	9 30 47	15.76	15.11	-0.65	-4.12%	213.85%	($0.19)	$4.40	10	9
20	10 31 47	11 30 47	15.43	14.99	-0.44	-2.85%	211.00%	($0.13)	$4.28	10	10
21	12 31 47	1 31 48	15.30	14.69	-0.61	-3.99%	207.01%	($0.17)	$4.11	10	11
22	3 31 48	11 30 48	15.08	14.75	-0.33	-2.19%	204.82%	($0.09)	$4.02	10	12
23	8 31 49	4 30 53	15.22	24.62	9.4	61.76%	266.59%	$2.48	$6.50	11	12
24	12 31 53	9 30 56	24.81	45.35	20.54	82.79%	349.37%	$5.38	$11.87	12	12
25	12 31 56	1 31 57	46.67	44.72	-1.95	-4.18%	345.20%	($0.50)	$11.38	12	13
26	5 31 57	8 31 57	47.43	45.22	-2.21	-4.66%	340.54%	($0.53)	$10.85	12	14
27	4 30 58	1 31 60	43.44	55.61	12.17	28.02%	368.55%	$3.04	$13.89	13	14
28	8 31 60	9 30 60	56.96	53.52	-3.44	-6.04%	362.51%	($0.84)	$13.05	13	15
29	12 31 60	4 30 62	58.11	65.24	7.13	12.27%	374.78%	$1.60	$14.65	14	15
30	12 31 62	6 30 65	63.10	84.12	21.02	33.31%	408.10%	$4.88	$19.53	15	15
31	8 31 65	3 31 66	87.17	89.23	2.06	2.36%	410.46%	$0.46	$19.99	16	15
32	4 30 66	5 31 66	91.06	86.13	-4.93	-5.41%	405.04%	($1.08)	$18.91	16	16
33	1 31 67	1 31 68	86.61	92.24	5.63	6.50%	411.54%	$1.23	$20.14	17	16
34	4 30 68	2 28 69	97.59	98.13	0.54	0.55%	412.10%	$0.11	$20.25	18	16
35	3 31 69	6 30 69	101.51	97.71	-3.8	-3.74%	408.35%	($0.76)	$19.49	18	17
36	11 30 70	10 31 71	87.20	94.23	7.03	8.06%	416.42%	$1.57	$21.06	19	17
37	12 31 71	3 31 73	102.09	111.52	9.43	9.24%	425.65%	$1.95	$23.01	20	17
38	2 28 75	1 31 77	81.59	102.03	20.44	25.05%	450.71%	$5.76	$28.77	21	17
39	4 30 78	10 31 78	96.83	93.15	-3.68	-3.80%	446.91%	($1.09)	$27.68	21	18
40	12 31 78	2 28 79	96.11	96.28	0.17	0.18%	447.08%	$0.05	$27.73	22	18
41	3 31 79	3 31 80	101.59	102.09	0.5	0.49%	447.57%	$0.14	$27.86	23	18
42	5 31 80	7 31 81	111.24	130.92	19.68	17.69%	465.27%	$4.93	$32.79	24	18
43	8 31 82	2 29 84	119.51	157.06	37.55	31.42%	496.69%	$10.30	$43.10	25	18
44	8 31 84	5 29 87	166.68	290.10	123.42	74.05%	570.73%	$31.91	$75.01	26	18

CHAPTER 9

FINE TUNING WITH WEEKLY DATA

Month-end closing data is easier to use than weekly data but is slow to respond to sudden changes in the market's trend. Therefore, if we run our tests on month-end closing price data only, equity drawdowns are often larger than we are comfortable with. If we use weekly data instead of monthly, sensitivity to the market's shifts and opportunities to adapt quickly to trend changes increase significantly. Thus, profitability and reward/risk ratios increase. Although trading activity (turnover or number of trades) increases, it does not increase proportionately to our number of data points. In sum, most performance measures are enhanced with weekly versus monthly trading opportunities. Therefore, we have chosen to test with weekly rather than monthly data wherever practical.

Ted C. Earle (*Market Timing Report*, P.O. Box 225, Tucson, AZ 85702) has assembled a long database of weekly New York Stock Exchange Composite Index data going back to 1885. In addition, he has developed computer testing software to manipulate the data. Earle's research has convinced him of the importance of studying as long a data history as possible, covering many cycles and all kinds of market conditions. Our research confirms Earle's view.

At our request, Earle searched for the optimal weekly simple moving average crossover rule from 1920 through 1986. He found that the 54-week simple moving average was best. This 54-week period is, of course, very close to the 12 months that proved best on the monthly data. Ignoring transaction costs, dividends, and interest, the 54-week long and short simple moving average rule provided a compound average annual rate of capital growth of 8.0%, versus 7.2% for the frequently used 40-week simple moving average and versus 5.2% for a buy-and-hold strategy. The total number of transactions in the 66 years was 165, or 2.5 per year. Although only 29.1% of the 165 trades resulted in a profit, losses were under control, with only 6.7% or 11 of the 165 trades producing a loss in excess of 5%. This could be improved with the addition of stop-loss strategy.

Earle didn't stop with the optimal simple moving average. He tested percentage bands around the moving average in an effort to speed up the signals, and he found a better model. For the downside crossover sell signal, sell and sell short when the ratio of price to the 54-week simple moving average falls to less than 1.006. For the upside crossover buy signal, cover shorts and buy long when the ratio of price to 54-week simple moving average rises to greater than .998. In other words, sell when price falls to within 0.6% of the moving average, and buy when price rises to within 0.2% of the moving average. Draw asymmetrical bands around the moving average of plus 0.6% and minus 0.2% and use those bands as your signal points rather than the moving average itself. With this refinement, the compound average annual rate of capital appreciation rose to 9.1% versus 8.0% for the basic crossover strategy. Also, the number of transactions decreased substantially to 127 versus 168 and the percentage of profitable trades increased to 41.7% from 29.1%.

In conclusion, test results of a simple decision rule can be improved by using more frequent data sampling and adding refined filters.

CHAPTER 10

HOW MUCH FINE TUNING?
KEEP IT SIMPLE

Former professional statistician Robert C. Pelletier, now president of Commodity Systems, Inc. (200 West Palmetto Park Road, Boca Raton, FL 33432) observed in *CSI News Journal,* February 1986, that many analysts make the error of ignoring the concept of loss of freedom in statistical testing and model building. Each additional parameter introduced into a model represents a measure of control that detracts from the predictive reliability of the model with unseen data. The greater the imposition of constraints (indicator signals) is, the less predictive reliability results. Moreover, many analysts fail to test the association present in the independent variables chosen. A well-designed statistical experiment will test for possible joint correlation among independent variables, and it will exclude redundant variables in order to avoid overstating results. Pelletier believes that the best trading models use a very low number of variables, no more than two to five.

A timing model should be tested over a long sample database, long enough to allow a minimum of 30 trades, thus approaching normality according to the Central Limit Theorem. The test period should include an integer multiple of a full low frequency cycle in order to eliminate a buy or sell bias. For example, given the well-known 4-year stock market cycle, the analyst should test at least 8 years of data (twice the cycle length) in order to eliminate performance bias. Models developed over shorter test periods or with more than five parameters simply are not trustworthy.

In conclusion, when testing market timing models, keep it simple and do extensive testing. Pelletier believes that this will save you time, trouble, and money. This is also our approach.

CHAPTER 11

SHORT-TERM TRADING
WITH DAILY DATA

Our focus has been on weekly and monthly data analysis for the determination of major trend changes relevant to investors. Most people ought to be investors rather than short-term traders, in our opinion, because of the well-known and substantial difficulties involved with adjusting to the greater day-to-day random nature of short-term trading. The same concepts used in this book, however, are equally relevant to short-term trading.

The highly leveraged futures and options markets demand a much more intense short-term focus. A substantial proportion of invested capital can be made or lost in hours. Building on the extensive moving average studies conducted by Frank L. Hochheimer of Merrill Lynch Commodities Research Department from 1978 to 1982, Louis Mendelsohn (Investment Growth Corporation, 50 Meadow Lane, Zephyrhills, FL 34249-9748) has developed a PC-based software package to develop, test, and implement short-term trend-following models geared toward futures and options. In contrast to some other trading software, the logic and decision rules of ProfitTaker are fully disclosed, so the timing model user is not expected to take a blind leap of faith with a "black box." The latter is usually quickly abandoned at the first sign of adversity, because the user could never gain solid confidence in the basic rationale in the first place.

Mendelsohn believes in keeping his timing model* as simple as possible. First, there is an oscillator of a short and long directional indicator, which in the case of a 1984–1986 optimization run gave a trend change signal when the 3-day simple moving average crossed the 11-day simple moving average of the close for the nearby Standard & Poor's 500 Index futures contract—3 day above 11 day is positive, while 3 day below 11 day is negative. Second, there is a momentum timing filter, which was the direction of a 2-day simple moving average of the close for the S&P contract—rising is positive,

---

*Reprinted with permission

falling is negative. Third, there are percentage "sensitivity" bands around the short directional indicator used for the placement of protective stops. These optimized parameters were equal to 0% (or the short indicator, 3-day moving average itself) for open short trades and 3% below the 3-day average for open long trades. Finally, the optimization process showed that entry of trades on the next day's open and exit from trades on the signal day's close were best. All of the above parameters were determined by testing and optimizing 2 years of historical daily data from January 1, 1984 through December 31, 1986. An allowance of $75 per trade was made for commissions and slippage. Over the 1984–1986 period, the model performed as follows:

Historical Daily Data
January 1, 1984 through December 31, 1986

Total closed out trades	75
Total winning trades	44%
Long winning trades	45%
Short winning trades	43%
Cumulative profit	$31,350
Cumulative net profit (− slippage and commissions)	$25,725
Maximum drawdown	$10,275
Ratio of net profit to maximum drawdown	2.50
Consecutive number of losing trades	6
Unrealized profit in open position	$1650

Mendelsohn has conducted important research in an attempt to find out how long such short-term market timing models perform well in real time before decaying. His early evidence seems to indicate that short-term models should be reoptimized fairly frequently. In the example of the 2-year Standard & Poor's futures model above, real-time results were very good 1 month after the optimization study, but performance gradually deteriorated in subsequent months. Although he is still working on this idea of determining an optimal time interval for optimizing his short-term timing models, he is fine tuning them monthly and has found that to be satisfactory for practical purposes. After using a short-term model for only 1 month, a short-term trader might be wise to conduct ongoing testing and reoptimizing in an effort to find a new model to use before the current model decays. In the example, this would involve moving the 2-year test window forward in time, dropping off the oldest price data and adding the most recent price data. This ongoing process of moving forward a test window of fixed size should help to keep the trader's models in tune with current market conditions, in Mendelsohn's opinion. The time-length size of the fixed window should be long enough to include at least two full trading cycles, but the optimal size also remains to be determined by future research.

CHAPTER 12

BUY-AND-HOLD
(PASSIVE) STRATEGY

Some researchers choose a passive buy-and-hold strategy as a standard for comparison against technical indicator performance. That is inadequate because it is not at all comparable. The buy-and-hold outcome is entirely dependent upon the time period selected. Almost any timing tool can outperform buy-and-hold in down markets, but obviously that does not mean that the indicator in question is a particularly effective one. Also, most timing tools cannot hope to keep pace with buy-and-hold in very strong bull markets, but that does not mean that they are worthless.

Since the history of the market in this century has enjoyed a strong bullish bias, it has not been easy to outperform a buy-and-hold strategy. Perhaps if we could be sure somehow that a strong and consistent bullish bias would dominate the years ahead, we really would not need technical indicators at all. But, of course, a severe bear market could always be just around the corner. Most investors would choose to protect their invested wealth from the possibility of a large loss. Although buy-and-hold has been fairly good over long periods in the past, we just cannot be sure about the future.

Over our basic 19-year test period for the New York Stock Exchange Composite Stock Price Index, buy-and-hold gained 85.01 points, or 158.69%. Buy-and-hold can be a risky strategy, however. From its closing high of 65.48 on January 11, 1973, to its closing low of 32.89 on October 3, 1974, buy-and-hold lost 32.59 points, or 49.77%. A 50% margined leveraged speculator would have been all but totally wiped out. The total profits to worst loss string ratio was 2.61 to 1, considerably below our standard.

In conclusion, we find buy-and-hold to be highly overrated as an investment approach, perhaps due to false confidence based on hindsight analysis and underestimation of the risks associated with long and severe equity drawdown (loss string) periods.

CHAPTER 13

A STANDARD OF COMPARISON— THE 40-WEEK SIMPLE MOVING AVERAGE CROSSOVER RULE

To judge the effectiveness of a technical indicator, we need some objective standard of comparison. We believe the best choice is the most common technical indicator: the 40-week simple moving average crossover rule. The 40-week (or 30-week) moving average is shown in many popular chart services, including *Daily Graphs, Market Charts,* Security Research Company's *Red Book of 5-Trend Security Charts, Trendline* and *Mansfield.* Also, it is followed by many advisory services and market letters.

The rule for interpretation is simple: Buy when price closes above its own 40-week simple moving average, then reverse position and go short when price closes below its own 40-week simple moving average.

How would this simple strategy have performed over the past 19 years of New York Stock Exchange Composite Index weekly data? We tested this indicator using Compu Trac software and two 9.75-year test periods of weekly data (consisting of high, low, close, and volume for each week) for the broad-based New York Stock Exchange Composite Index (NYSE). The first period ran from January 5, 1968 through September 30, 1977, and the second period ran from April 8, 1977 through December 31, 1986. The overlap in data is necessary to facilitate testing throughout the full time period.

When the weekly closing price crossed its own 40-week simple moving average, a trend change and a trade position change in the direction of the crossing were signaled. The 19-year results for this rule are shown in Exhibits 13, 14, 15, and 16 (pages 43–45).

Combined profits totaled 94.44 NYSE points, outperforming a 85.01 point gain for a buy-and-hold strategy before transaction costs. The number of transactions totaled 57 trades, about 3.2 per year. At an institutional rate of 10 cents per trade, profits would be reduced by 5.70 to 88.74. Interestingly, only 35% of the buy and sell signals resulted in a profit, but the best gain to worst loss ratio was 26.63 to 2.89, or 9.2 to 1. So this common trend-following rule adheres to the wisdom of the ages: Let your profits run and cut your losses short. The worst equity drawdown (loss string) in points was 15.40, or 10.60% of the price index level of 145.32 in 1986. The worst drawdown (loss) in percentage terms was 22.53% (or 13.57 NYSE points) of the price index level of 60.24 on September 8, 1978 to the equity low on May 23, 1980, nearly 22 months of unprofitability. The total profits to worst loss ratio was 6.13 to 1.

These are the standards by which we will compare some of the other simple investment timing models we have tested. Exhibit 17 in Chapter 14 summarizes some of these results, in which comparability appeared reasonably valid. Each of the models listed is fully discussed in alphabetical order in the second part of this book.

EXHIBIT 13:

Profit Summary for 40-Week Simple Moving Average Crossover Rule, 1968 to 1977

Item		Long	Short	Net
		-- Per Trade Ranges -------		
Per Trade Ranges				
Best Trade	(Closed position yielding maximum P/L)	6.84	16.70	16.70
.. Date		710730	750131	750131
Worst Trade	(Closed position yielding minimum P/L)	-1.92	-1.86	-1.92
.. Date		690221	690502	690221
Max Open P/L	(Maximum P/L occurring in an open position)	11.35	24.71	24.71
.. Date		710423	741004	741004
Min Open P/L	(Minimum P/L occurring in an open position)	-1.09	-0.98	-1.09
.. Date		690110	751219	690110
		----- Overall Ranges ------		
Overall Ranges				
Max P/L	(Maximum P/L from all closed positions during the run)	34.59	33.60	34.59
.. Date		761015	761029	761015
Min P/L	(Minimum P/L from all closed positions during the run)	-4.08	-3.78	-4.08
.. Date		690530	690502	690530
Max Equity	(Maximum P/L from all closed and open positions)	37.71	35.67	37.71
.. Date		760924	741004	760924
Min Equity	(Minimum P/L from all closed and open positions)	-4.08	-4.08	-4.08
.. Date		690530	690530	690530
		----- Statistics ------		
Statistics				
Periods	(The number of periods in each position and entire run)	281	228	509
Trades	(The number of trades in each position and entire run)	16	15	31
# Profitable	(The number of profitable trades...)	6	4	10
# Losing	(The number of unprofitable trades...)	10	11	21
% Profitable	(The percent of profitable trades to total trades)	37.50	26.67	32.26
% Losing	(The percent of unprofitable trades to total trades)	62.50	73.33	67.74
		------ Results ------		
Results				
Commission	(Total commission deducted from closed trades)	0.00	0.00	0.00
Slippage	(Total slippage deducted from closed trades)	0.00	0.00	0.00
Gross P/L	(Total points gained in closed positions)	12.12	16.23	28.35
Open P/L	(P/L in a position which remains open at the end)	0.00	1.31	1.31
P/L	(Net P/L: Gross P/L less Commission and Slippage)	12.12	16.23	28.35
Equity	(Net P/L plus Open P/L at the end of the run)	12.12	17.54	29.66

There are columns for Long trades, Short trades and Net. In the Long column, results are reported only for Long positions. In the Short column, results are reported for Short positions only. In the Net column for the "Per Trade Ranges" and "Overall Ranges," entries will be the extreme from either the Long or Short column. Net column entries for the "Statistics" and "Results" categories are the combined results of entries in the Long and Short columns.

43

EXHIBIT 14:

Profit Summary for 40-Week Simple Moving Average Crossover Rule, 1977 to 1986

Item		Long	Short	Net
		— Per Trade Ranges —		
Per Trade Ranges				
Best Trade	(Closed position yielding maximum P/L)	26.63	7.87	26.63
..Date		831216	820827	831216
Worst Trade	(Closed position yielding minimum P/L)	-1.48	-2.89	-2.89
..Date		810821	790105	790105
Max Open P/L	(Maximum P/L occurring in an open position)	37.17	15.56	37.17
..Date		860829	820813	860829
Min Open P/L	(Minimum P/L occurring in an open position)	-0.67	-2.00	-2.00
..Date		810306	861003	861003
		— Overall Ranges —		
Overall Ranges				
Max P/L	(Maximum P/L from all closed positions during the run)	64.79	61.90	64.79
..Date		860912	861010	860912
Min P/L	(Minimum P/L from all closed positions during the run)	-5.42	-6.57	-6.57
..Date		790511	800523	800523
Max Equity	(Maximum P/L from all closed and open positions)	77.30	64.79	77.30
..Date		860829	860912	860829
Min Equity	(Minimum P/L from all closed and open positions)	-6.57	-6.57	-6.57
..Date		800523	800523	800523
		— Statistics —		
Statistics				
Periods	(The number of periods in each position and entire run)	368	141	509
Trades	(The number of trades in each position and entire run)	13	13	26
# Profitable	(The number of profitable trades...)	8	2	10
# Losing	(The number of unprofitable trades...)	5	11	16
% Profitable	(The percent of profitable trades to total trades)	61.54	15.38	38.46
% Losing	(The percent of unprofitable trades to total trades)	38.46	84.62	61.54
		— Results —		
Results				
Commission	(Total commission deducted from closed trades)	0.00	0.00	0.00
Slippage	(Total slippage deducted from closed trades)	0.00	0.00	0.00
Gross P/L	(Total points gained in closed positions)	76.36	-11.58	64.78
Open P/L	(P/L in a position which remains open at the end)	0.00	0.00	0.00
P/L	(Net P/L: Gross P/L less Commission and Slippage)	76.36	-11.58	64.78
Equity	(Net P/L plus Open P/L at the end of the run)	76.36	-11.58	64.78

There are columns for Long trades, Short trades and Net. In the Long column, results are reported only for Long positions. In the Short column, results are reported for Short positions only. In the Net column for the "Per Trade Ranges" and "Overall Ranges," entries will be the extreme from either the Long or Short column. Net column entries for the "Statistics" and "Results" categories are the combined results of entries in the Long and Short columns.

44

EXHIBIT 15:

Total Equity for 40-Week Simple Moving Average Crossover Rule Applied to New York Stock Exchange Composite Index Data from 1968 to 1977

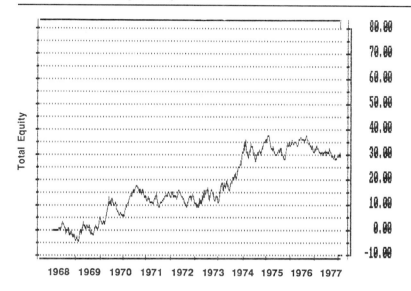

EXHIBIT 16:

Total Equity for 40-Week Simple Moving Average Crossover Rule Applied to New York Stock Exchange Composite Index Data from 1977 to 1986

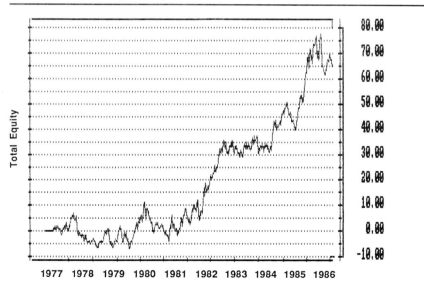

CHAPTER 14

SUMMARY OF INVESTMENT TIMING MODEL'S RESULTS: PRICE AND VOLUME MOMENTUM—SELECTED STUDIES

Exhibit 17 (pages 48–49) summarizes the results of some of our testing in which the results seemed reasonably comparable. We tested many other indicators that, for one reason or another, did not seem truly comparable, so we left them out of Exhibit 17.

With the exception of the first two indicators, which are used as unoptimized standards of comparison, the models are presented in alphabetical order. Next to each model is its optimal parameter, which produced the highest total profit in points of the New York Stock Exchange (NYSE) Composite Index using weekly data from January 1968 to December 1986. Note that several of the indicators presented were not optimized and that these naturally were the poorer performers.

The column headings should be fairly evident. Total profit was measured in cumulative points gained based on buying and shorting the NYSE Composite Index. Number of trades is the total number of transactions over the 19-year test period. Profit per trade is the total profit divided by the number of trades.

Percent trades right is the proportion of trades resulting in a profit and percent trades wrong is the proportion resulting in a loss. (Accuracy is overrated as a performance criterion, in our judgment. Total profits to maximum drawdown and profit per trade are more meaningful.)

Single trade reward to risk is the points of profit of the best single transaction divided by the points of loss on the worst single trade.

NYSE Composite Index points maximum drawdown is the worst decline in cumulative total profits, from peak to trough, over the entire test period. This is a key measure of risk. Percent maximum drawdown is the NYSE points maximum drawdown divided by the level of the NYSE Composite

Index just before the loss string started. Total profits divided by maximum drawdown in NYSE points is an important reward/risk ratio.

Finally, simple average annual percentage rate of return is total profit divided by the NYSE Composite Index level on December 31, 1967, which was 53.83, and that ratio is divided by the 19 years of the test period.

There is more behind this table than meets the eye. We recommend that you study the individual indicators listed before you choose an investment strategy. You should note that some of the fundamental models based on interest rates, net free reserves, dividends, and earnings also produced strong results, but they are not included in the exhibit because of an absence of complete comparability in the testing procedure.

EXHIBIT 17:
Summary of Investment Timing Model's Results—Selected Studies

INDICATOR: OPTIMIZED PARAMETERS	19 YEAR NYSE POINTS TOTAL PROFIT
Simple Moving Average: 40 Weeks -- Our Standard of Comparison	94.44
Buy-and-Hold Strategy	85.01
Arms Ease of Movement Value: 14 Weeks	83.50
Commodity Channel Index: 90 Weeks	62.25
Zero Commodity Channel Index: 53 Weeks	98.85
Demand Index (Not Optimized)	62.98
Demand Index Buying Power Oscillator: 1/49 Weeks Moving Average Oscillator	73.76
Directional Movement: 11 Weeks	60.26
Linear Regression Direction: 66 Weeks	127.39
Lowry's Simplified (Not Optimized)	12.26
Moving Average Convergence Divergence: .075/.15/.2 Constants (Not Optimized)	44.66
Moving Average Convergence Divergence: .05/.75/-- Constants	87.54
Exponential Moving Average: 42 Weeks or .0465 Constant	112.38
Simple Moving Average: 45 Weeks	111.79
Weighted Moving Average: 69 Weeks	118.21
Oscillator Difference Between Two Simple Moving Averages: 15 Weeks Versus 36 Weeks	95.46
Oscillator Difference Between Two Simple Moving Averages: 17 Weeks Versus 58 Weeks	101.08
Price Channel: 29 Week Breakout Rule	99.20
Rate of Change: 31 Weeks	111.31
Relative Strength Index (Wilder's): 21 Weeks, Crossing 50	110.72
K-39 Stochastics: 39 Weeks, K Crossing 50%	115.79
Volume Crossing Simple Moving Average: 105 Weeks	108.61
On Balance Volume Crossing Simple Moving Average: 9 Weeks	98.63
On Balance Volume Crossing Simple Moving Average: 66 Weeks	91.71
On Balance Volume Rate of Change: 24 Weeks	104.85
Volume Accumulation Oscillator: 1/21 Weeks Moving Average Oscillator	80.16

EXHIBIT 17 (continued)

NUMBER OF TRADES	PROFIT PER TRADE	ACCURACY		SINGLE TRADE REWARD TO RISK	NYSE POINTS MAXIMUM DRAW DOWN	% MAXIMUM DRAW DOWN	TOTAL PROFIT TO MAXIMUM DRAW DOWN	SIMPLE AVERAGE ANNUAL % RETURN
		% TRADES RIGHT	% TRADES WRONG					
57	1.66	35.00%	65.00%	9.20	15.40	24.35%	6.13	9.23%
1	85.01	100.00%	0.00%	85.01	32.59	49.77%	2.61	8.31%
80	1.04	46.25%	53.75%	4.53	17.37	28.83%	4.81	8.16%
30	2.08	40.00%	60.00%	6.63	15.73	39.88%	3.96	6.09%
40	2.47	30.00%	70.00%	6.99	14.41	23.92%	6.86	9.66%
105	0.60	33.33%	66.67%	5.87	20.76	21.46%	3.03	6.13%
73	1.01	32.88%	67.12%	3.60	30.10	49.97%	2.45	7.21%
54	1.12	48.15%	51.85%	2.53	7.96	13.92%	7.57	5.89%
57	2.23	43.86%	56.14%	6.50	15.48	25.70%	8.23	12.46%
35	0.35	31.43%	68.57%	2.41	48.25	99.14%	0.25	1.20%
76	0.59	42.11%	57.89%	2.77	18.18	34.62%	2.46	4.37%
59	1.48	30.51%	69.49%	6.47	13.83	27.00%	6.33	8.56%
71	1.58	26.76%	73.24%	11.39	15.93	31.41%	7.05	10.99%
50	2.24	30.00%	70.00%	9.53	17.21	28.57%	6.50	10.93%
40	2.96	27.50%	72.50%	7.04	15.43	25.61%	7.66	11.55%
24	3.98	66.67%	33.33%	-7.73	15.46	27.44%	6.17	9.33%
12	8.42	66.67%	33.33%	2.48	20.14	45.41%	5.02	9.88%
13	7.63	69.23%	30.77%	6.75	17.46	19.50%	5.68	9.70%
57	1.95	49.12%	50.88%	7.20	16.09	48.91%	6.92	10.88%
75	1.48	28.00%	72.00%	14.44	14.90	26.13%	7.43	10.83%
44	2.63	38.63%	61.36%	6.27	18.35	30.46%	6.31	11.32%
156	0.70	44.23%	55.77%	3.25	16.49	38.17%	6.59	10.62%
193	0.51	34.20%	65.80%	5.15	22.32	31.04%	4.42	9.64%
43	2.13	34.88%	65.12%	5.08	26.79	50.21%	3.42	8.97%
71	1.48	42.25%	57.75%	5.54	19.33	36.08%	5.42	10.25%
69	1.16	39.13%	60.87%	2.09	24.85	35.02%	3.23	7.84%

CHAPTER 15

A COMPLEMENTARY APPROACH— DAVID R. ARONSON ON THE CELLS METHOD OF INDICATOR EVALUATION

A complementary approach to optimization studies is the *cells method* of indicator evaluation, as explained here by David R. Aronson, President of Raden Research Group (P.O. Box 1809, Madison Square Station, New York, NY 10159). This approach is similar to that taken in our evaluation of many market breadth and sentiment indicators presented in Part II.

Does a given technical indicator have predictive value or not? This fundamental question must be answered before it is used in forecasting market trends or as an input to our trading decisions. An intuitively appealing way to answer this question is what we shall call the *signal event method*. This method evaluates the net profit or loss that would have resulted over some period of past data, had one acted on the buy and sell signals generated by the indicator. As profitability is the end toward which all investment analysis is ultimately directed, the signal event method is a reasonable approach to indicator analysis. The cells method for evaluating the utility of technical indicators is different from and complementary to the signal event method.

Applying the signal event method requires that the analyst define a rule (one or more conditions) that generates buy and sell signals from the indicator. For example, let us assume that the indicator we wish to test is a price momentum oscillator calculated by the difference between a 3-day and a 10-day moving average of price. The indicator takes on positive values when the value of the 3-day moving average is greater than the 10-day moving average, and it takes on negative values when the reverse is true. One possible signal rule could be as follows: Buy when the oscillator becomes positive; sell when it becomes negative.

As with any method of analysis, the signal event method has a number of limitations. First, it requires the analyst to define a signal rule. There are an infinite number of rules ranging from the simple to the highly complex that can be defined for any given indicator. Thus, a given signal event method analysis relates to the defined rule as much as it does to the indicator. It would be desirable to evaluate the indicator apart from any rules imposed on it. Second, in the quest for better results the analyst is often tempted to define complex multiple conditioned rules. Increasing complexity results in an ever-increasing probability of finding rules that are profitable on past data by chance alone. Such "overfitted" rules are not likely to do as well in the future. Third, much potentially useful information is lost, because the indicator is only examined when a signal event occurs. It may be the case that the oscillator has little information when the signal conditions are met (i.e., at a zero crossing), but it could be very informative when at a negative extreme. The signal event method would miss such information. Fourth, as signals do not happen everyday, the total number of data points is small relative to the total amount of history analyzed. Smaller sample size reduces the reliability of the conclusions that we draw from data analysis.

The cells method overcomes the above-mentioned limitations. The term *cells* refers to the fact that the historical data being analyzed are broken into ranges, or cells, in such a way that the observations with similar indicator readings will be grouped together. Thus, there will be a cell composed of days with high indicator readings, a cell of medium readings, and a cell of low readings.

The cells method differs from the signal event method in a number of important ways. First, the cells method focuses directly on an indicator's ability to forecast future market changes rather than the profitability of trading signals derived from the indicator. Second, the cells method evaluates the predictive information content of an indicator over its entire range of possible values rather than only at "signal event" points. Third, no buy/sell rules need to be defined to conduct cells method analysis. This avoids the whole problem of overly complex rules mentioned above. Fourth, since our analysis is no longer limited to specific action points, we have a larger sample of data points. Fifth, the indicator is evaluated with respect to a specific prediction horizon. For example, an indicator may be useful in forecasting the trend over the next 50 days, but useless for purposes of predicting it over the next 10 days. The cells method will reveal this. Typically, the analyst will examine an indicator with respect to a number of different horizons during the same analysis (e.g., 10 days, 20 days, 60 days, 120 days, and 250 days.)

The cells method determines the predictive power of the indicator by measuring the degree of association between the indicator's current level and the subsequent percentage change in the market. In other words, it discovers to what degree the market's future change depends upon or is predictable from the current level of the indicator.

The cells method rates the strength of this dependence on a continuous scale anywhere from 0% to 100%. A reading of 100% implies the ability to predict perfectly, while 0% indicates a total lack of predictive information. This rating is called *variance reduction.*

Based on our experience, indicators scoring 100 or anything close do not exist. Financial markets are too complex and too subject to random shocks to permit a single indicator to contain that degree of predictive power. Indicators typically score in the range of 0% to 10%, with many more scoring closer to zero than to 10. Achieving higher levels of variance reduction requires the proper integration of several complementary indicators into a multivariate model. This form of predictive modeling is quite sophisticated and complex, and it will be discussed later in this chapter.

A prime benefit of the cells method is that it permits a ranked comparison of many indicators with respect to specific time horizons. This is important as the market analyst often has a whole library of indicators but lacks an objective way of comparing predictive power for short-term, intermediate-term, and long-term forecasting.

HOW CELL METHOD ANALYSIS IS PERFORMED

To illustrate the underlying principle of the cells method, let's consider its application to one well-known indicator: the New York Stock Exchange smoothed advance/decline ratio (SADR). The ratio is defined as the net difference between the number of stocks advancing and the number of stocks declining divided by total issues traded. Since the daily ratio is erratic, many analysts smooth it with a moving average. Ten days is a common smoothing. For this analysis we used an equivalent exponential smoothing constant of .1818.

For our prediction horizon the 60-day future percent change in the Standard & Poor's 500 Index (S&P 500) was selected. In the parlance of statistical data analysis, this is known as the *dependent variable.* The implication of the word *dependent* is that the value of this variable depends to some degree on the current value of the indicator. The variance reduction rating provided by the cells method measures the strength of this dependence.

Variance reduction is determined statistically from historical data. For this particular analysis, daily data for the period January 1, 1945 through July 1, 1986 were used. This represents 10,708 observations. To reduce computing time, every other day was used for analysis, thus providing a total of 5354 observations. Each past day, or observation, was characterized by two pieces of information: the value of the SADR indicator on the given day and the value of the dependent variable (the percent change experienced by the S&P 500 over the following 60 days).

Central to the cells method is the grouping of observations with similar indicator values into bins, or cells. There are an almost unlimited number of ways of grouping data, but one common way is based on deciles. Decile grouping creates 10 equally populated cells, with 10% of the population in each cell. Quintile grouping is coarser and creates five cells, with 20% of the cases in each cell. Since the number of cells created can influence the results of the analysis, it is recommended that a number of different cell structures be tried. Typically, the strongest indicators will rank well for a variety of cell resolutions. For purposes of illustration, decile groups are used.

The grouping process begins by ranking all 5354 days according to their SADR values. Those days in the top decile (i.e., the 535 days with the highest SADR values) are placed in cell 10. Of the remaining 4819 cases, those 535 with the next highest SADR readings are placed in cell 9. Cell 8 gets the third highest SADR group. The process of grouping continues until the 535 observations with the lowest SADR reading are placed in cell 1. In the case of SADR, all days with readings of $+.13$ or higher qualified for cell 10. At the bottom of the ranking, we find that days with indicator readings of $-.146$ or less were assigned to cell 1. The following table shows the SADR levels separating the 10 cells.

Cell	SADR Level			Number of Cases
10	Greater than	$+.13$		535
9	Greater than	$+.094$	and	
	equal to or less than	$+.13$		535
8	Greater than	$+.064$	and	
	equal to or less than	$+.094$		535
7	Greater than	$+.038$	and	
	equal to or less than	$+.064$		535
6	Greater than	$+.013$	and	
	equal to or less than	$+.038$		535
5	Greater than	$-.014$	and	
	equal to or less than	$+.013$		535
4	Greater than	$-.047$	and	
	equal to or less than	$-.014$		535
3	Greater than	$-.088$	and	
	equal to or less than	$-.047$		535
2	Greater than	$-.146$	and	
	equal to or less than	$-.088$		535
1	Less than	$-.146$		535

After all 5354 observations have been placed in their proper cells based on the associated SADR value, the cells method turns its attention to the dependent variable. It is worth recalling that each observation has a second piece of information associated with it—its dependent variable, which in this case is the market's future percentage change. First, a "grand sample" dependent variable average for all 5354 observations is calculated. For the 40-year data set used in this analysis, the average dependent variable was +1.85%. In other words, for all 5354 cases, the average 60-day percent change for the S&P 500 was +1.85%. This positive value merely reflects the long-term upward trend in stock prices since 1945.

It so happens that this grand sample average can serve as the basis of a simplistic type of forecast. For this reason it is often referred to as the *naive prediction*. On any given day, without any other information, it is history's best estimate of what the market is likely to do over the next 60 days. By other information we refer to values of indicators available on the given day.

Next, the dependent variable average in each individual cell is calculated. In other words, an average dependent variable for just the 535 cases in cell 10 is calculated. The same is done for cell 9, cell 8, and so on until an average dependent variable has been computed for each cell. The cell dependent variable averages follow:

Cell	Average Dependent Variable
10	+3.22%
9	+2.29%
8	+2.34%
7	+1.82%
6	+1.55%
5	+1.23%
4	+1.31%
3	+1.66%
2	+1.37%
1	+1.70%

Notice that the cases falling into cell 10 had an average dependent variable of +3.22%. This means that for all 535 cases qualifying for cell 10, the average 60-day future change in the S&P 500 was +3.22%. The cell dependent variable can serve as the basis for a conditional forecast, which is *conditioned* on information other than the grand dependent variable average. It is potentially better than the naive forecast mentioned above. Whether or not it is truly better will be determined by the variance reduction measure.

To clarify how the conditional forecast is derived from the indicator's current level, suppose that on a given day SADR has a reading of + .24. Such a reading would qualify for cell 10. Given such information, one could say the historical data project a 60-day change in the S&P 500 of + 3.22% because that is the average future outcome of days falling into cell 10. The real question is whether forecasts of this type predict better than the grand dependent variable average. Does the conditional forecast beat the naive one? The answer to this question is the key to determining the predictive power of an indicator.

WHAT IS VARIANCE REDUCTION?

Note that we said that the conditional forecast was potentially better than the naive forecast. If the indicator on which the forecast is conditioned has predictive information, it will prove to be better than the naive forecast. In fact, the definition of an indicator with predictive information is one that can provide more accurate forecasts than the grand dependent variable average. The degree to which the conditional prediction is less erroneous than the naive one is called *variance reduction*.

It may seem counterintuitive to the reader that a naive forecast can be more accurate than one based on an indicator, but this is often the case. When the indicator is something as obviously absurd as the NDTI (noon-day temperature in Istanbul), we have no trouble understanding how the grand dependent variable average could be a better predictor. But when the indicator is something that sounds rational, such as SADR, it is not so obvious. In such cases the objective evidence provided by variance reduction is of enormous value.

In sum, variance reduction measures indicate how much less error-prone our predictions will be when using the dependent variable average of each decile cell, as compared to the grand dependent variable average. When the grand average dependent variable is a better estimate of the future than the individual cell averages, the variance reduction is zero or a negative number. When an indicator contains useful information, the variance reduction measure will be positive. The higher the variance reduction, the higher the predictive information content will be.

GUARDING AGAINST ACCIDENTAL VARIANCE REDUCTION

Unfortunately there is a complication—and not a minor one. Positive variance reduction readings can be achieved by chance. The larger the number of indicators being tested, the greater the chance will be of this occurring. While this problem can never be totally eliminated, there are two ways to minimize it: *cross-validation* and *significance testing*.

Cross-validation involves breaking the data up into two independent sets for learning and testing. The learning set is used to derive the cell dependent variable values. These values are then used to predict on the independent test set. In other words, we require that the predictive power be found in two independent sets of data. Thus, indicators that look good by chance on one set of data will be revealed as bogus when they fail to predict well on the test set.

Despite the inherent rigor of the cross-validation method, there is still a small probability of a bogus indicator doing well in both test and learning sets. So as an additional form of insurance, the variance reduction achieved by an indicator must exceed a threshold of significance. The threshold is derived by a complex statistical theory that calculates the amount of variance reduction that can be achieved by a useless indicator by chance alone 5% of the time. Indicators that can pass these two tests are likely to contain valid predictive information.

THE CELL METHOD'S EVALUATION OF THE ADVANCE/DECLINE RATIO

We utilized the cells method analysis on SADR. It was determined that it has very little predictive power. In addition, different smoothings other than a 10-day average were tested to determine if this would improve SADR's predictive power. Exhibit 18 shows the variance reduction for each version of SADR for each of five time horizons tested.

The indicator analyst can quickly see that SADR is devoid of predictive information on a stand-alone basis. However, this does not mean that it can not contribute to the variance reduction of a multivariate prediction model. That can only be determined by further investigation.

MULTIVARIATE ANALYSIS

In the previous analysis, the cells method was used to evaluate only single indicators. This entirely ignores the potential gain in information when indi-

EXHIBIT 18:
Variance Reduction of Several Versions of SADR for Several Time Horizons

Indicator	Time Horizon				
	10 days	20 days	60 days	120 days	250 days
SADR/10	+ 0.00 %	+ 0.00 %	+ 0.00 %	+ 0.00 %	+ 0.00 %
SADR/13	+ 0.00 %	+ 0.00 %	+ 0.00 %	+ 0.00 %	+ 0.00 %
SADR/20	+ 0.00 %	+ 0.00 %	+ 0.00 %	+ 0.00 %	+ 0.00 %
SADR/40	+ 0.00 %	+ 0.00 %	+ 0.00 %	+ 0.00 %	+ 0.00 %
SADR/52	+ 0.68 %	+ 0.00 %	+ 0.00 %	+ 0.00 %	+ 0.00 %
SADR/66	+ 0.00 %	+ 0.00 %	+ 0.00 %	+ 0.00 %	+ 0.00 %
SADR/100	+ 0.00 %	+ 0.00 %	+ 0.00 %	+ 0.00 %	+ 0.00 %
SADR/150	+ 0.00 %	+ 0.00 %	+ 0.00 %	+ 0.00 %	+ 0.00 %

cators are permitted to act in concert. The informational synergy that results can be significant. For example, sometimes several indicators that show no predictive power individually can, when properly combined, demonstrate a high level of predictive power. An entire branch of data analysis, known as *multivariate analysis,* is devoted to the discovery of such effects. Truly useful forecasting models can be derived by means of such methods.

COMPUTER IMPLEMENTATIONS

A number of cells method analysis routines have been implemented within the pattern recognition information synthesis modeling system (PRISM), a proprietary technology of the Raden Research Group. PRISM is used for the development of multivariate forecasting systems.

One cells method routine, EXAMINE, was the primary tool used in the analysis presented here. EXAMINE is one of a number of tools within PRISM that are employed in identifying candidate indicator variables that contain useful predictive information. This is necessary as potential indicators can easily number in the hundreds or thousands. The process of reducing the candidate indicators to a manageable number is referred to as *feature selection*. Other PRISM feature selection programs using the cells approach are SINGLES, PAIRS, and TRIPS. PAIRS evaluates the variance reduction of all possible pairs of indicators. This can be a very large number, as 200 candidate indicators produce 19,900 different pairs. TRIPS performs a similar analysis on three-way combinations. SINGLES, PAIRS, and TRIPS make extensive use of cross-validation and significance testing as described above.

Indicator Test Results

The EXAMINE program was used to determine the variance reduction of 284 indicators when employing them to forecast the S&P 500. Each indicator was evaluated with respect to five different dependent variables, or *prediction horizons*. The five dependent variables were defined as the percent change in the S&P 500 over the following periods: 10 days, 20 days, 60 days, 120 days, and 250 days.

The indicators fell into five broad types, with 50 or more indicators within each type:

50 indicators based on advance/decline statistics

82 indicators based on market volatility

50 indicators based on changes in short-term interest rates

50 indicators based on changes in long-term interest rates

50 indicators based on the slope of the term structure of interest rates (yield curve)

The analysis produced the following conclusions:

1. The longer-time horizons were the most predictable. Variance reductions of over 10% were achievable for 120-day and 250-day prediction, while the maximum achieved for 10-day and 20-day prediction was less than 3%. Sixty-day forecasting was the shortest horizon that seemed feasible with individual indicators.

2. While time horizons of less than 120 days are very difficult to forecast with single indicators, multiple indicators may be able to forecast short-term horizons to a meaningful degree.

3. Indicators based on market breadth (SADR) are not useful predictors on a stand-alone basis.

4. Indicators based on interest rate changes in both long-term bonds and short-term Treasury bills contain useful predictive information.

5. Indicators based on the slope of the yield curve and changes in it contain useful predictive information.

6. Long-term smoothings produced better results than short-term smoothings in enhancing the information of various indicators, even for short horizon prediction.

The Best Indicators

Our research identified the following indicators as having the best forecasting capability, given our test method and time horizons. (See Exhibit 19 for specific variance reduction ratings.)

1. Change In The Slope Of The Yield Curve

This indicator is created in the following manner. First, the yield curve slope is calculated by means of the following formula:

$$\frac{\text{(Yield on Long-Term Government Bonds)} - \text{(Yields on 3-Month Treasury Bill)}}{\text{Yield On Long-Term Government Bonds}}$$

Next, the yield curve slope is exponentially smoothed with a constant of .0137 (approximately equal to a 150-day simple moving average). The indicator is the change in the smoothed yield curve over the past 225 days.

2. Smoothed Change In Long-Term Government Bond Yields

This indicator is created in the following manner. First, the daily percent change in long-term government bond yields is calculated by means of the following formula:

$$\frac{\text{Yield Today} - \text{Yield Yesterday}}{\text{Yield Yesterday}}$$

The indicator is the daily percent change smoothed with an exponential smoothing constant of .0137 (approximately equal to a 150-day simple moving average).

3. Smoothed Change In 3-Month Treasury Bill Yields

This indicator is exactly the same as the one preceding it, except Treasury bill yields are used instead of long-term government bond yields.

4. Smoothed Yield Curve Slope

The yield curve is calculated as in indicator 1. The indicator is the expo-

EXHIBIT 19:
Variance Reduction Ratings Achieved for the Best Indicators

Indicator	Time Horizon				
	10 days	20 days	60 days	120 days	250 days
1. Change in the Slope of the Yield Curve	+0.92%	+1.87%*	+2.79%*	+10.30%*	+0.00%
2. Smoothed Change in Long-Term Government Bond Yields	+2.40%*	+2.92%*	+0.00%	+0.00%	+12.00%*
3. Smoothed Change in 3-Month Treasury Bill Yields	+2.35%*	+2.28%*	+0.00%	+0.00%	+9.22%*
4. Smoothed Yield Curve Slope	+0.00%	+0.00%	+0.00%	+2.04%*	+0.00%

* Passed significance test at the 5% level (i.e., there is less than a 5% probability that the variance reduction attained was due to chance).

nentially smoothed yield curve slope using a constant of .0137, which is approximately a 150-day moving average.

CONCLUSION

Because the information processing capacities of analysts and computers are different and complementary, there exists a great opportunity for synergy between the market analyst, his computer, and sound data analysis methods. Human creativity has not yet been, and may never be, replicated by the computer. So, the market analyst is crucial to the creation of indicator formulas. But the objective evaluation of an indicator's predictive power is best left to a computer programmed with rigorous data analysis methods, employing cross-validation and significance testing.

Particularly exciting is the rapid evolution in two of these areas: computer hardware and data analysis methods. The vast gains in the performance/price of computers has spawned a host of powerful data analysis methods that were not practical in the computer's earlier stages of development. The cells method and similar tools can help the market analyst objectively evaluate and compare the predictive utility of various indicators. Objective indicator evaluation methods are crucial to the development of sound prediction systems. In addition, advanced software is already allowing computers to inductively derive predictive rules and models directly from data. These are known as *self-organizing pattern recognition modeling* and are part of computer science's leading edge, *artificial intelligence*.

PART 2

TECHNICAL MARKET INDICATORS

ABSOLUTE BREADTH INDEX

The Absolute Breadth Index was developed by Norman Fosback (The Institute for Econometric Research, 3471 North Federal Highway, Fort Lauderdale, FL 33306). It is simply the absolute value of the number of advancing issues minus the number of declining issues. For example, if the number of advancing issues is 1400 and the number of declining issues is 400, the Absolute Breadth Index equals 1000. If the number of advancing issues is 500, and the number of declining issues is 900, the Absolute Breadth Index equals 400. (Remember, the sign is ignored in the calculation of an absolute number.) Daily or weekly New York Stock Exchange data normally is used in the calculation.

The theory behind the Absolute Breadth Index is that when the absolute difference between the number of advancing and declining stocks is high, you are more likely to be near a market bottom than a top since a selling climax with most stocks participating often occurs near a bottom.

On the other hand, a low Absolute Breadth Index reading is more likely to signify, according to the theory, the slow topping activity that frequently occurs at a market peak.

We tested the Absolute Breadth Index for the period from January 1928 to March 1987 on a daily and weekly basis. In addition, we applied a 10-period simple moving average to both the daily and weekly readings to smooth out any erratic movements. The results are shown in Exhibits A-1 through A-4 (pages 64–67).

The test process was as follows. The indicator readings for the test period were divided into 20 ranges with approximately the same number of occurrences in each range. For each reading in a range the gain or loss in four subsequent time periods (1 month later, 3 months later, 6 months later, and 12 months later) was calculated. The combined results for readings within each range were statistically compared, using chi-squared tests, to the performance of the overall market (as measured by the Standard & Poor's 500). Varying degrees of bullishness and bearishness were noted on the basis of that comparison.

Our results show a very slight bullish tendency at extremely high readings, as well as a very slight bearish tendency at extremely low readings. The indicator in the form tested is not recommended for market timing.

A variation of the Absolute Breadth Index that has been tested over a 40-year period by Norman Fosback is calculated by dividing the absolute value of the number of advancing issues minus the number of declining issues by the

EXHIBIT A-1:
Interpretation of Absolute Breadth Index's Daily Readings

```
================================================================================================
ABSOLUTE BREADTH INDEX - DAILY DATA
PERIOD ANALYZED:  JANUARY 1928 TO MARCH 1987
================================================================================================
```

INDICATOR RANGE		INTERPRETATION GIVEN INVESTOR'S TIME FRAME			
GREATER THAN	LESS THAN OR EQUAL TO	1 MONTH	3 MONTHS	6 MONTHS	12 MONTHS
0	18	NEUTRAL	NEUTRAL	NEUTRAL	NEUTRAL
18	36	SLIGHTLY BEARISH	NEUTRAL	NEUTRAL	NEUTRAL
36	54	NEUTRAL	NEUTRAL	NEUTRAL	NEUTRAL
54	74	NEUTRAL	NEUTRAL	NEUTRAL	NEUTRAL
74	93	NEUTRAL	NEUTRAL	NEUTRAL	NEUTRAL
93	113	NEUTRAL	NEUTRAL	NEUTRAL	NEUTRAL
113	133	NEUTRAL	NEUTRAL	NEUTRAL	SLIGHTLY BEARISH
133	156	NEUTRAL	NEUTRAL	NEUTRAL	NEUTRAL
156	181	NEUTRAL	SLIGHTLY BEARISH	SLIGHTLY BEARISH	NEUTRAL
181	206	NEUTRAL	NEUTRAL	NEUTRAL	NEUTRAL
206	233	NEUTRAL	NEUTRAL	NEUTRAL	NEUTRAL
233	262	NEUTRAL	NEUTRAL	NEUTRAL	NEUTRAL
262	297	NEUTRAL	NEUTRAL	NEUTRAL	NEUTRAL
297	335	NEUTRAL	NEUTRAL	NEUTRAL	NEUTRAL
335	377	NEUTRAL	NEUTRAL	NEUTRAL	NEUTRAL
377	426	NEUTRAL	NEUTRAL	NEUTRAL	NEUTRAL
426	488	NEUTRAL	NEUTRAL	NEUTRAL	NEUTRAL
488	635	NEUTRAL	NEUTRAL	NEUTRAL	NEUTRAL
635	713	SLIGHTLY BULLISH	NEUTRAL	NEUTRAL	NEUTRAL
713	1691	NEUTRAL	NEUTRAL	SLIGHTLY BULLISH	VERY BULLISH

```
================================================================================================
```

Definitions of Very Bullish, Bullish, Slightly Bullish, Neutral, Slightly Bearish, Bearish, and Very Bearish are provided in Appendix A.

total number of issues traded.[*] Fosback tested a 10-week moving average of the resulting Absolute Breadth Index, noting that readings under 15% preceded periods when market performance was below normal and often negative. Very bullish signals were given by readings over 40%.

---

*Reprinted with permission.

EXHIBIT A-2:

Interpretation of Absolute Breadth Index's 10-Day Simple Moving Average Readings

```
====================================================================================
ABSOLUTE BREADTH INDEX - 10 DAY MOVING AVERAGE
PERIOD ANALYZED:  JANUARY 1928 TO MARCH 1987
====================================================================================
```

INDICATOR RANGE		INTERPRETATION GIVEN INVESTOR'S TIME FRAME			
GREATER THAN	LESS THAN OR EQUAL TO	1 MONTH	3 MONTHS	6 MONTHS	12 MONTHS
0.0	114.1	BULLISH	SLIGHTLY BULLISH	NEUTRAL	BEARISH
114.1	135.8	SLIGHTLY BEARISH	NEUTRAL	NEUTRAL	VERY BEARISH
135.8	152.0	SLIGHTLY BEARISH	NEUTRAL	SLIGHTLY BEARISH	VERY BEARISH
152.0	166.5	BEARISH	NEUTRAL	NEUTRAL	SLIGHTLY BEARISH
166.5	179.4	NEUTRAL	NEUTRAL	NEUTRAL	NEUTRAL
179.4	191.2	NEUTRAL	NEUTRAL	BULLISH	SLIGHTLY BULLISH
191.2	203.8	NEUTRAL	NEUTRAL	SLIGHTLY BEARISH	NEUTRAL
203.8	215.9	SLIGHTLY BEARISH	NEUTRAL	SLIGHTLY BEARISH	SLIGHTLY BEARISH
215.9	228.6	NEUTRAL	NEUTRAL	NEUTRAL	NEUTRAL
228.6	242.4	NEUTRAL	NEUTRAL	NEUTRAL	NEUTRAL
242.4	256.5	NEUTRAL	NEUTRAL	NEUTRAL	NEUTRAL
256.5	271.9	NEUTRAL	NEUTRAL	SLIGHTLY BEARISH	NEUTRAL
271.9	289.3	NEUTRAL	NEUTRAL	NEUTRAL	NEUTRAL
289.3	308.6	NEUTRAL	NEUTRAL	NEUTRAL	NEUTRAL
308.6	329.3	NEUTRAL	NEUTRAL	NEUTRAL	NEUTRAL
329.3	352.3	NEUTRAL	NEUTRAL	SLIGHTLY BULLISH	BULLISH
352.3	380.7	NEUTRAL	SLIGHTLY BEARISH	NEUTRAL	BULLISH
380.7	420.1	BULLISH	NEUTRAL	NEUTRAL	BULLISH
420.1	480.8	BULLISH	NEUTRAL	NEUTRAL	BULLISH
480.8	938.2	NEUTRAL	VERY BULLISH	BULLISH	VERY BULLISH

```
====================================================================================
```

Definitions of Very Bullish, Bullish, Slightly Bullish, Neutral, Slightly Bearish, Bearish, and Very Bearish are provided in Appendix A.

EXHIBIT A-3:
Interpretation of Absolute Breadth Index's Weekly Readings

```
=====================================================================================
ABSOLUTE BREADTH INDEX - WEEKLY DATA
PERIOD ANALYZED:  JANUARY 1928 TO MARCH 1987
=====================================================================================
```

INDICATOR RANGE		INTERPRETATION GIVEN INVESTOR'S TIME FRAME			
GREATER THAN	LESS THAN OR EQUAL TO	1 MONTH	3 MONTHS	6 MONTHS	12 MONTHS
0	38	NEUTRAL	NEUTRAL	NEUTRAL	NEUTRAL
38	73	NEUTRAL	NEUTRAL	NEUTRAL	NEUTRAL
73	110	NEUTRAL	NEUTRAL	NEUTRAL	NEUTRAL
110	144	NEUTRAL	NEUTRAL	NEUTRAL	NEUTRAL
144	180	NEUTRAL	NEUTRAL	NEUTRAL	NEUTRAL
180	218	NEUTRAL	NEUTRAL	NEUTRAL	NEUTRAL
218	249	NEUTRAL	NEUTRAL	NEUTRAL	NEUTRAL
249	289	NEUTRAL	NEUTRAL	NEUTRAL	NEUTRAL
289	325	NEUTRAL	NEUTRAL	NEUTRAL	NEUTRAL
325	364	NEUTRAL	NEUTRAL	NEUTRAL	NEUTRAL
364	405	BULLISH	SLIGHTLY BULLISH	NEUTRAL	NEUTRAL
405	447	NEUTRAL	NEUTRAL	NEUTRAL	NEUTRAL
447	485	NEUTRAL	NEUTRAL	NEUTRAL	NEUTRAL
485	535	NEUTRAL	NEUTRAL	NEUTRAL	NEUTRAL
535	584	NEUTRAL	NEUTRAL	NEUTRAL	NEUTRAL
584	652	NEUTRAL	NEUTRAL	NEUTRAL	NEUTRAL
652	724	NEUTRAL	NEUTRAL	NEUTRAL	NEUTRAL
724	822	NEUTRAL	NEUTRAL	NEUTRAL	NEUTRAL
822	977	NEUTRAL	NEUTRAL	NEUTRAL	NEUTRAL
977	1910	NEUTRAL	NEUTRAL	NEUTRAL	SLIGHTLY BULLISH

```
=====================================================================================
```

Definitions of Very Bullish, Bullish, Slightly Bullish, Neutral, Slightly Bearish, Bearish, and Very Bearish are provided in Appendix A.

EXHIBIT A-4:
Interpretation of Absolute Breadth Index's 10-Week Simple Moving Average Readings

```
=========================================================================================
ABSOLUTE BREADTH INDEX - 10 WEEK MOVING AVERAGE
PERIOD ANALYZED: JANUARY 1928 TO MARCH 1987
=========================================================================================
```

INDICATOR RANGE		INTERPRETATION GIVEN INVESTOR'S TIME FRAME			
GREATER THAN	LESS THAN OR EQUAL TO	1 MONTH	3 MONTHS	6 MONTHS	12 MONTHS
0.0	210.8	NEUTRAL	SLIGHTLY BEARISH	NEUTRAL	SLIGHTLY BEARISH
210.8	243.9	NEUTRAL	BULLISH	NEUTRAL	NEUTRAL
243.9	265.6	NEUTRAL	NEUTRAL	NEUTRAL	NEUTRAL
265.6	288.1	NEUTRAL	NEUTRAL	NEUTRAL	SLIGHTLY BEARISH
288.1	307.4	NEUTRAL	SLIGHTLY BULLISH	VERY BULLISH	NEUTRAL
307.4	326.4	NEUTRAL	NEUTRAL	NEUTRAL	NEUTRAL
326.4	345.8	NEUTRAL	NEUTRAL	NEUTRAL	NEUTRAL
345.8	366.0	NEUTRAL	NEUTRAL	NEUTRAL	NEUTRAL
366.0	383.6	NEUTRAL	NEUTRAL	NEUTRAL	NEUTRAL
383.6	400.5	NEUTRAL	NEUTRAL	NEUTRAL	NEUTRAL
400.5	420.6	NEUTRAL	NEUTRAL	NEUTRAL	SLIGHTLY BEARISH
420.6	436.7	NEUTRAL	NEUTRAL	NEUTRAL	BEARISH
436.7	455.0	NEUTRAL	NEUTRAL	NEUTRAL	NEUTRAL
455.0	474.3	BULLISH	BEARISH	NEUTRAL	SLIGHTLY BULLISH
474.3	497.8	NEUTRAL	NEUTRAL	SLIGHTLY BEARISH	NEUTRAL
497.8	527.8	NEUTRAL	NEUTRAL	NEUTRAL	VERY BULLISH
527.8	563.6	NEUTRAL	NEUTRAL	NEUTRAL	VERY BULLISH
563.6	612.2	NEUTRAL	NEUTRAL	NEUTRAL	NEUTRAL
612.2	696.6	NEUTRAL	NEUTRAL	NEUTRAL	SLIGHTLY BULLISH
696.6	1030.3	NEUTRAL	NEUTRAL	NEUTRAL	SLIGHTLY BULLISH

```
=========================================================================================
```

Definitions of Very Bullish, Bullish, Slightly Bullish, Neutral, Slightly Bearish, Bearish, and Very Bearish are provided in Appendix A.

ADVANCE/DECLINE DIVERGENCE OSCILLATOR

One method of interpreting the Advance-Decline Line is to visually compare it to a broad market index, such as the Dow Jones Industrial Average. For example, if the Advance-Decline Line is decreasing while the market index is increasing, a divergence is noted and an expectation is formed that the market index will peak and change its trend to the downside. Unfortunately, there is a great deal of subjectivity in this type of eyeball analysis.

The Advance/Decline Divergence Oscillator was designed by Arthur Merrill (Merrill Analysis, Inc., Box 228, Chappaqua, NY 10514) with the intent of removing the subjective element of the analysis.[*] It is calculated in several steps. First, the daily number of advancing issues, declining issues and unchanged issues on the New York Stock Exchange are totalled for each week during the preceding year. A weekly ratio is then calculated by dividing the number of advancing issues minus the number of declining issues by the number of unchanged issues. Merrill credits Edmund Tabell for the concept of the ratio. The ratio is constructed to magnify market conviction. If conviction is high, the number of unchanged issues will be low and the ratio will be relatively high. If the market lacks conviction, the ratio will be relatively low as a result of a large number of unchanged issues.

Next, you sum up the ratio's values for the preceding 52 weeks. Using the calculated data and the weekly closing price of the Dow Jones Industrial Average (DJIA) for the preceding 52 weeks, regression analysis is performed and a regression line can be plotted, as illustrated in Exhibit A-5. The DJIA is on the Y axis; the cumulative ratio is on the X axis. To determine the expected value of the DJIA for a given value of the cumulative ratio, you simply locate the point on the regression line that is directly above the cumulative ratio value.

Finally, the Advance/Decline Divergence Oscillator is computed as the percent deviation of the current closing price of the DJIA from its expected value. As illustrated in Exhibit A-6, positive oscillator readings imply that stock prices are increasing at a rate greater than the underlying advance/decline data expected. Therefore, a downturn in market prices is likely. On the other hand, negative oscillator readings indicate that stock prices are decreasing at a less-than-expected rate, so an upward reversal in stock prices is likely.

Although the Advance/Decline Divergence Oscillator is not a simple indicator to calculate, Merrill has found it worth the effort.

---

[*]Reprinted with permission.

EXHIBIT A-5:
Regression Line for Advance/Decline Divergence Oscillator

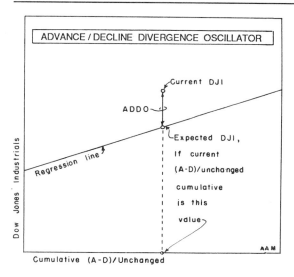

Source: By Permission of Merrill Analysis, Inc.

EXHIBIT A-6:
Sample Chart of Advance/Decline Divergence Oscillator

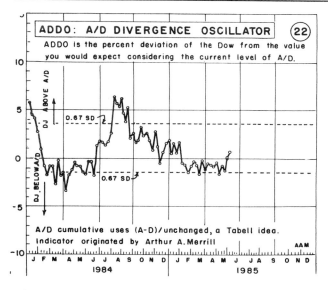

Source: By Permission of Merrill Analysis, Inc.

ADVANCE-DECLINE LINE

The Advance-Decline Line is a cumulative market breadth indicator. It is designed to facilitate comparison to a general market index, such as the Dow Jones Industrial Average.

The Advance-Decline Line's value or level is not as important as its trend. As a result, you can begin its calculation at any time. Customarily, a large base number such as +50,000 is used. Each day you calculate the difference between the number of advancing issues and number of declining issues and add that difference to the previous day's running total. Daily or weekly New York Stock Exchange data is typically used in the calculation. An example of the indicator's calculation follows:

Day	Number of Advancing Issues	Number of Declining Issues	Difference	Value of Advance/ Decline Line
1	400	800	−400	49,600
2	550	650	−100	49,500
3	780	490	+290	49,790
4	875	430	+445	50,235
5	575	645	−70	50,165

Exhibit A-7 shows a comparison of the Advance-Decline Line versus the Standard & Poor's 500 Index. Interpretation of the Advance-Decline Line is commonly performed as follows:

Market Index	Advance-Decline Line	Interpretation
Rising	Falling	Bearish
Near or at previous top	Significantly below corresponding top	Bearish
Near or at previous top	Significantly above corresponding top	Bullish
Falling	Rising	Bullish
Near or at previous bottom	Significantly above previous bottom	Bullish
Near or at previous bottom	Significantly below previous bottom	Bearish

EXHIBIT A-7:

Advance-Decline Line (top of chart) versus Standard & Poor's 500 Index (bottom of chart) from January 1984 to December 1986

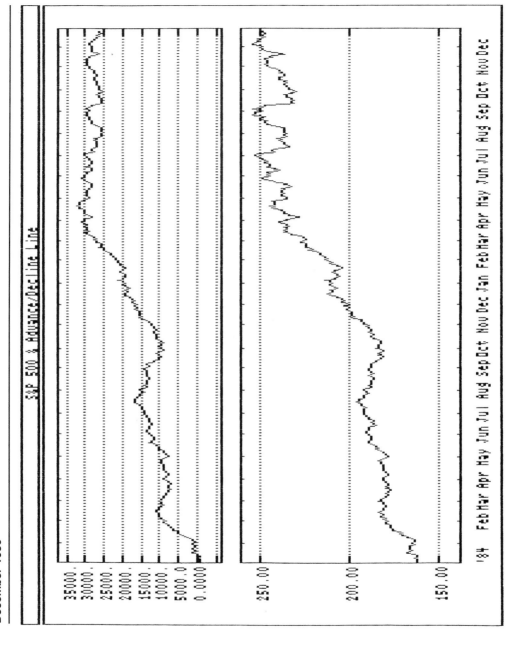

S&P 500 & Advance/Decline Line

The major criticism of the Advance-Decline Line is the subjectivity involved in its interpretation. Significant divergences between the trends of the Advance-Decline Line and a market index are easily seen in retrospect, but not so easily spotted while they are developing. In addition, a very large percentage of divergences prove to be misleading.

ADVANCE/DECLINE NONCUMULATIVE

The Advance/Decline Noncumulative (also known as Hughes Breadth Index) is calculated by dividing the number of advancing issues minus the number of declining issues by the total number of issues traded. Daily or weekly NYSE data is typically used in the calculation.

The theory behind the Advance/Decline Noncumulative is that increases in stock prices are preceded by strengthening in the internals of the market. The indicator is used to measure such market strength. Decreases in stock prices occur in a similar fashion, preceded by weakness in market internals.

We tested the Advance/Decline Noncumulative for the period of January 1928 to March 1987 on a daily and weekly basis. In addition, we applied a 10-period simple moving average to both the daily and weekly readings to smooth out any erratic movements. The results are shown in Exhibits A-8 through A-11 (pages 73–76).

The test process was as follows. The indicator readings for the test period were divided into 20 ranges with approximately the same number of occurrences in each range. For each reading in a range, the gain or loss in four subsequent time periods (1 month later, 3 months later, 6 months later, and 12 months later) was calculated. The combined results for earnings within each range were statistically compared, using chi-squared tests, to the performance of the overall market (as measured by the Standard & Poor's 500). Varying degrees of bullishness and bearishness were noted on the basis of that comparison.

Daily and weekly indicator readings without the use of a moving average showed little bullish or bearish tendencies. However, upon application of a 10-period moving average to both the daily and weekly data, a significant bullish pattern occurs at higher indicator readings.

In particular, during the past 40 years when the 10-day moving average of the Advance/Decline Noncumulative was .25 or greater, an average gain occurred in the overall market (as measured by the S&P 500) of 4.07% 1 month later, 8.05% 3 months later, 13.43% 6 months later, and 17.69% 12

EXHIBIT A-8:
Interpretation of Advance/Decline Noncumulative's Daily Readings

```
=====================================================================================
A/D NON-CUMULATIVE/HUGHES BREADTH INDEX - DAILY DATA
PERIOD ANALYZED:  JANUARY 1928 TO MARCH 1987
=====================================================================================
```

INDICATOR RANGE		INTERPRETATION GIVEN INVESTOR'S TIME FRAME			
GREATER THAN	LESS THAN OR EQUAL TO	1 MONTH	3 MONTHS	6 MONTHS	12 MONTHS
-0.910	-0.519	NEUTRAL	NEUTRAL	BEARISH	BEARISH
-0.519	-0.388	NEUTRAL	NEUTRAL	BEARISH	NEUTRAL
-0.388	-0.302	VERY BEARISH	BEARISH	BEARISH	VERY BEARISH
-0.302	-0.233	BEARISH	NEUTRAL	NEUTRAL	NEUTRAL
-0.233	-0.174	SLIGHTLY BEARISH	NEUTRAL	NEUTRAL	NEUTRAL
-0.174	-0.126	NEUTRAL	NEUTRAL	NEUTRAL	BULLISH
-0.126	-0.085	NEUTRAL	NEUTRAL	NEUTRAL	SLIGHTLY BEARISH
-0.085	-0.049	NEUTRAL	NEUTRAL	NEUTRAL	NEUTRAL
-0.049	-0.014	NEUTRAL	NEUTRAL	NEUTRAL	NEUTRAL
-0.014	0.018	NEUTRAL	NEUTRAL	NEUTRAL	NEUTRAL
0.018	0.050	NEUTRAL	NEUTRAL	NEUTRAL	NEUTRAL
0.050	0.083	NEUTRAL	NEUTRAL	NEUTRAL	NEUTRAL
0.083	0.116	NEUTRAL	NEUTRAL	NEUTRAL	NEUTRAL
0.116	0.152	NEUTRAL	NEUTRAL	NEUTRAL	NEUTRAL
0.152	0.190	NEUTRAL	SLIGHTLY BULLISH	SLIGHTLY BULLISH	NEUTRAL
0.190	0.232	BULLISH	NEUTRAL	NEUTRAL	NEUTRAL
0.232	0.284	BULLISH	NEUTRAL	NEUTRAL	NEUTRAL
0.284	0.353	NEUTRAL	SLIGHTLY BULLISH	NEUTRAL	NEUTRAL
0.353	0.457	SLIGHTLY BULLISH	BULLISH	BULLISH	BULLISH
0.457	0.887	NEUTRAL	NEUTRAL	NEUTRAL	NEUTRAL

```
=====================================================================================
```

Definitions of Very Bullish, Bullish, Slightly Bullish, Neutral, Slightly Bearish, Bearish, and Very Bearish are provided in Appendix A.

months later. Exhibit A-12 (page 77) shows the results in more detail. You should note that all signals generated within 3 months after an initial reading of .25 or greater were considered repeat signals and are not included in the results.

In addition, readings in the lowest 5% of observations when a 10-day moving average was used (−.219 and lower) were very bearish in the subsequent 1-, 3-, 6-, and 12-month periods.

EXHIBIT A-9:

Interpretation of Advance/Decline Noncumulative's 10-Day Simple Moving Average Readings

```
========================================================================================
A/D NON-CUMULATIVE/HUGHES BREADTH INDEX - 10 DAY MOVING AVERAGE
PERIOD ANALYZED: JANUARY 1928 TO MARCH 1987
========================================================================================
```

INDICATOR RANGE		INTERPRETATION GIVEN INVESTOR'S TIME FRAME			
GREATER THAN	LESS THAN OR EQUAL TO	1 MONTH	3 MONTHS	6 MONTHS	12 MONTHS
-0.750	-0.219	VERY BEARISH	VERY BEARISH	VERY BEARISH	VERY BEARISH
-0.219	-0.163	NEUTRAL	SLIGHTLY BEARISH	SLIGHTLY BEARISH	NEUTRAL
-0.163	-0.126	NEUTRAL	BEARISH	NEUTRAL	NEUTRAL
-0.126	-0.097	NEUTRAL	NEUTRAL	BEARISH	NEUTRAL
-0.097	-0.075	NEUTRAL	NEUTRAL	BEARISH	NEUTRAL
-0.075	-0.055	BEARISH	VERY BEARISH	BEARISH	BEARISH
-0.055	-0.036	NEUTRAL	NEUTRAL	NEUTRAL	NEUTRAL
-0.036	-0.020	SLIGHTLY BEARISH	NEUTRAL	NEUTRAL	NEUTRAL
-0.020	-0.005	BEARISH	NEUTRAL	NEUTRAL	SLIGHTLY BEARISH
-0.005	0.010	NEUTRAL	NEUTRAL	NEUTRAL	NEUTRAL
0.010	0.025	NEUTRAL	NEUTRAL	NEUTRAL	NEUTRAL
0.025	0.038	NEUTRAL	NEUTRAL	NEUTRAL	NEUTRAL
0.038	0.053	NEUTRAL	NEUTRAL	NEUTRAL	NEUTRAL
0.053	0.067	SLIGHTLY BULLISH	BULLISH	NEUTRAL	NEUTRAL
0.067	0.084	NEUTRAL	NEUTRAL	SLIGHTLY BULLISH	NEUTRAL
0.084	0.101	NEUTRAL	SLIGHTLY BULLISH	VERY BULLISH	SLIGHTLY BULLISH
0.101	0.122	NEUTRAL	SLIGHTLY BULLISH	BULLISH	BULLISH
0.122	0.146	BULLISH	NEUTRAL	BULLISH	SLIGHTLY BULLISH
0.146	0.185	BULLISH	SLIGHTLY BULLISH	SLIGHTLY BULLISH	SLIGHTLY BULLISH
0.185	0.505	VERY BULLISH	VERY BULLISH	VERY BULLISH	BULLISH

Definitions of Very Bullish, Bullish, Slightly Bullish, Neutral, Slightly Bearish, Bearish, and Very Bearish are provided in Appendix A.

EXHIBIT A-10:

Interpretation of Advance/Decline Noncumulative's Weekly Readings

```
==========================================================================================
A/D NON-CUMULATIVE/HUGHES BREADTH INDEX - WEEKLY DATA
PERIOD ANALYZED:  JANUARY 1928 TO MARCH 1987
==========================================================================================
```

INDICATOR RANGE		INTERPRETATION GIVEN INVESTOR'S TIME FRAME			
GREATER THAN	LESS THAN OR EQUAL TO	1 MONTH	3 MONTHS	6 MONTHS	12 MONTHS
-0.960	-0.613	SLIGHTLY BEARISH	NEUTRAL	NEUTRAL	NEUTRAL
-0.613	-0.467	NEUTRAL	NEUTRAL	NEUTRAL	NEUTRAL
-0.467	-0.374	NEUTRAL	NEUTRAL	NEUTRAL	NEUTRAL
-0.374	-0.300	SLIGHTLY BEARISH	SLIGHTLY BEARISH	BEARISH	NEUTRAL
-0.300	-0.228	NEUTRAL	NEUTRAL	NEUTRAL	NEUTRAL
-0.228	-0.164	NEUTRAL	NEUTRAL	NEUTRAL	NEUTRAL
-0.164	-0.108	NEUTRAL	NEUTRAL	NEUTRAL	NEUTRAL
-0.108	-0.055	NEUTRAL	NEUTRAL	SLIGHTLY BULLISH	NEUTRAL
-0.055	-0.001	NEUTRAL	NEUTRAL	NEUTRAL	NEUTRAL
-0.001	0.047	NEUTRAL	NEUTRAL	NEUTRAL	NEUTRAL
0.047	0.098	NEUTRAL	SLIGHTLY BEARISH	NEUTRAL	NEUTRAL
0.098	0.136	NEUTRAL	NEUTRAL	NEUTRAL	NEUTRAL
0.136	0.178	NEUTRAL	NEUTRAL	NEUTRAL	NEUTRAL
0.178	0.219	NEUTRAL	NEUTRAL	NEUTRAL	NEUTRAL
0.219	0.268	NEUTRAL	NEUTRAL	NEUTRAL	NEUTRAL
0.268	0.319	NEUTRAL	NEUTRAL	NEUTRAL	NEUTRAL
0.319	0.375	NEUTRAL	NEUTRAL	SLIGHTLY BULLISH	NEUTRAL
0.375	0.433	NEUTRAL	NEUTRAL	NEUTRAL	SLIGHTLY BULLISH
0.433	0.531	NEUTRAL	NEUTRAL	NEUTRAL	NEUTRAL
0.531	0.882	NEUTRAL	NEUTRAL	NEUTRAL	NEUTRAL

```
==========================================================================================
```

Definitions of Very Bullish, Bullish, Slightly Bullish, Neutral, Slightly Bearish, Bearish, and Very Bearish are provided in Appendix A.

EXHIBIT A-11:

Interpretation of Advance/Decline Noncumulative's 10-Week Simple Moving Average Readings

```
===============================================================================================
A/D NON-CUMULATIVE/HUGHES BREADTH INDEX - 10 WEEK MOVING AVERAGE
PERIOD ANALYZED:  JANUARY 1928 TO MARCH 1987
===============================================================================================
```

INDICATOR RANGE		INTERPRETATION GIVEN INVESTOR'S TIME FRAME			
GREATER THAN	LESS THAN OR EQUAL TO	1 MONTH	3 MONTHS	6 MONTHS	12 MONTHS
-0.450	-0.235	SLIGHTLY BEARISH	NEUTRAL	VERY BEARISH	SLIGHTLY BEARISH
-0.235	-0.178	NEUTRAL	BEARISH	VERY BEARISH	NEUTRAL
-0.178	-0.140	NEUTRAL	BEARISH	NEUTRAL	NEUTRAL
-0.140	-0.108	NEUTRAL	NEUTRAL	NEUTRAL	NEUTRAL
-0.108	-0.082	NEUTRAL	NEUTRAL	NEUTRAL	NEUTRAL
-0.082	-0.059	NEUTRAL	NEUTRAL	NEUTRAL	NEUTRAL
-0.059	-0.038	NEUTRAL	NEUTRAL	NEUTRAL	SLIGHTLY BEARISH
-0.038	-0.017	NEUTRAL	NEUTRAL	NEUTRAL	BEARISH
-0.017	0.005	SLIGHTLY BEARISH	NEUTRAL	NEUTRAL	NEUTRAL
0.005	0.024	BEARISH	VERY BEARISH	NEUTRAL	NEUTRAL
0.024	0.039	NEUTRAL	NEUTRAL	NEUTRAL	NEUTRAL
0.039	0.055	NEUTRAL	NEUTRAL	NEUTRAL	NEUTRAL
0.055	0.074	NEUTRAL	SLIGHTLY BULLISH	NEUTRAL	NEUTRAL
0.074	0.094	NEUTRAL	NEUTRAL	NEUTRAL	NEUTRAL
0.094	0.116	NEUTRAL	NEUTRAL	NEUTRAL	NEUTRAL
0.116	0.135	NEUTRAL	NEUTRAL	NEUTRAL	NEUTRAL
0.135	0.156	SLIGHTLY BULLISH	SLIGHTLY BULLISH	BULLISH	NEUTRAL
0.156	0.186	SLIGHTLY BULLISH	SLIGHTLY BULLISH	VERY BULLISH	VERY BULLISH
0.186	0.237	NEUTRAL	BULLISH	SLIGHTLY BULLISH	SLIGHTLY BULLISH
0.237	0.538	BULLISH	VERY BULLISH	VERY BULLISH	SLIGHTLY BULLISH

```
===============================================================================================
```

Definitions of Very Bullish, Bullish, Slightly Bullish, Neutral, Slightly Bearish, Bearish, and Very Bearish are provided in Appendix A.

EXHIBIT A-12:

Advance/Decline Noncumulative's 10-Day Simple Moving Average Readings Equal to or Greater than 0.25 from 1947 to 1986

```
================================================================
A/D NON-CUMULATIVE/HUGHES BREADTH INDEX - 10 DAY MOVING AVERAGE
================================================================
```

		PERCENTAGE CHANGE IN S&P 500			
DATE	INDICATOR VALUE	1 MONTH LATER	3 MONTHS LATER	6 MONTHS LATER	12 MONTHS LATER
JUN 23 1947	0.25	4.59	-0.46	-0.13	11.09
MAR 29 1948	0.27	5.71	14.49	7.62	1.56
JUL 13 1949	0.26	3.45	7.78	14.07	12.92
JUL 31 1950	0.25	3.98	11.27	22.03	26.18
NOV 20 1950	0.26	0.15	11.04	11.49	13.60
JAN 25 1954	0.25	-0.39	7.52	17.01	36.68
JAN 24 1958	0.27	-2.54	3.43	11.84	34.26
JUL 10 1962	0.27	0.54	-0.23	12.92	22.45
NOV 7 1962	0.26	7.41	12.71	19.83	24.02
JAN 13 1967	0.27	3.61	6.98	9.71	14.42
AUG 31 1970	0.26	3.30	6.97	18.96	23.26
DEC 3 1970	0.27	3.26	11.32	13.95	7.47
DEC 8 1971	0.28	6.76	12.42	11.07	21.32
SEP 27 1973	0.25	2.11	-10.40	-13.07	-38.05
JAN 8 1975	0.26	12.16	18.28	35.35	33.54
JAN 6 1976	0.27	8.96	10.67	10.70	14.40
AUG 23 1982	0.27	6.79	18.01	27.47	40.86
JAN 21 1985	0.25	3.40	3.12	10.93	18.43
AVERAGE CHANGE		4.07	8.05	13.43	17.69

```
================================================================
```

ADVANCE/DECLINE RATIO

The Advance/Decline Ratio displays market strength or weakness. It is calculated using daily or weekly NYSE data by dividing the number of advancing issues by the number of declining issues. It is used as both a momentum indicator and an overbought/oversold indicator.

The overbought/oversold interpretation holds that the higher the ratio becomes, the more excessive the rally and more likely a correction will occur. On the other hand, the lower the ratio becomes, the greater the chance that a technical rally will occur. A 10-day simple moving average often is used to smooth out random fluctuations. The conventional interpretation is that when the 10-day moving average of the ratio is above 1.25, the market is overbought (bearish); when it is below 0.75, it is oversold (bullish).

We tested the Advance/Decline Ratio for the period of January 1928 to March 1987 on a daily and weekly basis. In addition, we applied a 10-period simple moving average to both the daily and weekly readings to smooth out any erratic movements. The results are shown in Exhibits A-13 through A-16 (pages 78–81).

EXHIBIT A-13:
Interpretation of Advance/Decline Ratio's Daily Readings

```
================================================================================================
A/D RATIO - DAILY DATA
PERIOD ANALYZED: JANUARY 1928 TO MARCH 1987
================================================================================================
```

INDICATOR RANGE		INTERPRETATION GIVEN INVESTOR'S TIME FRAME			
GREATER THAN	LESS THAN OR EQUAL TO	1 MONTH	3 MONTHS	6 MONTHS	12 MONTHS
0.000	0.226	SLIGHTLY BEARISH	NEUTRAL	BEARISH	VERY BEARISH
0.226	0.349	NEUTRAL	NEUTRAL	BEARISH	NEUTRAL
0.349	0.450	BEARISH	BEARISH	BEARISH	BEARISH
0.450	0.540	VERY BEARISH	NEUTRAL	NEUTRAL	NEUTRAL
0.540	0.638	NEUTRAL	NEUTRAL	NEUTRAL	NEUTRAL
0.638	0.722	NEUTRAL	NEUTRAL	NEUTRAL	SLIGHTLY BULLISH
0.722	0.805	NEUTRAL	NEUTRAL	NEUTRAL	NEUTRAL
0.805	0.883	NEUTRAL	NEUTRAL	NEUTRAL	NEUTRAL
0.883	0.968	NEUTRAL	NEUTRAL	NEUTRAL	NEUTRAL
0.968	1.052	NEUTRAL	NEUTRAL	NEUTRAL	NEUTRAL
1.052	1.142	NEUTRAL	NEUTRAL	NEUTRAL	NEUTRAL
1.142	1.244	NEUTRAL	NEUTRAL	NEUTRAL	NEUTRAL
1.244	1.360	NEUTRAL	NEUTRAL	NEUTRAL	NEUTRAL
1.360	1.493	NEUTRAL	NEUTRAL	NEUTRAL	SLIGHTLY BEARISH
1.493	1.655	NEUTRAL	SLIGHTLY BULLISH	SLIGHTLY BULLISH	NEUTRAL
1.655	1.857	BULLISH	NEUTRAL	NEUTRAL	NEUTRAL
1.857	2.153	SLIGHTLY BULLISH	SLIGHTLY BULLISH	SLIGHTLY BULLISH	NEUTRAL
2.153	2.629	NEUTRAL	BULLISH	NEUTRAL	NEUTRAL
2.629	3.653	NEUTRAL	SLIGHTLY BULLISH	BULLISH	VERY BULLISH
3.653	39.111	NEUTRAL	NEUTRAL	NEUTRAL	NEUTRAL

```
================================================================================================
```

Definitions of Very Bullish, Bullish, Slightly Bullish, Neutral, Slightly Bearish, Bearish, and Very Bearish are provided in Appendix A.

EXHIBIT A-14:

Interpretation of Advance/Decline Ratio's 10-Day Simple Moving Average Readings

```
=================================================================================================
A/D RATIO - 10 DAY MOVING AVERAGE
PERIOD ANALYZED:  JANUARY 1928 TO MARCH 1987
=================================================================================================
```

INDICATOR RANGE		INTERPRETATION GIVEN INVESTOR'S TIME FRAME			
GREATER THAN	LESS THAN OR EQUAL TO	1 MONTH	3 MONTHS	6 MONTHS	12 MONTHS
0.000	0.724	VERY BEARISH	VERY BEARISH	VERY BEARISH	SLIGHTLY BEARISH
0.724	0.832	BEARISH	VERY BEARISH	VERY BEARISH	NEUTRAL
0.832	0.910	NEUTRAL	NEUTRAL	VERY BEARISH	SLIGHTLY BEARISH
0.910	0.970	NEUTRAL	NEUTRAL	NEUTRAL	NEUTRAL
0.970	1.023	NEUTRAL	NEUTRAL	NEUTRAL	NEUTRAL
1.023	1.074	BEARISH	NEUTRAL	SLIGHTLY BEARISH	SLIGHTLY BEARISH
1.074	1.121	NEUTRAL	NEUTRAL	NEUTRAL	SLIGHTLY BEARISH
1.121	1.168	BEARISH	NEUTRAL	NEUTRAL	NEUTRAL
1.168	1.215	NEUTRAL	NEUTRAL	NEUTRAL	NEUTRAL
1.215	1.263	NEUTRAL	NEUTRAL	NEUTRAL	NEUTRAL
1.263	1.313	NEUTRAL	NEUTRAL	NEUTRAL	NEUTRAL
1.313	1.367	NEUTRAL	NEUTRAL	NEUTRAL	NEUTRAL
1.367	1.423	NEUTRAL	NEUTRAL	SLIGHTLY BULLISH	NEUTRAL
1.423	1.489	VERY BULLISH	SLIGHTLY BULLISH	VERY BULLISH	BULLISH
1.489	1.571	VERY BULLISH	NEUTRAL	VERY BULLISH	VERY BULLISH
1.571	1.671	BULLISH	SLIGHTLY BULLISH	BULLISH	NEUTRAL
1.671	1.811	VERY BULLISH	SLIGHTLY BULLISH	VERY BULLISH	NEUTRAL
1.811	2.044	NEUTRAL	NEUTRAL	NEUTRAL	NEUTRAL
2.044	2.489	SLIGHTLY BULLISH	SLIGHTLY BULLISH	NEUTRAL	NEUTRAL
2.489	8.630	BEARISH	BEARISH	VERY BEARISH	BEARISH

```
=================================================================================================
```

Definitions of Very Bullish, Bullish, Slightly Bullish, Neutral, Slightly Bearish, Bearish, and Very Bearish are provided in Appendix A.

The test process was as follows. The indicator readings for the test period were divided into 20 ranges with approximately the same number of occurrences in each range. For each reading in a range, the gain or loss in four subsequent time periods (1 month later, 3 months later, 6 months later, and 12 months later) was calculated. The combined results for readings within each range were statistically compared, using chi-squared tests, to the

EXHIBIT A-15:
Interpretation of Advance/Decline Ratio's Weekly Readings

```
=======================================================================================
A/D RATIO - WEEKLY DATA
PERIOD ANALYZED:  JANUARY 1928 TO MARCH 1987
=======================================================================================
```

INDICATOR RANGE		INTERPRETATION GIVEN INVESTOR'S TIME FRAME			
GREATER THAN	LESS THAN OR EQUAL TO	1 MONTH	3 MONTHS	6 MONTHS	12 MONTHS
0.000	0.194	SLIGHTLY BEARISH	NEUTRAL	NEUTRAL	NEUTRAL
0.194	0.312	NEUTRAL	NEUTRAL	NEUTRAL	NEUTRAL
0.312	0.407	NEUTRAL	NEUTRAL	NEUTRAL	NEUTRAL
0.407	0.492	NEUTRAL	NEUTRAL	BEARISH	NEUTRAL
0.492	0.589	NEUTRAL	NEUTRAL	SLIGHTLY BEARISH	NEUTRAL
0.589	0.680	NEUTRAL	NEUTRAL	NEUTRAL	NEUTRAL
0.680	0.775	NEUTRAL	NEUTRAL	NEUTRAL	NEUTRAL
0.775	0.880	NEUTRAL	NEUTRAL	NEUTRAL	NEUTRAL
0.880	0.998	NEUTRAL	NEUTRAL	NEUTRAL	NEUTRAL
0.998	1.110	SLIGHTLY BEARISH	NEUTRAL	NEUTRAL	NEUTRAL
1.110	1.247	NEUTRAL	NEUTRAL	NEUTRAL	NEUTRAL
1.247	1.366	NEUTRAL	NEUTRAL	NEUTRAL	NEUTRAL
1.366	1.491	NEUTRAL	NEUTRAL	NEUTRAL	NEUTRAL
1.491	1.654	NEUTRAL	NEUTRAL	SLIGHTLY BULLISH	SLIGHTLY BULLISH
1.654	1.867	NEUTRAL	NEUTRAL	NEUTRAL	NEUTRAL
1.867	2.128	NEUTRAL	SLIGHTLY BULLISH	NEUTRAL	NEUTRAL
2.128	2.446	NEUTRAL	NEUTRAL	SLIGHTLY BULLISH	NEUTRAL
2.446	2.896	NEUTRAL	NEUTRAL	NEUTRAL	NEUTRAL
2.896	3.828	NEUTRAL	NEUTRAL	NEUTRAL	NEUTRAL
3.828	24.857	NEUTRAL	NEUTRAL	NEUTRAL	NEUTRAL

```
=======================================================================================
```

Definitions of Very Bullish, Bullish, Slightly Bullish, Neutral, Slightly Bearish, Bearish, and Very Bearish are provided in Appendix A.

performance of the overall market (as measured by the Standard & Poor's 500). Varying degrees of bullishness and bearishness were noted on the basis of that comparison.

Contrary to common interpretation, our research found the Advance/Decline Ratio to be of no value as an overbought/oversold indicator. High indicator readings using a 10-day moving average (between 1.423 and 2.489) proved to be bullish. Only at the most extreme 10-day level, in excess of

EXHIBIT A-16:

Interpretation of Advance/Decline Ratio's 10-Week Simple Moving Average Readings

```
=================================================================================
A/D RATIO - 10 WEEK MOVING AVERAGE
PERIOD ANALYZED:  JANUARY 1928 TO MARCH 1987
=================================================================================
```

INDICATOR RANGE		INTERPRETATION GIVEN INVESTOR'S TIME FRAME			
GREATER THAN	LESS THAN OR EQUAL TO	1 MONTH	3 MONTHS	6 MONTHS	12 MONTHS
0.000	0.795	NEUTRAL	NEUTRAL	VERY BEARISH	SLIGHTLY BEARISH
0.795	0.895	NEUTRAL	VERY BEARISH	BEARISH	NEUTRAL
0.895	0.968	NEUTRAL	SLIGHTLY BEARISH	NEUTRAL	NEUTRAL
0.968	1.036	NEUTRAL	NEUTRAL	NEUTRAL	NEUTRAL
1.036	1.093	SLIGHTLY BEARISH	NEUTRAL	SLIGHTLY BEARISH	SLIGHTLY BEARISH
1.093	1.152	NEUTRAL	NEUTRAL	NEUTRAL	NEUTRAL
1.152	1.203	SLIGHTLY BEARISH	SLIGHTLY BEARISH	NEUTRAL	SLIGHTLY BEARISH
1.203	1.257	NEUTRAL	NEUTRAL	NEUTRAL	NEUTRAL
1.257	1.314	NEUTRAL	NEUTRAL	NEUTRAL	NEUTRAL
1.314	1.368	NEUTRAL	NEUTRAL	BULLISH	NEUTRAL
1.368	1.425	NEUTRAL	NEUTRAL	NEUTRAL	NEUTRAL
1.425	1.475	NEUTRAL	SLIGHTLY BEARISH	NEUTRAL	NEUTRAL
1.475	1.545	NEUTRAL	NEUTRAL	SLIGHTLY BULLISH	NEUTRAL
1.545	1.621	NEUTRAL	NEUTRAL	NEUTRAL	NEUTRAL
1.621	1.722	NEUTRAL	NEUTRAL	NEUTRAL	NEUTRAL
1.722	1.834	NEUTRAL	NEUTRAL	NEUTRAL	NEUTRAL
1.834	1.960	NEUTRAL	NEUTRAL	BULLISH	VERY BULLISH
1.960	2.128	NEUTRAL	SLIGHTLY BULLISH	VERY BULLISH	NEUTRAL
2.128	2.540	BULLISH	VERY BULLISH	VERY BULLISH	NEUTRAL
2.540	5.332	NEUTRAL	NEUTRAL	NEUTRAL	NEUTRAL

```
=================================================================================
```

Definitions of Very Bullish, Bullish, Slightly Bullish, Neutral, Slightly Bearish, Bearish, and Very Bearish are provided in Appendix A.

2.489 (which occurred only 5% of the time), did the Advance/Decline Ratio correctly signal market vulnerability due to overbought excesses.

On the oversold side, the indicator was a total failure, in that extreme low 10-day moving average readings under 0.832 (which occurred 10% of the time) were followed by further market decline. This was also true when weekly data was used.

In conclusion, the Advance/Decline Ratio must be considered unreliable as an overbought/oversold indicator. It is better viewed as a breadth momentum, trend continuation indicator.

ADVISORY SENTIMENT INDEX

The Advisory Sentiment Index is a contrary opinion overbought/oversold indicator. It summarizes what stock market advisory services think the stock market will do.

The Advisory Sentiment Index was first developed by A.W. Cohen of Chartcraft, Inc., and it is reported on a weekly basis in a related publication, *Investors Intelligence* (1 West Avenue, Larchmont, NY 10538). Based on a careful reading of about 100 stock market newsletters, the proportion with bullish and bearish expectations on the stock market's future trend is tallied.

The most popular interpretation of the indicator is that, when taken in aggregate, advisory services tend to be wrong about the direction of stock prices at major turning points. When the vast majority of advisory services are bullish, it is viewed in a contrary fashion as bearish for stock prices. On the other hand, when the vast majority of advisory services is bearish, it is considered bullish for the stock market.

Exhibit A-17 shows a 2-week moving average of the percentage of bullish advisors and a 4-week moving average of bearish advisors along with the Dow Jones Industrial Average from 1974 to 1987. The moving averages are used for smoothing purposes.

We tested the proportion of bullish advisors for the period of January 1970 to March 1987 on a weekly basis. In addition, we applied a 4-period simple moving average to the weekly readings to smooth out any erratic movements. The results are shown in Exhibits A-18 and A-19 (pages 84– 85). A visual representation is presented in Exhibit A-20 (page 86).

The test process was as follows. The indicator readings for the test period were divided into 20 ranges with approximately the same number of occurrences in each range. For each reading in a range, the gain or loss in four subsequent time periods (1 month later, 3 months later, 6 months later, and 12 months later) was calculated. The combined results for readings within each range were statistically compared, using chi-squared tests, to the performance of the overall market (as measured by the Standard & Poor's 500). Varying degrees of bullishness and bearishness were noted on the basis of that comparison.

EXHIBIT A-17:
Bullish Advisors (bottom) and Bearish Advisors (middle) Versus the Dow Jones Industrial Average from 1974 to 1986

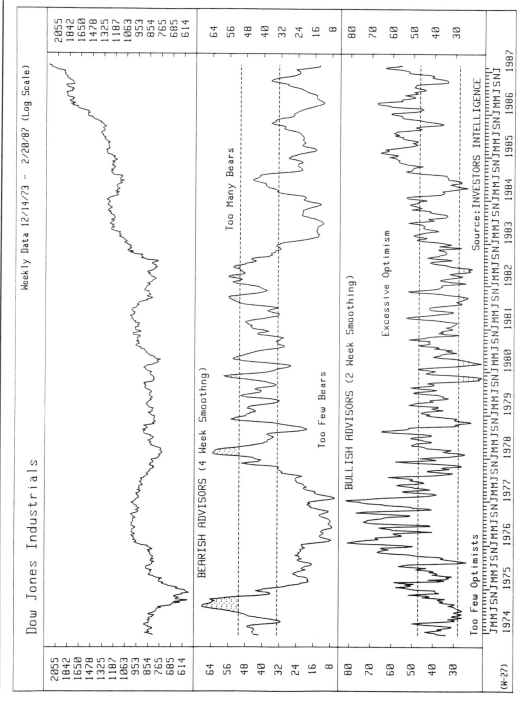

Source: By Permission of Ned Davis Research, Inc.

83

EXHIBIT A-18:
Interpretation of Bullish Sentiment's Weekly Readings

```
=================================================================================
BULLISH SENTIMENT - WEEKLY DATA
PERIOD ANALYZED:  JANUARY 1970 TO MARCH 1987
=================================================================================


INDICATOR RANGE                 INTERPRETATION GIVEN INVESTOR'S TIME FRAME
-----------------     -----------------------------------------------------------

          LESS
GREATER  THAN OR
 THAN    EQUAL TO   1 MONTH          3 MONTHS          6 MONTHS         12 MONTHS
-------  --------   ---------------  ----------------  ----------------  ---------------

 0.000    0.327     NEUTRAL          NEUTRAL           BULLISH           VERY BULLISH
 0.327    0.364     NEUTRAL          NEUTRAL           NEUTRAL           SLIGHTLY BULLISH
 0.364    0.405     NEUTRAL          NEUTRAL           NEUTRAL           NEUTRAL
 0.405    0.437     NEUTRAL          NEUTRAL           NEUTRAL           NEUTRAL
 0.437    0.461     NEUTRAL          NEUTRAL           NEUTRAL           NEUTRAL
 0.461    0.487     NEUTRAL          NEUTRAL           NEUTRAL           NEUTRAL
 0.487    0.515     NEUTRAL          NEUTRAL           NEUTRAL           NEUTRAL
 0.515    0.541     NEUTRAL          SLIGHTLY BEARISH  NEUTRAL           SLIGHTLY BULLISH
 0.541    0.562     NEUTRAL          NEUTRAL           NEUTRAL           NEUTRAL
 0.562    0.587     NEUTRAL          NEUTRAL           NEUTRAL           NEUTRAL
 0.587    0.621     BEARISH          NEUTRAL           NEUTRAL           SLIGHTLY BEARISH
 0.621    0.645     NEUTRAL          NEUTRAL           NEUTRAL           NEUTRAL
 0.645    0.677     NEUTRAL          SLIGHTLY BULLISH  NEUTRAL           NEUTRAL
 0.677    0.705     NEUTRAL          NEUTRAL           NEUTRAL           SLIGHTLY BULLISH
 0.705    0.722     NEUTRAL          NEUTRAL           NEUTRAL           NEUTRAL
 0.722    0.740     NEUTRAL          NEUTRAL           NEUTRAL           NEUTRAL
 0.740    0.768     NEUTRAL          NEUTRAL           NEUTRAL           NEUTRAL
 0.768    0.790     NEUTRAL          NEUTRAL           NEUTRAL           SLIGHTLY BEARISH
 0.790    0.830     NEUTRAL          NEUTRAL           NEUTRAL           NEUTRAL
 0.830    0.946     NEUTRAL          SLIGHTLY BEARISH  BEARISH           VERY BEARISH

=================================================================================
```

Definitions of Very Bullish, Bullish, Slightly Bullish, Neutral, Slightly Bearish, Bearish, and Very Bearish are provided in Appendix A.

Our research results confirm the common method of interpreting bullish sentiment for 6- and 12-month time horizons. When a relatively small percentage (37.5% or less) of advisory services were bullish, there was a significant bullish tendency for stock prices. On the other hand, when a relatively high percentage (greater than 78.2%) of advisory services were bullish, there was a significantly bearish tendency. Note, however, that this indicator proved meaningless for shorter time horizons of 1 and 3 months.

EXHIBIT A-19:

Interpretation of Bullish Sentiment's 4-Week Simple Moving Average Readings

```
=====================================================================================================
BULLISH SENTIMENT - 4 WEEK MOVING AVERAGE
PERIOD ANALYZED: JANUARY 1970 TO MARCH 1987
=====================================================================================================
```

INDICATOR RANGE		INTERPRETATION GIVEN INVESTOR'S TIME FRAME			
GREATER THAN	LESS THAN OR EQUAL TO	1 MONTH	3 MONTHS	6 MONTHS	12 MONTHS
0.000	0.341	NEUTRAL	NEUTRAL	BULLISH	VERY BULLISH
0.341	0.375	NEUTRAL	NEUTRAL	SLIGHTLY BULLISH	VERY BULLISH
0.375	0.417	NEUTRAL	NEUTRAL	NEUTRAL	NEUTRAL
0.417	0.438	NEUTRAL	NEUTRAL	SLIGHTLY BEARISH	NEUTRAL
0.438	0.468	NEUTRAL	NEUTRAL	NEUTRAL	NEUTRAL
0.468	0.493	NEUTRAL	NEUTRAL	NEUTRAL	NEUTRAL
0.493	0.519	NEUTRAL	NEUTRAL	NEUTRAL	NEUTRAL
0.519	0.538	NEUTRAL	NEUTRAL	NEUTRAL	NEUTRAL
0.538	0.561	SLIGHTLY BEARISH	BEARISH	NEUTRAL	NEUTRAL
0.561	0.587	NEUTRAL	NEUTRAL	NEUTRAL	BEARISH
0.587	0.617	NEUTRAL	NEUTRAL	NEUTRAL	NEUTRAL
0.617	0.656	NEUTRAL	NEUTRAL	NEUTRAL	NEUTRAL
0.656	0.683	NEUTRAL	NEUTRAL	NEUTRAL	SLIGHTLY BULLISH
0.683	0.701	NEUTRAL	SLIGHTLY BULLISH	VERY BULLISH	BULLISH
0.701	0.718	NEUTRAL	NEUTRAL	NEUTRAL	BULLISH
0.718	0.735	NEUTRAL	NEUTRAL	NEUTRAL	NEUTRAL
0.735	0.760	NEUTRAL	NEUTRAL	NEUTRAL	SLIGHTLY BEARISH
0.760	0.782	NEUTRAL	NEUTRAL	SLIGHTLY BULLISH	NEUTRAL
0.782	0.826	SLIGHTLY BEARISH	NEUTRAL	VERY BEARISH	VERY BEARISH
0.826	0.922	NEUTRAL	NEUTRAL	SLIGHTLY BEARISH	VERY BEARISH

```
=====================================================================================================
```

Definitions of Very Bullish, Bullish, Slightly Bullish, Neutral, Slightly Bearish, Bearish, and Very Bearish are provided in Appendix A.

EXHIBIT A-20:
Bullish Sentiment (bottom) Versus Dow Jones Industrial Average (top) from 1966 to 1986

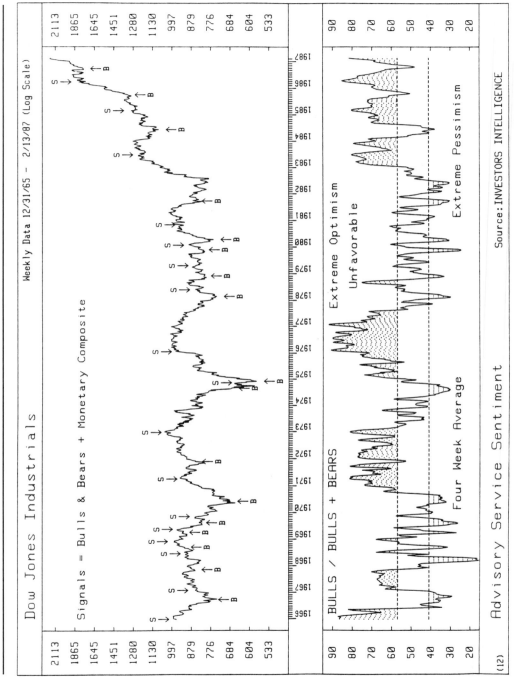

Source: By Permission of Ned Davis Research, Inc.

ARMS' EASE OF MOVEMENT VALUE

Arms' Ease of Movement Value (EMV) is a momentum indicator developed by Richard W. Arms, Jr., author of *Volume Cycles in the Stock Market: Market Timing through Equivolume Charting* (Dow Jones-Irwin, Homewood, IL, 1983). Arms has attempted to quantify volume and price changes in one indicator in order to determine the ease, or lack thereof, with which market price is able to move up or down.

The mathematical formula for EMV is as follows:

$$EMV = \left[\left(\frac{H + L}{2} \right) - \left(\frac{H_p + L_p}{2} \right) \right] \div \left(\frac{V}{H - L} \right)$$

where

H is the current period's high price.
L is the current period's low price.
H_p is the previous period's high price.
L_p is the previous period's low price.
V is the current period's volume.

For example, if this week's high was 18, low was 17, close was $17\frac{3}{4}$, volume was 2000 shares, and the previous week's high was $17\frac{1}{2}$, low $16\frac{3}{4}$, close $17\frac{1}{2}$ and volume 1500, then

$$EMV = \left[\left(\frac{18 + 17}{2} \right) - \left(\frac{17\frac{1}{2} + 16\frac{3}{4}}{2} \right) \right] \div \left(\frac{2000}{18 - 17} \right) = .0001875$$

An optimized simple moving average can be found for the basic EMV value. The decision rule is buy when the simple moving average rises above zero, then sell and sell short when the simple moving average falls below zero.

We tested this indicator using Compu Trac software and two 9.75-year test periods of weekly data (consisting of high, low, close, and volume for each week) for the broad-based NYSE Composite Index. The first period ran from January 5, 1968 through September 30, 1977, and the second period ran from April 8, 1977 through December 31, 1986. The overlap in data was necessary to facilitate testing of various moving averages throughout the full time period.

We tested simple moving average periods ranging between 1 and 25 weeks. Results were rather erratic as shown in Exhibits A-21 to A-24 (pages 88–91). The optimal period was 14 weeks for the simple moving average, but

EXHIBIT A-21:

Profitability Chart for Arms' Ease of Movement Values (Simple Moving Average Period Lengths of 1 to 25 Weeks from 1977 to 1986)

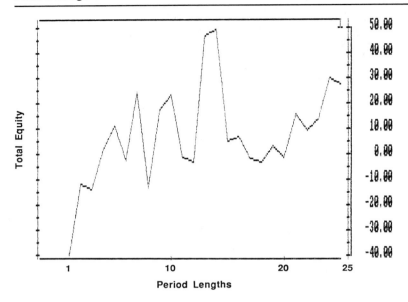

profits dropped nearly 50% on either side of 14 weeks suggesting unreliability of parameters. Results were poor with simple moving average periods less than 10 weeks and more than 40 weeks (not shown in Exhibits).

As shown in Exhibits A-25 through A-32 (pages 92–97), combined profits over 19 years were below our standard of comparison (results derived by use of the 40-week simple moving average crossover rule) at 83.50 NYSE points. Trading was relatively frequent at 80 total trades. Only 46% of these trades were profitable. Maximum drawdown of 17.37 points in 1978–1980 was somewhat worse than the standard 15.40.

In sum, optimized EMV proved to be below standard as a mechanical trading system. We suspect this is due to the erratic nature of volume itself as a technical indicator.

EXHIBIT A-22:
Profit Table for Arms' Ease of Movement Values (Simple Moving Average Period Lengths of 1 to 25 Weeks from 1977 to 1986)

Pass	Total Equity	Short Equity	Long Equity	Max. Equity	Min. Equity	P/L	Best Trade	Worst Trade	Max. Open P/L	Min. Open P/L
1	-54.76	-69.20	14.44	9.10	-66.32	-54.76	12.47	-7.58	15.56	-3.93
2	-12.13	-48.51	36.38	23.36	-24.64	-14.65	14.67	-9.41	15.56	-3.93
3	-14.06	-49.49	35.43	21.35	-16.66	-16.62	16.32	-9.41	18.71	-4.48
4	1.85	-41.21	43.06	45.88	-6.92	1.85	15.17	-9.41	16.19	-4.48
5	11.35	-36.55	47.90	39.30	-4.67	11.35	14.85	-9.41	17.74	-4.67
6	-2.22	-43.20	40.98	26.30	-9.18	-2.22	14.55	-11.07	17.18	-4.80
7	24.28	-30.81	55.09	52.11	-3.26	21.72	26.57	-12.51	29.32	-4.67
8	-13.16	-49.19	36.03	35.83	-13.16	-13.16	22.50	-11.08	27.93	-8.97
9	17.32	-33.73	51.05	36.23	-4.13	17.32	26.37	-4.47	31.59	-8.97
10	22.86	-30.54	53.40	41.37	-14.17	26.85	26.37	-7.53	32.73	-5.87
11	-1.00	-42.08	41.08	36.23	-8.39	2.99	27.57	-12.51	32.73	-8.69
12	-2.92	-43.29	40.37	33.69	-12.37	2.19	27.57	-11.08	32.73	-9.76
13	46.93	-18.42	65.35	58.60	-8.01	49.88	26.37	-5.87	32.73	-3.71
14	49.65	-16.97	66.62	61.90	-4.58	52.17	26.61	-5.87	31.59	-5.17
15	4.71	-39.08	43.79	32.88	-13.41	7.27	25.15	-9.41	30.31	-10.88
16	7.00	-38.73	45.73	39.69	-16.11	12.77	23.54	-11.07	30.31	-10.88
17	-1.68	-43.11	41.43	33.89	-20.64	4.09	25.02	-12.51	28.56	-10.88
18	-3.07	-44.02	40.95	26.30	-26.07	2.70	25.48	-9.77	30.31	-10.88
19	3.18	-41.01	44.19	28.43	-28.64	8.95	24.05	-9.77	30.31	-10.88
20	-1.04	-43.51	42.47	33.77	-27.94	4.73	24.02	-11.07	30.31	-11.60
21	15.55	-34.85	50.40	47.04	-17.15	21.32	27.05	-9.41	31.59	-10.88
22	9.34	-38.25	47.59	40.83	-20.93	15.11	27.05	-9.41	31.59	-10.88
23	13.51	-36.14	49.65	42.76	-22.00	19.28	27.05	-9.41	31.59	-10.88
24	29.79	-28.36	58.15	48.07	-20.60	35.56	27.05	-11.51	31.59	-11.11
25	27.49	-29.14	56.63	45.77	-18.30	33.26	27.05	-11.51	31.59	-11.11

Pass indicates period length.
Equity indicates the total number of points gained or lost.
Short equity indicates the number of points gained or lost on short positions.
Long equity indicates the number of points gained or lost on long positions.
Max. equity indicates the highest total profit recorded over the tested period.
Min. equity indicates the lowest total profit recorded over the tested period.
P/L indicates total number of points gained or lost in closed positions.
Best trade indicates the highest number of points gained in any closed trade.
Worst trade indicates the highest number of points lost in any closed trade.
Max. open P/L indicates the highest gain in a position which remains open at the end of the test run.
Min. open P/L indicates the highest loss in a position which remains open at the end of the test run.

EXHIBIT A-23:

Profitability Chart for Arms' Ease of Movement Values (Simple Moving Average Period Lengths of 1 to 25 Weeks from 1968 to 1977)

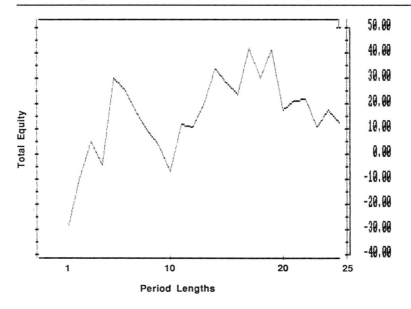

EXHIBIT A-24:

Profit Table for Arms' Ease of Movement Values (Simple Moving Average Period Lengths of 1 to 25 Weeks from 1968 to 1977)

Pass	Total Equity	Short Equity	Long Equity	Max. Equity	Min. Equity	P/L	Best Trade	Worst Trade	Max. Open P/L	Min. Open P/L
1	-28.92	-13.78	-15.14	11.73	-29.15	-28.92	9.87	-4.59	9.42	-2.00
2	-9.11	-4.21	-4.90	21.88	-10.52	-9.09	10.22	-4.59	10.28	-1.91
3	5.02	2.33	2.69	19.43	-4.95	3.71	9.15	-3.81	12.00	-2.84
4	-4.52	-2.83	-1.69	14.05	-5.83	-5.83	10.97	-3.81	12.00	-2.84
5	29.73	13.57	16.16	39.35	-1.57	28.42	9.83	-4.45	12.97	-2.76
6	25.74	11.57	14.17	39.57	-1.58	24.43	8.95	-4.45	12.97	-2.74
7	16.57	7.22	9.35	33.26	-1.11	15.34	9.39	-4.45	12.97	-2.90
8	9.47	3.12	6.35	22.61	-5.87	8.24	13.62	-3.63	17.01	-4.12
9	3.82	0.22	3.60	16.97	-11.62	2.59	14.82	-4.17	16.55	-3.18
10	-6.98	-5.16	-1.82	7.98	-13.86	-9.16	12.07	-5.68	16.65	-4.49
11	11.80	4.02	7.78	25.41	-13.37	8.90	12.40	-6.44	19.13	-5.55
12	10.44	3.84	6.60	25.99	-18.71	9.13	12.07	-5.01	17.31	-4.21
13	20.00	9.49	10.51	28.78	-17.01	17.82	13.62	-4.45	17.31	-4.73
14	33.85	17.32	16.53	35.60	-9.79	30.95	13.08	-3.49	17.31	-4.45
15	28.28	14.43	13.85	41.96	-9.51	26.97	14.85	-3.87	17.31	-2.58
16	23.97	12.71	11.26	31.68	-8.00	22.66	12.20	-3.42	16.65	-2.33
17	41.99	22.12	19.87	50.04	-4.92	40.68	18.13	-2.95	22.58	-2.43
18	30.23	16.28	13.95	36.30	-4.70	29.10	15.74	-4.64	20.19	-2.32
19	41.09	21.33	19.76	42.98	-7.32	39.96	14.52	-5.42	20.19	-4.13
20	17.56	9.69	7.87	24.12	-6.15	16.91	12.61	-7.33	18.32	-5.42
21	20.99	11.84	9.15	28.75	-6.08	20.11	15.23	-5.42	20.19	-3.23
22	22.16	13.23	8.93	39.16	-3.21	21.31	16.64	-4.78	22.58	-3.39
23	10.67	7.44	3.23	30.09	-3.12	9.82	12.18	-6.25	20.19	-4.37
24	17.70	10.83	6.87	28.92	-2.59	16.38	11.29	-7.16	20.19	-4.77
25	12.53	7.90	4.63	26.26	-1.90	10.94	10.93	-6.67	20.19	-5.49

Pass indicates period length.

Equity indicates the total number of points gained or lost.

Short equity indicates the number of points gained or lost on short positions.

Long equity indicates the number of points gained or lost on long positions.

Max. equity indicates the highest total profit recorded over the tested period.

Min. equity indicates the lowest total profit recorded over the tested period.

P/L indicates total number of points gained or lost in closed positions.

Best trade indicates the highest number of points gained in any closed trade.

Worst trade indicates the highest number of points lost in any closed trade.

Max. open P/L indicates the highest gain in a position which remains open at the end of the test run.

Min. open P/L indicates the highest loss in a position which remains open at the end of the test run.

EXHIBIT A-25:
New York Stock Exchange Composite Price Index Weekly High and Low from April 8, 1977 to December 31, 1986

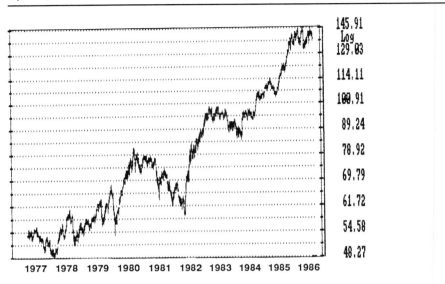

1977 1978 1979 1980 1981 1982 1983 1984 1985 1986

EXHIBIT A-26:
Arms' Ease of Movement Values, 1977 to 1986, Smoothed by 14-Week Simple Moving Average

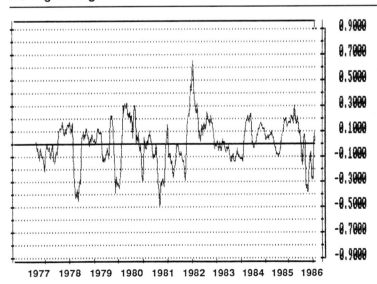

1977 1978 1979 1980 1981 1982 1983 1984 1985 1986

EXHIBIT A-27:

Total Equity for Arms' Ease of Movement Values, 1977 to 1986, Smoothed by 14-Week Simple Moving Average

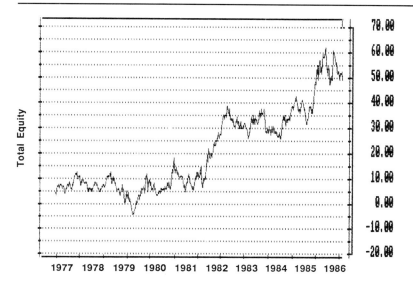

EXHIBIT A-28:
Profit Summary for Arms' Ease of Movement Values, 1977 to 1986, Smoothed by 14-Week Simple Moving Average

Item		Long	Short	Net
		— Per Trade Ranges —		
Per Trade Ranges				
Best Trade	(Closed position yielding maximum P/L)	26.61	5.10	26.61
.. Date		830812	811218	830812
Worst Trade	(Closed position yielding minimum P/L)	-4.46	-5.87	-5.87
.. Date		820115	851115	851115
Max Open P/L	(Maximum P/L occurring in an open position)	31.59	12.01	31.59
.. Date		830624	810925	830624
Min Open P/L	(Minimum P/L occurring in an open position)	-2.52	-5.17	-5.17
.. Date		861231	800613	800613
		— Overall Ranges —		
Overall Ranges				
Max P/L	(Maximum P/L from all closed positions during the run)	53.58	52.17	53.58
.. Date		860718	861219	860718
Min P/L	(Minimum P/L from all closed positions during the run)	0.59	-3.65	-3.65
.. Date		800307	800620	800620
Max Equity	(Maximum P/L from all closed and open positions)	61.90	60.46	61.90
.. Date		860704	860912	860704
Min Equity	(Minimum P/L from all closed and open positions)	-3.65	-4.58	-4.58
.. Date		800620	800613	800613
		— Statistics —		
Statistics				
Periods	(The number of periods in each position and entire run)	276	233	509
Trades	(The number of trades in each position and entire run)	19	19	38
# Profitable	(The number of profitable trades...)	13	7	20
# Losing	(The number of unprofitable trades...)	6	12	18
% Profitable	(The percent of profitable trades to total trades)	68.42	36.84	52.63
% Losing	(The percent of unprofitable trades to total trades)	31.58	63.16	47.37
		— Results —		
Results				
Commission	(Total commission deducted from closed trades)	0.00	0.00	0.00
Slippage	(Total slippage deducted from closed trades)	0.00	0.00	0.00
Gross P/L	(Total points gained in closed positions)	69.14	-16.97	52.17
Open P/L	(P/L in a position which remains open at the end)	-2.52	-0.00	-2.52
P/L	(Net P/L: Gross P/L less Commission and Slippage)	69.14	-16.97	52.17
Equity	(Net P/L plus Open P/L at the end of the run)	66.62	-16.97	49.65

There are columns for Long trades, Short trades and Net. In the Long column, results are reported only for Long positions. In the Short column, results are reported for Short positions only. In the Net column for the "Per Trade Ranges" and "Overall Ranges," entries will be the extreme from either the Long or Short column. Net column entries for the "Statistics" and "Results" categories are the combined results of entries in the Long and Short columns.

EXHIBIT A-29:

New York Stock Exchange Composite Price Index Weekly High and Low from January 5, 1968 to September 30, 1977

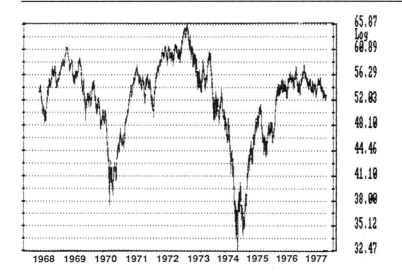

EXHIBIT A-30:

Arms' Ease of Movement Values, 1968 to 1977, Smoothed by 14-Week Simple Moving Average

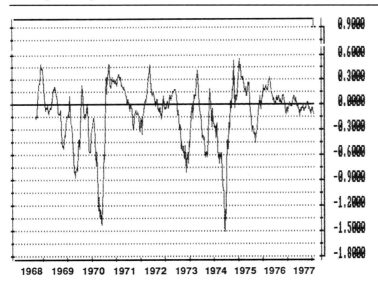

EXHIBIT A-31:

Total Equity for Arms' Ease of Movement Values, 1968 to 1977, Smoothed by 14-Week Simple Moving Average

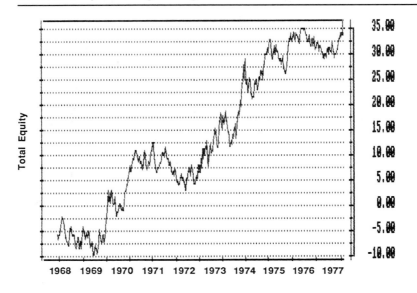

EXHIBIT A-32:

Profit Summary for Arms' Ease of Movement Values, 1968 to 1977, Smoothed by 14-Week Simple Moving Average

Item		Long	Short	Net
		Per Trade Ranges		
Per Trade Ranges				
Best Trade	(Closed position yielding maximum P/L)	10.15	13.08	13.08
..Date		710618	741129	741129
Worst Trade	(Closed position yielding minimum P/L)	-2.97	-3.49	-3.49
..Date		740329	681101	681101
Max Open P/L	(Maximum P/L occurring in an open position)	12.84	17.31	17.31
..Date		710423	741004	741004
Min Open P/L	(Minimum P/L occurring in an open position)	-2.70	-4.45	-4.45
..Date		770225	681018	681018
		Overall Ranges		
Overall Ranges				
Max P/L	(Maximum P/L from all closed positions during the run)	33.77	32.35	33.77
..Date		760827	760903	760827
Min P/L	(Minimum P/L from all closed positions during the run)	-9.79	-7.83	-9.79
..Date		691128	691031	691128
Max Equity	(Maximum P/L from all closed and open positions)	35.60	34.59	35.60
..Date		760709	770923	760709
Min Equity	(Minimum P/L from all closed and open positions)	-9.60	-9.79	-9.79
..Date		691121	691128	691128
		Statistics		
Statistics				
Periods	(The number of periods in each position and entire run)	224	285	509
Trades	(The number of trades in each position and entire run)	21	21	42
# Profitable	(The number of profitable trades...)	9	8	17
# Losing	(The number of unprofitable trades...)	12	13	25
% Profitable	(The percent of profitable trades to total trades)	42.86	38.10	40.48
% Losing	(The percent of unprofitable trades to total trades)	57.14	61.90	59.52
		Results		
Results				
Commission	(Total commission deducted from closed trades)	0.00	0.00	0.00
Slippage	(Total slippage deducted from closed trades)	0.00	0.00	0.00
Gross P/L	(Total points gained in closed positions)	16.53	14.42	30.95
Open P/L	(P/L in a position which remains open at the end)	0.00	2.90	2.90
P/L	(Net P/L: Gross P/L less Commission and Slippage)	16.53	14.42	30.95
Equity	(Net P/L plus Open P/L at the end of the run)	16.53	17.32	33.85

There are columns for Long trades, Short trades and Net. In the Long column, results are reported only for Long positions. In the Short column, results are reported for Short positions only. In the Net column for the "Per Trade Ranges" and "Overall Ranges," entries will be the extreme from either the Long or Short column. Net column entries for the "Statistics" and "Results" categories are the combined results of entries in the Long and Short columns.

97

ARMS' SHORT-TERM TRADING INDEX

Arms' Short-Term Trading Index was developed by Richard W. Arms, Jr. (Eppler, Guerin, Turner, 1650 University Boulevard N.E., Suite 300, Albequerque, NM 87102). It is also commonly referred to by its quote machine symbols, TRIN and MKDS. Arms' Index is calculated by dividing the ratio of the number of advancing issues to the number of declining issues by the ratio of the volume of advancing issues to the volume of declining issues. Daily NYSE data is used in the calculation.

Arms' Index is designed to measure the relative strength of the volume associated with advancing stocks versus that of declining stocks. If more volume goes into advancing stocks than declining stocks, Arms' Index will fall to a low level under 1.00. Alternatively, if more volume flows into declining stocks than advancing stocks, Arms' Index will rise to a high level over 1.00.

We tested Arms' Index for the period of January 1928 to March 1987 on a daily basis. In addition, we applied a 10-period simple moving average to the daily readings to smooth out erratic movements. The results are shown in Exhibits A-33 and A-34 (pages 99–100).

The test process was as follows. The indicator readings for the test period were divided into 20 ranges with approximately the same number of occurrences in each range. For each reading in a range, the gain or loss in four subsequent time periods (1 month later, 3 months later, 6 months later, and 12 months later) was calculated. The combined results for readings within each range were statistically compared, using chi-squared tests, to the performance of the overall market (as measured by the Standard & Poor's 500). Varying degrees of bullishness and bearishness were noted on the basis of that comparison.

Our results reveal a slight bullish tendency for up to 3 months after a daily Arms' Index reading of .523 or lower. When the indicator is smoothed using a 10-day simple moving average, bullish tendencies were also identified at extreme high readings (greater than 1.266) for time frames of 3 to 12 months after such readings. Low levels appeared insignificant.

Many other studies have been performed on Arms' Index with various conclusions. Based on our research and that of others, we can only conclude that Arms' Index has relatively limited forecasting value for stock prices.

One variation of Arms' Index that many technicians monitor is the Open 10 TRIN. It is also known as the Open 10 Trading Index. It is calculated by dividing a ratio of a 10-day total of the number of advancing issues to a 10-day total of the number of declining issues by a ratio of a 10-day total of the

EXHIBIT A-33:
Interpretation of the Arms' Index's Daily Readings

```
=========================================================================================
TRIN - DAILY DATA
PERIOD ANALYZED: MAY 1964 TO MARCH 1987
=========================================================================================

   INDICATOR RANGE              INTERPRETATION GIVEN INVESTOR'S TIME FRAME
------------------- ---------------------------------------------------------------------

            LESS
GREATER   THAN OR
 THAN    EQUAL TO    1 MONTH         3 MONTHS          6 MONTHS         12 MONTHS
-------  --------  ---------------  ----------------  ----------------  ----------------

 0.000    0.523    SLIGHTLY BULLISH  SLIGHTLY BULLISH  BULLISH          BULLISH
 0.523    0.586    NEUTRAL          NEUTRAL           NEUTRAL          NEUTRAL
 0.586    0.638    NEUTRAL          NEUTRAL           NEUTRAL          NEUTRAL
 0.638    0.679    NEUTRAL          NEUTRAL           NEUTRAL          NEUTRAL
 0.679    0.717    NEUTRAL          NEUTRAL           NEUTRAL          NEUTRAL
 0.717    0.753    NEUTRAL          NEUTRAL           NEUTRAL          NEUTRAL
 0.753    0.788    NEUTRAL          NEUTRAL           NEUTRAL          NEUTRAL
 0.788    0.821    NEUTRAL          NEUTRAL           NEUTRAL          NEUTRAL
 0.821    0.861    NEUTRAL          NEUTRAL           NEUTRAL          NEUTRAL
 0.861    0.898    NEUTRAL          NEUTRAL           NEUTRAL          NEUTRAL
 0.898    0.935    NEUTRAL          NEUTRAL           NEUTRAL          NEUTRAL
 0.935    0.981    NEUTRAL          NEUTRAL           NEUTRAL          SLIGHTLY BEARISH
 0.981    1.026    NEUTRAL          NEUTRAL           NEUTRAL          NEUTRAL
 1.026    1.081    NEUTRAL          BEARISH           NEUTRAL          NEUTRAL
 1.081    1.139    NEUTRAL          NEUTRAL           NEUTRAL          NEUTRAL
 1.139    1.215    NEUTRAL          NEUTRAL           NEUTRAL          NEUTRAL
 1.215    1.311    NEUTRAL          NEUTRAL           NEUTRAL          NEUTRAL
 1.311    1.444    NEUTRAL          NEUTRAL           NEUTRAL          NEUTRAL
 1.444    1.666    NEUTRAL          NEUTRAL           NEUTRAL          BULLISH
 1.666    4.453    NEUTRAL          SLIGHTLY BULLISH  NEUTRAL          BULLISH

=========================================================================================
```

Definitions of Very Bullish, Bullish, Slightly Bullish, Neutral, Slightly Bearish,
Bearish, and Very Bearish are provided in Appendix A.

volume of advancing issues to a 10-day total of the volume of declining issues. In addition, a 30-day version of the Open 10 TRIN is frequently used.

The Open 10 TRIN and Open 30 TRIN are displayed in Exhibit A-35 (page 101). High readings reflect an oversold condition and are generally considered bullish. Low readings reflect an overbought condition and are generally deemed bearish.

EXHIBIT A-34:
Interpretation of the Arms' Index's 10-Day Simple Moving Average Readings

```
===============================================================================================
TRIN - 10 DAY MOVING AVERAGE
PERIOD ANALYZED:  MAY 1964 TO MARCH 1987
===============================================================================================
```

INDICATOR RANGE		INTERPRETATION GIVEN INVESTOR'S TIME FRAME			
GREATER THAN	LESS THAN OR EQUAL TO	1 MONTH	3 MONTHS	6 MONTHS	12 MONTHS
0.000	0.760	NEUTRAL	SLIGHTLY BULLISH	NEUTRAL	SLIGHTLY BEARISH
0.760	0.793	NEUTRAL	BEARISH	NEUTRAL	SLIGHTLY BEARISH
0.793	0.819	NEUTRAL	SLIGHTLY BEARISH	NEUTRAL	NEUTRAL
0.819	0.839	NEUTRAL	SLIGHTLY BEARISH	NEUTRAL	NEUTRAL
0.839	0.858	NEUTRAL	NEUTRAL	NEUTRAL	SLIGHTLY BEARISH
0.858	0.877	NEUTRAL	NEUTRAL	NEUTRAL	NEUTRAL
0.877	0.894	NEUTRAL	NEUTRAL	NEUTRAL	NEUTRAL
0.894	0.913	NEUTRAL	NEUTRAL	NEUTRAL	NEUTRAL
0.913	0.930	NEUTRAL	NEUTRAL	NEUTRAL	NEUTRAL
0.930	0.947	NEUTRAL	SLIGHTLY BEARISH	NEUTRAL	NEUTRAL
0.947	0.966	NEUTRAL	SLIGHTLY BULLISH	SLIGHTLY BULLISH	NEUTRAL
0.966	0.986	NEUTRAL	NEUTRAL	NEUTRAL	NEUTRAL
0.986	1.009	NEUTRAL	SLIGHTLY BEARISH	NEUTRAL	NEUTRAL
1.009	1.036	NEUTRAL	NEUTRAL	NEUTRAL	NEUTRAL
1.036	1.064	NEUTRAL	NEUTRAL	NEUTRAL	NEUTRAL
1.064	1.094	SLIGHTLY BULLISH	NEUTRAL	NEUTRAL	NEUTRAL
1.094	1.136	NEUTRAL	NEUTRAL	SLIGHTLY BEARISH	NEUTRAL
1.136	1.192	NEUTRAL	NEUTRAL	NEUTRAL	NEUTRAL
1.192	1.266	NEUTRAL	NEUTRAL	NEUTRAL	SLIGHTLY BULLISH
1.266	1.760	NEUTRAL	VERY BULLISH	SLIGHTLY BULLISH	VERY BULLISH

```
===============================================================================================
```

Definitions of Very Bullish, Bullish, Slightly Bullish, Neutral, Slightly Bearish, Bearish, and Very Bearish are provided in Appendix A.

In view of the limited significance of the standard Arms' Index readings, we did not test the Open 10 TRIN or the Open 30 TRIN. We therefore reserve judgment on their effectiveness in market timing.

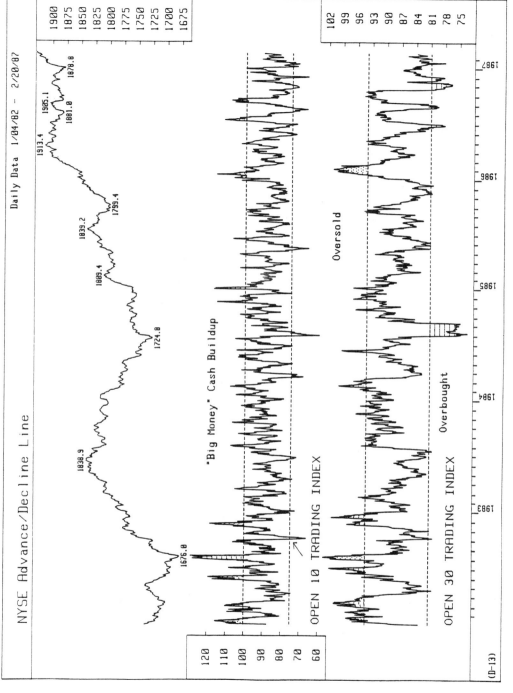

NYSE Advance/Decline Line

Daily Data 1/04/82 - 2/20/87

"Big Money" Cash Buildup

OPEN 10 TRADING INDEX

Oversold

Overbought

OPEN 30 TRADING INDEX

(D-13)

Source: By Permission of Ned Davis Research, Inc.

101

BOLTON-TREMBLAY INDICATOR

The Bolton-Tremblay Indicator is a cumulative advance-decline indicator that uses the number of unchanged issues as a basic component. It is computed in five steps. First, divide the number of advancing issues by the number of unchanged issues. Second, divide the number of declining issues by the number of unchanged issues. Third, subtract the declining ratio from the advancing ratio. Fourth, calculate the square root of the difference. Fifth, add the square root to the previous day's Bolton-Tremblay Indicator, respecting the sign (plus if there were more advances, minus if more declines).

For example, if there are 1400 advancing issues, 600 declining issues, and 200 unchanged issues, the Bolton-Tremblay Indicator is calculated as follows:

$$\text{Today's Bolton-Tremblay Indicator} =$$
$$\text{Yesterday's Bolton-Tremblay Indicator}$$
$$+ \text{ Square Root of } (1400/200 - 600/200)$$
$$= \text{Yesterday's Bolton-Tremblay Indicator } + 2$$

If, on the other hand, there are 600 advancing issues, 1400 declining issues, and 200 unchanged issues, today's Bolton-Tremblay Indicator equals yesterday's indicator value minus 2.

As with many cumulative indicators, you can begin calculating the Bolton-Tremblay Indicator at any point in time. Use a positive starting value (for example, 1000) to avoid having to chart negative numbers.

The Bolton-Tremblay Indicator can be charted and interpreted in a manner similar to the Advance-Decline Line. In interpretation, technical analysts commonly focus on divergences from a market index, such as the Dow Jones Industrial Average, to identify trend changes and underlying strength or weakness in the market. Keep in mind that the actual value of the indicator is less important than its trend.

BREADTH ADVANCE/DECLINE INDICATOR

The Breadth Advance/Decline Indicator was developed by Martin Zweig (The Zweig Forecast, P.O. Box 5345, New York, NY 10150).[*] It is calculated by

---

*Reprinted with permission.

taking a 10-day simple moving average of the number of advancing issues divided by the number of advancing issues plus the number of declining issues. NYSE data is normally used in the calculation.

We tested the Breadth Advance/Decline Indicator for the period of January 1928 to March 1987. The results are shown in Exhibit B-1.

The test process was as follows. The indicator readings for the test period were divided into 20 ranges with approximately the same number of

EXHIBIT B-1:
Interpretation of Breadth Advance/Decline Indicator Readings

```
=====================================================================================================
BREADTH THRUST - 10 DAY MOVING AVERAGE
PERIOD ANALYZED:  JANUARY 1928 TO MARCH 1987
=====================================================================================================
```

INDICATOR RANGE		INTERPRETATION GIVEN INVESTOR'S TIME FRAME			
GREATER THAN	LESS THAN OR EQUAL TO	1 MONTH	3 MONTHS	6 MONTHS	12 MONTHS
0.000	0.367	VERY BEARISH	VERY BEARISH	VERY BEARISH	VERY BEARISH
0.367	0.401	NEUTRAL	SLIGHTLY BEARISH	SLIGHTLY BEARISH	NEUTRAL
0.401	0.423	NEUTRAL	BEARISH	SLIGHTLY BEARISH	NEUTRAL
0.423	0.441	NEUTRAL	NEUTRAL	BEARISH	NEUTRAL
0.441	0.455	SLIGHTLY BEARISH	NEUTRAL	VERY BEARISH	SLIGHTLY BEARISH
0.455	0.467	NEUTRAL	SLIGHTLY BEARISH	NEUTRAL	NEUTRAL
0.467	0.478	NEUTRAL	NEUTRAL	NEUTRAL	NEUTRAL
0.478	0.488	NEUTRAL	NEUTRAL	NEUTRAL	NEUTRAL
0.488	0.497	VERY BEARISH	NEUTRAL	NEUTRAL	SLIGHTLY BEARISH
0.497	0.512	NEUTRAL	NEUTRAL	NEUTRAL	SLIGHTLY BEARISH
0.512	0.520	NEUTRAL	NEUTRAL	NEUTRAL	NEUTRAL
0.520	0.529	NEUTRAL	NEUTRAL	NEUTRAL	NEUTRAL
0.529	0.538	NEUTRAL	NEUTRAL	NEUTRAL	NEUTRAL
0.538	0.548	SLIGHTLY BULLISH	NEUTRAL	NEUTRAL	NEUTRAL
0.548	0.558	NEUTRAL	NEUTRAL	BULLISH	SLIGHTLY BULLISH
0.558	0.570	NEUTRAL	SLIGHTLY BULLISH	VERY BULLISH	SLIGHTLY BULLISH
0.570	0.584	VERY BULLISH	BULLISH	SLIGHTLY BULLISH	SLIGHTLY BULLISH
0.584	0.602	SLIGHTLY BULLISH	SLIGHTLY BULLISH	VERY BULLISH	BULLISH
0.602	0.639	VERY BULLISH	VERY BULLISH	VERY BULLISH	VERY BULLISH
0.639	0.795	VERY BULLISH	BULLISH	NEUTRAL	NEUTRAL

```
=====================================================================================================
```

Definitions of Very Bullish, Bullish, Slightly Bullish, Neutral, Slightly Bearish, Bearish, and Very Bearish are provided in Appendix A.

occurrences in each range. For each reading in a range, the gain or loss in four subsequent time periods (1 month later, 3 months later, 6 months later, and 12 months later) was calculated. The combined results for readings within each range were statistically compared, using chi-squared tests, to the performance of the overall market (as measured by the Standard & Poor's 500). Varying degrees of bullishness and bearishness were noted on the basis of that comparison.

The results show a very bullish tendency at high readings. In particular, readings of .66 or greater have produced significant gains with very few losses since the 1930s. Exhibit B-2 shows the results for the period of 1949 to 1986. As noted, an average gain occurred in the overall market (as measured by the S&P 500) of 3.55% 1 month later, 9.10% 3 months later, 15.06% 6 months later, and 22.13% 12 months later. You should note that all signals generated within 3 months of the initial reading of .66 or greater were considered repeat signals and are not included in the results. In addition, readings of .367 or lower were very bearish.

EXHIBIT B-2:

Breadth Advance/Decline Indicator Readings Equal to or Greater than 0.66 from 1949 to 1986

```
==================================================================
BREADTH THRUST - 10 DAY MOVING AVERAGE
==================================================================
```

		PERCENTAGE CHANGE IN S&P 500			
DATE	INDICATOR VALUE	1 MONTH LATER	3 MONTHS LATER	6 MONTHS LATER	12 MONTHS LATER
JUL 13 1949	0.67	3.45	7.78	14.07	12.92
NOV 20 1950	0.67	0.15	11.04	11.49	13.60
JAN 25 1954	0.67	-0.39	7.52	17.01	36.68
JAN 24 1958	0.67	-2.54	3.43	11.84	34.26
JUL 11 1962	0.67	-0.45	-0.92	12.09	21.06
NOV 9 1962	0.67	6.02	11.87	19.90	24.80
JAN 16 1967	0.67	4.58	8.02	10.01	14.36
DEC 4 1970	0.68	3.23	11.09	13.00	7.13
DEC 8 1971	0.66	6.76	12.42	11.07	21.32
JAN 10 1975	0.68	7.92	15.93	30.37	30.26
JAN 6 1976	0.67	8.96	10.67	10.70	14.40
AUG 24 1982	0.66	7.34	16.37	26.13	42.17
JAN 23 1985	0.66	1.16	3.03	8.05	14.77
AVERAGE CHANGE		3.55	9.10	15.06	22.13

```
==================================================================
```

CALL-PUT DOLLAR VALUE FLOW LINE

The Call-Put Dollar Value Flow Line is a longer term sentiment indicator developed by R. Bruce McCurtain, Chief Technical Analyst at Reid, Thunberg and Co. Inc., Westport, CT 06880. McCurtain first presented this idea in his article "Creating a Long-Term Indicator from Short-Term Statistics," *Futures*, Oster Communications, 219 Parkade, Cedar Falls, Iowa 50613, July 1986, pp. 62–63.

Using weekly data, as listed in *Barron's* and other newspapers, multiply the volume by the closing price for all Standard & Poor's 100 Index (OEX) call

EXHIBIT C-1:
Call-Put Dollar Value Flow Line

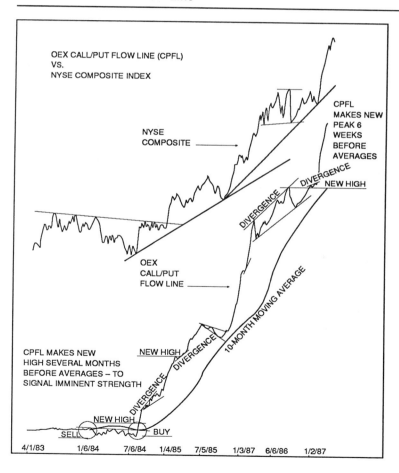

options traded on the Chicago Board Options Exchange. Sum these products to calculate *Call Dollar Value*. Next, multiply the volume by the closing price for all OEX puts. Then, sum these products to calculate *Put Dollar Value*. Subtract the Put Dollar Value from the Call Dollar Value. The resulting difference is called the *Weekly Net Call-Put Dollar Value*. Note that if Call Dollar Value is less than Put Dollar Value, the weekly Net Call-Put Dollar Value will carry a minus sign, signifying a negative number. Combine these Weekly Net Call-Put Dollar Values into a running total, which will rise when Call Dollar Value exceeds Put Dollar Value and will decline when Call Dollar Value is less than Put Dollar Value. Finally, calculate a 43-week simple moving average of this Cumulative Weekly Net Call-Put Dollar Value Flow Line (CPFL).

McCurtain's decision rule is simple: Buy when CPFL closes above its own 43-week simple moving average. Hold long until CPFL crosses under its own 43-week simple moving average, then sell and sell short.

This rule has a perfect record of accuracy in its short history since data became available in 1983. However, the data appears to have a strong upward bias and to be of little value for catching short-term trading moves.

CALL/PUT RATIO

The Call/Put Ratio is simply the inverse of the Put/Call Ratio. It is calculated by dividing the daily volume of call options by the daily volume of put options. Typically, volume statistics are taken from the Chicago Board Options Exchange (CBOE).

Interpretation of the Call/Put Ratio is based on the concept that option traders are usually wrong and, therefore, high readings are bearish and low readings are bullish. More detailed guidelines can be developed by referring to the section on the Put/Call Ratio and interpreting its signals in an opposite fashion. For example, if the Put/Call Ratio is considered bullish for a given range of values, the Call/Put Ratio should be interpreted as being bearish for that same range of values.

CHART PATTERN RECOGNITION (SHORT-TERM)

Back Trak PC software (MicroVest, P.O. Box 272, Macomb, IL 61455) is capable of testing simple pattern breakouts and/or trend reversal chart formations. Those are by nature different from the major trend-following indicator tools that fill most of these pages. Shorter-term chart patterns on the weekly charts appear to be more relevant to the swing trader than to the investor.

Shorter-term pattern trading requires the use of strict protective stops to protect capital and improve overall profitability. In all cases, a long-side protective sell stop just below the previous week's low and a short-side protective buy stop just above the previous week's high prove effective and improve results. All of the profit summary exhibits we present include those stops, except where specifically noted. Without stops, pattern trading not only is not worthwhile but, with most of the patterns, produces actual losses.

We tested numerous indicator patterns over a 19-year period of time using weekly data (consisting of high, low, close, and volume for each week) for the broad-based NYSE Composite Index. The period ran from January 5, 1968 through December 31, 1986. Note that test results provided in Exhibits C-2 through C-13 (pages 108–115) show profit and loss in cents rather than dollars.

The historical simulation results of trading the chart patterns were quite informative and even surprising. Some very popular chart formations did not test well under our assumptions. Others were quite effective. Note that some of these pattern recognition systems were out of the market much of the time, thus cutting their profitability potential. Also, a combination of these patterns might produce higher total profits than they produced separately, and this may be a fruitful area for further research.

PIVOT POINT REVERSE

Pivot points signal a change in direction. A top pivot point is characterized by a high that is higher than the previous high and higher than the next period's high. A bottom pivot point is characterized by a low that is lower than the previous low and lower than the next period's low. The Pivot Point Reverse system assumes that when one of these pivot points is formed, a reverse in direction will take place. When a top pivot point is formed, sell on the close.

EXHIBIT C-2:

Profit Summary for Pivot Point Reverse for New York Stock Exchange Composite Index Weekly Data from 1968 to 1986. (Enter Trades on Close; Exit Trades on Previous Period's High or Low Penetration)

Number Of Trades Made	> 387	Commissions Paid	> 0
Number Of Weeks In Market	> 835	Frequency Of Trades	> 0.85
Number Of Winning Trades	> 140	Largest Winning Trade	> 1245
Total Of Winning Trades	> 23431	Average Winning Trade	> 167
Number Of Losing Trades	> 239	Largest Losing Trade	> −487
Total Of Losing Trades	> −15780	Average Losing Trade	> −66
Largest Winning Streak	> 5	Largest Losing Streak	> 18
Win/Loss Ratio	> 0.59	Profit/Margin Ratio	> 3.83
Number Of Stops Hit	> 328	Stops Frequency	> 0.85
Largest Drawdown	> −2348	Largest Unrealized Loss	> −393
Largest Obtained Equity	> 9150	Number Of Tradeable Weeks	> 985
Short Profit Or Loss	> 3996	Long Profit Or Loss	> 3655
Total Profit Or Loss	> 7651	Average Weekly Gain/Loss	> 9.16

When a bottom pivot point is formed, buy on the close. As shown in Exhibit C-2, total profit of 76.51 NYSE points was below our standard of comparison (results derived by use of the 40-week simple moving average crossover rule). Nevertheless, it was fair for such a simple model.

PIVOT POINT CHANNELS

Pivot points are simply price-turning points thought to mark specific levels of support and resistance. A top or *resistance* pivot point is higher than the previous high and higher than the next period's high. The value of the middle highest high is resistance. A low or *support* pivot point is lower than the previous low and lower than the next period's low. By keeping track of the most recent upper and lower pivot points, we can easily construct a trading channel consisting of horizontal lines drawn to the right of the most recent pivots. Then, when prices break out above the most recent high pivot point, a resistance level has been penetrated—so we buy (go long). Conversely, when prices fall below the most recent low pivot point, a support area has been violated—so we sell and sell short.

We found that the minimum margin of resistance penetration or support violation of .001% maximized profits at 95.39 NYSE points, as shown in Exhibit C-3. Furthermore, results were optimized with a .75 point trailing stop from extreme high or low prices. As shown in Exhibit C-4, total profits of 125.16 NYSE points were relatively high among all the pattern recognition tests we conducted.

EXHIBIT C-3:

Profit Summary for Pivot Point Channel for New York Stock Exchange Composite Index Weekly Data from 1968 to 1986. (Enter Trades on Breakout Intraday; Exit Trades on Previous Period's High or Low Penetration)

Number Of Trades Made	> 213	Commissions Paid	> 0
Number Of Weeks In Market	> 763	Frequency Of Trades	> 0.79
Number Of Winning Trades	> 106	Largest Winning Trade	> 1097
Total Of Winning Trades	> 20553	Average Winning Trade	> 193
Number Of Losing Trades	> 105	Largest Losing Trade	> −557
Total Of Losing Trades	> −11014	Average Losing Trade	> −104
Largest Winning Streak	> 4	Largest Losing Streak	> 7
Win/Loss Ratio	> 1.01	Profit/Margin Ratio	> 4.77
Number Of Stops Hit	> 197	Stops Frequency	> 0.92
Largest Drawdown	> −1445	Largest Unrealized Loss	> −537
Largest Obtained Equity	> 10451	Number Of Tradeable Weeks	> 960
Short Profit Or Loss	> 1325	Long Profit Or Loss	> 8214
Total Profit Or Loss	> 9539	Average Weekly Gain/Loss	> 12.50

HEAD AND SHOULDERS REVERSAL PATTERN

A Head and Shoulders Top is defined simply as a series of three high price pivots with the second greater than the first and the third less than the second. You sell long positions and sell short on the third high pivot. A Head and Shoulders Bottom is defined as a series of three low price pivots, with the second lower than the first and the third higher than the second. You cover short positions and buy (long) on the third low pivot.

Computer testing the above definitions produced surprisingly low profits of only 8.85 NYSE points, as shown in Exhibit C-5. This may be due partially

EXHIBIT C-4:

Profit Summary for Pivot Point Channel for New York Stock Exchange Composite Index Weekly Data from 1968 to 1986. (Enter Trades on Breakout Intraday; Exit Trades on Touching 0.75 Trailing Stop from Extreme Price)

Number Of Trades Made	> 237	Commissions Paid	> 0
Number Of Weeks In Market	> 778	Frequency Of Trades	> 0.81
Number Of Winning Trades	> 130	Largest Winning Trade	> 822
Total Of Winning Trades	> 23312	Average Winning Trade	> 179
Number Of Losing Trades	> 107	Largest Losing Trade	> −453
Total Of Losing Trades	> −10796	Average Losing Trade	> −100
Largest Winning Streak	> 7	Largest Losing Streak	> 6
Win/Loss Ratio	> 1.21	Profit/Margin Ratio	> 6.26
Number Of Stops Hit	> 218	Stops Frequency	> 0.92
Largest Drawdown	> −1603	Largest Unrealized Loss	> −410
Largest Obtained Equity	> 12880	Number Of Tradeable Weeks	> 960
Short Profit Or Loss	> 2465	Long Profit Or Loss	> 10051
Total Profit Or Loss	> 12516	Average Weekly Gain/Loss	> 16.09

EXHIBIT C-5:
Profit Summary for Head and Shoulders Reversal Pattern for New York Stock Exchange Composite Index Weekly Data from 1968 to 1986. (Enter Trades on Close; Exit Trades on Previous Period's High or Low Penetration)

Number Of Trades Made	> 90	Commissions Paid	> 0
Number Of Weeks In Market	> 214	Frequency Of Trades	> 0.22
Number Of Winning Trades	> 31	Largest Winning Trade	> 700
Total Of Winning Trades	> 4964	Average Winning Trade	> 160
Number Of Losing Trades	> 58	Largest Losing Trade	> −309
Total Of Losing Trades	> −4079	Average Losing Trade	> −70
Largest Winning Streak	> 3	Largest Losing Streak	> 12
Win/Loss Ratio	> 0.53	Profit/Margin Ratio	> 0.44
Number Of Stops Hit	> 89	Stops Frequency	> 0.99
Largest Drawdown	> −1549	Largest Unrealized Loss	> −152
Largest Obtained Equity	> 1243	Number Of Tradeable Weeks	> 960
Short Profit Or Loss	> 328	Long Profit Or Loss	> 557
Total Profit Or Loss	> 885	Average Weekly Gain/Loss	> 4.14

to the oversimplicity of the definition. Many practicing technicians require that more conditions be met, such as symmetry of the pattern, neckline penetration, and volume confirmation (declining volume at tops and rising volume at bottoms).

KEY REVERSALS

Key Reversals are simple two-period chart patterns that are supposed to indicate turning points in the market. Bullish Key Reversals are characterized by a high that is higher than the previous high, a low that is lower than the previous low, and a close that is above the previous close. A bearish Key Reversal is characterized by a high that is higher than the previous high, a low that is lower than the previous low, and a close that is lower than the previous low.

The rationale for the Key Reversal is as follows: When highs are higher than their previous highs, bulls are extremely active and bullish. When lows are below the previous lows, bears are confident and active. The closing price will indicate whether the bulls or the bears have won the "tug of war." If the close is higher than the previous close, the bulls have won, indicating a pending upturn in the market. On the other hand, a lower close indicates that the bears have won, indicating a pending downturn in the market. Total profit of only 3.09 NYSE points from 1968 through 1986 (as shown in Exhibit C-6) for this popular pattern was surprisingly poor.

EXHIBIT C-6:

Profit Summary for Key Reversals for New York Stock Exchange Composite Index Weekly Data from 1968 to 1986. (Enter Trades on Close; Exit Trades on Previous Period's High or Low Penetration)

Number Of Trades Made	> 92	Commissions Paid	> 0
Number Of Weeks In Market	> 250	Frequency Of Trades	> 0.25
Number Of Winning Trades	> 39	Largest Winning Trade	> 944
Total Of Winning Trades	> 6502	Average Winning Trade	> 166
Number Of Losing Trades	> 53	Largest Losing Trade	> −331
Total Of Losing Trades	> −6193	Average Losing Trade	> −116
Largest Winning Streak	> 9	Largest Losing Streak	> 6
Win/Loss Ratio	> 0.74	Profit/Margin Ratio	> 0.15
Number Of Stops Hit	> 92	Stops Frequency	> 1.00
Largest Drawdown	> −2241	Largest Unrealized Loss	> −222
Largest Obtained Equity	> 1655	Number Of Tradeable Weeks	> 989
Short Profit Or Loss	> 914	Long Profit Or Loss	> −605
Total Profit Or Loss	> 309	Average Weekly Gain/Loss	> 1.24

BULL/BEAR HOOK REVERSALS

Bull/Bear Hooks are used to identify turning points in the market. A Bearish Hook is characterized by a higher high and lower close. A Bullish Hook is characterized by a lower low and a higher close.

The rationale for the Bearish Hook Reversal is this: The higher high indicates that bulls are extremely confident and active, but the lower close shows that their confidence withered as the week progressed. Since the bulls retreated as the closing bell approached, lower prices are assumed to be ahead. Opposite conditions explain the rationale for the Bullish Hook Reversals.

Exhibit C-7 shows that total profit of 87.24 NYSE points for the Hook Reversals was below our standard of comparison in our 19-year weekly data test. However, Exhibit C-8 shows that with an optimized stop requiring a 2.1% penetration of a simple 2-week moving average of the Friday closes, total profit jumped to an above-standard 107.00 NYSE points, and the average gain per week at .2202 points was quite high among our pattern recognition tests for this hook pattern, although it spent 51% of the time on the sidelines.

ISLAND REVERSAL

The Island Reversal is similar to a pivot point, but it also requires a gap. A bullish Island Reversal is characterized by a high that is lower than the previous low and lower than the subsequent low. A bearish Island Reversal

EXHIBIT C-7:

Profit Summary for Hook Reversals for New York Stock Exchange Composite Index Weekly Data from 1968 to 1986. (Enter Trades on Close; Exit Trades on Previous Period's High or Low Penetration)

Number Of Trades Made	> 253	Commissions Paid	> 0
Number Of Weeks In Market	> 585	Frequency Of Trades	> 0.59
Number Of Winning Trades	> 111	Largest Winning Trade	> 1040
Total Of Winning Trades	> 20865	Average Winning Trade	> 187
Number Of Losing Trades	> 142	Largest Losing Trade	> -331
Total Of Losing Trades	> -12141	Average Losing Trade	> -85
Largest Winning Streak	> 5	Largest Losing Streak	> 7
Win/Loss Ratio	> 0.78	Profit/Margin Ratio	> 4.36
Number Of Stops Hit	> 172	Stops Frequency	> 0.68
Largest Drawdown	> -1823	Largest Unrealized Loss	> -249
Largest Obtained Equity	> 8957	Number Of Tradeable Weeks	> 989
Short Profit Or Loss	> 5266	Long Profit Or Loss	> 3458
Total Profit Or Loss	> 8724	Average Weekly Gain/Loss	> 14.91

is characterized by a low that is higher than the previous high and higher than the subsequent high. There was only one Island Reversal in our 19-year weekly database. It produced a small loss of .10 NYSE points, as shown in Exhibit C-9.

MODIFIED CLOVER METHOD

The Modified Clover Method is used to identify new trends. The system consists of identifying key highs and lows and taking long and short positions when current prices surpass these highs and lows.

EXHIBIT C-8:

Profit Summary for Hook Reversals for New York Stock Exchange Composite Index Weekly Data from 1968 to 1986. (Enter Trades on Close; Exit Trades on a Stop 2.1% Either Side of a 2-Week Simple Moving Average of the Close)

Number Of Trades Made	> 252	Commissions Paid	> 0
Number Of Weeks In Market	> 486	Frequency Of Trades	> 0.49
Number Of Winning Trades	> 110	Largest Winning Trade	> 1040
Total Of Winning Trades	> 17383	Average Winning Trade	> 158
Number Of Losing Trades	> 142	Largest Losing Trade	> -174
Total Of Losing Trades	> -6683	Average Losing Trade	> -47
Largest Winning Streak	> 7	Largest Losing Streak	> 7
Win/Loss Ratio	> 0.77	Profit/Margin Ratio	> 5.35
Number Of Stops Hit	> 216	Stops Frequency	> 0.86
Largest Drawdown	> -825	Largest Unrealized Loss	> -138
Largest Obtained Equity	> 10812	Number Of Tradeable Weeks	> 989
Short Profit Or Loss	> 6091	Long Profit Or Loss	> 4609
Total Profit Or Loss	> 10700	Average Weekly Gain/Loss	> 22.02

EXHIBIT C-9:

Profit Summary for Island Reversals for New York Stock Exchange Composite Index Weekly Data from 1968 to 1986. (Enter Trades on Close; Exit Trades on Previous Period's High or Low Penetration)

Number Of Trades Made	> 1	Commissions Paid	> 0
Number Of Weeks In Market	> 1	Frequency Of Trades	> 0.00
Number Of Winning Trades	> 0	Largest Winning Trade	> 0
Total Of Winning Trades	> 0	Average Winning Trade	> 0
Number Of Losing Trades	> 1	Largest Losing Trade	> −10
Total Of Losing Trades	> −10	Average Losing Trade	> −10
Largest Winning Streak	> 0	Largest Losing Streak	> 1
Win/Loss Ratio	> 0.00	Profit/Margin Ratio	> −0.01
Number Of Stops Hit	> 1	Stops Frequency	> 1.00
Largest Drawdown	> −10	Largest Unrealized Loss	> 0
Largest Obtained Equity	> 0	Number Of Tradeable Weeks	> 989
Short Profit Or Loss	> −10	Long Profit Or Loss	> 0
Total Profit Or Loss	> −10	Average Weekly Gain/Loss	> −10.00

A key high is identified by a current high that is higher than the previous high and a current low that is higher than the previous low. A key low occurs when the current low is lower than the previous low and the current high is lower than the previous high.

A buy signal is generated when the current price rises above the last key high. A sell signal is generated when the current price falls below the last key low.

As shown in Exhibit C-10, 19-year total profits at 58.97 NYSE points were below our standard of comparison, and only 40% of the 250 total trades were profitable.

EXHIBIT C-10:

Profit Summary for Modified Clover for New York Stock Exchange Composite Index Weekly Data from 1968 to 1986. (Enter Trades on Close; Exit Trades on Previous Period's High or Low Penetration)

Number Of Trades Made	> 250	Commissions Paid	> 0
Number Of Weeks In Market	> 630	Frequency Of Trades	> 0.64
Number Of Winning Trades	> 100	Largest Winning Trade	> 1087
Total Of Winning Trades	> 16402	Average Winning Trade	> 164
Number Of Losing Trades	> 145	Largest Losing Trade	> −393
Total Of Losing Trades	> −10505	Average Losing Trade	> −72
Largest Winning Streak	> 10	Largest Losing Streak	> 8
Win/Loss Ratio	> 0.69	Profit/Margin Ratio	> 2.95
Number Of Stops Hit	> 245	Stops Frequency	> 0.98
Largest Drawdown	> −1651	Largest Unrealized Loss	> −393
Largest Obtained Equity	> 7089	Number Of Tradeable Weeks	> 989
Short Profit Or Loss	> 1265	Long Profit Or Loss	> 4632
Total Profit Or Loss	> 5897	Average Weekly Gain/Loss	> 9.36

RUNAWAY GAPS

A gap occurs when the current low is higher than the previous high, or the current high is lower than the previous low. The Runaway Gap is intended to signal future price movements in the direction of the gap itself. A gap between the previous high and the current low indicates that extreme strength is present and future price increases are likely. A gap between the current high and the previous low indicates that extreme weakness is present and prices are likely to fall further. As Exhibit C-11 shows, total profit of 37.40 NYSE points was not high, but profit per week of .1520 points was relatively good for this pattern, which was out of the market 75% of the time.

TWO-WEEK CLOSE PATTERN

When the current high is higher than the previous high and the close is higher than the midpoint of the weekly range for the second week in a row, a buy signal is generated. Opposite conditions indicate a sell signal. As Exhibit C-12 shows, total profits over the 19 years of 63.52 NYSE points were below our standard of comparison.

TRAILING REVERSE

The Trailing Reverse, used as a trend-following filter, is based on the observation that trends originating from a large countertrend movement tend to

EXHIBIT C-11:

Profit Summary for Runaway Gaps for New York Stock Exchange Composite Index Weekly Data from 1968 to 1986. (Enter Trades on Close; Exit Trades on Previous Period's High or Low Penetration)

Number Of Trades Made	> 91	Commissions Paid	> 0
Number Of Weeks In Market	> 246	Frequency Of Trades	> 0.25
Number Of Winning Trades	> 41	Largest Winning Trade	> 706
Total Of Winning Trades	> 6102	Average Winning Trade	> 148
Number Of Losing Trades	> 47	Largest Losing Trade	> −205
Total Of Losing Trades	> −2362	Average Losing Trade	> −50
Largest Winning Streak	> 7	Largest Losing Streak	> 7
Win/Loss Ratio	> 0.87	Profit/Margin Ratio	> 1.87
Number Of Stops Hit	> 91	Stops Frequency	> 1.00
Largest Drawdown	> −686	Largest Unrealized Loss	> −143
Largest Obtained Equity	> 3904	Number Of Tradeable Weeks	> 989
Short Profit Or Loss	> 1510	Long Profit Or Loss	> 2230
Total Profit Or Loss	> 3740	Average Weekly Gain/Loss	> 15.20

EXHIBIT C-12:

Profit Summary for 2-Week Close Pattern for New York Stock Exchange Composite Index Weekly Data from 1968 to 1986. (Enter Trades on Close; Exit Trades on Previous Period's High or Low Penetration)

Number Of Trades Made	> 230	Commissions Paid	> 0
Number Of Weeks In Market	> 640	Frequency Of Trades	> 0.65
Number Of Winning Trades	> 99	Largest Winning Trade	> 1245
Total Of Winning Trades	> 17714	Average Winning Trade	> 178
Number Of Losing Trades	> 130	Largest Losing Trade	> −289
Total Of Losing Trades	> −11362	Average Losing Trade	> −87
Largest Winning Streak	> 8	Largest Losing Streak	> 7
Win/Loss Ratio	> 0.76	Profit/Margin Ratio	> 3.18
Number Of Stops Hit	> 229	Stops Frequency	> 1.00
Largest Drawdown	> −1476	Largest Unrealized Loss	> −206
Largest Obtained Equity	> 7397	Number Of Tradeable Weeks	> 989
Short Profit Or Loss	> 2630	Long Profit Or Loss	> 3722
Total Profit Or Loss	> 6352	Average Weekly Gain/Loss	> 9.93

persist. Prices moving X percent from the most favorable price in the trend indicate a reversal. For example, if we buy at 1540 and the next high reaches 1556, our most favorable price will become 1556. As new highs are made, they replace the most favorable price. A reversal is indicated when prices finally drop below X percent of the most favorable (highest) price. Reversal of a short position in a downtrending market is signaled when price finally rises X percent above the most favorable price, which in the case of a bearish short-selling position is the lowest price during the time duration of the short trade. The value of the X percent filter can be optimized with Back Trak

EXHIBIT C-13:

Profit Summary for Trailing Reverse at 1.6% from Most Favorable Extreme Price for New York Stock Exchange Composite Index Weekly Data from 1968 to 1986. (Enter Trades on Intraday Signal Price; Exit and Reverse Trades at Intraday Signal Price)

Number Of Trades Made	> 512	Commissions Paid	> 0
Number Of Weeks In Market	> 988	Frequency Of Trades	> 1.00
Number Of Winning Trades	> 285	Largest Winning Trade	> 1402
Total Of Winning Trades	> 49082	Average Winning Trade	> 172
Number Of Losing Trades	> 227	Largest Losing Trade	> −638
Total Of Losing Trades	> −21512	Average Losing Trade	> −94
Largest Winning Streak	> 16	Largest Losing Streak	> 5
Win/Loss Ratio	> 1.26	Profit/Margin Ratio	> 13.79
Number Of Stops Hit	> 0	Stops Frequency	> 0.00
Largest Drawdown	> −1343	Largest Unrealized Loss	> −645
Largest Obtained Equity	> 27876	Number Of Tradeable Weeks	> 989
Short Profit Or Loss	> 9395	Long Profit Or Loss	> 18175
Total Profit Or Loss	> 27570	Average Weekly Gain/Loss	> 27.90

software. Note that the Back Trak software requires that entry into and exit from trades be made at the indicator prices intraday, as with stop orders, rather than at the close. So test results may not be directly comparable to tests conducted with weekly closing prices only.

In our 19-year weekly NYSE tests, the optimal Trailing Reversal X percent was 1.6%, and the results were remarkable. As Exhibit C-13 (page 115) shows, 19-year total profits were outstanding at 275.70 NYSE points. Moreover, 55.66% of the 512 trades produced a profit. The largest equity drawdown (or loss string) was relatively low at 13.43 points. This trend-following indicator appears to warrant further study.

COMMODITY CHANNEL INDEX

Commodity Channel Index (CCI) is a price momentum indicator developed by Donald R. Lambert.[*] Despite the word *commodity* in the name, this price momentum indicator is equally applicable to stocks. Mathematically, the CCI formula is represented as:

$$CCI = (M - \overline{M}) \div (.015\overline{D})$$

where

M = 1/3 (H + L + C) or mean price for a period.
H = the highest price for a period.
L = the lowest price for a period.
C = the closing price for a period.
$\overline{M}$ = the n-period simple moving average of M.

$$\overline{D} = \frac{1}{n} \sum_{i=1}^{n} |M_i - \overline{M}|$$

$\overline{D}$ = the mean deviation of the absolute value of the difference between mean price and the simple moving average of mean prices.

CCI creates an index similar to a statistical standard score measuring the price excursions from the mean price as a statistical variation. It can be calculated in six steps:

1. Calculate each period's mean, the high plus low plus close divided by 3.

---

*Reprinted by permission.

2. Calculate the *n*-period simple moving average of these means.

3. From each period's mean price, subtract the *n*-period simple moving average of mean prices.

4. Compute the mean deviation, which is the sum of the absolute values of the differences (the differences between each period's mean price and the *n*-period simple moving average of those mean prices).

5. Multiply the mean deviations by .015.

6. The mean price − moving average differences respecting sign (from Step 3) are then divided by .015 times the mean deviations (from Step 5).

Most of the random fluctuations of the CCI are supposed to fall within a +100% to −100% channel. Movements beyond ±100% are supposed to be nonrandom and create trading opportunities. The trading rules are: Buy long when CCI rises above +100%, then sell long when CCI falls below +100%; sell short when CCI falls below −100%, then cover shorts when CCI rises above −100%.

We set out to find the optimal *n* time period for calculation, and we found it to be 90 weeks, as shown in Exhibits C-14 through C-17 (pages 117–122). We used Compu Trac software and two 9.75-year test periods of weekly data (consisting of high, low, close, and volume for each week) for the broad-

EXHIBIT C-14:

Profitability Chart for Commodity Channel Index (Simple Moving Average Period Lengths of 1 to 100 from 1977 to 1986)

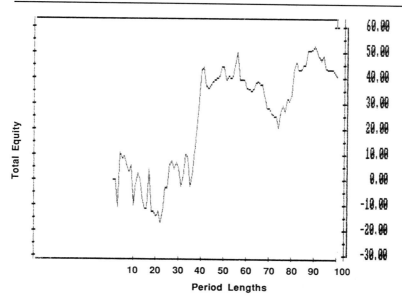

EXHIBIT C-15:

Profit Table for Commodity Channel Index (Simple Moving Average Period Lengths of 1 to 100 from 1977 to 1986)

Pass	Total Equity	Short Equity	Long Equity	Max. Equity	Min. Equity	P/L	Best Trade	Worst Trade	Max. Open P/L	Min. Open P/L
1	0.00	0.00	0.00	0.00	0.00	0.00	N/A	N/A	0.00	0.00
2	0.00	0.00	0.00	0.00	0.00	0.00	N/A	N/A	0.00	0.00
3	-10.87	-13.37	2.50	2.33	-12.76	-10.87	5.61	-5.40	3.99	0.00
4	10.67	-2.13	12.80	17.19	-13.88	10.67	8.61	-4.17	7.28	-0.19
5	9.03	-9.57	18.60	22.14	-5.45	9.03	8.40	-4.96	8.13	-1.13
6	9.54	-6.16	15.70	23.33	-2.77	9.54	8.40	-4.96	8.61	-1.37
7	5.38	-10.80	16.18	24.74	-2.82	5.38	8.63	-5.16	8.41	-1.82
8	3.26	-10.03	13.29	21.84	-5.87	3.26	8.29	-5.16	8.41	-2.06
9	5.76	-14.89	20.65	25.42	-5.18	5.76	10.07	-5.16	13.98	-2.06
10	-10.07	-27.22	17.15	14.95	-13.64	-10.07	10.07	-7.02	13.98	-1.82
11	-1.30	-25.15	23.85	23.16	-5.43	-1.30	10.07	-7.02	13.98	-1.82
12	2.32	-20.08	22.40	25.66	-3.48	2.32	10.07	-5.81	13.98	-1.82
13	0.13	-15.53	15.66	18.78	-8.42	0.13	8.68	-4.96	13.98	-1.98
14	-7.32	-19.03	11.71	22.41	-8.23	-7.32	9.56	-12.51	13.98	-1.98
15	-10.96	-25.07	14.11	15.76	-11.33	-10.96	8.58	-12.51	13.98	-1.98
16	-11.02	-30.45	19.43	15.13	-11.96	-11.02	8.58	-11.07	13.98	-1.82
17	4.63	-21.77	26.40	30.78	-5.36	4.63	12.09	-11.07	14.60	-1.98
18	-12.74	-29.55	16.81	9.69	-14.10	-12.74	12.51	-11.07	13.98	-1.82
19	-12.29	-28.96	16.67	10.14	-13.65	-12.29	12.51	-11.07	13.98	-2.89
20	-14.59	-27.75	13.16	10.08	-15.88	-14.59	11.68	-11.07	16.16	-2.89
21	-12.38	-27.24	14.86	12.29	-14.73	-12.38	11.68	-11.07	16.16	-2.89
22	-16.93	-30.16	13.23	7.74	-18.78	-16.93	11.68	-11.07	16.16	-2.89
23	-12.21	-28.73	16.52	10.30	-16.92	-12.21	11.68	-11.07	16.16	-2.89
24	-3.31	-24.33	21.02	19.20	-11.77	-3.31	11.71	-11.07	16.16	-1.80
25	-3.24	-23.95	20.71	20.74	-8.59	-3.24	11.71	-11.07	16.16	-1.80
26	6.35	-18.76	25.11	29.46	-4.49	6.35	13.26	-11.07	17.74	-1.80
27	7.33	-15.21	22.54	27.82	-3.09	7.33	14.99	-11.07	17.74	-1.80
28	4.37	-19.34	23.71	23.37	-8.11	4.37	14.99	-11.07	17.74	-1.80
29	6.80	-19.56	26.36	25.80	-5.01	6.80	14.99	-11.07	17.74	-2.26
30	4.67	-20.01	24.68	23.22	-7.65	4.67	14.99	-11.07	17.74	-2.26
31	-2.41	-16.69	14.28	18.30	-12.57	-2.41	14.99	-11.07	17.74	-1.80
32	1.48	-16.69	18.17	24.87	-8.97	1.48	22.50	-11.07	27.93	-1.80
33	9.71	-13.82	23.53	33.10	-8.16	9.71	22.50	-11.07	27.93	-2.89
34	8.86	-12.92	21.78	32.25	-7.88	8.86	22.50	-11.07	27.93	-2.89
35	-2.49	-17.55	15.06	19.16	-16.27	-2.49	22.50	-12.51	27.93	-2.89
36	2.14	-17.55	19.69	22.26	-13.17	2.14	22.50	-12.51	27.93	-2.89
37	11.10	-17.55	28.65	31.22	-9.01	11.10	22.50	-12.51	27.93	-2.89
38	20.65	-11.13	31.78	40.77	-9.01	20.65	22.50	-12.51	27.93	-1.52
39	31.54	-5.86	37.40	51.37	-5.80	31.54	27.57	-12.51	32.73	-1.52
40	43.42	-7.98	51.40	52.17	-5.84	43.42	27.57	-5.33	32.73	-1.52
41	44.37	-7.34	51.71	53.12	-5.75	44.37	27.57	-4.17	32.73	-1.52
42	36.80	-10.92	47.72	45.55	-5.83	36.80	27.57	-3.67	32.73	-1.66
43	36.12	-10.26	46.38	44.87	-6.49	36.12	27.57	-3.67	32.73	-1.66
44	36.75	-10.20	46.95	45.50	-6.91	36.75	27.57	-3.67	32.73	-1.66
45	38.94	-11.31	50.25	47.69	-6.81	38.94	27.57	-3.67	32.73	-1.66
46	39.46	-9.42	48.88	48.21	-6.84	39.46	27.57	-3.67	32.73	-1.98
47	39.79	-10.61	50.40	48.54	-7.36	39.79	27.57	-3.67	32.73	-1.98
48	40.60	-9.80	50.40	49.35	-6.55	40.60	27.57	-3.67	32.73	-1.98
49	44.08	-8.64	52.72	52.83	-6.38	44.08	27.57	-3.67	32.73	-1.98
50	44.54	-9.03	53.57	53.29	-5.92	44.54	27.57	-3.67	32.73	-1.98
51	39.28	-12.24	51.52	49.03	-6.97	39.28	24.41	-3.67	32.73	-2.79
52	40.64	-13.76	54.40	50.39	-6.04	40.64	24.41	-3.67	32.73	-3.00
53	39.91	-15.38	55.29	49.66	-6.04	39.91	24.41	-3.67	32.73	-2.46
54	40.62	-14.67	55.29	50.37	-6.04	40.62	24.41	-3.67	32.73	-1.41
55	45.69	-11.04	56.73	54.00	-4.91	45.69	24.41	-3.67	32.73	-1.41
56	50.29	-7.20	57.49	58.60	-6.18	50.29	24.41	-3.67	32.73	-1.28

EXHIBIT C-15: (continued)

Pass	Total Equity	Short Equity	Long Equity	Max. Equity	Min. Equity	P/L	Best Trade	Worst Trade	Max. Open P/L	Min. Open P/L
57	39.21	-7.20	46.41	58.60	-6.18	39.21	24.41	-11.07	32.73	-1.28
58	39.32	-7.09	46.41	58.71	-6.18	39.32	24.41	-11.07	32.73	-1.28
59	39.48	-7.09	46.57	58.87	-6.02	39.48	24.41	-11.07	32.73	-1.28
60	36.20	-7.09	43.29	55.59	-6.02	36.20	24.41	-11.07	32.73	-1.28
61	35.77	-7.24	43.01	55.16	-6.30	35.77	24.41	-11.07	32.73	-1.28
62	34.76	-9.53	44.29	54.15	-5.02	34.76	24.41	-11.07	32.73	-2.21
63	35.66	-9.53	45.19	55.05	-4.12	35.66	24.41	-11.07	32.73	-2.21
64	38.36	-9.53	47.89	57.75	-4.12	38.36	24.41	-11.07	32.73	-2.21
65	38.68	-9.13	47.81	56.41	-4.12	38.68	24.41	-9.41	32.73	-2.21
66	37.53	-9.13	46.66	55.26	-4.12	37.53	24.41	-9.41	32.73	-2.21
67	37.53	-9.13	46.66	55.26	-4.12	37.53	24.41	-9.41	32.73	-2.21
68	32.70	-12.29	44.99	50.43	-5.79	32.70	24.41	-9.41	32.73	-2.89
69	28.00	-14.83	42.83	45.73	-7.95	28.00	24.41	-9.41	32.73	-2.89
70	28.34	-13.79	42.13	47.13	-8.14	28.34	23.35	-9.41	32.73	-2.89
71	26.37	-13.40	39.77	45.16	-8.67	26.37	23.35	-9.41	32.73	-2.89
72	25.03	-14.58	39.61	43.82	-8.83	25.03	23.35	-9.41	32.73	-3.90
73	24.93	-15.00	39.93	43.72	-8.15	24.93	23.35	-9.41	32.73	-3.90
74	20.53	-15.00	35.53	39.32	-10.29	20.53	23.35	-9.41	32.73	-3.90
75	26.73	-12.11	38.84	45.52	-7.64	26.73	23.35	-9.41	32.73	-3.90
76	29.64	-10.64	40.28	48.43	-6.20	29.64	23.35	-9.41	32.73	-0.65
77	26.65	-12.50	39.15	45.44	-6.61	26.65	23.35	-9.41	32.73	-0.80
78	31.89	-8.60	40.49	50.68	-7.17	31.89	23.35	-9.41	32.73	-0.80
79	31.32	-8.60	39.92	50.11	-7.76	31.32	23.35	-9.41	32.73	-0.80
80	33.54	-10.55	44.09	52.33	-3.59	33.54	23.35	-9.41	32.73	-1.98
81	43.54	-3.53	47.07	62.33	-3.59	43.54	23.35	-9.41	32.73	-1.98
82	46.01	-3.53	49.54	63.68	-2.24	46.01	24.47	-9.41	32.73	-1.98
83	43.03	-3.53	46.56	60.70	-2.24	43.03	24.47	-9.41	32.73	-1.98
84	43.03	-3.53	46.56	60.70	-2.24	43.03	24.47	-9.41	32.73	-1.98
85	44.75	-1.81	46.56	62.42	-2.24	44.75	24.47	-9.41	32.73	-1.98
86	44.75	-1.81	46.56	62.42	-2.24	44.75	24.47	-9.41	32.73	-1.98
87	50.52	-1.81	52.33	63.03	-2.24	50.52	20.87	-1.71	33.38	-1.98
88	50.38	-4.04	54.42	62.89	-2.71	50.38	20.87	-2.61	33.38	-0.04
89	51.30	-4.04	55.34	63.81	-2.35	51.30	20.87	-2.61	33.38	-0.04
90	52.19	-4.04	56.23	64.70	-1.75	52.19	20.87	-2.61	33.38	0.00
91	50.93	-3.13	54.06	63.44	-1.75	50.93	20.87	-2.16	33.38	-2.73
92	47.88	-3.13	51.01	62.55	-2.39	47.88	20.87	-2.16	33.38	-2.73
93	47.10	-3.13	50.23	62.55	-2.39	47.10	20.87	-2.16	33.38	-2.73
94	48.49	-3.13	51.62	63.94	-2.39	48.49	22.26	-2.16	34.77	-2.73
95	43.66	-3.13	46.79	59.11	-2.34	43.66	22.26	-2.73	34.77	-3.69
96	42.92	-2.80	45.72	58.37	-2.34	42.92	22.26	-2.73	34.77	-3.69
97	42.92	-2.80	45.72	58.37	-2.34	42.92	22.26	-2.73	34.77	-3.69
98	42.92	-2.80	45.72	58.37	-2.34	42.92	22.26	-2.73	34.77	-3.69
99	41.97	-2.53	44.50	56.30	-2.03	41.97	22.26	-2.73	34.77	-3.69
100	40.47	-4.25	44.72	54.58	-3.14	40.47	22.26	-2.73	34.77	-3.69

Pass indicates period length.
Equity indicates the total number of points gained or lost.
Short equity indicates the number of points gained or lost on short positions.
Long equity indicates the number of points gained or lost on long positions.
Max. equity indicates the highest total profit recorded over the tested period.
Min. equity indicates the lowest total profit recorded over the tested period.
P/L indicates total number of points gained or lost in closed positions.
Best trade indicates the highest number of points gained in any closed trade.
Worst trade indicates the highest number of points lost in any closed trade.
Max. open P/L indicates the highest gain in a position which remains open at the end of the test run.
Min. open P/L indicates the highest loss in a position which remains open at the end of the test run.

EXHIBIT C-16:
Profitability Chart for Commodity Channel Index (Simple Moving Average Period Length
100 from 1968 to 1977)

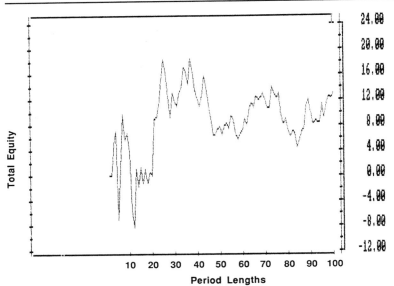

based NYSE Composite Index. The first period ran from January 5, 1968 through September 30, 1977, and the second period ran from April 8, 1977 through December 31, 1986. The overlap in data was necessary to facilitate testing of various moving averages throughout the full time period.

As shown in Exhibits C-18 through C-25 (pages 123–128), combined profits of 62.25 NYSE points were below our 40-week simple moving average crossover rule standard of comparison. The neutral band between $+100$ and -100 kept the system out of the market part of the time, particularly at some critical turning points. This caused CCI to miss the very early phases of new trends. These phases are often the most dynamic.

By relaxing the ±100 filter and using crossings of zero as the signal, the above problem was overcome. Reoptimizing the calculation period n for the zero crossover rule resulted in n equal to 53 weeks as an above standard, reasonably profitable (total profits of 98.85 NYSE points), and effective trading system. We call this new indicator Zero CCI. Test results are shown in Exhibits C-26 through C-33 (pages 129–134).

EXHIBIT C-17:

Profit Table for Commodity Channel Index (Simple Moving Average Period Lengths of 1 to 100 from 1968 to 1977)

Pass	Total Equity	Short Equity	Long Equity	Max. Equity	Min. Equity	P/L	Best Trade	Worst Trade	Max. Open P/L	Min. Open P/L
1	0.00	0.00	0.00	0.00	0.00	0.00	N/A	N/A	0.00	0.00
2	0.00	0.00	0.00	0.00	0.00	0.00	N/A	N/A	0.00	0.00
3	4.93	-2.05	6.98	19.87	0.00	4.93	4.22	-4.59	3.40	-0.14
4	6.91	-0.72	7.63	24.18	-0.35	6.91	6.26	-4.59	6.43	-0.02
5	-6.93	-10.87	3.94	22.44	-6.93	-6.93	6.26	-4.59	7.85	-0.42
6	1.25	-9.62	10.87	23.87	-0.51	1.25	6.89	-4.59	7.85	-0.42
7	9.87	-11.74	21.61	24.25	-0.04	9.87	6.89	-4.59	7.85	-2.00
8	5.86	-10.23	16.09	20.84	-0.04	5.86	6.89	-4.59	7.85	-2.00
9	6.80	-11.61	18.41	17.53	-0.04	6.80	5.80	-4.59	7.85	-2.00
10	3.67	-11.95	15.62	16.00	0.00	3.67	5.80	-4.59	7.85	-2.00
11	-5.41	-14.13	8.72	13.82	-5.41	-5.41	5.80	-4.59	7.85	-2.00
12	-8.34	-14.48	6.14	12.02	-8.91	-8.34	5.63	-4.59	7.85	-2.00
13	0.88	-8.84	9.72	11.05	-4.31	0.88	5.63	-2.15	7.85	-2.00
14	-1.64	-8.93	7.29	14.31	-2.45	-1.64	8.38	-2.75	12.97	-2.00
15	1.36	-7.84	9.20	14.57	-2.67	1.36	7.41	-2.75	12.00	-2.00
16	-1.17	-6.35	5.18	10.91	-5.35	-1.17	7.41	-2.97	12.00	-2.00
17	0.99	-2.97	3.96	12.06	-5.20	1.01	8.38	-2.97	12.97	-2.00
18	-1.13	-3.10	1.97	10.43	-5.12	-1.13	8.38	-2.40	12.97	-2.00
19	0.40	-5.95	6.35	12.46	-6.06	0.40	8.38	-2.21	12.97	-2.00
20	0.12	-5.70	5.82	11.20	-6.94	0.14	8.38	-2.21	12.97	-2.00
21	8.93	-1.93	10.86	19.98	-5.09	9.14	8.38	-2.39	12.97	-1.91
22	9.13	-3.00	12.13	20.67	-5.37	9.34	8.38	-2.39	12.97	-1.91
23	11.06	-0.96	12.02	22.93	-2.89	11.27	8.38	-1.59	12.97	-1.91
24	15.03	0.90	14.13	26.52	-1.24	15.24	8.38	-1.67	12.97	-1.50
25	18.29	2.07	16.22	28.46	0.00	18.50	8.38	-1.67	12.97	-1.50
26	16.59	1.27	15.32	26.05	-0.52	16.02	8.38	-1.66	12.97	-1.50
27	12.41	-3.42	15.83	21.17	-2.10	11.84	8.02	-1.73	12.97	-1.91
28	9.14	-4.16	13.30	18.13	-2.37	8.57	8.02	-2.31	12.97	-1.91
29	12.96	-3.61	16.57	21.95	-0.44	12.39	8.02	-2.31	12.97	-1.91
30	11.84	-3.97	15.81	21.32	-0.68	11.27	8.02	-2.64	12.97	-2.15
31	10.96	-4.53	15.49	19.96	-1.43	10.39	7.79	-2.64	12.97	-2.15
32	12.90	-2.95	15.85	22.01	-1.43	12.33	7.79	-2.15	12.97	-1.91
33	14.02	-2.20	16.22	22.76	-0.68	13.45	7.79	-2.15	12.97	-1.91
34	17.03	-1.14	18.17	23.40	-1.46	16.46	7.79	-2.15	12.97	-1.91
35	16.61	0.00	16.61	22.84	-0.88	16.04	7.79	-2.15	12.97	-1.91
36	14.51	-0.15	14.66	20.74	-1.35	13.94	7.79	-2.15	12.97	-1.91
37	18.53	3.00	15.53	24.76	-1.11	17.96	7.79	-2.15	12.97	-1.91
38	16.54	3.39	13.15	23.13	-1.11	15.97	7.79	-2.15	12.97	-1.91
39	13.44	3.39	10.05	20.86	-1.87	12.87	7.79	-2.15	12.97	-1.91
40	12.14	2.98	9.16	19.25	-2.29	11.57	7.79	-2.03	12.97	-1.91
41	10.93	1.77	9.16	18.13	-3.68	10.36	7.79	-2.03	12.97	-1.91
42	12.41	2.97	9.44	19.61	-3.67	11.84	8.80	-2.03	12.97	-1.91
43	15.87	3.55	12.32	20.85	-0.87	15.30	6.93	-2.03	12.97	-1.91
44	14.03	2.87	11.16	20.02	-1.39	13.46	6.93	-2.03	12.97	-1.91
45	11.15	0.25	10.90	16.70	-2.57	10.58	6.93	-2.08	12.97	-1.91
46	9.20	-1.03	10.23	15.50	-3.75	8.63	6.93	-2.08	12.97	-1.91
47	6.52	-2.34	8.86	13.01	-4.93	5.95	6.93	-2.66	12.97	-1.91
48	6.45	0.19	6.26	14.52	-4.23	5.88	6.93	-2.66	12.97	-1.91
49	7.59	1.51	6.08	16.04	-4.16	7.02	6.93	-2.66	12.97	-1.91
50	7.72	1.59	6.13	16.17	-3.50	7.15	6.93	-3.04	12.97	-1.91
51	6.46	-1.03	7.49	17.00	-2.56	5.89	6.24	-3.04	12.97	-1.91
52	8.00	1.75	6.25	17.34	-2.09	7.43	6.24	-2.94	12.97	-1.91
53	8.26	1.75	6.51	17.53	-2.09	7.69	6.24	-2.94	12.97	-1.91
54	7.41	2.27	5.14	16.68	-2.09	6.84	6.24	-1.96	12.97	-1.91
55	9.51	4.37	5.14	17.94	-2.09	8.94	6.24	-1.50	12.97	-1.91
56	8.85	4.37	4.48	17.92	-2.09	8.28	6.24	-1.50	12.97	-1.91

EXHIBIT C-17: (continued)

Pass	Total Equity	Short Equity	Long Equity	Max. Equity	Min. Equity	P/L	Best Trade	Worst Trade	Max. Open P/L	Min. Open P/L
57	6.49	3.40	3.09	16.95	-2.09	5.92	6.24	-1.73	12.97	-1.91
58	5.71	5.51	0.20	18.11	-2.09	5.14	10.58	-1.52	17.31	-1.91
59	6.66	5.84	0.82	18.29	-2.09	6.09	10.58	-1.52	17.31	-1.91
60	7.27	7.27	-0.00	19.72	-2.09	6.70	10.58	-1.52	17.31	-1.91
61	9.10	10.30	-1.20	19.72	-2.09	8.53	10.58	-1.52	17.31	-1.91
62	7.92	10.30	-2.38	18.54	-2.09	7.35	10.58	-1.52	17.31	-1.91
63	10.77	11.02	-0.25	21.39	-2.23	10.20	10.58	-1.81	17.31	-1.91
64	11.58	12.51	-0.93	20.71	-2.23	11.01	12.86	-1.81	17.31	-1.91
65	10.77	12.51	-1.74	20.13	-2.23	10.20	12.86	-2.75	17.31	-1.91
66	12.52	14.81	-2.29	21.78	-2.00	11.95	12.86	-2.75	17.31	-1.91
67	12.00	15.01	-3.01	21.26	-2.00	11.43	12.86	-2.75	17.31	-1.91
68	12.33	15.01	-2.68	21.26	-2.00	11.76	12.86	-2.75	17.31	-1.91
69	13.05	16.62	-3.57	21.55	-0.67	12.48	12.86	-2.75	17.31	-1.91
70	11.90	14.93	-3.03	21.62	-1.14	11.33	11.64	-2.75	17.31	-1.91
71	10.79	14.93	-4.14	20.34	-1.14	10.22	11.64	-2.58	17.31	-1.91
72	10.79	14.93	-4.14	20.34	-1.14	10.22	11.64	-2.58	17.31	-1.91
73	14.09	14.73	-0.64	19.29	-1.14	13.52	11.64	-3.40	17.31	-2.13
74	12.99	15.17	-2.18	18.01	-2.40	12.42	11.64	-3.40	17.31	-2.13
75	12.20	15.17	-2.97	17.22	-3.19	11.63	11.64	-3.40	17.31	-2.13
76	13.01	15.17	-2.16	18.03	-2.38	12.44	11.64	-3.40	17.31	-2.13
77	9.39	12.44	-3.05	14.14	-5.47	8.82	11.64	-3.40	17.31	-2.13
78	8.25	11.30	-3.05	13.00	-6.61	7.68	11.64	-3.40	17.31	-2.13
79	9.09	12.14	-3.05	13.84	-5.77	8.52	11.64	-3.40	17.31	-2.13
80	7.24	11.63	-4.39	12.77	-6.84	7.45	11.64	-3.40	17.31	-2.13
81	6.25	11.17	-4.92	12.31	-7.30	6.46	11.64	-3.40	17.31	-2.13
82	6.96	12.36	-5.40	13.50	-6.11	7.17	11.64	-3.40	17.31	-2.13
83	6.81	12.64	-5.83	13.78	-5.83	7.02	11.64	-3.40	17.31	-2.13
84	4.41	11.27	-6.86	11.38	-8.23	4.62	11.64	-3.50	17.31	-2.23
85	5.54	12.40	-6.86	12.51	-7.10	5.75	11.64	-3.50	17.31	-2.23
86	7.05	12.95	-5.90	13.31	-6.30	7.26	12.35	-2.53	17.31	-1.43
87	7.53	13.43	-5.90	14.38	-5.23	7.60	12.35	-2.53	17.31	-1.19
88	11.07	17.33	-6.26	17.19	-2.42	11.14	12.35	-2.53	17.31	-1.19
89	11.91	17.38	-5.47	17.98	-1.63	11.93	12.35	-2.53	17.31	-1.19
90	10.06	16.65	-6.59	17.25	-4.18	10.08	14.17	-3.15	19.13	-1.54
91	8.36	14.95	-6.59	17.25	-4.18	9.10	13.19	-3.15	19.13	-1.54
92	8.78	15.16	-6.38	17.46	-3.97	9.52	13.19	-3.15	19.13	-1.54
93	8.58	14.96	-6.38	17.26	-4.17	9.32	13.19	-2.53	19.13	-1.19
94	8.44	14.82	-6.38	16.38	-5.05	8.44	13.19	-2.53	19.13	-1.19
95	11.33	16.63	-5.30	17.72	-3.71	11.33	13.19	-2.53	19.13	-1.19
96	9.26	14.56	-5.30	17.72	-3.71	9.26	11.12	-2.53	19.13	-1.19
97	11.60	16.73	-5.13	20.06	-1.37	11.60	11.12	-1.52	19.13	-1.19
98	12.44	17.01	-4.57	19.95	-1.48	12.44	11.12	-1.52	19.13	-1.19
99	12.15	16.61	-4.46	19.66	-1.77	12.15	11.12	-1.52	19.13	-1.19
100	12.88	16.35	-3.47	20.39	-2.19	12.88	14.57	-1.76	22.58	-1.19

Pass indicates period length.

Equity indicates the total number of points gained or lost.

Short equity indicates the number of points gained or lost on short positions.

Long equity indicates the number of points gained or lost on long positions.

Max. equity indicates the highest total profit recorded over the tested period.

Min. equity indicates the lowest total profit recorded over the tested period.

P/L indicates total number of points gained or lost in closed positions.

Best trade indicates the highest number of points gained in any closed trade.

Worst trade indicates the highest number of points lost in any closed trade.

Max. open P/L indicates the highest gain in a position which remains open at the end of the test run.

Min. open P/L indicates the highest loss in a position which remains open at the end of the test run.

EXHIBIT C-18:

New York Stock Exchange Composite Price Index Weekly High and Low from April 8, 1977 to December 31, 1986

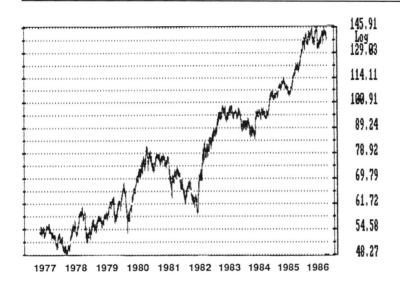

EXHIBIT C-19:

Commodity Channel Index, 1977 to 1986, Smoothed by 90-Week Simple Moving Average

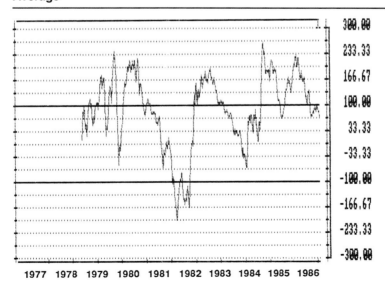

EXHIBIT C-20:

Total Equity for Commodity Channel Index, 1977 to 1986, Smoothed by 90-Week Simple Moving Average

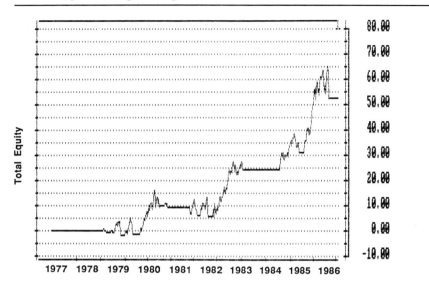

EXHIBIT C-21:

Profit Summary for Commodity Channel Index, 1977 to 1986, Smoothed by 90-Week Simple Moving Average

Item	Long	Short	Net
	--- Per Trade Ranges ---		
Per Trade Ranges			
Best Trade (Closed position yielding maximum P/L)	20.87	-0.46	20.87
..Date	860912	820423	860912
Worst Trade (Closed position yielding minimum P/L)	-1.11	-2.61	-2.61
..Date	791019	820129	820129
Max Open P/L (Maximum P/L occurring in an open position)	33.38	6.72	33.38
..Date	860829	820813	860829
Min Open P/L (Minimum P/L occurring in an open position)	0.00	0.00	0.00
..Date	770408	820122	770408
Overall Ranges	--- Overall Ranges ---		
Max P/L (Maximum P/L from all closed positions during the run)	52.19	6.94	52.19
..Date	860912	820129	860912
Min P/L (Minimum P/L from all closed positions during the run)	-1.75	5.51	-1.75
..Date	791019	820827	791019
Max Equity (Maximum P/L from all closed and open positions)	64.70	13.20	64.70
..Date	860829	820813	860829
Min Equity (Minimum P/L from all closed and open positions)	-1.75	5.51	-1.75
..Date	791019	820827	791019
Statistics	--- Statistics ---		
Periods (The number of periods in each position and entire run)	311	26	509
Trades (The number of trades in each position and entire run)	10	3	13
# Profitable (The number of profitable trades. . .)	6	0	6
# Losing (The number of unprofitable trades. . .)	4	3	7
% Profitable (The percent of profitable trades to total trades)	60.00	0.00	46.15
% Losing (The percent of unprofitable trades to total trades)	40.00	100.00	53.85
Results	--- Results ---		
Commission (Total commission deducted from closed trades)	0.00	0.00	0.00
Slippage (Total slippage deducted from closed trades)	0.00	0.00	0.00
Gross P/L (Total points gained in closed positions)	56.23	-4.04	52.19
Open P/L (P/L in a position which remains open at the end)	0.00	0.00	0.00
P/L (Net P/L: Gross P/L less Commission and Slippage)	56.23	-4.04	52.19
Equity (Net P/L plus Open P/L at the end of the run)	56.23	-4.04	52.19

There are columns for Long trades, Short trades and Net. In the Long column, results are reported only for Long positions. In the Short column, results are reported for Short positions only. In the Net column for the "Per Trade Ranges" and "Overall Ranges," entries will be the extreme from either the Long or Short column. Net column entries for the "Statistics" and "Results" categories are the combined results of entries in the Long and Short columns.

EXHIBIT C-22:
New York Stock Exchange Composite Price Index Weekly High and Low from January 5, 1968 to September 30, 1977

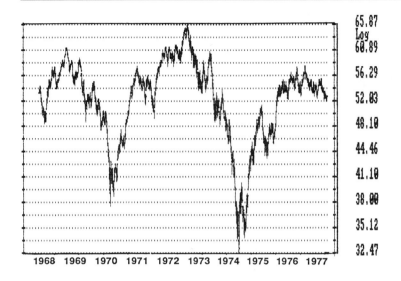

EXHIBIT C-23:
Commodity Channel Index, 1968 to 1977, Smoothed by 90-Week Simple Moving Average

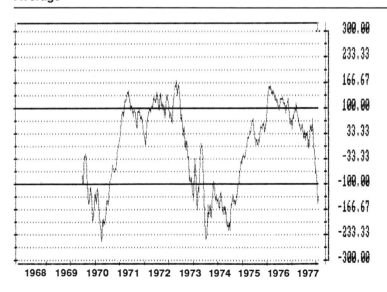

EXHIBIT C-24:

Total Equity for Commodity Channel Index, 1968 to 1977, Smoothed by 90-Week Simple Moving Average

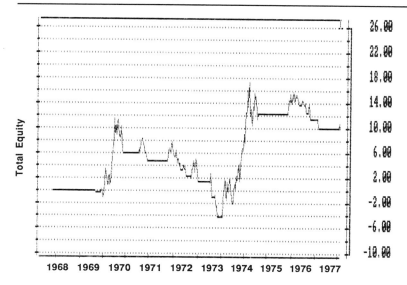

EXHIBIT C-25:
Profit Summary for Commodity Channel Index, 1977 to 1986, Smoothed by 90-Week Simple Moving Average

Item		Long	Short	Net
Per Trade Ranges				
Best Trade	(Closed position yielding maximum P/L)	1.37	14.17	14.17
..Date		760604	750117	750117
Worst Trade	(Closed position yielding minimum P/L)	-1.52	-3.15	-3.15
..Date		770114	730921	730921
Max Open P/L	(Maximum P/L occurring in an open position)	3.46	19.13	19.13
..Date		760326	741004	741004
Min Open P/L	(Minimum P/L occurring in an open position)	-1.19	-1.54	-1.54
..Date		720609	730907	730907
Overall Ranges				
Max P/L	(Maximum P/L from all closed positions during the run)	13.66	12.29	13.66
..Date		760604	750117	760604
Min P/L	(Minimum P/L from all closed positions during the run)	1.50	-4.18	-4.18
..Date		730202	730921	730921
Max Equity	(Maximum P/L from all closed and open positions)	15.75	17.25	17.25
..Date		760326	741004	741004
Min Equity	(Minimum P/L from all closed and open positions)	0.00	-4.18	-4.18
..Date		680105	730921	730921
Statistics				
Periods	(The number of periods in each position and entire run)	180	112	509
Trades	(The number of trades in each position and entire run)	11	6	17
# Profitable	(The number of profitable trades...)	3	3	6
# Losing	(The number of unprofitable trades...)	8	3	11
% Profitable	(The percent of profitable trades to total trades)	27.27	50.00	35.29
% Losing	(The percent of unprofitable trades to total trades)	72.73	50.00	64.71
Results				
Commission	(Total commission deducted from closed trades)	0.00	0.00	0.00
Slippage	(Total slippage deducted from closed trades)	0.00	0.00	0.00
Gross P/L	(Total points gained in closed positions)	-6.59	16.67	10.08
Open P/L	(P/L in a position which remains open at the end)	0.00	-0.02	-0.02
P/L	(Net P/L: Gross P/L less Commission and Slippage)	-6.59	16.67	10.08
Equity	(Net P/L plus Open P/L at the end of the run)	-6.59	16.65	10.06

There are columns for Long trades, Short trades and Net. In the Long column, results are reported only for Long positions. In the Short column, results are reported for Short positions only. In the Net column for the "Per Trade Ranges" and "Overall Ranges," entries will be the extreme from either the Long or Short column. Net column entries for the "Statistics" and "Results" categories are the combined results of entries in the Long and Short columns.

EXHIBIT C-26:

New York Stock Exchange Composite Price Index Weekly High and Low from April 8, 1977 to December 31, 1986

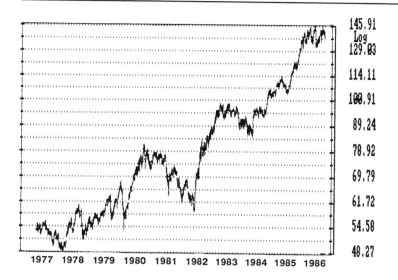

1977 1978 1979 1980 1981 1982 1983 1984 1985 1986

EXHIBIT C-27:

Zero Commodity Channel Index, 1977 to 1986, Smoothed by 53-Week Simple Moving Average

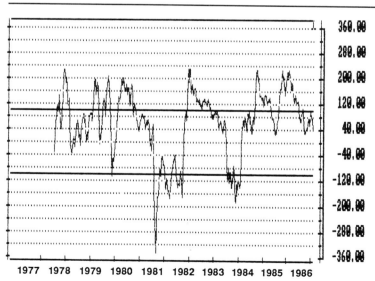

1977 1978 1979 1980 1981 1982 1983 1984 1985 1986

EXHIBIT C-28:

Total Equity for Zero Commodity Channel Index, 1977 to 1986, Smoothed by 53-Week Simple Moving Average

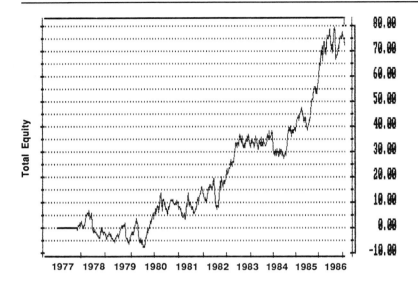

EXHIBIT C-29:

Profit Summary for Zero Commodity Channel Index, 1977 to 1986, Smoothed by 53-Week Simple Moving Average

Item	Long	Short	Net
Per Trade Ranges	--- Per Trade Ranges ---		
Best Trade (Closed position yielding maximum P/L)	22.72	4.84	22.72
.. Date	840203	820903	840203
Worst Trade (Closed position yielding minimum P/L)	-1.36	-2.10	-2.10
.. Date	810724	840810	840810
Max Open P/L (Maximum P/L occurring in an open position)	50.24	15.56	50.24
.. Date	860829	820813	860829
Min Open P/L (Minimum P/L occurring in an open position)	-1.56	-1.81	-1.81
.. Date	841207	800502	800502
Overall Ranges	--- Overall Ranges ---		
Max P/L (Maximum P/L from all closed positions during the run)	31.28	29.18	31.28
.. Date	840203	840810	840203
Min P/L (Minimum P/L from all closed positions during the run)	-5.72	-7.27	-7.27
.. Date	800321	800509	800509
Max Equity (Maximum P/L from all closed and open positions)	79.42	38.09	79.42
.. Date	860829	840615	860829
Min Equity (Minimum P/L from all closed and open positions)	-7.27	-7.53	-7.53
.. Date	800509	800502	800502
Statistics	--- Statistics ---		
Periods (The number of periods in each position and entire run)	407	102	509
Trades (The number of trades in each position and entire run)	10	11	21
# Profitable (The number of profitable trades...)	5	1	6
# Losing (The number of unprofitable trades...)	5	10	15
% Profitable (The percent of profitable trades to total trades)	50.00	9.09	28.57
% Losing (The percent of unprofitable trades to total trades)	50.00	90.91	71.43
Results	--- Results ---		
Commission (Total commission deducted from closed trades)	0.00	0.00	0.00
Slippage (Total slippage deducted from closed trades)	0.00	0.00	0.00
Gross P/L (Total points gained in closed positions)	36.16	-6.98	29.18
Open P/L (P/L in a position which remains open at the end)	43.50	0.00	43.50
P/L (Net P/L: Gross P/L less Commission and Slippage)	36.16	-6.98	29.18
Equity (Net P/L plus Open P/L at the end of the run)	79.66	-6.98	72.68

There are columns for Long trades, Short trades and Net. In the Long column, results are reported only for Long positions. In the Short column, results are reported for Short positions only. In the Net column for the "Per Trade Ranges" and "Overall Ranges," entries will be the extreme from either the Long or Short column. Net column entries for the "Statistics" and "Results" categories are the combined results of entries in the Long and Short columns.

EXHIBIT C-30:

New York Stock Exchange Composite Price Index Weekly High and Low from January 5, 1968 to September 30, 1977

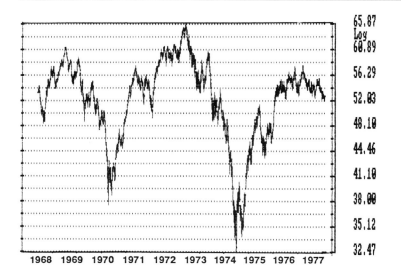

65.87
Log
60.89
56.29
52.83
48.10
44.46
41.10
38.00
35.12
32.47

1968 1969 1970 1971 1972 1973 1974 1975 1976 1977

EXHIBIT C-31:

Zero Commodity Channel Index, 1968 to 1977, Smoothed by 53-Week Simple Moving Average

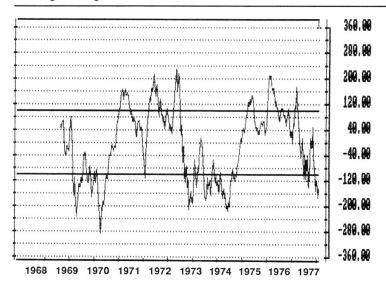

360.00
280.00
200.00
120.00
40.00
-40.00
-120.00
-200.00
-280.00
-360.00

1968 1969 1970 1971 1972 1973 1974 1975 1976 1977

EXHIBIT C-32:

Total Equity for Zero Commodity Channel Index, 1968 to 1977, Smoothed by 53-Week Simple Moving Average

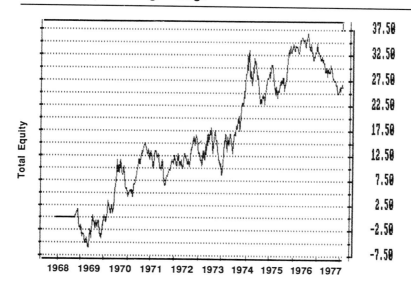

EXHIBIT C-33:
Profit Summary for Zero Commodity Channel Index, 1968 to 1977, Smoothed by 53-Week Simple Moving Average

Item		Long	Short	Net
		Per Trade Ranges		
Per Trade Ranges				
Best Trade	(Closed position yielding maximum P/L)	9.89	14.40	14.40
.. Date		761112	750214	750214
Worst Trade	(Closed position yielding minimum P/L)	-2.64	-3.25	-3.25
.. Date		731102	711217	711217
Max Open P/L	(Maximum P/L occurring in an open position)	13.81	24.71	24.71
.. Date		760924	741004	741004
Min Open P/L	(Minimum P/L occurring in an open position)	-0.83	-1.92	-1.92
.. Date		690221	711210	711210
		Overall Ranges		
Overall Ranges				
Max P/L	(Maximum P/L from all closed positions during the run)	33.02	31.51	33.02
.. Date		761119	761119	761112
Min P/L	(Minimum P/L from all closed positions during the run)	-6.02	-4.93	-6.02
.. Date		690606	690502	690606
Max Equity	(Maximum P/L from all closed and open positions)	36.94	33.44	36.94
.. Date		760924	741004	760924
Min Equity	(Minimum P/L from all closed and open positions)	-6.02	-6.02	-6.02
.. Date		690606	690606	690606
		Statistics		
Statistics				
Periods	(The number of periods in each position and entire run)	287	222	509
Trades	(The number of trades in each position and entire run)	10	9	19
# Profitable	(The number of profitable trades...)	4	2	6
# Losing	(The number of unprofitable trades...)	6	7	13
% Profitable	(The percent of profitable trades to total trades)	40.00	22.22	31.58
% Losing	(The percent of unprofitable trades to total trades)	60.00	77.78	68.42
		Results		
Results				
Commission	(Total commission deducted from closed trades)	0.00	0.00	0.00
Slippage	(Total slippage deducted from closed trades)	0.00	0.00	0.00
Gross P/L	(Total points gained in closed positions)	10.92	13.94	24.86
Open P/L	(P/L in a position which remains open at the end)	0.00	1.31	1.31
P/L	(Net P/L: Gross P/L less Commission and Slippage)	10.92	13.94	24.86
Equity	(Net P/L plus Open P/L at the end of the run)	10.92	15.25	26.17

There are columns for Long trades, Short trades and Net. In the Long column, results are reported only for Long positions. In the Short column, results are reported for Short positions only. In the Net column for the "Per Trade Ranges" and "Overall Ranges," entries will be the extreme from either the Long or Short column. Net column entries for the "Statistics" and "Results" categories are the combined results of entries in the Long and Short columns.

CONFIDENCE INDEX

The Confidence Index, developed in 1932 by *Barron's*, is one of the oldest sentiment indicators. It is calculated by dividing the average yield of high grade conservative bonds by the average yield of intermediate grade speculative bonds.

The Confidence Index is based on the concept that when investors are confident of economic conditions, they are more likely to put their money in riskier, more speculative bonds. As a result, the prices of such bonds increase, the yields decrease, and the Confidence Index rises.

Alternatively, when investors lack confidence in the future of the economy, they shift their funds from more speculative bonds to conservative bonds. The effect is a decrease in the Confidence Index.

The theory further assumes a positive correlation between the bond and stock markets. When investors are confident in the economy, not only do they buy riskier bonds, they also invest in stocks bidding up their prices.

A change in the trend of the Confidence Index is supposed to be a leading indicator of a change in the trend of the stock market by approximately 2 to 4 months. However, the record of the Confidence Index as a leading indicator has not been good in the past decade. It has frequently changed its trend without a subsequent change in trend in the stock market. As a result, many market technicians now doubt its value in stock market forecasting.

CUMULATIVE VOLUME INDEX

The Cumulative Volume Index is simply a running total of net upside-downside volume. It is calculated on a daily basis in two steps. First, you subtract the volume of declining issues traded on the New York Stock Exchange from the volume of advancing issues traded on the New York Stock Exchange. That net volume is then added to the cumulative value for the preceding day.

The value of this indicator is limited by the subjective method in which it is normally interpreted. Interpretation typically is accomplished by visually comparing the Cumulative Volume Index (as shown in Exhibit C-34) to a market index (such as the Standard & Poor's 500 Index) for divergences.

As with most cumulative indicators, the trend of the Cumulative Volume Index is more important than its actual value. If the market index is rising at a time when the Cumulative Volume Index is declining, underlying market

EXHIBIT C-34:
Cumulative Volume Index (top) Versus the Standard & Poor's 500 Index (bottom) from 1984 to 1986

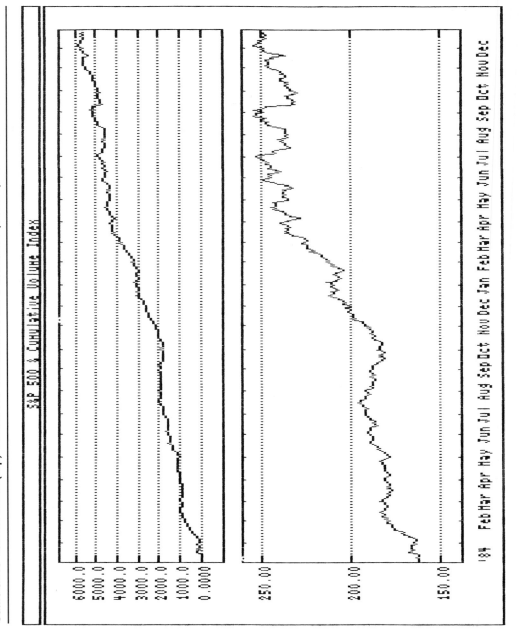

weakness is suggested—a bearish sign for stock prices. On the other hand, if the market index is declining while the Cumulative Volume Index rises, underlying market strength is in place—a bullish sign for stock prices.

CYCLES

Ian S. Notley, President of Yelton Fiscal, Inc., 90 Grove Street, Ridge-field, CT 06877, has been a student of cycles since 1958. The following introduction to his research has been condensed from his May, 1977 manual, *Trend and Cycle Analysis*, Toronto, Ontario, Canada: Dominion Securities Limited.*

A cycle is defined as a period of time within which a round of regularly recurring events or phenomena is completed. The following is a short list of historic data sets in which the element of periodicity has been substantiated by the Foundation for the Study of Cycles (124 South Highland Avenue, Pittsburgh, PA).

Salmon Cycle and Abundance in Canada

Tent Caterpillar Cycle

The 17.7-Year Cycle in War, 600 B.C.–A.D. 1957

17.33-Year Cycle in the Flood Stages of the River Nile

Cycles in Viscose Rayon Filament Yarn Production

Fluctuations in the Number of Birds in the Toronto Region

Cycles in Stock Prices

Pig Iron Cycle

Circadian Rhythms in Respiratory Functions

The 18-Year Cycle in Bituminous Coal Production

Wages in England

The 19.75-Month Cycle in Soybean Prices

Rabbit Abundance in Canada

17.5-Year Cycle in U.S. Wholesale Prices

The 5.9-Year Cotton Cycle

Sugar Cycle

---

*Reprinted with permission.

Cycles in Shoe Production

Recurring Cycles of Fashion

Rhythms in Nature: Daily, Lunar, Annual, and Sunspot Cycles

5.9-Year Grouse Abundance in Aberdeenshire

Cycles in Copper Prices

Cycles in Sedimentary Rock Deposits

The 19.89-Month (1.66-Year) Cycle in Barron's Oil Group

Long Weather Cycles

Cycles in Industrial Bond Yields

Incidence of Influenza

Cycle of Automobile Factory Sales

45-Year Drought Cycle

Standard & Poor's Combined Index

7.65-Year Cycle in American Wheat Production

Cycle of Society Trends in Great Britain

Cycles in Japanese Bamboo

Cycle analysis has a long history. Sir William Herschel wrote an essay about cycle phenomena called "The Nature of the Sun," which appeared in *Philosophical Transactions of the Royal Society*, April 16, 1801. In 1847, Dr. Clarke cited a 50-year-plus cycle in economics, which was later described by W.S. Jevons and N.D. Kondratieff.

In 1860, Clemant Juglar observed a general economic cycle lasting 8 to 10 years. He also discovered the fundamental mechanism of alternating prosperities and liquidations, the latter of which he interpreted as a reaction of the economic system to the events of the former. Eventually he discounted the "crisis" role and focused on the wave. Juglar's findings were calculated on banking figures, interest rates, stock prices, business failures, patents issued, pig iron prices, and a variety of other phenomena. On Wall Street it became known as the Decennial Pattern or the Juglar Wave, a 9.25-year cycle in stock prices. This cycle has repeated itself 16 times since 1834. According to the Bartels test of probability, the 9.25-year cycle could not occur by chance more than once in 5000 times.

The Kitchin Wave or Four-Year Cycle was thought to have been used by the Rothschilds for trading British Consols. In 1923, Professor W.L. Crum of Harvard published an analysis of monthly commercial paper rates in New York from 1866 to 1922. Crum demonstrated the presence of recurring 40-month periods. The importance of the contribution was that it established, at least for one series, the existence of a cycle which could be observed with remarkable regularity. Simultaneously, Professor Joseph Kitchin, also of Harvard, showed cyclic influences in bank clearings, wholesale prices, and interest rates in Great Britain and in the U.S. for the period 1890 to 1922. The "4-year cycle," although at first none too favorably received, has acquired acceptance over the years.

In his book *Profit Magic of Stock Market Transaction Timing* (Prentice Hall, New York, 1960), J.M. Hurst described the stock market as a number of wave rhythms that act together in cycles of nominal length. The nominal cycle lengths, or wave averages, can be utilized to form a predictive model indicating the probable occurrence of cyclic lows. A proportionate relationship was found to exist between the cycles: two 10-week nominal cycles make one 20-week normal length; two 20-week cycles comprise a 39-week rhythm; and two 39-week cycles correspond to a 78-week cycle. Over time, the cyclic rhythms tend to come together, or "nest," at major bottoms. The more rhythms of the various waves nesting together, the greater is the tendency for a major cyclic bottom to form (examples: August 1982, June 1983, February 1984, December 1984, and September 1985).

There are many other cycles. Shorter-term daily chart cycles have durations of less than 30 days. The short-term trend structure (minute rhythm) is subject to directional domination by the (major) long-term trend structure and the (minor) intermediate trend structure, particularly at times of correction or recovery against the underlying dominant force.

Cycle analysis can become quite complex. Cycles are often skewed, and they can be distorted by random events. Occasionally, the cycles themselves can miss a beat, give us an extra wave or two, or aberrate somewhat before they get back into course again.

DAYS OF THE MONTH

When are the best times in the month to buy and sell stock? In a recent study, Arthur Merrill (Merrill Analysis Inc., Box 228, Chappaqua, NY 10514) examined the period from 1897 to 1983 and determined the proportion of trading days that were up or down as measured by the Dow Jones Industrial Average (DJIA).* His results are visually displayed in Exhibit D-1.

Merrill found a definite bullish bias in the first 6 trading days of the month, particularly in the first 2 days. The first and second days rose 60.5% and 59.7% of the time, respectively, while on average the DJIA increased only 52.5% of the time.

---

*Reprinted with permission.

EXHIBIT D-1:
Percent of Months from 1897 to 1983 that the Dow Jones Industrial Average Posted an Increase for the Day

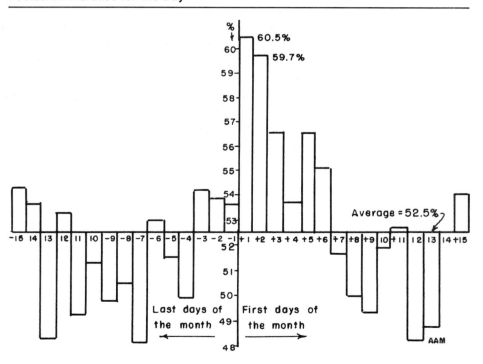

Source: By Permission of Merrill Analysis, Inc.

On average, the stock market performed relatively poorly during the second and third weeks of the month. The last week of the month was average, but improved in the final three trading days.

Sophisticated short-term traders can benefit from knowledge that stock market prices tend to rise at a greater than expected rate during the first few days of each month. One investment strategy is to buy stocks in the last week of the month and sell them in the second week of the month. Be aware, however, that seasonal tendencies and minor cycles are often overwhelmed by major trend forces.

DAYS OF THE WEEK

When are the best times in the week to buy and sell stocks? In a recent study, Arthur Merrill (Merrill Analysis Inc., Box 228, Chappaqua, NY 10514) determined the proportion of days that were up or down as measured by the Dow Jones Industrial Average (DJIA).* His test period covered the 32 years between 1952 and 1983.

Merrill discovered that on average the DJIA increased 52.1% of the time. Tuesdays, Wednesdays, and Thursdays did not deviate significantly from the norm, rising 50.5%, 55.2%, and 53.2% of the time, respectively. Mondays and Fridays were more significant. Mondays were bearish with the market rising only 43.6% of the time. On the other hand, Fridays were bullish with the market up 57.7% of the time. Obviously, these minor calendar tendencies can be easily overwhelmed by major trend momentum which should dominate an investor's strategy.

DEMAND INDEX

The Demand Index is a price and volume momentum indicator developed by James Sibbet (Sibbet Publications, 61 South Lake Avenue, Suite 301, Pasadena, CA 91101). It was designed to be a leading indicator of price trend change. Divergencies mark trend changes. Crossings of an index reading of 1.0 are a lagging indicator of trend change. Readings near 1.0 indicate

---

*Reprinted with permission.

EXHIBIT D-2:
New York Stock Exchange Composite Price Index Weekly High and Low from April 8, 1977 to December 31, 1986

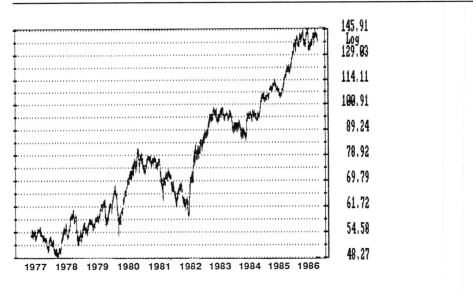

145.91
Log
129.03

114.11

100.91

89.24

78.92

69.79

61.72

54.58

48.27

1977 1978 1979 1980 1981 1982 1983 1984 1985 1986

EXHIBIT D-3:
Demand Index, 1977 to 1986

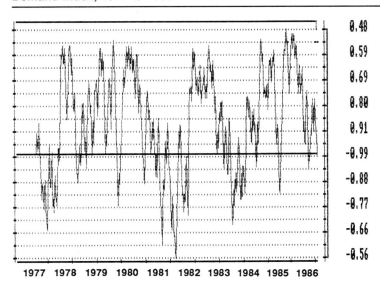

0.48

0.59

0.69

0.80

0.91

-0.99

-0.88

-0.77

-0.66

-0.56

1977 1978 1979 1980 1981 1982 1983 1984 1985 1986

low momentum. The copyrighted proprietary formula is complex, involving moving totals and ratios of volume weighted by price change.

As shown in Exhibits D-2 through D-9 (pages 142–147), profits for the Demand Index over our 19 years of weekly NYSE Composite Index data totalled 62.98 points, well below our 40-week simple moving average crossover rule standard of comparison.

Computer optimization uncovered a slightly more profitable 1/49-week simple moving average differential oscillator of the formula's Buying Power, but here, too, results were below standard. We optimized this indicator using Compu Trac software and two 9.75-year test periods of weekly data (consisting of high, low, close, and volume for each week) for the broad-based NYSE Composite Index. The first period ran from January 5, 1968 through September 30, 1977, and the second period ran from April 8, 1977 through December 31, 1986. The overlap in data was necessary to facilitate testing of various moving averages throughout the full time period. Our basic statistical testing technique was the simple moving average crossover rule for univariate analysis of time series data to isolate the trend. When the Buying Power crossed its own *n*-period simple moving average, a trend

EXHIBIT D-4:
Total Equity for Demand Index, 1977 to 1986

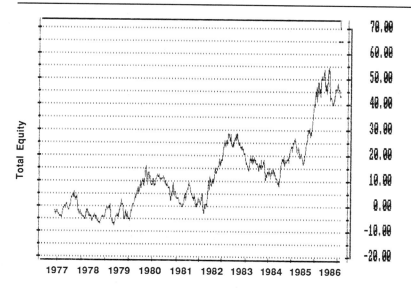

EXHIBIT D-5:

Profit Summary for Demand Index, 1977 to 1986

Item	Long	Short	Net
	— Per Trade Ranges —		
Per Trade Ranges			
Best Trade (Closed position yielding maximum P/L)	27.05	3.62	27.05
..Date	831028	820423	831028
Worst Trade (Closed position yielding minimum P/L)	-4.61	-3.85	-4.61
..Date	810828	840106	810828
Max Open P/L (Maximum P/L occurring in an open position)	37.17	9.35	37.17
..Date	860829	820312	860829
Min Open P/L (Minimum P/L occurring in an open position)	-1.99	-1.32	-1.99
..Date	820521	831230	820521
	— Overall Ranges —		
Overall Ranges			
Max P/L (Maximum P/L from all closed positions during the run)	43.14	40.26	43.14
..Date	861231	861010	861231
Min P/L (Minimum P/L from all closed positions during the run)	-5.84	-7.07	-7.07
..Date	791026	791102	791102
Max Equity (Maximum P/L from all closed and open positions)	54.30	43.14	54.30
..Date	860829	861231	860829
Min Equity (Minimum P/L from all closed and open positions)	-7.52	-7.07	-7.52
..Date	791109	791102	791109
	— Statistics —		
Statistics			
Periods (The number of periods in each position and entire run)	367	142	509
Trades (The number of trades in each position and entire run)	24	23	47
# Profitable (The number of profitable trades...)	11	6	17
# Losing (The number of unprofitable trades...)	13	17	30
% Profitable (The percent of profitable trades to total trades)	45.83	26.09	36.17
% Losing (The percent of unprofitable trades to total trades)	54.17	73.91	63.83
	— Results —		
Results			
Commission (Total commission deducted from closed trades)	0.00	0.00	0.00
Slippage (Total slippage deducted from closed trades)	0.00	0.00	0.00
Gross P/L (Total points gained in closed positions)	63.15	-20.01	43.14
Open P/L (P/L in a position which remains open at the end)	0.00	0.00	0.00
P/L (Net P/L: Gross P/L less Commission and Slippage)	63.15	-20.01	43.14
Equity (Net P/L plus Open P/L at the end of the run)	63.15	-20.01	43.14

There are columns for Long trades, Short trades and Net. In the Long column, results are reported only for Long positions. In the Short column, results are reported for Short positions only. In the Net column for the "Per Trade Ranges" and "Overall Ranges," entries will be the extreme from either the Long or Short column. Net column entries for the "Statistics" and "Results" categories are the combined results of entries in the Long and Short columns.

EXHIBIT D-6:

New York Stock Exchange Composite Price Index Weekly High and Low from January 5, 1968 to September 30, 1977

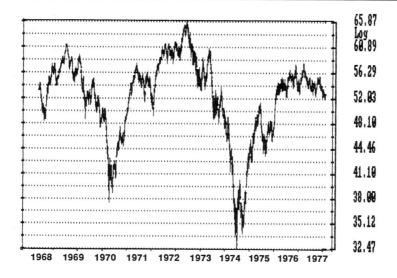

1968   1969   1970   1971   1972   1973   1974   1975   1976   1977

EXHIBIT D-7:

Demand Index, 1968 to 1977

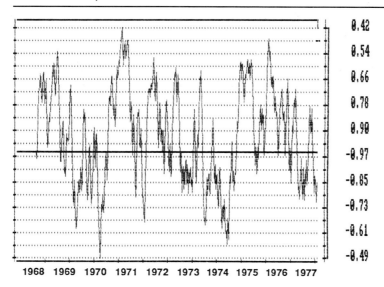

1968   1969   1970   1971   1972   1973   1974   1975   1976   1977

EXHIBIT D-8:
Total Equity for Demand Index, 1968 to 1977

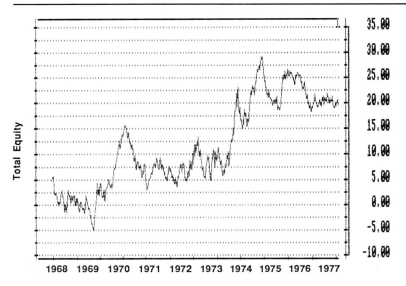

change and thus a trade position change in the direction of the crossing were signaled. We displayed this indicator as a differential oscillator: Buying Power minus its own 49-week simple moving average, as shown in Exhibits D-16 (page 153) and D-20 (page 156). As noted in Exhibit D-10 through D-14 (pages 148–152), combined profits peaked at 73.76 NYSE points at the 49-week simple moving average. Not only was this below our 40-week simple moving average crossover rule standard, but maximum drawdown at 30.10 points (see Exhibit D-17, page 154) was 1.95 times worse than our standard of comparison.

EXHIBIT D-9:

Profit Summary for Demand Index, 1968 to 1977

Item	Long	Short	Net
Per Trade Ranges	--- Per Trade Ranges ---		
Best Trade (Closed position yielding maximum P/L)	11.25	10.58	11.25
.. Date	710625	741108	710625
Worst Trade (Closed position yielding minimum P/L)	-2.91	-2.50	-2.91
.. Date	690228	711217	690228
Max Open P/L (Maximum P/L occurring in an open position)	14.47	17.31	17.31
.. Date	710423	741004	741004
Min Open P/L (Minimum P/L occurring in an open position)	-1.79	-1.17	-1.79
.. Date	690221	711210	690221
Overall Ranges	--- Overall Ranges ---		
Max P/L (Maximum P/L from all closed positions during the run)	24.57	23.62	24.57
.. Date	760604	760611	760604
Min P/L (Minimum P/L from all closed positions during the run)	-4.97	-3.80	-4.97
.. Date	700410	700327	700410
Max Equity (Maximum P/L from all closed and open positions)	29.14	24.57	29.14
.. Date	750711	760604	750711
Min Equity (Minimum P/L from all closed and open positions)	-4.97	-4.97	-4.97
.. Date	700410	700410	700410
Statistics	--- Statistics ---		
Periods (The number of periods in each position and entire run)	310	199	509
Trades (The number of trades in each position and entire run)	29	29	58
# Profitable (The number of profitable trades...)	9	9	18
# Losing (The number of unprofitable trades...)	20	20	40
% Profitable (The percent of profitable trades to total trades)	31.03	31.03	31.03
% Losing (The percent of unprofitable trades to total trades)	68.97	68.97	68.97
Results	--- Results ---		
Commission (Total commission deducted from closed trades)	0.00	0.00	0.00
Slippage (Total slippage deducted from closed trades)	0.00	0.00	0.00
Gross P/L (Total points gained in closed positions)	11.80	7.24	19.04
Open P/L (P/L in a position which remains open at the end)	0.00	0.80	0.80
P/L (Net P/L: Gross P/L less Commission and Slippage)	11.80	7.24	19.04
Equity (Net P/L plus Open P/L at the end of the run)	11.80	8.04	19.84

There are columns for Long trades, Short trades and Net. In the Long column, results are reported only for Long positions. In the Short column, results are reported for Short positions only. In the Net column for the "Per Trade Ranges" and "Overall Ranges," entries will be the extreme from either the Long or Short column. Net column entries for the "Statistics" and "Results" categories are the combined results of entries in the Long and Short columns.

EXHIBIT D-10:

Profitability Chart for Demand Index Buying Power 1/n Oscillator (for Period Lengths of $n = 1$ to $n = 50$ from 1977 to 1986)

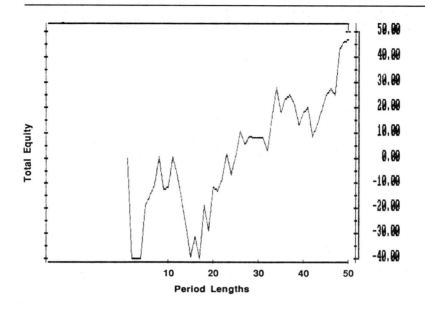

EXHIBIT D-11:

Profitability Chart for Demand Index Buying Power 1/n Oscillator (for Period Lengths of $n = 51$ to $n = 100$ from 1977 to 1986)

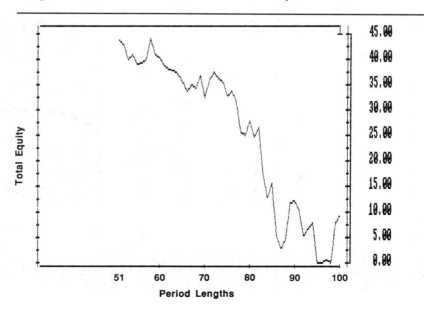

EXHIBIT D-12:

Profit Table for Demand Index Buying Power 1/n Oscillator (for Period Lengths of 1 to 100 from 1977 to 1986)

Pass	Total Equity	Short Equity	Long Equity	Max. Equity	Min. Equity	P/L	Best Trade	Worst Trade	Max. Open P/L	Min. Open P/L
1	0.00	0.00	0.00	0.00	0.00	0.00	N/A	N/A	0.00	0.00
2	-41.80	-62.48	20.68	9.29	-46.52	-41.80	15.80	-6.67	16.49	-3.49
3	-40.00	-61.83	21.83	9.03	-47.28	-42.95	14.67	-7.58	15.56	-3.93
4	-51.89	-67.83	15.94	19.46	-56.06	-54.84	14.67	-7.23	15.56	-7.58
5	-18.53	-51.06	32.53	18.36	-28.20	-21.48	14.67	-10.89	15.36	-9.77
6	-15.25	-49.06	33.81	19.60	-24.03	-18.20	14.67	-10.89	17.18	-9.77
7	-10.64	-47.55	36.91	20.91	-19.42	-13.59	15.55	-11.07	17.18	-9.77
8	0.40	-42.07	42.47	32.89	-8.38	-2.55	15.55	-12.38	17.18	-10.89
9	-12.65	-48.81	36.16	26.98	-20.57	-15.17	14.67	-12.38	17.18	-10.89
10	-12.12	-48.66	36.54	29.71	-20.04	-14.64	14.67	-12.51	17.18	-10.89
11	0.70	-42.64	43.34	26.61	-8.95	-1.82	14.67	-13.03	17.18	-12.38
12	-6.01	-45.63	39.62	27.30	-13.93	-8.53	13.67	-13.03	17.18	-12.38
13	-17.10	-51.47	34.37	24.75	-19.98	-17.10	13.67	-13.03	17.18	-12.38
14	-27.01	-56.40	29.39	13.28	-29.89	-27.01	13.49	-12.51	17.18	-7.30
15	-39.41	-62.96	23.55	8.94	-40.71	-39.41	13.49	-12.51	17.18	-9.28
16	-31.15	-58.46	27.31	6.74	-32.45	-31.15	15.40	-11.08	17.18	-9.93
17	-41.55	-63.77	22.22	4.20	-42.85	-41.55	14.55	-11.08	17.18	-9.93
18	-18.76	-53.05	34.29	0.97	-40.17	-18.76	23.93	-9.43	29.33	-9.93
19	-29.03	-58.50	29.47	0.34	-50.84	-29.03	23.93	-9.43	29.33	-9.93
20	-11.77	-49.79	38.02	0.50	-33.58	-11.77	23.93	-8.24	29.33	-9.93
21	-13.17	-50.74	37.57	0.00	-42.71	-13.17	27.03	-6.12	31.51	-9.93
22	-7.92	-46.90	38.98	0.24	-37.35	-7.92	27.03	-7.49	31.51	-9.93
23	1.95	-42.06	44.01	7.06	-26.92	1.95	24.84	-6.64	29.32	-9.93
24	-6.41	-45.83	39.42	4.99	-25.18	-6.41	24.84	-6.64	29.32	-9.93
25	1.26	-42.49	43.75	12.61	-22.95	1.26	24.84	-7.90	29.32	-9.93
26	10.92	-37.97	48.89	22.27	-21.35	10.92	24.84	-7.90	29.32	-9.93
27	5.41	-40.78	46.19	16.76	-21.80	5.41	24.84	-7.90	29.32	-9.93
28	8.64	-38.84	47.48	19.99	-20.55	8.64	24.84	-7.90	29.32	-9.93
29	8.42	-38.83	47.25	19.77	-11.85	8.42	24.84	-7.90	29.32	-9.93
30	8.00	-39.97	47.97	19.35	-16.52	8.00	24.84	-7.90	29.32	-9.93
31	7.87	-40.57	48.44	19.22	-16.65	7.87	24.84	-7.90	29.32	-9.93
32	3.33	-42.76	46.09	16.84	-19.03	3.33	24.84	-7.90	29.32	-9.93
33	16.08	-36.72	52.80	29.59	-6.61	16.08	24.84	-7.90	29.32	-9.93
34	28.18	-30.34	58.52	39.79	-0.93	28.18	26.57	-7.90	29.32	-8.20
35	18.15	-35.21	53.36	33.56	-1.31	18.15	23.89	-7.90	29.32	-10.88
36	24.00	-32.84	56.84	42.75	-2.97	24.00	23.89	-7.06	29.32	-10.88
37	24.83	-32.28	57.11	43.58	-3.38	24.83	23.89	-7.06	29.32	-10.88
38	21.49	-34.21	55.70	35.12	-3.90	18.97	23.22	-7.06	27.93	-10.88
39	12.82	-38.14	50.96	26.71	-10.83	9.87	23.22	-9.25	27.93	-10.88
40	18.13	-35.10	53.23	32.02	-7.96	15.18	23.22	-9.25	27.93	-10.88
41	19.80	-34.46	54.26	33.69	-10.95	16.85	23.22	-9.25	27.93	-10.88
42	8.83	-39.95	48.78	22.72	-21.92	5.88	23.22	-9.25	27.93	-10.88
43	13.25	-37.46	50.71	27.14	-24.12	10.30	29.80	-9.25	30.82	-10.88
44	18.78	-33.93	52.71	32.67	-25.69	15.83	33.26	-9.25	34.17	-10.88
45	25.15	-30.39	55.54	39.04	-24.76	22.20	33.26	-9.25	34.17	-10.88
46	27.80	-28.44	56.24	41.69	-24.83	24.85	33.26	-9.25	34.17	-10.88
47	25.05	-29.78	54.83	38.94	-27.58	22.10	33.26	-9.25	34.17	-10.88
48	43.25	-20.24	63.49	57.14	-18.66	40.30	33.26	-9.25	34.17	-10.88
49	46.43	-18.60	65.03	60.32	-24.81	43.48	33.26	-9.25	34.17	-10.88
50	46.62	-18.91	65.53	60.51	-19.86	43.67	33.26	-9.25	34.17	-10.88
51	43.87	-19.84	63.71	57.76	-22.51	40.92	33.26	-9.25	34.17	-10.88
52	42.82	-19.84	62.66	56.71	-23.56	39.87	33.26	-9.25	34.17	-10.88
53	39.90	-21.94	61.84	53.79	-22.28	36.95	32.24	-9.25	34.17	-10.88
54	40.80	-21.94	62.74	54.69	-21.38	37.85	32.24	-9.25	34.17	-10.88
55	39.06	-22.93	61.99	52.95	-21.85	36.11	32.24	-9.25	34.17	-10.88

Pass	Total Equity	Short Equity	Long Equity	Max. Equity	Min. Equity	P/L	Best Trade	Worst Trade	Max. Open P/L	Min. Open P/L
56	39.38	-22.93	62.31	53.27	-21.53	36.43	32.24	-9.25	34.17	-10.88
57	40.14	-21.81	61.95	54.03	-22.30	37.19	32.24	-9.25	34.17	-10.88
58	44.15	-19.76	63.91	58.04	-19.43	41.20	32.24	-9.25	34.17	-10.88
59	40.82	-20.79	61.61	54.71	-20.70	37.87	32.24	-9.25	34.17	-10.88
60	40.40	-19.92	60.32	54.29	-22.24	37.45	32.24	-9.25	34.17	-10.88
61	38.65	-20.70	59.35	54.10	-22.43	35.70	32.24	-7.06	34.17	-10.88
62	38.12	-20.70	58.82	53.57	-22.96	35.17	32.24	-7.06	34.17	-10.88
63	37.88	-20.74	58.62	52.89	-23.12	34.93	32.24	-7.06	34.17	-10.88
64	37.26	-21.39	58.65	52.27	-23.59	34.31	32.24	-7.06	34.17	-10.88
65	35.56	-21.39	56.95	50.57	-25.29	32.61	32.24	-7.06	34.17	-10.88
66	33.77	-23.00	56.77	48.78	-23.86	30.82	30.63	-7.06	34.17	-10.88
67	34.93	-23.14	58.07	49.94	-23.83	31.98	30.63	-7.06	34.17	-10.88
68	34.52	-23.14	57.66	49.53	-24.24	31.57	30.63	-7.06	34.17	-10.88
69	36.72	-21.76	58.48	49.49	-24.80	33.77	30.63	-7.06	34.17	-10.88
70	32.55	-23.55	56.10	45.32	-25.39	29.60	30.63	-7.06	34.17	-10.88
71	36.02	-23.90	59.92	48.79	-23.62	33.07	30.63	-7.06	34.17	-10.88
72	37.42	-24.32	61.74	50.19	-25.86	34.47	30.63	-7.06	34.17	-10.88
73	36.25	-24.42	60.67	51.26	-24.79	33.30	30.63	-7.06	34.17	-10.88
74	35.48	-25.19	60.67	50.49	-25.56	32.53	30.63	-7.06	34.17	-10.88
75	32.96	-26.54	59.50	47.97	-22.40	30.01	30.63	-7.06	34.17	-10.88
76	33.86	-25.64	59.50	48.87	-21.50	30.91	30.63	-7.06	34.17	-10.88
77	31.55	-26.63	58.18	46.56	-22.75	28.60	30.63	-7.06	34.17	-10.88
78	25.66	-29.43	55.09	42.83	-20.07	22.71	30.63	-7.62	34.17	-4.45
79	24.91	-30.18	55.09	42.08	-20.82	21.96	30.63	-7.62	34.17	-4.45
80	27.77	-28.52	56.29	44.94	-17.96	24.82	30.63	-7.62	34.17	-4.45
81	24.82	-30.07	54.89	41.99	-18.11	21.87	30.63	-7.62	34.17	-4.45
82	26.61	-28.28	54.89	43.78	-16.32	23.66	30.63	-7.62	34.17	-4.45
83	17.27	-32.20	49.47	44.76	-14.82	14.32	30.63	-7.62	34.17	-5.81
84	12.71	-35.01	47.72	40.20	-15.88	9.76	30.63	-7.62	34.17	-5.81
85	15.75	-32.92	48.67	43.24	-17.22	12.80	30.63	-7.62	34.17	-5.81
86	5.21	-38.79	44.00	32.70	-19.58	2.26	30.63	-7.62	34.17	-5.81
87	2.85	-40.43	43.28	30.34	-20.50	-0.10	30.63	-7.62	34.17	-5.81
88	4.77	-39.22	43.99	32.26	-18.58	1.82	30.63	-7.62	34.17	-5.81
89	11.84	-35.93	47.77	39.33	-19.07	8.89	30.63	-7.62	34.17	-5.81
90	12.11	-36.05	48.16	39.60	-19.58	9.16	29.62	-7.62	34.17	-5.81
91	10.19	-36.29	46.48	37.68	-18.14	7.24	29.62	-7.62	34.17	-5.81
92	5.33	-38.35	43.68	33.26	-17.40	2.38	27.04	-7.62	31.59	-5.81
93	6.96	-37.27	44.23	33.33	-16.87	4.01	27.04	-7.62	31.59	-5.81
94	7.67	-36.89	44.56	34.04	-18.34	4.72	27.04	-7.62	31.59	-5.81
95	-0.28	-40.41	40.13	26.09	-21.64	-3.23	27.04	-7.62	31.59	-5.81
96	-6.05	-43.55	37.50	21.88	-21.13	-9.00	27.04	-7.62	31.59	-5.81
97	0.55	-40.47	41.02	19.60	-22.63	-2.40	30.52	-5.72	31.59	-5.81
98	-0.42	-40.80	40.38	18.63	-23.60	-3.37	30.52	-5.72	31.59	-5.81
99	7.74	-37.04	44.78	22.62	-21.80	4.79	32.62	-5.72	33.70	-5.81
100	9.46	-36.82	46.28	23.90	-20.52	6.51	32.62	-5.72	33.70	-5.81

Pass indicates period length.

Equity indicates the total number of points gained or lost.

Short equity indicates the number of points gained or lost on short positions.

Long equity indicates the number of points gained or lost on long positions.

Max. equity indicates the highest total profit recorded over the tested period.

Min. equity indicates the lowest total profit recorded over the tested period.

P/L indicates total number of points gained or lost in closed positions.

Best trade indicates the highest number of points gained in any closed trade.

Worst trade indicates the highest number of points lost in any closed trade.

Max. open P/L indicates the highest gain in a position which remains open at the end of the test run.

Min. open P/L indicates the highest loss in a position which remains open at the end of the test run.

EXHIBIT D-13:

Profitability Chart for Demand Index Buying Power 1/n **Oscillator (for Period Lengths of** $n = 21$ **to** $n = 61$ **from 1968 to 1977)**

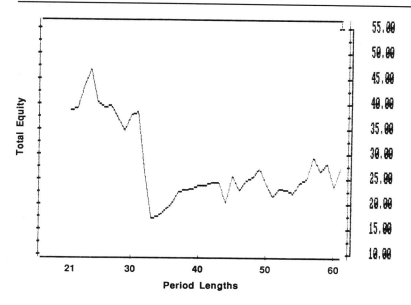

EXHIBIT D-14:

Profit Table for Demand Index Buying Power 1/n Oscillator (for Period Lengths of 21 to 61 from 1968 to 1977)

Pass	Total Equity	Short Equity	Long Equity	Max. Equity	Min. Equity	P/L	Best Trade	Worst Trade	Max. Open P/L	Min. Open P/L
21	38.77	20.07	18.70	44.37	-4.85	38.20	13.04	-4.05	13.54	-3.29
22	38.93	20.29	18.64	47.41	-6.86	38.36	13.47	-3.77	16.10	-3.28
23	43.50	23.02	20.48	51.98	-5.89	42.93	13.47	-3.61	16.10	-3.28
24	46.74	24.66	22.08	56.90	-7.71	46.17	13.43	-3.61	17.31	-3.28
25	40.45	21.54	18.91	50.61	-6.94	39.88	14.52	-3.61	17.31	-3.28
26	39.40	21.61	17.79	50.43	-4.94	38.83	13.43	-3.61	17.31	-3.28
27	39.61	21.65	17.96	50.36	-5.51	39.04	14.54	-3.47	19.13	-3.14
28	37.06	20.64	16.42	46.94	-4.98	36.49	14.52	-3.47	15.17	-3.14
29	34.70	19.68	15.02	44.58	-4.54	34.13	14.52	-3.47	15.17	-3.14
30	37.68	21.55	16.13	46.72	-3.78	36.88	14.39	-3.22	15.04	-3.47
31	38.29	21.73	16.56	47.33	-4.03	37.49	14.39	-3.22	17.31	-3.47
32	26.46	16.28	10.18	35.50	-5.25	25.66	13.82	-3.32	17.31	-3.47
33	17.04	11.43	5.61	27.53	-4.97	16.24	13.82	-3.32	17.31	-3.47
34	17.64	11.39	6.25	28.85	-4.29	16.84	13.82	-3.32	17.31	-3.04
35	18.68	12.17	6.51	28.05	-3.77	17.88	13.82	-4.64	17.31	-3.04
36	19.86	13.35	6.51	29.23	-2.59	19.06	13.82	-4.64	17.31	-3.04
37	22.54	14.91	7.63	29.03	-2.15	21.74	13.50	-4.64	17.31	-3.04
38	22.92	15.69	7.23	29.41	-0.97	22.12	13.50	-4.64	17.31	-3.63
39	23.16	15.69	7.47	29.65	-0.73	22.36	13.50	-4.64	17.31	-3.63
40	23.83	15.99	7.84	30.94	-0.66	23.03	13.50	-4.64	17.31	-3.63
41	23.89	15.69	8.20	31.00	0.00	23.09	13.50	-4.64	17.31	-3.63
42	24.35	15.48	8.87	29.62	0.00	23.55	13.50	-4.64	17.31	-3.63
43	24.34	15.24	9.10	31.45	-0.09	23.54	13.50	-4.64	17.31	-3.63
44	20.23	12.28	7.95	27.16	-3.84	19.43	13.50	-4.64	17.31	-3.63
45	25.63	15.29	10.34	32.56	-3.22	24.83	13.50	-3.03	17.31	-3.63
46	22.67	13.98	8.69	30.61	-2.88	21.87	12.74	-3.19	17.31	-3.63
47	24.61	15.09	9.52	32.55	-2.60	23.81	12.74	-3.19	17.31	-3.63
48	25.29	15.56	9.73	32.81	-2.34	24.49	12.74	-3.19	17.31	-3.63
49	27.33	16.58	10.75	32.81	-2.34	26.53	12.74	-3.19	17.31	-3.63
50	24.20	13.85	10.35	29.68	-5.47	23.40	12.74	-3.19	17.31	-3.63
51	21.46	11.92	9.54	26.94	-6.59	20.66	12.74	-3.97	17.31	-3.63
52	23.18	12.85	10.33	28.66	-4.51	22.38	12.74	-3.83	17.31	-3.83
53	22.78	12.45	10.33	28.26	-4.91	21.98	12.74	-4.23	17.31	-3.83
54	22.12	12.59	9.53	27.60	-3.97	21.32	12.74	-3.29	17.31	-3.63
55	24.46	14.25	10.21	29.94	-2.31	23.66	12.74	-3.19	17.31	-3.63
56	25.07	14.31	10.76	30.31	-2.80	24.27	12.74	-3.19	17.31	-3.63
57	29.43	16.72	12.71	34.67	-2.64	28.63	12.74	-3.19	17.31	-3.63
58	26.53	15.14	11.39	34.41	-2.90	25.73	12.74	-3.19	17.31	-3.63
59	28.13	16.08	12.05	36.01	-2.62	27.33	12.74	-3.19	17.31	-3.63
60	23.46	14.41	9.05	33.70	-1.29	22.66	12.13	-4.37	17.31	-3.63
61	27.19	16.57	10.62	37.43	-0.70	26.39	12.13	-4.37	17.31	-3.63

Pass indicates period length.

Equity indicates the total number of points gained or lost.

Short equity indicates the number of points gained or lost on short positions.

Long equity indicates the number of points gained or lost on long positions.

Max. equity indicates the highest total profit recorded over the tested period.

Min. equity indicates the lowest total profit recorded over the tested period.

P/L indicates total number of points gained or lost in closed positions.

Best trade indicates the highest number of points gained in any closed trade.

Worst trade indicates the highest number of points lost in any closed trade.

Max. open P/L indicates the highest gain in a position which remains open at the end of the test run.

Min. open P/L indicates the highest loss in a position which remains open at the end of the test run.

EXHIBIT D-15:
New York Stock Exchange Composite Price Index Weekly High and Low from April 8, 1977 to December 31, 1986

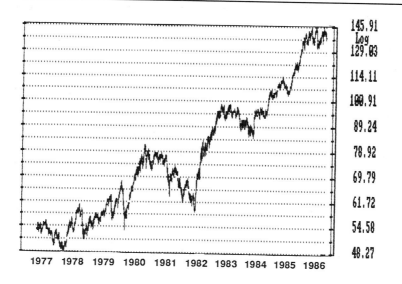

EXHIBIT D-16:
Demand Index Buying Power 1/49 Week Oscillator, 1977 to 1986

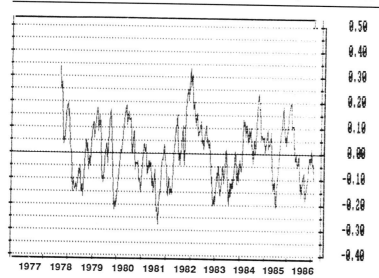

EXHIBIT D-17:
Total Equity for Demand Index Buying Power 1/49 Week Oscillator, 1977 to 1986

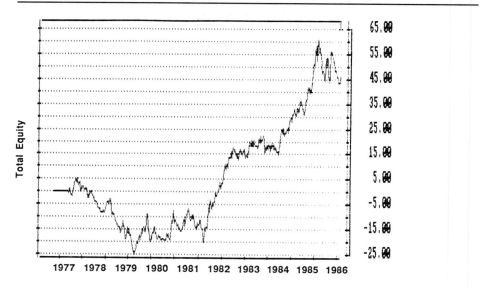

EXHIBIT D-18:

Profit Summary for Demand Index Buying Power 1/49 Week Oscillator, 1977 to 1986

Item		Long	Short	Net
Per Trade Ranges	— Per Trade Ranges —			
Best Trade	(Closed position yielding maximum P/L)	33.26	4.98	33.26
. . Date		830701	820409	830701
Worst Trade	(Closed position yielding minimum P/L)	-3.47	-9.25	-9.25
. . Date		820604	861205	861205
Max Open P/L	(Maximum P/L occurring in an open position)	34.17	11.79	34.17
. . Date		830624	810925	830624
Min Open P/L	(Minimum P/L occurring in an open position)	-2.35	-10.88	-10.88
. . Date		820528	860829	860829
Overall Ranges	— Overall Ranges —			
Max P/L	(Maximum P/L from all closed positions during the run)	54.89	45.64	54.89
. . Date		860516	861205	860516
Min P/L	(Minimum P/L from all closed positions during the run)	-19.12	-23.88	-23.88
. . Date		810501	800613	800613
Max Equity	(Maximum P/L from all closed and open positions)	60.32	56.52	60.32
. . Date		860418	860912	860418
Min Equity	(Minimum P/L from all closed and open positions)	-24.81	-23.88	-24.81
. . Date		800620	800613	800620
Statistics	— Statistics —			
Periods	(The number of periods in each position and entire run)	287	222	509
Trades	(The number of trades in each position and entire run)	17	16	33
# Profitable	(The number of profitable trades. . .)	5	6	11
# Losing	(The number of unprofitable trades. . .)	12	10	22
% Profitable	(The percent of profitable trades to total trades)	29.41	37.50	33.33
% Losing	(The percent of unprofitable trades to total trades)	70.59	62.50	66.67
Results	— Results —			
Commission	(Total commission deducted from closed trades)	0.00	0.00	0.00
Slippage	(Total slippage deducted from closed trades)	0.00	0.00	0.00
Gross P/L	(Total points gained in closed positions)	65.03	-21.55	43.48
Open P/L	(P/L in a position which remains open at the end)	0.00	2.95	2.95
P/L	(Net P/L: Gross P/L less Commission and Slippage)	65.03	-21.55	43.48
Equity	(Net P/L plus Open P/L at the end of the run)	65.03	-18.60	46.43

There are columns for Long trades, Short trades and Net. In the Long column, results are reported only for Long positions. In the Short column, results are reported for Short positions only. In the Net column for the "Per Trade Ranges" and "Overall Ranges," entries will be the extreme from either the Long or Short column. Net column entries for the "Statistics" and "Results" categories are the combined results of entries in the Long and Short columns.

EXHIBIT D-19:

New York Stock Exchange Composite Price Index Weekly High and Low from January 5, 1968 to September 30, 1977

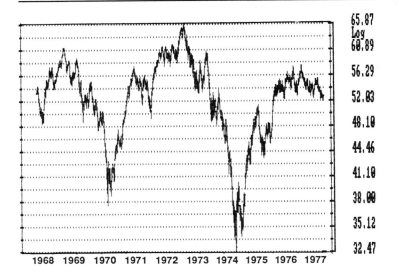

EXHIBIT D-20:

Demand Index Buying Power 1/49 Week Oscillator, 1968 to 1977

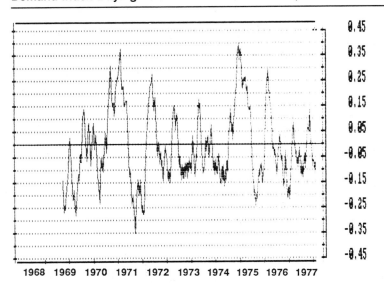

EXHIBIT D-21:
Total Equity for Demand Index Buying Power 1/49 Week Oscillator, 1968 to 1977

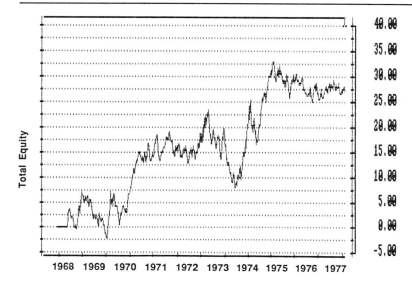

EXHIBIT D-22:
Profit Summary for Demand Index Buying Power 1/49 Week Oscillator, 1968 to 1977

Item	Long	Short	Net
	-- Per Trade Ranges --		
Per Trade Ranges			
Best Trade (Closed position yielding maximum P/L)	12.74	12.13	12.74
.. Date	710521	741018	710521
Worst Trade (Closed position yielding minimum P/L)	-2.76	-3.19	-3.19
.. Date	740111	760109	760109
Max Open P/L (Maximum P/L occurring in an open position)	14.47	17.31	17.31
.. Date	710423	741004	741004
Min Open P/L (Minimum P/L occurring in an open position)	-3.63	-2.02	-3.63
.. Date	741206	760702	741206
	-- Overall Ranges --		
Overall Ranges			
Max P/L (Maximum P/L from all closed positions during the run)	29.27	27.56	29.27
.. Date	760416	770617	760416
Min P/L (Minimum P/L from all closed positions during the run)	-2.34	-1.17	-2.34
.. Date	700410	700327	700410
Max Equity (Maximum P/L from all closed and open positions)	32.81	32.04	32.81
.. Date	750711	750912	750711
Min Equity (Minimum P/L from all closed and open positions)	-2.34	-2.34	-2.34
.. Date	700410	700410	700410
	-- Statistics --		
Statistics			
Periods (The number of periods in each position and entire run)	236	273	509
Trades (The number of trades in each position and entire run)	20	20	40
# Profitable (The number of profitable trades. . .)	6	7	13
# Losing (The number of unprofitable trades. . . .)	14	13	27
% Profitable (The percent of profitable trades to total trades)	30.00	35.00	32.50
% Losing (The percent of unprofitable trades to total trades)	70.00	65.00	67.50
	-- Results --		
Results			
Commission (Total commission deducted from closed trades)	0.00	0.00	0.00
Slippage (Total slippage deducted from closed trades)	0.00	0.00	0.00
Gross P/L (Total points gained in closed positions)	10.75	15.78	26.53
Open P/L (P/L in a position which remains open at the end)	0.00	0.80	0.80
P/L (Net P/L: Gross P/L less Commission and Slippage)	10.75	15.78	26.53
Equity (Net P/L plus Open P/L at the end of the run)	10.75	16.58	27.33

There are columns for Long trades, Short trades and Net. In the Long column, results are reported only for Long positions. In the Short column, results are reported for Short positions only. In the Net column for the "Per Trade Ranges" and "Overall Ranges," entries will be the extreme from either the Long or Short column. Net column entries for the "Statistics" and "Results" categories are the combined results of entries in the Long and Short columns.

DIRECTIONAL MOVEMENT INDEX

The Directional Movement Index (DMI) is a unique filtered momentum indicator published by J. Welles Wilder, Jr., in his 1978 book *New Concepts in Technical Trading Systems* (Trend Research, P.O. Box 128, McLeansville, NC 27301). DMI is a rather complex trend-following indicator. Wilder has asserted that markets exhibit strong trends only about 30% of the time. To avoid the unprofitable frustration of trend following in a sideways market, he devised DMI as a filter that permits entry into trades only when markets exhibit significant trending characteristics. When a market fails to exhibit significant trending or directional behavior, DMI keeps investors out of the market.

By use of exponential moving averages and ratios, DMI tames high, low, and close price data down to a scale that ranges from zero to 100. Directional Movement (DM) is defined as the largest part of the current period's price range that lies outside the previous period's price range. Thus,

$$PDM = H - H_p$$
$$MDM = L - L_p$$

where

PDM is positive or plus DM.
MDM is negative or minus DM.
H is the highest price of the current period.
H_p is the highest price of the previous period.
L is the lowest price of the current period.
L_p is the lowest price of the previous period.

The *lesser* of the above two absolute values is reset to equal zero. On an inside day (with lower high and higher low), both PDM and MDM are reset to equal zero.

True Range (TR) is defined as the largest absolute value of the following three possibilities:

$$TR = H - L, \text{ or } TR = H - C_p, \text{ or } TR = L - C_p$$

where

C_p is the closing price of the previous period.

Before proceeding, all of the above data is smoothed by optimized exponential smoothing constants (also known as exponential moving averages) approximating an 11-week simple moving average. This smoothed data is used in all of the following calculations.

The Positive Directional Indicator (PDI) is the exponentially smoothed Plus Directional Movement divided by the smoothed True Range. Thus,

$$\text{PDI} = \frac{\text{SPDM}}{\text{STR}} = \frac{\text{Smoothed Plus Directional Movement}}{\text{Smoothed True Range}}$$

Remember, when the absolute value of $L - L_p$ is greater than the absolute value of $H - H_p$, then PDM is reset to zero, so PDI must decline.

The Minus Directional Indicator (MDI) is defined by the following exponentially smoothed data:

$$\text{MDI} = \frac{\text{SMDM}}{\text{STR}} = \frac{\text{Smoothed Minus Directional Movement}}{\text{Smoothed True Range}}$$

Remember, when the absolute value of $L - L_p$ is less than the absolute value of $H - H_p$, then MDM is reset to zero, so MDI must decline.

Now, Directional Movement (DX) is defined by the following:

$$\text{DX} = \frac{\text{PDI} - \text{MDI}}{\text{PDI} + \text{MDI}}$$

Average directional movement (ADX) is an exponential smooth of DX.

An example of a four-period smoothed DMI calculation should make Wilder's exact formulas clear (pages 162–163).

We tested several decision rule variations for interpreting directional movement on our 19-year weekly NYSE Composite Index database. One resulted in an excellent profit to maximum drawdown ratio. This rule only enters a trade when ADX is rising, indicating significant Directional Movement. We bought when PDI crossed above MDI. We sold when PDI crossed below MDI, or when ADX turned lower, thus indicating diminishing directional movement. We entered a short sale trade when ADX was rising and PDI crossed below MDI. We covered (or closed out) a short sale trade when PDI crossed above MDI or ADX turned lower, thus indicating diminishing directional movement.

We tested Directional Movement using Compu Trac software and two 9.75-year test periods of weekly data (consisting of high, low, close, and volume for each week) for the broad-based NYSE Composite Common Stock Price Index. The first period ran from January 5, 1968 through September 30, 1977, and the second period ran from April 8, 1977 through December 31, 1986. The overlap in data was necessary to facilitate testing of various moving averages throughout the full time period.

As shown in Exhibits D-23 through D-26 (pages 161–166), the optimal time period parameter for calculating this trend-following indicator was 11 weeks. As detailed in Exhibits D-27 through D-36 (pages 167–172). combined total profit of 60.26 NYSE points was below our 40-week simple moving average crossover rule standard of comparison, due largely to the fact that DMI was out of the market in sideways trends and often misses the very early dynamic phase of a new trend. No doubt, responsiveness to new trends would improve significantly if we used daily rather than weekly data. It is well worth noting, however, that the total profit to maximum drawdown ratio of 7.57 to 1 was well above average. Moreover, the worst case loss string or maximum equity drawdown of 7.96 NYSE points was the lowest of all indicators tested. This illustrates the value of DMI to risk-adverse investors. We believe that Wilder's Directional Movement concept is worthy of further study.

EXHIBIT D-23:

Profitability Chart for Directional Movement (Smoothing Period Lengths of 1 to 50 from 1977 to 1986)

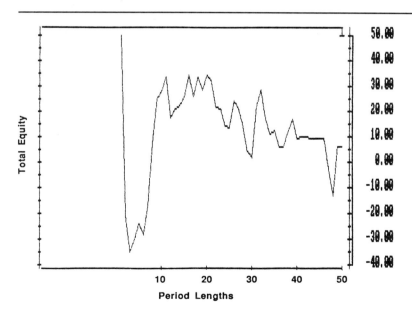

Example of Directional Movement: 4 Periods; 0.75 Smoothing Constant

	NYSE Composite Annual Prices			True Range	$H-H_p$	$L-L_p$	Smoothed Data (0.75 × previous + New Data)		
Date	High	Low	Close	TR	PDM	MDM	STR	SPDM	SMDM
68/12/31	61.34	48.50	58.90	– –	– –	– –			
69/12/31	59.32	48.82	51.53	10.50	0	0			
70/12/31	52.39	37.69	50.23	14.70	0	11.13			
71/12/31	57.84	49.35	56.43	8.49	5.45	0	33.69*	5.45*	11.13*
72/12/29	65.16	56.07	64.48	9.09	7.32	0	34.36	11.41	8.35
73/12/31	65.87	48.71	51.82	17.16	0	7.36	42.93	8.56	13.62
74/12/31	53.77	32.47	36.13	21.30	0	16.24	53.50	6.42	26.46
75/12/31	51.39	36.49	47.64	15.26	0	0	55.39	4.82	19.85
76/12/31	57.88	47.67	57.88	10.24	6.49	0	51.78	10.11	14.89
77/12/30	57.92	49.61	52.50	8.31	0.04	0	47.15	7.62	11.17
78/12/29	60.60	48.27	53.62	12.33	2.68	0	47.69	8.39	8.38
79/12/31	63.58	53.42	61.95	10.16	2.98	0	45.93	9.27	6.28
80/12/31	81.29	53.66	77.86	27.63	17.71	0	62.08	24.66	4.71
81/12/31	79.44	63.75	71.11	15.69	0	0	62.25	18.50	3.53
82/12/31	83.13	58.78	81.03	24.35	0	4.97	71.04	13.87	7.62
83/12/30	99.63	79.63	95.18	20.00	16.50	0	73.28	26.90	5.72
84/12/31	98.12	84.81	96.38	13.31	0	0	68.27	20.18	4.29
85/12/31	122.44	94.41	121.58	28.03	24.32	0	79.23	39.45	3.21
86/12/31	145.91	117.30	138.58	28.61	23.47	0	88.03	53.06	2.41

* Wilder uses Simple Moving Totals and Averages to establish first smoothings; Exponential-Type Smoothings are used thereafter.

SPDM ÷ STR PDI	SMDM ÷ STR MDI	PDI − MDI Difference	÷	PDI + MDI Sum	=	Difference ÷ Sum DX	+	3ADX$_p$	=	DX + 3ADX$_p$	÷	4	=	ADX
.3321	.2430	.0891	÷	.5751	=	.1549								
.1994	.3173	.1179	÷	.5187	=	.2273								
.1200	.4946	.3746	÷	.6146	=	.6095								
.0870	.3584	.2714	÷	.4454	=	.6093								.4003*
.1952	.2875	.0923	÷	.4827	=	.1912	+	1.2009	=	1.3921	÷	4	=	.3480
.1616	.2369	.0753	÷	.3985	=	.1890	+	1.0440	=	1.2330	÷	4	=	.3083
.1759	.1757	.0002	÷	.3516	=	.0006	+	.9248	=	.8254	÷	4	=	.2064
.2018	.1367	.0651	÷	.3385	=	.1923	+	.6191	=	.8114	÷	4	=	.2029
.3972	.0759	.3213	÷	.4731	=	.6791	+	.6086	=	1.2877	÷	4	=	.3219
.2972	.0567	.2405	÷	.3539	=	.6795	+	.9658	=	1.6453	÷	4	=	.4113
.1952	.1073	.0879	÷	.3025	=	.2906	+	1.2339	=	1.5245	÷	4	=	.3811
.3671	.0781	.2890	÷	.4452	=	.6491	+	1.1433	=	1.7924	÷	4	=	.4481
.2956	.0628	.2328	÷	.3584	=	.6495	+	1.3443	=	1.9938	÷	4	=	.4984
.4979	.0405	.4574	÷	.5384	=	.8496	+	1.4954	=	2.3450	÷	4	=	.5862
.6027	.0274	.5753	÷	.6301	=	.9130	+	1.7588	=	2.6718	÷	4	=	.6680

EXHIBIT D-24:
Profit Table for Directional Movement (Smoothing Period Lengths of 1 to 50 from 1977 to 1986)

Pass	Total Equity	Short Equity	Long Equity	Max. Equity	Min. Equity	P/L	Best Trade	Worst Trade	Max. Open P/L	Min. Open P/L
1	63.35	-82.59	145.94	142.68	-7.60	63.35	45.70	-21.61	49.08	0.00
2	-20.85	-24.89	4.04	17.49	-20.85	-20.85	12.47	-11.07	13.98	-2.22
3	-34.96	-32.93	-2.03	5.54	-34.96	-34.96	12.26	-12.51	13.98	-2.16
4	-30.29	-24.84	-5.45	5.77	-30.29	-30.29	10.07	-12.51	13.98	-2.16
5	-24.02	-30.33	6.31	11.61	-24.02	-24.02	11.69	-12.51	11.76	-2.89
6	-28.22	-29.76	1.54	4.88	-28.22	-28.22	11.30	-12.51	11.37	-1.58
7	-16.90	-21.85	4.95	14.17	-16.90	-16.90	10.07	-12.51	11.57	-1.83
8	7.58	-11.77	19.35	19.27	-2.96	7.58	9.06	-5.16	11.57	-1.83
9	25.17	-10.73	35.90	26.64	-3.26	25.17	9.88	-6.11	11.49	-2.21
10	28.01	-13.50	41.51	29.48	-3.78	28.01	9.57	-6.11	11.49	-2.26
11	34.02	-6.90	40.92	38.50	-2.93	34.02	9.28	-3.67	13.22	-2.91
12	17.40	-11.58	28.98	21.88	-10.29	17.40	9.52	-6.11	13.22	-2.91
13	21.09	-10.58	31.67	25.57	-11.23	21.09	11.81	-6.11	14.22	-2.91
14	22.32	-11.88	34.20	26.80	-12.28	22.32	11.81	-6.11	14.22	-2.91
15	26.54	-12.22	38.76	31.02	-13.35	26.54	11.81	-6.11	14.22	-2.91
16	34.27	-10.60	44.87	38.75	-10.64	34.27	20.28	-6.11	23.82	-3.23
17	26.25	-11.32	37.57	30.73	-9.75	26.25	19.27	-6.11	23.82	-3.23
18	33.96	-11.68	45.64	39.39	-7.27	33.96	20.08	-6.11	25.51	-3.23
19	28.54	-11.08	39.62	33.97	-10.40	28.54	20.08	-5.07	25.51	-1.98
20	34.41	-13.72	48.13	39.57	-8.56	34.41	25.15	-6.11	30.31	-3.16
21	32.14	-13.19	45.33	37.30	-10.23	32.14	23.27	-5.07	28.43	-3.16
22	21.67	-17.80	39.47	26.83	-15.11	21.67	23.27	-7.02	28.43	-3.16
23	21.47	-18.32	39.79	26.63	-16.11	21.47	23.27	-6.22	28.43	-2.92
24	14.52	-23.50	38.02	19.68	-22.90	14.52	23.27	-8.07	28.43	-6.22
25	13.83	-20.49	34.32	18.99	-22.13	13.83	23.27	-8.07	28.43	-6.22
26	24.21	-2.27	26.48	32.53	-16.98	24.21	20.11	-6.01	28.43	-8.28
27	21.23	-2.27	23.50	29.55	-19.96	21.23	20.11	-6.01	28.43	-8.28
28	14.59	-2.27	16.86	22.91	-23.93	14.59	20.11	-7.50	28.43	-8.28
29	4.32	-4.71	9.03	12.64	-19.03	4.32	19.80	-9.33	28.12	-7.50
30	1.91	-7.54	9.45	10.23	-19.81	1.91	19.36	-7.90	27.68	-6.07
31	21.83	-7.69	29.52	30.15	-12.06	21.83	32.34	-7.69	40.66	-5.11
32	28.65	0.00	28.65	38.03	-7.95	28.65	31.47	-6.01	40.85	-3.77
33	16.66	0.00	16.66	24.92	-14.93	16.66	27.54	-6.70	35.80	-4.46
34	11.26	0.00	11.26	23.77	-16.73	11.26	22.84	-7.72	35.35	-5.48
35	12.46	0.00	12.46	24.97	-15.53	12.46	22.84	-5.40	35.35	-6.29
36	6.37	0.00	6.37	18.88	-7.62	6.37	11.98	-5.40	24.49	-2.49
37	6.37	0.00	6.37	18.88	-7.62	6.37	11.98	-5.40	24.49	-2.49
38	11.64	0.00	11.64	23.47	-3.03	11.64	12.66	-1.02	24.49	-2.01
39	16.73	0.00	16.73	23.47	-3.03	-1.02	-1.02	-1.02	24.49	-2.01
40	9.07	0.00	9.07	15.81	-10.69	-8.20	-8.20	-8.20	24.01	-7.72
41	10.28	0.00	10.28	17.02	-9.48	-6.99	-6.99	-6.99	24.01	-6.51
42	10.28	0.00	10.28	17.02	-9.48	-6.99	-6.99	-6.99	24.01	-6.51
43	9.07	0.00	9.07	15.81	-10.69	-8.20	-8.20	-8.20	24.01	-7.72
44	9.07	0.00	9.07	15.81	-10.69	-8.20	-8.20	-8.20	24.01	-7.72
45	9.07	0.00	9.07	15.81	-10.69	-8.20	-8.20	-8.20	24.01	-7.72

EXHIBIT D-24: (continued)

Pass	Total Equity	Short Equity	Long Equity	Max. Equity	Min. Equity	P/L	Best Trade	Worst Trade	Max. Open P/L	Min. Open P/L
46	9.07	0.00	9.07	15.81	-10.69	-8.20	-8.20	-8.20	24.01	-7.72
47	-2.63	0.00	-2.63	4.11	-22.39	-19.90	-8.20	-11.70	24.01	-9.88
48	-13.15	0.00	-13.15	0.85	-22.32	-22.32	-10.62	-11.70	15.91	-9.88
49	6.28	0.00	6.28	13.02	-13.48	-11.47	-11.47	-11.47	24.49	-9.05
50	6.28	0.00	6.28	13.02	-13.48	-11.47	-11.47	-11.47	24.49	-9.05

Pass indicates period length.
Equity indicates the total number of points gained or lost.
Short equity indicates the number of points gained or lost on short positions.
Long equity indicates the number of points gained or lost on long positions.
Max. equity indicates the highest total profit recorded over the tested period.
Min. equity indicates the lowest total profit recorded over the tested period.
P/L indicates total number of points gained or lost in closed positions.
Best trade indicates the highest number of points gained in any closed trade.
Worst trade indicates the highest number of points lost in any closed trade.
Max. open P/L indicates the highest gain in a position which remains open at the end of the test run.
Min. open P/L indicates the highest gain in a position which remains open at the end of the test run.

EXHIBIT D-25:

Profitability Chart for Directional Movement (Smoothing Period Lengths of 1 to 25 from 1968 to 1977)

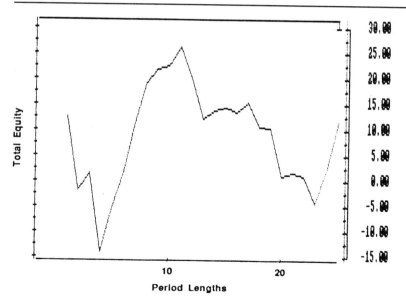

EXHIBIT D-26:
Profit Table for Directional Movement (Smoothing Period Lengths of 1 to 25 from 1968 to 1977)

Pass	Total Equity	Short Equity	Long Equity	Max. Equity	Min. Equity	P/L	Best Trade	Worst Trade	Max. Open P/L	Min. Open P/L
1	12.37	6.66	5.71	22.69	-5.70	12.58	10.60	-3.90	15.56	-3.31
2	-1.95	-14.45	12.50	12.37	-3.23	-1.95	7.99	-4.59	7.85	-2.00
3	1.41	-13.53	14.94	16.46	-0.47	1.41	6.89	-2.90	7.85	-1.91
4	-14.09	-21.05	6.96	1.67	-14.71	-14.09	6.89	-2.90	7.85	-1.91
5	-5.46	-17.99	12.53	4.83	-8.76	-5.44	6.55	-2.97	7.85	-1.91
6	1.55	-11.27	12.82	11.45	-6.79	0.98	6.55	-2.97	7.85	-1.91
7	11.37	-1.06	12.43	21.49	-5.02	11.58	8.38	-2.90	12.97	-1.50
8	19.07	5.21	13.86	30.26	-2.14	19.28	8.38	-2.90	12.97	-1.50
9	21.75	8.44	13.31	32.73	-1.34	21.96	10.03	-2.75	12.97	-1.50
10	22.40	9.65	12.75	30.41	-1.03	22.61	8.38	-2.75	12.97	-1.50
11	26.24	8.80	17.44	32.78	-1.95	26.45	8.38	-2.41	12.97	-1.50
12	20.11	7.17	12.94	26.91	-1.73	20.32	8.38	-2.15	12.97	-1.57
13	12.21	2.77	9.44	19.91	-2.61	12.42	8.38	-2.49	12.97	-1.57
14	13.76	3.50	10.26	21.78	-0.59	13.97	8.38	-2.39	12.97	-2.15
15	14.53	6.14	8.39	22.65	-0.59	14.74	9.07	-2.39	13.66	-2.15
16	13.57	10.14	3.43	21.90	-1.35	14.31	8.48	-2.42	13.66	-2.39
17	15.32	10.20	5.12	20.07	-3.16	15.32	8.48	-2.66	13.66	-2.15
18	10.63	6.36	4.27	13.69	-4.28	10.63	8.48	-2.98	13.66	-2.15
19	10.40	7.31	3.09	12.23	-4.87	10.40	9.52	-3.57	13.69	-2.98
20	0.95	0.81	0.14	5.03	-10.78	0.95	7.65	-3.57	13.69	-2.98
21	1.48	0.81	0.67	4.70	-11.11	1.48	7.65	-3.57	13.69	-2.98
22	0.94	3.06	-2.12	5.41	-10.40	0.94	6.96	-3.57	13.69	-2.98
23	-4.35	1.40	-5.75	2.03	-10.18	-4.35	3.97	-3.43	10.70	-2.84
24	2.31	10.85	-8.54	7.63	-12.65	2.31	12.61	-3.89	18.28	-3.40
25	11.59	18.55	-6.96	16.91	-3.37	11.59	12.78	-3.11	18.45	-3.40

Pass indicates period length.

Equity indicates the total number of points gained or lost.

Short equity indicates the number of points gained or lost on short positions.

Long equity indicates the number of points gained or lost on long positions.

Max. equity indicates the highest total profit recorded over the tested period.

Min. equity indicates the lowest total profit recorded over the tested period.

P/L indicates total number of points gained or lost in closed positions.

Best trade indicates the highest number of points gained in any closed trade.

Worst trade indicates the highest number of points lost in any closed trade.

Max. open P/L indicates the highest gain in a position which remains open at the end of the test run.

Min. open P/L indicates the highest loss in a position which remains open at the end of the test run.

EXHIBIT D-27:

New York Stock Exchange Composite Price Index Weekly High and Low from April 8, 1977 to December 31, 1986

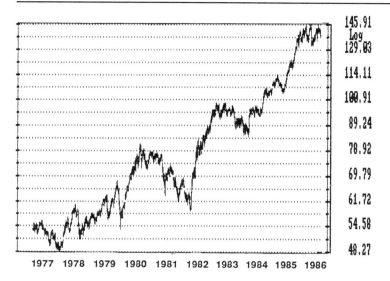

1977 1978 1979 1980 1981 1982 1983 1984 1985 1986

EXHIBIT D-28:

Spread Between Plus Directional Movement and Minus Directional Movement, 1977 to 1986 (Smoothed by 11-Week Moving Average)

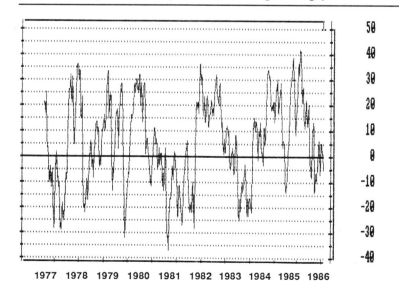

1977 1978 1979 1980 1981 1982 1983 1984 1985 1986

EXHIBIT D-29:
Average Directional Movement, 1977 to 1986, Smoothed by 11-Week Moving Average

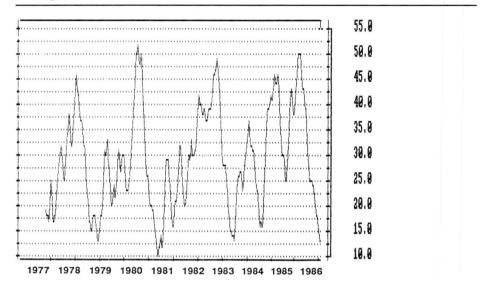

EXHIBIT D-30:
Total Equity for Directional Movement Index, 1977 to 1986, Smoothed by 11-Week Moving Average

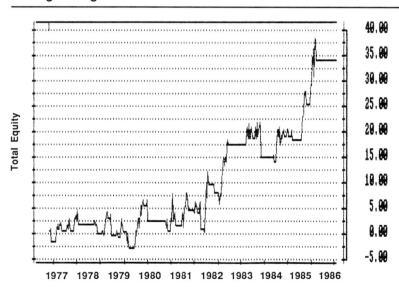

EXHIBIT D-31:

Profit Summary for Directional Movement Index, 1977 to 1986, Smoothed by 11-Week Moving Average

Item		Long	Short	Net
Per Trade Ranges		*Per Trade Ranges*		
Best Trade	(Closed position yielding maximum P/L)	9.28	3.14	9.28
.. Date		830701	820402	830701
Worst Trade	(Closed position yielding minimum P/L)	-3.59	-3.67	-3.67
.. Date		791012	840803	840803
Max Open P/L	(Maximum P/L occurring in an open position)	13.22	7.01	13.22
.. Date		860418	810925	860418
Min Open P/L	(Minimum P/L occurring in an open position)	-2.26	-2.91	-2.91
.. Date		830318	800425	800425
Overall Ranges		*Overall Ranges*		
Max P/L	(Maximum P/L from all closed positions during the run)	34.02	18.60	34.02
.. Date		860502	840427	860502
Min P/L	(Minimum P/L from all closed positions during the run)	-0.71	-2.93	-2.93
.. Date		800104	800502	800502
Max Equity	(Maximum P/L from all closed and open positions)	38.50	21.99	38.50
.. Date		860418	840615	860418
Min Equity	(Minimum P/L from all closed and open positions)	-2.93	-2.93	-2.93
.. Date		800627	800502	800502
Statistics		*Statistics*		
Periods	(The number of periods in each position and entire run)	162	81	509
Trades	(The number of trades in each position and entire run)	17	10	27
# Profitable	(The number of profitable trades...)	10	4	14
# Losing	(The number of unprofitable trades...)	7	6	13
% Profitable	(The percent of profitable trades to total trades)	58.82	40.00	51.85
% Losing	(The percent of unprofitable trades to total trades)	41.18	60.00	48.15
Results		*Results*		
Commission	(Total commission deducted from closed trades)	0.00	0.00	0.00
Slippage	(Total slippage deducted from closed trades)	0.00	0.00	0.00
Gross P/L	(Total points gained in closed positions)	40.92	-6.90	34.02
Open P/L	(P/L in a position which remains open at the end)	0.00	0.00	0.00
P/L	(Net P/L: Gross P/L less Commission and Slippage)	40.92	-6.90	34.02
Equity	(Net P/L plus Open P/L at the end of the run)	40.92	-6.90	34.02

There are columns for Long trades, Short trades and Net. In the Long column, results are reported only for Long positions. In the Short column, results are reported for Short positions only. In the Net column for the "Per Trade Ranges" and "Overall Ranges," entries will be the extreme from either the Long or Short column. Net column entries for the "Statistics" and "Results" categories are the combined results of entries in the Long and Short columns.

EXHIBIT D-32:

New York Stock Exchange Composite Price Index Weekly High and Low from January 5, 1968 to September 30, 1977

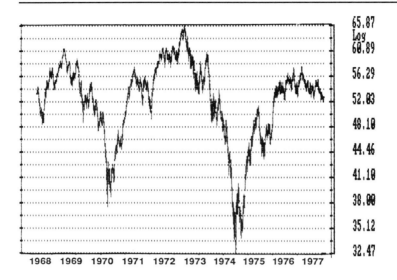

EXHIBIT D-33:

Spread Between Plus Directional Movement and Minus Directional Movement, 1968 to 1977, (Smoothed by 11-Week Moving Average)

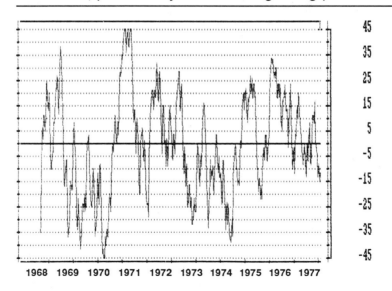

EXHIBIT D-34:

Average Directional Movement, 1968 to 1977, Smoothed by 11-Week Moving Average

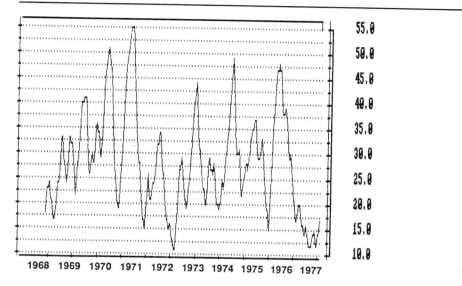

EXHIBIT D-35:

Total Equity for Directional Movement Index, 1968 to 1977, Smoothed by 11-Week Moving Average

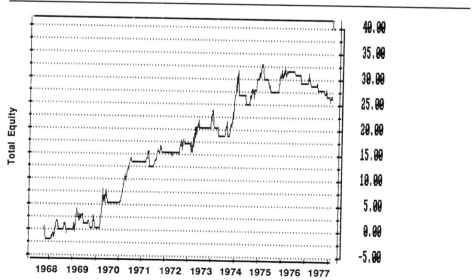

EXHIBIT D-36:
Profit Summary for Directional Movement Index, 1968 to 1977, Smoothed by 11-Week Moving Average

Item		Long	Short	Net
Per Trade Ranges		Per Trade Ranges		
Best Trade	(Closed position yielding maximum P/L)	8.02	8.38	8.38
..Date		710507	741011	741011
Worst Trade	(Closed position yielding minimum P/L)	-1.95	-2.41	-2.41
..Date		680726	751010	751010
Max Open P/L	(Maximum P/L occurring in an open position)	8.67	12.97	12.97
..Date		710423	741004	741004
Min Open P/L	(Minimum P/L occurring in an open position)	-1.03	-1.50	-1.50
..Date		680628	730413	730413
Overall Ranges		Overall Ranges		
Max P/L	(Maximum P/L from all closed positions during the run)	31.50	27.75	31.50
..Date		760507	770415	760507
Min P/L	(Minimum P/L from all closed positions during the run)	-1.95	-0.05	-1.95
..Date		680726	690404	680726
Max Equity	(Maximum P/L from all closed and open positions)	32.78	31.60	32.78
..Date		750711	741004	750711
Min Equity	(Minimum P/L from all closed and open positions)	-1.95	-0.54	-1.95
..Date		680726	690328	680726
Statistics		Statistics		
Periods	(The number of periods in each position and entire run)	147	110	509
Trades	(The number of trades in each position and entire run)	13	14	27
# Profitable	(The number of profitable trades. . .)	7	5	12
# Losing	(The number of unprofitable trades. . .)	6	9	15
% Profitable	(The percent of profitable trades to total trades)	53.85	35.71	44.44
% Losing	(The percent of unprofitable trades to total trades)	46.15	64.29	55.56
Results		Results		
Commission	(Total commission deducted from closed trades)	0.00	0.00	0.00
Slippage	(Total slippage deducted from closed trades)	0.00	0.00	0.00
Gross P/L	(Total points gained in closed positions)	17.44	9.01	26.45
Open P/L	(P/L in a position which remains open at the end)	0.00	-0.21	-0.21
P/L	(Net P/L: Gross P/L less Commission and Slippage)	17.44	9.01	26.45
Equity	(Net P/L plus Open P/L at the end of the run)	17.44	8.80	26.24

There are columns for Long trades, Short trades and Net. In the Long column, results are reported only for Long positions. In the Short column, results are reported for Short positions only. In the Net column for the "Per Trade Ranges" and "Overall Ranges," entries will be the extreme from either the Long or Short column. Net column entries for the "Statistics" and "Results" categories are the combined results of entries in the Long and Short columns.

DIVERGENCE ANALYSIS

A technical divergence is present when the price of something (stock, index, or contract) makes a significant movement unconfirmed or unaccompanied by a similar movement in a logically selected companion indicator. For example, in the classic Dow Theory, if the Dow Jones Industrial Average makes a new high, but the Dow Jones Transportation Average does not make a new high, then a negative divergence is present. This often has bearish implications for the near future. Conversely, if the industrials make a new low and the transports do not, then a positive divergence is present. This often has bullish implications for the immediate future. Other indexes and especially momentum indicators are also compared against the Dow Jones Industrials and other general price indexes (such as the Standard & Poor's 500 Index) for divergence analysis. In actual current practice, a wide variety of indicators are used for divergence analysis. The larger the number of indicators that confirm or diverge, the more significant it is generally thought to be.

In narrow and rigorous chi-squared statistical testing, David A. Glickstein and Rolf Wubbels ("Dow Theory is Alive and Well!", *Journal of Portfolio Management*, Spring 1983) concluded that daily relationships from 1971 through 1980 between the Dow Jones Industrials and Transports and the cumulative Daily Advance-Decline Line were not random but instead were statistically significant.

Testing weekly data from 1961 through 1980, Joseph E. Kalish[1] found the Dow Jones Industrial Average's divergencies versus transports, New York Stock Exchange cumulative daily advance-decline line, 20 most active stocks, cumulative weekly advance-decline line, and 5% and 10% reversals of *Trendline*'s percentage of stocks above their own 30-week moving averages were all statistically significant. Moreover, a composite chi-squared test showed that the more valid indicators confirming or diverging, the more meaningful it was, thus confirming conventional wisdom. Contrary to popular belief, however, Kalish was unable to demonstrate statistical significance of divergencies by the Dow Jones Utility Average, probably due to its long and variable lead times. (The study required indicator confirmation of the Dow Jones Industrial Average's new high or low within one week.) Finally, Kalish found that by combining the statistically valid signals into a composite indicator, confirmation and divergence signals were highly significant statistically beyond the .005 level. This means that the observed results should occur by

---

[1] "Divergence Analysis: Several Empirical Tests," *Market Technicians Association Journal*, May 1986.

chance less than 0.5% of the time. Or, it is more than 99.5% certain that these relationships did not occur by chance.

Our observations confirm that divergence analysis is a powerful technical analysis tool when properly used, particularly in conjunction with other statistically valid techniques. Unfortunately, the capability to test for divergence has not yet been incorporated into readily available personal computer software at this time.

DIVIDEND YIELDS

Most of the large and mature companies that dominate the capitalization-weighted market price indexes (such as the Standard & Poor's 500 Index) pay out a portion of their earnings to shareholders in the form of dividends that generally are paid quarterly. The Dividend Yield Indicator is simply the most recent four-quarter total of dividends per share for the S & P 500 stocks divided by the S & P 500 Index. Our studies showed that when Dividend Yields were relatively high (more than 5.2%), the stock market was undervalued or cheap and, therefore, offered potential for price appreciation. Conversely, when Dividend Yields were relatively low (less than 3.4%), the stock market was overvalued or too expensive and, therefore, was vulnerable to price decline.

Testing month-end data from 1944 through 1986 showed best and most consistent results when using Dividend Yields in conjunction with the 12-month simple moving average price crossover rule (12 SMA). The optimal rules are as follows:

1. Buy long when the S&P month-end close is greater than 12 SMA and when the S&P dividend yield is 3.4% or greater.

2. Sell long positions when the S&P month-end close is less than 12 SMA or the S&P dividend yield is less than 3.4%.

3. Sell short when the S&P month-end close is less than 12 SMA and the S&P dividend yield is less than 3.0%.

4. Cover short positions when the S&P month-end close is greater than 12 SMA or the S&P dividend yield is greater than 5.2%.

As shown in Exhibits D-37 through D-41 (pages 175–178), total profits of 284.11 S&P 500 points were better than the basic 12 SMA rule alone, with less than half the number of trades. Moreover, equity drawdown was smaller. Thus, the Reward/Risk Ratio is enhanced using 12 SMA with the dividend yield filter.

EXHIBIT D-37:

Standard & Poor's 500 Index Month-End Data, 1944 to 1986, with 12-Month Simple Moving Average

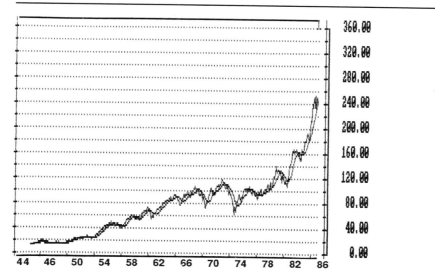

EXHIBIT D-38:

Dividend Yields (Four Quarter Trailing Dividends) Divided by Standard & Poor's 500 Composite Index, 1944 to 1986

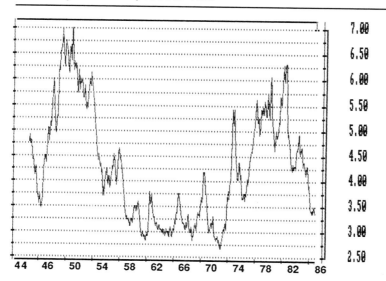

EXHIBIT D-39:

Total Equity for Dividend Yield and Standard & Poor's 500 Index 12-Month Simple Moving Average Crossover Rules Combined, 1944 to 1986

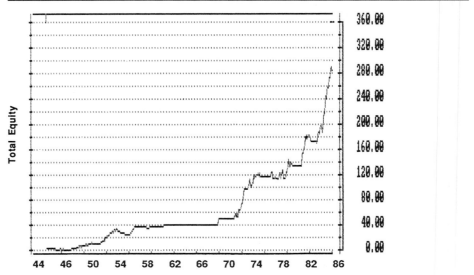

Note from Exhibits D-39 and D-41 that the growth in equity (cumulative profit) was fairly smooth with no substantial or prolonged drawdowns. This obviously is a highly desirable characteristic in an investment timing model.

EXHIBIT D-40:

Profit Summary for Dividend Yield and Standard & Poor's 500 Index Simple Moving Average Crossover Rules Combined, 1944 to 1986

Item		Long	Short	Net
Per Trade Ranges				
Best Trade	(Closed position yielding maximum P/L)	84.12	47.98	84.12
..Date		860630	740930	860630
Worst Trade	(Closed position yielding minimum P/L)	-3.68	47.98	-3.68
..Date		781031	740930	781031
Max Open P/L	(Maximum P/L occurring in an open position)	80.67	39.37	80.67
..Date		860531	740831	860531
Min Open P/L	(Minimum P/L occurring in an open position)	-3.10	0.00	-3.10
..Date		841130	730331	841130
Overall Ranges				
Max P/L	(Maximum P/L from all closed positions during the run)	284.11	97.67	284.11
..Date		861231	740930	861231
Min P/L	(Minimum P/L from all closed positions during the run)	-0.04	97.67	-0.04
..Date		481130	740930	481130
Max Equity	(Maximum P/L from all closed and open positions)	291.16	97.67	291.16
..Date		861130	740930	861130
Min Equity	(Minimum P/L from all closed and open positions)	-0.04	49.69	-0.04
..Date		481130	730331	481130
Statistics				
Periods	(The number of periods in each position and entire run)	232	18	509
Trades	(The number of trades in each position and entire run)	24	1	25
# Profitable	(The number of profitable trades. . .)	16	1	17
# Losing	(The number of unprofitable trades. . .)	8	0	8
% Profitable	(The percent of profitable trades to total trades)	66.67	100.00	68.00
% Losing	(The percent of unprofitable trades to total trades)	33.33	0.00	32.00
Results				
Commission	(Total commission deducted from closed trades)	0.00	0.00	0.00
Slippage	(Total slippage deducted from closed trades)	0.00	0.00	0.00
Gross P/L	(Total points gained in closed positions)	236.13	47.98	284.11
Open P/L	(P/L in a position which remains open at the end)	0.00	0.00	0.00
P/L	(Net P/L: Gross P/L less Commission and Slippage)	236.13	47.98	284.11
Equity	(Net P/L plus Open P/L at the end of the run)	236.13	47.98	284.11

There are columns for Long trades, Short trades and Net. In the Long column, results are reported only for Long positions. In the Short column, results are reported for Short positions only. In the Net column for the "Per Trade Ranges" and "Overall Ranges," entries will be the extreme from either the Long or Short column. Net column entries for the "Statistics" and "Results" categories are the combined results of entries in the Long and Short columns.

EXHIBIT D-41:

Transaction Dates and Prices for Dividend Yields and Standard & Poor's 500 Index Simple Moving Average Crossover Rules Combined, 1944 to 1986

Exit Date	Entry Date	Short or Long*	Entry Price	Exit Price	Maximum P/L	Minimum P/L	Gross P/L	Net P/L	Maximum Equity	Minimum Equity	Cumulative Profit or Equity
460831	450731	Lc	14.66	16.65	4.52	0.00	1.99	1.99	4.52	0.00	1.99
470930	470731	Lc	15.76	15.11	0.00	-0.65	-0.65	-0.65	4.52	0.00	1.34
471130	471031	Lc	15.43	14.99	0.00	-0.44	-0.44	-0.44	4.52	0.00	0.90
480131	471231	Lc	15.30	14.69	0.00	-0.61	-0.61	-0.61	4.52	0.00	0.29
481130	480331	Lc	15.08	14.75	1.66	-0.33	-0.33	-0.33	4.52	-0.04	-0.04
530430	490831	Lc	15.22	24.62	11.35	0.00	9.40	9.40	11.31	-0.04	9.36
560930	531231	Lc	24.81	45.35	24.58	0.00	20.54	20.54	33.94	-0.04	29.90
570131	561231	Lc	46.67	44.72	0.00	-1.95	-1.95	-1.95	33.94	-0.04	27.95
570831	570531	Lc	47.43	45.22	0.48	-2.21	-2.21	-2.21	33.94	-0.04	25.74
581231	580430	Lc	43.44	55.21	11.77	0.00	11.77	11.77	37.51	-0.04	37.51
600930	600831	Lc	56.96	53.52	0.00	-3.44	-3.44	-3.44	37.51	-0.04	34.07
610131	601231	Lc	58.11	61.78	3.67	0.00	3.67	3.67	37.74	-0.04	37.74
630131	621231	Lc	63.10	66.20	3.10	0.00	3.10	3.10	40.84	-0.04	40.84
670228	670131	Lc	86.61	86.78	0.17	0.00	0.17	0.17	41.01	-0.04	41.01
710131	701130	Lc	87.20	95.88	8.68	0.00	8.68	8.68	49.69	-0.04	49.69
740930	730331	Sc	111.52	63.54	47.98	0.00	47.98	47.98	97.67	-0.04	97.67
770131	750228	Lc	81.59	102.03	25.87	0.00	20.44	20.44	123.54	-0.04	118.11
781031	780430	Lc	96.83	93.15	6.46	-3.68	-3.68	-3.68	124.57	-0.04	114.43
790228	781231	Lc	96.11	96.28	3.82	0.00	0.17	0.17	124.57	-0.04	114.60
800331	790331	Lc	101.59	102.09	12.57	-2.51	0.50	0.50	127.17	-0.04	115.10
810731	800531	Lc	111.24	130.92	29.28	0.00	19.68	19.68	144.38	-0.04	134.78
840229	820831	Lc	119.51	157.06	48.60	0.00	37.55	37.55	183.38	-0.04	172.33
860630	840831	Lc	166.68	250.80	84.12	-3.10	84.12	84.12	256.45	-0.04	256.45
860831	860731	Lc	236.12	252.93	16.81	0.00	16.81	16.81	273.26	-0.04	273.26
861231	860930	Lc	231.32	242.17	17.90	0.00	10.85	10.85	291.16	-0.04	284.11

*Lc indicates a long position that has been closed. Sc indicates a short position that has been closed.

Exit Date indicates the date a trade is closed out.

Entry Date indicates the date a trade is opened or begun.

P/L indicates profit or loss on the trade.

Equity is the total cumulative P/L.

THE DOW THEORY

The Dow Theory is one of the oldest methods used to determine the major trend of prices in the stock market. It was derived from the writings of Charles H. Dow during the late 1800s.

The Dow Theory utilizes two market indexes, namely the Dow Jones Industrial Average and the Dow Jones Transportation Average. It is comprised of the following seven basic principles:

1. Everything is discounted by the averages. Since the averages reflect the activities of all stock market investors, everything that could possibly affect the demand for or supply of stocks is discounted by the averages.

2. There are three trends in the market. A primary trend is the long-term trend in the price of stocks. A secondary reaction is corrective in nature, interrupting and acting in the opposite direction of the primary trend. Minor trends are day-to-day fluctuations that are disregarded in the Dow Theory.

3. Primary up trends (bull markets) usually have three up moves. The first move up in stock prices is the result of far-sighted investors accumulating stocks at a time when business is slow but anticipated to improve. The second move up is a result of investors buying stocks based on increased company earnings. The final up move occurs when the general public jumps in buying stocks at a time when all the financial news is good. During the final up move, speculation becomes rampant.

4. Primary down trends (bear markets) usually have three down moves. The first move down in stock prices occurs when far-sighted investors recognize that business earnings are too high to be maintained and they sell stocks. The second move down reflects panic as buyers become scarce and sellers rush to get out of the market. The final move down results from distress selling and the need to raise cash.

5. The two averages must confirm each other. To signal a bear trend, both the Dow Jones Industrial Average and the Dow Jones Transportation Average must drop below their respective lows of previous secondary reactions. To signal a bull trend, both averages must rise above their respective highs of previous upward secondary reactions.

Normally one average signals a change in trend before the other. The Dow Theory does not stipulate a time period beyond which a confirmation becomes invalid.

6. Only closing prices are considered.

7. A trend remains in effect until a reversal has been signaled by both averages.

Exhibit D-42 provides a record of bull market signals since 1897. Bear market signals are reflected in Exhibit D-43.

Although the Dow Theory has been successful, it is criticized for several reasons. The major criticism is that it is frequently late in giving signals, thus depriving investors of profits that could be earned during the beginning and end of major moves.

For a more detailed discussion of the Dow Theory, refer to the classic book, *Technical Analysis of Stock Trends*, by Robert D. Edwards and John Magee (John Magee Inc., 103 State Street, Boston, MA 02109).

EXHIBIT D-42:
Dow Theory Bull Market Signals from 1897 to 1986

Date	Dow Jones Industrial Average	Percent Gain
JUL 1897	44	43
OCT 1900	59	0
JUL 1904	51	80
APR 1908	70	21
OCT 1910	82	3
APR 1915	65	32
MAY 1918	82	22
FEB 1922	84	8
DEC 1923	94	226
MAY 1933	84	95
JUN 1938	127	7
JUL 1939	143	(7)
FEB 1943	126	52
APR 1948	184	(6)
OCT 1950	229	22
JAN 1954	288	63
APR 1958	450	36
NOV 1960	602	13
NOV 1962	625	43
JAN 1967	823	9
DEC 1970	823	12
JAN 1975	680	18
APR 1978	780	23
AUG 1982	840	?

EXHIBIT D-43:
Dow Theory Bear Market Signals from 1897 to 1986

Date	Dow Jones Industrial Average	Percent Gain
DEC 1899	63	6
JUN 1903	59	14
APR 1906	92	24
MAY 1910	85	4
JAN 1913	85	24
AUG 1917	86	5
FEB 1920	99	16
JUN 1923	91	(3)
OCT 1929	306	73
SEP 1937	164	23
MAR 1939	136	5
MAY 1940	138	8
AUG 1946	191	4
NOV 1948	173	(32)
APR 1953	280	(3)
OCT 1956	468	4
MAR 1960	612	2
APR 1962	683	8
MAY 1966	900	9
JUN 1969	900	9
APR 1973	921	26
OCT 1977	801	3
JUL 1981	960	13

EARNINGS FORECASTS

It is generally accepted on Wall Street that earnings are important to stock prices. Moreover, given the consensus that the stock market leads economic conditions by about 6 months, it stands to reason that if we could correctly forecast the direction of earnings two quarters in advance, our investment performance ought to be good.

Assuming perfect earnings forecasting ability and using the four-quarter moving total of trailing earnings for the S&P 500, as published in *Standard & Poor's Statistical Record*, our decision rule was to buy two quarters before an upturn in earnings and to sell and sell short two quarters before a downturn in earnings. Surprisingly, the historical results of perfect earnings forecasting were very poor, particularly after 1973. As shown in Exhibits E-1 and E-2, equity or total cumulative profit amounted to only 21.47 S&P points from 1944 through 1986—only 8% of the profits of our combined price and divided model (refer to section on Dividend Yields). As shown in Exhibit E-2, from maximum equity of 70.95 S&P points on December 31, 1972 to minimum equity of −26.68 S&P points on December 31, 1985, the maximum equity drawdown was 97.63 S&P points. These results would be devastating to virtually any investor.

EXHIBIT E-1:
Total Equity for Perfect Earnings Forecasting Model Direction of Earnings, 1944 to 1986, Using Standard & Poor's 500 Index Month-End Closing Data

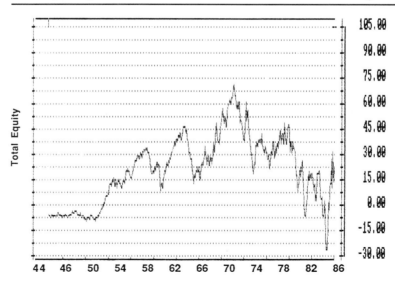

EXHIBIT E-2:

Perfect Earnings Forecasting Model Direction of Earnings, 1944 to 1986, Using Standard & Poor's 500 Index Month-End Closing Data

Item		Long	Short	Net
Per Trade Ranges	*— Per Trade Ranges —*			
Best Trade	(Closed position yielding maximum P/L)	39.52	13.50	39.52
.. Date		860630	700930	860630
Worst Trade	(Closed position yielding minimum P/L)	-19.58	-45.18	-45.18
.. Date		810930	851231	851231
Max Open P/L	(Maximum P/L occurring in an open position)	36.07	24.99	36.07
.. Date		860531	700630	860531
Min Open P/L	(Minimum P/L occurring in an open position)	-12.97	-36.07	-36.07
.. Date		810831	851130	851130
Overall Ranges	*— Overall Ranges —*			
Max P/L	(Maximum P/L from all closed positions during the run)	47.38	37.11	47.38
.. Date		800930	700930	800930
Min P/L	(Minimum P/L from all closed positions during the run)	-8.44	-26.68	-26.68
.. Date		530630	851231	851231
Max Equity	(Maximum P/L from all closed and open positions)	70.95	61.36	70.95
.. Date		721231	740930	721231
Min Equity	(Minimum P/L from all closed and open positions)	-26.68	-26.68	-26.68
.. Date		851231	851231	851231
Statistics	*— Statistics —*			
Periods	(The number of periods in each position and entire run)	349	160	509
Trades	(The number of trades in each position and entire run)	16	15	31
# Profitable	(The number of profitable trades...)	12	4	16
# Losing	(The number of unprofitable trades....)	4	11	15
% Profitable	(The percent of profitable trades to total trades)	75.00	26.67	51.61
% Losing	(The percent of unprofitable trades to total trades)	25.00	73.33	48.39
Results	*— Results —*			
Commission	(Total commission deducted from closed trades)	0.00	0.00	0.00
Slippage	(Total slippage deducted from closed trades)	0.00	0.00	0.00
Gross P/L	(Total points gained in closed positions)	125.41	-112.57	12.84
Open P/L	(P/L in a position which remains open at the end)	0.00	8.63	8.63
P/L	(Net P/L: Gross P/L less Commission and Slippage)	125.41	-112.57	12.84
Equity	(Net P/L plus Open P/L at the end of the run)	125.41	-103.94	21.47

There are columns for Long trades, Short trades and Net. In the Long column, results are reported only for Long positions. In the Short column, results are reported for Short positions only. In the Net column for the "Per Trade Ranges" and "Overall Ranges," entries will be the extreme from either the Long or Short column. Net column entries for the "Statistics" and "Results" categories are the combined results of entries in the Long and Short columns.

EXPONENTIAL MOVING AVERAGE: EXPONENTIAL SMOOTHING

Mathematically, a single exponential smoothing is calculated as follows:

$$X = (C - X_p)K + X_p$$

where

X is the exponential smoothing for the current period.

C is the closing price for the current period.

X_p is the exponential smoothing for the previous period.

K is the smoothing constant, equal to $2/n + 1$ for Compu Trac and $2/n$ for Back Trak.

n is the total number of periods in a simple moving average to be roughly aproximated by X (see example, page 185).

There are other slightly different representations of exponential smoothing formulas. They all involve multiplying by constants, and they all result in a front-loaded (or front-weighted) smoothed line that gives more weight to recent prices and ever decreasing weight to the oldest data, which theoretically never totally goes away, no matter what its age. John Carder and other technicians consider this "tail weighting" of stale data to be a disadvantage, sometimes holding the exponentially smoothed average back too long following a large move in prices. For practical purposes, however, exponential average disadvantages do not appear severe by our testing. It is certain that exponentially smoothed averages are somewhat more responsive or sensitive than equivalent length simple moving averages, but they are somewhat less responsive than equivalent length weighted moving averages.

The only parameter to be optimized was n, which determines the smoothing constant, K. For this, we used Compu Trac software and two 9.75-year test periods of weekly data (consisting of high, low, close, and volume for each week) for the broad-based NYSE Composite Index. The first period ran from January 5, 1968 through September 30, 1977, and the second period ran from April 8, 1977 through December 31, 1986. The overlap in data was necessary to facilitate testing of various moving averages throughout the full time period.

Optimal values were determined by a systematic trial-and-error procedure on the computer. We tested for n equal to 1 through 75, roughly equivalent to simple moving averages ranging in length from 1 week (which is the indicator data itself) up to 75 weeks. The results of optimization runs for each n-week time length are shown in Exhibits E-3 through E-6 (pages 186–191).

**Example of Exponential Smoothing
Approximating a Four-Day Simple Moving Average**

Year End	NYSE Close	Previous Periods EMA	Difference Close Minus EMA Previous (D)	Multiply by	Smoothing Constant (K) Equals $2 \div (n+1) =$ $2 \div (4+1) =$	Difference Times Smoothing Constant $D \times K$	Plus New EMA Previous	Current New EMA
1968	58.90	58.90	0.00	×	.4	0.00	58.90 =	58.90
1969	51.53	58.90	−7.37	×	.4 =	−2.95	+58.90 =	55.95
1970	50.23	55.95	−5.72	×	.4 =	−2.29	+55.95 =	53.66
1971	56.43	53.66	+2.77	×	.4 =	+1.11	+53.66 =	54.77
1972	64.48	54.77	+9.71	×	.4 =	+3.88	+54.77 =	58.65
1973	51.82	58.65	−6.83	×	.4 =	−2.73	+58.65 =	55.92
1974	36.13	55.92	−19.79	×	.4 =	−7.92	+55.92 =	48.00
1975	47.64	48.00	−0.36	×	.4 =	−0.14	+48.00 =	47.86
1976	57.88	47.86	+10.02	×	.4 =	+4.01	+47.86 =	51.87
1977	52.50	51.87	+0.63	×	.4 =	+0.25	+51.87 =	52.12
1978	53.62	52.12	+1.51	×	.4 =	+0.60	+52.12 =	52.72
1979	61.95	52.72	+9.23	×	.4 =	+3.69	+52.72 =	56.41
1980	77.86	56.41	+21.45	×	.4 =	+8.58	+56.41 =	64.99
1981	71.11	64.99	+6.12	×	.4 =	+2.45	+64.99 =	67.44
1982	81.03	67.44	+13.59	×	.4 =	+5.44	+67.44 =	72.88
1983	95.18	72.88	+22.30	×	.4 =	+8.92	+72.88 =	81.80
1984	96.38	81.80	+14.58	×	.4 =	+5.83	+81.80 =	87.63
1985	121.58	87.63	+33.95	×	.4 =	+13.58	+87.63 =	101.21
1986	138.58	101.21	+37.37	×	.4 =	+14.95	+101.21 =	116.16
1987		116.16		×	.4 =		+116.16 =	

Equity signifies total profits or losses accumulated for each pass (length of *n*).

The highest combined profit for both optimization runs 1968–1977 and 1977–1986 was produced by the 42-week exponential moving average crossover rule. There were fairly good results for periods from 31 to 52 weeks but some poor results for less than 10 weeks. Note that the results take on the shape of a non-random bell-shaped curve. As shown in Exhibits E-7 through E-14 (pages 192–197), combined profit of 112.38 NYSE points exceeded that of our 40-week simple moving average crossover rule standard of comparison.

The 42-week exponential moving average (smoothing constant = 2 ÷ (42 + 1) = .0465) crossover rule produced very similar results to the optimal simple moving average of nearly equivalent length, as one might expect. (See Simple Moving Average.) Note in Exhibits E-10 and E-14 that the combined 19-year number of trades with the exponential moving average was 71, or 42% more than the optimal 45-week simple moving average total of 50. As a result of this larger number of transactions, profit per trade at 1.58 NYSE points was not only below 2.24 for the 45-week simple

EXHIBIT E-3:

Profitability Chart for Exponential Moving Average (Period Lengths of 1 to 75 Weeks from 1977 to 1986)

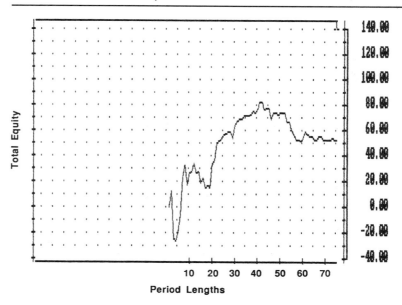

EXHIBIT E-4:

Profit Table for Exponential Moving Average (Period Lengths of 1 to 75 Weeks from 1977 to 1986)

Pass	Total Equity	Short Equity	Long Equity	Max. Equity	Min. Equity	P/L	Best Trade	Worst Trade	Max. Open P/L	Min. Open P/L
1	0.00	0.00	0.00	0.00	0.00	0.00	N/A	N/A	0.00	0.00
2	12.62	-35.51	48.13	12.62	-19.82	9.67	14.67	-4.99	15.56	-1.13
3	-24.76	-54.20	29.44	12.69	-33.54	-27.71	12.87	-9.41	15.56	-2.00
4	-25.98	-54.81	28.83	22.75	-34.76	-28.93	14.67	-9.41	17.18	-2.00
5	-19.66	-51.65	31.99	27.19	-26.86	-22.61	13.49	-9.41	17.18	-2.89
6	-6.00	-44.82	38.82	37.36	-12.34	-8.52	14.89	-9.41	18.43	-2.89
7	22.34	-30.65	52.99	51.37	-8.23	19.82	30.63	-9.41	34.17	-2.89
8	33.04	-25.30	59.44	61.43	-7.90	33.04	30.63	-9.41	34.17	-2.89
9	17.06	-33.29	51.45	41.99	-8.88	17.06	30.63	-9.41	34.17	-2.89
10	26.36	-28.64	56.10	51.29	-9.72	26.36	30.63	-9.41	34.17	-2.89
11	28.10	-27.77	56.97	53.03	-11.88	28.10	30.63	-9.41	34.17	-2.89
12	33.36	-25.14	56.66	60.49	-11.96	33.36	31.36	-9.41	36.52	-2.89
13	26.78	-28.43	53.37	60.23	-11.90	26.78	29.62	-9.41	36.52	-2.89
14	27.10	-28.27	53.53	60.55	-10.54	27.10	29.62	-9.41	36.52	-2.89
15	19.18	-32.23	49.57	58.87	-9.24	19.18	29.62	-9.41	36.52	-2.89
16	21.98	-30.83	50.97	61.67	-9.72	21.98	29.62	-9.41	36.52	-2.89
17	15.16	-34.24	47.56	54.85	-5.98	15.16	28.95	-9.41	36.52	-2.89
18	15.76	-33.94	47.86	55.45	-5.98	15.76	28.95	-9.41	36.52	-2.89
19	14.52	-34.56	47.24	54.21	-5.28	14.52	28.95	-9.41	36.52	-2.89
20	34.22	-24.71	60.03	67.63	-6.92	34.22	29.63	-9.41	36.52	-2.89
21	36.46	-23.59	61.15	69.87	-9.98	36.46	29.63	-9.41	36.52	-2.89
22	49.48	-17.08	67.66	67.15	-9.98	49.48	29.63	-4.67	36.52	-2.89
23	50.64	-16.50	68.24	68.31	-9.98	50.64	29.63	-4.67	36.52	-2.89
24	54.02	-14.81	69.93	71.69	-6.26	54.02	29.63	-4.67	36.52	-2.89
25	55.74	-13.95	70.79	71.82	-5.88	55.74	29.63	-4.67	37.17	-2.89
26	57.00	-13.32	71.42	73.08	-5.88	57.00	29.63	-4.67	37.17	-2.89
27	59.22	-12.21	72.53	75.30	-5.88	59.22	29.63	-4.67	37.17	-2.89
28	58.76	-12.44	72.30	74.84	-5.88	58.76	29.12	-4.67	37.17	-2.89
29	53.60	-15.02	69.72	69.68	-5.88	53.60	26.54	-4.67	37.17	-2.89
30	63.48	-10.08	73.56	76.00	-4.65	60.60	26.54	-2.89	37.17	-2.00
31	67.46	-8.09	75.55	79.98	-4.65	64.58	26.63	-2.89	37.17	-2.00
32	69.32	-7.16	76.48	81.84	-4.65	66.44	26.63	-2.89	38.76	-2.00
33	69.32	-7.16	76.48	81.84	-4.65	66.44	26.63	-2.89	38.76	-2.00
34	71.72	-5.96	77.68	82.46	-4.65	67.95	26.25	-2.33	38.76	-1.28
35	71.72	-5.96	77.68	82.46	-4.65	67.95	26.25	-2.33	38.76	-1.28
36	70.86	-6.39	77.25	81.60	-5.51	67.09	26.25	-2.33	38.76	-1.28
37	72.88	-5.38	78.26	83.62	-5.51	69.11	26.86	-2.33	39.37	-1.28
38	75.22	-4.21	79.43	84.22	-5.51	70.58	26.86	-2.68	39.37	-1.28
39	74.30	-4.67	78.97	83.30	-5.51	69.66	26.86	-2.68	39.37	-1.28
40	76.82	-3.41	80.23	84.92	-5.51	71.73	26.86	-2.68	39.37	-1.28
41	82.18	-0.73	82.91	90.28	-5.51	77.09	26.86	-2.26	39.37	-1.28
42	82.40	-0.62	83.02	89.14	-5.51	49.77	25.75	-2.26	39.37	-1.28
43	76.14	-3.75	79.89	82.88	-5.51	43.51	25.75	-3.98	39.37	-1.28
44	76.96	-3.34	80.30	83.70	-5.53	44.33	25.75	-3.98	39.37	-1.28
45	76.96	-3.34	80.30	83.70	-5.53	44.33	25.75	-3.98	39.37	-1.28
46	69.36	-7.14	76.50	76.10	-5.63	36.73	22.84	-3.98	39.37	-1.87
47	73.94	-4.85	78.79	80.68	-5.63	28.59	22.84	-2.26	52.09	-1.66
48	73.94	-4.85	78.79	80.68	-5.63	28.59	22.84	-2.26	52.09	-1.66
49	73.04	-5.30	78.34	79.78	-6.53	27.69	22.84	-2.26	52.09	-1.66
50	73.56	-5.04	78.60	80.30	-4.97	28.21	22.84	-2.26	52.09	-1.66

EXHIBIT E-4: (continued)

Pass	Total Equity	Short Equity	Long Equity	Max. Equity	Min. Equity	P/L	Best Trade	Worst Trade	Max. Open P/L	Min. Open P/L
51	73.56	-5.04	78.60	80.30	-4.97	28.21	22.84	-2.26	52.09	-1.66
52	73.56	-5.04	78.60	80.30	-4.97	28.21	22.84	-2.26	52.09	-1.66
53	65.90	-8.87	74.77	72.64	-5.49	20.55	22.84	-2.46	52.09	-1.60
54	65.90	-8.87	74.77	72.64	-5.49	20.55	22.84	-2.46	52.09	-1.60
55	60.44	-11.60	72.04	67.18	-5.49	15.09	22.84	-2.79	52.09	-1.41
56	55.96	-13.84	69.80	62.70	-9.97	10.61	22.84	-2.89	52.09	-1.54
57	52.62	-15.51	68.13	59.36	-9.97	7.27	22.84	-3.67	52.09	-1.54
58	52.62	-15.51	68.13	59.36	-9.97	7.27	22.84	-3.67	52.09	-1.54
59	51.50	-16.07	67.57	58.24	-9.97	6.15	22.84	-3.67	52.09	-1.54
60	54.24	-14.70	68.94	60.98	-9.00	8.89	22.84	-3.67	52.09	-1.54
61	59.22	-12.21	71.43	65.96	-9.00	13.87	22.84	-3.67	52.09	-1.54
62	56.20	-13.72	69.92	62.94	-9.00	10.85	22.84	-3.67	52.09	-1.54
63	54.88	-14.38	69.26	61.62	-10.19	9.53	22.84	-3.67	52.09	-1.54
64	54.88	-14.38	69.26	61.62	-10.19	9.53	22.84	-3.67	52.09	-1.54
65	51.94	-15.85	67.79	58.68	-10.19	6.59	19.81	-3.67	52.09	-1.54
66	51.94	-15.85	67.79	58.68	-10.19	6.59	19.81	-3.67	52.09	-1.54
67	54.58	-14.53	69.11	61.32	-10.19	9.23	19.81	-3.67	52.09	-1.54
68	54.58	-14.53	69.11	61.32	-10.19	9.23	19.81	-3.67	52.09	-1.54
69	52.20	-15.72	67.92	58.94	-11.61	6.85	19.33	-3.67	52.09	-1.54
70	52.20	-15.72	67.92	58.94	-11.61	6.85	19.33	-3.67	52.09	-1.54
71	52.20	-15.72	67.92	58.94	-11.61	6.85	19.33	-3.67	52.09	-1.54
72	52.20	-15.72	67.92	58.94	-11.61	6.85	19.33	-3.67	52.09	-1.54
73	54.00	-14.82	68.82	60.74	-11.61	8.65	18.68	-3.67	52.09	-1.54
74	52.48	-15.58	68.06	59.22	-11.61	7.13	18.68	-3.67	52.09	-1.54
75	52.48	-15.58	68.06	59.22	-11.61	7.13	18.68	-3.67	52.09	-1.54

Pass indicates period length.
Equity indicates the total number of points gained or lost.
Short equity indicates the number of points gained or lost on short positions.
Long equity indicates the number of points gained or lost on long positions.
Max. equity indicates the highest total profit recorded over the tested period.
Min. equity indicates the lowest total profit recorded over the tested period.
P/L indicates total number of points gained or lost in closed positions.
Best trade indicates the highest number of points gained in any closed trade.
Worst trade indicates the highest number of points lost in any closed trade.
Max. open P/L indicates the highest gain in a position which remains open at the end of the test run.
Min. open P/L indicates the highest gain in a position which remains open at the end of the test run.

moving average, but was also lower than 1.66 for our 40-week simple moving average crossover rule standard. Moreover, exponential moving averages underperformed simple moving averages in our testing of 42 years of month-end data (not shown). Our conclusion is that for price crossover decision rules, exponential smoothing offers no worthwhile advantages and may offer moderate performance disadvantages compared to simple moving averages.

EXHIBIT E-5:

Profitability Chart for Exponential Moving Average (Period Lengths of 1 to 75 Weeks from 1968 to 1977)

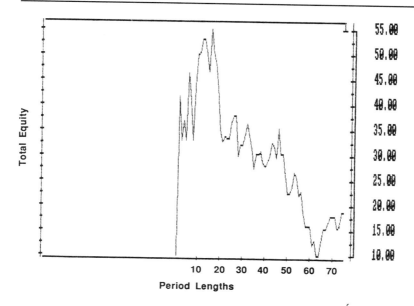

DIRECTION OF EXPONENTIAL MOVING AVERAGE

Mathematically, an n-period exponential moving average changes direction, from falling to rising or from rising to falling, at the same time that the new data crosses the n-period exponential moving average. Therefore, it would be redundant to optimize and follow both the direction and the crossover of an exponential moving average.

EXHIBIT E-6:
Profit Table for Exponential Moving Average (Period Lengths of 1 to 75 Weeks from 1968 to 1977)

Pass	Total Equity	Short Equity	Long Equity	Max. Equity	Min. Equity	P/L	Best Trade	Worst Trade	Max. Open P/L	Min. Open P/L
1	0.00	0.00	0.00	0.00	0.00	0.00	N/A	N/A	0.00	0.00
2	41.70	21.53	20.17	53.06	-0.67	41.70	7.08	-3.24	9.42	-0.73
3	33.10	17.23	15.87	41.88	-0.67	33.10	7.08	-3.24	9.42	-0.73
4	36.80	19.08	17.72	44.42	-0.67	36.80	10.03	-3.24	11.76	-0.73
5	33.12	17.24	15.88	41.62	-0.67	33.12	10.03	-2.84	12.97	-1.04
6	46.14	23.75	22.39	53.38	-0.67	44.83	9.71	-2.84	12.97	-1.04
7	40.96	21.16	19.80	48.22	-0.67	39.65	9.71	-2.84	12.97	-1.04
8	33.14	17.25	15.89	40.40	-0.67	31.83	8.95	-2.84	12.97	-1.54
9	43.70	22.53	21.17	52.64	-0.67	42.39	10.49	-2.76	15.08	-1.54
10	50.00	25.68	24.32	59.93	-0.67	48.69	12.74	-2.35	15.08	-1.12
11	50.18	25.77	24.41	59.75	-0.67	48.87	12.74	-2.35	15.08	-1.12
12	53.22	27.29	25.93	62.79	-0.67	51.91	12.74	-2.17	15.08	-1.12
13	53.26	27.31	25.95	62.83	-0.67	51.95	12.07	-2.17	15.08	-1.12
14	49.90	25.63	24.27	57.05	-0.67	48.59	12.07	-2.17	15.08	-0.98
15	46.48	23.92	22.56	53.63	-0.67	45.17	12.07	-2.33	17.31	-0.98
16	55.38	28.37	27.01	62.53	-0.67	54.07	13.09	-2.33	19.13	-0.98
17	50.24	25.80	24.44	58.10	-0.77	48.93	12.40	-2.33	19.13	-1.24
18	48.10	24.73	23.37	56.92	-0.77	46.79	12.40	-2.33	19.13	-1.24
19	43.44	22.40	21.04	52.26	-2.73	42.13	12.40	-2.33	19.13	-1.24
20	35.00	18.18	16.82	45.72	-2.73	33.69	12.40	-2.37	19.13	-1.24
21	32.72	17.04	15.68	43.44	-2.21	31.41	13.46	-2.37	19.13	-0.96
22	33.70	17.53	16.17	42.27	-2.21	32.39	13.46	-2.37	19.13	-0.96
23	33.52	17.44	16.08	42.09	-2.21	32.21	13.46	-2.37	19.13	-0.96
24	33.52	17.44	16.08	42.09	-2.21	32.21	13.46	-2.37	19.13	-0.96
25	36.56	18.96	17.60	45.21	-2.21	35.25	13.46	-2.07	19.13	-0.96
26	37.66	19.51	18.15	48.09	-1.67	36.35	13.19	-2.21	19.13	-0.71
27	37.66	19.51	18.15	48.09	-1.67	36.35	13.19	-2.21	19.13	-0.71
28	30.04	15.70	14.34	40.47	-5.29	28.73	11.12	-2.21	19.13	-0.71
29	32.34	16.85	15.49	42.77	-5.29	31.03	16.70	-2.21	24.71	-0.71
30	32.34	16.85	15.49	42.77	-5.29	31.03	16.70	-2.21	24.71	-0.71
31	34.12	17.74	16.38	44.55	-2.83	32.81	16.70	-2.21	24.71	-0.71
32	36.30	18.83	17.47	46.73	-2.83	34.99	16.70	-2.21	24.71	-0.71
33	33.96	17.66	16.30	45.34	-2.83	32.65	16.70	-2.21	24.71	-0.71
34	31.68	16.52	15.16	42.86	-2.83	30.37	16.70	-2.21	24.71	-0.71
35	27.38	14.37	13.01	39.50	-2.83	26.07	16.70	-2.21	24.71	-0.71
36	30.40	15.88	14.52	42.52	-2.81	29.09	16.70	-1.86	24.71	-0.71
37	30.18	15.77	14.41	41.18	-2.81	28.87	16.70	-1.86	24.71	-0.71
38	30.98	16.17	14.81	41.98	-2.81	29.67	16.70	-1.86	24.71	-0.71
39	28.34	14.85	13.49	41.98	-2.81	27.03	16.70	-1.86	24.71	-0.95
40	27.82	14.59	13.23	41.46	-2.81	26.51	16.70	-1.86	24.71	-0.95
41	28.72	15.04	13.68	42.31	-2.25	27.41	16.70	-1.86	24.71	-0.95
42	29.98	15.67	14.31	44.60	-1.01	28.67	16.70	-2.03	24.71	-0.95
43	32.38	16.87	15.51	45.87	-1.01	31.07	15.81	-2.03	24.71	-0.95
44	31.76	16.56	15.20	45.25	-1.01	30.45	15.81	-2.03	24.71	-0.95
45	29.80	15.58	14.22	43.07	-1.01	28.49	15.81	-2.03	24.71	-0.95
46	35.40	18.38	17.02	45.73	-0.98	34.09	15.81	-2.03	24.71	-0.73
47	30.46	15.91	14.55	44.23	-0.98	29.15	15.81	-2.03	24.71	-1.12
48	30.46	15.91	14.55	44.23	-0.98	29.15	15.81	-2.03	24.71	-1.12
49	26.30	13.83	12.47	40.07	-3.62	24.99	15.81	-2.03	24.71	-1.12
50	22.58	11.97	10.61	39.47	-3.62	21.27	14.40	-2.03	24.71	-1.12

EXHIBIT E-6: (continued)

Pass	Total Equity	Short Equity	Long Equity	Max. Equity	Min. Equity	P/L	Best Trade	Worst Trade	Max. Open P/L	Min. Open P/L
51	22.58	11.97	10.61	39.47	-3.62	21.27	14.40	-2.03	24.71	-1.12
52	23.64	12.50	11.14	40.53	-3.62	22.33	14.40	-2.03	24.71	-1.12
53	26.66	14.01	12.65	40.53	-3.62	25.35	14.40	-2.03	24.71	-1.12
54	25.66	13.51	12.15	39.53	-3.62	24.35	14.40	-2.03	24.71	-1.12
55	22.24	11.80	10.44	34.33	-3.62	20.93	14.40	-2.87	24.71	-1.50
56	22.78	12.07	10.71	34.33	-3.62	21.47	14.40	-2.87	24.71	-1.50
57	18.76	10.06	8.70	30.31	-3.62	17.45	14.40	-2.87	24.71	-1.50
58	16.06	8.71	7.35	30.87	-3.06	14.75	14.40	-2.87	24.71	-1.50
59	16.06	8.71	7.35	30.87	-3.06	14.75	14.40	-2.87	24.71	-1.50
60	16.06	8.71	7.35	30.87	-3.06	14.75	14.40	-2.87	24.71	-1.50
61	12.10	6.73	5.37	30.99	-3.06	10.87	14.40	-2.87	24.71	-1.50
62	13.02	7.19	5.83	31.87	-2.18	11.79	14.40	-2.87	24.71	-1.50
63	9.68	5.52	4.16	31.87	-2.18	8.45	13.91	-2.87	24.71	-1.50
64	8.82	5.09	3.73	31.87	-2.18	8.02	13.91	-2.87	24.71	-1.50
65	13.10	7.23	5.87	31.87	-2.18	12.30	13.91	-2.87	24.71	-1.50
66	15.38	8.37	7.01	34.49	-1.26	14.58	13.91	-1.85	24.71	-1.50
67	15.38	8.37	7.01	34.49	-1.26	14.58	13.91	-1.85	24.71	-1.50
68	16.58	8.97	7.61	34.49	-1.26	15.78	13.06	-1.85	24.71	-1.50
69	17.88	9.62	8.26	34.49	-1.26	17.08	13.06	-2.26	24.71	-1.50
70	17.88	9.62	8.26	34.49	-1.26	17.08	13.06	-2.26	24.71	-1.50
71	17.88	9.62	8.26	34.49	-1.26	17.08	13.06	-2.26	24.71	-1.50
72	15.64	8.50	7.14	32.25	-3.50	14.84	13.06	-2.26	24.71	-1.50
73	16.06	8.71	7.35	32.25	-3.50	15.26	13.06	-2.26	24.71	-1.50
74	18.62	9.99	8.63	32.25	-3.50	17.82	13.06	-1.85	24.71	-1.50
75	18.62	9.99	8.63	32.25	-3.50	17.82	13.06	-1.85	24.71	-1.50

Pass indicates period length.

Equity indicates the total number of points gained or lost.

Short equity indicates the number of points gained or lost on short positions.

Long equity indicates the number of points gained or lost on long positions.

Max. equity indicates the highest total profit recorded over the tested period.

Min. equity indicates the lowest total profit recorded over the tested period.

P/L indicates total number of points gained or lost in closed positions.

Best trade indicates the highest number of points gained in any closed trade.

Worst trade indicates the highest number of points lost in any closed trade.

Max. open P/L indicates the highest gain in a position which remains open at the end of the test run.

Min. open P/L indicates the highest loss in a position which remains open at the end of the test run.

EXHIBIT E-7:
New York Stock Exchange Composite Index, 1977 to 1986, with 42-Week Exponential Moving Average

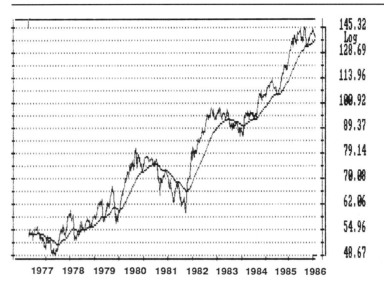

EXHIBIT E-8:
Ratio Oscillator: New York Stock Exchange Composite Index Close to 42-Week Exponential Moving Average, 1977 to 1986

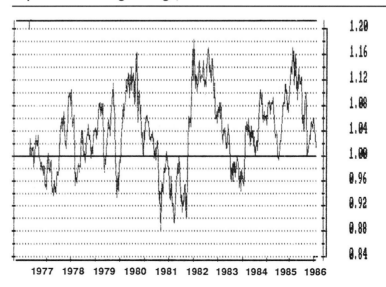

EXHIBIT E-9:

Total Equity for 42-Week Exponential Moving Average Crossover, 1977 to 1986

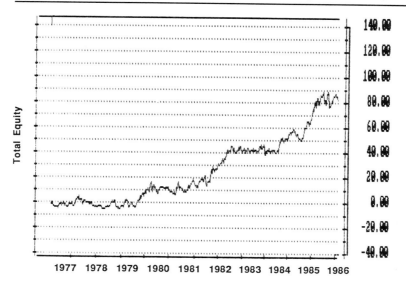

EXHIBIT E-10:
Profit Summary for 42-Week Exponential Moving Average Crossover, 1977 to 1986

Item		Long	Short	Net
Per Trade Ranges		-- Per Trade Ranges --		
Best Trade	(Closed position yielding maximum P/L)	25.75	5.20	25.75
. . Date		840203	820827	840203
Worst Trade	(Closed position yielding minimum P/L)	-2.26	-1.49	-2.26
. . Date		770527	791116	770527
Max Open P/L	(Maximum P/L occurring in an open position)	39.37	12.89	39.37
. . Date		860829	820813	860829
Min Open P/L	(Minimum P/L occurring in an open position)	-1.28	-0.68	-1.28
. . Date		770429	770603	770429
Overall Ranges		---- Overall Ranges ----		
Max P/L	(Maximum P/L from all closed positions during the run)	50.90	49.77	50.90
. . Date		850927	851004	850927
Min P/L	(Minimum P/L from all closed positions during the run)	-4.50	-5.41	-5.41
. . Date		790511	791116	791116
Max Equity	(Maximum P/L from all closed and open positions)	89.14	50.90	89.14
. . Date		860829	850927	860829
Min Equity	(Minimum P/L from all closed and open positions)	-5.51	-5.41	-5.51
. . Date		790601	791116	790601
Statistics		------ Statistics ------		
Periods	(The number of periods in each position and entire run)	364	145	509
Trades	(The number of trades in each position and entire run)	15	15	30
# Profitable	(The number of profitable trades. . .)	6	4	10
# Losing	(The number of unprofitable trades. . .)	9	11	20
% Profitable	(The percent of profitable trades to total trades)	40.00	26.67	33.33
% Losing	(The percent of unprofitable trades to total trades)	60.00	73.33	66.67
Results		------ Results ------		
Commission	(Total commission deducted from closed trades)	0.00	0.00	0.00
Slippage	(Total slippage deducted from closed trades)	0.00	0.00	0.00
Gross P/L	(Total points gained in closed positions)	50.39	-0.62	49.77
Open P/L	(P/L in a position which remains open at the end)	32.63	0.00	32.63
P/L	(Net P/L: Gross P/L less Commission and Slippage)	50.39	-0.62	49.77
Equity	(Net P/L plus Open P/L at the end of the run)	83.02	-0.62	82.40

There are columns for Long trades, Short trades and Net. In the Long column, results are reported only for Long positions. In the Short column, results are reported for Short positions only. In the Net column for the "Per Trade Ranges" and "Overall Ranges," entries will be the extreme from either the Long or Short column. Net column entries for the "Statistics" and "Results" categories are the combined results of entries in the Long and Short columns.

EXHIBIT E-11:

New York Stock Exchange Composite Index, 1968 to 1977, with 42-Week Exponential Moving Average

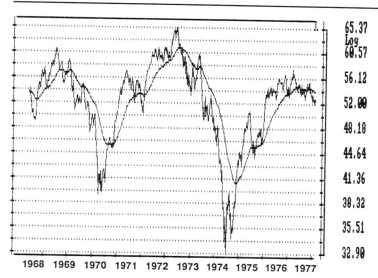

EXHIBIT E-12:

Ratio Oscillator: New York Stock Exchange Composite Index Close to 42-Week Exponential Moving Average, 1968 to 1977

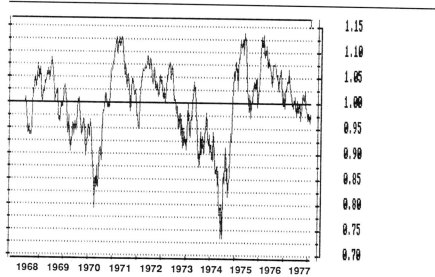

EXHIBIT E-13:
Total Equity for 42-Week Exponential Moving Average Crossover, 1968 to 1977

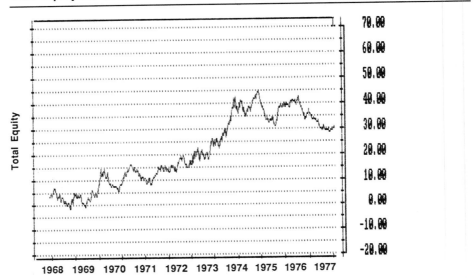

EXHIBIT E-14:

Profit Summary for 42-Week Exponential Moving Average Crossover, 1968 to 1977

Item	Long	Short	Net
	-- Per Trade Ranges -----		
Per Trade Ranges			
Best Trade (Closed position yielding maximum P/L)	7.31	16.70	16.70
.. Date	730223	750131	750131
Worst Trade (Closed position yielding minimum P/L)	-2.03	-1.86	-2.03
.. Date	750912	690502	750912
Max Open P/L (Maximum P/L occurring in an open position)	11.86	24.71	24.71
.. Date	730105	741004	741004
Min Open P/L (Minimum P/L occurring in an open position)	-0.95	-0.71	-0.95
.. Date	761105	770520	761105
	----- Overall Ranges -----		
Overall Ranges			
Max P/L (Maximum P/L from all closed positions during the run)	38.74	37.30	38.74
.. Date	750822	750829	750822
Min P/L (Minimum P/L from all closed positions during the run)	-1.01	-0.77	-1.01
.. Date	690606	680412	690606
Max Equity (Maximum P/L from all closed and open positions)	44.60	42.81	44.60
.. Date	750711	741004	750711
Min Equity (Minimum P/L from all closed and open positions)	-1.01	-1.01	-1.01
.. Date	690606	690606	690606
	------ Statistics ------		
Statistics			
Periods (The number of periods in each position and entire run)	283	226	509
Trades (The number of trades in each position and entire run)	21	20	41
# Profitable (The number of profitable trades. . .)	5	4	9
# Losing (The number of unprofitable trades. . .)	16	16	32
% Profitable (The percent of profitable trades to total trades)	23.81	20.00	21.95
% Losing (The percent of unprofitable trades to total trades)	76.19	80.00	78.05
	------ Results ------		
Results			
Commission (Total commission deducted from closed trades)	0.00	0.00	0.00
Slippage (Total slippage deducted from closed trades)	0.00	0.00	0.00
Gross P/L (Total points gained in closed positions)	14.31	14.36	28.67
Open P/L (P/L in a position which remains open at the end)	0.00	1.31	1.31
P/L (Net P/L: Gross P/L less Commission and Slippage)	14.31	14.36	28.67
Equity (Net P/L plus Open P/L at the end of the run)	14.31	15.67	29.98

There are columns for Long trades, Short trades and Net. In the Long column, results are reported only for Long positions. In the Short column, results are reported for Short positions only. In the Net column for the "Per Trade Ranges" and "Overall Ranges," entries will be the extreme from either the Long or Short column. Net column entries for the "Statistics" and "Results" categories are the combined results of entries in the Long and Short columns.

FED FUNDS-DISCOUNT RATE SPREAD INDEX

The Fed Funds-Discount Rate Spread is simply the difference between the Federal Funds Rate and the Discount Rate. Discount Rate increases and cuts normally follow changes in the Federal Funds Rate. Therefore, as the spread widens, the probability increases that the Discount Rate will be increased or cut. The direction of the change in the Discount Rate depends on whether the spread is positive or negative. If the spread is positive (the Federal Funds Rate is above the Discount Rate), the Discount Rate is likely to be increased. On the other hand, a negative spread (the Federal Funds Rate is below the Discount Rate) indicates the likelihood of a cut in the Discount Rate.

Increases in the Discount Rate are generally bearish for stock prices; therefore, a positive spread is viewed as bearish. Decreases in the Discount Rate are generally bullish for stock prices; thus, a negative spread is considered bullish.

A visual comparison of the Federal Funds Rate to the Discount Rate is provided in Exhibit F-1.

We tested the Fed Funds-Discount Rate Spread Index for the period of May 1978 to March 1987 on a weekly basis. The results are shown in Exhibit F-2 (page 200).

The test process was as follows. The spread values for the test period were divided into 20 ranges with approximately the same number of occurrences in each range. For each value in a range, the gain or loss in four subsequent time periods (1 month later, 3 months later, 6 months later, and 12 months later) was calculated. The combined results for values within each range were statistically compared, using chi-squared tests, to the performance of the overall market (as measured by the S&P 500). Varying degrees of bullishness and bearishness were noted on the basis of that comparison.

Our research results revealed only moderate bullish tendencies at extreme negative spread values. On the other hand, positive spread readings over 4.71 were very bearish for 6-month and 12-month time horizons.

EXHIBIT F-1:

Comparison of Federal Funds Rate to Discount Rate (Middle and Bottom) Versus the Value Line Composite from 1979 to 1986

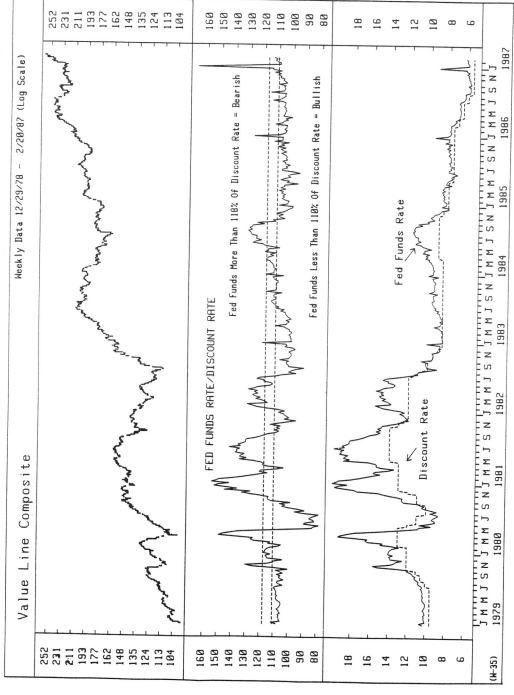

Weekly Data 12/29/78 – 2/20/87 (Log Scale)

Value Line Composite

FED FUNDS RATE/DISCOUNT RATE

Fed Funds More Than 110% Of Discount Rate = Bearish

Fed Funds Less Than 110% Of Discount Rate = Bullish

Fed Funds Rate

Discount Rate

(H-35)

Source: By Permission of Ned Davis Research, Inc.

EXHIBIT F-2:

Interpretation of Fed Funds-Discount Rate Spread Index's Weekly Readings

```
===================================================================================
FED FUNDS - DISCOUNT RATE SPREAD INDEX - WEEKLY DATA
PERIOD ANALYZED: MAY 1978 TO MARCH 1987
===================================================================================
```

INDICATOR RANGE		INTERPRETATION GIVEN INVESTOR'S TIME FRAME			
GREATER THAN	LESS THAN OR EQUAL TO	1 MONTH	3 MONTHS	6 MONTHS	12 MONTHS
-2.54	-0.31	SLIGHTLY BULLISH	BULLISH	BULLISH	NEUTRAL
-0.31	-0.01	NEUTRAL	NEUTRAL	SLIGHTLY BULLISH	NEUTRAL
-0.01	0.17	NEUTRAL	NEUTRAL	NEUTRAL	NEUTRAL
0.17	0.27	NEUTRAL	NEUTRAL	NEUTRAL	NEUTRAL
0.27	0.35	NEUTRAL	NEUTRAL	NEUTRAL	NEUTRAL
0.35	0.39	NEUTRAL	NEUTRAL	NEUTRAL	NEUTRAL
0.39	0.46	NEUTRAL	NEUTRAL	NEUTRAL	NEUTRAL
0.46	0.51	NEUTRAL	SLIGHTLY BULLISH	NEUTRAL	NEUTRAL
0.51	0.57	NEUTRAL	NEUTRAL	NEUTRAL	NEUTRAL
0.57	0.64	NEUTRAL	NEUTRAL	NEUTRAL	NEUTRAL
0.64	0.75	BULLISH	SLIGHTLY BULLISH	SLIGHTLY BULLISH	SLIGHTLY BULLISH
0.75	0.86	NEUTRAL	NEUTRAL	SLIGHTLY BEARISH	SLIGHTLY BULLISH
0.86	0.98	NEUTRAL	SLIGHTLY BEARISH	VERY BEARISH	NEUTRAL
0.98	1.16	NEUTRAL	BEARISH	SLIGHTLY BEARISH	NEUTRAL
1.16	1.55	NEUTRAL	NEUTRAL	NEUTRAL	NEUTRAL
1.55	1.93	NEUTRAL	NEUTRAL	NEUTRAL	NEUTRAL
1.93	2.47	NEUTRAL	NEUTRAL	NEUTRAL	NEUTRAL
2.47	2.99	NEUTRAL	NEUTRAL	NEUTRAL	NEUTRAL
2.99	4.71	SLIGHTLY BEARISH	SLIGHTLY BEARISH	SLIGHTLY BEARISH	SLIGHTLY BEARISH
4.71	7.06	NEUTRAL	NEUTRAL	VERY BEARISH	VERY BEARISH

```
===================================================================================
```

Definitions of Very Bullish, Bullish, Slightly Bullish, Neutral, Slightly Bearish, Bearish, and Very Bearish are provided in Appendix A.

FED FUNDS-PRIME RATE SPREAD INDEX

The Fed Funds-Prime Rate Spread Index is simply the difference between the Federal Funds Rate and the Prime Rate. Prime Rate increases and cuts normally follow changes in the Federal Funds Rate. Therefore, as the spread widens, the probability increases that the Prime Rate will be increased or cut. The direction of the change in the Prime Rate depends on whether the spread is positive or negative. If the spread is positive (the Federal Funds rate is above the Prime Rate), the Prime Rate is likely to be increased. On the other hand, a negative spread (the Federal Funds Rate is below the Prime Rate) indicates the likelihood of a cut in the Prime Rate.

Increases in the Prime Rate are considered bearish for stock prices; therefore, a positive spread is viewed as bearish. Decreases in the Prime Rate are seen as bullish for stock prices; thus, a negative spread is considered bullish.

We tested the Fed Funds-Prime Rate Spread Index for the period of May 1978 to March 1987 on a weekly basis. The results are shown in Exhibit F-3 (page 202).

The test process was as follows. The indicator spread values for the test period were divided into 20 ranges with approximately the same number of occurrences in each range. For each value in a range, the gain or loss in four subsequent time periods (1 month later, 3 months later, 6 months later, and 12 months later) was calculated. The combined results for values within each range were statistically compared, using chi-squared tests, to the performance of the overall market (as measured by the Standard & Poor's 500). Varying degrees of bullishness and bearishness were noted on the basis of that comparison.

For time horizons of 6 and 12 months forward, our research results revealed a very bearish tendency when the Fed Funds-Prime Rate Spread Index rose to -0.86 or higher. Such a reading occurs only 5% of the time, but when it does, take warning.

EXHIBIT F-3:
Interpretation of Fed Funds-Prime Rate Spread Index's Weekly Readings

```
===================================================================================
FED FUNDS - PRIME RATE SPREAD INDEX - WEEKLY DATA
PERIOD ANALYZED:  MAY 1978 TO MARCH 1987
===================================================================================
```

INDICATOR RANGE		INTERPRETATION GIVEN INVESTOR'S TIME FRAME			
GREATER THAN	LESS THAN OR EQUAL TO	1 MONTH	3 MONTHS	6 MONTHS	12 MONTHS
-5.890	-3.360	NEUTRAL	NEUTRAL	NEUTRAL	NEUTRAL
-3.360	-2.810	NEUTRAL	NEUTRAL	NEUTRAL	NEUTRAL
-2.810	-2.590	NEUTRAL	NEUTRAL	NEUTRAL	NEUTRAL
-2.590	-2.310	NEUTRAL	NEUTRAL	SLIGHTLY BULLISH	NEUTRAL
-2.310	-2.130	NEUTRAL	SLIGHTLY BULLISH	SLIGHTLY BULLISH	NEUTRAL
-2.130	-2.005	SLIGHTLY BEARISH	NEUTRAL	NEUTRAL	NEUTRAL
-2.005	-1.880	NEUTRAL	NEUTRAL	NEUTRAL	BEARISH
-1.880	-1.750	NEUTRAL	NEUTRAL	NEUTRAL	NEUTRAL
-1.750	-1.680	NEUTRAL	NEUTRAL	NEUTRAL	NEUTRAL
-1.680	-1.630	NEUTRAL	NEUTRAL	NEUTRAL	NEUTRAL
-1.630	-1.600	NEUTRAL	NEUTRAL	NEUTRAL	NEUTRAL
-1.600	-1.540	NEUTRAL	NEUTRAL	NEUTRAL	NEUTRAL
-1.540	-1.490	NEUTRAL	SLIGHTLY BULLISH	NEUTRAL	NEUTRAL
-1.490	-1.450	NEUTRAL	NEUTRAL	NEUTRAL	NEUTRAL
-1.450	-1.380	NEUTRAL	NEUTRAL	NEUTRAL	NEUTRAL
-1.380	-1.310	NEUTRAL	NEUTRAL	NEUTRAL	NEUTRAL
-1.310	-1.220	NEUTRAL	NEUTRAL	NEUTRAL	NEUTRAL
-1.220	-1.070	NEUTRAL	SLIGHTLY BEARISH	NEUTRAL	NEUTRAL
-1.070	-0.860	NEUTRAL	NEUTRAL	BEARISH	NEUTRAL
-0.860	1.700	NEUTRAL	NEUTRAL	VERY BEARISH	VERY BEARISH

```
===================================================================================
```

Definitions of Very Bullish, Bullish, Slightly Bullish, Neutral, Slightly Bearish, Bearish, and Very Bearish are provided in Appendix A.

FED INDICATOR

The Fed Indicator is a long-term monetary indicator developed by Martin Zweig (The Zweig Forecast, P.O. Box 5345, New York, NY 10150).* It

---

*Reprinted with permission.

is designed to track Federal Reserve activity in a manner that will signal a bullish or bearish condition for the stock market.

To calculate the Fed Indicator, you must first grade two components, the discount rate and reserve requirements, on a point system. Each component is graded in the same manner and the total points for each are added together for interpretation purposes.

Two positive points are given for an initial decrease in the discount rate or reserve requirements (a bullish sign) while one positive point is rewarded for subsequent cuts in either component. One negative point is earned for each increase in the discount rate or reserve requirements (a bearish sign).

One initial positive point is considered stale and lost 6 months after a cut in the discount rate or reserve requirement. The other initial positive point is lost 12 months after the cut. Each subsequent positive point is given up 6 months after its associated discount rate or reserve requirements cut. Each negative point is considered stale and lost 6 months after it is earned. Finally, when any positive point is earned, all negative points are eliminated and, vice versa, when any negative point is earned, all positive points are eliminated.

After grading each component and adding the two point totals together, interpretation is as follows:

+2 or more points   —Extremely Bullish
0 or +1 point   —Neutral
−1 or −2 points   —Moderately Bearish
−3 or more points   —Extremely Bearish

Zweig tested the Fed Indicator for the period of January 1958 to November 1984 with the following results:

Fed Indicator Rating	Total Number of Years	Percent of Cases S & P 500 Index Rose	Annualized Return
Extremely Bullish	7.6	83	+25.6%
Neutral	9.4	60	+2.0%
Moderately Bearish	7.4	43	−5.2%
Extremely Bearish	2.5	22	−4.8%

As shown, investing in stocks when the Fed Indicator was rated extremely bullish would have produced significant returns for an investor, well in excess of the average 5% annual returns (excluding dividends) of a passive buy-and-hold strategy.

Further discussion of the Fed Indicator appears in Zweig's 1986 book entitled *Winning On Wall Street* (Warner Books, New York, NY).

FIRST FIVE DAYS IN JANUARY

Yale Hirsch (The Hirsch Organization, Inc., Six Deer Trail, Old Tappan, NJ 07675) has researched a correlation between what happens in the stock market during the first 5 trading days in January and throughout the year as a whole.* If the market goes up during the first 5 days, the market for the year tends to go up. Likewise, if market prices decline during the first 5 days, the market typically ends the year at a lower level.

As shown in Exhibit F-4, years that began with early January gains were more successful indicators of what would occur during the rest of the year than those beginning with losses. Of the 22 years since 1950 in which gains occurred during the first 5 trading days, only 2 years ended with overall losses. This produces a track record of 91% accuracy for signals given by early January gains.

Signals given by early January losses, however, were not quite as consistent, having a track record of only 62% accuracy of prediction. Market prices increased for the overall year during 5 of the 13 years in which there were losses during the first 5 trading days in January.

Overall, this indicator offers surprisingly high historical accuracy. Since the underlying rationale is far from clear, however, it is perhaps best used in conjunction with other more logical indicators.

For a discussion of a similar indicator, refer to the section on the January Barometer.

---

*Reprinted with permission.

EXHIBIT F-4:
The First Five Days in January from 1950 to 1985

	Chronologic Data				Ranked By Performance		
Year	Previous Year's Close	5th Day in January	Change 1st 5 Days	Rank	Year	Change 1st 5 Days	Change for Year
1950	16.76*	17.09*	2.0%	1.	1976	4.9%	19.1%
1951	20.41	20.88	2.3	2.	1983	3.2	17.3
1952	23.77	23.91	0.6	3.	1967	3.1	20.1
1953	26.57	26.33	−0.9	4.	1979	2.8	12.3
1954	24.81	24.93	0.5	5.	1963	2.6	18.9
1955	35.98	35.33	−1.8	6.	1958	2.5	38.1
1956	45.48	44.51	−2.1	7.	1984	2.4	1.4
1957	46.67	46.25	−0.9	8.	1951	2.3	16.5
1958	39.99	40.99	2.5	9.	1975	2.2	31.5
1959	55.21	55.40	0.3	10.	1950	2.0	21.8
1960	59.89	59.50	−0.7	11.	1973	1.5	−17.4
1961	58.11	58.81	1.2	12.	1972	1.4	15.6
1962	71.55	69.12	−3.4	13.	1964	1.3	13.0
1963	63.10	64.74	2.6	14.	1961	1.2	23.1
1964	75.02	76.00	1.3	15.	1980	0.9	25.8
1965	84.75	85.37	0.7	16.	1966	0.8	−13.1
1966	92.43	93.14	0.8	17.	1965	0.7	9.1
1967	80.33	82.81	3.1	18.	1970	0.7	0.1
1968	96.47	96.62	0.2	19.	1952	0.6	11.8
1969	103.86	100.80	−2.9	20.	1954	0.5	45.0
1970	92.06	92.68	0.7	21.	1959	0.3	8.5
1971	92.15	92.19	0.0	22.	1968	0.2	7.7
1972	102.09	103.47	1.4	23.	1971	0.0	10.8
1973	118.05	119.85	1.5	24.	1960	−0.7	−3.0
1974	97.55	96.12	−1.5	25.	1953	−0.9	−6.6
1975	68.56	70.04	2.2	26.	1957	−0.9	−14.3
1976	90.19	94.58	4.9	27.	1974	−1.5	−29.7
1977	107.46	105.01	−2.3	28.	1955	−1.8	26.4
1978	95.10	90.69	−4.6	29.	1985	−1.9	26.3
1979	96.11	98.80	2.8	30.	1981	−2.0	−9.7
1980	107.94	108.95	0.9	31.	1956	−2.1	2.6
1981	135.76	133.06	−2.0	32.	1977	−2.3	−11.5
1982	122.55	119.55	−2.4	33.	1982	−2.4	14.8
1983	140.64	145.18	3.2	34.	1969	−2.9	−11.4
1984	164.93	168.90	2.4	35.	1962	−3.4	−11.8
1985	167.24	163.99	−1.9	36.	1978	−4.6	1.1

*S & P Composite Index

Source: By permission of the Hirsch Organization, Inc.

FUNDS NET PURCHASES INDEX

The Funds Net Purchases Index is a sentiment indicator developed by Arthur Merrill (Merrill Analysis, Inc., Box 228, Chappaqua, NY 10514).*

Merrill's theory is that investment funds are managed by astute analysts who fall into the "smart money" category. In other words, these analysts should be right about the direction of stock prices more often than they are wrong. By analyzing their behavior, one should be able to discover their market expectations.

Three pieces of mutual fund information are required to compute the Funds Net Purchases Index: purchases of common stock, sales of common stocks, and total fund assets for stock, bond and income funds. The data appears in *Barron's* on a monthly basis about 1 month late. More timely information is available on a subscription basis from the Investment Company Institute (1600 M Street NW, Washington, DC 20036).

To compute the Funds Net Purchases Index, you first subtract sales of common stock from purchases of common stock. The calculated value is then divided by total fund assets. For smoothing purposes a 33% exponential (the equivalent of about a 5-month simple moving average) is applied. Finally, the number is divided by the standard deviation.

Merrill tested the Funds Net Purchases Index over a 10-year period. He concluded that a positive index reading greater than two thirds of the standard deviation from the mean should be interpreted as bullish for 13, 26, and 52 weeks into the future. A negative reading of greater than two thirds of the standard deviation from the mean should be viewed as bearish for 13, 26, and 52 weeks into the future. Refer to Exhibit F-5 for a visual display of the Funds Net Purchases Index.

———————

*Reprinted with permission.

EXHIBIT F-5:
Sample Chart of Funds Net Purchases Index

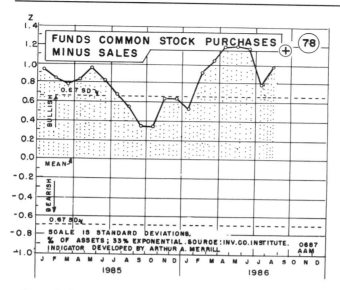

Source: By Permission of Merrill Analysis, Inc.

GENERAL MOTORS AS A BELLWETHER STOCK

Over the years, certain stocks have been viewed as stock market bellwethers. Therefore, it is widely believed to be advantageous to monitor their activity for signs of what will happen to prices in the overall stock market. The perennial favorite has been General Motors (GM). The belief is that since GM is one of the largest industrial companies in the world, whatever is good for GM must be good for business in general.

The theory that General Motors is a bellwether stock provides buy-and-sell signals for the overall stock market. A buy signal is given during a declining market whenever the price of GM's common stock fails to reach a new low within a 4-month period. A sell signal is given during an upward trending market whenever the price of GM's common stock fails to reach a new high within a 4-month period.

The actual market performance following buy and sell signals are shown in Exhibit G-1 for the period of 1940 to 1984. Buy signals produced on average a significant 24.2% gain before the next sell signal was given. Sell signal results are unimpressive, averaging a gain of only 4.1%.

It should be noted that the indicator was not successful in the latest 10-year period (April 1974 to May 1984). During that time, the stock market rose 38%, but following the signals generated by this indicator would have resulted in a net 1.7% loss.

General Motors As A Bellwether Stock is an interesting indicator, but its inconsistent record makes its value in market timing questionable.

EXHIBIT G-1:

Buy-and-Sell Signal Results from 1942 to 1984 Following General Motors as a Bellwether Stock Theory

	Buy Signals			Sell Signals	
Date	Dow Jones Industrial Average	Percent Decrease from Previous Sell Signal	Date	Dow Jones Industrial Average	Percent Increase from Previous Buy Signal
APR 1942	96.92	34.5	JUN 1946	211.47	118.2
JUL 1948	185.90	12.1	MAR 1956	503.88	171.0
APR 1958	450.72	10.5	NOV 1959	650.92	44.4
APR 1961	672.66	(3.3)	APR 1962	687.90	2.3
OCT 1962	569.02	17.3	MAR 1964	802.75	41.1
AUG 1964	840.35	(4.7)	FEB 1966	951.89	13.3
MAY 1967	892.93	6.2	JAN 1968	863.67	(3.3)
JUL 1968	883.36	2.3	FEB 1969	903.97	2.3
SEP 1970	758.97	16.0	AUG 1971	901.43	18.8
MAR 1972	928.66	(3.0)	AUG 1972	953.12	2.6
APR 1974	847.54	11.1	OCT 1974	658.17	(22.3)
APR 1975	842.88	(28.1)	APR 1976	986.00	17.0
DEC 1976	996.09	(1.0)	MAY 1977	931.22	(6.5)
JUN 1978	836.97	10.1	DEC 1978	817.65	(2.3)
JUN 1979	843.04	(3.1)	JAN 1980	879.95	4.4
AUG 1980	955.03	(8.5)	JAN 1981	970.99	1.7
MAY 1981	976.86	(0.6)	OCT 1981	851.69	(12.8)
MAR 1982	805.65	5.4	MAY 1984	1167.19	44.9
	Average	4.1		Average	24.2

GROSS TRINITY INDEX

The Gross Trinity Index was developed by Robert Gross, editor of the *Professional Investor* market newsletter (P.O. Box 2144, Pompano Beach, FL 33061). It is also referred to as the *Professional Investor*'s Trinity Index.

The Gross Trinity Index combines three short indicators in a manner that smooths out erratic moves. It is designed to compare professional or sophisticated shorting activity with that of the supposedly less knowledgeable public. The index is relatively complex in its construction. It is best calculated in two steps on a weekly basis. First, calculate the three components of the index as follows:

Specialist Short Ratio = Specialist Shorts/Total Shorts
Member Short Ratio = Member Shorts/Total Shorts
Public Short Ratio = Public Shorts/Total Shorts

(Refer to the appropriate section in this book for a complete discussion of each of these three indicators.)

In the second step, you combine the three components using exponential averages for smoothing purposes. The Gross Trinity Index equals an 18% exponential average (equivalent to a 10-week simple moving average) of the Specialist Short Ratio plus a 29% exponential average (equivalent to a 6-week simple moving average) of the Member Short Ratio, with the total then divided by an 18% exponential average (equivalent to a 10-week simple moving Average) of the Public Short Ratio.

Ned Davis (Ned Davis Research, Inc., P.O. Box 2089, Venice, FL 34284) has performed extensive tests of the Gross Trinity Index. As illustrated in Exhibit G-2, he has determined that high readings (over 108%) represent heavy professional shorting compared to public shorting and should be interpreted as bearish. On the other hand, low readings (less than 85%) imply light professional shorting versus public shorting and should be considered bullish, according to Davis.

EXHIBIT G-2:

Gross Trinity Index (Bottom) Versus Dow Jones Industrial Average from 1980 to 1986

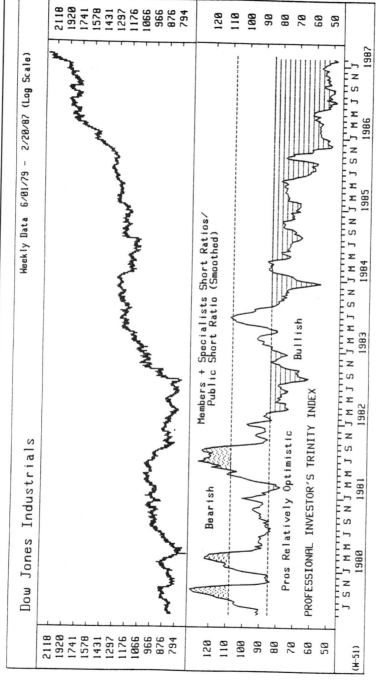

Source: By permission of Ned Davis Research, Inc.

HAURLAN INDEX

The Haurlan Index is a market breadth indicator developed by P.N. Haurlan (Trade Levels, Inc., 22801 Ventura Boulevard, Suite 210, Woodland Hills, CA 91364). It consists of three components, each with a different purpose and interpretation.

The short-term component is a 3-day exponential moving average of the net difference between the number of advancing issues and the number of declining issues. The intermediate-term component is a 20-day exponential moving average of the net difference between the number of advancing issues and the number of declining issues. The long-term component is a 200-day exponential moving average of the net difference between the number of advancing issues and the number of declining issues. NYSE data is used in the calculations.

Each of the three components is interpreted differently. When the short-term component moves above +100, a short-term buy signal is given. The buy signal remains in effect until a level of −150 is reached. At that time, a short-term sell signal is generated and remains in effect until the next short-term buy signal. These decision rules lend themselves to active short-term trading. The intermediate-component is interpreted subjectively with buy and sell signals given when trend lines or support and resistence levels are crossed. The long-term component is not used to generate specific buy and sell signals. Rather, it is intended to be used to determine the primary trend of stock prices.

HIGH LOW LOGIC INDEX

The High Low Logic Index was developed by Normal Fosback (The Institute for Econometric Research, 3471 North Federal Highway, Fort Lauderdale, FL 33306).* It is computed as the lesser of the number of new highs or of new lows divided by the total number of issues traded. Daily or weekly NYSE data typically is used in the calculation.

The concept behind the indicator is that either a large number of stocks will reach new highs or a large number will establish new lows, but normally not both at the same time. Since the High Low Logic Index is the lesser of the two ratios, high readings are infrequent.

---

*Reprinted with permission.

When a high indicator reading does occur, it signifies that market internals are inconsistent with many stocks reaching new highs at the same time that many stocks establish new lows. Such a condition is considered bearish for stock prices.

Extreme low indicator readings reveal a uniform market. They are considered bullish for stock prices.

We tested the High Low Logic Index for the period of January 1962 to March 1987 on a daily basis and January 1937 to March 1987 on a weekly basis. In addition, we applied a 10-period simple moving average to both the daily and weekly readings to smooth out any erratic movements. The results are shown in Exhibits H-1 through H-4 (pages 214–217).

The test process was as follows. The indicator readings for the test period were divided into 20 ranges with approximately the same number of occurrences in each range. For each reading in a range, the gain or loss in four subsequent time periods (1 month later, 3 months later, 6 months later, and 12 months later) was calculated. The combined results for readings within each range were statistically compared, using chi-squared tests, to the performance of the overall market (as measured by the Standard & Poor's 500). Varying degrees of bullishness and bearishness were noted on the basis of that comparison.

Keep in mind that since early 1978, new highs and new lows have been defined as issues reaching new extremes in price on a 52-week basis. Prior to that time, the base period ranged from 2 1/2 to 14 1/2 months. For a date between January 1 and mid-March of a given year, a new high or new low was based on the period from January 1 of the previous year to the current date. For dates after mid-March, a new high or new low was determined on the basis of the period from January 1 of the current year to the current date.

Our research confirmed a definite bullish tendency at low readings of the High Low Logic Index and bearish tendency at high readings of the indicator. Superior results were achieved by using a 10-day simple moving average.

Fosback tested weekly High Low Logic Index readings using a 10-week exponential moving average over a 40-year period. He concluded that readings above .05 are bearish and below .01 are particularly bullish.

EXHIBIT H-1:
Interpretation of High Low Logic Index's Daily Readings

```
================================================================================
HIGH LOW LOGIC INDEX - DAILY DATA
PERIOD ANALYZED:  JANUARY 1962 TO MARCH 1987
================================================================================
```

INDICATOR RANGE		INTERPRETATION GIVEN INVESTOR'S TIME FRAME			
GREATER THAN	LESS THAN OR EQUAL TO	1 MONTH	3 MONTHS	6 MONTHS	12 MONTHS
0.000	0.001	VERY BULLISH	VERY BULLISH	VERY BULLISH	VERY BULLISH
0.001	0.002	VERY BULLISH	VERY BULLISH	VERY BULLISH	SLIGHTLY BULLISH
0.002	0.003	NEUTRAL	NEUTRAL	NEUTRAL	NEUTRAL
0.003	0.004	NEUTRAL	NEUTRAL	NEUTRAL	NEUTRAL
0.004	0.005	NEUTRAL	NEUTRAL	NEUTRAL	NEUTRAL
0.005	0.006	BEARISH	NEUTRAL	BEARISH	NEUTRAL
0.006	0.007	NEUTRAL	NEUTRAL	NEUTRAL	NEUTRAL
0.007	0.008	NEUTRAL	NEUTRAL	NEUTRAL	NEUTRAL
0.008	0.009	NEUTRAL	SLIGHTLY BEARISH	BEARISH	NEUTRAL
0.009	0.010	NEUTRAL	NEUTRAL	NEUTRAL	NEUTRAL
0.010	0.011	NEUTRAL	NEUTRAL	NEUTRAL	NEUTRAL
0.011	0.012	NEUTRAL	NEUTRAL	NEUTRAL	NEUTRAL
0.012	0.013	NEUTRAL	NEUTRAL	NEUTRAL	NEUTRAL
0.013	0.014	SLIGHTLY BEARISH	NEUTRAL	SLIGHTLY BEARISH	NEUTRAL
0.014	0.015	NEUTRAL	NEUTRAL	NEUTRAL	NEUTRAL
0.015	0.016	NEUTRAL	BEARISH	NEUTRAL	NEUTRAL
0.016	0.018	NEUTRAL	NEUTRAL	BEARISH	NEUTRAL
0.018	0.020	VERY BEARISH	SLIGHTLY BEARISH	NEUTRAL	NEUTRAL
0.020	0.024	VERY BEARISH	VERY BEARISH	VERY BEARISH	NEUTRAL
0.024	0.063	VERY BEARISH	VERY BEARISH	NEUTRAL	VERY BEARISH

```
================================================================================
```

Definitions of Very Bullish, Bullish, Slightly Bullish, Neutral, Slightly Bearish, Bearish, and Very Bearish are provided in Appendix A.

EXHIBIT H-2:

Interpretation of High Low Logic Index's 10-Day Simple Moving Average Readings

```
=======================================================================================
HIGH LOW LOGIC INDEX - 10 DAY MOVING AVERAGE
PERIOD ANALYZED:  JANUARY 1962 TO MARCH 1987
=======================================================================================


    INDICATOR RANGE                INTERPRETATION GIVEN INVESTOR'S TIME FRAME
    ---------------    ----------------------------------------------------------------

           LESS
GREATER  THAN OR
 THAN    EQUAL TO    1 MONTH            3 MONTHS           6 MONTHS          12 MONTHS
-------  --------   ----------------   ----------------   ----------------  ----------------

 0.000    0.001     VERY BULLISH       VERY BULLISH       VERY BULLISH      VERY BULLISH
 0.001    0.002     VERY BULLISH       VERY BULLISH       VERY BULLISH      VERY BULLISH
 0.002    0.003     VERY BULLISH       SLIGHTLY BULLISH   NEUTRAL           NEUTRAL
 0.003    0.004     NEUTRAL            NEUTRAL            NEUTRAL           NEUTRAL
 0.004    0.005     NEUTRAL            NEUTRAL            NEUTRAL           NEUTRAL
 0.005    0.006     NEUTRAL            SLIGHTLY BEARISH   NEUTRAL           NEUTRAL
 0.006    0.007     NEUTRAL            VERY BEARISH       SLIGHTLY BEARISH  NEUTRAL
 0.007    0.008     NEUTRAL            BEARISH            BEARISH           SLIGHTLY BEARISH
 0.008    0.009     SLIGHTLY BEARISH   BEARISH            BEARISH           NEUTRAL
 0.009    0.010     VERY BEARISH       SLIGHTLY BEARISH   VERY BEARISH      SLIGHTLY BEARISH
 0.010    0.011     NEUTRAL            NEUTRAL            NEUTRAL           NEUTRAL
 0.011    0.012     NEUTRAL            NEUTRAL            NEUTRAL           NEUTRAL
 0.012    0.013     NEUTRAL            NEUTRAL            NEUTRAL           NEUTRAL
 0.013    0.014     NEUTRAL            NEUTRAL            SLIGHTLY BEARISH  NEUTRAL
 0.014    0.015     NEUTRAL            NEUTRAL            NEUTRAL           NEUTRAL
 0.015    0.016     NEUTRAL            NEUTRAL            NEUTRAL           NEUTRAL
 0.016    0.018     NEUTRAL            BEARISH            NEUTRAL           NEUTRAL
 0.018    0.020     BEARISH            NEUTRAL            BEARISH           NEUTRAL
 0.020    0.022     NEUTRAL            VERY BEARISH       VERY BEARISH      VERY BEARISH
 0.022    0.037     VERY BEARISH       VERY BEARISH       NEUTRAL           VERY BEARISH

=======================================================================================
```

Definitions of Very Bullish, Bullish, Slightly Bullish, Neutral, Slightly Bearish, Bearish, and Very Bearish are provided in Appendix A.

EXHIBIT H-3:
Interpretation of High Low Logic Index's Weekly Readings

```
================================================================================
HIGH LOW LOGIC INDEX - WEEKLY DATA
PERIOD ANALYZED: JANUARY 1937 TO MARCH 1987
================================================================================

INDICATOR RANGE              INTERPRETATION GIVEN INVESTOR'S TIME FRAME
----------------    ------------------------------------------------------------

         LESS
GREATER  THAN OR
THAN     EQUAL TO   1 MONTH          3 MONTHS         6 MONTHS        12 MONTHS
-------  --------   ---------------  ---------------  --------------- ---------------

0.000    0.003      NEUTRAL          VERY BULLISH     BULLISH         BULLISH
0.003    0.004      NEUTRAL          SLIGHTLY BULLISH NEUTRAL         NEUTRAL
0.004    0.006      VERY BULLISH     BULLISH          BULLISH         SLIGHTLY BULLISH
0.006    0.007      BULLISH          NEUTRAL          NEUTRAL         NEUTRAL
0.007    0.009      BULLISH          SLIGHTLY BULLISH NEUTRAL         NEUTRAL
0.009    0.011      NEUTRAL          NEUTRAL          NEUTRAL         NEUTRAL
0.011    0.013      NEUTRAL          NEUTRAL          NEUTRAL         NEUTRAL
0.013    0.015      NEUTRAL          NEUTRAL          NEUTRAL         NEUTRAL
0.015    0.017      NEUTRAL          NEUTRAL          NEUTRAL         NEUTRAL
0.017    0.019      SLIGHTLY BEARISH NEUTRAL          NEUTRAL         NEUTRAL
0.019    0.022      NEUTRAL          NEUTRAL          NEUTRAL         NEUTRAL
0.022    0.024      SLIGHTLY BEARISH SLIGHTLY BEARISH NEUTRAL         NEUTRAL
0.024    0.027      NEUTRAL          NEUTRAL          NEUTRAL         NEUTRAL
0.027    0.031      NEUTRAL          NEUTRAL          NEUTRAL         NEUTRAL
0.031    0.034      NEUTRAL          NEUTRAL          NEUTRAL         NEUTRAL
0.034    0.039      NEUTRAL          NEUTRAL          NEUTRAL         SLIGHTLY BEARISH
0.039    0.046      NEUTRAL          NEUTRAL          NEUTRAL         NEUTRAL
0.046    0.056      NEUTRAL          NEUTRAL          NEUTRAL         NEUTRAL
0.056    0.070      NEUTRAL          SLIGHTLY BEARISH SLIGHTLY BEARISH NEUTRAL
0.070    0.162      VERY BEARISH     VERY BEARISH     BEARISH         SLIGHTLY BEARISH

================================================================================
```

Definitions of Very Bullish, Bullish, Slightly Bullish, Neutral, Slightly Bearish, Bearish, and Very Bearish are provided in Appendix A.

EXHIBIT H-4:

Interpretation of High Low Logic Index's 10-Week Simple Moving Average Readings

```
=================================================================================================
HIGH LOW LOGIC INDEX - 10 WEEK MOVING AVERAGE
PERIOD ANALYZED:  JANUARY 1937 TO MARCH 1987
=================================================================================================
```

INDICATOR RANGE		INTERPRETATION GIVEN INVESTOR'S TIME FRAME			
GREATER THAN	LESS THAN OR EQUAL TO	1 MONTH	3 MONTHS	6 MONTHS	12 MONTHS
0.000	0.005	BULLISH	VERY BULLISH	NEUTRAL	VERY BULLISH
0.005	0.007	VERY BULLISH	SLIGHTLY BULLISH	VERY BULLISH	NEUTRAL
0.007	0.009	BULLISH	VERY BULLISH	VERY BULLISH	NEUTRAL
0.009	0.011	NEUTRAL	BULLISH	NEUTRAL	BULLISH
0.011	0.013	NEUTRAL	NEUTRAL	NEUTRAL	NEUTRAL
0.013	0.015	NEUTRAL	NEUTRAL	NEUTRAL	NEUTRAL
0.015	0.017	NEUTRAL	NEUTRAL	NEUTRAL	NEUTRAL
0.017	0.019	NEUTRAL	BEARISH	NEUTRAL	NEUTRAL
0.019	0.021	NEUTRAL	NEUTRAL	SLIGHTLY BEARISH	NEUTRAL
0.021	0.023	NEUTRAL	NEUTRAL	NEUTRAL	SLIGHTLY BEARISH
0.023	0.025	NEUTRAL	NEUTRAL	NEUTRAL	NEUTRAL
0.025	0.027	NEUTRAL	NEUTRAL	NEUTRAL	NEUTRAL
0.027	0.029	NEUTRAL	NEUTRAL	NEUTRAL	NEUTRAL
0.029	0.031	NEUTRAL	NEUTRAL	NEUTRAL	NEUTRAL
0.031	0.034	NEUTRAL	NEUTRAL	NEUTRAL	NEUTRAL
0.034	0.037	NEUTRAL	NEUTRAL	NEUTRAL	NEUTRAL
0.037	0.041	NEUTRAL	NEUTRAL	NEUTRAL	NEUTRAL
0.041	0.047	SLIGHTLY BEARISH	BEARISH	SLIGHTLY BEARISH	SLIGHTLY BEARISH
0.047	0.058	BEARISH	BEARISH	NEUTRAL	NEUTRAL
0.058	0.093	BEARISH	VERY BEARISH	BEARISH	BEARISH

```
=================================================================================================
```

Definitions of Very Bullish, Bullish, Slightly Bullish, Neutral, Slightly Bearish, Bearish, and Very Bearish are provided in Appendix A.

INSIDERS' SELL/BUY RATIO

An insider is an officer, director, or beneficial owner of a company's stock. Insiders of companies with publicly traded securities are required to report any changes in direct or indirect holdings to the Securities and Exchange Commission no later than the tenth day of the month following the month of the transaction.

In order to prevent insiders from taking advantage of access to information before it is made available to the public, insiders are not allowed to realize a profit from their transactions until at least 6 months following the transaction. If they do realize a profit within this period, any shareholder may challenge the publicly reported transaction and require the insider to return any profits to the company.

The rationale behind this indicator is that insiders have superior insight into their companies. As a result, they consistently profit by buying and selling stock in the companies with which they are associated at the right time.

Insiders are thought to buy stocks in three situations: when a development is about to improve a company's fortunes, when the stock price has fallen so far below its intrinsic value that the shares seem irresistibly cheap, and when buying stock is part of a regular program.

On the other hand, insider selling is not necessarily an indication that a company is in trouble. People often sell stocks to raise funds for personal reasons.

Vickers Stock Research Corporation offers an Insiders' Sell/Buy Ratio to quantify insiders' actions in aggregate and to identify specific points at which the overall stock market is likely to go up. Interpretation of the ratio is simple. Buy when it hits 1.5 or less. Sell when both of the following conditions are met: The stock market has retreated 5% from the buy level or 5% from a subsequent high, and the Insiders' Sell/Buy Ratio is 2 or more.

Suppose you had used the insiders' sell/buy ratio for the period of January 1976 to May 1986, as shown in Exhibit I-1. Following its signals resulted in a 1077 point gain in the Dow Jones Industrial Average (DJIA). During that same 10-year period, a buy-and-hold strategy produced 7% less, an 892 point gain in the DJIA. Losses from bad signals were minimal. In addition, the signals kept you out of the market for 48 months, a period in which funds could have earned interest, increasing your overall profit.

A visual presentation of the Insiders' Sell/Buy Ratio versus the DJIA from 1975 to 1987 is provided in Exhibit I-2 (page 220).

The key to employing effective strategies based on the actions of insiders is having access to timely information. A suggested source of such information is Vickers Stock Research Corporation (P.O. Box 59, Brookside, NJ 07926).

EXHIBIT I-1:

10-Year Performance Evaluation of the Insiders' Sell/Buy Ratio

Action B-buy S-sell	Date	S/B	DJIA	Appreciation in points (Depreciation)
B	1/5/76	1.35	865	
	Subsequent high 1014 stop loss at 963 (1014-5%)			
S	10/15/76	2.57	963	98
B	12/8/76	1.50	963	
	Subsequent high 995 stop loss at 945 (995-5%)			
S	2/15/77	2.74	945	(15)
B	7/25/77	1.49	888	
	Stop loss at 843 (888-5%)			
S	9/19/77	2.08	843	(45)
B	3/6/78	1.43	751	
	Stop loss at 820			
S	7/3/78	2.83	820	69
B	12/4/78	1.40	822	
	Stop loss at 842			
S	10/15/79	3.09	842	20
B	12/17/79	1.46	839	
	Stop loss at 859			
S	2/12/80	2.26	859	20
B	4/28/80	1.41	817	
	Stop loss at 941			
S	12/23/80	2.62	941	124
B	2/23/81	1.49	954	
	Stop loss at 964			
S	7/15/81	2.53	964	10
B	9/21/81	1.42	841	
	Stop loss at 844			
S	1/29/82	2.00	844	3
B	3/8/82	1.26	805	
	Stop loss at 821			
S	6/22/82	2.04	*797	(8)
B	8/2/82	1.36	803	
	Stop loss at 1012			
S	10/20/82	2.82	1012	209
B	4/15/84	1.48	1165	
	Stop loss at 1757			
S	5/21/86	6.33	1757	592

*S/B below 2 at DOW 821 — so stop-loss not executed.

Total Appreciation   1077

EXHIBIT I-2:
Insiders' Sell/Buy Ratio

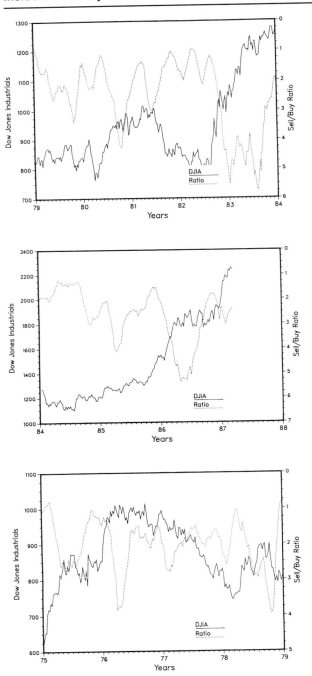

Source: By Permission of Vickers Stock Research Corporation.

INSTALLMENT DEBT INDICATOR

The Installment Debt Indicator is a long-term monetary indicator developed by Martin Zweig (The Zweig Forecast, P.O. Box 5345, New York, NY 10150).*

The basic premise behind the indicator is that when demand for loans increases, interest rates increase—a bearish sign for the stock market. On the other hand, when demand for loans decreases, interest rates decrease—a bullish sign.

One measure of loan demand is consumer installment debt. It is reported on a monthly basis by the Federal Reserve about 6 weeks after the end of a given month, on both a seasonally and a nonseasonally adjusted basis. For the Installment Debt Indicator, use the nonseasonally adjusted number.

The Installment Debt Indicator is calculated by dividing the total consumer installment debt for a given month by the total consumer installment debt for the same month 1 year earlier. (In other words, you are comparing January to January, February to February, etc.). To arrive at the percentage gain or loss in consumer installment debt on a year-to-year basis, you subtract 1.00 from the calculated ratio.

Exhibit I-3 visually shows the relationship between consumer installment debt and the Standard & Poor's 500 Index. Consumer installment debt is plotted for a 20-year period on a year-to-year basis. As Zweig noted in his research, an expansion in consumer installment debt tends to be bearish for stock prices, and a contraction in consumer installment debt is bullish.

In developing a more objective measure, Zweig asked: How much of a year-to-year change in consumer installment debt is required to signal a bullish or bearish condition for the stock market? His research concluded that 9% is the key level.

A buy signal occurs when the year-to-year change is falling and it drops below 9%. A sell signal is given when the year-to-year change is rising and it goes above 9%.

Zweig's test results for the period of 1951 to 1984 show that the Installment Debt Indicator is not infallible. Buy signals were better than sell signals, producing average annualized gains of 13.6% (as measured by the S&P 500) and significantly outperforming a buy-and-hold return of 6.0% during the same period. Sell signals were less successful, producing average annual gains of only 0.3% (as measured by the S&P 500), much less than buy-and-hold results.

Further discussion of the Installment Debt Indicator appears in Zweig's 1986 book entitled *Winning On Wall Street* (Warner Books, New York, NY).

---

*Reprinted with permission.

EXHIBIT I-3:
Consumer Installment Debt (bottom) Versus Standard & Poor's 500 Index from 1966 to 1986

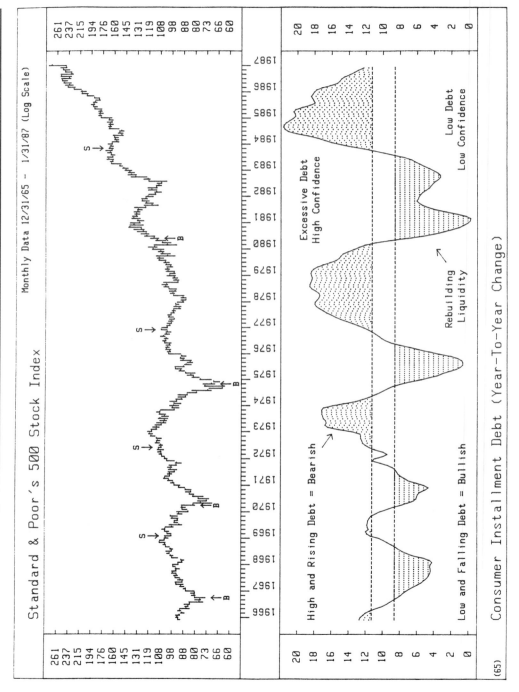

Source: By Permission of Ned Davis Research, Inc.

INTEREST RATES AND STOCK PRICES

Using monthly average data from January 1946 through December 1986, one of the best predictors of Standard & Poor's U.S. Government securities' short-term interest rates is simply the monthly direction of movement, that is, the 1-month rate of change. Using weekly futures price data for both U.S. Treasury bill and bond perpetual contracts from 1977, the 2-week rate of change (the price on Friday divided by the price 2 weeks earlier) was most effective.

We applied this knowledge to our Standard & Poor's 500 Index month-end and the NYSE Composite Index week-end databases to see if an effective interest rate indicator would be profitable for stock market trading.

As shown in Exhibits I-7 and I-8 (pages 225–226), the 1-month rate of change produced profits of 229.21 S&P points. Thus, the monthly indicator was only 1.1% more profitable than our 12-month Simple Moving Average of Price Crossover Rule over the same 1946–1986 period. Trading activity was 3.37 times greater, however, and the worst loss was 58% larger. Moreover, as Exhibit I-7 shows, the 1-month change in interest rates model was counter-productive between 1946 and May 31, 1969, when it lost 40.32 S&P points. And, it really was not until 1979 that the model produced worthwhile returns. We suspect that this is because prior to their take off to double digits in 1979, rates were not high (or painful) enough to make much difference to the equity market. This seems to imply that interest rates might not be a consistent indicator of stock prices in the future—particularly during periods of relatively low and stable rates.

As shown in Exhibits I-9 to I-13 (pages 227–229), using the weekly NYSE file and the 2-week change of Treasury bill futures, profits of 95.11 NYSE points were 18.6% better than our 45-week simple moving average of price crossover rule. Trading was 6.86 times more frequent, however, and the worst trade was 2.27 times greater. In our view, the latter disadvantages offset the higher profit.

Next, we optimized 42 years of monthly average data for Standard & Poor's U.S. Government yields for short-term maturities of 3 to 4 years against the S&P month-end close. The ratio of the yield to the 15-month simple moving average yield produced maximum and consistent profits with the following decision rules: Buy when the ratio of yield to its 15-month simple moving average (shown in Exhibit I-16, page 231) crosses below 1, indicating a declining trend of interest rates; sell and sell short when the same yield to moving average ratio crosses above 1, indicating a rising trend of interest rates.

Exhibits I-17 and I-18 (pages 231–232) show total profits at 241.62 S&P points, better than our 12-month S&P price crossover rule for the

Text continued on p. 234.

EXHIBIT I-4:
Standard & Poor's 500 Index Month-End Close, 1946 to 1986

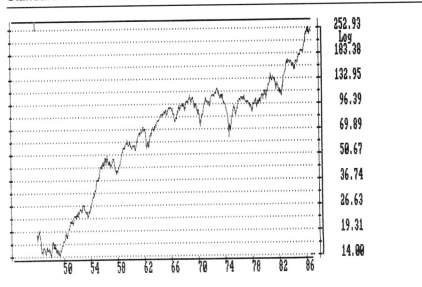

EXHIBIT I-5:
Short-Term Yields on 3- to 4-Year U.S. Government Securities, Monthly Averages, 1946 to 1986

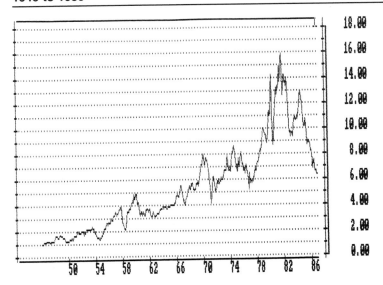

EXHIBIT I-6:
One Month Rate of Change of Short-Term Yields

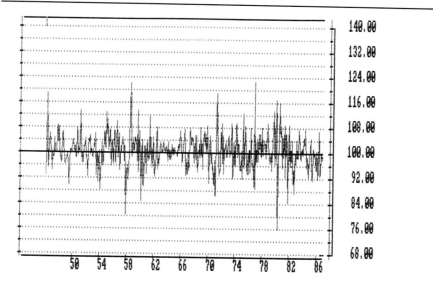

EXHIBIT I-7:
Total Equity in S&P Points for 1-Month Rate of Change of Short-Term Yields

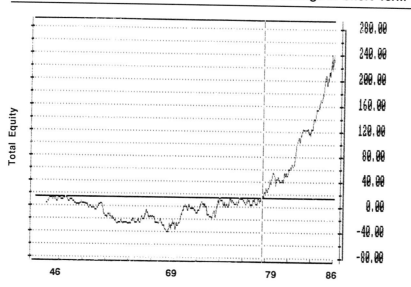

EXHIBIT I-8:
Profit Summary for 1-Month Rate of Change of Short-Term Yields Using the Standard & Poor's 500 Index Month-End Close, 1946 to 1986

Item		Long	Short	Net
		Per Trade Ranges		
Per Trade Ranges				
Best Trade	(Closed position yielding maximum P/L)	40.97	15.77	40.97
.. Date		830228	740930	830228
Worst Trade	(Closed position yielding minimum P/L)	-15.21	-15.14	-15.21
.. Date		620630	860228	620630
Max Open P/L	(Maximum P/L occurring in an open position)	38.21	18.44	38.21
.. Date		830131	700131	830131
Min Open P/L	(Minimum P/L occurring in an open position)	-10.33	-18.85	-18.85
.. Date		620531	801130	801130
		Overall Ranges		
Overall Ranges				
Max P/L	(Maximum P/L from all closed positions during the run)	211.93	223.16	223.16
.. Date		860531	860731	860731
Min P/L	(Minimum P/L from all closed positions during the run)	-40.32	-40.09	-40.32
.. Date		690531	690430	690531
Max Equity	(Maximum P/L from all closed and open positions)	239.97	223.16	239.97
.. Date		860831	860731	860831
Min Equity	(Minimum P/L from all closed and open positions)	-40.32	-40.32	-40.32
.. Date		690531	690531	690531
		Statistics		
Statistics				
Periods	(The number of periods in each position and entire run)	224	268	492
Trades	(The number of trades in each position and entire run)	86	86	172
# Profitable	(The number of profitable trades...)	50	40	90
# Losing	(The number of unprofitable trades...)	36	46	82
% Profitable	(The percent of profitable trades to total trades)	58.14	46.51	52.33
% Losing	(The percent of unprofitable trades to total trades)	41.86	53.49	47.67
		Results		
Results				
Commission	(Total commission deducted from closed trades)	0.00	0.00	0.00
Slippage	(Total slippage deducted from closed trades)	0.00	0.00	0.00
Gross P/L	(Total points gained in closed positions)	221.00	2.16	223.16
Open P/L	(P/L in a position which remains open at the end)	6.05	0.00	6.05
P/L	(Net P/L: Gross P/L less Commission and Slippage)	221.00	2.16	223.16
Equity	(Net P/L plus Open P/L at the end of the run)	227.05	2.16	229.21

There are columns for Long trades, Short trades and Net. In the Long column, results are reported only for Long positions. In the Short column, results are reported for Short positions only. In the Net column for the "Per Trade Ranges" and "Overall Ranges," entries will be the extreme from either the Long or Short column. Net column entries for the "Statistics" and "Results" categories are the combined results of entries in the Long and Short columns.

EXHIBIT I-9:

New York Stock Exchange Composite Price Index Weekly High and Low from April 8, 1977 to December 31, 1986

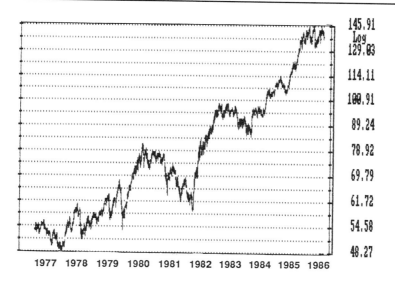

1977 1978 1979 1980 1981 1982 1983 1984 1985 1986

EXHIBIT I-10:

U.S. Treasury Bill Futures Contract Prices, 1977 to 1986

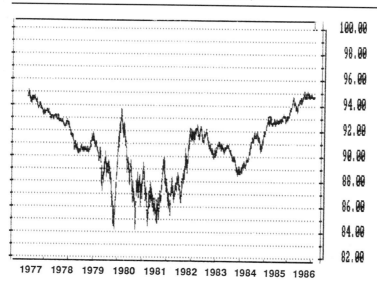

1977 1978 1979 1980 1981 1982 1983 1984 1985 1986

EXHIBIT I-11:
2-Week Rate of Change of U.S. Treasury Bill Futures Contract Prices, 1976 to 1986

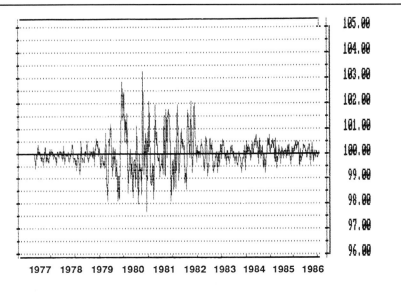

EXHIBIT I-12:
Total Equity in NYSE Points for 2-Week Rate of Change of U.S. Treasury Bill Futures Contract Prices, 1977 to 1986

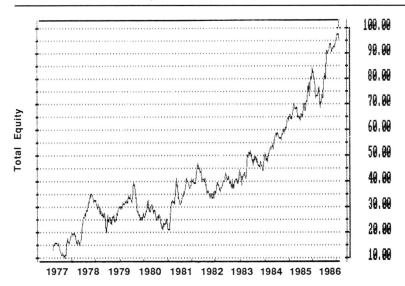

EXHIBIT I-13:

Profit Summary for 2-Week Rate of Change of U.S. Treasury Bill Futures Contract Prices, 1977 to 1986, Using New York Stock Exchange Composite Index Weekly Closing Data

Item	Long	Short	Net
Per Trade Ranges			
Best Trade (Closed position yielding maximum P/L)	12.87	9.95	12.87
.. Date	860425	860926	860425
Worst Trade (Closed position yielding minimum P/L)	-5.36	-6.56	-6.56
.. Date	810925	860613	860613
Max Open P/L (Maximum P/L occurring in an open position)	13.22	11.08	13.22
.. Date	860418	860912	860418
Min Open P/L (Minimum P/L occurring in an open position)	-4.65	-7.62	-7.62
.. Date	860718	860530	860530
Overall Ranges			
Max P/L (Maximum P/L from all closed positions during the run)	95.12	97.67	97.67
.. Date	861205	861226	861226
Min P/L (Minimum P/L from all closed positions during the run)	-0.03	0.95	-0.03
.. Date	770429	770527	770429
Max Equity (Maximum P/L from all closed and open positions)	97.67	97.71	97.71
.. Date	861226	861219	861219
Min Equity (Minimum P/L from all closed and open positions)	-0.03	-0.77	-0.77
.. Date	770429	770520	770520
Statistics			
Periods (The number of periods in each position and entire run)	249	260	509
Trades (The number of trades in each position and entire run)	72	72	144
# Profitable (The number of profitable trades. . .)	44	34	78
# Losing (The number of unprofitable trades. . .)	28	38	66
% Profitable (The percent of profitable trades to total trades)	61.11	47.22	54.17
% Losing (The percent of unprofitable trades to total trades)	38.89	52.78	45.83
Results			
Commission (Total commission deducted from closed trades)	0.00	0.00	0.00
Slippage (Total slippage deducted from closed trades)	0.00	0.00	0.00
Gross P/L (Total points gained in closed positions)	92.56	5.11	97.67
Open P/L (P/L in a position which remains open at the end)	-2.56	0.00	-2.56
P/L (Net P/L: Gross P/L less Commission and Slippage)	92.56	5.11	97.67
Equity (Net P/L plus Open P/L at the end of the run)	90.00	5.11	95.11

There are columns for Long trades, Short trades and Net. In the Long column, results are reported only for Long trades. In the Short column, results are reported for Short positions only. In the Net column for the "Per Trade Ranges" and "Overall Ranges," entries will be the extreme from either the Long or Short column. Net column entries for the "Statistics" and "Results" categories are the combined results of entries in the Long and Short columns.

EXHIBIT I-14:
Standard & Poor's 500 Index Month-End Close, 1944 to 1986

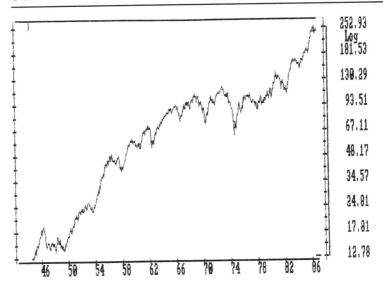

EXHIBIT I-15:
Short-Term Yields on 3- to 4-Year U.S. Government Securities with 15-Month Simple Moving Average, 1944 to 1986

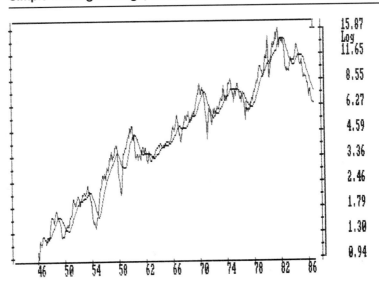

EXHIBIT I-16:

Ratio of Short-Term Interest Rate Yield Divided by its 15-Month Simple Moving Average

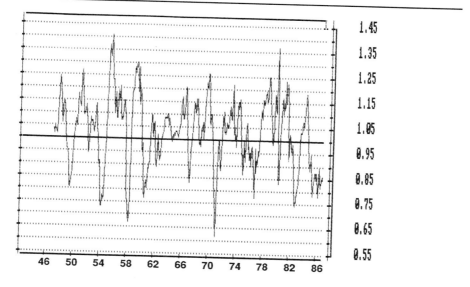

EXHIBIT I-17:

Total Equity in S&P Points for Short-Term Yield Versus 15-Month Average Cross-over Rule

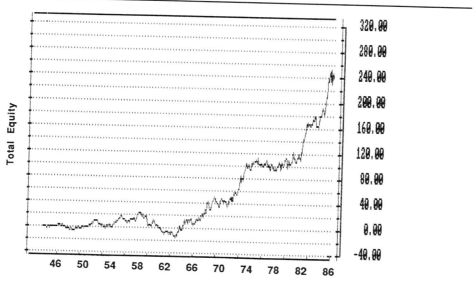

EXHIBIT I-18:
Profit Summary for Short-Term Yield Versus 15-Month Average Crossover Using Standard & Poor's 500 Index Month-End Closing Data, 1946 to 1986

Item		Long	Short	Net
		Per Trade Ranges		
Per Trade Ranges				
Best Trade	(Closed position yielding maximum P/L)	52.44	24.01	52.44
..Date		830831	741130	830831
Worst Trade	(Closed position yielding minimum P/L)	-11.32	-17.54	-17.54
..Date		620731	640831	640831
Max Open P/L	(Maximum P/L occurring in an open position)	86.84	31.14	86.84
..Date		860831	700630	860831
Min Open P/L	(Minimum P/L occurring in an open position)	-14.80	-18.89	-18.89
..Date		620630	640731	640731
		Overall Ranges		
Overall Ranges				
Max P/L	(Maximum P/L from all closed positions during the run)	167.23	165.54	167.23
..Date		830831	841031	830831
Min P/L	(Minimum P/L from all closed positions during the run)	-5.37	-7.72	-7.72
..Date		640930	640831	640831
Max Equity	(Maximum P/L from all closed and open positions)	252.38	181.08	252.38
..Date		860831	840531	860831
Min Equity	(Minimum P/L from all closed and open positions)	-7.72	-14.07	-14.07
..Date		640831	660131	660131
		Statistics		
Statistics				
Periods	(The number of periods in each position and entire run)	208	301	509
Trades	(The number of trades in each position and entire run)	19	20	39
# Profitable	(The number of profitable trades. . .)	16	6	22
# Losing	(The number of unprofitable trades. . .)	3	14	17
% Profitable	(The percent of profitable trades to total trades)	84.21	30.00	56.41
% Losing	(The percent of unprofitable trades to total trades)	15.79	70.00	43.59
		Results		
Results				
Commission	(Total commission deducted from closed trades)	0.00	0.00	0.00
Slippage	(Total slippage deducted from closed trades)	0.00	0.00	0.00
Gross P/L	(Total points gained in closed positions)	158.23	7.31	165.54
Open P/L	(P/L in a position which remains open at the end)	76.08	0.00	76.08
P/L	(Net P/L: Gross P/L less Commission and Slippage)	158.23	7.31	165.54
Equity	(Net P/L plus Open P/L at the end of the run)	234.31	7.31	241.62

There are columns for Long trades, Short trades and Net. In the Long column, results are reported only for Long positions. In the Short column, results are reported for Short positions only. In the Net column for the "Per Trade Ranges" and "Overall Ranges," entries will be the extreme from either the Long or Short column. Net column entries for the "Statistics" and "Results" categories are the combined results of entries in the Long and Short columns.

EXHIBIT I-19:

Transaction Dates and Prices for Short-Term Yields Versus 15-Month Simple Moving Average Crossover Rule Using Standard & Poor's 500 Index Month-End Closing Data

Exit Date	Entry Date	Short or Long*	Entry Price	Exit Price	Maximum P/L	Minimum P/L	Gross P/L	Net P/L	Maximum Equity	Minimum Equity	Cumulative Profit or Equity
490131	470331	Sc	15.17	15.22	1.17	-1.57	-0.05	-0.05	1.17	-1.57	-0.05
500331	490131	Lc	15.22	17.29	2.07	-1.06	2.07	2.07	2.02	-1.57	2.02
520430	500331	Sc	17.29	23.32	0.00	-7.08	-6.03	-6.03	2.02	-5.06	-4.01
520731	520430	Lc	23.32	25.40	2.08	0.00	2.08	2.08	2.02	-5.06	-1.93
531031	520731	Sc	25.40	24.54	2.08	-1.17	0.86	0.86	2.02	-5.06	-1.07
550131	531031	Lc	24.54	36.63	12.09	0.00	12.09	12.09	11.02	-5.06	11.02
571231	550131	Sc	36.63	39.98	0.05	-12.76	-3.35	-3.35	11.07	-5.06	7.67
580930	571231	Lc	39.98	50.06	10.08	0.00	10.08	10.08	17.75	-5.06	17.75
600331	580930	Sc	50.06	55.34	0.00	-10.45	-5.28	-5.28	17.75	-5.06	12.47
610630	600331	Lc	55.34	64.64	11.22	-1.95	9.30	9.30	23.69	-5.06	21.77
620331	610630	Sc	64.64	69.55	0.00	-6.91	-4.91	-4.91	23.69	-5.06	16.86
620831	620731	Lc	69.55	58.23	0.00	-14.80	-11.32	-11.32	23.69	-5.06	5.54
630228	620831	Sc	58.23	59.12	0.00	-0.89	-0.89	-0.89	23.69	-5.06	4.65
640831	630228	Lc	59.12	64.29	7.08	-2.85	5.17	5.17	23.69	-5.06	9.82
640930	640831	Sc	64.29	81.83	0.00	-18.89	-17.54	-17.54	23.69	-9.07	-7.72
661231	640930	Lc	81.83	84.18	2.35	0.00	2.35	2.35	23.69	-9.07	-5.37
670831	661231	Sc	84.18	80.33	7.62	-8.70	3.85	3.85	23.69	-14.07	-1.52
680831	670831	Lc	80.33	93.64	14.42	0.00	13.31	13.31	23.69	-14.07	11.79
681231	680831	Sc	93.64	98.86	4.28	-5.94	-5.22	-5.22	23.69	-14.07	6.57
700930	681231	Lc	98.86	103.86	9.51	0.00	5.00	5.00	23.69	-14.07	11.57
710731	700930	Sc	103.86	84.21	31.14	0.00	19.65	19.65	42.71	-14.07	31.22
710831	710731	Lc	84.21	95.58	19.74	-0.96	11.37	11.37	50.96	-14.07	42.59
720229	710831	Sc	95.58	99.03	0.00	-3.45	-3.45	-3.45	50.96	-14.07	39.14
740228	720229	Lc	99.03	106.57	7.54	-5.04	7.54	7.54	50.96	-14.07	46.68
740331	740228	Sc	106.57	96.22	10.61	-11.48	10.35	10.35	57.29	-14.07	57.03
741130	740331	Lc	96.22	93.98	0.00	-2.24	-2.24	-2.24	57.29	-14.07	54.79
750731	741130	Sc	93.98	69.97	30.44	0.00	24.01	24.01	85.23	-14.07	78.80
751130	750731	Lc	69.97	88.75	25.22	-1.41	18.78	18.78	104.02	-14.07	97.58
770831	751130	Sc	88.75	91.24	4.88	-2.49	-2.49	-2.49	104.02	-14.07	95.09
790630	770831	Lc	91.24	96.77	16.22	-1.05	5.53	5.53	111.31	-14.07	100.62
790831	790630	Sc	96.77	102.91	9.73	-6.52	-6.14	-6.14	111.31	-14.07	94.48
800531	790831	Lc	102.91	109.32	6.41	0.00	6.41	6.41	111.31	-14.07	100.89
800930	800531	Sc	109.32	111.24	7.50	-4.84	-1.92	-1.92	111.31	-14.07	98.97
811130	800930	Lc	111.24	125.46	14.22	0.00	14.22	14.22	113.19	-14.07	113.19
820131	811130	Sc	125.46	126.35	9.28	-15.06	-0.89	-0.89	122.47	-14.07	112.30
820331	820131	Lc	126.35	120.40	0.00	-5.95	-5.95	-5.95	122.47	-14.07	106.35
830831	820331	Sc	120.40	111.96	8.44	0.00	8.44	8.44	122.47	-14.07	114.79
841031	830831	Lc	111.96	164.40	56.15	-4.87	52.44	52.44	170.94	-14.07	167.23
861231	841031	Sc	164.40	166.09	13.85	-2.28	-1.69	-1.69	181.08	-14.07	165.54
	841031	oL	166.09	242.17	86.84	-2.51	76.08	76.08	252.38	-14.07	241.62

*Lc indicates a long position that has been closed. oL indicates a long position that is opened or begun. Sc indicates a short position that has been closed.

Exit Date indicates the date a trade is closed out.

Entry Date indicates the date a trade is opened or begun.

P/L indicates profit or loss on the trade.

Equity is the total cumulative P/L.

same period. Moreover, there was a 56.41% majority of profitable trades. The model was unprofitable from 1944 to January 1966, however, when it lost 14.07 S&P points. Also, there was a long stagnation in profitability from December 1976 through January 1982.

We also tried other widely used data, including the Fed's discount rate directional changes, the prime rate directional changes, and Treasury bill futures trend changes. As shown in Exhibits I-20 and I-21 (pages 235–236), using monthly data from 1944 through 1986, total profit of 217.36 S&P points was nearly as great using changes in the Fed's discount rate—buy and hold when the rate is falling, sell and sell short when the rate is rising. Moreover, the number of trades was cut to only 19, accuracy improved with 63.16% profitable trades, and the nine long-side transactions were all profitable—a perfect record.

As shown in Exhibits I-22 and I-23 (pages 237–238), even better monthly data results were obtained with prime rate data. Here, total profits jumped to 296.31 S&P points, and the percent of profitable trades increased to a very high 70.27%. Trading was 95% more active than the discount rate model but only slightly less active than the short-term government rates trend model. Here again, results were unprofitable from 1944 to 1954, and there were three significant equity drawdowns (loss strings) of 21.16% to 25.30% of the S&P thereafter.

Testing more sensitive weekly prime rate data from April 1977 through December 1986 showed better consistency and more moderate equity drawdowns, as shown in Exhibits I-24 to I-27 (pages 239–242).

In conclusion, interest rate trends have been well worth following during most of the 1970s and 1980s, a time of generally higher interest rates. But in earlier times, interest rates were a poor indicator for the stock market. A simple visual inspection of the data suggests that the stock market pays little attention to interest rates when they are very low, under 4.5% for the discount rate and under 6% for the prime rate.

INTEREST RATES WITH AN ADDITIONAL OPTIMIZED THRESHOLD FILTER RULE

A further test of our idea that the market ignores interest rates when they are very low resulted in the addition of a filter. A logical filter is to not turn aggressively bearish (selling short) when rates are rising if they are below a certain low threshold level of $X\%$. One should exit long positions and not sell short until rates rise to a significantly high threshold of pain.

EXHIBIT I-20:

Total Equity in S&P Points for Discount Rate Direction, 1946 to 1986

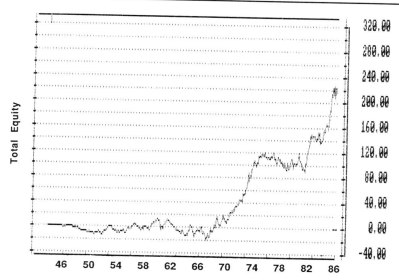

We programmed our computer to find that threshold by testing all S&P short-term government interest rates from .5% to 16%. Fine tuning the result to the nearest .1%, the threshold of pain was reached when interest rates rose to 4.9% or higher (See Exhibit I-28.)

Our previous decision rule was modified as follows: Buy the S&P when the ratio of interest rates to their own 15-month simple moving average crosses below 1, indicating a declining trend of interest rates; sell when the same ratio crosses above 1; sell short when the ratio crosses above 1 and interest rates are 4.9% or higher; cover short and go long when interest rates cross back down below their own 15-month simple moving average and the ratio crosses below 1.

As shown in Exhibits I-30 and I-31 (pages 244–245), total profits rose to 290.46 S&P points, and they were considerably smoother and more consistent in those early years. Moreover, equity drawdowns (loss strings) were considerably less severe and prolonged. On the whole, a worthwhile improvement was attained with the 4.9% filter versus the similar unfiltered model.

As shown in Exhibits I-33 and I-34 (pages 247–248), an unoptimized 6% threshold filter for the prime rate model failed to improve total profits. Nevertheless, consistency of profits was enhanced, with milder and less pro-

EXHIBIT I-21:
Profit Summary in S&P Points for Discount Rate Direction, 1946 to 1986, Using S&P 500 Month-End Closing Data

Item		Long	Short	Net
		--- Per Trade Ranges ---		
Per Trade Ranges				
Best Trade	(Closed position yielding maximum P/L)	33.70	47.47	47.47
..Date		840430	741231	741231
Worst Trade	(Closed position yielding minimum P/L)	4.92	-19.95	-19.95
..Date		671130	670531	670531
Max Open P/L	(Maximum P/L occurring in an open position)	89.35	52.49	89.35
..Date		860831	740930	860831
Min Open P/L	(Minimum P/L occurring in an open position)	-19.26	-24.88	-24.88
..Date		820731	670430	670430
		--- Overall Ranges ---		
Overall Ranges				
Max P/L	(Maximum P/L from all closed positions during the run)	142.30	138.77	142.30
..Date		840430	841130	840430
Min P/L	(Minimum P/L from all closed positions during the run)	-4.75	-11.46	-11.46
..Date		671130	540228	540228
Max Equity	(Maximum P/L from all closed and open positions)	228.12	151.80	228.12
..Date		860831	860531	860831
Min Equity	(Minimum P/L from all closed and open positions)	-11.46	-19.12	-19.12
..Date		540228	681130	681130
		--- Statistics ---		
Statistics				
Periods	(The number of periods in each position and entire run)	221	288	509
Trades	(The number of trades in each position and entire run)	9	10	19
# Profitable	(The number of profitable trades...)	9	3	12
# Losing	(The number of unprofitable trades...)	0	7	7
% Profitable	(The percent of profitable trades to total trades)	100.00	30.00	63.16
% Losing	(The percent of unprofitable trades to total trades)	0.00	70.00	36.84
		--- Results ---		
Results				
Commission	(Total commission deducted from closed trades)	0.00	0.00	0.00
Slippage	(Total slippage deducted from closed trades)	0.00	0.00	0.00
Gross P/L	(Total points gained in closed positions)	143.83	-5.06	138.77
Open P/L	(P/L in a position which remains open at the end)	78.59	0.00	78.59
P/L	(Net P/L: Gross P/L less Commission and Slippage)	143.83	-5.06	138.77
Equity	(Net P/L plus Open P/L at the end of the run)	222.42	-5.06	217.36

There are columns for Long trades, Short trades and Net. In the Long column, results are reported only for Long positions. In the Short column, results are reported for Short positions only. In the Net column for the "Per Trade Ranges" and "Overall Ranges," entries will be the extreme from either the Long or Short column. Net column entries for the "Statistics" and "Results" categories are the combined results of entries in the Long and Short columns.

EXHIBIT I-22:

Total Equity in S&P Points for Prime Rate Direction, 1946 to 1986

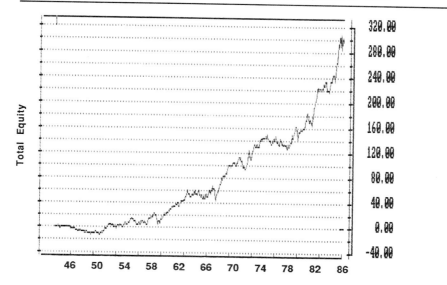

longed equity drawdowns in the early years of low interest rates, and that is a worthwhile improvement.

In conclusion, interest rate trends have proved to be very effective stock market timing tools, particularly over the past 7 years.

EXHIBIT I-23:
Profit Summary in S&P Points for Prime Rate Direction, 1946 to 1986, Using S&P 500 Month-End Closing Data

Item		Long	Short	Net
		------ Per Trade Ranges ------		
Per Trade Ranges				
Best Trade	(Closed position yielding maximum P/L)	48.22	20.08	48.22
.. Date		830831	741031	830831
Worst Trade	(Closed position yielding minimum P/L)	-14.31	-11.64	-14.31
.. Date		740331	540331	740331
Max Open P/L	(Maximum P/L occurring in an open position)	86.83	30.44	86.83
.. Date		860831	740930	860831
Min Open P/L	(Minimum P/L occurring in an open position)	-16.91	-18.14	-18.14
.. Date		700630	801130	801130
		------ Overall Ranges ------		
Overall Ranges				
Max P/L	(Maximum P/L from all closed positions during the run)	221.94	220.24	221.94
.. Date		830831	840930	830831
Min P/L	(Minimum P/L from all closed positions during the run)	4.60	-11.64	-11.64
.. Date		550831	540331	540331
Max Equity	(Maximum P/L from all closed and open positions)	307.07	235.79	307.07
.. Date		860831	840531	860831
Min Equity	(Minimum P/L from all closed and open positions)	-11.64	-11.64	-11.64
.. Date		540331	540331	540331
		------ Statistics ------		
Statistics				
Periods	(The number of periods in each position and entire run)	259	250	509
Trades	(The number of trades in each position and entire run)	18	19	37
# Profitable	(The number of profitable trades...)	15	11	26
# Losing	(The number of unprofitable trades...)	3	8	11
% Profitable	(The percent of profitable trades to total trades)	83.33	57.89	70.27
% Losing	(The percent of unprofitable trades to total trades)	16.67	42.11	29.73
		------ Results ------		
Results				
Commission	(Total commission deducted from closed trades)	0.00	0.00	0.00
Slippage	(Total slippage deducted from closed trades)	0.00	0.00	0.00
Gross P/L	(Total points gained in closed positions)	185.52	34.72	220.24
Open P/L	(P/L in a position which remains open at the end)	76.07	0.00	76.07
P/L	(Net P/L: Gross P/L less Commission and Slippage)	185.52	34.72	220.24
Equity	(Net P/L plus Open P/L at the end of the run)	261.59	34.72	296.31

There are columns for Long trades, Short trades and Net. In the Long column, results are reported only for Long positions. In the Short column, results are reported for Short positions only. In the Net column for the "Per Trade Ranges" and "Overall Ranges," entries will be the extreme from either the Long or Short column. Net column entries for the "Statistics" and "Results" categories are the combined results of entries in the Long and Short columns.

EXHIBIT I-24:
Prime Rate and New York Stock Exchange Composite Index, 1979 to 1986, Weekly Data

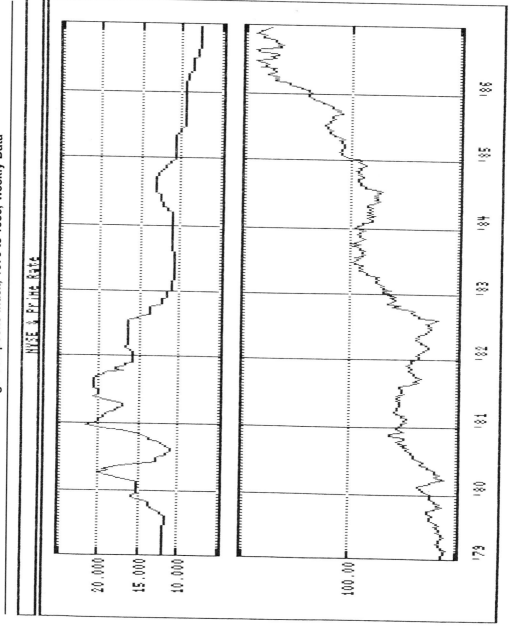

EXHIBIT I-25:
Total Equity in NYSE Points for Prime Rate Direction, 1977 to 1986, Using New York Stock Exchange Composite Index Weekly Data

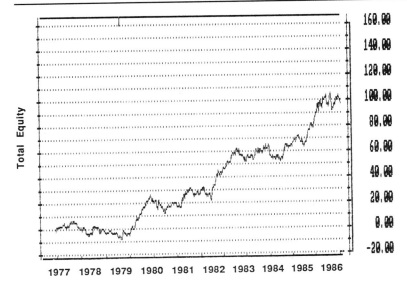

EXHIBIT I-26:

Profit Summary in NYSE Points for Prime Rate Direction, 1977 to 1986, Using NYSE Composite Index Weekly Data

Item		Long	Short	Net
		Per Trade Ranges		
Per Trade Ranges				
Best Trade	(Closed position yielding maximum P/L)	28.51	8.59	28.51
..Date		830812	800418	830812
Worst Trade	(Closed position yielding minimum P/L)	-1.58	-5.79	-5.79
..Date		810710	810102	810102
Max Open P/L	(Maximum P/L occurring in an open position)	49.55	8.98	49.55
..Date		860829	800328	860829
Min Open P/L	(Minimum P/L occurring in an open position)	-5.81	-8.55	-8.55
..Date		810220	801128	801128
		Overall Ranges		
Overall Ranges				
Max P/L	(Maximum P/L from all closed positions during the run)	57.18	55.25	57.18
..Date		830812	840928	830812
Min P/L	(Minimum P/L from all closed positions during the run)	-2.89	-4.87	-4.87
..Date		790727	791130	791130
Max Equity	(Maximum P/L from all closed and open positions)	104.80	64.85	104.80
..Date		860829	840615	860829
Min Equity	(Minimum P/L from all closed and open positions)	-4.87	-7.55	-7.55
..Date		791130	791005	791005
		Statistics		
Statistics				
Periods	(The number of periods in each position and entire run)	276	233	509
Trades	(The number of trades in each position and entire run)	8	8	16
# Profitable	(The number of profitable trades. . .)	6	4	10
# Losing	(The number of unprofitable trades. . .)	2	4	6
% Profitable	(The percent of profitable trades to total trades)	75.00	50.00	62.50
% Losing	(The percent of unprofitable trades to total trades)	25.00	50.00	37.50
		Results		
Results				
Commission	(Total commission deducted from closed trades)	0.00	0.00	0.00
Slippage	(Total slippage deducted from closed trades)	0.00	0.00	0.00
Gross P/L	(Total points gained in closed positions)	48.78	6.47	55.25
Open P/L	(P/L in a position which remains open at the end)	42.81	0.00	42.81
P/L	(Net P/L: Gross P/L less Commission and Slippage)	48.78	6.47	55.25
Equity	(Net P/L plus Open P/L at the end of the run)	91.59	6.47	98.06

There are columns for Long trades, Short trades and Net. In the Long column, results are reported only for Long positions. In the Short column, results are reported for Short positions only. In the Net column for the "Per Trade Ranges" and "Overall Ranges," entries will be the extreme from either the Long or Short column. Net column entries for the "Statistics" and "Results" categories are the combined results of entries in the Long and Short columns.

EXHIBIT I-27:

Transaction Dates and Prices for Prime Rate Direction Using New York Stock Exchange Composite Index Weekly Data, 1977 to 1986

Exit Date	Short or Long*	Entry Date	Entry Price	Exit Price	Maximum P/L	Minimum P/L	Gross P/L	Net P/L	Maximum Equity	Minimum Equity	Cumulative Profit or Equity
770513	Lc	770408	53.46	54.13	1.48	0.00	0.67	0.67	1.48	0.00	0.67
790622	Sc	770513	54.13	58.21	5.46	-6.11	-4.08	-4.08	6.13	-5.44	-3.41
790727	Lc	790622	58.21	58.73	0.61	-0.32	0.52	0.52	6.13	-5.44	-2.89
791130	Sc	790727	58.73	60.71	1.77	-4.66	-1.98	-1.98	6.13	-7.55	-4.87
800222	Lc	791130	60.71	65.80	6.86	0.00	5.09	5.09	6.13	-7.55	0.22
800418	Sc	800222	65.80	57.21	8.98	0.00	8.59	8.59	9.20	-7.55	8.81
800822	Lc	800418	57.21	72.47	15.26	0.00	15.26	15.26	24.07	-7.55	24.07
810102	Sc	800822	72.47	78.26	1.94	-8.55	-5.79	-5.79	26.01	-7.55	18.28
810424	Lc	810102	78.26	78.05	0.00	-5.81	-0.21	-0.21	26.01	-7.55	18.07
810605	Sc	810424	78.05	76.73	1.92	0.00	1.32	1.32	26.01	-7.55	19.39
810710	Lc	810605	76.73	75.15	0.87	-2.00	-1.58	-1.58	26.01	-7.55	17.81
810918	Sc	810710	75.15	67.27	7.88	-1.85	7.88	7.88	26.01	-7.55	25.69
820205	Lc	810918	67.27	67.79	5.97	-2.31	0.52	0.52	31.66	-7.55	26.21
820226	Sc	820205	67.79	65.33	2.46	0.00	2.46	2.46	31.66	-7.55	28.67
830812	Lc	820226	65.33	93.84	33.49	-5.79	28.51	28.51	62.16	-7.55	57.18
840928	Sc	830812	93.84	95.77	7.67	-4.88	-1.93	-1.93	64.85	-7.55	55.25
861231	oL	840928	95.77	138.58	49.55	-2.25	42.81	42.81	104.80	-7.55	98.06

*Lc Indicates a long position that has been closed. oL Indicates a long position that remains open. Sc Indicates a short position that has been closed.

Exit Date Indicates the date a trade is closed out.

Entry Date Indicates the date a trade is opened or begun.

P/L Indicates profit or loss on the trade.

Equity is the total cumulative P/L.

EXHIBIT I-28:

Profitability Chart for Short-Term Yield 1/15 Oscillator with .5% to 16% Minimum Yield to Enter Short Side

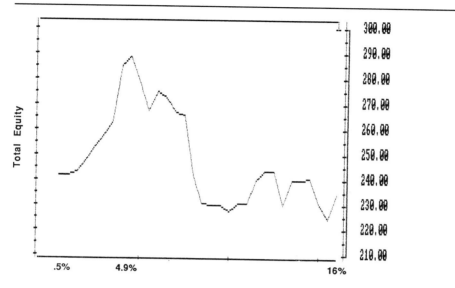

EXHIBIT I-29:

Short-Term Yields on 3- to 4-Year U.S. Government Securities with 15-Month Simple Moving Average, 1944 to 1986

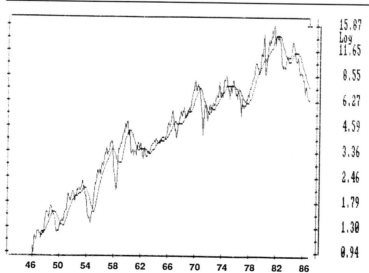

EXHIBIT I-30:

Total Equity in S&P Points for Short-Term Yield 1/15 Oscillator with 4.9% Short Side Minimum

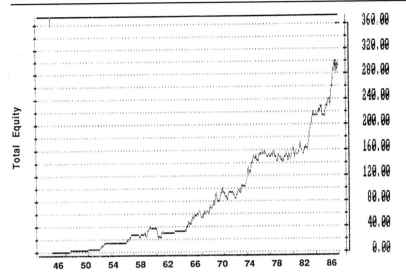

EXHIBIT I-31:
Profit Summary in S&P Points for Short-Term Yield 1/15 Oscillator with 4.9% Minimum Level for Entering Short Sales, 1946 to 1986, Using Standard & Poor's 500 Index Month-End Data

Item		Long	Short	Net
Per Trade Ranges				
Best Trade	(Closed position yielding maximum P/L)	52.44	24.01	52.44
. . Date		830831	741130	830831
Worst Trade	(Closed position yielding minimum P/L)	-11.32	-6.14	-11.32
. . Date		620731	790630	620731
Max Open P/L	(Maximum P/L occurring in an open position)	86.84	31.14	86.84
. . Date		860831	700630	860831
Min Open P/L	(Minimum P/L occurring in an open position)	-14.80	-15.06	-15.06
. . Date		620630	801130	801130
Overall Ranges				
Max P/L	(Maximum P/L from all closed positions during the run)	216.07	214.38	216.07
. . Date		830831	841031	830831
Min P/L	(Minimum P/L from all closed positions during the run)	2.07	27.86	2.07
. . Date		500331	600331	500331
Max Equity	(Maximum P/L from all closed and open positions)	301.22	229.92	301.22
. . Date		860831	840531	860831
Min Equity	(Minimum P/L from all closed and open positions)	-1.06	23.40	-1.06
. . Date		490630	591231	490630
Statistics				
Periods	(The number of periods in each position and entire run)	213	146	492
Trades	(The number of trades in each position and entire run)	19	13	32
# Profitable	(The number of profitable trades. . .)	16	6	22
# Losing	(The number of unprofitable trades. . .)	3	7	10
% Profitable	(The percent of profitable trades to total trades)	84.21	46.15	68.75
% Losing	(The percent of unprofitable trades to total trades)	15.79	53.85	31.25
Results				
Commission	(Total commission deducted from closed trades)	0.00	0.00	0.00
Slippage	(Total slippage deducted from closed trades)	0.00	0.00	0.00
Gross P/L	(Total points gained in closed positions)	158.23	56.15	214.38
Open P/L	(P/L in a position which remains open at the end)	76.08	0.00	76.08
P/L	(Net P/L: Gross P/L less Commission and Slippage)	158.23	56.15	214.38
Equity	(Net P/L plus Open P/L at the end of the run)	234.31	56.15	290.46

There are columns for Long trades, Short trades and Net. In the Long column, results are reported only for Long positions. In the Short column, results are reported for Short positions only. In the Net column for the "Per Trade Ranges" and "Overall Ranges," entries will be the extreme from either the Long or Short column. Net column entries for the "Statistics" and "Results" categories are the combined results of entries in the Long and Short columns.

EXHIBIT I-32:

Transaction Dates and Prices for Short-Term Yields 1/15 Oscillator With 4.9% Minimum to Enter Short Sales, 1946 to 1986, Using Standard & Poor's 500 Index Data

Exit Date	Short or Long*	Entry Date	Entry Price	Exit Price	Maximum P/L	Minimum P/L	Gross P/L	Net P/L	Maximum Equity	Minimum Equity	Cumulative Profit or Equity
500331	Lc	490131	15.22	17.29	2.07	-1.06	2.07	2.07	2.07	-1.06	2.07
520731	Lc	520430	23.32	25.40	2.08	0.00	2.08	2.08	4.15	-1.06	4.15
550131	Lc	531031	24.54	36.63	12.09	0.00	12.09	12.09	16.24	-1.06	16.24
580930	Lc	571231	39.98	50.06	10.08	0.00	10.08	10.08	26.32	-1.06	26.32
600331	Sc	590930	56.88	55.34	1.54	-2.92	1.54	1.54	27.86	-1.06	27.86
610630	Lc	600331	55.34	64.64	11.22	-1.95	9.30	9.30	39.08	-1.06	37.16
620731	Lc	620331	69.55	58.23	0.00	-14.80	-11.32	-11.32	39.08	-1.06	25.84
630228	Lc	620831	59.12	64.29	7.08	-2.85	5.17	5.17	39.08	-1.06	31.01
640930	Lc	640831	81.83	84.18	2.35	0.00	2.35	2.35	39.08	-1.06	33.36
661231	Sc	660228	91.22	80.33	14.66	0.00	10.89	10.89	48.02	-1.06	44.25
670831	Lc	661231	80.33	93.64	14.42	0.00	13.31	13.31	58.67	-1.06	57.56
680831	Sc	670930	96.71	98.86	7.35	-2.87	-2.15	-2.15	64.91	-1.06	55.41
681231	Lc	680831	98.86	103.86	9.51	0.00	5.00	5.00	64.92	-1.06	60.41
700930	Sc	681231	103.86	84.21	31.14	0.00	19.65	19.65	91.55	-1.06	80.06
710731	Lc	700930	84.21	95.58	19.74	-0.96	11.37	11.37	99.80	-1.06	91.43
710831	Sc	710731	95.58	99.03	0.00	-3.45	-3.45	-3.45	99.80	-1.06	87.98
720229	Lc	710831	99.03	106.57	7.54	-5.04	7.54	7.54	99.80	-1.06	95.52
740228	Sc	720229	106.57	96.22	10.61	-11.48	10.35	10.35	106.13	-1.06	105.87
740331	Lc	740228	96.22	93.98	0.00	-2.24	-2.24	-2.24	106.13	-1.06	103.63
741130	Sc	740331	93.98	69.97	30.44	0.00	24.01	24.01	134.07	-1.06	127.64
750731	Lc	741130	69.97	88.75	25.22	-1.41	18.78	18.78	152.86	-1.06	146.42
751130	Sc	750731	88.75	91.24	4.88	-2.49	-2.49	-2.49	152.86	-1.06	143.93
770831	Lc	751130	91.24	96.77	16.22	-1.05	5.53	5.53	160.15	-1.06	149.46
790630	Sc	770831	96.77	102.91	9.73	-6.52	-6.14	-6.14	160.15	-1.06	143.32
790831	Lc	790630	102.91	109.32	6.41	0.00	6.41	6.41	160.15	-1.06	149.73
800531	Sc	790831	109.32	111.24	7.50	-4.84	-1.92	-1.92	160.15	-1.06	147.81
800930	Lc	800531	111.24	125.46	14.22	0.00	14.22	14.22	162.03	-1.06	162.03
811130	Sc	800930	125.46	126.35	9.28	-15.06	-0.89	-0.89	171.31	-1.06	161.14
820131	Lc	811130	126.35	120.40	0.00	-5.95	-5.95	-5.95	171.31	-1.06	155.19
820331	Sc	820131	120.40	111.96	8.44	0.00	8.44	8.44	171.31	-1.06	163.63
830831	Lc	820331	111.96	164.40	56.15	-4.87	52.44	52.44	219.78	-1.06	216.07
841031	Sc	830831	164.40	166.09	13.85	-2.28	-1.69	-1.69	229.92	-1.06	214.38
861231	oL	841031	166.09	242.17	86.84	-2.51	76.08	76.08	301.22	-1.06	290.46

*Lc Indicates a long position that has been closed. oL Indicates a long position that remains open. Sc Indicates a short position that has been closed.

Exit Date Indicates the date a trade is closed out.

Entry Date Indicates the date a trade is opened or begun.

P/L Indicates profit or loss on the trade.

Equity Is the total cumulative P/L.

EXHIBIT I-33:

Total Equity in S&P Points for Prime Rate Direction Filtering Out Short Sales When Prime Rate is 6% or Less, 1946 to 1986, Using Standard & Poor's 500 Index Month-End Closing Data

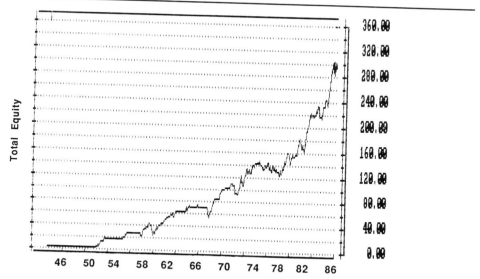

EXHIBIT I-34:

Profit Summary in S&P Points for Prime Rate Direction Filtering Out Short Sales When Prime Rate is 6% or Less, 1946 to 1986, Using Standard & Poor's 500 Index Month-End Closing Data

Item		Long	Short	Net
		Per Trade Ranges		
Per Trade Ranges				
Best Trade	(Closed position yielding maximum P/L)	48.22	20.08	48.22
.. Date		830831	741031	830831
Worst Trade	(Closed position yielding minimum P/L)	-14.31	-7.17	-14.31
.. Date		740331	810131	740331
Max Open P/L	(Maximum P/L occurring in an open position)	86.83	30.44	86.83
.. Date		860831	740930	860831
Min Open P/L	(Minimum P/L occurring in an open position)	-16.91	-18.14	-18.14
.. Date		700630	801130	801130
		Overall Ranges		
Overall Ranges				
Max P/L	(Maximum P/L from all closed positions during the run)	219.95	218.25	219.95
.. Date		830831	840930	830831
Min P/L	(Minimum P/L from all closed positions during the run)	2.48	106.72	2.48
.. Date		471231	731031	471231
Max Equity	(Maximum P/L from all closed and open positions)	305.08	233.80	305.08
.. Date		860831	860531	860831
Min Equity	(Minimum P/L from all closed and open positions)	-0.04	92.41	-0.04
.. Date		440930	740331	440930
		Statistics		
Statistics				
Periods	(The number of periods in each position and entire run)	259	73	509
Trades	(The number of trades in each position and entire run)	19	11	30
# Profitable	(The number of profitable trades. . .)	16	6	22
# Losing	(The number of unprofitable trades. . .)	3	5	8
% Profitable	(The percent of profitable trades to total trades)	84.21	54.55	73.33
% Losing	(The percent of unprofitable trades to total trades)	15.79	45.45	26.67
		Results		
Results				
Commission	(Total commission deducted from closed trades)	0.00	0.00	0.00
Slippage	(Total slippage deducted from closed trades)	0.00	0.00	0.00
Gross P/L	(Total points gained in closed positions)	188.00	30.25	218.25
Open P/L	(P/L in a position which remains open at the end)	76.07	0.00	76.07
P/L	(Net P/L: Gross P/L less Commission and Slippage)	188.00	30.25	218.25
Equity	(Net P/L plus Open P/L at the end of the run)	264.07	30.25	294.32

There are columns for Long trades, Short trades and Net. In the Long column, results are reported only for Long positions. In the Short column, results are reported for Short positions only. In the Net column for the "Per Trade Ranges" and "Overall Ranges," entries will be the extreme from either the Long or Short column. Net column entries for the "Statistics" and "Results" categories are the combined results of entries in the Long and Short columns.

EXHIBIT I-35:

Transaction Dates and Prices for Prime Rate Direction With 6% Short Sales Filter, 1946 to 1986, Using Standard & Poor's 500 Index Month-End Close

Exit Date	Entry Date	Short or Long*	Entry Price	Exit Price	Maximum P/L	Minimum P/L	Gross P/L	Net P/L	Maximum Equity	Minimum Equity	Cumulative Profit or Equity
471231	440831	Lc	12.82	15.30	6.36	-0.04	2.48	2.48	6.36	-0.04	2.48
550831	540331	Lc	26.94	43.18	16.58	0.00	16.24	16.24	19.06	-0.04	18.72
580930	580131	Lc	41.70	50.06	8.36	-0.86	8.36	8.36	27.08	-0.04	27.08
651231	600831	Lc	56.96	92.43	35.47	-3.57	35.47	35.47	62.55	-0.04	62.55
671130	670131	Lc	86.61	94.00	10.10	0.00	7.39	7.39	72.65	-0.04	69.94
681231	680930	Lc	102.67	103.86	5.70	0.00	1.19	1.19	75.64	-0.04	71.13
710430	700331	Lc	89.63	103.95	14.32	-16.91	14.32	14.32	85.45	-0.04	85.45
720430	711031	Lc	94.23	107.67	13.44	-0.24	13.44	13.44	98.89	-0.04	98.89
721031	720630	Lc	107.14	111.58	4.44	0.00	4.44	4.44	103.33	-0.04	103.33
731031	730228	Sc	111.68	108.29	7.43	0.00	3.39	3.39	110.76	-0.04	106.72
740331	731031	Lc	108.29	93.98	0.00	-14.31	-14.31	-14.31	110.76	-0.04	92.41
741031	740331	Sc	93.98	73.90	30.44	0.00	20.08	20.08	122.85	-0.04	112.49
750731	741031	Lc	73.90	88.75	21.29	-5.34	14.85	14.85	133.78	-0.04	127.34
751031	750731	Sc	88.75	89.04	4.88	-0.29	-0.29	-0.29	133.78	-0.04	127.05
760630	751031	Lc	89.04	104.28	15.24	0.00	15.24	15.24	142.29	-0.04	142.29
760831	760630	Sc	104.28	102.91	1.37	0.00	1.37	1.37	143.66	-0.04	143.66
770531	760831	Lc	102.91	96.12	4.55	-6.79	-6.79	-6.79	143.66	-0.04	136.87
790630	770531	Sc	96.12	102.91	9.08	-7.17	-6.79	-6.79	148.21	-0.04	130.08
790731	790630	Lc	102.91	103.81	0.90	0.00	0.90	0.90	148.21	-0.04	130.98
791130	790731	Sc	103.81	106.16	1.99	-5.51	-2.35	-2.35	148.21	-0.04	128.63
800229	791130	Lc	106.16	113.66	8.00	0.00	7.50	7.50	148.21	-0.04	136.13
800430	800229	Sc	113.66	106.29	11.57	0.00	7.37	7.37	148.21	-0.04	143.50
800831	800430	Lc	106.29	122.38	16.09	0.00	16.09	16.09	159.59	-0.04	159.59
810131	800831	Sc	122.38	129.55	0.00	-18.14	-7.17	-7.17	159.59	-0.04	152.42
810430	810131	Lc	129.55	132.81	6.45	0.00	3.26	3.26	159.59	-0.04	155.68
810630	810430	Sc	132.81	131.21	1.60	0.00	1.60	1.60	159.59	-0.04	157.28
810731	810630	Lc	131.21	130.92	0.00	-0.29	-0.29	-0.29	159.59	-0.04	156.99
810930	810731	Sc	130.92	116.18	14.74	0.00	14.74	14.74	171.73	-0.04	171.73
830831	810930	Lc	116.18	164.40	51.93	-9.09	48.22	48.22	223.66	-0.04	219.95
840930	830831	Sc	164.40	166.10	13.85	-2.28	-1.70	-1.70	233.80	-0.04	218.25
861231	840930	oL	166.10	242.17	86.83	-2.52	76.07	76.07	305.08	-0.04	294.32

*Lc indicates a long position that has been closed. oL indicates a long position that remains open. Sc indicates a short position that has been closed.

Exit Date indicates the date a trade is closed out.

Entry Date indicates the date a trade is opened or begun.

P/L indicates profit or loss on the trade.

Equity is the total cumulative P/L.

JANUARY BAROMETER

Yale Hirsch (The Hirsch Organization, Inc., Six Deer Trail, Old Tappan, NJ 07675), among others, contends that the January Barometer has consistently predicted the annual direction of stock market prices.* Between 1950 and 1985, January's market action correctly predicted the direction of the stock market for the entire year 31 times (86% accuracy).

As shown in Exhibit J-1, years beginning with January gains were more successful indicators of what would occur during the rest of the year than those beginning with losses. Of the 21 years since 1950 with gains during January, only 1 year ended with a loss.

For each of the 20 correct signals, remarkable gains of 5% to 38% in market prices occurred between the end of January, when the signal is given, and the end of the year. On average for those 20 years, 77% of each year's market gains occurred between the end of January and December 31.

Signals given by January losses were not as consistent with an accuracy record of 60%. Market prices increased for the overall year during 6 of the 15 years in which there were losses in January.

The January Barometer accuracy is better than many other indicators. However, due to the total absence of rationale for the indicator's performance, the use of other indicators to confirm its signals is highly recommended.

For a discussion of a similar indicator, refer to the section on the First Five Days in January.

---

*Reprinted with permission.

EXHIBIT J-1:
The January Barometer from 1950 to 1985

Market Performance in January					January Performance by Rank			
Year	Previous Year's Close	January Close	January Change		Rank	Year	January Change	Year's Change
1950	16.76*	17.05*	1.7%		1.	1975	12.3%	31.5%
1951	20.41	21.66	6.1		2.	1976	11.8	19.1
1952	23.77	24.14	1.6		3.	1967	7.8	20.1
1953	26.57	26.38	−0.7		4.	1985	7.4	26.3
1954	24.81	26.08	5.1		5.	1961	6.3	23.1
1955	35.98	36.63	1.8		6.	1951	6.1	16.5
1956	45.48	43.82	−3.7		7.	1980	5.8	25.8
1957	46.67	44.72	−4.2		8.	1954	5.1	45.0
1958	39.99	41.70	4.3		9.	1963	4.9	18.9
1959	55.21	55.42	0.4		10.	1958	4.3	38.1
1960	59.89	55.61	−7.1		11.	1971	4.0	10.8
1961	58.11	61.78	6.3		12.	1979	4.0	12.3
1962	71.55	68.84	−3.8		13.	1983	3.3	17.3
1963	63.10	66.20	4.9		14.	1965	3.3	9.1
1964	75.02	77.04	2.7		15.	1964	2.7	13.0
1965	84.75	87.56	3.3		16.	1955	1.8	26.4
1966	92.43	92.88	0.5		17.	1972	1.8	15.6
1967	80.33	86.61	7.8		18.	1950	1.7	21.8
1968	96.47	92.24	−4.4		19.	1952	1.6	11.8
1969	103.86	103.01	−0.8		20.	1966	0.5	−13.1
1970	92.06	85.02	−7.6		21.	1959	0.4	8.5
1971	92.15	95.88	4.0		22.	1953	−0.7	−6.6
1972	102.09	103.94	1.8		23.	1969	−0.8	−11.4
1973	118.05	116.03	−1.7		24.	1984	−0.9	1.4
1974	97.55	96.57	−1.0		25.	1974	−1.0	−29.7
1975	68.56	76.98	12.3		26.	1973	−1.7	−17.4
1976	90.19	100.86	11.8		27.	1982	−1.8	14.8
1977	107.46	102.03	−5.1		28.	1956	−3.6	2.6
1978	95.10	89.25	−6.2		29.	1962	−3.8	−11.8
1979	96.11	99.93	4.0		30.	1957	−4.2	−14.3
1980	107.94	114.16	5.8		31.	1968	−4.4	7.7
1981	135.76	129.55	−4.6		32.	1981	−4.6	−9.7
1982	122.55	120.40	−1.8		33.	1977	−5.1	−11.5
1983	140.64	145.30	3.3		34.	1978	−6.2	1.1
1984	164.93	163.41	−0.9		35.	1960	−7.1	−3.0
1985	167.24	179.63	7.4		36.	1970	−7.6	0.1

*S & P Composite Index

Source: By permission of the Hirsch Organization, Inc.

LARGE BLOCK RATIO

Large blocks are defined as trades of more than 10,000 shares that occur on the New York Stock Exchange. The Large Block Ratio (also known as the Big Block Index) is calculated by dividing the volume of large block trades by the total volume on the New York Stock Exchange.

The Large Block Ratio is a sentiment indicator that reflects institutional behavior. It is used to identify major reversal points in the stock market. The theory is that it takes sustained buying or selling to reach an overbought or oversold condition. Such buying or selling can be monitored using the Large Block Ratio. Once a legitimate overbought or oversold condition is reached, stock prices will reverse their direction.

Common usage smooths the Large Block Ratio with a 5-week simple moving average. When the 5-week moving average of the Large Block Ratio exceeds 50% (or .50), it is considered overbought and a market reverse to the downside is anticipated. On the other hand, when the 5-week moving average of the ratio drops below the 20% (or .20) level, an oversold condition is in effect warning that a market turn to the upside may be forthcoming.

LINEAR REGRESSION

Linear regression is a statistical method of following trends. For practical purposes, its results are similar to the more familiar moving averages.

Mathematically the linear regression formula is represented as:

$$y = a + bx$$

where

$y =$ the closing price.

$x =$ the position of the current time period in the database.

$a = 1/n(\sum y - b\sum x)$

$b = \dfrac{n\sum xy - \sum x \sum y}{n\sum x^2 - (\sum x)^2}$

$n =$ number of time periods in the summations.

We tested the linear regression approach using Compu Trac software and two 9.75-year test periods of weekly data (consisting of high, low, close, and volume for each week) for the broad-based NYSE Composite Index. The first period ran from January 5, 1968 through September 30, 1977, and the second period ran from April 8, 1977 through December 31, 1986. The overlap in data was necessary to facilitate testing throughout the full time period.

We obtained our best results by following the direction (rising is bullish, falling is bearish) of the linear regression line. Prices crossing the linear regression line proved less profitable. The only variable to be optimized is n, the number of time periods that go into the calculation. As shown in Exhibits L-1 to L-4 (pages 253–256), the results for the 66-week optimal parameter were quite good, but profitability was noticeably reduced when 66 weeks was varied slightly, indicating somewhat greater instability than moving average crossover rules.

As shown in Exhibits L-6, L-7, L-9, and L-10 (pages 257–260), combined equity (cumulative profit) of 127.39 NYSE points was relatively high and well above our 40-week simple moving average crossover rule standard of comparison. Combined with moderate loss strings, the ratio of total profits to maximum drawdowns was relatively high. In sum, the direction of the 66-week linear regression line has been an effective indicator over the past 19 years.

EXHIBIT L-1:
Profitability Chart for Direction of Linear Regression Line (Period Lengths of 50 to 80 Weeks from 1977 to 1986)

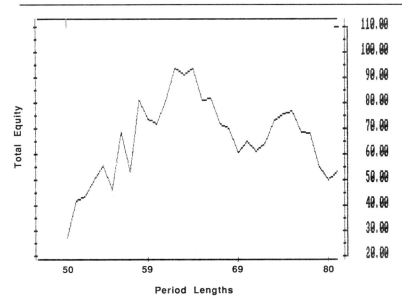

EXHIBIT L-2:
Profit Table for Direction of Linear Regression Line (Period Lengths of 50 to 80 Weeks from 1977 to 1986)

Pass	Short Equity	Long Equity	Total Equity	Max. Equity	Min. Equity	P/L	Best Trade	Worst Trade	Max. Open P/L	Min. Open P/L
50	27.80	-30.46	58.26	48.16	-12.72	24.85	27.04	-9.76	34.77	-8.69
51	41.73	-23.50	65.23	64.33	-14.68	38.78	29.62	-10.88	34.77	-9.76
52	43.51	-22.33	65.84	61.79	-16.36	49.28	29.62	-4.44	34.77	-10.88
53	50.30	-18.17	68.47	72.90	-16.89	47.35	28.95	-10.88	36.96	-9.76
54	55.55	-15.19	70.74	78.15	-11.54	52.60	29.19	-10.88	34.77	-9.76
55	46.48	-19.10	65.58	69.08	-8.93	43.53	30.27	-10.88	34.77	-9.76
56	68.93	-7.84	76.77	87.21	-9.10	74.70	29.15	-4.27	38.76	-10.88
57	53.23	-15.25	68.48	71.51	-10.45	59.00	29.15	-4.27	37.17	-10.88
58	81.27	-1.18	82.45	99.55	-8.79	87.04	31.52	-2.98	37.17	-10.88
59	74.00	-5.22	79.22	92.28	-7.24	79.77	28.94	-2.98	38.76	-10.88
60	71.99	-5.78	77.77	88.31	-11.01	69.85	31.59	-6.93	37.17	-3.99
61	81.24	-0.63	81.87	93.54	-16.10	79.10	31.59	-3.56	38.76	-2.97
62	93.76	4.99	88.77	102.06	-9.22	91.40	33.35	-3.14	37.17	-2.75
63	91.26	3.29	87.97	92.10	-10.90	88.31	33.38	-2.30	37.17	-1.45
64	93.46	4.27	89.19	94.30	-11.54	90.51	33.17	-2.51	36.96	-2.30
65	81.16	-2.04	83.20	82.00	-10.70	78.21	30.98	-4.70	34.77	-2.51
66	81.64	-1.06	82.70	83.34	-10.06	79.12	30.55	-4.70	34.77	-2.51
67	72.09	-5.79	77.88	73.71	-14.16	69.53	30.59	-4.70	34.77	-2.51
68	69.70	-6.35	76.05	76.44	-16.39	69.70	28.51	-3.66	34.77	-1.97
69	60.88	-9.68	70.56	67.62	-17.17	60.88	30.43	-5.82	37.17	-3.58
70	64.93	-7.56	72.49	71.67	-17.42	64.93	30.22	-6.01	36.96	-3.77
71	61.54	-8.99	70.53	69.64	-15.13	61.54	27.05	-6.54	34.77	-4.30
72	64.24	-7.56	71.80	70.98	-17.19	64.24	30.43	-6.70	37.17	-4.46
73	73.38	-3.33	76.71	80.12	-13.57	73.38	43.89	-6.02	50.63	-3.78
74	75.48	-1.43	76.91	82.22	-13.03	33.95	28.23	-7.72	48.27	-5.48
75	76.59	-1.59	78.18	83.33	-13.08	35.06	28.43	-6.29	48.27	-4.05
76	68.69	-6.26	74.95	75.43	-11.20	24.90	28.43	-4.85	50.53	-2.99
77	68.12	-6.34	74.46	74.86	-13.95	24.33	25.14	-5.26	50.53	-3.02
78	54.88	-12.68	67.56	61.62	-15.51	11.09	23.60	-5.84	50.53	-4.02
79	49.87	-14.89	64.76	56.61	-15.16	8.15	23.60	-6.41	48.46	-4.17
80	53.04	-15.39	68.43	59.78	-12.61	11.32	23.60	-3.98	48.46	-3.34

Pass indicates period length.
Equity indicates the total number of points gained or lost.
Short equity indicates the number of points gained or lost on short positions.
Long equity indicates the number of points gained or lost on long positions.
Max. equity indicates the highest total profit recorded over the tested period.
Min. equity indicates the lowest total profit recorded over the tested period.
P/L indicates total number of points gained or lost in closed positions.
Best trade indicates the highest number of points gained in any closed trade.
Worst trade indicates the highest number of points lost in any closed trade.
Max. open P/L indicates the highest gain in a position which remains open at the end of the test run.
Min. open P/L indicates the highest loss in a position which remains open at the end of the test run.

EXHIBIT L-3:

Profitability Chart for Direction of Linear Regression Line (Period Lengths of 50 to 80 Weeks from 1968 to 1977)

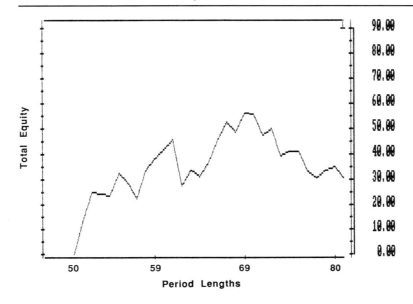

EXHIBIT L-4:
Profit Table for Direction of Linear Regression Line (Period Lengths of 50 to 80 Weeks from 1968 to 1977)

Pass	Short Equity	Long Equity	Total Equity	Max. Equity	Min. Equity	P/L	Best Trade	Worst Trade	Max. Open P/L	Min. Open P/L
50	0.15	3.82	-3.67	19.75	-6.48	-1.16	11.12	-3.86	19.13	-2.83
51	13.97	10.29	3.68	32.47	-4.28	12.66	14.34	-4.17	20.28	-3.22
52	24.96	15.55	9.41	34.68	-1.81	23.65	13.19	-3.42	19.13	-1.81
53	24.23	14.28	9.95	38.01	0.00	22.92	11.12	-4.03	19.13	-2.91
54	23.85	14.40	9.45	38.89	-4.79	22.54	11.12	-5.57	19.13	-4.45
55	32.71	19.00	13.71	42.59	-5.93	31.40	13.19	-5.57	19.13	-4.45
56	29.01	17.29	11.72	40.61	-5.60	27.70	11.12	-5.57	19.13	-4.45
57	22.31	14.07	8.24	36.37	-5.86	21.00	12.51	-5.57	19.13	-4.45
58	33.61	19.72	13.89	41.91	-5.18	32.30	11.12	-4.45	19.13	-2.85
59	38.10	20.80	17.30	43.84	-2.85	35.99	11.12	-2.85	19.13	-2.85
60	41.66	22.02	19.64	47.41	-3.97	39.55	11.12	-2.75	19.13	-3.97
61	45.68	24.10	21.58	51.83	-3.83	44.37	10.22	-2.43	17.31	-3.83
62	27.56	14.84	12.72	35.96	-4.23	26.25	11.64	-2.97	17.31	-4.23
63	33.60	18.33	15.27	42.11	-4.27	32.29	11.64	-2.97	17.31	-2.80
64	31.08	17.56	13.52	43.79	-3.29	29.77	13.46	-2.75	19.13	-2.80
65	37.11	20.33	16.78	45.85	-2.33	35.80	13.65	-4.45	19.32	-2.20
66	45.75	24.88	20.87	51.13	-1.35	44.44	14.00	-2.29	19.13	-1.39
67	52.57	28.16	24.41	61.56	-0.28	51.26	18.77	-2.23	24.71	-1.51
68	48.53	26.28	22.25	50.40	-1.63	47.22	18.77	-2.37	24.71	-1.56
69	56.14	30.75	25.39	59.45	-0.30	54.83	16.70	-2.64	24.71	-0.76
70	55.45	30.70	24.75	59.76	-0.89	54.14	16.70	-2.37	24.71	-1.56
71	47.71	27.03	20.68	51.24	-2.08	46.40	16.70	-3.15	24.71	-2.37
72	49.75	27.71	22.04	53.06	-1.40	48.44	15.81	-2.27	24.71	-1.49
73	39.26	22.16	17.10	42.13	-3.08	37.95	15.81	-3.16	24.71	-3.15
74	41.23	22.75	18.48	44.96	0.00	39.92	15.81	-4.39	24.71	-3.61
75	41.37	21.78	19.59	44.68	-0.21	40.06	15.81	-3.61	24.71	-2.80
76	33.04	16.94	16.10	36.86	-1.56	31.73	14.40	-3.61	24.71	-2.80
77	30.39	15.73	14.66	34.21	-1.33	29.08	14.40	-5.14	24.71	-4.36
78	33.68	18.04	15.64	38.38	0.00	31.03	15.81	-3.25	24.71	-1.92
79	34.88	17.56	17.32	38.50	-2.02	33.12	15.81	-3.46	24.71	-3.16
80	30.93	15.35	15.58	36.62	-2.49	29.17	15.81	-4.47	24.71	-3.14

Pass indicates period length.

Equity indicates the total number of points gained or lost.

Short equity indicates the number of points gained or lost on short positions.

Long equity indicates the number of points gained or lost on long positions.

Max. equity indicates the highest total profit recorded over the tested period.

Min. equity indicates the lowest total profit recorded over the tested period.

P/L indicates total number of points gained or lost in closed positions.

Best trade indicates the highest number of points gained in any closed trade.

Worst trade indicates the highest number of points lost in any closed trade.

Max. open P/L indicates the highest gain in a position which remains open at the end of the test run.

Min. open P/L indicates the highest loss in a position which remains open at the end of the test run.

EXHIBIT L-5:

Linear Regression Line (Solid) and New York Stock Exchange Composite Index (Dashes), 1977 to 1986, Weekly Data

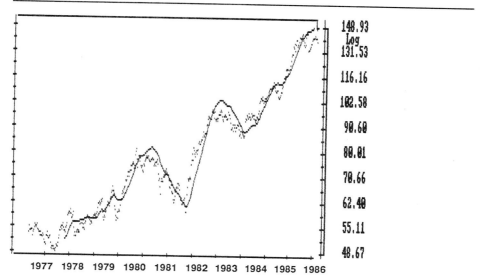

EXHIBIT L-6:

Total Equity for Direction of Linear Regression Line, 66 Weeks, 1977 to 1986

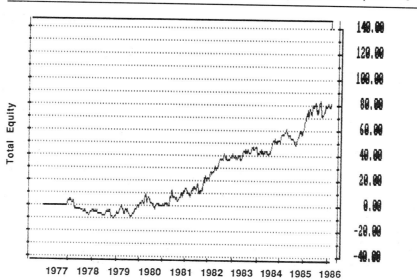

EXHIBIT L-7:

Profit Summary for Direction of Linear Regression Line, 66 Weeks, 1977 to 1986

Item		Long	Short	Net
		-- Per Trade Ranges --		
Per Trade Ranges				
Best Trade	(Closed position yielding maximum P/L)	30.55	9.52	30.55
.. Date		861219	820827	861219
Worst Trade	(Closed position yielding minimum P/L)	-2.10	-4.70	-4.70
.. Date		781110	851101	851101
Max Open P/L	(Maximum P/L occurring in an open position)	34.77	17.21	34.77
.. Date		860829	820813	860829
Min Open P/L	(Minimum P/L occurring in an open position)	-2.30	-2.51	-2.51
.. Date		781027	851025	851025
		-- Overall Ranges --		
Overall Ranges				
Max P/L	(Maximum P/L from all closed positions during the run)	79.12	48.57	79.12
.. Date		861219	851101	861219
Min P/L	(Minimum P/L from all closed positions during the run)	-9.04	-9.61	-9.61
.. Date		791019	791102	791102
Max Equity	(Maximum P/L from all closed and open positions)	83.34	81.64	83.34
.. Date		860829	861231	860829
Min Equity	(Minimum P/L from all closed and open positions)	-10.06	-9.61	-10.06
.. Date		791109	791102	791109
		-- Statistics --		
Statistics				
Periods	(The number of periods in each position and entire run)	366	143	509
Trades	(The number of trades in each position and entire run)	14	13	27
# Profitable	(The number of profitable trades. . .)	8	2	10
# Losing	(The number of unprofitable trades. . .)	6	11	17
% Profitable	(The percent of profitable trades to total trades)	57.14	15.38	37.04
% Losing	(The percent of unprofitable trades to total trades)	42.86	84.62	62.96
		-- Results --		
Results				
Commission	(Total commission deducted from closed trades)	0.00	0.00	0.00
Slippage	(Total slippage deducted from closed trades)	0.00	0.00	0.00
Gross P/L	(Total points gained in closed positions)	82.70	-3.58	79.12
Open P/L	(P/L in a position which remains open at the end)	0.00	2.52	2.52
P/L	(Net P/L: Gross P/L less Commission and Slippage)	82.70	-3.58	79.12
Equity	(Net P/L plus Open P/L at the end of the run)	82.70	-1.06	81.64

There are columns for Long trades, Short trades and Net. In the Long column, results are reported only for Long positions. In the Short column, results are reported for Short positions only. In the Net column for the "Per Trade Ranges" and "Overall Ranges," entries will be the extreme from either the Long or Short column. Net column entries for the "Statistics" and "Results" categories are the combined results of entries in the Long and Short columns.

EXHIBIT L-8:

Linear Regression Line (Solid) and New York Stock Exchange Composite Index (Dashes), 1968 to 1977, Weekly Data

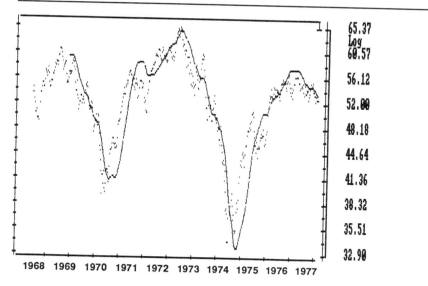

EXHIBIT L-9:

Total Equity for Direction of Linear Regression Line, 66 Weeks, 1968 to 1977

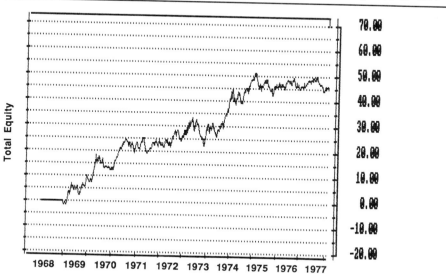

EXHIBIT L-10:

Profit Summary for Direction of Linear Regression Line, 66 Weeks, 1968 to 1977

Item		Long	Short	Net
Per Trade Ranges		*--- Per Trade Ranges ---*		
Best Trade	(Closed position yielding maximum P/L)	8.79	14.00	14.00
.. Date		710924	700828	700828
Worst Trade	(Closed position yielding minimum P/L)	-2.29	-2.25	-2.29
.. Date		731102	760109	731102
Max Open P/L	(Maximum P/L occurring in an open position)	11.87	19.13	19.13
.. Date		750711	741004	741004
Min Open P/L	(Minimum P/L occurring in an open position)	-0.50	-1.39	-1.39
.. Date		770701	761126	761126
Overall Ranges		*--- Overall Ranges ---*		
Max P/L	(Maximum P/L from all closed positions during the run)	46.93	47.54	47.54
.. Date		770708	770624	770624
Min P/L	(Minimum P/L from all closed positions during the run)	-1.04	-1.35	-1.35
.. Date		690523	690502	690502
Max Equity	(Maximum P/L from all closed and open positions)	51.13	50.28	51.13
.. Date		750711	770527	750711
Min Equity	(Minimum P/L from all closed and open positions)	-1.35	-1.35	-1.35
.. Date		690502	690502	690502
Statistics		*--- Statistics ---*		
Periods	(The number of periods in each position and entire run)	276	233	509
Trades	(The number of trades in each position and entire run)	15	15	30
# Profitable	(The number of profitable trades...)	9	6	15
# Losing	(The number of unprofitable trades...)	6	9	15
% Profitable	(The percent of profitable trades to total trades)	60.00	40.00	50.00
% Losing	(The percent of unprofitable trades to total trades)	40.00	60.00	50.00
Results		*--- Results ---*		
Commission	(Total commission deducted from closed trades)	0.00	0.00	0.00
Slippage	(Total slippage deducted from closed trades)	0.00	0.00	0.00
Gross P/L	(Total points gained in closed positions)	20.87	23.57	44.44
Open P/L	(P/L in a position which remains open at the end)	0.00	1.31	1.31
P/L	(Net P/L: Gross P/L less Commission and Slippage)	20.87	23.57	44.44
Equity	(Net P/L plus Open P/L at the end of the run)	20.87	24.88	45.75

There are columns for Long trades, Short trades and Net. In the Long column, results are reported only for Long positions. In the Short column, results are reported for Short positions only. In the Net column for the "Per Trade Ranges" and "Overall Ranges," entries will be the extreme from either the Long or Short column. Net column entries for the "Statistics" and "Results" categories are the combined results of entries in the Long and Short columns.

LOWRY'S REPORTS (SIMPLIFIED)

Lowry's Reports, Inc. (701 North Federal Highway, North Palm Beach, FL 33408) is one of the oldest technical investment advisory services. It has been dispensing specific data and buy and sell advice on a daily and weekly basis since 1937. Lowry's specific formulas for calculating its Buying Power (demand) and Selling Pressure (supply) are proprietary, but they are based on stock price changes and the volume behind those price changes. The full set of Lowry's decision rules is complex—too complex, in fact, for our "Keep It Simple" purposes in this book.

Stan Lipstadt (PSM Investors Inc., 121 Judy Farm Road, Carlisle, MA 01741) suggested in the *Market Technician's Association Journal* (May 1978) a greatly simplified set of interpretative rules that performed well in his testing of weekly data (Friday's closing only) over the 32 years between January 1946 and December 1977. His rules were:

1. Buy when the Buying Power line rises above the Selling Pressure line for 2 consecutive weeks, with the extent of the crossing larger after the second week than after the first.
2. Alternatively, whenever the point spread between the Buying and Selling curves reaches an extreme of -20.0% or greater, buy after the first improvement as of Friday following such a registration.
3. Sell when the Buying Power line falls below the Selling Pressure line for 2 consecutive weeks, with the second week showing a crossing of greater extent than the first.

We tested these decision rules using Compu Trac software and two 9.75-year test periods of weekly data (consisting of high, low, close, and volume for each week) for the broad-based NYSE Composite Index. The first period ran from January 5, 1968 through September 30, 1977 and the second period ran from April 8, 1977 through December 31, 1986. The overlap in data was necessary to facilitate testing throughout the full time period.

Lipstadt warned of the dangers of facile decision rules and especially of the effect of secular changes in market statistics. Indeed, market changes apparently have detracted significantly from the effectiveness of the above decision rules since 1975. As shown in Exhibits L-11 to L-16 (pages 262–265), combined profits of 12.26 NYSE points were well below our 40-week simple moving average crossover rule standard of comparison. Results for an unbiased and aggressive long buying and short selling strategy were quite poor from 1976 through 1986 as shown in Exhibits L-12 and L-15. Even ignoring the quite unprofitable short side and counting long-side trades

Text continued on page 266.

EXHIBIT L-11:

New York Stock Exchange Composite Price Index Weekly High and Low from April 8, 1977 to December 31, 1986

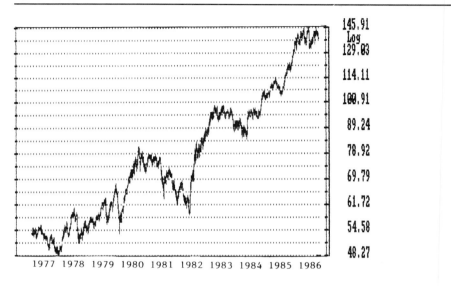

1977 1978 1979 1980 1981 1982 1983 1984 1985 1986

EXHIBIT L-12:

Total Equity for Lowry's Simplified, 1977 to 1986

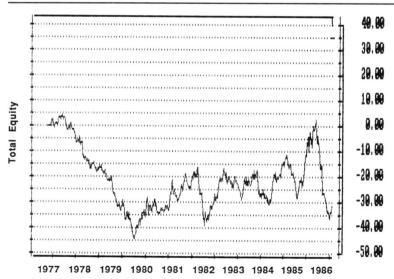

1977 1978 1979 1980 1981 1982 1983 1984 1985 1986

EXHIBIT L-13:
Profit Summary for Lowry's Simplified, 1977 to 1986

Item		Long Per Trade Ranges	Short	Net
Per Trade Ranges				
Best Trade	(Closed position yielding maximum P/L)	20.93	-1.16	20.93
. . Date		860801	780505	860801
Worst Trade	(Closed position yielding minimum P/L)	-10.40	-9.18	-10.40
. . Date		860919	790817	860919
Max Open P/L	(Maximum P/L occurring in an open position)	30.31	16.90	30.31
. . Date		860704	820813	860704
Min Open P/L	(Minimum P/L occurring in an open position)	-11.08	-10.20	-11.08
. . Date		860912	861205	860912
Overall Ranges		Overall Ranges		
Max P/L	(Maximum P/L from all closed positions during the run)	-1.47	-1.16	-1.16
. . Date		780630	780505	780505
Min P/L	(Minimum P/L from all closed positions during the run)	-37.12	-43.18	-43.18
. . Date		800314	800613	800613
Max Equity	(Maximum P/L from all closed and open positions)	2.38	4.14	4.14
. . Date		860704	780303	780303
Min Equity	(Minimum P/L from all closed and open positions)	-44.11	-43.18	-44.11
. . Date		800620	800613	800620
Statistics		Statistics		
Periods	(The number of periods in each position and entire run)	223	286	509
Trades	(The number of trades in each position and entire run)	10	10	20
# Profitable	(The number of profitable trades. . .)	4	0	4
# Losing	(The number of unprofitable trades. . .)	6	10	16
% Profitable	(The percent of profitable trades to total trades)	40.00	0.00	20.00
% Losing	(The percent of unprofitable trades to total trades)	60.00	100.00	80.00
Results		Results		
Commission	(Total commission deducted from closed trades)	0.00	0.00	0.00
Slippage	(Total slippage deducted from closed trades)	0.00	0.00	0.00
Gross P/L	(Total points gained in closed positions)	27.34	-53.34	-26.00
Open P/L	(P/L in a position which remains open at the end)	0.00	-5.09	-5.09
P/L	(Net P/L: Gross P/L less Commission and Slippage)	27.34	-53.34	-26.00
Equity	(Net P/L plus Open P/L at the end of the run)	27.34	-58.43	-31.09

There are columns for Long trades, Short trades and Net. In the Long column, results
are reported only for Long positions. In the Short column, results are reported for
Short positions only. In the Net column for the "Per Trade Ranges" and "Overall
Ranges," entries will be the extreme from either the Long or Short column. Net column
entries for the "Statistics" and "Results" categories are the combined results of entries
in the Long and Short columns.

EXHIBIT L-14:

New York Stock Exchange Composite Price Index Weekly High and Low from January 5, 1968 to September 30, 1977

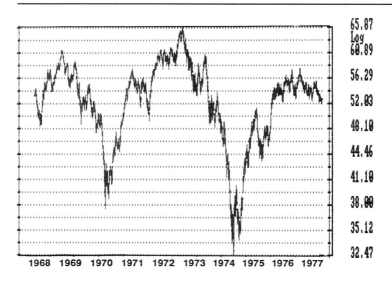

EXHIBIT L-15:

Total Equity for Lowry's Simplified, 1968 to 1977

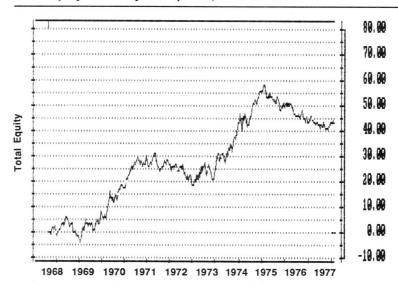

EXHIBIT L-16:
Profit Summary for Lowry's Simplified, 1968 to 1977

Item		Long	Short	Net
Per Trade Ranges		*Per Trade Ranges*		
Best Trade	(Closed position yielding maximum P/L)	13.19	25.05	25.05
. . Date		710716	740920	740920
Worst Trade	(Closed position yielding minimum P/L)	-2.50	-5.39	-5.39
. . Date		730202	760116	760116
Max Open P/L	(Maximum P/L occurring in an open position)	15.54	27.68	27.68
. . Date		710423	740913	740913
Min Open P/L	(Minimum P/L occurring in an open position)	-3.84	-4.93	-4.93
. . Date		741004	721124	721124
Overall Ranges		*Overall Ranges*		
Max P/L	(Maximum P/L from all closed positions during the run)	53.38	47.99	53.38
. . Date		750815	760116	750815
Min P/L	(Minimum P/L from all closed positions during the run)	0.19	13.74	0.19
. . Date		690307	700529	690307
Max Equity	(Maximum P/L from all closed and open positions)	58.07	55.14	58.07
. . Date		750711	750912	750711
Min Equity	(Minimum P/L from all closed and open positions)	-0.96	-3.64	-3.64
. . Date		680802	690516	690516
Statistics		*Statistics*		
Periods	(The number of periods in each position and entire run)	242	267	509
Trades	(The number of trades in each position and entire run)	8	7	15
# Profitable	(The number of profitable trades...)	5	2	7
# Losing	(The number of unprofitable trades...)	3	5	8
% Profitable	(The percent of profitable trades to total trades)	62.50	28.57	46.67
% Losing	(The percent of unprofitable trades to total trades)	37.50	71.43	53.33
Results		*Results*		
Commission	(Total commission deducted from closed trades)	0.00	0.00	0.00
Slippage	(Total slippage deducted from closed trades)	0.00	0.00	0.00
Gross P/L	(Total points gained in closed positions)	20.51	21.71	42.22
Open P/L	(P/L in a position which remains open at the end)	0.00	1.13	1.13
P/L	(Net P/L: Gross P/L less Commission and Slippage)	20.51	21.71	42.22
Equity	(Net P/L plus Open P/L at the end of the run)	20.51	22.84	43.35

There are columns for Long trades, Short trades and Net. In the Long column, results are reported only for Long positions. In the Short column, results are reported for Short positions only. In the Net column for the "Per Trade Ranges" and "Overall Ranges," entries will be the extreme from either the Long or Short column. Net column entries for the "Statistics" and "Results" categories are the combined results of entries in the Long and Short columns.

only, total results were improved but were still well below standard. Lipstadt claims to have devised proprietary daily calculations based on Lowry's data that are better suited to current trading patterns. In conclusion, beware of outmoded decision rules that were once successful.

MARGIN DEBT

Margin Debt represents the total amount that customers owe their brokerage firms as a result of borrowing through their stock margin accounts. Margin Debt statistics are released on a monthly basis by the New York Stock Exchange.

Margin Debt can be utilized in two ways as an indicator of future stock prices. First, investors can examine the percentage of debt included in "troubled" margin accounts with equity under 40%. These accounts represent customers who have less potential stock purchasing power, as well as those who are vulnerable to forced liquidation through margin calls in the event of a decline in stock prices.

A low percentage of debt included in "troubled" margin accounts with equity under 40% implies a healthy market. When the percentage of debt in "troubled" accounts rises to the 40% to 50% range, the stock market is ripe for a selling climax. Typically, such high readings are registered late in a bear market.

The second method that analysts use to view Margin Debt is to study the trend of the total amount relative to the trend in an overall market index, such as the Dow Jones Industrial Average. As illustrated in Exhibit M-1 (page 268), however, the direction of margin debt closely correlates with the stock market, making it of limited value as a leading indicator. Major changes in the trend of stock prices occur at the same time that margin debt peaks and bottoms out. Its value as a leading indicator is further diminished by the fact that margin debt can remain at record levels for years at a time. However, visual inspection of the 12-month moving average crossings appear to offer some value as a lagging indicator of the major stock market trend.

EXHIBIT M-1:
Margin Debt (bottom) Versus The Dow Jones Industrial Average (top) from 1966 to 1986

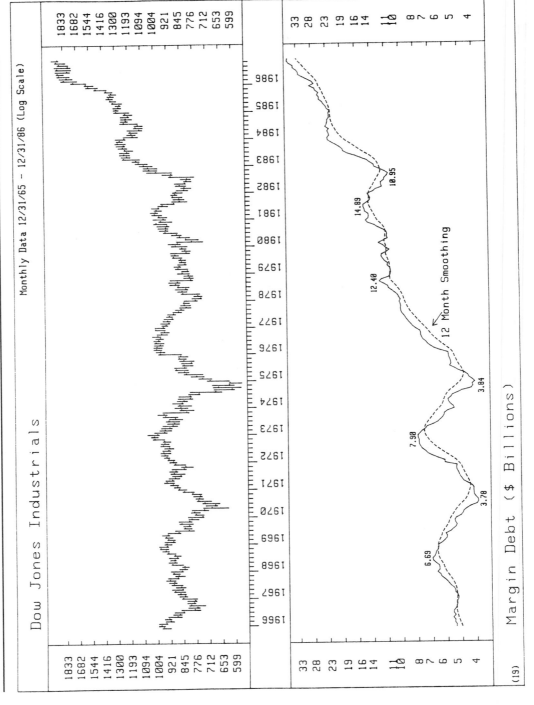

Source: By Permission of Ned Davis Research, Inc.

MARGIN REQUIREMENT

The Margin Requirement is the minimum percentage of a total stock purchase price that an investor is required to put up as equity. For example, assume an investor wants to buy $10,000 worth of stock. If the Margin Requirement is 50%, the investor is required to pay at least $5000 in cash (or check) to his stockbroker. He can then borrow the remaining $5000 "on margin" from his stockbroker, using his paid equity as collateral.

The Federal Reserve sets the Margin Requirement. Since it was empowered to do so in 1934, it has increased the Margin Requirement 12 times and lowered it 10 times. The current rate of 50% has been effective since January 1974.

Norman Fosback points out in his 1976 book *Stock Market Logic* (The Institute for Econometric Research, 3471 North Federal Highway, Fort Lauderdale, FL 33306) that although several years have passed since the Federal Reserve's last adjustment in the Margin Requirement, the stock market's reaction to past changes has been so significant that investors should note the historical record in the event of future changes.[*]

The Federal Reserve increases the Margin Requirement in order to decrease speculation and force investors to put up more money to buy stock. In theory, this should have a bearish impact on the stock market, because investors are less likely to buy stock.

According to Fosback's research, the stock market's initial reaction to these increases in the Margin Requirement is negative. However, contrary to the theory, by the end of the first month after an increase, the overall stock market (as measured by the Standard & Poor's 500 Index) recovers and is up an average of 1.1%. One year after an increase, the overall stock market (as measured by the S&P 500) rises an average of 14.4%, a rate of gain significantly above normal.

The Federal Reserve usually reduces the Margin Requirement after significant declines in the stock market. In theory, increased purchases of stock should occur and the stock market should rise.

Fosback discovered that, contrary to the theory, the stock market initially declines after a reduction in the Margin Requirement with the overall stock market (as measured by the S&P 500) being down on average 2.3% after 3 months. However, the overall stock market then increases significantly and is up an average of 12.5%, 16.3%, and 18.5% (as measured by the S&P 500),

---

[*]Reprinted with permission.

1 year, 15 months, and 18 months after a reduction, respectively. Thus, it appears that reductions in the Margin Requirement can be used profitably as a leading indicator.

McCLELLAN OSCILLATOR

The McClellan Oscillator is a short-term to intermediate-term market breadth indicator. It is calculated by subtracting a 39-day exponential moving average of the net difference between the number of advancing issues and the number of declining issues from a 19-day exponential moving average of the net difference between the number of advancing issues and the number of declining issues. NYSE data is used in the calculation.

The McClellan Oscillator signals when the market is overbought or oversold. The oscillator typically reaches an extreme reading prior to a change in the trend of stock prices.

A bear market selling climax is indicated by an oscillator reading of approximately -150. A surge of buying activity, implying an overbought condition, is signaled by an oscillator reading above 100.

The McClellan Oscillator normally passes through zero near market tops and bottoms. As illustrated in Exhibit M-2, when the oscillator goes from below to above zero, it is considered bullish for stock prices. On the other hand, when it goes from above to below zero, it is interpreted as bearish for the stock market.

Numerous chart patterns in the indicator are supposed to signal various market conditions. A detailed explanation of these chart formations are beyond the scope of this book. However, a full description of how to interpret the McClellan Oscillator is included in *Patterns for Profit: The McClellan Oscillator and Summation Index*, (Trade Levels, Inc., 22801 Ventura Boulevard, Suite 210, Woodland Hills, CA 91364).

EXHIBIT M-2:
McClellan Oscillator (top) Versus the Standard & Poor's 500 Index (bottom) from 1984 to 1986

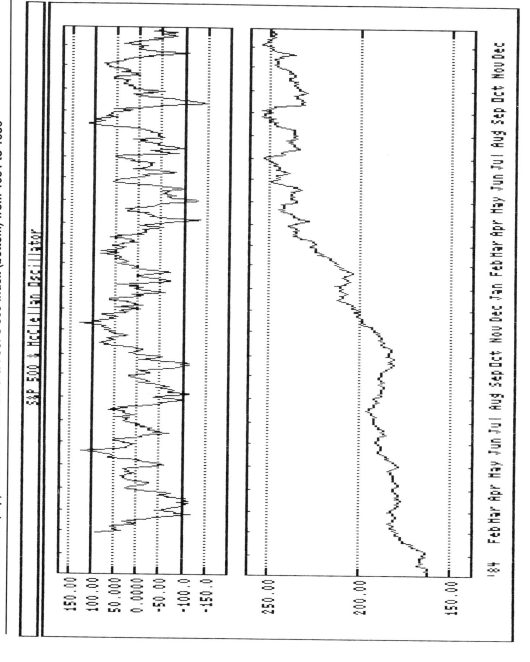

McCLELLAN SUMMATION INDEX

The McClellan Summation Index is simply a cumulative total of the McClellan Oscillator. It is used for interpreting intermediate to long-term moves in the stock market.

Similar to the McClellan Oscillator, the McClellan Summation Index gives buy and sell signals when it crosses zero. As illustrated in Exhibit M-3, when the index goes from below to above zero, it is considered bullish for stock prices. When it crosses from above to below zero, it is interpreted as a bearish sign for the stock market.

An extensive explanation of the McClellan Summation Index is included in *Patterns for Profit: The McClellan Oscillator and Summation Index* (Trade Levels, Inc., 22801 Ventura Boulevard, Suite 210, Woodland Hills, CA 91364).

EXHIBIT M-3:
McClellan Summation Index (top) Versus the Standard & Poor's 500 Index (bottom) from 1984 to 1986

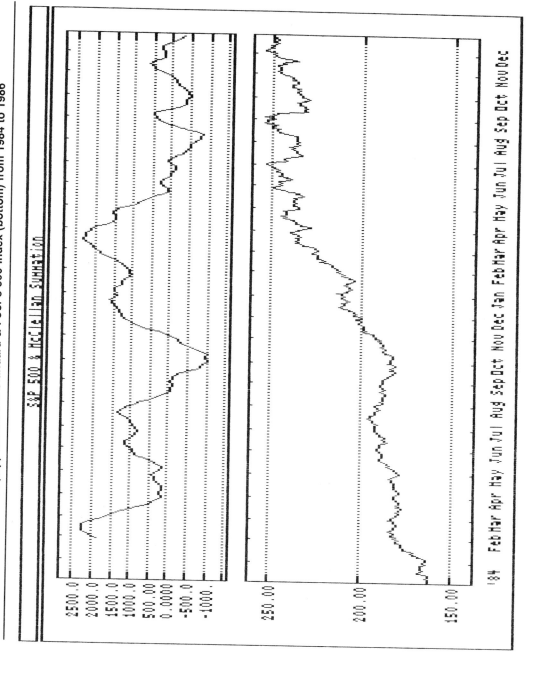

MEMBER SHORT RATIO

Investors sell short stock when they anticipate its price going lower. At a later date, they must cover their short sales and buy the stock back. A profit is made if the stock is bought back at a lower price than when it was sold short.

On a weekly basis, the New York Stock Exchange releases information on short sales, including those made by stock exchange members and those made by nonmembers. The Member Short Ratio is computed by dividing total member short sales by total short sales. A 2-week moving average of the indicator is graphically displayed in Exhibit M-4.

Since the professionals are generally right about the trend of stock prices, low Member Short Ratio readings are viewed as bullish. Alternatively, high readings are considered bearish.

We tested the Member Short Ratio for the period of January 1946 to March 1987 on a weekly basis. In addition, we applied a 10-period simple moving average to the weekly readings to smooth out any erratic movements. The results are shown in Exhibits M-5 and M-6 (pages 276–277).

The test process was as follows. The indicator readings for the test period were divided into 20 ranges with approximately the same number of occurrences in each range. For each reading in a range, the gain or loss in four subsequent time periods (1 month later, 3 months later, 6 months later, and 12 months later) was calculated. The combined results for readings within each range were statistically compared, using chi-squared tests, to the performance of the overall market (as measured by the S&P 500). Varying degrees of bullishness and bearishness were noted on the basis of that comparison.

Our research results confirm that low indicator readings are very bullish and high readings are very bearish. In particular, during the past 40 years, when the 10-week moving average of the Member Short Ratio was 0.66 or lower, an average gain occurred in the overall market (as measured by the Standard & Poor's 500 Index) of 1.59% 1 month later, 5.63% 3 months later, 12.03% 6 months later, and 24.30% 12 months later. Exhibit M-7 (page 278) shows the results in greater detail. You should note that all signals generated within 3 months after an initial reading of 0.66 or lower were considered repeat signals and are not included in the results. It should also be noted that no readings of 0.66 or lower have occurred since 1974, suggesting that the value of this indicator may be diminishing.

EXHIBIT M-4:
Member Short Ratio (bottom) Versus Dow Jones Industrial Average (top) from 1979 to 1986

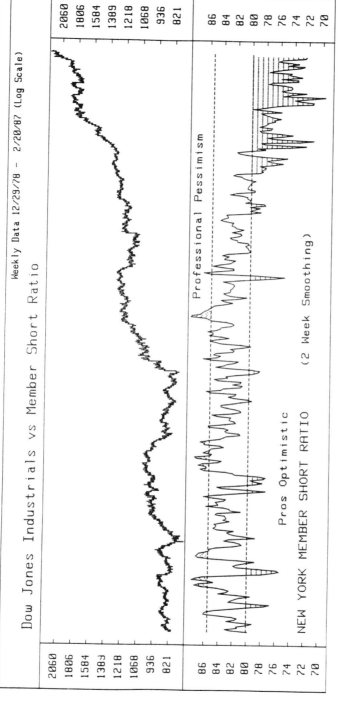

Source: By Permission of Ned Davis Research, Inc.

275

EXHIBIT M-5:
Interpretation of Member Short Ratio's Weekly Readings

```
=================================================================================
MEMBER SHORT RATIO - WEEKLY DATA
PERIOD ANALYZED:  JANUARY 1946 TO MARCH 1987
=================================================================================
```

INDICATOR RANGE		INTERPRETATION GIVEN INVESTOR'S TIME FRAME			
GREATER THAN	LESS THAN OR EQUAL TO	1 MONTH	3 MONTHS	6 MONTHS	12 MONTHS
0.000	0.593	BULLISH	VERY BULLISH	VERY BULLISH	VERY BULLISH
0.593	0.647	NEUTRAL	BULLISH	BULLISH	VERY BULLISH
0.647	0.677	SLIGHTLY BULLISH	VERY BULLISH	VERY BULLISH	VERY BULLISH
0.677	0.700	SLIGHTLY BULLISH	NEUTRAL	NEUTRAL	SLIGHTLY BULLISH
0.700	0.718	NEUTRAL	NEUTRAL	NEUTRAL	NEUTRAL
0.718	0.734	NEUTRAL	NEUTRAL	NEUTRAL	NEUTRAL
0.734	0.747	NEUTRAL	SLIGHTLY BULLISH	NEUTRAL	SLIGHTLY BULLISH
0.747	0.761	NEUTRAL	NEUTRAL	NEUTRAL	NEUTRAL
0.761	0.773	NEUTRAL	NEUTRAL	NEUTRAL	NEUTRAL
0.773	0.782	NEUTRAL	NEUTRAL	NEUTRAL	NEUTRAL
0.782	0.792	NEUTRAL	NEUTRAL	NEUTRAL	NEUTRAL
0.792	0.800	NEUTRAL	NEUTRAL	NEUTRAL	NEUTRAL
0.800	0.808	NEUTRAL	NEUTRAL	NEUTRAL	NEUTRAL
0.808	0.815	NEUTRAL	NEUTRAL	NEUTRAL	SLIGHTLY BEARISH
0.815	0.823	NEUTRAL	NEUTRAL	NEUTRAL	SLIGHTLY BEARISH
0.823	0.832	NEUTRAL	NEUTRAL	NEUTRAL	NEUTRAL
0.832	0.840	NEUTRAL	VERY BEARISH	NEUTRAL	NEUTRAL
0.840	0.852	NEUTRAL	VERY BEARISH	SLIGHTLY BEARISH	VERY BEARISH
0.852	0.868	BEARISH	VERY BEARISH	BEARISH	SLIGHTLY BEARISH
0.868	1.000	VERY BEARISH	VERY BEARISH	BEARISH	VERY BEARISH

```
=================================================================================
```

Definitions of Very Bullish, Bullish, Slightly Bullish, Neutral, Slightly Bearish, Bearish, and Very Bearish are provided in Appendix A.

EXHIBIT M-6:

Interpretation of Member Short Ratio's 10-Week Simple Moving Average Readings

```
=================================================================================
MEMBER SHORT RATIO - 10 WEEK MOVING AVERAGE
PERIOD ANALYZED: JANUARY 1946 TO MARCH 1987
=================================================================================
```

INDICATOR RANGE		INTERPRETATION GIVEN INVESTOR'S TIME FRAME			
GREATER THAN	LESS THAN OR EQUAL TO	1 MONTH	3 MONTHS	6 MONTHS	12 MONTHS
0.000	0.613	VERY BULLISH	VERY BULLISH	VERY BULLISH	VERY BULLISH
0.613	0.664	BULLISH	VERY BULLISH	VERY BULLISH	VERY BULLISH
0.664	0.692	BULLISH	SLIGHTLY BULLISH	SLIGHTLY BULLISH	NEUTRAL
0.692	0.713	NEUTRAL	NEUTRAL	NEUTRAL	SLIGHTLY BULLISH
0.713	0.727	NEUTRAL	NEUTRAL	NEUTRAL	SLIGHTLY BULLISH
0.727	0.738	BULLISH	BULLISH	NEUTRAL	NEUTRAL
0.738	0.748	NEUTRAL	NEUTRAL	NEUTRAL	NEUTRAL
0.748	0.758	NEUTRAL	NEUTRAL	NEUTRAL	NEUTRAL
0.758	0.769	SLIGHTLY BEARISH	NEUTRAL	NEUTRAL	NEUTRAL
0.769	0.780	NEUTRAL	NEUTRAL	NEUTRAL	NEUTRAL
0.780	0.789	NEUTRAL	NEUTRAL	NEUTRAL	NEUTRAL
0.789	0.796	NEUTRAL	NEUTRAL	BEARISH	BEARISH
0.796	0.802	NEUTRAL	SLIGHTLY BEARISH	NEUTRAL	NEUTRAL
0.802	0.810	NEUTRAL	NEUTRAL	NEUTRAL	NEUTRAL
0.810	0.817	NEUTRAL	NEUTRAL	NEUTRAL	NEUTRAL
0.817	0.824	NEUTRAL	BEARISH	NEUTRAL	NEUTRAL
0.824	0.830	VERY BEARISH	NEUTRAL	NEUTRAL	NEUTRAL
0.830	0.838	NEUTRAL	BEARISH	NEUTRAL	NEUTRAL
0.838	0.850	SLIGHTLY BEARISH	VERY BEARISH	BEARISH	VERY BEARISH
0.850	0.884	VERY BEARISH	VERY BEARISH	VERY BEARISH	VERY BEARISH

```
=================================================================================
```

Definitions of Very Bullish, Bullish, Slightly Bullish, Neutral, Slightly Bearish, Bearish, and Very Bearish are provided in Appendix A.

EXHIBIT M-7:

Member Short Ratio's 10-Week Simple Moving Average Readings Less Than or Equal to 0.66 from 1947 to 1986

```
=====================================================================
MEMBER SHORT RATIO - 10 WEEK MOVING AVERAGE
=====================================================================
```

DATE	INDICATOR VALUE	PERCENTAGE CHANGE IN S&P 500			
		1 MONTH LATER	3 MONTHS LATER	6 MONTHS LATER	12 MONTHS LATER
APR 12 1947	0.66	0.69	9.41	8.24	5.08
AUG 1 1947	0.62	-4.43	-2.91	-7.47	0.63
FEB 11 1949	0.65	3.50	2.20	5.01	17.17
JUN 3 1949	0.55	3.27	11.96	18.43	32.38
OCT 1 1949	0.56	3.35	8.18	12.50	26.68
JAN 7 1950	0.65	1.52	2.57	3.22	23.58
JAN 20 1951	0.66	1.96	3.18	2.01	14.25
SEP 4 1953	0.66	-0.76	5.39	13.24	30.17
JAN 8 1954	0.65	5.21	9.83	20.90	40.55
NOV 15 1957	0.66	-2.35	1.83	7.41	30.86
JAN 17 1958	0.66	0.02	2.80	10.83	35.79
MAY 2 1958	0.58	1.76	8.70	17.35	31.95
JUN 22 1962	0.65	6.99	9.51	18.91	33.35
OCT 5 1962	0.64	2.24	13.44	20.06	27.65
OCT 14 1966	0.65	6.64	11.28	19.92	25.33
MAR 22 1968	0.65	9.27	13.07	17.63	17.07
MAY 1 1970	0.66	-4.42	-4.14	2.44	28.65
SEP 4 1970	0.61	4.85	8.00	19.98	19.87
SEP 6 1974	0.66	-9.06	-7.41	18.03	20.69
AVERAGE CHANGE		1.59	5.63	12.03	24.30

```
=====================================================================
```

MISERY INDEX

The Misery Index is an interesting indicator, but it is of limited value in determining the future direction of the overall stock market. It is calculated easily by summing the prime rate, inflation rate, and unemployment rate.

As can be seen in Exhibit M-8, the Misery Index acts in an inverse fashion to the overall stock market. It tends to peak at market lows and bottom out at market highs.

Changes in the trend of the Misery Index do not lead or lag changes in the trend of the overall stock market. Rather they occur concurrently, minimizing the indicator's value in market timing.

EXHIBIT M-8:
Misery Index (bottom) Versus The Standard & Poor's 500 Index (top) from 1953 to 1986

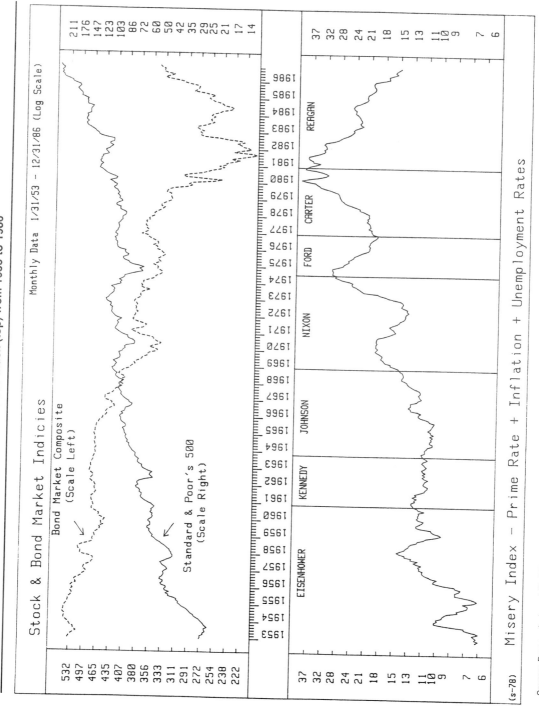

Source: By permission of Ned David Research, Inc.

MONEY SUPPLY

Money Supply can be defined in its simplest form as all the money held by the public. The Federal Reserve uses more precise definitions of Money Supply (such as M1, M2, M3, and L) that include a variety of types of currency, deposits, bonds, etc.

According to Norman Fosback (The Institute for Econometric Research, 3471 North Federal Highway, Fort Lauderdale, FL 33306), Money Supply is a key economic factor. However, when it comes to using it as an indicator to predict future moves in the stock market, it is of little use. At best, it acts coincidentally to the stock market. Increases in the Money Supply normally accompany increases in stock prices and vice versa. In addition, the extent to which Money Supply increases or decreases has no direct correlation to how far the stock market rises or falls.

Other factors under the control of the Federal Reserve are better stock market indicators. Refer to the sections on Interest Rates and Stock Prices, Margin Requirement, and Reserve Requirement.

MONTHS

What are the best months in the year to invest in stocks? In a recent study, Arthur Merrill (Merrill Analysis Inc., Box 228, Chappaqua, NY 10514) analyzed monthly stock market activity from 1897 to 1983.[*] His results are visually shown in Exhibit M-9.

On average, December has been the best month of the year with the stock market increasing 68% of the time. Next, comes August and January with market prices rising 67% and 64.3% of the time, respectively. The most bearish months are June and September, rising only 44.9% and 44.3% of the time, respectively.

One investment strategy that has been devised to take advantage of the monthly tendency of the market is to buy at Thanksgiving and sell at the New Year. Merrill discovered a highly significant success rate of 72% for the test period of 1897 to 1983.

A slightly less accurate strategy is to buy on July 4th and sell on Labor Day. Merrill's study shows that the market rose during this "summer rally" period 66.2% of the time between 1897 and 1983.

---

[*]Reprinted with permission.

EXHIBIT M-9:

Percent of Years from 1897 to 1983 that the Dow Jones Industrial Average Posted an Increase for the Month

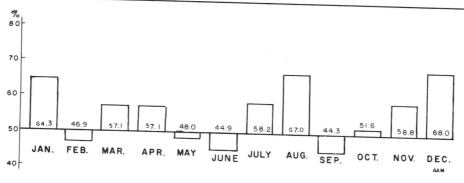

Source: By Permission of Merrill Analysis, Inc.

MOVING AVERAGE CONVERGENCE– DIVERGENCE TRADING METHOD

The Moving Average Convergence-Divergence Trading Method (MACDTM) is a price momentum indicator developed by Gerald Appel, publisher of *Systems and Forecasts* (Signalert Corporation, 150 Great Neck Road, Great Neck, NY 11021). It is an oscillator based on the point spread difference between two exponential moving averages (EMA) of the closing price—a slower, 26-week EMA (with a smoothing constant of .075) and a faster 12-week EMA (with a smoothing constant of 0.15). This difference itself is smoothed by an even faster 9-week EMA (with a smoothing constant of .2). This is called the *signal line*. Appel further calculates a second oscillator by subtracting from the first difference its own .2 EMA signal line.

The simplest possible MACDTM decision rule is: Buy when the second differential oscillator is positive (above zero), and sell and sell short when the second differential oscillator is negative (below zero). This is the only rule we tested. Note that the indicator's inventor, Gerald Appel, does not advocate this simple rule but instead has devised other proprietary (and much more complex) decision rules that he offers for sale.

Our basic unoptimized MACDTM decision rule substantially under-performed our 40-week simple moving average crossover rule standard of comparison. For our two 9.75-year test periods (January 1968 through September 1977 and April 1977 through December 1986) using NYSE Composite Index weekly closing price data, combined profits totaled only 44.66 NYSE points, less than half our standard. Moreover, number of trades and maximum drawdown were both significantly higher than our standard of comparison. Full details are presented in Exhibits M-10 to M-17 (pages 282–287).

The smoothing constants can be optimized. We discovered an accelerated version that outperformed our basic version, but it still did not perform as well as the basic optimized single moving average crossover rules. Our fast MACDTM consists of a slow, 39-week EMA (with a smoothing constant of 0.05), a fast 1.67-week EMA (with a smoothing constant of 0.75), and no signal line. Therefore, the decision rule is: Buy when the 0.75 EMA minus the 0.05 EMA differential oscillator crosses above zero, and sell and sell short when the oscillator crosses below zero. With this formula and rule, combined profits for both weekly test periods 1968–1977 and 1977–1986 more than doubled to 87.54 NYSE points, as shown in Exhibits M-18 to M-25 (pages 288–293). The number of trades and maximum drawdown declined significantly, and the reward/risk ratio (total profit divided by maximum drawdown) rose to slightly above standard. Still, we see no real advantage to this simplified MACDTM concept versus the simple moving average crossover rules, and there is a disadvantage of somewhat greater computational complexity.

EXHIBIT M-10:
New York Stock Exchange Composite Price Index Weekly High and Low from April 8, 1977 to December 31, 1986

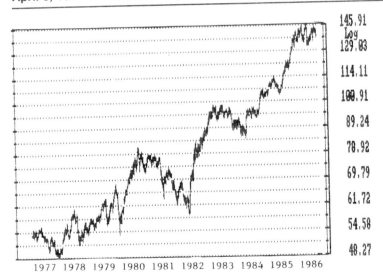

EXHIBIT M-11:

Moving Average Convergence-Divergence Trading Method .075/.15/.2, 1977 to 1986

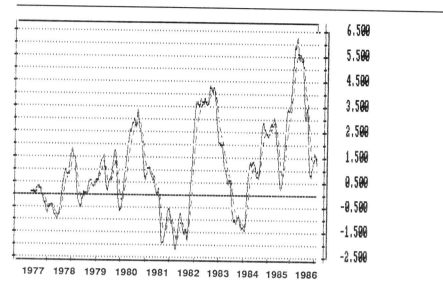

EXHIBIT M-12:

Total Equity for Moving Average Convergence-Divergence Trading Method .075/.15/.2, 1977 to 1986

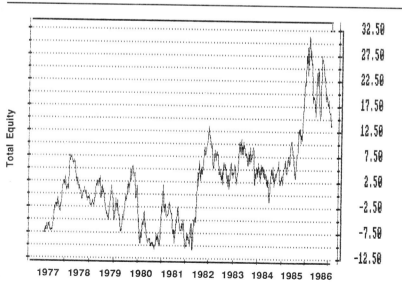

EXHIBIT M-13:

Profit Summary for Moving Average Convergence-Divergence Trading Method .075/.15/.2, 1977 to 1986

Item		Long	Short	Net
		--- Per Trade Ranges ---		
Per Trade Ranges				
Best Trade	(Closed position yielding maximum P/L)	22.50	5.90	22.50
.. Date		860516	811113	860516
Worst Trade	(Closed position yielding minimum P/L)	-4.80	-8.13	-8.13
.. Date		801212	861128	861128
Max Open P/L	(Maximum P/L occurring in an open position)	27.93	11.79	27.93
.. Date		860418	810925	860418
Min Open P/L	(Minimum P/L occurring in an open position)	-3.47	-10.88	-10.88
.. Date		820604	860829	860829
		--- Overall Ranges ---		
Overall Ranges				
Max P/L	(Maximum P/L from all closed positions during the run)	25.91	17.78	25.91
.. Date		860516	861128	860516
Min P/L	(Minimum P/L from all closed positions during the run)	-9.90	-10.58	-10.58
.. Date		810501	820820	820820
Max Equity	(Maximum P/L from all closed and open positions)	31.34	27.54	31.34
.. Date		860418	860912	860418
Min Equity	(Minimum P/L from all closed and open positions)	-10.58	-10.75	-10.75
.. Date		820820	810612	810612
		--- Statistics ---		
Statistics				
Periods	(The number of periods in each position and entire run)	257	252	509
Trades	(The number of trades in each position and entire run)	22	22	44
# Profitable	(The number of profitable trades...)	10	6	16
# Losing	(The number of unprofitable trades...)	12	16	28
% Profitable	(The percent of profitable trades to total trades)	45.45	27.27	36.36
% Losing	(The percent of unprofitable trades to total trades)	54.55	72.73	63.64
		--- Results ---		
Results				
Commission	(Total commission deducted from closed trades)	0.00	0.00	0.00
Slippage	(Total slippage deducted from closed trades)	0.00	0.00	0.00
Gross P/L	(Total points gained in closed positions)	49.34	-35.55	13.79
Open P/L	(P/L in a position which remains open at the end)	0.00	0.00	0.00
P/L	(Net P/L: Gross P/L less Commission and Slippage)	49.34	-35.55	13.79
Equity	(Net P/L plus Open P/L at the end of the run)	49.34	-35.55	13.79

There are columns for Long trades, Short trades and Net. In the Long column, results
are reported only for Long positions. In the Short column, results are reported for
Short positions only. In the Net column for the "Per Trade Ranges" and "Overall
Ranges," entries will be the extreme from either the Long or Short column. Net column
entries for the "Statistics" and "Results" categories are the combined results of entries
in the Long and Short columns.

EXHIBIT M-14:

New York Stock Exchange Composite Price Index Weekly High and Low from January 5, 1968 to September 30, 1977

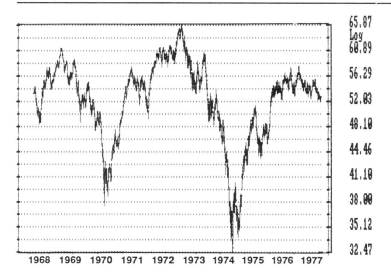

Moving Average Convergence-Divergence Trading Method .075/.15/.2, 1968 to 1977

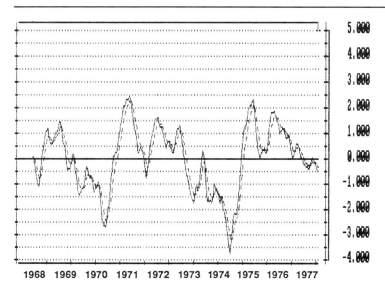

EXHIBIT M-16:

Total Equity for Moving Average Convergence-Divergence Trading Method .075/.15/.2, 1968 to 1977

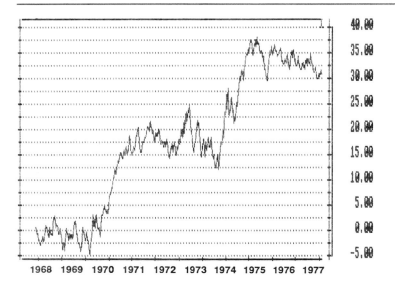

EXHIBIT M-17:

Profit Summary for Moving Average Convergence-Divergence Trading Method .075/.15/2, 1968 to 1977

Item		Long	Short	Net
Per Trade Ranges	—— Per Trade Ranges ——			
Best Trade	(Closed position yielding maximum P/L)	14.07	10.77	14.07
.. Date		710514	741025	710514
Worst Trade	(Closed position yielding minimum P/L)	-5.27	-3.29	-5.27
.. Date		731123	680927	731123
Max Open P/L	(Maximum P/L occurring in an open position)	15.04	14.94	15.04
.. Date		710423	741004	710423
Min Open P/L	(Minimum P/L occurring in an open position)	-4.18	-3.47	-4.18
.. Date		730824	760924	730824
Overall Ranges	—— Overall Ranges ——			
Max P/L	(Maximum P/L from all closed positions during the run)	35.31	34.32	35.31
.. Date		760416	751114	760416
Min P/L	(Minimum P/L from all closed positions during the run)	-4.63	-2.81	-4.63
.. Date		700417	680927	700417
Max Equity	(Maximum P/L from all closed and open positions)	37.45	38.22	38.22
.. Date		750711	750912	750912
Min Equity	(Minimum P/L from all closed and open positions)	-4.63	-4.63	-4.63
.. Date		700417	700417	700417
Statistics	—— Statistics ——			
Periods	(The number of periods in each position and entire run)	223	286	509
Trades	(The number of trades in each position and entire run)	16	16	32
# Profitable	(The number of profitable trades. . .)	7	9	16
# Losing	(The number of unprofitable trades. . .)	9	7	16
% Profitable	(The percent of profitable trades to total trades)	43.75	56.25	50.00
% Losing	(The percent of unprofitable trades to total trades)	56.25	43.75	50.00
Results	—— Results ——			
Commission	(Total commission deducted from closed trades)	0.00	0.00	0.00
Slippage	(Total slippage deducted from closed trades)	0.00	0.00	0.00
Gross P/L	(Total points gained in closed positions)	15.09	14.98	30.07
Open P/L	(P/L in a position which remains open at the end)	0.00	0.80	0.80
P/L	(Net P/L: Gross P/L less Commission and Slippage)	15.09	14.98	30.07
Equity	(Net P/L plus Open P/L at the end of the run)	15.09	15.78	30.87

There are columns for Long trades, Short trades and Net. In the Long column, results
are reported only for Long positions. In the Short column, results are reported for
Short positions only. In the Net column for the "Per Trade Ranges" and "Overall
Ranges," entries will be the extreme from either the Long or Short column. Net column
entries for the "Statistics" and "Results" categories are the combined results of entries
in the Long and Short columns.

EXHIBIT M-18:

New York Stock Exchange Composite Price Index Weekly High and Low from April 8, 1977 to December 31, 1986

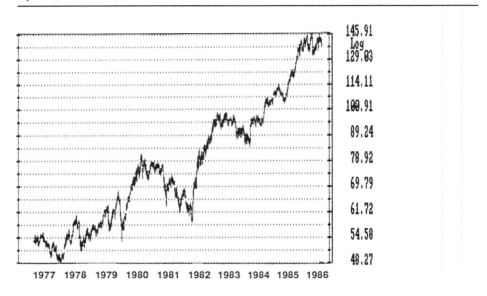

EXHIBIT M-19:

Moving Average Convergence-Divergence Trading Method .05/0.75/--, 1977 to 1986

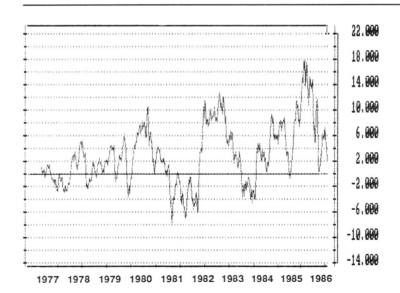

EXHIBIT M-20:

**Total Equity for Moving Average Convergence-Divergence Trading Method
.05/0.75/--, 1977 to 1986**

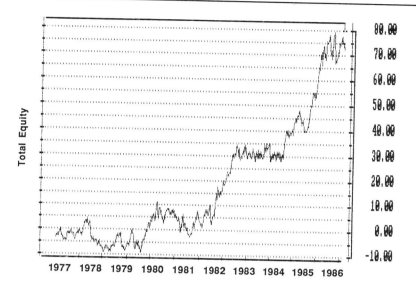

EXHIBIT M-21:

Profit Summary for Moving Average Convergence-Divergence Trading Method .05/0.75/--, 1977 to 1986

Item		Long	Short	Net
		--- Per Trade Ranges ---		
Per Trade Ranges				
Best Trade	(Closed position yielding maximum P/L)	25.75	5.20	25.75
. . Date		840203	820827	840203
Worst Trade	(Closed position yielding minimum P/L)	-3.98	-2.89	-3.98
. . Date		810828	790105	810828
Max Open P/L	(Maximum P/L occurring in an open position)	39.37	12.89	39.37
. . Date		860829	820813	860829
Min Open P/L	(Minimum P/L occurring in an open position)	-1.28	-1.54	-1.54
. . Date		770429	781208	781208
		--- Overall Ranges ---		
Overall Ranges				
Max P/L	(Maximum P/L from all closed positions during the run)	40.27	39.71	40.27
. . Date		850920	851004	850920
Min P/L	(Minimum P/L from all closed positions during the run)	-7.39	-8.67	-8.67
. . Date		800314	790309	790309
Max Equity	(Maximum P/L from all closed and open positions)	79.08	40.84	79.08
. . Date		860829	850927	860829
Min Equity	(Minimum P/L from all closed and open positions)	-9.00	-8.67	-9.00
. . Date		790511	790309	790511
		--- Statistics ---		
Statistics				
Periods	(The number of periods in each position and entire run)	369	140	509
Trades	(The number of trades in each position and entire run)	12	12	24
# Profitable	(The number of profitable trades. . .)	6	3	9
# Losing	(The number of unprofitable trades. . .)	6	9	15
% Profitable	(The percent of profitable trades to total trades)	50.00	25.00	37.50
% Losing	(The percent of unprofitable trades to total trades)	50.00	75.00	62.50
		--- Results ---		
Results				
Commission	(Total commission deducted from closed trades)	0.00	0.00	0.00
Slippage	(Total slippage deducted from closed trades)	0.00	0.00	0.00
Gross P/L	(Total points gained in closed positions)	45.36	-5.65	39.71
Open P/L	(P/L in a position which remains open at the end)	32.63	0.00	32.63
P/L	(Net P/L: Gross P/L less Commission and Slippage)	45.36	-5.65	39.71
Equity	(Net P/L plus Open P/L at the end of the run)	77.99	-5.65	72.34

There are columns for Long trades, Short trades and Net. In the Long column, results are reported only for Long positions. In the Short column, results are reported for Short positions only. In the Net column for the "Per Trade Ranges" and "Overall Ranges," entries will be the extreme from either the Long or Short column. Net column entries for the "Statistics" and "Results" categories are the combined results of entries in the Long and Short columns.

EXHIBIT M-22:

New York Stock Exchange Composite Price Index Weekly High and Low from
January 5, 1968 to September 30, 1977

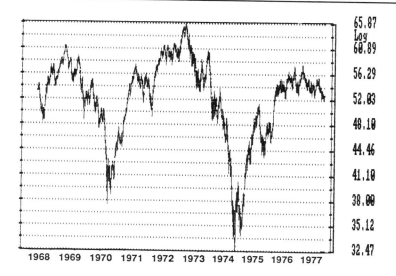

EXHIBIT M-23:

Moving Average Convergence-Divergence Trading Method .05/0.75/--, 1968 to
1977

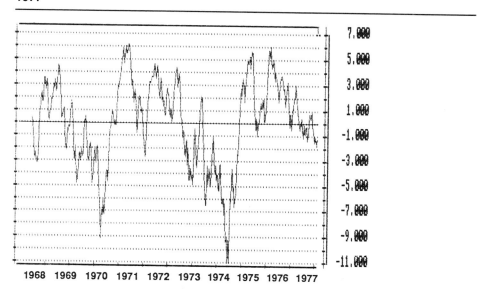

EXHIBIT M-24:

Total Equity for Moving Average Convergence-Divergence Trading Method .05/0.75/--, 1968 to 1977

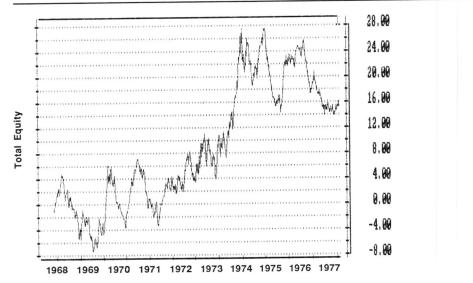

EXHIBIT M-25:

Profit Summary for Moving Average Convergence-Divergence Trading Method, .05/0.75/--, 1968 to 1977

Item		Long	Short	Net
Per Trade Ranges		--- Per Trade Ranges ---		
Best Trade	(Closed position yielding maximum P/L)	6.83	14.71	14.71
.. Date		730223	750207	750207
Worst Trade	(Closed position yielding minimum P/L)	-3.17	-2.31	-3.17
.. Date		690613	710820	690613
Max Open P/L	(Maximum P/L occurring in an open position)	11.38	23.61	23.61
.. Date		730105	741004	741004
Min Open P/L	(Minimum P/L occurring in an open position)	-1.09	-1.27	-1.27
.. Date		690606	750919	750919
Overall Ranges		--- Overall Ranges ---		
Max P/L	(Maximum P/L from all closed positions during the run)	22.17	20.70	22.17
.. Date		761022	761029	761022
Min P/L	(Minimum P/L from all closed positions during the run)	-7.29	-5.08	-7.29
.. Date		691121	691024	691121
Max Equity	(Maximum P/L from all closed and open positions)	27.58	27.57	27.58
.. Date		750711	741004	750711
Min Equity	(Minimum P/L from all closed and open positions)	-7.29	-7.29	-7.29
.. Date		691121	691121	691121
Statistics		--- Statistics ---		
Periods	(The number of periods in each position and entire run)	284	225	509
Trades	(The number of trades in each position and entire run)	18	17	35
# Profitable	(The number of profitable trades...)	5	4	9
# Losing	(The number of unprofitable trades...)	13	13	26
% Profitable	(The percent of profitable trades to total trades)	27.78	23.53	25.71
% Losing	(The percent of unprofitable trades to total trades)	72.22	76.47	74.29
Results		--- Results ---		
Commission	(Total commission deducted from closed trades)	0.00	0.00	0.00
Slippage	(Total slippage deducted from closed trades)	0.00	0.00	0.00
Gross P/L	(Total points gained in closed positions)	6.92	6.97	13.89
Open P/L	(P/L in a position which remains open at the end)	0.00	1.31	1.31
P/L	(Net P/L: Gross P/L less Commission and Slippage)	6.92	6.97	13.89
Equity	(Net P/L plus Open P/L at the end of the run)	6.92	8.28	15.20

There are columns for Long trades, Short trades and Net. In the Long column, results are reported only for Long positions. In the Short column, results are reported for Short positions only. In the Net column for the "Per Trade Ranges" and "Overall Ranges," entries will be the extreme from either the Long or Short column. Net column entries for the "Statistics" and "Results" categories are the combined results of entries in the Long and Short columns.

MUTUAL FUNDS CASH/ASSETS RATIO

On a monthly basis, the Investment Company Institute (1775 K Street, N.W., Washington, DC 20006) collects detailed statistics on the portfolios of hundreds of mutual funds. The compiled data is used by technicians in the calculation of the Mutual Funds Cash/Assets Ratio. As you would expect, the ratio is computed by dividing cash and cash equivalents held in mutual funds by the total assets of all the mutual funds.

The Mutual Funds Cash/Assets Ratio is a sentiment indicator that reflects the activity of portfolios under professional management. It is interpreted in a contrary fashion since stock market history shows that professional money managers tend to be wrong at market extremes. Therefore, when the ratio is high and stock prices are expected to drop, it is viewed as a bullish sign. On the other hand, when the ratio is low, it is interpreted as bearish for stock prices. Exhibit M-26 graphically displays the Mutual Funds Cash/Assets Ratio from 1966 to 1987.

The Mutual Funds Cash/Assets Ratio may also be viewed as representing available buying power. When the ratio is high, more cash is available to buy stocks and to drive up prices than when it is low.

EXHIBIT M-26:

Mutual Funds Cash/Assets Ratio (bottom) Versus the Dow Jones Industrial Average (top) from 1966 to 1986

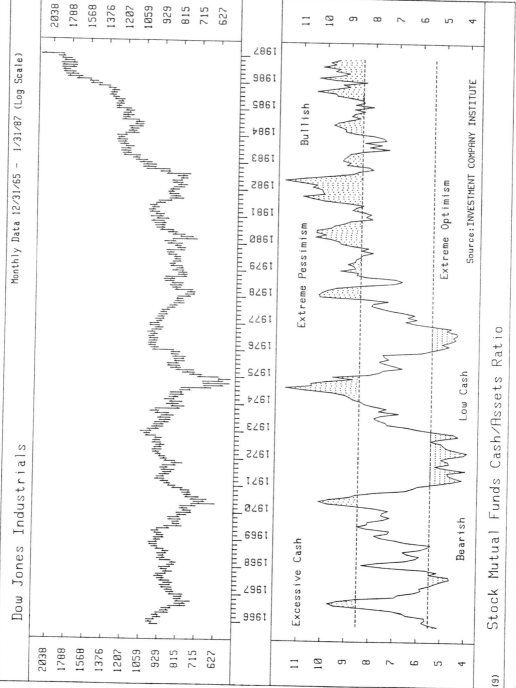

Source: By Permission of Ned Davis Research, Inc.

NEGATIVE VOLUME INDEX

The Negative Volume Index focuses on market action during periods of declining volume. The concept behind the indicator is that "smart" investors buy and sell during relatively quiet periods of declining volume, while unsophisticated investors tend to buy and sell on days when volume rises significantly. Therefore, market activity on days when a negative change in volume occurs will reflect buying or selling of stocks by sophisticated investors.

The Negative Volume Index is a cumulative indicator that can be calculated using any market index (such as the Dow Jones Industrial Average) or the net difference between the number of advancing and declining issues, along with volume statistics from the New York Stock Exchange. Daily or weekly data can be used in the computation.

The first step in calculating the Negative Volume Index is to compare the current day's volume to the previous day's volume. If the current day's volume is greater than the previous day's volume, there is no decline and, therefore, the Negative Volume Index remains at the previous day's value. If the current day's volume is less than the previous day's volume, a decline has occurred. As a result, the Negative Volume Index is calculated by dividing the gain (or loss) in a market index from the previous day to the current day by the market index for the previous day. Since the indicator is cumulative in nature, the calculated value is then added to the previous day's value of the Negative Volume Index.

Using an arbitrary base index level of 100.00, the following table illustrates how to calculate the indicator:

Day	Volume (Millions of Shares)	Volume Change	Percent Change In Market Index	Negative Volume Index
1	168	--		100.00
2	137	Down	+0.67	100.67
3	141	Up		100.67
4	138	Down	-1.23	99.44
5	181	Up		99.44
6	161	Down	+0.41	101.59
7	145	Down	+1.74	101.59
8	183	Up		101.59
9	189	Up		101.59
10	178	Down	+0.47	102.06

On Day 2, volume declined to 137 million shares. Since the change in volume from Day 1 was negative, the Negative Volume Index was increased by the percent change in the market index (any market index can be used). The indicator's rise implies that sophisticated investors were buying leading to higher stock prices. On Day 3, no change to the indicator reading was made since the change in volume was not negative.

A visual display of the Negative Volume Index from 1984 to 1986 versus the Standard & Poor's 500 Index is shown in Exhibit N-1 (page 298).

The common method of interpreting the Negative Volume Index is rather subjective. You use technical analysis tools, such as trendlines, to determine the direction stock prices are going based on whether the "smart" money is buying or selling.

Norman Fosback (The Institute for Econometric Research, 3471 North Federal Highway, Forth Lauderdale, FL 33306) suggests that a simple moving average crossover rule be used for more objective interpretation of the Negative Volume Index.[*] His approach is to average indicator readings over the past year and then compare the current period's (day or week) reading to the 1 year average. If it is above the average, an uptrend in the Negative Volume Index is in progress and stock prices should continue to rise. If it is below the average, a downtrend signals selling is in progress and stock rices are likely to go lower.

Using weekly data, Fosback tested his method of interpretation over a period of 35 years (1941 to 1975). He concluded that when the current weekly Negative Volume Index is above its 1 year average, the odds are greater than 95% that the stock market is in a major bull market. On the other hand, when the current weekly Negative Volume Index is below its 1 year average, the odds are little more than 50% that the stock market is in a bear market. Thus, the Negative Volume Index is of greatest value as a bull market indicator.

For a discussion of a related indicator, refer to the section on the Positive Volume Index.

---

*Reprinted with permission.

EXHIBIT N-1:
Negative Volume Index (top) Versus The Standard & Poor's 500 Index (bottom) from 1984 to 1986

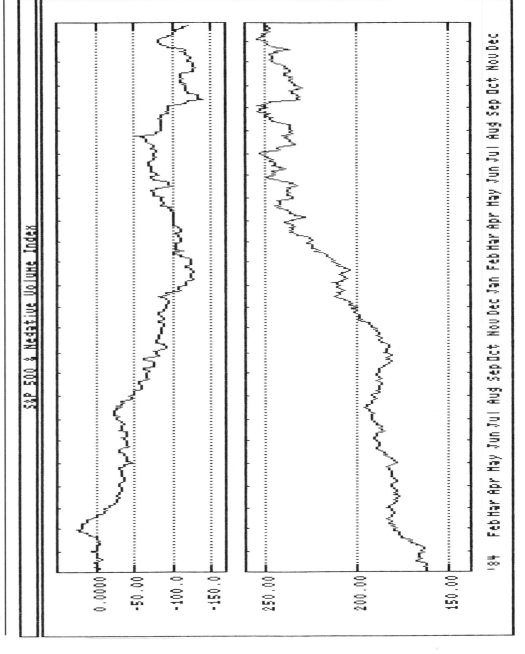

NET FREE RESERVES OF THE BANKING SYSTEM

When the banking system enjoys rising Net Free Reserves, the Federal Reserve Board's monetary policy generally is thought to be more accommodative or expansionary, and banking liquidity is increasing. Conversely, when the banking system is in a worsening (falling) free reserve position (with rising net borrowings from the Fed), the Federal Reserve Board's monetary policy is thought to be growing tighter or more restrictive, and banking liquidity is deteriorating.

Using month-end closing prices for the Standard & Poor's 500 Index and Net Free Reserves data (borrowings exclude extended credits), we tested various decision rules. After manipulating this data many different ways, the best decision rule we found was to buy the S&P stocks when the spread between Net Free Reserves minus the 19-month simple moving average of Net Free Reserves turned positive by crossing above zero, thus indicating a positive trend for banking system liquidity. Conversely, we sold and sold short when the spread turned negative by crossing below zero, thus indicating a worsening trend of banking system liquidity. (see Exhibits N-2, N-4, and N-5, pages 300–301.)

Total profit over the 42 years from 1944 through 1986 was quite good at 308.23 S&P points, as shown in Exhibits N-6 and N-7. Note from Exhibit N-6 (page 302) that the 19-month free reserves spread rule was unprofitable before December 31, 1960, and consistency of performance was poor before December 31, 1968. Since then, results have been quite consistent. The largest equity drawdown (loss period) since 1968 was from December 31, 1978 through February 29, 1980 when the equity fell 18.69 points or 19.45% of the S&P index value of 96.11 in December 1968—a relatively satisfactory performance for a relatively insensitive monthly indicator. In sum, the Net Free Reserve 19-month Simple Moving Average spread rule appears to have value for stock market forecasting.

EXHIBIT N-2:
Profitability Chart for Net Free Reserves, Simple Moving Average Crossover Rule

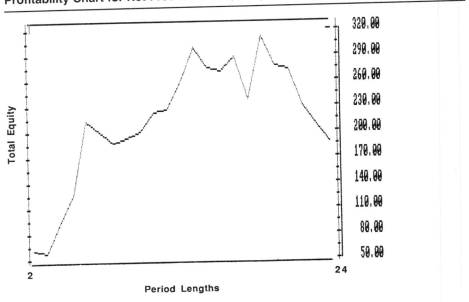

Total Equity

320.00
290.00
260.00
230.00
200.00
170.00
140.00
110.00
80.00
50.00

2   24

Period Lengths

EXHIBIT N-3:
Standard & Poor's 500 Index, Month-End Close, 1944 to 1986

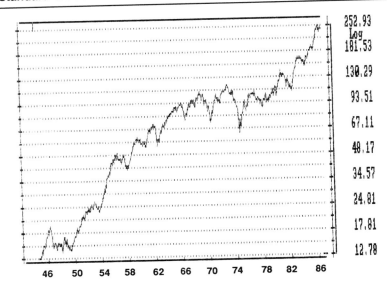

252.93
Log
181.53
130.29
93.51
67.11
48.17
34.57
24.81
17.81
12.78

46   50   54   58   62   66   70   74   78   82   86

EXHIBIT N-4:

Net Free Reserves (Solid Line) and 19-Month Simple Moving Average (Dashed Line)

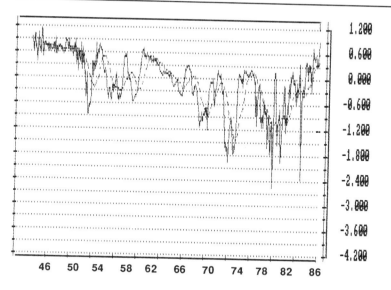

EXHIBIT N-5:

Spread: Net Free Reserves Minus Their 19-Month Simple Moving Average

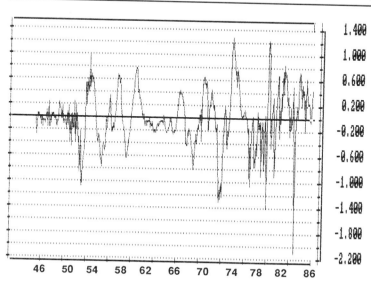

EXHIBIT N-6:
Total Equity for Net Free Reserves Versus 19-Month Simple Moving Average Crossover Rule

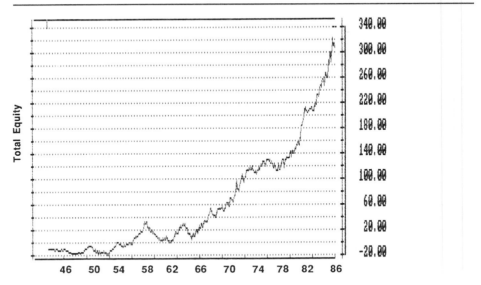

EXHIBIT N-7:

Profit Summary for Net Free Reserves Versus 19-Month Simple Moving Average Crossover Rule Using Standard & Poor's 500 Index Month-End Data, 1944 to 1986

Item	Long	Short	Net
Per Trade Ranges	*Per Trade Ranges*		
Best Trade (Closed position yielding maximum P/L)	51.51	20.08	51.51
.. Date	851130	741031	851130
Worst Trade (Closed position yielding minimum P/L)	-4.97	-18.05	-18.05
.. Date	700531	800131	800131
Max Open P/L (Maximum P/L occurring in an open position)	56.23	30.44	56.23
.. Date	830630	740930	830630
Min Open P/L (Minimum P/L occurring in an open position)	-6.61	-19.01	-19.01
.. Date	810930	681130	681130
Overall Ranges	*Overall Ranges*		
Max P/L (Maximum P/L from all closed positions during the run)	301.09	310.04	310.04
.. Date	860831	861031	861031
Min P/L (Minimum P/L from all closed positions during the run)	-15.45	-16.22	-16.22
.. Date	570331	530630	530630
Max Equity (Maximum P/L from all closed and open positions)	315.28	322.70	322.70
.. Date	861130	860930	860930
Min Equity (Minimum P/L from all closed and open positions)	-17.04	-19.25	-19.25
.. Date	530831	570731	570731
Statistics	*Statistics*		
Periods (The number of periods in each position and entire run)	237	272	509
Trades (The number of trades in each position and entire run)	43	43	86
# Profitable (The number of profitable trades...)	27	18	45
# Losing (The number of unprofitable trades...)	16	25	41
% Profitable (The percent of profitable trades to total trades)	62.79	41.86	52.33
% Losing (The percent of unprofitable trades to total trades)	37.21	58.14	47.67
Results	*Results*		
Commission (Total commission deducted from closed trades)	0.00	0.00	0.00
Slippage (Total slippage deducted from closed trades)	0.00	0.00	0.00
Gross P/L (Total points gained in closed positions)	268.37	41.67	310.04
Open P/L (P/L in a position which remains open at the end)	-1.81	0.00	-1.81
P/L (Net P/L: Gross P/L less Commission and Slippage)	268.37	41.67	310.04
Equity (Net P/L plus Open P/L at the end of the run)	266.56	41.67	308.23

There are columns for Long trades, Short trades and Net. In the Long column, results are reported only for Long positions. In the Short column, results are reported for Short positions only. In the Net column for the "Per Trade Ranges" and "Overall Ranges," entries will be the extreme from either the Long or Short column. Net column entries for the "Statistics" and "Results" categories are the combined results of entries in the Long and Short columns.

NEW HIGH/NEW LOW RATIO

The New High/New Low Ratio is simply the number of issues reaching new highs in price divided by the number of issues reaching new lows in price. Daily or weekly NYSE data typically is used in the calculation.

Since early 1978, new highs and new lows have been defined as issues reaching new extremes in price on a 52-week basis. Prior to that time, the base period ranged from 2 1/2 to 14 1/2 months. For a date between January 1 and mid-March of a given year, a new high or new low was based on the period from January 1 of the previous year to the current date. For dates after mid-March, a new high or new low was determined on the basis of the period from January 1 of the current year to the current date.

With full knowledge that the method of determining new highs and new lows has been inconsistent, we tested the New High/New Low Ratio for the period of January 1962 to March 1987 on a daily basis and January 1937 to March 1987 on a weekly basis. We also applied a 10-period simple moving average to both the daily and weekly readings to smooth out any erratic movements. The results are shown in Exhibits N-8 through N-11 (pages 305–308).

The test process was as follows. The indicator readings for the test period were divided into 20 ranges with approximately the same number of occurrences in each range. For each reading in a range, the gain or loss in four subsequent time periods (1 month later, 3 months later, 6 months later, and 12 months later) was calculated. The combined results for readings within each range were statistically compared, using chi-squared tests, to the performance of the overall market (as measured by the Standard & Poor's 500 Index). Varying degrees of bullishness and bearishness were noted on the basis of that comparison.

Our research results revealed a bullish tendency at extreme high readings and a slightly bearish tendency at extreme low readings. In particular, during the last 25 years when the 10-day moving average of the New High/New Low Ratio was 40 or greater, average gains (as measured by the S&P 500) occurred of 0.58% 1 month later, 2.17% 3 months later, 4.16% 6 months later, and 9.24% 12 months later. Exhibit N-12 (page 309) shows the results in more detail. You should note that all signals generated within 3 months after an initial reading of 40 or greater were considered repeat signals and are not included in the results.

EXHIBIT N-8:

Interpretation of New High/New Low Ratio's Daily Readings

```
===================================================================================================
NEW HIGH/NEW LOW RATIO - DAILY DATA
PERIOD ANALYZED:  JANUARY 1962 TO MARCH 1987
===================================================================================================

INDICATOR RANGE               INTERPRETATION GIVEN INVESTOR'S TIME FRAME
----------------     ----------------------------------------------------------------------

          LESS
GREATER  THAN OR
 THAN    EQUAL TO    1 MONTH            3 MONTHS           6 MONTHS           12 MONTHS
-------  --------    ----------------   ----------------   ----------------   ----------------

 0.000    0.020     NEUTRAL            NEUTRAL            NEUTRAL            NEUTRAL
 0.020    0.060     NEUTRAL            BEARISH            VERY BEARISH       NEUTRAL
 0.060    0.122     NEUTRAL            NEUTRAL            NEUTRAL            NEUTRAL
 0.122    0.209     NEUTRAL            NEUTRAL            NEUTRAL            NEUTRAL
 0.209    0.328     SLIGHTLY BEARISH   NEUTRAL            NEUTRAL            NEUTRAL
 0.328    0.500     NEUTRAL            NEUTRAL            SLIGHTLY BEARISH   NEUTRAL
 0.500    0.714     NEUTRAL            NEUTRAL            NEUTRAL            NEUTRAL
 0.714    1.000     NEUTRAL            NEUTRAL            NEUTRAL            NEUTRAL
 1.000    1.350     NEUTRAL            NEUTRAL            NEUTRAL            NEUTRAL
 1.350    1.867     NEUTRAL            NEUTRAL            NEUTRAL            NEUTRAL
 1.867    2.452     BEARISH            NEUTRAL            BEARISH            SLIGHTLY BEARISH
 2.452    3.167     SLIGHTLY BEARISH   NEUTRAL            NEUTRAL            NEUTRAL
 3.167    4.077     SLIGHTLY BEARISH   NEUTRAL            NEUTRAL            NEUTRAL
 4.077    5.364     NEUTRAL            NEUTRAL            NEUTRAL            NEUTRAL
 5.364    7.182     NEUTRAL            NEUTRAL            NEUTRAL            NEUTRAL
 7.182    9.833     NEUTRAL            NEUTRAL            NEUTRAL            SLIGHTLY BEARISH
 9.833   14.455     VERY BULLISH       NEUTRAL            NEUTRAL            NEUTRAL
14.455   21.667     NEUTRAL            NEUTRAL            NEUTRAL            NEUTRAL
21.667   43.000     BULLISH            NEUTRAL            SLIGHTLY BULLISH   NEUTRAL
43.000  527.000     VERY BULLISH       VERY BULLISH       VERY BULLISH       NEUTRAL

===================================================================================================
```

Definitions of Very Bullish, Bullish, Slightly Bullish, Neutral, Slightly Bearish, Bearish, and Very Bearish are provided in Appendix A.

EXHIBIT N-9:
Interpretation of New High/New Low Ratio's 10-Day Simple Moving Average Readings

```
===================================================================================
NEW HIGH/NEW LOW RATIO - 10 DAY MOVING AVERAGE
PERIOD ANALYZED: JANUARY 1962 TO MARCH 1987
===================================================================================
```

INDICATOR RANGE		INTERPRETATION GIVEN INVESTOR'S TIME FRAME			
GREATER THAN	LESS THAN OR EQUAL TO	1 MONTH	3 MONTHS	6 MONTHS	12 MONTHS
0.000	0.059	NEUTRAL	SLIGHTLY BULLISH	NEUTRAL	VERY BULLISH
0.059	0.118	NEUTRAL	NEUTRAL	SLIGHTLY BEARISH	NEUTRAL
0.118	0.215	NEUTRAL	VERY BEARISH	BEARISH	NEUTRAL
0.215	0.344	BEARISH	VERY BEARISH	NEUTRAL	NEUTRAL
0.344	0.495	SLIGHTLY BEARISH	BEARISH	NEUTRAL	NEUTRAL
0.495	0.688	NEUTRAL	NEUTRAL	NEUTRAL	SLIGHTLY BULLISH
0.688	1.011	NEUTRAL	NEUTRAL	NEUTRAL	NEUTRAL
1.011	1.401	NEUTRAL	NEUTRAL	NEUTRAL	NEUTRAL
1.401	1.839	NEUTRAL	NEUTRAL	NEUTRAL	NEUTRAL
1.839	2.446	NEUTRAL	NEUTRAL	VERY BEARISH	NEUTRAL
2.446	3.129	NEUTRAL	NEUTRAL	NEUTRAL	BEARISH
3.129	3.872	VERY BEARISH	SLIGHTLY BEARISH	NEUTRAL	VERY BEARISH
3.872	5.027	NEUTRAL	BULLISH	BULLISH	BULLISH
5.027	6.389	NEUTRAL	NEUTRAL	NEUTRAL	NEUTRAL
6.389	8.187	NEUTRAL	NEUTRAL	SLIGHTLY BEARISH	VERY BEARISH
8.187	11.357	BEARISH	SLIGHTLY BEARISH	SLIGHTLY BEARISH	NEUTRAL
11.357	16.098	NEUTRAL	NEUTRAL	NEUTRAL	NEUTRAL
16.098	24.782	SLIGHTLY BULLISH	NEUTRAL	VERY BULLISH	NEUTRAL
24.782	42.748	VERY BULLISH	SLIGHTLY BULLISH	NEUTRAL	NEUTRAL
42.748	184.967	VERY BULLISH	VERY BULLISH	VERY BULLISH	SLIGHTLY BEARISH

```
===================================================================================
```

Definitions of Very Bullish, Bullish, Slightly Bullish, Neutral, Slightly Bearish, Bearish, and Very Bearish are provided in Appendix A.

EXHIBIT N-10:
Interpretation of New High/New Low Ratio's Weekly Readings

```
=================================================================================================
NEW HIGH/NEW LOW RATIO - WEEKLY DATA
PERIOD ANALYZED:  JANUARY 1937 TO MARCH 1987
=================================================================================================

   INDICATOR RANGE              INTERPRETATION GIVEN INVESTOR'S TIME FRAME
-------------------    --------------------------------------------------------------------------

           LESS
GREATER  THAN OR
 THAN    EQUAL TO    1 MONTH              3 MONTHS           6 MONTHS           12 MONTHS
-------  --------    ----------------     ----------------   ----------------   ----------------

 0.000    0.029      NEUTRAL              NEUTRAL            NEUTRAL            SLIGHTLY BULLISH
 0.029    0.078      NEUTRAL              NEUTRAL            NEUTRAL            NEUTRAL
 0.078    0.145      NEUTRAL              BEARISH            NEUTRAL            NEUTRAL
 0.145    0.226      NEUTRAL              NEUTRAL            NEUTRAL            NEUTRAL
 0.226    0.345      NEUTRAL              NEUTRAL            NEUTRAL            NEUTRAL
 0.345    0.483      NEUTRAL              NEUTRAL            NEUTRAL            NEUTRAL
 0.483    0.724      NEUTRAL              NEUTRAL            BEARISH            NEUTRAL
 0.724    1.024      NEUTRAL              NEUTRAL            NEUTRAL            NEUTRAL
 1.024    1.395      NEUTRAL              NEUTRAL            SLIGHTLY BEARISH   NEUTRAL
 1.395    1.780      NEUTRAL              NEUTRAL            NEUTRAL            NEUTRAL
 1.780    2.362      NEUTRAL              NEUTRAL            NEUTRAL            SLIGHTLY BEARISH
 2.362    3.129      NEUTRAL              NEUTRAL            NEUTRAL            NEUTRAL
 3.129    4.171      NEUTRAL              NEUTRAL            NEUTRAL            NEUTRAL
 4.171    5.444      NEUTRAL              NEUTRAL            NEUTRAL            NEUTRAL
 5.444    7.000      NEUTRAL              NEUTRAL            NEUTRAL            SLIGHTLY BEARISH
 7.000   10.265      NEUTRAL              NEUTRAL            NEUTRAL            NEUTRAL
10.265   14.800      SLIGHTLY BULLISH     NEUTRAL            NEUTRAL            NEUTRAL
14.800   23.667      BULLISH              SLIGHTLY BULLISH   VERY BULLISH       NEUTRAL
23.667   48.000      BULLISH              VERY BULLISH       VERY BULLISH       NEUTRAL
48.000  498.000      NEUTRAL              VERY BULLISH       VERY BULLISH       NEUTRAL

=================================================================================================
```

Definitions of Very Bullish, Bullish, Slightly Bullish, Neutral, Slightly Bearish, Bearish, and Very Bearish are provided in Appendix A.

EXHIBIT N-11:

Interpretation of New High/New Low Ratio's 10-Week Simple Moving Average Readings

```
=================================================================================
NEW HIGH/NEW LOW RATIO - 10 WEEK MOVING AVERAGE
PERIOD ANALYZED: JANUARY 1937 TO MARCH 1987
=================================================================================
```

INDICATOR RANGE		INTERPRETATION GIVEN INVESTOR'S TIME FRAME			
GREATER THAN	LESS THAN OR EQUAL TO	1 MONTH	3 MONTHS	6 MONTHS	12 MONTHS
0.000	0.127	NEUTRAL	NEUTRAL	BEARISH	NEUTRAL
0.127	0.236	NEUTRAL	SLIGHTLY BEARISH	NEUTRAL	VERY BULLISH
0.236	0.363	NEUTRAL	BEARISH	NEUTRAL	NEUTRAL
0.363	0.527	NEUTRAL	NEUTRAL	NEUTRAL	NEUTRAL
0.527	0.711	NEUTRAL	BEARISH	BEARISH	NEUTRAL
0.711	1.032	NEUTRAL	VERY BEARISH	NEUTRAL	NEUTRAL
1.032	1.378	NEUTRAL	NEUTRAL	NEUTRAL	NEUTRAL
1.378	1.813	NEUTRAL	NEUTRAL	NEUTRAL	NEUTRAL
1.813	2.283	SLIGHTLY BULLISH	NEUTRAL	NEUTRAL	NEUTRAL
2.283	2.819	NEUTRAL	NEUTRAL	NEUTRAL	BEARISH
2.819	3.375	BEARISH	NEUTRAL	BEARISH	NEUTRAL
3.375	4.089	NEUTRAL	NEUTRAL	NEUTRAL	NEUTRAL
4.089	5.190	NEUTRAL	NEUTRAL	NEUTRAL	NEUTRAL
5.190	7.048	NEUTRAL	NEUTRAL	NEUTRAL	NEUTRAL
7.048	9.463	NEUTRAL	VERY BEARISH	BEARISH	VERY BEARISH
9.463	12.885	NEUTRAL	SLIGHTLY BULLISH	SLIGHTLY BULLISH	SLIGHTLY BULLISH
12.885	19.321	SLIGHTLY BULLISH	SLIGHTLY BULLISH	VERY BULLISH	SLIGHTLY BULLISH
19.321	30.686	BULLISH	VERY BULLISH	VERY BULLISH	NEUTRAL
30.686	54.164	SLIGHTLY BULLISH	VERY BULLISH	BULLISH	NEUTRAL
54.164	161.155	SLIGHTLY BULLISH	BULLISH	SLIGHTLY BULLISH	NEUTRAL

```
=================================================================================
```

Definitions of Very Bullish, Bullish, Slightly Bullish, Neutral, Slightly Bearish, Bearish, and Very Bearish are provided in Appendix A.

EXHIBIT N-12:

New High/New Low Ratio's 10-Day Simple Moving Average Readings Equal to or Greater than 40 from 1962 to 1986

```
====================================================================
NEW HIGH/NEW LOW RATIO - 10 DAY MOVING AVERAGE
====================================================================
```

		PERCENTAGE CHANGE IN S&P 500			
DATE	INDICATOR VALUE	1 MONTH LATER	3 MONTHS LATER	6 MONTHS LATER	12 MONTHS LATER
JAN 24 1963	41.25	-0.44	6.10	3.82	17.28
MAR 10 1967	44.07	-0.01	3.00	6.15	1.39
JAN 7 1971	43.23	4.93	10.39	8.62	10.51
MAR 8 1972	40.94	0.61	-1.20	1.46	4.43
MAR 18 1975	53.25	2.49	6.40	-3.57	17.23
JUL 1 1975	127.47	-6.43	-11.58	-5.36	9.05
JAN 12 1976	55.11	4.30	4.17	9.93	9.01
DEC 29 1976	43.44	-4.28	-6.25	-5.83	-10.96
JAN 4 1977	63.40	-3.16	-7.07	-5.31	-11.24
AUG 14 1978	43.16	2.28	-8.85	-5.55	2.34
JUL 14 1980	40.58	3.15	8.57	11.07	8.02
SEP 2 1982	40.03	1.02	15.41	27.60	35.17
JAN 10 1983	51.33	-0.74	5.70	14.53	15.33
MAY 2 1983	42.75	0.27	-0.04	0.78	-1.37
JAN 24 1985	48.09	1.43	3.80	8.69	15.58
MAR 21 1986	40.65	3.89	6.10	-0.48	26.03
AVERAGE CHANGE		0.58	2.17	4.16	9.24

```
====================================================================
```

NEW HIGHS

The number of issues attaining new highs during a given day or week are used by some technicians as a market indicator. Since early 1978, new highs have been defined as issues reaching a new high in price on a 52-week basis. Prior to that time, the base period ranged from 2 1/2 to 14 1/2 months. For a date between January 1 and mid-March of a given year, a new high was based on the period from January 1 of the previous year to the current date. For dates after mid-March, a new high was determined on the basis of the period from January 1 of the current year to the current date.

With full knowledge that new highs were not reported consistently, we tested the number of new highs for the period of January 1962 to March 1987 on a daily basis and January 1937 to March 1987 on a weekly basis. In addition, we applied a 10-period simple moving average to both the daily and weekly readings to smooth out any erratic movements. The results are shown in Exhibits N-13 through N-16 (pages 311–314).

The test process was as follows. The indicator readings for the test period were divided into 20 ranges with approximately the same number of occurrences in each range. For each reading in a range, the gain or loss in four subsequent time periods (1 month later, 3 months later, 6 months later, and 12 months later) was calculated. The combined results for readings within each range were statistically compared to the performance of the overall market (as measured by the Standard & Poor's 500 Index). Varying degrees of bullishness and bearishness were noted on the basis of that comparison.

Our testing yielded few significant results. Slightly bullish tendencies did occur at both extreme high and low readings. However, most indicator readings were neither bullish nor bearish.

We did note that when the 10-day moving average of new highs was very low, equal to or less than 3.70, market prices rose at a faster than normal pace. (See Exhibit N-17, page 315. Repeat readings of 3.70 or less occurring within 3 months after an initial signal are not included). However, only three such readings have occurred since the 1978 change in the method of determining new highs, and the latest signal produced mixed results in varying time periods.

In conclusion, new highs by themselves are of questionable value as a predictor of stock market prices. For a discussion of related indicators, refer to the sections on the High Low Logic Index, New Highs–New Lows, and New High/New Low Ratio.

EXHIBIT N-13:
Interpretation of New Highs' Daily Readings

```
============================================================================================
NEW HIGHS - DAILY DATA
PERIOD ANALYZED: JANUARY 1962 TO MARCH 1987
============================================================================================
```

INDICATOR RANGE		INTERPRETATION GIVEN INVESTOR'S TIME FRAME			
GREATER THAN	LESS THAN OR EQUAL TO	1 MONTH	3 MONTHS	6 MONTHS	12 MONTHS
0	3	BULLISH	VERY BULLISH	NEUTRAL	VERY BULLISH
3	5	NEUTRAL	NEUTRAL	NEUTRAL	BULLISH
5	8	NEUTRAL	NEUTRAL	NEUTRAL	NEUTRAL
8	11	NEUTRAL	NEUTRAL	NEUTRAL	BULLISH
11	15	NEUTRAL	NEUTRAL	NEUTRAL	SLIGHTLY BULLISH
15	19	NEUTRAL	NEUTRAL	SLIGHTLY BEARISH	NEUTRAL
19	23	NEUTRAL	NEUTRAL	NEUTRAL	NEUTRAL
23	27	NEUTRAL	NEUTRAL	BEARISH	NEUTRAL
27	32	NEUTRAL	NEUTRAL	SLIGHTLY BEARISH	NEUTRAL
32	38	NEUTRAL	NEUTRAL	NEUTRAL	NEUTRAL
38	45	NEUTRAL	NEUTRAL	NEUTRAL	NEUTRAL
45	52	NEUTRAL	BULLISH	NEUTRAL	NEUTRAL
52	61	NEUTRAL	NEUTRAL	SLIGHTLY BULLISH	NEUTRAL
61	72	NEUTRAL	NEUTRAL	NEUTRAL	NEUTRAL
72	83	NEUTRAL	NEUTRAL	NEUTRAL	NEUTRAL
83	97	NEUTRAL	NEUTRAL	NEUTRAL	BEARISH
97	114	NEUTRAL	NEUTRAL	NEUTRAL	BEARISH
114	138	NEUTRAL	BEARISH	NEUTRAL	BEARISH
138	184	NEUTRAL	VERY BEARISH	NEUTRAL	VERY BEARISH
184	653	SLIGHTLY BULLISH	NEUTRAL	VERY BULLISH	NEUTRAL

```
============================================================================================
```

Definitions of Very Bullish, Bullish, Slightly Bullish, Neutral, Slightly Bearish, Bearish, and Very Bearish are provided in Appendix A.

EXHIBIT N-14:
Interpretation of New Highs' 10-Day Simple Moving Average Readings

```
=====================================================================================
NEW HIGHS - 10 DAY MOVING AVERAGE
PERIOD ANALYZED: JANUARY 1962 TO MARCH 1987
=====================================================================================

INDICATOR RANGE              INTERPRETATION GIVEN INVESTOR'S TIME FRAME
-----------------  --------------------------------------------------------------
           LESS
GREATER  THAN OR
 THAN   EQUAL TO  1 MONTH          3 MONTHS           6 MONTHS           12 MONTHS
-------  --------  ---------------  ----------------   ----------------   ----------------
```

GREATER THAN	LESS THAN OR EQUAL TO	1 MONTH	3 MONTHS	6 MONTHS	12 MONTHS
0.0	4.2	VERY BULLISH	VERY BULLISH	VERY BULLISH	VERY BULLISH
4.2	7.3	NEUTRAL	NEUTRAL	NEUTRAL	NEUTRAL
7.3	10.4	NEUTRAL	NEUTRAL	NEUTRAL	SLIGHTLY BULLISH
10.4	13.8	NEUTRAL	VERY BEARISH	VERY BEARISH	NEUTRAL
13.8	17.8	NEUTRAL	SLIGHTLY BEARISH	NEUTRAL	BULLISH
17.8	22.0	NEUTRAL	NEUTRAL	NEUTRAL	BULLISH
22.0	26.6	NEUTRAL	NEUTRAL	NEUTRAL	SLIGHTLY BULLISH
26.6	31.2	NEUTRAL	NEUTRAL	SLIGHTLY BEARISH	NEUTRAL
31.2	36.0	NEUTRAL	SLIGHTLY BEARISH	VERY BEARISH	NEUTRAL
36.0	41.8	NEUTRAL	NEUTRAL	NEUTRAL	NEUTRAL
41.8	50.1	NEUTRAL	BULLISH	SLIGHTLY BULLISH	NEUTRAL
50.1	57.2	NEUTRAL	NEUTRAL	NEUTRAL	NEUTRAL
57.2	64.5	NEUTRAL	NEUTRAL	NEUTRAL	NEUTRAL
64.5	74.0	NEUTRAL	NEUTRAL	NEUTRAL	NEUTRAL
74.0	85.7	NEUTRAL	NEUTRAL	NEUTRAL	SLIGHTLY BEARISH
85.7	98.8	VERY BEARISH	BEARISH	SLIGHTLY BEARISH	VERY BEARISH
98.8	114.3	NEUTRAL	VERY BEARISH	VERY BEARISH	VERY BEARISH
114.3	131.6	NEUTRAL	SLIGHTLY BEARISH	NEUTRAL	SLIGHTLY BEARISH
131.6	164.3	NEUTRAL	BEARISH	NEUTRAL	NEUTRAL
164.3	366.9	BULLISH	VERY BULLISH	VERY BULLISH	NEUTRAL

```
=====================================================================================
```

**Definitions of Very Bullish, Bullish, Slightly Bullish, Neutral, Slightly Bearish,
Bearish, and Very Bearish are provided in Appendix A.**

EXHIBIT N-15:
Interpretation of New Highs' Weekly Readings

```
===================================================================================
NEW HIGHS - WEEKLY DATA
PERIOD ANALYZED: JANUARY 1937 TO MARCH 1987
===================================================================================
```

INDICATOR RANGE		INTERPRETATION GIVEN INVESTOR'S TIME FRAME			
GREATER THAN	LESS THAN OR EQUAL TO	1 MONTH	3 MONTHS	6 MONTHS	12 MONTHS
0	8	NEUTRAL	NEUTRAL	NEUTRAL	BULLISH
8	15	NEUTRAL	NEUTRAL	NEUTRAL	NEUTRAL
15	23	NEUTRAL	NEUTRAL	NEUTRAL	NEUTRAL
23	30	NEUTRAL	NEUTRAL	NEUTRAL	NEUTRAL
30	39	NEUTRAL	SLIGHTLY BEARISH	NEUTRAL	NEUTRAL
39	49	NEUTRAL	SLIGHTLY BEARISH	SLIGHTLY BEARISH	NEUTRAL
49	60	NEUTRAL	NEUTRAL	NEUTRAL	NEUTRAL
60	73	NEUTRAL	NEUTRAL	NEUTRAL	NEUTRAL
73	85	NEUTRAL	NEUTRAL	NEUTRAL	NEUTRAL
85	100	NEUTRAL	NEUTRAL	NEUTRAL	NEUTRAL
100	117	NEUTRAL	NEUTRAL	NEUTRAL	NEUTRAL
117	135	NEUTRAL	NEUTRAL	NEUTRAL	NEUTRAL
135	155	NEUTRAL	NEUTRAL	NEUTRAL	NEUTRAL
155	178	NEUTRAL	NEUTRAL	NEUTRAL	NEUTRAL
178	205	NEUTRAL	SLIGHTLY BULLISH	NEUTRAL	NEUTRAL
205	234	NEUTRAL	NEUTRAL	NEUTRAL	NEUTRAL
234	273	NEUTRAL	NEUTRAL	NEUTRAL	NEUTRAL
273	318	NEUTRAL	NEUTRAL	NEUTRAL	NEUTRAL
318	396	NEUTRAL	NEUTRAL	BULLISH	NEUTRAL
396	1040	NEUTRAL	NEUTRAL	SLIGHTLY BULLISH	NEUTRAL

```
===================================================================================
```

Definitions of Very Bullish, Bullish, Slightly Bullish, Neutral, Slightly Bearish, Bearish, and Very Bearish are provided in Appendix A.

EXHIBIT N-16:
Interpretation of New Highs' 10-Week Simple Moving Average

```
=====================================================================================
NEW HIGHS - 10 WEEK MOVING AVERAGE
PERIOD ANALYZED: JANUARY 1937 TO MARCH 1987
=====================================================================================
```

INDICATOR RANGE		INTERPRETATION GIVEN INVESTOR'S TIME FRAME			
GREATER THAN	LESS THAN OR EQUAL TO	1 MONTH	3 MONTHS	6 MONTHS	12 MONTHS
0	16	NEUTRAL	NEUTRAL	NEUTRAL	SLIGHTLY BULLISH
16	26	NEUTRAL	NEUTRAL	NEUTRAL	VERY BULLISH
26	37	NEUTRAL	NEUTRAL	NEUTRAL	NEUTRAL
37	45	NEUTRAL	SLIGHTLY BEARISH	NEUTRAL	BEARISH
45	56	NEUTRAL	NEUTRAL	NEUTRAL	NEUTRAL
56	66	NEUTRAL	NEUTRAL	NEUTRAL	NEUTRAL
66	77	NEUTRAL	NEUTRAL	NEUTRAL	NEUTRAL
77	91	NEUTRAL	NEUTRAL	NEUTRAL	NEUTRAL
91	103	NEUTRAL	NEUTRAL	NEUTRAL	NEUTRAL
103	114	NEUTRAL	NEUTRAL	NEUTRAL	NEUTRAL
114	125	NEUTRAL	NEUTRAL	NEUTRAL	NEUTRAL
125	143	NEUTRAL	SLIGHTLY BEARISH	NEUTRAL	NEUTRAL
143	160	NEUTRAL	NEUTRAL	BEARISH	NEUTRAL
160	180	BULLISH	NEUTRAL	NEUTRAL	NEUTRAL
180	201	SLIGHTLY BULLISH	SLIGHTLY BULLISH	NEUTRAL	NEUTRAL
201	224	NEUTRAL	NEUTRAL	NEUTRAL	NEUTRAL
224	251	NEUTRAL	NEUTRAL	NEUTRAL	NEUTRAL
251	287	NEUTRAL	NEUTRAL	NEUTRAL	NEUTRAL
287	341	NEUTRAL	VERY BULLISH	SLIGHTLY BULLISH	NEUTRAL
341	648	SLIGHTLY BULLISH	NEUTRAL	SLIGHTLY BULLISH	NEUTRAL

```
=====================================================================================
```

Definitions of Very Bullish, Bullish, Slightly Bullish, Neutral, Slightly Bearish, Bearish, and Very Bearish are provided in Appendix A.

EXHIBIT N-17:

New Highs' 10-Day Simple Moving Average Readings Less than or Equal to 3.70 from 1962 to 1986

```
================================================================================
NEW HIGHS - 10 DAY MOVING AVERAGE
================================================================================
```

| | | PERCENTAGE CHANGE IN S&P 500 | | | |
DATE	INDICATOR VALUE	1 MONTH LATER	3 MONTHS LATER	6 MONTHS LATER	12 MONTHS LATER
JUN 20 1962	3.50	3.71	7.61	14.24	29.43
OCT 2 1962	3.40	0.93	13.58	20.07	28.73
JUL 1 1965	3.70	1.11	6.49	9.41	0.45
MAY 18 1966	3.70	1.63	-4.63	-3.23	9.00
SEP 1 1966	1.00	-3.60	3.13	13.38	20.51
MAR 7 1969	3.70	2.40	2.58	-5.34	-10.28
JUL 18 1969	2.70	0.13	1.38	-5.58	-19.60
FEB 6 1970	3.30	2.80	-7.98	-10.71	11.93
JUN 1 1970	2.90	-6.58	5.16	10.39	27.70
AUG 9 1971	3.70	8.35	0.99	12.11	17.76
JUN 27 1973	3.10	5.76	5.03	-7.60	-14.13
MAY 30 1974	3.70	-1.64	-19.07	-20.54	2.61
SEP 5 1974	3.70	-12.04	-4.88	18.09	21.39
JAN 2 1975	3.10	9.61	16.06	34.10	27.82
OCT 31 1978	3.60	1.66	7.28	9.20	8.12
MAR 18 1980	3.30	-2.93	11.46	21.75	28.65
SEP 4 1981	3.50	-0.57	5.16	-10.60	0.17
AVERAGE CHANGE		0.63	2.90	5.83	11.19

```
================================================================================
```

NEW HIGHS–NEW LOWS

New Highs — New Lows is simply the difference between the number of issues reaching new highs and the number of issues reaching new lows. Daily or weekly NYSE data normally is used in the calculation. A visual display of New Highs — New Lows is shown in Exhibit N-18 (page 316).

Since early 1978, new highs and new lows have been defined as issues reaching a new high or new low in price on a 52-week basis. Prior to that time, the base period ranged from 2 1/2 to 14 1/2 months. For a date between January 1 and mid-March of a given year, a new high or new low was based on the period from January 1 of the previous year to the current date. For dates

EXHIBIT N-18:

New Highs—New Lows (bottom) Versus Dow Jones Industrial Average (top) from 1977 to 1986

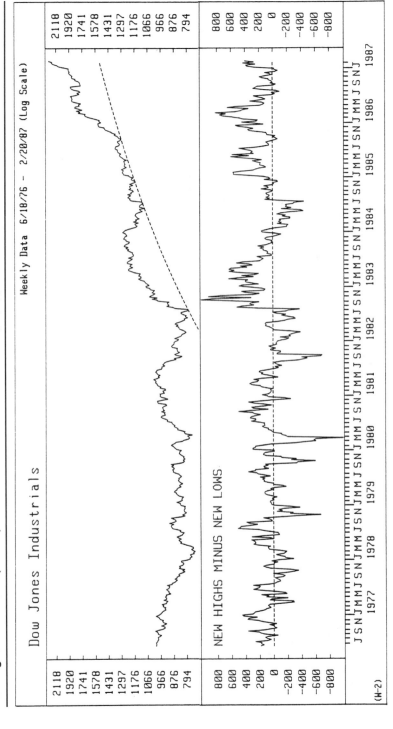

Source: By Permission of Ned Davis Research, Inc.

316

after mid-March, a new high or new low was determined on the basis of the period from January 1 of the current year to the current date.

With full knowledge that the method of determining new highs and new lows has been inconsistent, we tested New Highs—New Lows for the period of January 1962 to March 1987 on a daily basis and January 1937 to March 1987 on a weekly basis. In addition, we applied a 10-period simple moving average to both the daily and weekly readings to smooth out any erratic movements. The results are shown in Exhibits N-19 through N-22 (pages 318–321).

The test process was as follows. The indicator readings for the test period were divided into 20 ranges with approximately the same number of occurrences in each range. For each reading in a range, the gain or loss in four subsequent time periods (1 month later, 3 months later, 6 months later, and 12 months later) was calculated. The combined results for readings within each range were statistically compared, using chi-squared tests, to the performance of the overall market (as measured by the Standard & Poor's 500 Index). Varying degrees of bullishness and bearishness were noted on the basis of that comparison.

Our research results revealed a slight bullish tendency at extreme high readings and a slight bearish tendency at extreme low readings. However, results were not significant enough to warrant reliance on New Highs—New Lows for market timing.

EXHIBIT N-19:
Interpretation of New Highs—New Lows' Daily Readings

```
==============================================================================================
NEW HIGHS-NEW LOWS - DAILY DATA
PERIOD ANALYZED:  JANUARY 1962 TO MARCH 1987
==============================================================================================
```

INDICATOR RANGE		INTERPRETATION GIVEN INVESTOR'S TIME FRAME			
GREATER THAN	LESS THAN OR EQUAL TO	1 MONTH	3 MONTHS	6 MONTHS	12 MONTHS
-1030	-168	VERY BEARISH	BEARISH	VERY BEARISH	NEUTRAL
-168	-99	NEUTRAL	VERY BEARISH	VERY BEARISH	NEUTRAL
-99	-68	NEUTRAL	NEUTRAL	SLIGHTLY BEARISH	NEUTRAL
-68	-44	BEARISH	VERY BEARISH	NEUTRAL	NEUTRAL
-44	-28	NEUTRAL	NEUTRAL	NEUTRAL	NEUTRAL
-28	-16	NEUTRAL	NEUTRAL	NEUTRAL	NEUTRAL
-16	-7	NEUTRAL	NEUTRAL	NEUTRAL	NEUTRAL
-7	1	NEUTRAL	NEUTRAL	NEUTRAL	BULLISH
1	8	SLIGHTLY BULLISH	BULLISH	NEUTRAL	BULLISH
8	17	NEUTRAL	NEUTRAL	NEUTRAL	SLIGHTLY BULLISH
17	25	NEUTRAL	NEUTRAL	NEUTRAL	NEUTRAL
25	34	NEUTRAL	NEUTRAL	NEUTRAL	NEUTRAL
34	44	NEUTRAL	NEUTRAL	NEUTRAL	NEUTRAL
44	55	NEUTRAL	SLIGHTLY BULLISH	SLIGHTLY BULLISH	SLIGHTLY BULLISH
55	68	NEUTRAL	NEUTRAL	NEUTRAL	NEUTRAL
68	83	NEUTRAL	NEUTRAL	NEUTRAL	SLIGHTLY BEARISH
83	100	NEUTRAL	NEUTRAL	NEUTRAL	NEUTRAL
100	127	NEUTRAL	SLIGHTLY BEARISH	NEUTRAL	SLIGHTLY BEARISH
127	175	NEUTRAL	BEARISH	NEUTRAL	VERY BEARISH
175	646	BULLISH	SLIGHTLY BULLISH	VERY BULLISH	NEUTRAL

```
==============================================================================================
```

Definitions of Very Bullish, Bullish, Slightly Bullish, Neutral, Slightly Bearish, Bearish, and Very Bearish are provided in Appendix A.

EXHIBIT N-20:

Interpretation of New Highs—New Lows' 10-Day Simple Moving Average Readings

```
===========================================================================================
NEW HIGHS-NEW LOWS - 10 DAY MOVING AVERAGE
PERIOD ANALYZED:  JANUARY 1962 TO MARCH 1987
===========================================================================================
```

INDICATOR RANGE		INTERPRETATION GIVEN INVESTOR'S TIME FRAME			
GREATER THAN	LESS THAN OR EQUAL TO	1 MONTH	3 MONTHS	6 MONTHS	12 MONTHS
-589.1	-160.8	VERY BEARISH	VERY BEARISH	VERY BEARISH	NEUTRAL
-160.8	-106.3	NEUTRAL	NEUTRAL	NEUTRAL	NEUTRAL
-106.3	-70.4	NEUTRAL	VERY BEARISH	NEUTRAL	NEUTRAL
-70.4	-49.8	NEUTRAL	BEARISH	SLIGHTLY BEARISH	NEUTRAL
-49.8	-29.2	NEUTRAL	NEUTRAL	NEUTRAL	SLIGHTLY BULL
-29.2	-17.1	NEUTRAL	NEUTRAL	NEUTRAL	BULLISH
-17.1	-7.4	NEUTRAL	SLIGHTLY BULLISH	NEUTRAL	VERY BULLISH
-7.4	2.4	NEUTRAL	SLIGHTLY BULLISH	NEUTRAL	NEUTRAL
2.4	11.9	VERY BULLISH	VERY BULLISH	NEUTRAL	VERY BULLISH
11.9	18.9	NEUTRAL	VERY BULLISH	NEUTRAL	NEUTRAL
18.9	26.2	NEUTRAL	NEUTRAL	NEUTRAL	NEUTRAL
26.2	36.3	NEUTRAL	NEUTRAL	SLIGHTLY BULLISH	NEUTRAL
36.3	46.8	NEUTRAL	SLIGHTLY BULLISH	NEUTRAL	NEUTRAL
46.8	57.3	NEUTRAL	NEUTRAL	NEUTRAL	NEUTRAL
57.3	68.3	NEUTRAL	NEUTRAL	NEUTRAL	SLIGHTLY BEAR
68.3	84.0	NEUTRAL	NEUTRAL	NEUTRAL	BEARISH
84.0	100.4	NEUTRAL	NEUTRAL	SLIGHTLY BEARISH	BEARISH
100.4	120.0	NEUTRAL	SLIGHTLY BEARISH	NEUTRAL	NEUTRAL
120.0	155.3	SLIGHTLY BULLISH	SLIGHTLY BEARISH	NEUTRAL	SLIGHTLY BEAR
155.3	363.7	BULLISH	VERY BULLISH	VERY BULLISH	NEUTRAL

```
===========================================================================================
```

Definitions of Very Bullish, Bullish, Slightly Bullish, Neutral, Slightly Bearish, Bearish, and Very Bearish are provided in Appendix A.

EXHIBIT N-21:

Interpretation of New Highs—New Lows' Weekly Readings

```
============================================================================================

NEW HIGHS-NEW LOWS - WEEKLY DATA
PERIOD ANALYZED:  JANUARY 1937 TO MARCH 1987

============================================================================================

   INDICATOR RANGE                   INTERPRETATION GIVEN INVESTOR'S TIME FRAME
------------------- -------------------------------------------------------------------------

          LESS
GREATER  THAN OR
 THAN    EQUAL TO   1 MONTH            3 MONTHS           6 MONTHS          12 MONTHS
-------  --------  ----------------   ----------------   ----------------  ----------------
```

GREATER THAN	LESS THAN OR EQUAL TO	1 MONTH	3 MONTHS	6 MONTHS	12 MONTHS
-1314	-249	NEUTRAL	SLIGHTLY BEARISH	NEUTRAL	NEUTRAL
-249	-209	NEUTRAL	NEUTRAL	NEUTRAL	NEUTRAL
-209	-169	NEUTRAL	NEUTRAL	NEUTRAL	SLIGHTLY BULLISH
-169	-116	NEUTRAL	SLIGHTLY BEARISH	NEUTRAL	NEUTRAL
-116	-72	NEUTRAL	NEUTRAL	NEUTRAL	NEUTRAL
-72	-46	NEUTRAL	NEUTRAL	NEUTRAL	NEUTRAL
-46	-20	NEUTRAL	NEUTRAL	NEUTRAL	NEUTRAL
-20	1	NEUTRAL	NEUTRAL	NEUTRAL	NEUTRAL
1	21	NEUTRAL	NEUTRAL	NEUTRAL	NEUTRAL
21	41	NEUTRAL	NEUTRAL	NEUTRAL	NEUTRAL
41	59	NEUTRAL	SLIGHTLY BULLISH	NEUTRAL	NEUTRAL
59	80	NEUTRAL	NEUTRAL	NEUTRAL	NEUTRAL
80	106	SLIGHTLY BEARISH	NEUTRAL	NEUTRAL	NEUTRAL
106	131	NEUTRAL	NEUTRAL	NEUTRAL	NEUTRAL
131	158	NEUTRAL	NEUTRAL	NEUTRAL	NEUTRAL
158	196	SLIGHTLY BULLISH	NEUTRAL	NEUTRAL	NEUTRAL
196	237	SLIGHTLY BULLISH	SLIGHTLY BULLISH	NEUTRAL	NEUTRAL
237	285	NEUTRAL	NEUTRAL	NEUTRAL	NEUTRAL
285	368	NEUTRAL	NEUTRAL	NEUTRAL	NEUTRAL
368	1030	SLIGHTLY BULLISH	NEUTRAL	BULLISH	NEUTRAL

```
============================================================================================
```

Definitions of Very Bullish, Bullish, Slightly Bullish, Neutral, Slightly Bearish, Bearish, and Very Bearish are provided in Appendix A.

EXHIBIT N-22:

Interpretation of New Highs — New Lows' 10-Week Simple Moving Average Readings

```
======================================================================================
NEW HIGHS-NEW LOWS - 10 WEEK MOVING AVERAGE
PERIOD ANALYZED:  JANUARY 1937 TO MARCH 1987
======================================================================================
```

INDICATOR RANGE		INTERPRETATION GIVEN INVESTOR'S TIME FRAME			
GREATER THAN	LESS THAN OR EQUAL TO	1 MONTH	3 MONTHS	6 MONTHS	12 MONTHS
-705.6	-328.3	BEARISH	NEUTRAL	SLIGHTLY BEARISH	NEUTRAL
-328.3	-215.4	NEUTRAL	SLIGHTLY BEARISH	NEUTRAL	SLIGHTLY BULLISH
-215.4	-160.4	NEUTRAL	NEUTRAL	NEUTRAL	VERY BULLISH
-160.4	-127.2	NEUTRAL	BEARISH	NEUTRAL	NEUTRAL
-127.2	-91.8	NEUTRAL	NEUTRAL	NEUTRAL	NEUTRAL
-91.8	-62.3	NEUTRAL	NEUTRAL	NEUTRAL	NEUTRAL
-62.3	-32.6	NEUTRAL	NEUTRAL	NEUTRAL	NEUTRAL
-32.6	-3.0	SLIGHTLY BEARISH	NEUTRAL	NEUTRAL	NEUTRAL
-3.0	20.0	NEUTRAL	NEUTRAL	NEUTRAL	NEUTRAL
20.0	38.9	NEUTRAL	NEUTRAL	BEARISH	VERY BEARISH
38.9	56.4	NEUTRAL	NEUTRAL	SLIGHTLY BEARISH	SLIGHTLY BEARISH
56.4	79.2	NEUTRAL	NEUTRAL	NEUTRAL	SLIGHTLY BEARISH
79.2	100.5	NEUTRAL	NEUTRAL	SLIGHTLY BEARISH	NEUTRAL
100.5	120.3	NEUTRAL	NEUTRAL	NEUTRAL	NEUTRAL
120.3	149.8	SLIGHTLY BULLISH	NEUTRAL	NEUTRAL	NEUTRAL
149.8	179.4	NEUTRAL	NEUTRAL	NEUTRAL	NEUTRAL
179.4	213.5	SLIGHTLY BULLISH	VERY BULLISH	SLIGHTLY BULLISH	NEUTRAL
213.5	260.9	SLIGHTLY BEARISH	BULLISH	SLIGHTLY BULLISH	NEUTRAL
260.9	314.5	NEUTRAL	SLIGHTLY BULLISH	BULLISH	NEUTRAL
314.5	596.9	BULLISH	NEUTRAL	SLIGHTLY BULLISH	NEUTRAL

```
======================================================================================
```

Definitions of Very Bullish, Bullish, Slightly Bullish, Neutral, Slightly Bearish, Bearish, and Very Bearish are provided in Appendix A.

NEW LOWS

The number of issues making new lows during a given day or week are used by some technicians as a market indicator. Since early 1978, new lows have been defined as issues reaching a new low in price on a 52-week basis. Prior to that time, the base period ranged from 2 1/2 to 14 1/2 months. For a date between January 1 and mid-March of a given year, a new low was based on the period from January 1 of the previous year to the current date. For dates after mid-March, a new low was determined on the basis of the period from January 1 of the current year to the current date.

With full knowledge that new lows were not reported consistently, we tested the number of new lows for the period of January 1962 to March 1987 on a daily basis and January 1937 to March 1987 on a weekly basis. We also applied a 10-period simple moving average to both the daily and weekly readings to smooth out any erratic movements. The results are shown in Exhibits N-23 through N-26 (pages 323–326).

The test process was as follows. The indicator readings for the test period were divided into 20 ranges with approximately the same number of occurrences in each range. For each reading in a range, the gain or loss in four subsequent time periods (1 month later, 3 months later, 6 months later, and 12 months later) was calculated. The combined results for readings within each range were statistically compared, using chi-squared tests, to the performance of the overall market (as measured by the Standard & Poor's 500 Index). Varying degrees of bullishness and bearishness were noted on the basis of that comparison.

Our results show that daily data is more suitable for analysis than weekly data. In addition, better results were obtained by using a 10-period moving average of daily data.

As illustrated in Exhibit N-27 (page 327), extreme low readings of the 10-day moving average (equal to or less than 4) produced very bullish results for the period before and after the 1978 change in the method of determining new lows. You should note that all signals generated within 3 months of the initial reading of 4 or less were considered repeat signals and are not included in the results.

For a discussion of related indicators, refer to the sections on the High Low Logic Index, New Highs—New Lows, and New High/New Low Ratio.

EXHIBIT N-23:

Interpretation of New Lows' Daily Readings

```
==================================================================================================
NEW LOWS - DAILY DATA
PERIOD ANALYZED:  JANUARY 1962 TO MARCH 1987
==================================================================================================
```

INDICATOR RANGE		INTERPRETATION GIVEN INVESTOR'S TIME FRAME			
GREATER THAN	LESS THAN OR EQUAL TO	1 MONTH	3 MONTHS	6 MONTHS	12 MONTHS
0	2	VERY BULLISH	VERY BULLISH	VERY BULLISH	VERY BULLISH
2	4	VERY BULLISH	VERY BULLISH	VERY BULLISH	NEUTRAL
4	5	SLIGHTLY BULLISH	NEUTRAL	NEUTRAL	NEUTRAL
5	7	NEUTRAL	NEUTRAL	NEUTRAL	NEUTRAL
7	9	BEARISH	NEUTRAL	NEUTRAL	SLIGHTLY BEARISH
9	11	NEUTRAL	NEUTRAL	NEUTRAL	NEUTRAL
11	13	NEUTRAL	NEUTRAL	NEUTRAL	NEUTRAL
13	15	NEUTRAL	NEUTRAL	NEUTRAL	NEUTRAL
15	18	NEUTRAL	NEUTRAL	NEUTRAL	NEUTRAL
18	21	NEUTRAL	SLIGHTLY BULLISH	NEUTRAL	NEUTRAL
21	25	SLIGHTLY BULLISH	NEUTRAL	NEUTRAL	NEUTRAL
25	29	NEUTRAL	NEUTRAL	SLIGHTLY BEARISH	NEUTRAL
29	35	NEUTRAL	SLIGHTLY BEARISH	SLIGHTLY BEARISH	NEUTRAL
35	42	BEARISH	NEUTRAL	BEARISH	NEUTRAL
42	51	NEUTRAL	NEUTRAL	NEUTRAL	NEUTRAL
51	65	VERY BEARISH	VERY BEARISH	NEUTRAL	NEUTRAL
65	83	NEUTRAL	VERY BEARISH	BEARISH	NEUTRAL
83	113	SLIGHTLY BEARISH	BEARISH	BEARISH	SLIGHTLY BEARISH
113	175	NEUTRAL	VERY BEARISH	VERY BEARISH	NEUTRAL
175	1032	VERY BEARISH	VERY BEARISH	VERY BEARISH	NEUTRAL

```
==================================================================================================
```

Definitions of Very Bullish, Bullish, Slightly Bullish, Neutral, Slightly Bearish, Bearish, and Very Bearish are provided in Appendix A.

EXHIBIT N-24:
Interpretation of New Lows' 10-Day Simple Moving Average Readings

```
=================================================================================
NEW LOWS - 10 DAY MOVING AVERAGE
PERIOD ANALYZED: JANUARY 1962 TO MARCH 1987
=================================================================================
```

INDICATOR RANGE		INTERPRETATION GIVEN INVESTOR'S TIME FRAME			
GREATER THAN	LESS THAN OR EQUAL TO	1 MONTH	3 MONTHS	6 MONTHS	12 MONTHS
0.0	2.7	VERY BULLISH	VERY BULLISH	VERY BULLISH	VERY BULLISH
2.7	4.5	VERY BULLISH	VERY BULLISH	VERY BULLISH	NEUTRAL
4.5	6.3	BULLISH	NEUTRAL	NEUTRAL	NEUTRAL
6.3	9.1	SLIGHTLY BEARISH	NEUTRAL	NEUTRAL	NEUTRAL
9.1	11.2	NEUTRAL	NEUTRAL	NEUTRAL	NEUTRAL
11.2	13.0	NEUTRAL	NEUTRAL	NEUTRAL	NEUTRAL
13.0	14.8	SLIGHTLY BEARISH	NEUTRAL	SLIGHTLY BEARISH	VERY BEARISH
14.8	16.8	NEUTRAL	NEUTRAL	NEUTRAL	SLIGHTLY BEARISH
16.8	19.5	NEUTRAL	VERY BULLISH	NEUTRAL	NEUTRAL
19.5	22.7	SLIGHTLY BULLISH	BULLISH	NEUTRAL	NEUTRAL
22.7	26.5	BULLISH	NEUTRAL	NEUTRAL	NEUTRAL
26.5	31.7	NEUTRAL	VERY BEARISH	VERY BEARISH	NEUTRAL
31.7	37.7	NEUTRAL	NEUTRAL	NEUTRAL	NEUTRAL
37.7	45.2	NEUTRAL	NEUTRAL	NEUTRAL	VERY BULLISH
45.2	57.5	VERY BEARISH	VERY BEARISH	NEUTRAL	SLIGHTLY BEARISH
57.5	72.3	VERY BEARISH	VERY BEARISH	NEUTRAL	NEUTRAL
72.3	89.0	NEUTRAL	VERY BEARISH	BEARISH	BEARISH
89.0	117.1	NEUTRAL	VERY BEARISH	NEUTRAL	NEUTRAL
117.1	168.1	NEUTRAL	NEUTRAL	SLIGHTLY BEARISH	NEUTRAL
168.1	590.4	VERY BEARISH	VERY BEARISH	VERY BEARISH	NEUTRAL

```
=================================================================================
```

Definitions of Very Bullish, Bullish, Slightly Bullish, Neutral, Slightly Bearish, Bearish, and Very Bearish are provided in Appendix A.

EXHIBIT N-25:
Interpretation of New Lows' Weekly Readings

```
==============================================================================================
NEW LOWS - WEEKLY DATA
PERIOD ANALYZED:  JANUARY 1937 TO MARCH 1987
==============================================================================================
```

INDICATOR RANGE		INTERPRETATION GIVEN INVESTOR'S TIME FRAME			
GREATER THAN	LESS THAN OR EQUAL TO	1 MONTH	3 MONTHS	6 MONTHS	12 MONTHS
0	5	NEUTRAL	BULLISH	SLIGHTLY BULLISH	NEUTRAL
5	9	BULLISH	VERY BULLISH	VERY BULLISH	NEUTRAL
9	13	VERY BULLISH	SLIGHTLY BULLISH	SLIGHTLY BULLISH	NEUTRAL
13	17	VERY BULLISH	SLIGHTLY BULLISH	BULLISH	NEUTRAL
17	22	NEUTRAL	NEUTRAL	NEUTRAL	NEUTRAL
22	28	NEUTRAL	NEUTRAL	NEUTRAL	SLIGHTLY BEARISH
28	35	NEUTRAL	NEUTRAL	NEUTRAL	NEUTRAL
35	41	NEUTRAL	NEUTRAL	NEUTRAL	NEUTRAL
41	48	NEUTRAL	NEUTRAL	NEUTRAL	NEUTRAL
48	56	NEUTRAL	NEUTRAL	NEUTRAL	NEUTRAL
56	67	NEUTRAL	NEUTRAL	NEUTRAL	NEUTRAL
67	81	NEUTRAL	NEUTRAL	NEUTRAL	NEUTRAL
81	96	NEUTRAL	NEUTRAL	NEUTRAL	NEUTRAL
96	116	NEUTRAL	SLIGHTLY BEARISH	NEUTRAL	NEUTRAL
116	139	NEUTRAL	NEUTRAL	NEUTRAL	NEUTRAL
139	173	SLIGHTLY BEARISH	SLIGHTLY BEARISH	NEUTRAL	NEUTRAL
173	215	SLIGHTLY BEARISH	BEARISH	SLIGHTLY BEARISH	NEUTRAL
215	292	NEUTRAL	BEARISH	NEUTRAL	NEUTRAL
292	427	NEUTRAL	NEUTRAL	NEUTRAL	NEUTRAL
427	1322	SLIGHTLY BEARISH	NEUTRAL	SLIGHTLY BEARISH	NEUTRAL

```
==============================================================================================
```

Definitions of Very Bullish, Bullish, Slightly Bullish, Neutral, Slightly Bearish, Bearish, and Very Bearish are provided in Appendix A.

EXHIBIT N-26:
Interpretation of New Lows' 10-Week Simple Moving Average Readings

```
=================================================================================================
NEW LOWS - 10 WEEK MOVING AVERAGE
PERIOD ANALYZED: JANUARY 1937 TO MARCH 1987
=================================================================================================
```

INDICATOR RANGE		INTERPRETATION GIVEN INVESTOR'S TIME FRAME			
GREATER THAN	LESS THAN OR EQUAL TO	1 MONTH	3 MONTHS	6 MONTHS	12 MONTHS
0.0	9.1	BULLISH	VERY BULLISH	NEUTRAL	NEUTRAL
9.1	12.6	NEUTRAL	VERY BULLISH	VERY BULLISH	NEUTRAL
12.6	18.0	BULLISH	NEUTRAL	NEUTRAL	NEUTRAL
18.0	25.1	NEUTRAL	NEUTRAL	NEUTRAL	NEUTRAL
25.1	32.5	NEUTRAL	NEUTRAL	NEUTRAL	NEUTRAL
32.5	42.3	NEUTRAL	NEUTRAL	NEUTRAL	NEUTRAL
42.3	49.5	NEUTRAL	SLIGHTLY BULLISH	NEUTRAL	NEUTRAL
49.5	55.9	NEUTRAL	NEUTRAL	NEUTRAL	NEUTRAL
55.9	62.8	NEUTRAL	BULLISH	SLIGHTLY BULLISH	NEUTRAL
62.8	74.6	NEUTRAL	NEUTRAL	NEUTRAL	BEARISH
74.6	88.5	NEUTRAL	NEUTRAL	NEUTRAL	SLIGHTLY BEARISH
88.5	101.4	SLIGHTLY BEARISH	BEARISH	VERY BEARISH	SLIGHTLY BEARISH
101.4	118.9	VERY BEARISH	SLIGHTLY BEARISH	SLIGHTLY BEARISH	NEUTRAL
118.9	139.6	NEUTRAL	NEUTRAL	SLIGHTLY BULLISH	BULLISH
139.6	164.6	NEUTRAL	NEUTRAL	NEUTRAL	NEUTRAL
164.6	187.7	NEUTRAL	VERY BEARISH	NEUTRAL	NEUTRAL
187.7	216.3	NEUTRAL	SLIGHTLY BEARISH	NEUTRAL	NEUTRAL
216.3	263.6	NEUTRAL	NEUTRAL	NEUTRAL	NEUTRAL
263.6	358.2	NEUTRAL	SLIGHTLY BEARISH	NEUTRAL	SLIGHTLY BULLISH
358.2	726.1	BEARISH	NEUTRAL	BEARISH	NEUTRAL

```
=================================================================================================
```

Definitions of Very Bullish, Bullish, Slightly Bullish, Neutral, Slightly Bearish, Bearish, and Very Bearish are provided in Appendix A.

EXHIBIT N-27:

New Lows' 10-Day Simple Moving Average Readings Less than or Equal to 4.0 from 1962 to 1986

```
=====================================================================
NEW LOWS - 10 DAY MOVING AVERAGE
=====================================================================
```

| | | PERCENTAGE CHANGE IN S&P 500 | | | |
| | INDICATOR | 1 MONTH | 3 MONTHS | 6 MONTHS | 12 MONTHS |
DATE	VALUE	LATER	LATER	LATER	LATER
NOV 16 1962	3.70	3.17	10.57	16.29	20.26
JAN 2 1963	3.70	5.60	6.62	10.80	20.32
JAN 18 1967	2.80	2.41	7.17	9.16	11.48
SEP 10 1970	3.70	3.38	8.80	20.77	23.13
JAN 4 1971	2.40	5.79	10.32	9.47	11.66
DEC 31 1971	4.00	1.81	5.01	4.63	15.63
JAN 3 1972	3.60	2.30	5.71	5.38	17.14
JAN 21 1975	4.00	16.28	23.18	29.35	39.07
JUN 18 1975	3.70	3.11	-8.87	-1.62	12.25
JAN 8 1976	2.70	5.16	8.07	9.85	10.76
DEC 31 1976	3.90	-5.05	-8.41	-6.50	-11.65
JAN 3 1977	3.40	-4.17	-7.28	-6.45	-11.12
AUG 18 1978	4.00	-2.10	-10.52	-5.79	3.21
AUG 14 1979	3.80	0.31	-3.73	9.65	16.05
MAY 27 1980	3.80	4.78	12.35	24.16	19.18
SEP 2 1980	3.30	2.74	10.69	5.75	-0.77
SEP 13 1982	4.00	9.98	14.18	23.72	37.25
JAN 4 1983	3.70	1.33	7.46	17.86	16.68
MAY 11 1983	4.00	-1.38	-2.07	-1.94	-2.69
JAN 30 1985	3.80	2.14	-0.57	6.43	17.23
AVERAGE CHANGE		2.88	4.43	9.05	13.25

```
=====================================================================
```

NUMBER OF ADVANCING ISSUES

The number of advancing issues is simply the total number of stocks traded on the New York Stock Exchange that ended on a given day at a higher share price than the previous day's closing price.

We tested the number of advancing issues for the period of January 1928 to March 1987. In addition, we applied a 10-period simple moving average to the daily numbers to smooth out any erratic movements. The results are shown in Exhibits N-28 and N-29 (pages 328–329).

The test process was as follows. The daily numbers of advancing issues

EXHIBIT N-28:
Interpretation of Number of Advancing Issues' Daily Readings

```
===============================================================================================
NUMBER OF ADVANCING ISSUES - DAILY DATA
PERIOD ANALYZED: JANUARY 1928 TO MARCH 1987
===============================================================================================
```

INDICATOR RANGE		INTERPRETATION GIVEN INVESTOR'S TIME FRAME			
GREATER THAN	LESS THAN OR EQUAL TO	1 MONTH	3 MONTHS	6 MONTHS	12 MONTHS
0	122	VERY BEARISH	VERY BEARISH	VERY BEARISH	VERY BEARISH
122	176	NEUTRAL	NEUTRAL	SLIGHTLY BEARISH	NEUTRAL
176	222	BEARISH	SLIGHTLY BEARISH	BEARISH	VERY BEARISH
222	257	SLIGHTLY BEARISH	SLIGHTLY BEARISH	SLIGHTLY BEARISH	NEUTRAL
257	294	NEUTRAL	SLIGHTLY BEARISH	NEUTRAL	NEUTRAL
294	327	NEUTRAL	NEUTRAL	NEUTRAL	NEUTRAL
327	360	NEUTRAL	NEUTRAL	NEUTRAL	NEUTRAL
360	391	NEUTRAL	NEUTRAL	NEUTRAL	VERY BEARISH
391	424	NEUTRAL	NEUTRAL	NEUTRAL	NEUTRAL
424	457	NEUTRAL	NEUTRAL	SLIGHTLY BULLISH	NEUTRAL
457	490	NEUTRAL	NEUTRAL	NEUTRAL	SLIGHTLY BULLISH
490	526	SLIGHTLY BULLISH	BULLISH	VERY BULLISH	BULLISH
526	562	NEUTRAL	NEUTRAL	BULLISH	SLIGHTLY BULLISH
562	601	SLIGHTLY BULLISH	BULLISH	BULLISH	SLIGHTLY BULLISH
601	645	NEUTRAL	SLIGHTLY BULLISH	BULLISH	NEUTRAL
645	694	NEUTRAL	NEUTRAL	NEUTRAL	BULLISH
694	757	NEUTRAL	NEUTRAL	NEUTRAL	NEUTRAL
757	838	BULLISH	NEUTRAL	NEUTRAL	SLIGHTLY BULLISH
838	967	NEUTRAL	VERY BEARISH	NEUTRAL	NEUTRAL
967	1613	NEUTRAL	NEUTRAL	BULLISH	VERY BULLISH

```
===============================================================================================
```

Definitions of Very Bullish, Bullish, Slightly Bullish, Neutral, Slightly Bearish, Bearish, and Very Bearish are provided in Appendix A.

for the test period were divided into 20 ranges with approximately the same number of occurrences in each range. For each number in a range, the gain or loss in four subsequent time periods (1 month later, 3 months later, 6 months later, and 12 months later) was calculated. The combined results for numbers within each range were statistically compared, using chi-squared tests, to the performance of the overall market (as measured by the Standard & Poor's 500 Index). Varying degrees of bullishness and bearishness were noted on the basis of that comparison.

EXHIBIT N-29:

Interpretation of Number of Advancing Issues' 10-Day Simple Moving Average Readings

```
================================================================================
NUMBER OF ADVANCING ISSUES - 10 DAY MOVING AVERAGE
PERIOD ANALYZED:  JANUARY 1928 TO MARCH 1987
================================================================================
```

INDICATOR RANGE		INTERPRETATION GIVEN INVESTOR'S TIME FRAME			
GREATER THAN	LESS THAN OR EQUAL TO	1 MONTH	3 MONTHS	6 MONTHS	12 MONTHS
0.0	200.4	VERY BEARISH	VERY BEARISH	VERY BEARISH	VERY BEARISH
200.4	242.3	SLIGHTLY BEARISH	VERY BEARISH	VERY BEARISH	VERY BEARISH
242.3	272.7	NEUTRAL	VERY BEARISH	VERY BEARISH	VERY BEARISH
272.7	300.3	NEUTRAL	BEARISH	VERY BEARISH	VERY BEARISH
300.3	325.3	NEUTRAL	NEUTRAL	NEUTRAL	VERY BEARISH
325.3	349.4	BEARISH	NEUTRAL	NEUTRAL	NEUTRAL
349.4	374.4	NEUTRAL	NEUTRAL	NEUTRAL	NEUTRAL
374.4	404.1	NEUTRAL	NEUTRAL	BULLISH	VERY BULLISH
404.1	431.2	NEUTRAL	SLIGHTLY BULLISH	SLIGHTLY BULLISH	SLIGHTLY BULLISH
431.2	458.9	SLIGHTLY BULLISH	BULLISH	VERY BULLISH	SLIGHTLY BULLISH
458.9	487.6	NEUTRAL	NEUTRAL	BULLISH	VERY BULLISH
487.6	516.9	VERY BULLISH	VERY BULLISH	VERY BULLISH	VERY BULLISH
516.9	548.3	NEUTRAL	VERY BULLISH	VERY BULLISH	VERY BULLISH
548.3	583.4	BULLISH	VERY BULLISH	VERY BULLISH	NEUTRAL
583.4	632.8	NEUTRAL	BULLISH	NEUTRAL	NEUTRAL
632.8	680.9	NEUTRAL	BEARISH	VERY BEARISH	NEUTRAL
680.9	732.1	NEUTRAL	NEUTRAL	SLIGHTLY BEARISH	NEUTRAL
732.1	788.5	BEARISH	VERY BEARISH	NEUTRAL	SLIGHTLY BULLISH
788.5	849.5	NEUTRAL	BEARISH	NEUTRAL	NEUTRAL
849.5	1184.9	VERY BULLISH	NEUTRAL	VERY BULLISH	VERY BULLISH

```
================================================================================
```

Definitions of Very Bullish, Bullish, Slightly Bullish, Neutral, Slightly Bearish, Bearish, and Very Bearish are provided in Appendix A.

Our test results revealed no clear-cut patterns in the daily data. However, the 10-day moving average of the number of advancing issues displayed a very bullish pattern for midrange values (450 to 550). A similar bullish pattern appeared for the 10-day moving average of the number of declining issues. This implies that when the net difference between the number of advancing issues and the number of declining issues is low, market internals are at a standoff that is likely to be resolved with stock prices moving to the upside.

An extremely low number of advancing issues should be considered as very bearish, especially for the 10-day moving average. On the other hand, extremely high numbers of declining issues produce mixed signals and are not useful for market timing.

NUMBER OF DECLINING ISSUES

The number of declining issues is simply the total number of stocks traded on the New York Stock Exchange that ended on a given day at a lower share price than the previous day's closing price.

We tested the number of declining issues for the period of January 1928 to March 1987. In addition, we applied a 10-period simple moving average to the daily numbers to smooth out any erratic movements. The results are shown in Exhibits N-30 and N-31 (pages 331–332).

The test process was as follows. The daily numbers of declining issues for the test period were divided into 20 ranges with approximately the same number of occurrences in each range. For each number in a range, the gain or loss in four subsequent time periods (1 month later, 3 months later, 6 months later, and 12 months later) was calculated. The combined results for numbers within each range were statistically compared, using chi-squared tests, to the performance of the overall market (as measured by the Standard & Poor's 500 Index). Varying degrees of bullishness and bearishness were noted on the basis of that comparison.

Our test results were quite interesting. The daily data revealed no clear-cut patterns. However, the 10-day moving average of the number of declining issues displayed a very bullish pattern for midrange values (450 to 550). A similar bullish pattern appeared for the 10-day moving average of the number of advancing issues. This implies that when the net difference between the number of advancing issues and the number of declining issues is low, market internals are at a standoff that is likely to be resolved with stock prices moving to the upside.

An extremely low number of declining issues should be considered as slightly bearish. On the other hand, extremely high numbers of declining issues produce mixed signals and are not useful for market timing.

EXHIBIT N-30:

Interpretation of Number of Declining Issues' Daily Readings

```
================================================================================
NUMBER OF DECLINING ISSUES - DAILY DATA
PERIOD ANALYZED: JANUARY 1928 TO MARCH 1987
================================================================================
```

INDICATOR RANGE		INTERPRETATION GIVEN INVESTOR'S TIME FRAME			
GREATER THAN	LESS THAN OR EQUAL TO	1 MONTH	3 MONTHS	6 MONTHS	12 MONTHS
0	136	NEUTRAL	VERY BEARISH	BEARISH	VERY BEARISH
136	181	NEUTRAL	SLIGHTLY BULLISH	NEUTRAL	NEUTRAL
181	218	NEUTRAL	NEUTRAL	NEUTRAL	NEUTRAL
218	253	NEUTRAL	NEUTRAL	NEUTRAL	SLIGHTLY BEARISH
253	286	NEUTRAL	NEUTRAL	NEUTRAL	NEUTRAL
286	320	NEUTRAL	NEUTRAL	NEUTRAL	NEUTRAL
320	353	SLIGHTLY BULLISH	NEUTRAL	NEUTRAL	NEUTRAL
353	397	SLIGHTLY BULLISH	NEUTRAL	NEUTRAL	NEUTRAL
387	419	NEUTRAL	SLIGHTLY BULLISH	NEUTRAL	NEUTRAL
419	453	NEUTRAL	NEUTRAL	NEUTRAL	NEUTRAL
453	476	NEUTRAL	SLIGHTLY BULLISH	NEUTRAL	NEUTRAL
476	521	SLIGHTLY BULLISH	SLIGHTLY BULLISH	VERY BULLISH	NEUTRAL
521	558	NEUTRAL	NEUTRAL	NEUTRAL	NEUTRAL
558	597	NEUTRAL	NEUTRAL	NEUTRAL	NEUTRAL
597	644	NEUTRAL	NEUTRAL	NEUTRAL	NEUTRAL
644	698	NEUTRAL	BEARISH	NEUTRAL	NEUTRAL
698	765	NEUTRAL	SLIGHTLY BEARISH	NEUTRAL	NEUTRAL
765	849	NEUTRAL	NEUTRAL	NEUTRAL	SLIGHTLY BULLISH
849	978	NEUTRAL	SLIGHTLY BEARISH	NEUTRAL	SLIGHTLY BULLISH
978	1765	NEUTRAL	NEUTRAL	NEUTRAL	NEUTRAL

```
================================================================================
```

Definitions of Very Bullish, Bullish, Slightly Bullish, Neutral, Slightly Bearish, Bearish, and Very Bearish are provided in Appendix A.

EXHIBIT N-31:

Interpretation of Number of Declining Issues' 10-Day Simple Moving Average Readings

```
================================================================================
NUMBER OF DECLINING ISSUES - 10 DAY MOVING AVERAGE
PERIOD ANALYZED: JANUARY 1928 TO MARCH 1987
================================================================================
```

INDICATOR RANGE		INTERPRETATION GIVEN INVESTOR'S TIME FRAME			
GREATER THAN	LESS THAN OR EQUAL TO	1 MONTH	3 MONTHS	6 MONTHS	12 MONTHS
0.0	208.1	SLIGHTLY BEARISH	NEUTRAL	NEUTRAL	NEUTRAL
208.1	242.2	BEARISH	VERY BEARISH	VERY BEARISH	VERY BEARISH
242.2	269.2	NEUTRAL	NEUTRAL	NEUTRAL	SLIGHTLY BEARISH
269.2	295.4	NEUTRAL	NEUTRAL	NEUTRAL	VERY BEARISH
295.4	319.3	VERY BEARISH	BEARISH	BEARISH	VERY BEARISH
319.3	343.4	NEUTRAL	NEUTRAL	NEUTRAL	VERY BEARISH
343.4	368.7	NEUTRAL	NEUTRAL	NEUTRAL	NEUTRAL
368.7	394.3	NEUTRAL	NEUTRAL	NEUTRAL	NEUTRAL
394.3	421.6	BULLISH	BULLISH	SLIGHTLY BULLISH	SLIGHTLY BULLISH
421.6	452.4	SLIGHTLY BULLISH	VERY BULLISH	VERY BULLISH	BULLISH
452.4	487.6	BULLISH	VERY BULLISH	VERY BULLISH	VERY BULLISH
487.6	522.3	SLIGHTLY BULLISH	VERY BULLISH	VERY BULLISH	VERY BULLISH
522.3	560.3	NEUTRAL	VERY BULLISH	VERY BULLISH	VERY BULLISH
560.3	602.5	NEUTRAL	NEUTRAL	NEUTRAL	NEUTRAL
602.5	650.2	NEUTRAL	VERY BEARISH	NEUTRAL	NEUTRAL
650.2	692.3	NEUTRAL	VERY BEARISH	NEUTRAL	SLIGHTLY BULLISH
692.3	736.4	NEUTRAL	BEARISH	NEUTRAL	SLIGHTLY BULLISH
736.4	781.9	VERY BEARISH	SLIGHTLY BEARISH	NEUTRAL	NEUTRAL
781.9	844.0	NEUTRAL	NEUTRAL	SLIGHTLY BEARISH	NEUTRAL
844.0	1264.1	NEUTRAL	NEUTRAL	VERY BEARISH	SLIGHTLY BULLISH

```
================================================================================
```

Definitions of Very Bullish, Bullish, Slightly Bullish, Neutral, Slightly Bearish, Bearish, and Very Bearish are provided in Appendix A.

ODD LOT BALANCE INDEX

The Odd Lot Balance Index is a market sentiment indicator. It is calculated by dividing odd lot sales by odd lot purchases. Daily NYSE data normally is used in the calculation.

An odd lot is a small order of less than 100 shares of a stock. Traditionally, it was thought that odd lot purchases and sales were made by small investors who could not afford to buy 100 shares of stock. These investors supposedly were wrong about the direction of stock prices at market turns. Therefore, the Odd Lot Balance Index was considered to be a contrary opinion sentiment indicator.

We tested the Odd Lot Balance Index for the period of January 1962 to March 1987 on a daily basis. In addition, we applied a 10-period simple moving average to the daily readings to smooth out any erratic movements. The results are shown in Exhibits O-1 and O-2 (pages 334–335).

The test process was as follows. The indicator readings for the test period were divided into 20 ranges with approximately the same number of occurrences in each range. For each reading in a range, the gain or loss in four subsequent time periods (1 month later, 3 months later, 6 months later, and 12 months later) was calculated. The combined results for readings within each range were statistically compared, using chi-squared tests, to the performance of the overall market (as measured by the Standard & Poor's 500 Index). Varying degrees of bullishness and bearishness were noted on the basis of that comparison.

Our research results show a strong bullish tendency at high indicator readings, especially when a 10-day moving average is used. In particular, during the past 25 years when the 10-day moving average of the Odd Lot Balance Index was 2.75 or greater, an average gain occurred in the overall market (as measured by the S&P 500) of 3.03% 1 month later, 6.01% 3 months later, 10.55% 6 months later, and 19.97% 12 months later. Exhibit O-3 (page 336) shows the results in greater detail. You should note that all signals generated within 3 months after an initial reading of 2.75 or greater were considered repeat signals and are not included in the results.

EXHIBIT O-1:
Interpretation of Odd Lot Balance Index's Daily Readings

```
========================================================================================
ODD LOT BALANCE INDEX - DAILY DATA
PERIOD ANALYZED: JANUARY 1962 TO MARCH 1987
========================================================================================
```

INDICATOR RANGE		INTERPRETATION GIVEN INVESTOR'S TIME FRAME			
GREATER THAN	LESS THAN OR EQUAL TO	1 MONTH	3 MONTHS	6 MONTHS	12 MONTHS
0.000	0.876	NEUTRAL	NEUTRAL	NEUTRAL	VERY BULLISH
0.876	0.973	NEUTRAL	SLIGHTLY BEARISH	SLIGHTLY BEARISH	NEUTRAL
0.973	1.032	NEUTRAL	NEUTRAL	NEUTRAL	NEUTRAL
1.032	1.082	NEUTRAL	NEUTRAL	BULLISH	NEUTRAL
1.082	1.151	NEUTRAL	NEUTRAL	NEUTRAL	NEUTRAL
1.151	1.216	NEUTRAL	VERY BULLISH	NEUTRAL	NEUTRAL
1.216	1.293	NEUTRAL	NEUTRAL	NEUTRAL	SLIGHTLY BEARISH
1.293	1.411	VERY BEARISH	SLIGHTLY BEARISH	VERY BEARISH	VERY BEARISH
1.411	1.593	VERY BEARISH	BEARISH	VERY BEARISH	VERY BEARISH
1.593	1.729	NEUTRAL	VERY BULLISH	SLIGHTLY BULLISH	SLIGHTLY BEARISH
1.729	1.846	NEUTRAL	NEUTRAL	NEUTRAL	NEUTRAL
1.846	1.936	NEUTRAL	VERY BEARISH	NEUTRAL	NEUTRAL
1.936	2.023	NEUTRAL	VERY BEARISH	NEUTRAL	NEUTRAL
2.023	2.116	BULLISH	VERY BEARISH	NEUTRAL	NEUTRAL
2.116	2.195	NEUTRAL	NEUTRAL	NEUTRAL	NEUTRAL
2.195	2.293	SLIGHTLY BULLISH	NEUTRAL	NEUTRAL	NEUTRAL
2.293	2.399	NEUTRAL	NEUTRAL	NEUTRAL	NEUTRAL
2.399	2.517	NEUTRAL	NEUTRAL	NEUTRAL	NEUTRAL
2.517	2.739	NEUTRAL	SLIGHTLY BULLISH	NEUTRAL	VERY BULLISH
2.739	5.397	NEUTRAL	VERY BULLISH	VERY BULLISH	VERY BULLISH

```
========================================================================================
```

Definitions of Very Bullish, Bullish, Slightly Bullish, Neutral, Slightly Bearish, Bearish, and Very Bearish are provided in Appendix A.

EXHIBIT O-2:

Interpretation of Odd Lot Balance Index's 10-Day Simple Moving Average Readings

```
================================================================================
ODD LOT BALANCE INDEX - 10 DAY MOVING AVERAGE
PERIOD ANALYZED: JANUARY 1962 TO MARCH 1987
================================================================================
```

INDICATOR RANGE		INTERPRETATION GIVEN INVESTOR'S TIME FRAME			
GREATER THAN	LESS THAN OR EQUAL TO	1 MONTH	3 MONTHS	6 MONTHS	12 MONTHS
0.000	0.898	VERY BULLISH	NEUTRAL	NEUTRAL	VERY BULLISH
0.898	0.990	VERY BEARISH	BEARISH	BEARISH	SLIGHTLY BULLISH
0.990	1.034	NEUTRAL	NEUTRAL	NEUTRAL	NEUTRAL
1.034	1.090	NEUTRAL	SLIGHTLY BULLISH	BULLISH	NEUTRAL
1.090	1.160	BULLISH	VERY BULLISH	VERY BULLISH	NEUTRAL
1.160	1.217	NEUTRAL	VERY BULLISH	SLIGHTLY BEARISH	BULLISH
1.217	1.286	BEARISH	NEUTRAL	BEARISH	VERY BEARISH
1.286	1.427	VERY BEARISH	VERY BEARISH	VERY BEARISH	VERY BEARISH
1.427	1.652	NEUTRAL	NEUTRAL	NEUTRAL	VERY BEARISH
1.652	1.783	NEUTRAL	SLIGHTLY BULLISH	VERY BULLISH	NEUTRAL
1.783	1.865	NEUTRAL	NEUTRAL	VERY BULLISH	NEUTRAL
1.865	1.967	BULLISH	VERY BEARISH	SLIGHTLY BEARISH	NEUTRAL
1.967	2.047	NEUTRAL	VERY BEARISH	BEARISH	VERY BULLISH
2.047	2.122	BULLISH	NEUTRAL	NEUTRAL	SLIGHTLY BULLISH
2.122	2.195	NEUTRAL	NEUTRAL	SLIGHTLY BEARISH	BEARISH
2.195	2.269	NEUTRAL	NEUTRAL	NEUTRAL	NEUTRAL
2.269	2.350	NEUTRAL	NEUTRAL	NEUTRAL	NEUTRAL
2.350	2.464	NEUTRAL	BULLISH	NEUTRAL	NEUTRAL
2.464	2.646	VERY BEARISH	NEUTRAL	NEUTRAL	VERY BULLISH
2.646	3.625	BULLISH	VERY BULLISH	VERY BULLISH	VERY BULLISH

```
================================================================================
```

Definitions of Very Bullish, Bullish, Slightly Bullish, Neutral, Slightly Bearish, Bearish, and Very Bearish are provided in Appendix A.

EXHIBIT O-3:

Odd Lot Balance Index's 10-Day Simple Moving Average Readings Equal to or Greater than 2.75 from 1962 to 1986

```
=================================================================
ODD LOT BALANCE INDEX - 10 DAY MOVING AVERAGE
=================================================================
```

		PERCENTAGE CHANGE IN S&P 500			
DATE	INDICATOR VALUE	1 MONTH LATER	3 MONTHS LATER	6 MONTHS LATER	12 MONTHS LATER
DEC 29 1975	2.81	9.32	13.62	14.76	17.67
JAN 2 1976	2.86	10.97	12.48	13.96	17.58
AUG 4 1978	2.76	0.55	-8.00	-4.25	0.17
SEP 6 1979	2.76	4.14	0.37	1.68	17.60
DEC 14 1981	2.78	-5.90	-11.00	-10.66	13.67
JAN 4 1982	3.00	-3.85	-6.21	-12.29	14.33
SEP 1 1982	2.83	3.15	17.31	28.79	37.21
JAN 3 1983	2.78	3.34	10.61	22.10	19.17
JUL 24 1984	2.96	13.02	13.22	18.71	31.50
NOV 1 1984	3.25	-2.79	6.65	7.52	13.33
JAN 2 1985	3.58	8.62	9.17	16.11	27.76
SEP 4 1985	2.79	-2.21	9.00	20.15	33.47
JAN 2 1986	2.81	1.04	10.92	20.57	16.12
AVERAGE CHANGE		3.03	6.01	10.55	19.97

```
=================================================================
```

ODD LOT SHORT RATIO

Investors sell short stock when they anticipate its price going lower. At a later date, they must cover their short sales by buying the stock back. A profit is made if the stock is bought back at a lower price than when it was sold short.

An odd lot is a small order of less than 100 shares of a stock. Traditionally, odd lot purchases and sales were thought to be made by small investors who could not afford to buy 100 shares of stock. These investors were supposed to be wrong about the direction of stock prices at market turns.

The Odd Lot Short Ratio reflects the shorting activity of small investors. According to Arthur Merrill (Merrill Analysis, Inc., Box 228, Chappaqua, NY 10514) it is calculated by dividing odd lot short sales by the average of odd lot purchases and odd lot sales.

Readings generated by the Odd Lot Short Ratio commonly are interpreted in a contrary manner. If small investors believe stock prices are headed lower

EXHIBIT O-4:

Interpretation of Odd Lot Short Ratio's Daily Readings

```
===========================================================================
ODD LOT SHORT RATIO - DAILY DATA
PERIOD ANALYZED:  JANUARY 1962 TO MARCH 1987
===========================================================================
```

INDICATOR RANGE		INTERPRETATION GIVEN INVESTOR'S TIME FRAME			
GREATER THAN	LESS THAN OR EQUAL TO	1 MONTH	3 MONTHS	6 MONTHS	12 MONTHS
0.000	0.001	NEUTRAL	NEUTRAL	NEUTRAL	NEUTRAL
0.001	0.002	NEUTRAL	NEUTRAL	SLIGHTLY BULLISH	NEUTRAL
0.002	0.003	NEUTRAL	NEUTRAL	NEUTRAL	NEUTRAL
0.003	0.004	SLIGHTLY BEARISH	VERY BEARISH	NEUTRAL	NEUTRAL
0.004	0.005	BEARISH	VERY BEARISH	SLIGHTLY BEARISH	NEUTRAL
0.005	0.006	BEARISH	SLIGHTLY BEARISH	SLIGHTLY BEARISH	BEARISH
0.006	0.007	NEUTRAL	NEUTRAL	NEUTRAL	NEUTRAL
0.007	0.008	SLIGHTLY BULLISH	NEUTRAL	NEUTRAL	NEUTRAL
0.008	0.009	NEUTRAL	NEUTRAL	NEUTRAL	BEARISH
0.009	0.010	NEUTRAL	NEUTRAL	NEUTRAL	VERY BEARISH
0.010	0.011	NEUTRAL	NEUTRAL	NEUTRAL	NEUTRAL
0.011	0.012	NEUTRAL	NEUTRAL	NEUTRAL	NEUTRAL
0.012	0.013	BULLISH	BULLISH	NEUTRAL	NEUTRAL
0.013	0.014	SLIGHTLY BULLISH	NEUTRAL	NEUTRAL	NEUTRAL
0.014	0.015	BULLISH	NEUTRAL	NEUTRAL	NEUTRAL
0.015	0.018	NEUTRAL	NEUTRAL	NEUTRAL	NEUTRAL
0.018	0.021	NEUTRAL	NEUTRAL	NEUTRAL	NEUTRAL
0.021	0.027	VERY BEARISH	NEUTRAL	NEUTRAL	NEUTRAL
0.027	0.042	NEUTRAL	NEUTRAL	NEUTRAL	VERY BULLISH
0.042	0.738	VERY BULLISH	VERY BULLISH	VERY BULLISH	VERY BULLISH

```
===========================================================================
```

Definitions of Very Bullish, Bullish, Slightly Bullish, Neutral, Slightly Bearish, Bearish, and Very Bearish are provided in Appendix A.

and therefore increase their shorting activity, it is viewed as bullish. On the other hand, a reduction in odd lot short selling activity is considered bearish for the stock market.

We tested the Odd Lot Short Ratio for the period of January 1962 to March 1987 on a daily basis. In addition, we applied a 10-period simple moving average to both the daily and weekly readings to smooth out any erratic movements. The results are shown in Exhibits O-4 and O-5 (pages 337–338).

EXHIBIT O-5:
Interpretation of Odd Lot Short Ratio's 10-Day Simple Moving Average Readings

```
===========================================================================================
ODD LOT SHORT RATIO - 10 DAY MOVING AVERAGE
PERIOD ANALYZED:  JANUARY 1962 TO MARCH 1987
===========================================================================================
```

INDICATOR RANGE		INTERPRETATION GIVEN INVESTOR'S TIME FRAME			
GREATER THAN	LESS THAN OR EQUAL TO	1 MONTH	3 MONTHS	6 MONTHS	12 MONTHS
0.000	0.003	VERY BEARISH	VERY BEARISH	VERY BEARISH	NEUTRAL
0.003	0.004	VERY BEARISH	VERY BEARISH	NEUTRAL	NEUTRAL
0.004	0.005	NEUTRAL	NEUTRAL	NEUTRAL	BULLISH
0.005	0.006	SLIGHTLY BEARISH	VERY BEARISH	VERY BEARISH	NEUTRAL
0.006	0.007	VERY BEARISH	VERY BEARISH	BEARISH	NEUTRAL
0.007	0.008	NEUTRAL	NEUTRAL	NEUTRAL	BEARISH
0.008	0.009	NEUTRAL	NEUTRAL	NEUTRAL	SLIGHTLY BEARISH
0.009	0.010	SLIGHTLY BULLISH	NEUTRAL	NEUTRAL	NEUTRAL
0.010	0.011	SLIGHTLY BULLISH	BULLISH	NEUTRAL	NEUTRAL
0.011	0.012	BULLISH	NEUTRAL	NEUTRAL	NEUTRAL
0.012	0.013	VERY BULLISH	NEUTRAL	NEUTRAL	NEUTRAL
0.013	0.014	NEUTRAL	NEUTRAL	NEUTRAL	NEUTRAL
0.014	0.015	VERY BULLISH	VERY BULLISH	SLIGHTLY BULLISH	SLIGHTLY BULLISH
0.015	0.016	BULLISH	BULLISH	BULLISH	NEUTRAL
0.016	0.017	NEUTRAL	NEUTRAL	NEUTRAL	NEUTRAL
0.017	0.018	NEUTRAL	NEUTRAL	NEUTRAL	NEUTRAL
0.018	0.022	NEUTRAL	NEUTRAL	NEUTRAL	NEUTRAL
0.022	0.029	VERY BEARISH	NEUTRAL	VERY BEARISH	NEUTRAL
0.029	0.042	NEUTRAL	BULLISH	VERY BULLISH	VERY BULLISH
0.042	0.320	VERY BULLISH	VERY BULLISH	VERY BULLISH	VERY BULLISH

```
===========================================================================================
```

Definitions of Very Bullish, Bullish, Slightly Bullish, Neutral, Slightly Bearish, Bearish, and Very Bearish are provided in Appendix A.

The test process was as follows. The indicator readings for the test period were divided into 20 ranges with approximately the same number of occurrences in each range. For each reading in a range, the gain or loss in four subsequent time periods (1 month later, 3 months later, 6 months later, and 12 months later) was calculated. The combined results for readings within each range were statistically compared, using chi-squared tests, to the performance of the overall market (as measured by the Standard & Poor's 500 Index).

EXHIBIT O-6:

Odd Lot Short Ratio's 10-Day Simple Moving Average Readings Equal to or Greater than 0.042 from 1962 to 1986

```
===============================================================
ODD LOT SHORT RATIO - 10 DAY MOVING AVERAGE
===============================================================
```

		PERCENTAGE CHANGE IN S&P 500			
DATE	INDICATOR VALUE	1 MONTH LATER	3 MONTHS LATER	6 MONTHS LATER	12 MONTHS LATER
JUN 6 1962	0.04	-3.80	-0.46	6.85	20.79
OCT 1 1962	0.06	1.89	12.98	20.45	29.21
SEP 8 1966	0.05	-3.75	7.89	16.88	24.04
MAR 7 1968	0.04	4.70	13.66	14.83	12.94
JUN 29 1970	0.04	7.07	15.05	24.97	34.44
AUG 19 1974	0.04	-9.19	-3.57	8.53	15.81
OCT 24 1985	0.04	6.91	9.51	28.54	25.34
JAN 20 1986	0.05	5.89	17.93	13.83	28.31
AVERAGE CHANGE		1.22	9.12	16.86	23.86

```
===============================================================
```

Varying degrees of bullishness and bearishness were noted on the basis of that comparison.

Our research results confirm that the common interpretation of the Odd Lot Short Ratio is correct. Low readings were bearish and high readings were bullish for stock prices. In particular, during the last 25 years when the 10-day moving average of the Odd Lot Short Ratio was .042 or greater, an average gain occurred in the overall market (as measured by the S&P 500) of 1.22% 1 month later, 9.12% 3 months later, 16.86% 6 months later, and 23.86% 12 months later. Exhibit O-6 shows the results in greater detail. You should note that all signals generated within 3 months after an initial reading of .042 or greater were considered repeat signals and are not included in the results.

ON BALANCE VOLUME

On Balance Volume (OBV) is a volume trend quantification most closely identified with Joseph E. Granville, author of *A New Strategy of Daily Stock Market Timing for Maximum Profit* (Prentice-Hall, Englewood Cliffs, NJ, 1976). Mathematically, the cumulative OBV formula is represented as:

$$\text{OBV} = \sum \left[\left(\frac{C - C_p}{|C - C_p|} \right) * V \right]$$

where

C is the current period's closing price.

C_p is the previous period's closing price.

$|C - C_p|$ is the absolute value of the difference between the two closing prices.

V is the current period's volume.

Since any positive number divided by the absolute value of itself is 1, the expression in parentheses only determines the sign, plus or minus. Thus, if the current period is an up period, with C greater than Cp, volume is assigned a plus sign for the period. But if C is less than Cp, the price has fallen and volume is assigned a minus sign for that period. Finally, a running total is maintained, respecting sign, for the cumulative OBV line. For example, if the NYSE Composite Index rises for the current period, the volume is added to the cumulative total. If the NYSE Index closes lower, the volume is subtracted.

There are several ways to analyze OBV, primarily variations of trend assessment and divergence analysis. Using Compu Trac computer software, a logical way to find an objective decision rule would be to test for the optimal simple moving average crossover rule or differential oscillator (refer to the section on Oscillators). Using our price research experience as a guide, we tested the difference between the cumulative OBV line and its own *n*-week simple moving average, with the value of *n* ranging between 1 and 100 weeks. Using weekly NYSE Composite Index price and volume data, the results of this study for our two 9.75-year test periods (1968–1977 and 1977–1986) were near our 40-week simple moving average crossover rule standard of comparison, as shown in Exhibits O-7 to O-28 (pages 341–358). Note that the 1–9-week oscillator produced maximum total profits (equity), smaller maximum equity drawdown, and better reward/risk ratios. However, the 1–66-week oscillator produced only 22% as many trades, 4.18 times the profit per trade, and higher total profits in the more recent 9.75 years. Neither version, however, appears to offer any advantage over simpler moving average price crossover models.

Using Back Trak computer software to find an objective decision rule, we calculated an *n*-period point-to-point differential momentum or rate of change of the cumulative OBV line. Expressed in a mathematically equivalent way, we calculated an *n*-period moving total or moving average of the OBV for each period, then bought when the moving total or average rose following a previous decline, and we sold and sold short when the moving total or average

EXHIBIT O-7:

Profitability Chart for On Balance Volume 1–n Differential Oscillator, (Period Lengths of 1 to 100 Weeks from 1977 to 1986)

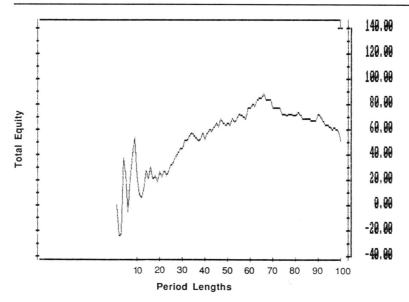

fell following a previous advance. Using weekly closing and volume data for the NYSE Composite Index from January 1968 through December 1986 and testing periods from 1 to 100 weeks showed best results for 24 weeks, as shown in Exhibit O-29 (page 359). At total profits of 104.85 NYSE points, this OBV rate of change produced better results than the OBV oscillators but it still was not as good as price-based moving average crossover rules.

EXHIBIT O-8:
Profit Table for On Balance Volume 1–n Differential Oscillator, (Period Lengths of 1 to 100 Weeks from 1977 to 1986)

Pass	Total Equity	Short Equity	Long Equity	Max. Equity	Min. Equity	P/L	Best Trade	Worst Trade	Max. Open P/L	Min. Open P/L
1	0.00	0.00	0.00	0.00	0.00	0.00	N/A	N/A	0.00	0.00
2	-23.20	-53.42	30.22	0.00	-41.20	-23.20	14.67	-5.79	15.36	0.00
3	-22.31	-53.60	31.29	0.03	-40.31	-22.31	14.67	-5.79	15.36	-0.77
4	37.34	-23.79	61.13	37.48	-30.72	34.82	16.05	-5.43	17.18	-2.73
5	25.61	-29.33	54.94	32.90	-23.08	23.09	16.05	-5.43	17.18	-3.16
6	-4.47	-44.46	39.99	27.80	-10.24	-4.47	14.67	-5.40	17.18	-1.38
7	20.72	-31.73	52.45	47.83	-7.13	20.72	14.74	-5.33	17.18	-2.87
8	39.82	-23.04	62.86	66.93	-8.16	39.82	14.74	-5.33	17.18	-2.87
9	53.42	-15.90	69.32	70.65	-6.02	53.42	28.83	-5.60	33.31	-3.55
10	23.80	-30.49	54.29	41.03	-10.62	23.80	28.83	-5.60	33.31	-3.88
11	8.30	-37.82	46.12	25.53	-24.95	3.21	27.24	-5.60	31.72	-3.88
12	5.86	-38.65	44.51	20.85	-33.11	0.77	27.24	-6.07	31.72	-3.88
13	12.54	-35.56	48.10	27.53	-29.57	7.45	27.24	-6.07	31.72	-3.88
14	27.77	-28.00	55.77	39.30	-21.40	22.68	26.29	-6.07	31.72	-3.59
15	20.71	-31.44	52.15	30.88	-30.36	21.01	29.80	-5.60	31.72	-6.07
16	29.71	-26.58	56.29	36.45	-33.64	-0.72	32.24	-6.41	37.17	-3.99
17	21.46	-31.50	52.96	28.20	-36.19	-8.97	32.24	-6.70	37.17	-4.85
18	23.32	-30.61	53.93	30.06	-35.11	-7.11	30.63	-6.40	37.17	-3.98
19	19.17	-32.90	52.07	25.91	-31.22	-11.26	30.63	-6.70	37.17	-4.85
20	26.72	-29.24	55.96	33.46	-23.67	-3.71	30.63	-6.70	37.17	-4.85
21	22.22	-31.88	54.10	28.96	-17.57	-8.21	30.63	-6.70	37.17	-4.85
22	27.19	-29.03	56.22	33.93	-16.62	-3.24	30.63	-6.70	37.17	-4.85
23	23.90	-30.97	54.87	30.64	-21.89	-8.12	30.63	-6.70	38.76	-4.85
24	26.97	-29.41	56.38	33.71	-17.02	-5.05	30.63	-6.70	38.76	-4.85
25	32.99	-26.76	59.75	39.73	-18.44	0.97	29.62	-6.70	38.76	-4.85
26	33.53	-26.12	59.65	40.27	-21.82	1.51	29.62	-5.60	38.76	-3.88
27	38.45	-23.77	62.22	45.19	-21.84	5.82	28.95	-5.60	39.37	-3.88
28	40.76	-23.29	64.05	47.50	-19.53	8.13	28.95	-5.60	39.37	-3.88
29	44.43	-21.77	66.20	51.17	-18.02	11.80	28.95	-7.88	39.37	-5.60
30	44.97	-21.42	66.39	51.71	-17.86	12.34	28.95	-7.88	39.37	-5.60
31	51.73	-18.29	70.02	58.47	-18.78	19.10	28.95	-10.19	39.37	-7.88
32	51.76	-17.06	68.82	58.50	-16.77	7.97	31.09	-10.19	50.53	-7.88
33	55.29	-15.39	70.68	62.03	-13.24	11.50	31.09	-10.19	50.53	-7.88
34	57.57	-13.84	71.41	64.31	-10.96	13.78	31.09	-10.19	50.53	-7.88
35	55.42	-15.41	70.83	62.16	-13.11	11.63	31.09	-10.19	50.53	-7.88
36	53.42	-16.72	70.14	60.16	-15.11	9.63	31.09	-10.19	50.53	-7.88
37	50.97	-18.00	68.97	57.71	-13.92	7.18	31.09	-10.19	50.53	-7.88
38	52.40	-16.96	69.36	59.14	-12.49	8.61	31.09	-10.19	50.53	-7.88
39	57.98	-14.05	72.03	64.72	-4.15	14.19	29.63	-10.19	50.53	-7.88
40	53.06	-17.44	70.50	59.80	-6.33	9.27	27.05	-10.19	50.53	-7.88
41	57.03	-15.99	73.02	63.77	-2.37	13.24	27.05	-10.19	50.53	-7.88
42	59.97	-14.44	74.41	66.71	-2.21	16.18	27.05	-10.19	50.53	-7.88
43	59.30	-15.11	74.41	66.04	-2.88	15.51	27.05	-10.19	50.53	-7.88
44	63.06	-12.90	75.96	69.80	-2.22	19.27	27.05	-5.72	50.53	-3.43
45	64.67	-11.95	76.62	71.41	-1.93	20.88	27.05	-5.72	50.53	-3.43
46	62.54	-13.57	76.11	69.28	-3.04	18.75	26.54	-5.72	50.53	-3.94
47	69.35	-10.02	79.37	76.09	-2.75	25.56	26.54	-5.72	50.53	-3.94
48	64.73	-12.59	77.32	71.47	-3.27	23.01	26.54	-5.72	48.46	-3.34
49	63.76	-12.67	76.43	70.50	-2.46	22.04	26.54	-5.72	48.46	-3.34
50	64.53	-11.90	76.43	71.27	-1.69	22.81	26.54	-5.72	48.46	-3.34
51	64.14	-12.29	76.43	70.88	-2.08	22.42	26.54	-5.72	48.46	-3.34
52	68.23	-10.25	78.48	74.97	-2.09	26.51	28.23	-5.72	48.46	-3.34
53	66.69	-10.74	77.43	73.43	-1.53	24.97	28.23	-5.72	48.46	-3.34
54	68.22	-9.21	77.43	74.96	0.00	26.50	28.23	-5.72	48.46	-3.34
55	71.93	-7.00	78.93	78.67	-0.13	29.86	28.43	-3.90	48.81	-2.99
56	70.68	-7.00	77.68	77.42	-1.38	28.61	28.43	-3.90	48.81	-2.99

Pass	Total Equity	Short Equity	Long Equity	Max. Equity	Min. Equity	P/L	Best Trade	Worst Trade	Max. Open P/L	Min. Open P/L
57	70.61	-7.00	77.61	77.35	-1.45	28.54	28.43	-3.90	48.81	-2.99
58	69.21	-7.26	76.47	75.95	-2.33	27.14	28.17	-3.90	48.81	-2.99
59	76.91	-3.36	80.27	83.65	-2.43	34.84	28.17	-2.31	48.81	-2.99
60	77.72	-3.36	81.08	84.46	-1.62	35.65	28.17	-2.31	48.81	-2.99
61	79.65	-1.95	81.60	86.39	-2.51	34.99	28.17	-2.99	51.40	-2.51
62	78.60	-1.95	80.55	85.34	-3.56	33.94	28.17	-2.99	51.40	-3.56
63	83.88	0.05	83.83	90.62	-2.28	39.22	28.17	-2.99	51.40	-2.28
64	84.78	0.05	84.73	91.52	-1.38	40.12	28.17	-2.99	51.40	-2.21
65	85.02	0.05	84.97	91.76	-1.14	40.36	28.17	-2.99	51.40	-2.21
66	88.38	1.57	86.81	95.12	-0.82	43.72	28.17	-2.99	51.40	-2.21
67	83.82	0.03	83.79	90.56	-2.30	39.16	26.63	-2.99	51.40	-2.30
68	83.73	0.03	83.70	90.47	-2.39	39.07	26.63	-2.99	51.40	-2.39
69	84.04	0.82	83.22	90.78	-3.66	39.38	26.63	-3.21	51.40	-3.66
70	77.98	-1.13	79.11	84.72	-5.82	33.32	26.63	-3.21	51.40	-5.82
71	77.79	-1.13	78.92	84.53	-6.01	33.13	26.63	-3.21	51.40	-6.01
72	77.26	-1.13	78.39	84.00	-6.54	32.60	26.63	-3.21	51.40	-6.54
73	77.10	-1.13	78.23	83.84	-6.70	32.44	26.63	-3.21	51.40	-6.70
74	72.26	-3.89	76.15	79.00	-6.02	27.60	26.63	-2.58	51.40	-6.02
75	72.74	-2.80	75.54	79.48	-7.72	28.08	27.54	-2.03	51.40	-7.72
76	70.89	-4.44	75.33	77.63	-6.29	27.87	27.54	-2.03	49.76	-6.29
77	72.33	-4.44	76.77	79.07	-4.85	29.31	27.54	-2.03	49.76	-4.85
78	71.92	-4.44	76.36	78.66	-5.26	28.90	27.54	-2.03	49.76	-5.26
79	71.36	-4.44	75.80	78.10	-5.82	28.34	27.54	-2.03	49.76	-5.82
80	70.77	-4.44	75.21	77.51	-6.41	27.75	27.54	-2.03	49.76	-6.41
81	73.68	-5.07	78.75	80.42	-2.24	30.66	27.54	-2.03	49.76	-2.61
82	72.72	-6.67	79.39	79.46	0.00	29.70	27.54	-2.61	49.76	-2.28
83	68.17	-8.46	76.63	74.91	-0.95	25.15	25.75	-3.75	49.76	-4.07
84	68.94	-8.46	77.40	75.68	-0.18	25.92	25.75	-3.75	49.76	-4.07
85	69.12	-8.46	77.58	75.86	0.00	26.10	25.75	-3.75	49.76	-4.07
86	68.22	-8.46	76.68	74.96	-0.13	25.20	25.75	-3.75	49.76	-4.07
87	67.89	-8.46	76.35	74.63	-0.46	24.87	25.75	-3.75	49.76	-4.07
88	67.22	-8.65	75.87	73.96	-0.75	24.20	25.75	-4.98	49.76	-5.30
89	67.97	-8.65	76.62	74.71	0.00	24.95	25.75	-4.98	49.76	-5.30
90	72.73	-6.04	78.77	79.47	-0.15	29.71	25.75	-4.98	49.76	-5.30
91	69.48	-7.74	77.22	76.22	0.00	26.46	25.75	-4.98	49.76	-5.30
92	67.69	-7.74	75.43	74.43	-1.04	24.67	25.75	-4.98	49.76	-5.30
93	63.85	-8.91	72.76	70.59	-2.54	20.83	25.75	-4.98	49.76	-5.30
94	63.61	-9.56	73.17	70.35	-1.48	20.59	25.75	-4.98	49.76	-5.30
95	62.47	-9.56	72.03	69.21	-2.62	19.45	25.75	-4.98	49.76	-5.30
96	59.95	-11.42	71.37	66.69	-1.42	16.93	22.84	-4.98	49.76	-5.30
97	60.87	-11.42	72.29	67.61	-0.50	17.85	22.84	-4.98	49.76	-5.30
98	60.37	-11.42	71.79	67.11	-1.00	17.35	22.84	-4.98	49.76	-5.30
99	58.50	-12.60	71.10	65.24	-0.51	15.48	22.84	-5.50	49.76	-5.82
100	50.79	-16.71	67.50	57.53	0.00	7.77	22.84	-5.50	49.76	-5.82

Pass indicates period length.

Equity indicates the total number of points gained or lost.

Short equity indicates the number of points gained or lost on short positions.

Long equity indicates the number of points gained or lost on long positions.

Max. equity indicates the highest total profit recorded over the tested period.

Min. equity indicates the lowest total profit recorded over the tested period.

P/L indicates total number of points gained or lost in closed positions.

Best trade indicates the highest number of points gained in any closed trade.

Worst trade indicates the highest number of points lost in any closed trade.

Max. open P/L indicates the highest gain in a position which remains open at the end of the test run.

Min. open P/L indicates the highest loss in a position which remains open at the end of the test run.

EXHIBIT O-9:

Profitability Chart for On Balance Volume 1–n Differential Oscillator, (Period Lengths of 1 to 100 Weeks from 1968 to 1977)

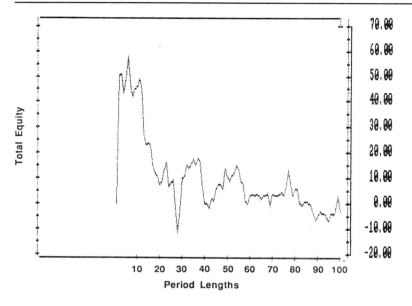

EXHIBIT O-10:

Profit Table for On Balance Volume 1−n Differential Oscillator, (Period Lengths of 1 to 100 Weeks from 1968 to 1977)

Pass	Total Equity	Short Equity	Long Equity	Max. Equity	Min. Equity	P/L	Best Trade	Worst Trade	Max. Open P/L	Min. Open P/L
1	0.00	0.00	0.00	0.00	0.00	0.00	N/A	N/A	0.00	0.00
2	50.52	25.94	24.58	72.18	-0.67	50.52	9.51	-3.24	10.26	0.00
3	51.19	25.94	25.25	72.85	0.00	51.19	9.51	-3.24	10.26	0.00
4	43.40	21.52	21.88	58.30	0.00	43.40	9.29	-3.24	10.26	-1.28
5	49.24	24.05	25.19	64.62	0.00	49.24	9.29	-3.24	9.82	-1.57
6	58.21	27.81	30.40	76.01	-0.46	58.21	14.71	-2.91	15.35	-1.79
7	46.46	21.93	24.53	63.54	-0.47	46.46	14.71	-2.91	15.35	-1.79
8	41.93	19.90	22.03	60.47	0.00	41.93	12.51	-3.19	15.35	-2.07
9	45.21	20.99	24.22	60.25	-2.21	43.98	12.51	-3.19	15.35	-2.32
10	45.84	21.23	24.61	59.46	-2.36	44.61	12.51	-3.45	15.35	-2.33
11	49.52	23.09	26.43	61.72	-2.32	48.29	12.51	-3.55	15.35	-3.45
12	45.30	20.77	24.53	59.82	-2.74	44.50	12.51	-3.55	16.65	-3.45
13	26.62	11.93	14.69	41.14	-1.74	25.82	11.74	-2.76	16.65	-1.73
14	23.06	11.02	12.04	37.42	0.00	22.26	11.74	-2.76	16.65	-2.08
15	23.61	12.20	11.41	34.58	-0.21	22.81	11.74	-2.76	15.35	-2.08
16	22.72	11.65	11.07	34.03	0.00	21.92	11.74	-2.76	15.35	-2.08
17	14.75	8.10	6.65	24.98	0.00	13.95	10.56	-2.76	15.35	-1.73
18	11.93	7.09	4.84	20.10	-2.27	11.13	10.56	-2.76	15.35	-1.45
19	10.73	6.53	4.20	21.50	-3.66	9.93	10.56	-2.76	15.39	-1.82
20	7.77	4.67	3.10	21.56	-4.92	6.97	9.49	-3.04	15.39	-1.82
21	8.96	5.39	3.57	23.49	-4.91	8.39	9.49	-3.39	15.39	-2.14
22	12.99	7.84	5.15	24.99	-4.82	12.42	11.32	-3.45	15.39	-2.76
23	16.16	10.23	5.93	26.73	-6.17	15.59	11.32	-4.64	15.39	-2.76
24	6.85	5.53	1.32	18.45	-9.48	6.28	10.20	-4.64	15.39	-3.45
25	8.00	5.98	2.02	21.46	-9.07	7.43	10.15	-4.64	15.39	-2.32
26	9.11	6.19	2.92	23.33	-6.66	8.54	10.15	-4.64	15.39	-2.32
27	-1.67	1.20	-2.87	14.94	-9.14	-2.24	10.15	-4.64	15.08	-2.70
28	-11.42	-3.29	-8.13	10.59	-20.47	-11.99	10.63	-4.64	15.08	-3.47
29	-2.63	0.55	-3.18	16.96	-14.04	-3.20	10.63	-4.64	15.08	-2.36
30	10.23	6.29	3.94	21.33	-6.82	9.66	15.43	-4.64	17.52	-2.32
31	10.91	6.14	4.77	21.91	-6.24	10.11	15.43	-4.64	17.52	-2.32
32	14.81	8.23	6.58	25.41	-3.77	14.01	15.43	-4.64	17.52	-2.32
33	13.86	8.20	5.66	23.75	-5.59	13.06	16.88	-4.64	18.71	-2.32
34	15.56	9.07	6.49	25.45	-3.89	14.76	16.88	-4.64	18.71	-2.32
35	17.25	9.94	7.31	27.14	-3.40	16.45	16.88	-4.64	18.71	-2.91
36	14.90	9.36	5.54	24.79	-5.28	14.10	16.88	-4.64	18.71	-2.91
37	17.49	10.59	6.90	25.50	-5.53	16.69	16.07	-4.64	19.67	-3.17
38	16.48	10.35	6.13	26.05	-2.70	15.68	14.85	-4.64	18.45	-3.17
39	6.26	5.46	0.80	15.83	-12.03	5.46	14.85	-4.64	18.45	-3.17
40	0.22	2.82	-2.60	8.93	-16.97	-1.01	14.58	-4.64	18.18	-3.17
41	0.03	2.60	-2.57	8.74	-17.16	-1.20	14.58	-5.42	18.18	-3.91
42	-1.64	2.23	-3.87	6.85	-19.05	-2.87	14.58	-5.42	18.18	-3.91
43	2.08	3.95	-1.87	10.57	-15.33	0.85	14.58	-5.42	18.18	-3.91
44	1.22	3.18	-1.96	9.71	-16.19	-0.01	14.58	-5.42	18.18	-3.91
45	5.60	5.63	-0.03	11.15	-14.75	4.37	15.10	-5.19	18.18	-3.91
46	7.30	7.07	0.23	14.29	-11.61	6.07	15.10	-5.19	18.18	-3.91
47	7.40	7.34	0.06	14.39	-11.51	6.17	15.10	-5.19	18.18	-3.91
48	5.78	7.12	-1.34	14.45	-11.45	4.55	14.26	-7.62	18.18	-6.34
49	13.48	10.85	2.63	20.71	-9.37	12.25	14.26	-7.38	18.18	-6.10
50	10.53	9.34	1.19	17.76	-9.30	9.30	14.26	-7.31	18.18	-6.03
51	8.51	8.00	0.51	15.74	-10.16	7.28	14.26	-6.65	18.18	-5.37
52	11.55	9.08	2.47	16.52	-9.38	10.32	14.26	-6.84	18.18	-6.37
53	11.68	8.91	2.77	16.15	-11.17	10.45	14.26	-6.37	18.18	-5.90
54	15.17	9.75	5.42	19.48	-7.84	13.86	14.26	-4.56	18.18	-4.09
55	12.85	8.90	3.95	17.16	-9.04	11.54	15.45	-5.18	16.97	-4.71
56	8.99	7.14	1.85	13.30	-12.90	7.68	15.45	-7.28	16.97	

Pass	Total Equity	Short Equity	Long Equity	Max. Equity	Min. Equity	P/L	Best Trade	Worst Trade	Max. Open P/L	Min. Open P/L
57	7.71	6.64	1.07	12.02	-14.18	6.40	15.45	-7.56	16.97	-5.80
58	0.93	3.38	-2.45	5.24	-20.54	-0.38	15.24	-7.82	16.97	-6.06
59	0.23	3.03	-2.80	4.54	-21.24	-1.08	15.24	-7.82	16.97	-6.06
60	2.92	3.21	-0.29	10.35	-16.44	1.61	15.24	-5.49	16.97	-3.73
61	4.04	3.21	0.83	11.47	-15.32	2.73	15.24	-4.44	16.97	-3.16
62	3.36	2.94	0.42	10.79	-16.00	2.05	15.24	-4.51	16.97	-3.16
63	3.76	2.94	0.82	11.19	-15.60	2.45	15.24	-4.44	16.97	-3.16
64	3.04	3.05	-0.01	10.47	-16.32	1.73	15.24	-5.05	16.97	-3.29
65	2.06	3.05	-0.99	9.49	-17.30	0.75	15.24	-6.03	16.97	-4.27
66	3.33	3.44	-0.11	10.76	-16.03	2.02	15.24	-5.54	16.97	-3.78
67	2.87	3.44	-0.57	10.30	-16.49	1.56	15.24	-6.00	16.97	-4.24
68	4.51	4.13	0.38	11.18	-13.53	3.20	14.58	-5.74	16.97	-3.98
69	-0.97	1.53	-2.50	8.13	-19.01	-2.28	14.58	-6.02	16.97	-4.26
70	3.52	4.44	-0.92	8.40	-16.63	2.21	14.58	-7.51	16.97	-7.35
71	3.37	4.66	-1.29	7.81	-16.78	2.06	14.58	-8.10	16.97	-7.94
72	2.85	4.60	-1.75	7.41	-17.30	1.54	14.58	-8.50	16.97	-8.34
73	3.53	4.60	-1.07	8.09	-16.62	2.22	14.58	-7.82	16.97	-7.66
74	4.14	4.60	-0.46	8.70	-16.01	2.83	14.58	-7.21	16.97	-7.05
75	2.85	3.56	-0.71	9.49	-17.30	1.54	14.58	-6.42	16.97	-6.26
76	5.99	4.09	1.90	12.63	-14.16	4.68	14.58	-4.44	16.97	-4.18
77	13.04	6.94	6.10	17.35	-7.11	11.73	14.58	-4.44	16.97	-3.16
78	7.35	4.21	3.14	13.75	-12.80	6.04	14.58	-4.44	16.97	-3.16
79	3.34	2.87	0.47	12.42	-16.81	2.03	14.58	-4.55	16.97	-4.39
80	5.44	2.84	2.60	14.58	-14.65	4.13	14.55	-4.44	16.97	-3.16
81	5.91	2.84	3.07	15.05	-14.18	4.60	14.55	-4.44	16.97	-3.16
82	0.25	-0.87	1.12	12.53	-19.84	-1.06	14.55	-4.44	16.97	-3.16
83	-0.55	-0.87	0.32	11.73	-20.64	-1.86	14.55	-4.44	16.97	-3.16
84	0.61	-0.15	0.76	12.89	-19.48	-0.70	14.55	-4.44	16.97	-3.16
85	0.53	-0.15	0.68	12.81	-19.56	-0.78	14.55	-4.44	16.97	-3.16
86	0.08	0.19	-0.11	12.36	-20.01	-1.23	14.55	-5.57	16.97	-3.18
87	-0.87	-0.37	-0.50	12.53	-20.96	-2.18	14.55	-5.40	16.97	-3.16
88	-3.93	-2.47	-1.46	13.67	-24.02	-5.24	14.55	-4.44	16.97	-3.16
89	-6.34	-3.48	-2.86	13.28	-26.27	-7.57	14.55	-4.65	16.97	-3.16
90	-5.13	-2.55	-2.58	12.63	-26.28	-6.36	14.55	-5.30	16.97	-3.16
91	-2.96	-1.77	-1.19	13.24	-25.67	-4.19	14.55	-4.69	16.97	-3.16
92	-3.56	-2.30	-1.26	12.64	-26.27	-4.79	14.55	-4.44	16.97	-3.16
93	-3.77	-2.30	-1.47	12.43	-26.48	-5.00	14.55	-4.44	16.97	-3.16
94	-5.51	-2.30	-3.21	10.69	-28.22	-6.74	14.55	-6.18	16.97	-3.79
95	-6.68	-2.30	-4.38	9.52	-29.39	-7.91	14.55	-7.35	16.97	-4.96
96	-3.60	-0.98	-2.62	9.96	-24.53	-4.83	13.66	-6.91	16.97	-4.52
97	-4.22	-0.98	-3.24	9.34	-25.15	-5.45	13.66	-7.53	16.97	-5.14
98	-2.32	-0.40	-1.92	12.54	-22.07	-3.55	13.66	-5.47	16.97	-6.79
99	3.07	1.47	1.60	14.19	-16.68	1.84	13.66	-4.44	16.97	-5.14
100	-3.36	-1.84	-1.52	11.24	-22.59	-4.59	13.66	-5.20	16.97	-4.95

Pass indicates period length.

Equity indicates the total number of points gained or lost.

Short equity indicates the number of points gained or lost on short positions.

Long equity indicates the number of points gained or lost on long positions.

Max. equity indicates the highest total profit recorded over the tested period.

Min. equity indicates the lowest total profit recorded over the tested period.

P/L indicates total number of points gained or lost in closed positions.

Best trade indicates the highest number of points gained in any closed trade.

Worst trade indicates the highest number of points lost in any closed trade.

Max. open P/L indicates the highest gain in a position which remains open at the end of the test run.

Min. open P/L indicates the highest loss in a position which remains open at the end of the test run.

EXHIBIT O-11:

New York Stock Exchange Composite Price Index Weekly High and Low from April 8, 1977 to December 31, 1986

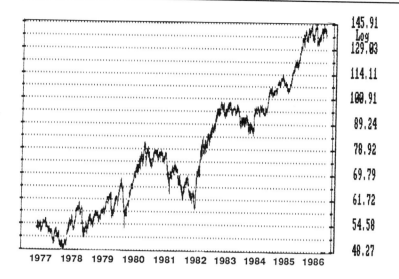

EXHIBIT O-12:

On Balance Volume Cumulative Line, 1977 to 1986

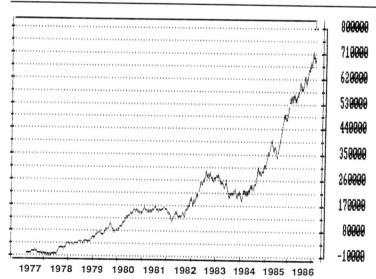

EXHIBIT O-13:
On Balance Volume 1–66-Week Simple Moving Average Differential Oscillator, 1977 to 1986

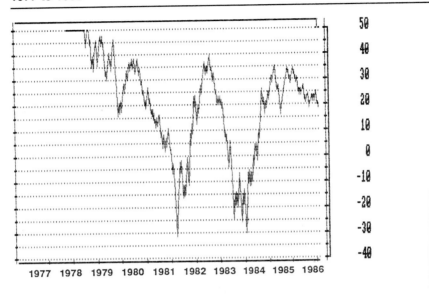

EXHIBIT O-14:
Total Equity for On Balance Volume 1–66-Week Simple Moving Average Differential Oscillator, 1977 to 1986

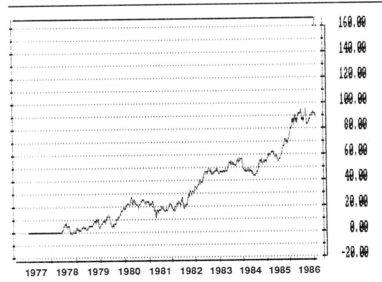

EXHIBIT O-15:

Profit Summary for On Balance Volume 1–66-Week Simple Moving Average Differential Oscillator, 1977 to 1986

Item		Long	Short	Net
Per Trade Ranges				
Best Trade	(Closed position yielding maximum P/L)	28.17	2.13	28.17
.. Date		831209	820827	831209
Worst Trade	(Closed position yielding minimum P/L)	-2.99	-0.40	-2.99
.. Date		841207	841214	841207
Max Open P/L	(Maximum P/L occurring in an open position)	51.40	9.96	51.40
.. Date		860829	840615	860829
Min Open P/L	(Minimum P/L occurring in an open position)	-2.21	-0.92	-2.21
.. Date		841130	840914	841130
Overall Ranges				
Max P/L	(Maximum P/L from all closed positions during the run)	47.49	47.11	47.49
.. Date		840120	841102	840120
Min P/L	(Minimum P/L from all closed positions during the run)	16.02	18.15	16.02
.. Date		820108	820827	820108
Max Equity	(Maximum P/L from all closed and open positions)	95.12	57.45	95.12
.. Date		860829	840615	860829
Min Equity	(Minimum P/L from all closed and open positions)	-0.82	15.99	-0.82
.. Date		781027	820129	781027
Statistics				
Periods	(The number of periods in each position and entire run)	431	78	509
Trades	(The number of trades in each position and entire run)	4	4	8
# Profitable	(The number of profitable trades...)	3	2	5
# Losing	(The number of unprofitable trades...)	1	2	3
% Profitable	(The percent of profitable trades to total trades)	75.00	50.00	62.50
% Losing	(The percent of unprofitable trades to total trades)	25.00	50.00	37.50
Results				
Commission	(Total commission deducted from closed trades)	0.00	0.00	0.00
Slippage	(Total slippage deducted from closed trades)	0.00	0.00	0.00
Gross P/L	(Total points gained in closed positions)	42.15	1.57	43.72
Open P/L	(P/L in a position which remains open at the end)	44.66	0.00	44.66
P/L	(Net P/L: Gross P/L less Commission and Slippage)	42.15	1.57	43.72
Equity	(Net P/L plus Open P/L at the end of the run)	86.81	1.57	88.38

There are columns for Long trades, Short trades and Net. In the Long column, results are reported only for Long positions. In the Short column, results are reported for Short positions only. In the Net column for the "Per Trade Ranges" and "Overall Ranges," entries will be the extreme from either the Long or Short column. Net column entries for the "Statistics" and "Results" categories are the combined results of entries in the Long and Short columns.

EXHIBIT O-16:

New York Stock Exchange Composite Price Index Weekly High and Low from January 5, 1968 to September 30, 1977

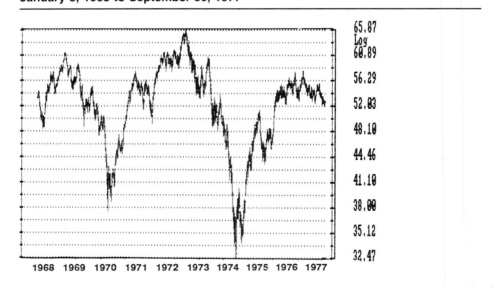

EXHIBIT O-17:

On Balance Volume Cumulative Line, 1968 to 1977

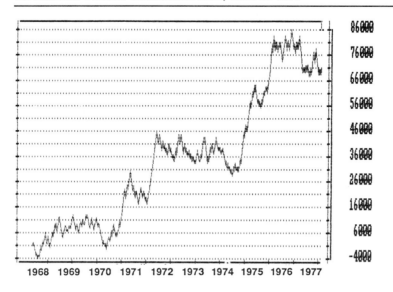

EXHIBIT O-18:

On Balance Volume 1–66-Week Simple Moving Average Differential Oscillator, 1968 to 1977

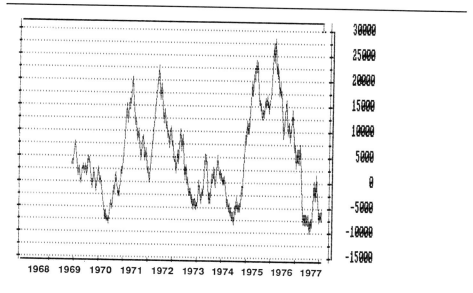

EXHIBIT O-19:

Total Equity for On Balance Volume 1–66-Week Simple Moving Average Differential Oscillator, 1968 to 1977

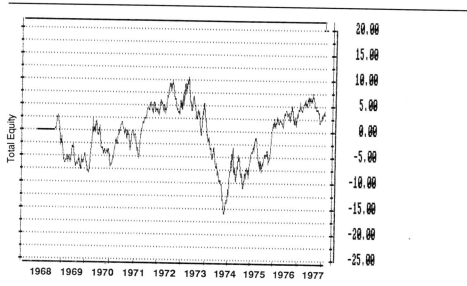

EXHIBIT O-20:

Profit Summary for On Balance Volume 1–66-Week Simple Moving Average Differential Oscillator, 1968 to 1977

Item		Long	Short	Net
		-- Per Trade Ranges --		
Per Trade Ranges				
Best Trade	(Closed position yielding maximum P/L)	15.24	4.96	15.24
.. Date		770121	750131	770121
Worst Trade	(Closed position yielding minimum P/L)	-5.54	-2.79	-5.54
.. Date		690725	740607	690725
Max Open P/L	(Maximum P/L occurring in an open position)	16.97	12.97	16.97
.. Date		761231	741004	761231
Min Open P/L	(Minimum P/L occurring in an open position)	-3.78	-0.94	-3.78
.. Date		690718	730921	690718
		--- Overall Ranges ---		
Overall Ranges				
Max P/L	(Maximum P/L from all closed positions during the run)	4.49	5.76	5.76
.. Date		730302	730727	730727
Min P/L	(Minimum P/L from all closed positions during the run)	-16.03	-13.19	-16.03
.. Date		740621	740607	740621
Max Equity	(Maximum P/L from all closed and open positions)	9.69	10.76	10.76
.. Date		730105	730706	730706
Min Equity	(Minimum P/L from all closed and open positions)	-16.03	-16.03	-16.03
.. Date		740621	740621	740621
		----- Statistics -----		
Statistics				
Periods	(The number of periods in each position and entire run)	364	145	509
Trades	(The number of trades in each position and entire run)	18	17	35
# Profitable	(The number of profitable trades...)	3	7	10
# Losing	(The number of unprofitable trades...)	15	10	25
% Profitable	(The percent of profitable trades to total trades)	16.67	41.18	28.57
% Losing	(The percent of unprofitable trades to total trades)	83.33	58.82	71.43
		----- Results -----		
Results				
Commission	(Total commission deducted from closed trades)	0.00	0.00	0.00
Slippage	(Total slippage deducted from closed trades)	0.00	0.00	0.00
Gross P/L	(Total points gained in closed positions)	-0.11	2.13	2.02
Open P/L	(P/L in a position which remains open at the end)	0.00	1.31	1.31
P/L	(Net P/L: Gross P/L less Commission and Slippage)	-0.11	2.13	2.02
Equity	(Net P/L plus Open P/L at the end of the run)	-0.11	3.44	3.33

There are columns for Long trades, Short trades and Net. In the Long column, results are reported only for Long positions. In the Short column, results are reported for Short positions only. In the Net column for the "Per Trade Ranges" and "Overall Ranges," entries will be the extreme from either the Long or Short column. Net column entries for the "Statistics" and "Results" categories are the combined results of entries in the Long and Short columns.

EXHIBIT O-21:

New York Stock Exchange Composite Price Index Weekly High and Low from April 8, 1977 to December 31, 1986

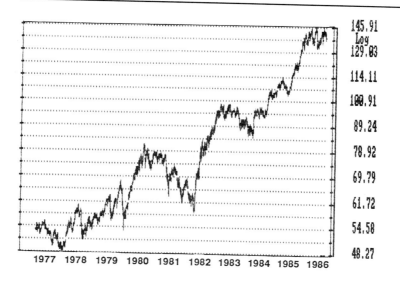

EXHIBIT O-22:

On Balance Volume 1–9-Week Simple Moving Average Differential Oscillator, 1977 to 1986

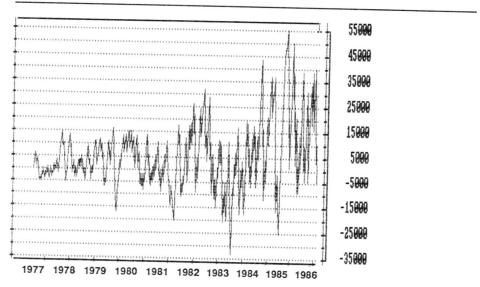

EXHIBIT O-23

Total Equity for 1–9-Week Simple Moving Average Differential Oscillator, 1977 to 1986

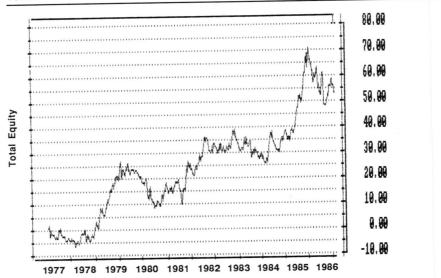

EXHIBIT O-24

Profit Summary for 1-9-Week Simple Moving Average Differential Oscillator, 1977 to 1986

Item		Long	Short	Net
		-- Per Trade Ranges --		
Per Trade Ranges				
Best Trade	(Closed position yielding maximum P/L)	28.83	4.90	28.83
.. Date		860502	800502	860502
Worst Trade	(Closed position yielding minimum P/L)	-5.60	-5.11	-5.60
.. Date		810904	820820	810904
Max Open P/L	(Maximum P/L occurring in an open position)	33.31	8.59	33.31
.. Date		860418	820312	860418
Min Open P/L	(Minimum P/L occurring in an open position)	-3.18	-3.55	-3.55
.. Date		810828	830617	830617
		---- Overall Ranges ----		
Overall Ranges				
Max P/L	(Maximum P/L from all closed positions during the run)	66.17	64.44	66.17
.. Date		860502	860509	860502
Min P/L	(Minimum P/L from all closed positions during the run)	-4.63	-6.02	-6.02
.. Date		790601	790608	790608
Max Equity	(Maximum P/L from all closed and open positions)	70.65	66.17	70.65
.. Date		860418	860502	860418
Min Equity	(Minimum P/L from all closed and open positions)	-6.02	-6.02	-6.02
.. Date		790608	790608	790608
		----- Statistics -----		
Statistics				
Periods	(The number of periods in each position and entire run)	339	170	509
Trades	(The number of trades in each position and entire run)	47	46	93
# Profitable	(The number of profitable trades. . .)	22	13	35
# Losing	(The number of unprofitable trades. . .)	25	33	58
% Profitable	(The percent of profitable trades to total trades)	46.81	28.26	37.63
% Losing	(The percent of unprofitable trades to total trades)	53.19	71.74	62.37
		----- Results -----		
Results				
Commission	(Total commission deducted from closed trades)	0.00	0.00	0.00
Slippage	(Total slippage deducted from closed trades)	0.00	0.00	0.00
Gross P/L	(Total points gained in closed positions)	69.32	-15.90	53.42
Open P/L	(P/L in a position which remains open at the end)	0.00	0.00	0.00
P/L	(Net P/L: Gross P/L less Commission and Slippage)	69.32	-15.90	53.42
Equity	(Net P/L plus Open P/L at the end of the run)	69.32	-15.90	53.42

There are columns for Long trades, Short trades and Net. In the Long column, results are reported only for Long positions. In the Short column, results are reported for Short positions only. In the Net column for the "Per Trade Ranges" and "Overall Ranges," entries will be the extreme from either the Long or Short column. Net column entries for the "Statistics" and "Results" categories are the combined results of entries in the Long and Short columns.

355

EXHIBIT O-25:

New York Stock Exchange Composite Price Index Weekly High and Low from January 5, 1968 to September 30, 1977

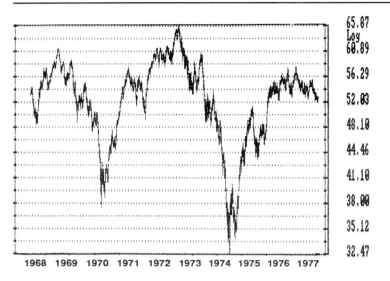

EXHIBIT O-26:

On Balance Volume 1–9-Week Simple Moving Average Differential Oscillator, 1968 to 1977

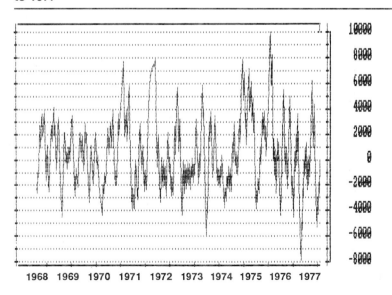

EXHIBIT O-27:

Total Equity for On Balance Volume 1–9-Week Simple Moving Average Differential Oscillator, 1968 to 1977

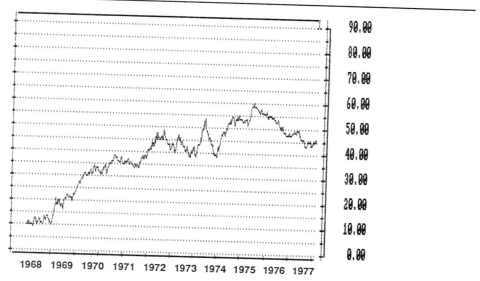

EXHIBIT O-28:
Profit Summary for On Balance Volume 1–9-Week Simple Moving Average Differential Oscillator, 1968 to 1977

Item	Long	Short	Net
	-- Per Trade Ranges --		
Per Trade Ranges			
Best Trade (Closed position yielding maximum P/L)	12.51	9.90	12.51
. . Date	750725	741018	750725
Worst Trade (Closed position yielding minimum P/L)	-3.19	-2.21	-3.19
. . Date	690228	680405	690228
Max Open P/L (Maximum P/L occurring in an open position)	15.35	15.08	15.35
. . Date	750711	741004	750711
Min Open P/L (Minimum P/L occurring in an open position)	-2.32	-1.67	-2.32
. . Date	740208	740222	740208
	-- Overall Ranges --		
Overall Ranges			
Max P/L (Maximum P/L from all closed positions during the run)	58.69	57.83	58.69
. . Date	760305	760312	760305
Min P/L (Minimum P/L from all closed positions during the run)	0.78	-2.21	-2.21
. . Date	680719	680405	680405
Max Equity (Maximum P/L from all closed and open positions)	60.25	58.69	60.25
. . Date	760220	760305	760220
Min Equity (Minimum P/L from all closed and open positions)	-2.21	-2.21	-2.21
. . Date	680405	680405	680405
	-- Statistics --		
Statistics			
Periods (The number of periods in each position and entire run)	273	236	509
Trades (The number of trades in each position and entire run)	50	50	100
# Profitable (The number of profitable trades. . .)	14	17	31
# Losing (The number of unprofitable trades. . .)	36	33	69
% Profitable (The percent of profitable trades to total trades)	28.00	34.00	31.00
% Losing (The percent of unprofitable trades to total trades)	72.00	66.00	69.00
	-- Results --		
Results			
Commission (Total commission deducted from closed trades)	0.00	0.00	0.00
Slippage (Total slippage deducted from closed trades)	0.00	0.00	0.00
Gross P/L (Total points gained in closed positions)	24.22	19.76	43.98
Open P/L (P/L in a position which remains open at the end)	0.00	1.23	1.23
P/L (Net P/L: Gross P/L less Commission and Slippage)	24.22	19.76	43.98
Equity (Net P/L plus Open P/L at the end of the run)	24.22	20.99	45.21

There are columns for Long trades, Short trades and Net. In the Long column, results are reported only for Long positions. In the Short column, results are reported for Short positions only. In the Net column for the "Per Trade Ranges" and "Overall Ranges," entries will be the extreme from either the Long or Short column. Net column entries for the "Statistics" and "Results" categories are the combined results of entries in the Long and Short columns.

EXHIBIT O-29:
Profit Summary for On Balance Volume 24-Week Rate of Change, 1968 to 1986

Number Of Trades Made	> 71	Commissions Paid	> 0
Number Of Weeks In Market	> 966	Frequency Of Trades	> 1.00
Number Of Winning Trades	> 30	Largest Winning Trade	> 4429
Total Of Winning Trades	> 17773	Average Winning Trade	> 592
Number Of Losing Trades	> 41	Largest Losing Trade	> −800
Total Of Losing Trades	> -7288	Average Losing Trade	> −177
Largest Winning Streak	> 6	Largest Losing Streak	> 7
Win/Loss Ratio	> 0.73	Profit/Margin Ratio	> 5.24
Number Of Stops Hit	> 0	Stops Frequency	> 0.00
Largest Drawdown	> −1933	Largest Unrealized Loss	> −800
Largest Obtained Equity	> 10903	Number Of Tradeable Weeks	> 966
Short Profit Or Loss	> 1024	Long Profit Or Loss	> 9461
Total Profit Or Loss	> 10485	Average Weekly Gain/Loss	> 10.85

OSCILLATORS: MOVING AVERAGE OSCILLATORS

Oscillators measure and quantify momentum, the velocity or speed at which a data series (usually price but often breadth or volume) is moving. An oscillator is defined as an indicator that swings to and fro, often varying between maximum and minimum limits. Generally set up as differences or ratios, oscillators move above and below a threshold of 0 or 1 that serves as a signal point.

The difference between two simple moving averages can tame raw market price data sufficiently to smooth out some of the erratic, random fluctuation that is all too common (and confusing) in the stock market. Technical analysis computer software generally will plot the point difference, percentage difference, or ratio between any two simple moving averages. For price data, we prefer the ratio or percentage difference representations because they automatically adjust over time to large differences in price levels. For example, a 100-point move was 10%, or a ratio of 1.1 to 1, when the Dow Jones Industrial Average was at 1000, but a 100-point swing was only 5%, or a ratio of 1.05 to 1, when the Dow was at 2000. While a point difference would show both movements as being of equal magnitude, a percentage difference or ratio more accurately portrays the comparative significance.

Exhibit O-30 (page 360) illustrates the NYSE Composite weekly high, low, and close, together with the popular 40-week (200-day) simple moving average of the close. Exhibit O-31 is the ratio of the closing price to the 40-week simple moving average. Note that a simple moving average of one period length is simply the raw data itself. Therefore, a 1/40 week ratio

EXHIBIT O-30:
New York Stock Exchange Composite Price Index with 40-Week Simple Moving Average, 1977 to 1986

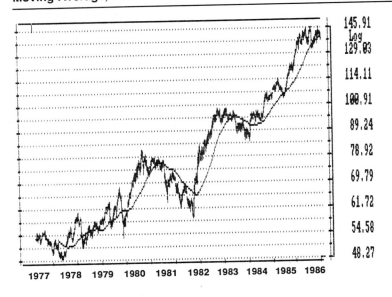

EXHIBIT O-31:
1/40 Week Ratio Oscillator, 1977 to 1986

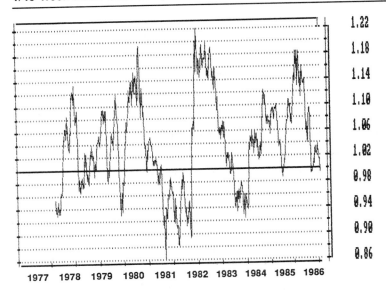

oscillator is simply the weekly closing price itself, divided by the 40-week simple moving average of weekly closing prices. When the 1/40 oscillator ratio crosses above the 1.00 level, the closing price moves above its own 40-week simple moving average, and that is interpreted as a buy signal. Conversely, when closing price moves below its own 40-week simple moving average, the 1/40 oscillator ratio also crosses below the 1.00 level, and that is taken as a signal to sell (close out) long positions and establish short positions.

There are three advantages to viewing moving average crossovers as differential or ratio oscillators moving above and below 0 or 1: We can often see crossings more clearly; we can better anticipate crossings; and we can subjectively interpret momentum divergences clearly from an oscillator chart—although such divergences might not be at all noticeable on a price with moving average chart.

There are two parameters to be optimized: the time length, n, of a shorter simple moving average and the time length, p, of a longer one. We tested many oscillators using Compu Trac software and two 9.75-year test periods of weekly data (consisting of high, low, close, and volume for each week) for the broad-based NYSE Composite Index. The first period ran from January 5, 1968 through September 30, 1977, and the second period ran from April 8, 1977 through December 31, 1986. The overlap in data was necessary to facilitate testing of various oscillators throughout the full time period.

When the ratio of the two simple moving averages crossed 1.00, a trend change, and thus a trade position change, was signalled in the direction of the crossing. The number of observations (n) that should be included in a moving average designed to isolate a trend depends on the length of the cyclical movements in the time series. Optimal values were determined by a systematic trial-and-error procedure on the computer. There are 10,000 (100 × 100) combinations of two simple moving averages ranging in length from 1 week (which is the indicator data itself) up to 100 weeks. We used a broad scanning and fine tuning testing procedure that did not test every possible combination of averages but instead narrowed down the field to the more promising areas of investigation.

The highest profit for combined optimization runs from 1968–1977 and 1977–1986 was produced by the 1/45 week moving average oscillator ratio. (See Simple Moving Average for further details.)

Extensive computer optimization studies also uncovered the 15/36 week moving average ratio oscillator as a very effective one that seems to pick up a relatively consistent intermediate-term cycle in the market. Using crossings of 1 as signal points to reverse positions, over the past 9.75 years the 15/36 week ratio oscillator has given only 11 buy long and sell short signals, and 7

EXHIBIT O-32:

New York Stock Exchange Composite Price Index Weekly High and Low from April 8, 1977 to December 31, 1986

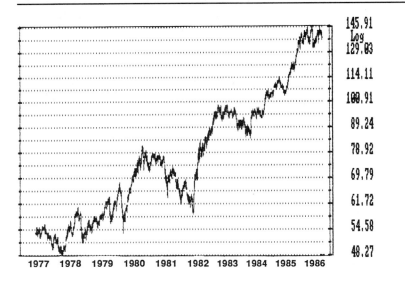

EXHIBIT O-33:

15/36 Week Ratio Oscillator, 1977 to 1986

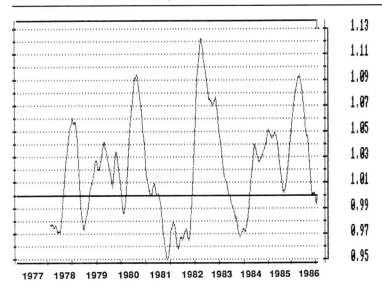

of the 11, or 63.64%, have been profitable. Of the 5 buy long signals, 4, or 80%, have been profitable. Total profits at a 9.33% simple annual rate were only slightly above our standard, but trading frequency was only 42.11% of the 1/40 oscillator standard, at 24 trades for the 15/36 versus 57 trades for the 1/40. See details in Exhibits O-32 to O-39 (pages 362–367).

Even fewer trades totaling 12 in 19 years (less frequent than one every year and a half) and higher combined profits for 1968–1977 and 1977–1986 were obtained by the 17/58 week moving average oscillator, as shown in Exhibits O-40 to O-47 (pages 368–373). The simple average annual return was 9.88%. Here, however, risk increased as maximum percentage drawdown rose to 45.41% versus only 27.44% for the 15/36 week oscillator. Moreover, the 15/36 has a higher total profit over the most recent 9.75-year period.

EXHIBIT O-34:
Total Equity for 15/36 Week Ratio Oscillator, 1977 to 1986

EXHIBIT O-35:

Profit Summary for 15/36 Week Ratio Oscillator, 1977 to 1986

Item	Long	Short	Net
	— Per Trade Ranges —		
Per Trade Ranges			
Best Trade (Closed position yielding maximum P/L)	48.02	5.11	48.02
..Date	861205	861231	861205
Worst Trade (Closed position yielding minimum P/L)	-0.37	-6.21	-6.21
..Date	800711	800711	800711
Max Open P/L (Maximum P/L occurring in an open position)	49.65	15.56	49.65
..Date	860829	820813	860829
Min Open P/L (Minimum P/L occurring in an open position)	-2.15	-5.84	-5.84
..Date	841207	800704	800704
	— Overall Ranges —		
Overall Ranges			
Max P/L (Maximum P/L from all closed positions during the run)	68.31	73.42	73.42
..Date	861205	861231	861231
Min P/L (Minimum P/L from all closed positions during the run)	-2.85	-9.06	-9.06
..Date	800516	800711	800711
Max Equity (Maximum P/L from all closed and open positions)	73.42	73.42	73.42
..Date	861231	861231	861231
Min Equity (Minimum P/L from all closed and open positions)	-9.06	-9.06	-9.06
..Date	800711	800711	800711
	— Statistics —		
Statistics			
Periods (The number of periods in each position and entire run)	363	146	509
Trades (The number of trades in each position and entire run)	5	6	11
# Profitable (The number of profitable trades...)	4	3	7
# Losing (The number of unprofitable trades...)	1	3	4
% Profitable (The percent of profitable trades to total trades)	80.00	50.00	63.64
% Losing (The percent of unprofitable trades to total trades)	20.00	50.00	36.36
	— Results —		
Results			
Commission (Total commission deducted from closed trades)	0.00	0.00	0.00
Slippage (Total slippage deducted from closed trades)	0.00	0.00	0.00
Gross P/L (Total points gained in closed positions)	80.14	-6.72	73.42
Open P/L (P/L in a position which remains open at the end)	0.00	0.00	0.00
P/L (Net P/L: Gross P/L less Commission and Slippage)	80.14	-6.72	73.42
Equity (Net P/L plus Open P/L at the end of the run)	80.14	-6.72	73.42

There are columns for Long trades, Short trades and Net. In the Long column, results are reported only for Long positions. In the Short column, results are reported for Short positions only. In the Net column for the "Per Trade Ranges" and "Overall Ranges," entries will be the extreme from either the Long or Short column. Net column entries for the "Statistics" and "Results" categories are the combined results of entries in the Long and Short columns.

EXHIBIT O-36:

New York Stock Exchange Composite Price Index Weekly High and Low from January 5, 1968 to September 30, 1977

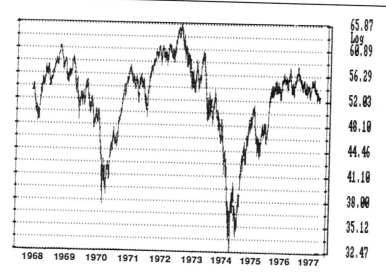

EXHIBIT O-37:

15/36 Week Ratio Oscillator, 1968 to 1977

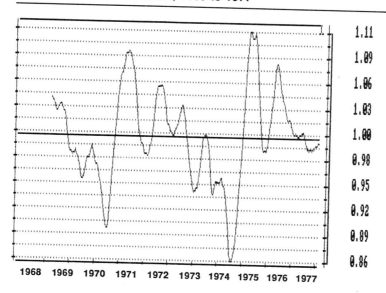

EXHIBIT O-38:
Total Equity for 15/36 Week Ratio Oscillator, 1968 to 1977

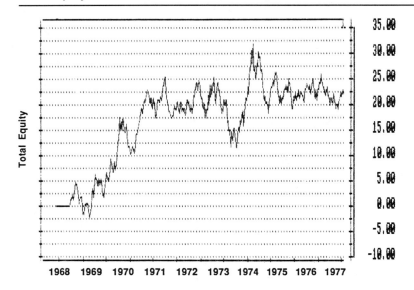

EXHIBIT O-39:

Profit Summary for 15/36 Week Ratio Oscillator, 1968 to 1977

Item		Long	Short	Net
Per Trade Ranges				
Best Trade	(Closed position yielding maximum P/L)	9.39	11.00	11.00
..Date		710917	701106	701106
Worst Trade	(Closed position yielding minimum P/L)	-5.86	-3.84	-5.86
..Date		731214	760116	731214
Max Open P/L	(Maximum P/L occurring in an open position)	11.47	17.41	17.41
..Date		710423	700522	700522
Min Open P/L	(Minimum P/L occurring in an open position)	-4.30	-3.56	-4.30
..Date		731130	740315	731130
Overall Ranges				
Max P/L	(Maximum P/L from all closed positions during the run)	23.18	21.02	23.18
..Date		751024	731102	751024
Min P/L	(Minimum P/L from all closed positions during the run)	0.22	11.22	0.22
..Date		690328	701106	690328
Max Equity	(Maximum P/L from all closed and open positions)	26.32	31.81	31.81
..Date		750711	741004	741004
Min Equity	(Minimum P/L from all closed and open positions)	-1.70	-2.09	-2.09
..Date		690314	690516	690516
Statistics				
Periods	(The number of periods in each position and entire run)	273	236	509
Trades	(The number of trades in each position and entire run)	7	6	13
# Profitable	(The number of profitable trades...)	5	4	9
# Losing	(The number of unprofitable trades...)	2	2	4
% Profitable	(The percent of profitable trades to total trades)	71.43	66.67	69.23
% Losing	(The percent of unprofitable trades to total trades)	28.57	33.33	30.77
Results				
Commission	(Total commission deducted from closed trades)	0.00	0.00	0.00
Slippage	(Total slippage deducted from closed trades)	0.00	0.00	0.00
Gross P/L	(Total points gained in closed positions)	9.11	12.28	21.39
Open P/L	(P/L in a position which remains open at the end)	0.00	0.65	0.65
P/L	(Net P/L: Gross P/L less Commission and Slippage)	9.11	12.28	21.39
Equity	(Net P/L plus Open P/L at the end of the run)	9.11	12.93	22.04

There are columns for Long trades, Short trades and Net. In the Long column, results are reported only for Long positions. In the Short column, results are reported for Short positions only. In the Net column for the "Per Trade Ranges" and "Overall Ranges," entries will be the extreme from either the Long or Short column. Net column entries for the "Statistics" and "Results" categories are the combined results of entries in the Long and Short columns.

EXHIBIT O-40:

New York Stock Exchange Composite Price Index Weekly High and Low from April 8, 1977 to December 31, 1986

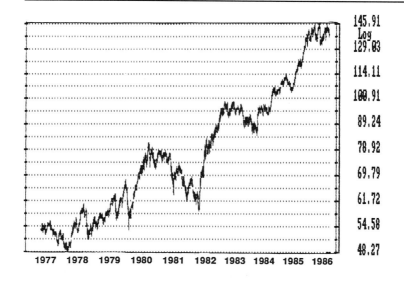

EXHIBIT O-41:

17/58 Week Ratio Oscillator, 1977 to 1986

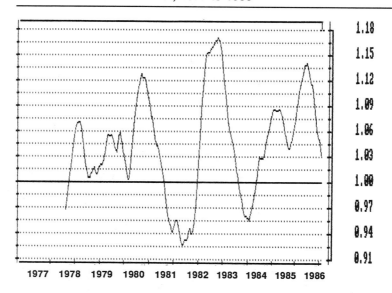

EXHIBIT O-42:

Total Equity for 17/58 Week Ratio Oscillator, 1977 to 1986

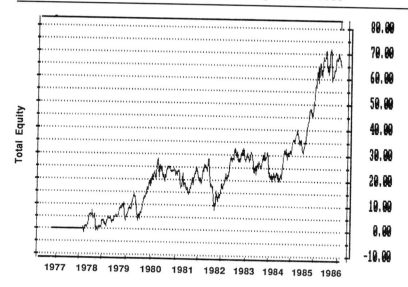

EXHIBIT O-43:
Profit Summary for 17/58 Week Ratio Oscillator, 1977 to 1986

Item		Long	Short	Net
		-- Per Trade Ranges --		
Per Trade Ranges				
Best Trade	(Closed position yielding maximum P/L)	16.42	0.95	16.42
.. Date		810911	780623	810911
Worst Trade	(Closed position yielding minimum P/L)	14.78	-6.63	-6.63
.. Date		840316	821029	821029
Max Open P/L	(Maximum P/L occurring in an open position)	49.98	10.78	49.98
.. Date		860829	820813	860829
Min Open P/L	(Minimum P/L occurring in an open position)	-1.82	-9.36	-9.36
.. Date		841022	821022	821022
		----- Overall Ranges -----		
Overall Ranges				
Max P/L	(Maximum P/L from all closed positions during the run)	25.52	21.91	25.52
.. Date		840316	841026	840316
Min P/L	(Minimum P/L from all closed positions during the run)	17.37	0.95	0.95
.. Date		810911	780623	780623
Max Equity	(Maximum P/L from all closed and open positions)	71.89	31.08	71.89
.. Date		860829	840615	860829
Min Equity	(Minimum P/L from all closed and open positions)	-0.43	-1.23	-1.23
.. Date		781027	780609	780609
		------ Statistics ------		
Statistics				
Periods	(The number of periods in each position and entire run)	412	97	509
Trades	(The number of trades in each position and entire run)	2	3	5
# Profitable	(The number of profitable trades. . .)	2	1	3
# Losing	(The number of unprofitable trades. . .)	0	2	2
% Profitable	(The percent of profitable trades to total trades)	100.00	33.33	60.00
% Losing	(The percent of unprofitable trades to total trades)	0.00	66.67	40.00
		------ Results ------		
Results				
Commission	(Total commission deducted from closed trades)	0.00	0.00	0.00
Slippage	(Total slippage deducted from closed trades)	0.00	0.00	0.00
Gross P/L	(Total points gained in closed positions)	31.20	-9.29	21.91
Open P/L	(P/L in a position which remains open at the end)	43.24	0.00	43.24
P/L	(Net P/L: Gross P/L less Commission and Slippage)	31.20	-9.29	21.91
Equity	(Net P/L plus Open P/L at the end of the run)	74.44		65.15

There are columns for Long trades, Short trades and Net. In the Long column, results are reported only for Long positions. In the Short column, results are reported for Short positions only. In the Net column for the "Per Trade Ranges" and "Overall Ranges," entries will be the extreme from either the Long or Short column. Net column entries for the "Statistics" and "Results" categories are the combined results of entries in the Long and Short columns.

EXHIBIT O-44:

New York Stock Exchange Composite Price Index Weekly High and Low from January 5, 1968 to September 30, 1977

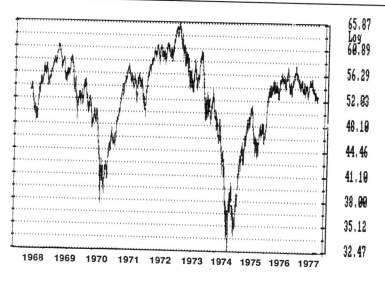

EXHIBIT O-45:

17/58 Week Ratio Oscillator, 1968 to 1977

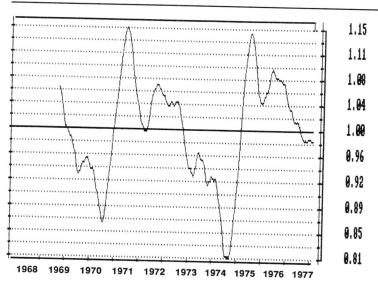

EXHIBIT O-46:
Total Equity for 17/58 Week Ratio Oscillator, 1968 to 1977

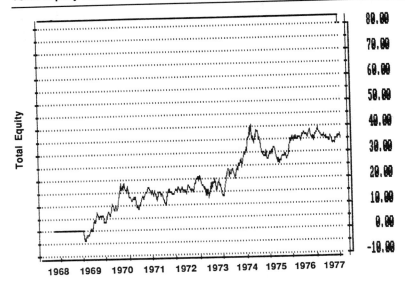

EXHIBIT O-47:

Profit Summary for 17/58 Week Ratio Oscillator, 1968 to 1977

Item	Long	Short	Net
Per Trade Ranges	---- Per Trade Ranges ----		
Best Trade (Closed position yielding maximum P/L)	7.71	12.82	12.82
.. Date	770429	750425	750425
Worst Trade (Closed position yielding minimum P/L)	-0.16	-1.90	-1.90
.. Date	690523	720211	720211
Max Open P/L (Maximum P/L occurring in an open position)	11.93	25.87	25.87
.. Date	761231	741004	741004
Min Open P/L (Minimum P/L occurring in an open position)	-3.71	-2.05	-3.71
.. Date	690314	770722	690314
Overall Ranges	---- Overall Ranges ----		
Max P/L (Maximum P/L from all closed positions during the run)	35.08	27.37	35.08
.. Date	770429	750425	770429
Min P/L (Minimum P/L from all closed positions during the run)	-0.16	8.95	-0.16
.. Date	690523	701225	690523
Max Equity (Maximum P/L from all closed and open positions)	39.30	40.42	40.42
.. Date	761231	741004	690523
Min Equity (Minimum P/L from all closed and open positions)	-3.71	-0.16	-3.71
.. Date	690314	690523	690314
Statistics	---- Statistics ----		
Periods (The number of periods in each position and entire run)	294	215	509
Trades (The number of trades in each position and entire run)	4	3	7
# Profitable (The number of profitable trades...)	3	2	5
# Losing (The number of unprofitable trades...)	1	1	2
% Profitable (The percent of profitable trades to total trades)	75.00	66.67	71.43
% Losing (The percent of unprofitable trades to total trades)	25.00	33.33	28.57
Results	---- Results ----		
Commission (Total commission deducted from closed trades)	0.00	0.00	0.00
Slippage (Total slippage deducted from closed trades)	0.00	0.00	0.00
Gross P/L (Total points gained in closed positions)	15.05	20.03	35.08
Open P/L (P/L in a position which remains open at the end)	0.00	0.85	0.85
P/L (Net P/L: Gross P/L less Commission and Slippage)	15.05	20.03	35.08
Equity (Net P/L plus Open P/L at the end of the run)	15.05	20.88	35.93

There are columns for Long trades, Short trades and Net. In the Long column, results are reported only for Long positions. In the Short column, results are reported for Short positions only. In the Net column for the "Per Trade Ranges" and "Overall Ranges," entries will be the extreme from either the Long or Short column. Net column entries for the "Statistics" and "Results" categories are the combined results of entries in the Long and Short columns.

OVERBOUGHT/OVERSOLD INDICATORS

There are many indicators that are thought to signal unsustainable market extremes. Excessively high readings are known as *overbought* and supposedly warn of vulnerability to downward correction. Excessively low readings, on the other hand, are called *oversold* and supposedly alert the technician of the potential for a sharp upward correction.

Not everyone finds these concepts very helpful. Legendary trader Richard Dennis, for instance, has been quoted as saying he is skeptical. Veteran technical analyst Alan R. Shaw of Smith Barney says the concept is often misused or not clearly expressed. In Shaw's view, "The ability of the market to register an extremely overbought condition during an advance is not a negative, but a positive sign of the vitality of the advance. On the other hand, the lack of an overbought reading during an advance often indicates the weakness of the rally, thus making it suspicious." It seems clear that the novice should approach this overbought/oversold concept with great care.

An example of the difficulties with the overbought/oversold concept is illustrated by the popular 12-month rate of change +30%/−10% rule. The specific decision rules are as follows: Buy when the 12-month rate of change for the Standard & Poor's 500 Index is less than −10%, and hold until the 12-month rate of change exceeds +30%, at which time you sell and sell short. Hold short until the 12-month rate of change declines to −10%, then reverse position again and go long.

Applying this rule mechanically since 1946 produced extremely poor results, as shown in Exhibits O-48 to O-52 (pages 375–378). This rule allows losses to run and cuts profits short. Total profit over 42 years came to only 2.24 S&P points. Obviously, no one would want to follow this rule mechanically, although it could conceivably be used as a filter in conjunction with other decision rules and indicators.

EXHIBIT O-48:
Standard & Poor's 500 Index, 1944 to 1986, Month-End Closing Price

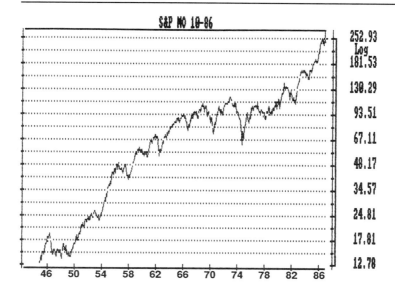

EXHIBIT O-49:
12-Month Rate of Change for Standard & Poor's 500 Index, 1944 to 1986

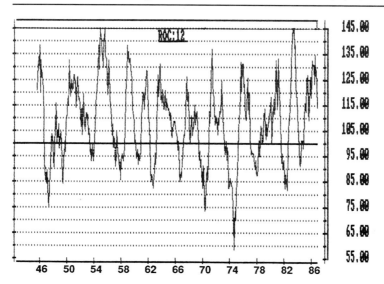

EXHIBIT O-50:

Total Equity for +30% / −10% Rule for Standard & Poor's 500 Index 12-Month Rate of Change, 1944 to 1986

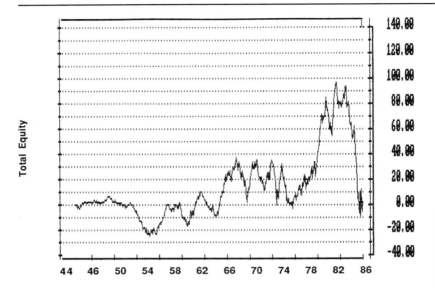

EXHIBIT O-51:
Profit Summary for + 30% / −10% Rule for 12-Month Rate of Change for Standard & Poor's 500 Index, 1944 to 1986

Item		Long — Per Trade Ranges —	Short	Net
Per Trade Ranges				
Best Trade	(Closed position yielding maximum P/L)	48.18	14.17	48.18
.. Date		801130	811130	801130
Worst Trade	(Closed position yielding minimum P/L)	-12.09	-21.20	-21.20
.. Date		750930	571231	571231
Max Open P/L	(Maximum P/L occurring in an open position)	35.13	24.34	35.13
.. Date		801031	810930	801031
Min Open P/L	(Minimum P/L occurring in an open position)	-32.42	-104.87	-104.87
.. Date		740930	860831	860831
Overall Ranges		— Overall Ranges —		
Max P/L	(Maximum P/L from all closed positions during the run)	96.35	74.64	96.35
.. Date		830228	811130	830228
Min P/L	(Minimum P/L from all closed positions during the run)	-0.22	-15.45	-15.45
.. Date		581231	571231	571231
Max Equity	(Maximum P/L from all closed and open positions)	93.59	96.35	96.35
.. Date		830131	830228	830228
Min Equity	(Minimum P/L from all closed and open positions)	-15.45	-24.86	-24.86
.. Date		571231	560731	560731
Statistics		— Statistics —		
Periods	(The number of periods in each position and entire run)	217	292	509
Trades	(The number of trades in each position and entire run)	7	7	14
# Profitable	(The number of profitable trades...)	6	3	9
# Losing	(The number of unprofitable trades...)	1	4	5
% Profitable	(The percent of profitable trades to total trades)	85.71	42.86	64.29
% Losing	(The percent of unprofitable trades to total trades)	14.29	57.14	35.71
Results		— Results —		
Commission	(Total commission deducted from closed trades)	0.00	0.00	0.00
Slippage	(Total slippage deducted from closed trades)	0.00	0.00	0.00
Gross P/L	(Total points gained in closed positions)	113.88	-17.53	96.35
Open P/L	(P/L in a position which remains open at the end)	0.00	-94.11	-94.11
P/L	(Net P/L: Gross P/L less Commission and Slippage)	113.88	-17.53	96.35
Equity	(Net P/L plus Open P/L at the end of the run)	113.88	-111.64	2.24

There are columns for Long trades, Short trades and Net. In the Long column, results are reported only for Long positions. In the Short column, results are reported for Short positions only. In the Net column for the "Per Trade Ranges" and "Overall Ranges," entries will be the extreme from either the Long or Short column. Net column entries for the "Statistics" and "Results" categories are the combined results of entries in the Long and Short columns.

EXHIBIT O-52:
Transaction Dates and Prices for + 30% / −10% Rule for 12-Month Rate of Change for Standard & Poor's 500 Index, 1944 to 1986

Exit Date	Entry Date	Short or Long*	Entry Price	Exit Price	Maximum P/L	Minimum P/L	Gross P/L	Net P/L	Maximum Equity	Minimum Equity	Cumulative Profit or Equity
461031	451031	Sc	16.65	14.84	1.81	-2.53	1.81	1.81	1.69	-2.53	1.81
500531	461031	Lc	14.84	18.78	3.94	-0.84	3.94	3.94	5.04	-2.53	5.75
571231	500531	Sc	18.78	39.98	1.09	-30.61	-21.20	-21.20	6.84	-24.86	-15.45
581231	571231	Lc	39.98	55.21	15.23	0.00	15.23	15.23	6.84	-24.86	-0.22
620531	581231	Sc	55.21	59.63	1.82	-16.34	-4.42	-4.42	6.84	-24.86	-4.64
631031	620531	Lc	59.63	74.01	14.38	-4.88	14.38	14.38	8.23	-24.86	9.74
660831	631031	Sc	74.01	77.10	0.78	-18.87	-3.09	-3.09	10.52	-24.86	6.65
710531	660831	Lc	77.10	99.63	31.27	-4.38	22.53	22.53	37.92	-24.86	29.18
731130	710531	Sc	99.63	95.96	5.64	-18.42	3.67	3.67	37.92	-24.86	32.85
750930	731130	Lc	95.96	83.87	1.59	-32.42	-12.09	-12.09	37.92	-24.86	20.76
771031	750930	Sc	83.87	92.34	0.00	-23.59	-8.47	-8.47	37.92	-24.86	12.29
801130	771031	Lc	92.34	140.52	48.18	-5.30	48.18	48.18	47.42	-24.86	60.47
811130	801130	Sc	140.52	126.35	24.34	0.00	14.17	14.17	84.81	-24.86	74.64
830228	811130	Lc	126.35	148.06	21.71	-19.26	21.71	21.71	93.59	-24.86	96.35
861231	830228	oS	148.06	242.17	0.00	-104.87	-94.11	-94.11	96.35	-24.86	2.24

*Lc indicates a long position that has been closed. oS indicates a short position that remains open. Sc indicates a short position that has been closed.

Exit Date indicates the date a trade is closed out.

Entry Date indicates the date a trade is opened or begun.

P/L indicates profit or loss on the trade.

Equity is the total cumulative P/L.

PARABOLIC TIME/PRICE SYSTEM

The Parabolic Time/Price System is a unique and complete stop-setting entry and exit trading system described by J. Welles Wilder, Jr. in *New Concepts In Technical Trading Systems* (Trend Research, Box 128, McLeansville, NC 27301, 1978).* The system is designed to allow more leeway or tolerance for contratrend price fluctuation early in a new trade, then to progressively tighten a protective trailing stop order as the trend matures. To accomplish this, it employs a series of progressively shorter, exponentially smoothed moving averages each period that price moves to a new extreme in the expected trend direction. These exponential smoothing constants, called *Acceleration Factors* (AF), rise from an initial minimum of .02 (or 50 days) to a maximum of .20 (or 5 days) in order to adjust a *stop and reverse price* (SAR) ever closer to the price trend. Thus, the Parabolic Time/Price System rides the trend until the SAR price is penetrated. Then the existing position is closed out and the reverse position is opened.

SAR calculations begin anew on each fresh SAR signal. On the day of the initial signal when a new position is opened, SAR is equal to the *Extreme Price* (EP) in the direction of the freshly closed previous position's trend. Thereafter, SAR is adjusted by an AF in the new expected trend direction.

On the positive side, for new buy signals, the initial SAR price is equal to the lowest price recorded during the previously closed short position. On the second day and thereafter, the SAR is adjusted as follows:

$$SAR_l = SAR_p + AF(H - SAR_p)$$

where

SAR_l is the long-side sell stop price at which you sell and sell short.

SAR_p is the previous period's SAR_l.

AF is an acceleration factor that begins at .02 for the period after the initial SAR buy stop order opens the long trade and is increased by .02 each period that price rises to the highest level (H) since the current long trade was opened. For periods when price does not set a new high within the current long trade time duration, AF is left unchanged from its previous period's level.

H is a new highest price high since the current long trade was opened on a stop buy order.

---

* Reprinted with permission.

On the negative side, for new sell short signals, the initial SAR price is equal to the highest price recorded during the previously closed long position. On the second day and thereafter, the SAR is adjusted as follows:

$$SAR_s = SAR_p - AF(L - SAR_p)$$

where

SAR_s is the short-side buy stop at which you buy and go long.

SAR_p is the previous period's SAR_s.

AF is an acceleration factor that beings at .02 for the period after the initial SAR sell stop order opens the short trade and is increased by .02 for each period that price falls to a lowest level (L) since the current short trade was opened. For periods when price does not set a new low within the current short trade time duration, AF is left unchanged from its previous period's level.

L is a new lowest price low since the current short trade was opened on a stop sell order.

On both the long side and the short side, SAR must lie at or outside the latest two periods' high-low price ranges, and never inside these ranges. If in a long position and SAR is greater than the two most recent lows, then reset SAR to the lower of those two lows. If in a short position and SAR is lower than the two most recent highs, then reset SAR to the higher of those two highs.

The table on page 381 presents an example of the Parabolic Time/Price System.

We tested these rules with weekly NYSE Composite Index data over the 19 years between January 5, 1968 and December 31, 1986, using Back Trak software, and we found below-standard profit of 59.41 NYSE points, as shown in Exhibit P-1 (page 382). Limited optimization, however, dramatically improved results. Note in Exhibit P-2 that by boosting the acceleration factor increment from the standard .02 up to .2, profits more than doubled to 147.59 NYSE points, well above our 40-week simple moving average crossover rule standard of comparison. This is a relatively active trading system that assumes intraweek execution of orders on actual stops. Therefore, commission and slippage become more important than with less active systems. In conclusion, Wilder's Parabolic Time/Price System appears worthy of consideration.

Example of Parabolic Time Price-System (AF begin at .02, increment .02, maximum 0.2)

Position Long or Short	Date	NYSE Annual Prices High	NYSE Annual Prices Low	Extreme High or Low Price*		SAR_p		Diff	×	AF		AF×Diff	+	SAR_p	=	SAR
Long	73/12/31	65.87	48.71	65.87	—											
Short	74/12/31	53.77	32.47	32.47	—	65.87	=	−33.40	×	.02	=	−.67	+	65.87	=	65.20
Short	75/12/31	51.39	36.49	32.47	—	65.20	=	−32.73	×	.02	=	−.65	+	65.20	=	64.55
Short	76/12/31	57.88	47.67	32.47	—	64.55	=	−32.08	×	.02	=	−.64	+	64.55	=	63.91
Short	77/12/30	57.92	49.61	32.47	—	63.91	=	−31.44	×	.02	=	−.63	+	63.91	=	63.28
Short	78/12/29	60.60	48.27	32.47	—	63.28	=	−30.81	×	.02	=	−.62	+	63.28	=	62.66
Long	79/12/31	63.58	53.42	63.58	—	32.47	=	+31.11	×	.02	=	+.62	+	32.47	=	33.09
Long	80/12/31	81.29	53.66	81.29	—	33.09	=	+48.20	×	.04	=	+1.93	+	33.09	=	35.02
Long	81/12/31	79.44	63.75	81.29	—	35.02	=	+46.27	×	.04	=	+1.85	+	35.02	=	36.87
Long	82/12/31	83.13	58.78	83.13	—	36.87	=	+46.26	×	.06	=	+2.78	+	36.87	=	39.65
Long	83/12/30	99.63	79.63	99.63	—	39.65	=	+59.98	×	.08	=	+4.80	+	39.65	=	44.45
Long	84/12/31	98.12	84.81	99.63	—	44.45	=	+55.18	×	.08	=	+4.41	+	44.45	=	48.86
Long	85/12/31	122.44	94.41	122.44	—	48.86	=	+73.58	×	.10	=	+7.36	+	48.86	=	56.22
Long	86/12/31	145.91	117.30	145.91	—	56.22	=	+89.69	×	.12	=	+10.76	+	56.22	=	66.98
Long	87/12/31					66.98									=	

*During the duration of the position.

EXHIBIT P-1:

Profit Summary for Parabolic Time/Price System .02/.02/.2, Wilder's Parameters, 1968 to 1986

Number Of Trades Made	> 99	Commissions Paid	> 0
Number Of Weeks In Market	> 989	Frequency Of Trades	> 1.00
Number Of Winning Trades	> 42	Largest Winning Trade	> 1516
Total Of Winning Trades	> 19767	Average Winning Trade	> 470
Number Of Losing Trades	> 57	Largest Losing Trade	> −816
Total Of Losing Trades	> −13826	Average Losing Trade	> −242
Largest Winning Streak	> 5	Largest Losing Streak	> 6
Win/Loss Ratio	> 0.74	Profit/Margin Ratio	> 2.97
Number Of Stops Hit	> 0	Stops Frequency	> 0.00
Largest Drawdown	> −3957	Largest Unrealized Loss	> −642
Largest Obtained Equity	> 9856	Number Of Tradeable Weeks	> 989
Short Profit Or Loss	> −1378	Long Profit Or Loss	> 7319
Total Profit Or Loss	> 5941	Average Weekly Gain/Loss	> 6.01

EXHIBIT P-2:

Profit Summary for Parabolic Time/Price System .02/.2/.2, Optimized Parameters

Number Of Trades Made	> 157	Commissions Paid	> 0
Number Of Weeks In Market	> 989	Frequency Of Trades	> 1.00
Number Of Winning Trades	> 82	Largest Winning Trade	> 1586
Total Of Winning Trades	> 27003	Average Winning Trade	> 329
Number Of Losing Trades	> 75	Largest Losing Trade	> −778
Total Of Losing Trades	> −12244	Average Losing Trade	> −163
Largest Winning Streak	> 5	Largest Losing Streak	> 7
Win/Loss Ratio	> 1.09	Profit/Margin Ratio	> 7.38
Number Of Stops Hit	> 0	Stops Frequency	> 0.00
Largest Drawdown	> −2622	Largest Unrealized Loss	> −778
Largest Obtained Equity	> 16996	Number Of Tradeable Weeks	> 989
Short Profit Or Loss	> 3031	Long Profit Or Loss	> 11728
Total Profit Or Loss	> 14759	Average Weekly Gain/Loss	> 14.92

PERCENTAGE OF STANDARD & POOR'S 500 STOCKS ABOVE THEIR OWN 200-DAY SIMPLE MOVING AVERAGES

The Percentage of Standard & Poor's Stocks Above their own 200-Day Simple Moving Averages is a popular breadth momentum indicator that is followed by *Trendline Daily Action Stock Charts, Investors Intelligence, Technical Trends, Indicator Digest,* and *Systems & Forecasts,* among other publications. It measures the percentage of 500 stocks in the S&P 500 Index that are trading above their own trailing 200-day simple moving averages of price. There are three steps in its computation. First, calculate simple 200-day moving averages for the 500 individual stocks. Second, calculate the percentage of those 500 stocks that are trading above their own 200-day moving averages. Third, calculate a 5-week moving average of the percentage above their own 200-day moving averages.

The percentage above their 200-day moving averages measurement could be regarded as a "head counting" type of statistic that represents the breadth of the market from a different vantage point than the advance-decline numbers. The percentage shows the proportion of stocks that can be considered strong or upward biased relative to their own most recent 200-day trading history. It can be viewed as both a trend-following indicator and as a momentum gauge with leading indicator characteristics.

Like most momentum indicators, the percentage often peaks and troughs before tops and bottoms in the price indexes. Excellent positive and negative examples of such momentum divergencies can be seen in 1982 and 1983, respectively.

One purely mechanical trend-following decision rule for this data is: Follow the direction of the 5-week moving average of the weekly percentage above 200 data. When the 5-week moving average turns up, buy the S&P 500 Index. Hold until the 5-week moving average turns down, then sell longs and sell short the S&P 500 Index. Stay short until the 5-week moving average turns up, then cover shorts and go long. There are no other rules and no subjective judgment is necessary.

Exhibit P-3 (page 384) shows the complete results, trade by trade, over the past 9.5 years. The first column shows that there have been a total of 85 trades since June 1977, an average of nine trades per year. Next, we present the date of the buy or sell signal. "Buy" means the 5-week moving average changed direction from down to up. "Sell" means the 5-week moving average changed direction from up to down. "S&P 500 CL"

EXHIBIT P-3:
Trade-By-Trade Results Using 5-Week Moving Average of Weekly Percentage of Standard & Poor's 500 Stocks Above Their Own 200-Day Simple Moving Average, 1977 to 1987

NUMBER	DATE	SIGNAL		S&P500 CL	POINTS	CHANGE %	TOTAL %	$ GAIN	PORTFOLIO VALUE	NUMBER RIGHT	NUMBER WRONG
0	JUN 17 77	BUY		99.97					100000.00	0	
1	JUL 29 77	SELL	1	98.85	-1.12	-1.12%	-1.12%	-1120.34	98879.66	0	1
2	SEP 30 77	BUY	0	96.53	2.32	2.35%	1.23%	2320.70	101200.36	1	1
3	OCT 7 77	SELL	1	95.97	-0.56	-0.58%	0.65%	-587.09	100613.27	1	2
4	NOV 11 77	BUY	0	95.98	-0.01	-0.01%	0.64%	-10.48	100602.78	1	3
5	DEC 16 77	SELL	1	93.40	-2.58	-2.69%	-2.05%	-2704.26	97898.52	1	4
6	FEB 17 78	BUY	0	87.96	5.44	5.82%	3.77%	5702.01	103600.53	2	4
7	JUN 16 78	SELL	1	97.42	9.46	10.75%	14.53%	11142.12	114742.65	3	4
8	JUL 28 78	BUY	0	100.00	-2.58	-2.65%	11.88%	-3038.76	111703.89	3	5
9	SEP 22 78	SELL	1	101.84	1.84	1.84%	13.72%	2055.35	113759.24	4	5
10	DEC 1 78	BUY	0	96.28	5.56	5.46%	19.18%	6210.74	119969.98	5	5
11	DEC 29 78	SELL	1	96.11	-0.17	-0.18%	19.00%	-211.83	119758.15	5	6
12	JAN 5 79	BUY	0	99.13	-3.02	-3.14%	15.86%	-3763.08	115995.07	5	7
13	FEB 9 79	SELL	1	97.87	-1.26	-1.27%	14.59%	-1474.36	114520.71	5	8
14	MAR 16 79	BUY	0	100.69	-2.82	-2.88%	11.71%	-3299.77	111220.94	5	9
15	MAY 4 79	SELL	1	100.69	0.00	0.00%	11.71%	0.00	111220.94	5	9
16	JUN 8 79	BUY	0	101.49	-0.8	-0.79%	10.91%	-883.67	110337.27	5	10
17	SEP 14 79	SELL	1	108.76	7.27	7.16%	18.08%	7903.75	118241.02	6	10
18	NOV 23 79	BUY	0	104.67	4.09	3.76%	21.84%	4446.54	122687.56	7	10
19	FEB 15 80	SELL	1	115.41	10.74	10.26%	32.10%	12588.75	135276.31	8	10
20	APR 25 80	BUY	0	105.16	10.25	8.88%	40.98%	12014.40	147290.71	9	10
21	SEP 26 80	SELL	1	126.35	21.19	20.15%	61.13%	29679.44	176970.16	10	10
22	JAN 9 81	BUY	0	133.48	-7.13	-5.64%	55.49%	-9986.52	166983.63	10	11
23	JAN 30 81	SELL	1	129.55	-3.93	-2.94%	52.54%	-4916.43	162067.20	10	12
24	MAR 6 81	BUY	0	129.85	-0.3	-0.23%	52.31%	-375.30	161691.90	10	13
25	APR 24 81	SELL	1	135.14	5.29	4.07%	56.38%	6587.22	168279.12	11	13
26	JUN 12 81	BUY	0	133.49	1.65	1.22%	57.61%	2054.61	170333.73	12	13
27	JUL 2 81	SELL	1	128.64	-4.85	-3.63%	53.97%	-6188.62	164145.11	12	14
28	OCT 9 81	BUY	0	121.45	7.19	5.59%	59.56%	9174.47	173319.58	13	14
29	DEC 18 81	SELL	1	124.00	2.55	2.10%	61.66%	3639.07	176958.65	14	14
30	FEB 19 82	BUY	0	113.22	10.78	8.69%	70.35%	15383.99	192342.63	15	14
31	MAR 5 82	SELL	1	109.34	-3.88	-3.43%	66.93%	-6591.50	185751.13	15	15
32	MAR 19 82	BUY	0	110.61	-1.27	-1.16%	65.77%	-2157.53	183593.61	15	16
33	MAY 21 82	SELL	1	114.89	4.28	3.78%	74.13%	7271.03	199613.67	16	16
34	JUL 9 82	BUY	0	108.83	6.06	5.27%	79.41%	10528.84	210142.51	17	16
35	JUL 30 82	SELL	1	107.09	-1.74	-1.60%	77.81%	-3359.81	206782.70	17	17
36	AUG 20 82	BUY	0	113.02	-5.93	-5.54%	72.27%	-11450.38	195332.32	17	18
37	NOV 26 82	SELL	1	134.88	21.86	19.34%	91.61%	37780.61	233112.93	18	18
38	DEC 31 82	BUY	0	140.64	-5.76	-4.27%	87.34%	-9955.00	223157.93	18	19
39	FEB 11 83	SELL	1	147.63	6.99	4.97%	92.31%	11091.25	234249.18	19	19
40	MAR 4 83	BUY	0	153.67	-6.04	-4.09%	88.22%	-9583.86	224665.32	19	20
41	MAR 18 83	SELL	1	149.90	-3.77	-2.45%	85.77%	-5511.73	219153.59	19	21
42	MAR 25 83	BUY	0	152.67	-2.77	-1.85%	83.92%	-4049.74	215103.85	19	22
43	MAR 31 83	SELL	1	152.96	0.29	0.19%	84.11%	408.59	215512.45	20	22
44	APR 22 83	BUY	0	160.42	-7.46	-4.88%	79.23%	-10510.74	205001.71	20	23

NUMBER	DATE	SIGNAL		S&P500 CL	POINTS	CHANGE %	TOTAL %	$ GAIN	PORTFOLIO VALUE	NUMBER RIGHT	NUMBER WRONG
45	JUN 3 83	SELL	1	164.42	4	2.49%	81.73%	5111.62	210113.33	21	23
46	SEP 9 83	BUY	0	166.92	-2.5	-1.52%	80.21%	-3194.77	206918.57	21	24
47	OCT 21 83	SELL	1	165.95	-0.97	-0.58%	79.63%	-1202.44	205716.13	21	25
48	DEC 2 83	BUY	0	165.44	0.51	0.31%	79.93%	632.21	206348.34	22	25
49	DEC 16 83	SELL	1	162.39	-3.05	-1.84%	78.09%	-3804.17	202544.16	22	26
50	JAN 20 84	BUY	0	166.21	-3.82	-2.35%	75.74%	-4764.57	197779.59	22	27
51	JAN 27 84	SELL	1	163.94	-2.27	-1.37%	74.37%	-2701.16	195078.43	22	28
52	MAR 16 84	BUY	0	159.27	4.67	2.85%	77.22%	5557.01	200635.44	23	28
53	APR 6 84	SELL	1	155.48	-3.79	-2.38%	74.84%	-4774.33	195861.11	23	29
54	APR 13 84	BUY	0	157.31	-1.83	-1.18%	73.66%	-2305.29	193555.82	23	30
55	MAY 18 84	SELL	1	155.78	-1.53	-0.97%	72.69%	-1882.53	191673.30	23	31
56	JUN 22 84	BUY	0	154.46	1.32	0.85%	73.54%	1624.14	193297.44	24	31
57	JUL 13 84	SELL	1	150.88	-3.58	-2.32%	71.22%	-4480.16	188817.28	24	32
58	JUL 20 84	BUY	0	149.55	1.33	0.88%	72.10%	1664.42	190481.70	25	32
59	JUL 27 84	SELL	1	151.19	1.64	1.06%	74.60%	2052.36	195349.80	26	32
60	AUG 3 84	BUY	0	162.35	-11.16	-7.38%	67.22%	-14419.63	180930.17	26	33
61	SEP 28 84	SELL	1	166.10	3.75	2.31%	69.53%	4179.17	185109.34	27	33
62	NOV 2 84	BUY	0	167.42	-1.32	-0.79%	68.73%	-1471.07	183638.27	27	34
63	DEC 7 84	SELL	1	162.26	-5.16	-3.08%	65.65%	-5659.86	177978.41	27	35
64	DEC 21 84	BUY	0	165.51	-3.25	-2.00%	63.65%	-3564.83	174413.58	27	36
65	DEC 28 84	SELL	1	166.26	0.75	0.45%	64.10%	790.35	175203.93	28	36
66	JAN 4 85	BUY	0	163.68	2.58	1.55%	65.65%	2718.79	177922.72	29	36
67	MAR 8 85	SELL	1	179.10	15.42	9.42%	75.08%	16761.78	194684.50	30	36
68	MAY 10 85	BUY	0	184.28	-5.18	-2.89%	72.18%	-5630.74	189053.76	30	37
69	JUN 14 85	SELL	1	187.10	2.82	1.53%	73.71%	2893.05	191946.81	31	37
70	JUL 5 85	BUY	0	192.52	-5.42	-2.90%	70.82%	-5560.40	186386.40	31	38
71	AUG 9 85	SELL	1	188.32	-4.2	-2.18%	68.63%	-4066.19	182320.21	31	39
72	OCT 18 85	BUY	0	187.04	1.28	0.68%	69.31%	1239.22	183559.43	32	39
73	JAN 17 86	SELL	1	208.43	21.39	11.44%	80.75%	20991.96	204551.39	33	39
74	JAN 31 86	BUY	0	211.78	-3.35	-1.61%	79.14%	-3287.66	201263.73	33	40
75	APR 4 86	SELL	1	228.69	16.91	7.98%	87.13%	16070.31	217334.04	34	40
76	APR 11 86	BUY	0	235.97	-7.28	-3.18%	83.94%	-6918.50	210415.54	34	41
77	APR 18 86	SELL	1	242.38	6.41	2.72%	86.66%	5715.83	216131.37	35	41
78	MAY 9 86	BUY	0	237.85	4.53	1.87%	88.53%	4039.42	220170.79	36	41
79	MAY 16 86	SELL	1	232.76	-5.09	-2.14%	86.39%	-4711.66	215459.12	36	42
80	AUG 22 86	BUY	0	250.19	-17.43	-7.49%	78.90%	-16134.44	199324.68	36	43
81	SEP 5 86	SELL	1	250.47	0.28	0.11%	79.01%	223.07	199547.76	37	43
82	OCT 10 86	BUY	0	235.48	14.99	5.98%	85.00%	11942.43	211490.19	38	43
83	DEC 12 86	SELL	1	247.35	11.87	5.04%	90.04%	10660.73	222150.92	39	43
84	JAN 9 87	BUY	0	258.73	-11.38	-4.60%	85.44%	-10220.65	211930.27	39	44
85	MAR 6 87	BUY	1	290.52	31.79	12.29%	97.73%	26039.75	237970.02	40	44

120.03

*THURSDAY'S CLOSING PRICES DUE TO HOLIDAYS

indicates the level of the S&P 500 Index closing on the date of the signal. "Points" shows the change of the S&P 500 Index between signals. A plus sign ($+$) indicates a profitable trade, while a minus sign ($-$) indicates a loss. Note the total gain of 120.03 points, which is 63% of the 190.55 total up move in the S&P 500 Index. Next, the point change is converted into percentage movement, cumulated, then converted to portfolio value dollars (base value $100,000). Total cumulative portfolio value is the bottom line, and it grew 138% to 237,970.02 over the 9.5 years. This underperformed a gain of 191% for a passive buy-and-hold strategy. Moreover, a significant criticism of the decision rule used is that portfolio value fell nearly 26% from February 11, 1983 to December 21, 1984, although the S&P 500 Index itself advanced 23%. Also, this rule has not added significantly to portfolio value since February 11, 1983. Finally, the last two columns show that 40 (or 47% of the 85 trades) produced positive results, 44 (or 52%) produced losses, and one produced no change. Obviously, this indicator has not performed up to our 40-week simple moving average crossover rule standard of comparison.

POSITIVE VOLUME INDEX

The Positive Volume Index focuses on market action during periods of increasing volume. It is a cumulative indicator that can be calculated using any market index (such as the Dow Jones Industrial Average) or the net difference between the number of advancing and declining issues along with volume statistics from the New York Stock Exchange. Daily or weekly data can be used in the computation.

The first step in calculating the Positive Volume Index is to compare the current day's volume to the previous day's volume. If the current day's volume is less than the previous day's volume, there is no advance and therefore the Positive Volume Index remains at the value it had on the previous day.

If the current day's volume is greater than the previous day's, an advance in volume has occurred. As a result, the Positive Volume Index is calculated by dividing the current day's gain (or loss) in a market index by the market index on the previous day. Since the indicator is cumulative in nature, the calculated value is then added to the previous day's value of the Positive Volume Index.

Using an arbitrary base index level of 100.00, the following example illustrates how to calculate the indicator.

Day	Volume (Millions of Shares)	Volume Change	Percent Change In Market Index	Negative Volume Index
1	168	– –		100.00
2	137	Down		100.00
3	141	Up	+ 0.57	100.57
4	138	Down		100.57
5	181	Up	– 1.54	99.03
6	161	Down		99.03
7	145	Down		99.03
8	183	Up	+ 1.02	100.05
9	189	Up	+ 0.22	100.27
10	178	Down		100.27

On Day 3, volume advanced to 141 million shares. Since the change in volume from Day 2 was positive, the positive volume index was increased by the percent change in the market index. The indicator's use implies that sophisticated investors were buying, leading to higher stock prices. On Day 4, no change to the indicator reading was made since the change in volume was not positive.

A visual display of the Positive Volume Index from 1984 to 1986 versus the Standard & Poor's 500 Index is shown in Exhibit P-4 (page 388).

The common method of interpreting the Positive Volume Index is rather subjective. You use technical analysis tools, such as trendlines, to determine the direction in which stock prices are going based on whether the "smart" money is buying or selling.

Norman Fosback (The Institute for Econometric Research, 3471 North Federal Highway, Fort Lauderdale, FL 33306) recommends that a simple moving average crossover rule be used for more objective interpretation of the Positive Volume Index.* His approach is to average indicator readings over the past year and then compare the current period's (day or week) reading to the 1 year average. If it is above the average, an uptrend in the Positive Volume Index is in progress and stock prices should continue to rise. If it is below the average, a downtrend signaling selling is in progress and stock prices are likely to go lower.

---

*Reprinted with permission.

EXHIBIT P-4:
Positive Volume Index (top) Versus The Standard & Poor's 500 Index (bottom) from 1984 to 1986

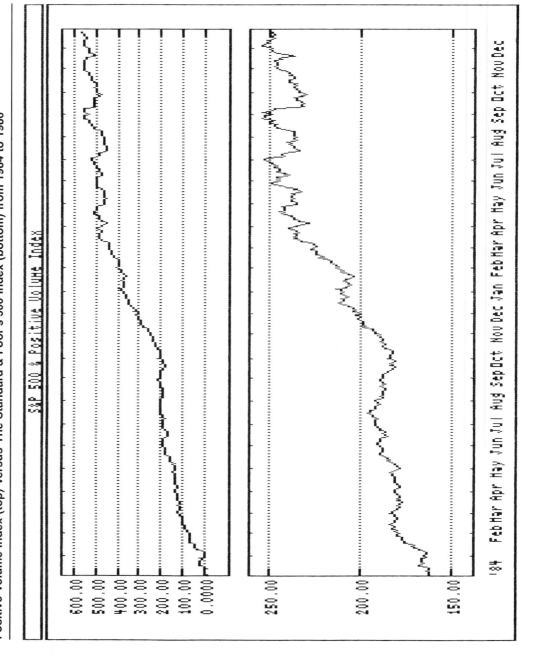

Using weekly data, Fosback tested his method of interpretation over a period of 35 years (1941 to 1975). He concluded that when the current weekly Positive Volume Index is above its 1 year average, the odds are approximately 80% that the stock market is in a major bull market. On the other hand, when the current weekly Positive Volume Index is below its 1 year average, the odds are slightly less than 70% that the stock market is in a bear market.

For a discussion of a related indicator, refer to section on the Negative Volume Index.

PREHOLIDAY SEASONALITY

History shows that stock market prices tend to rise on the last trading day before holidays. Arthur Merrill (Merrill Analysis, Inc., Box 228, Chappaqua, NY 10514) first revealed this phenomenon in his 1966 book *Behavior of Prices on Wall Street*. Recently, Merrill updated his preholiday price study to cover the period from 1897 and 1986.* He discovered that on the last trading day before eight annual holidays, the Dow Jones Industrial Average (DJIA) has risen 67.9% of the time. For all trading days during the same period of time, the DJIA increased only 52.5% of the time.

The percentage of times the DJIA has risen on the last trading day before each of the eight holidays follows:

New Year's Day	70.8%
Washington's Birthday	48.9%
Good Friday	61.5%
Memorial Day	75.0%
July 4	75.3%
Labor Day	79.6%
Thanksgiving	60.2%
Christmas	72.2%

Since the rationale behind this bullish bias before holidays is not clear, we recommend the use of this knowledge in conjunction with other indicators.

---

*Reprinted with permission.

PRESIDENTIAL ELECTION CYCLE

The United States Presidential Election Cycle is based on the observation that every 4 years the incumbent President tends to behave in a political manner so as to get reelected or keep his party in power. As a result, stock prices tend to rise in the last 2 years of an administration far more significantly than in the first 2 years.

Yale Hirsch has performed extensive research with regard to the Presidential Election Cycle. His results, summarized in Exhibit P-5, provide a convincing argument that the cycle does work. The total net market gain for the last 2 years (election year and pre-election year) of the 38 administrations since 1832 was 515%.* This compares to an insignificant 8% total net market gain for the first 2 years of these administrations.

Some caution is warranted. Although the total gains confirm the theory behind the Presidential Election Cycle, extreme variation does occur. For example, in 1985 and 1986, 2 years when we expected stock prices to be flat or down, they were up significantly (25% and 19%, respectively).

The most consistent return has been provided during the pre-election year. Double-digit gains have been experienced toward the end of the last nine administrations.

One investment strategy utilizing the Presidential Election Cycle was developed in 1973 by David MacNeill. He noted that excellent results could be produced by investing in stocks for the 2 years prior to the election and switching to Treasury bills for the next 2 years. As shown in Exhibit P-6 (page 392), the strategy resulted in a total return of 1860% between 1962 and 1984. A buy-and-hold strategy for that same period resulted in less than one third of that return (518%).

An update of the Presidential Election Cycle is provided annually in Yale Hirsch's *Stock Traders Almanac*, along with other interesting and useful investment statistics (The Hirsch Organization, Inc., Six Deer Trail, Old Tappan, NJ 07675).

---

*Reprinted with permission.

EXHIBIT P-5:

Stock Market Action Since 1832 (Net change from year to year based on average December prices)

President Elected	4-year cycle beginning	Election Year	Post-Election Year	Mid-term	Pre-Election Year
Jackson (D)	1832	15%	− 3%	10%	2%
Van Buren (D)	1836	− 8	− 8	1	−13
W.H. Harrison (W)**	1840*	5	−14	−13	36
Polk (D)	1844*	8	6	−15	1
Taylor (W)**	1848*	− 4	0	19	− 3
Pierce (D)	1852*	20	−13	−30	1
Buchanan (D)	1856	4	−30	− 7	− 7
Lincoln (R)	1860*	− 4	− 4	43	30
Lincoln (R)**	1864	0	−14	− 3	− 6
Grant (R)	1868	2	− 7	− 4	7
Grant (R)	1872	7	−13	3	− 4
Hayes (R)	1876	−18	−10	6	43
Garfield (R)**	1880	19	3	− 3	− 9
Cleveland (D)	1884*	−19	20	9	− 7
B. Harrison (R)	1888*	− 2	3	−14	18
Cleveland (D)	1892*	1	−20	− 3	1
McKinley (R)	1896*	− 2	13	19	7
McKinley (R)**	1900	14	16	1	−19
1832–1903 totals		38%	−75%	19%	78%
T. Roosevelt (R)	1904	25	16	3	−33
Taft (R)	1908	37	14	−12	1
Wilson (D)	1912*	3	−14	− 9	32
Wilson (D)	1916	3	−31	16	13
Harding (R)**	1920*	−24	7	20	− 3
Coolidge (R)	1924	19	23	5	26
Hoover (R)	1928	36	−15	−29	−47
F. Roosevelt (D)	1932*	−18	48	− 2	39
F. Roosevelt (D)	1936	28	−34	13	0
F. Roosevelt (D)	1940	−12	−15	6	21
F. Roosevelt (D)**	1944	14	33	−10	− 2
Truman (D)	1948	− 2	11	20	15
Eisenhower (R)	1952*	7	− 3	39	23
Eisenhower (R)	1956	4	−13	33	11
Kennedy (D)**	1960*	− 4	27	−13	18
Johnson (D)	1964	13	9	−11	17
Nixon (R)	1968*	12	−14	− 1	10
Nixon (R)***	1972	12	−19	−32	32
Carter (D)	1976*	18	−10	2	11
Reagan (R)	1980*	26	− 7	13	18
Reagan (R)	1984	0	25	19	
1904–1986 totals		197%	−38%	70%	202%
1832–1986 totals		235%	−37%	89%	280%

* Party in power ousted   ** Death in office   *** Resigned
D—Democrat, W—Whig, R—Republican

Source: By permission of the Hirsch Organization, Inc.

EXHIBIT P-6:
Political Investment Switching Strategy

POLITICAL INVESTMENT SWITCHING STRATEGY

Date:	S&P 500 Price	Annual Dividend	Annual Price Apprec.	Annual Total Return	Treasury Bills Risk-Free Return	2 Year S&P 500 Apprec.	2 Year S&P 500 Total Return	2 Year Risk-Free Return
11/30/62	62.26							
11/30/63	72.23	2.28	16.0%	19.7%	3.2%			
11/30/64	84.42	2.50	16.9%	20.3%	3.5%	35.6%	44.0%*	6.8%
11/30/65	91.61	2.72	8.5%	11.7%	3.9%			
11/30/66	80.45	2.87	−12.2%	− 9.0%	4.8%	− 4.7%	1.6%	8.9%*
11/30/67	94.00	2.92	16.8%	20.5%	4.2%			
11/30/68	108.37	3.07	15.3%	18.6%	5.2%	34.7%	42.9%*	9.6%
11/30/69	93.81	3.16	−13.4%	−10.5%	6.6%			
11/30/70	87.20	3.14	− 7.0%	− 3.7%	6.5%	−19.5%	−13.8%	13.5%*
11/30/71	93.99	3.07	7.8%	11.3%	4.4%			
11/30/72	116.67	3.15	24.1%	27.5%	3.8%	33.8%	41.9%*	8.4%
11/30/73	95.96	3.38	−17.8%	−14.9%	6.9%			
11/30/74	69.97	3.60	−27.1%	−23.3%	8.0%	−40.0%	−34.7%	15.5%*
11/30/75	91.24	3.68	30.4%	35.7%	5.8%			
11/30/76	102.10	4.05	11.9%	16.3%	5.1%	45.9%	57.8%*	11.2%
11/30/77	94.83	4.67	− 7.1%	− 2.5%	5.1%			
11/30/78	94.70	5.07	− 0.1%	5.2%	7.2%	− 7.2%	2.6%	12.7%*
11/30/79	106.16	5.65	12.1%	18.1%	9.8%			
11/30/80	140.52	6.16	32.4%	38.2%	11.9%	48.4%	63.2%*	22.9%
11/30/81	126.35	6.63	−10.1%	− 5.4%	13.9%			
11/30/82	138.54	6.87	9.6%	15.0%	10.5%	− 1.4%	8.8%	25.9%*
11/30/83	166.40	7.09	20.1%	25.2%	10.5%			
11/30/84	163.58	7.53	− 1.7%	2.8%	9.7%	18.0%	28.7%*	21.2%*
				22-Year Total Return	162.7%		517.8%	325.7%

* 2 Years Stocks/2 Years Treasuries 1860.4% *

Source: By Permission of The Hirsch Organization, Inc.

PRICE CHANNEL TRADING RANGE BREAKOUT RULE

According to Steven L. Kille's *Back Trak Software Manual* (PO Box 272, Macomb, IL 61455), Price Channel is one of the simplest and oldest trend-following models. It requires no calculations. The rules are: Buy when the weekly closing price moves up to a new n-period high; sell and sell short when the weekly closing price moves down to a new n-period low. In other words, when price moves out of its n-period range, go in the direction of this new trend.

EXHIBIT P-7:
Profit Summary for Price Channel of 29 Weeks, 1968 to 1986

Number Of Trades Made	> 13		Commissions Paid	> 0
Number Of Weeks In Market	> 952		Frequency Of Trades	> 0.99
Number Of Winning Trades	> 9		Largest Winning Trade	> 4547
Total Of Winning Trades	> 11673		Average Winning Trade	> 1297
Number Of Losing Trades	> 4		Largest Losing Trade	> −674
Total Of Losing Trades	> −1753		Average Losing Trade	> −438
Largest Winning Streak	> 3		Largest Losing Streak	> 1
Win/Loss Ratio	> 2.25		Profit/Margin Ratio	> 4.96
Number Of Stops Hit	> 0		Stops Frequency	> 0.00
Largest Drawdown	> −1746		Largest Unrealized Loss	> −665
Largest Obtained Equity	> 10338		Number Of Tradeable Weeks	> 961
Short Profit Or Loss	> 802		Long Profit Or Loss	> 9118
Total Profit Or Loss	> 9920		Average Weekly Gain/Loss	> 10.42

We tested this indicator using Back Trak software and a 19-year test period of weekly data (consisting of high, low, close, and volume for each week) for the broad-based NYSE Composite Index. The period ran from January 5, 1968 through December 31, 1986.

We optimized n by testing weekly periods of 1 to 78 weeks. We assumed execution of trades on the close at week's end. Highest total profit was demonstrated by the 29-week trading range breakout rule, as shown in Exhibits P-7 and P-8. Total profit of 99.20 NYSE points was somewhat above our 40-week simple moving average crossover rule standard of comparison. Trading frequency was low—only 13 trades in 18 years—so average profit per trade was an impressive 7.63. Also, 9 of those 13 trades, or 69.23%, produced a profit, while only 4, or 30.77%, produced a loss.

EXHIBIT P-8:
Transaction Dates and Prices for Price Channel of 29 Weeks, 1968 to 1986

Date	Exit	Enter	Pos.	Drdwn	OpnEq	Net	Total	Contracts
681004	0	5798	Long	0	25	0	0	1
690620	5388	5388	Shrt	−716	23	−410	−410	1
701204	4908	4908	Long	−1007	−43	480	70	1
711112	5047	5047	Shrt	−863	−38	139	209	1
711231	5721	5721	Long	−1577	−78	−674	−465	1
730323	5958	5958	Shrt	−1119	143	237	−228	1
750221	4307	4307	Long	−954	63	1651	1423	1
770527	5336	5336	Shrt	−384	68	1029	2452	1
780428	5397	5397	Long	−537	−7	−61	2391	1
810828	6955	6955	Shrt	−1389	−242	1558	3949	1
820903	6941	6941	Long	−1048	85	14	3963	1
840210	8959	8959	Shrt	−971	−48	2018	5981	1
840914	9567	9567	Long	−1393	138	−608	5373	1
861226	14114	9567	−Lng	−418	4547	4547	9920	1

Clearly, this model needs a trend to follow. In the choppy years from 1968 to March 23, 1973, cumulative results fluctuated narrowly up and down and stood at a loss of 2.28 NYSE points after 5 years. Equity has jumped strongly since 1982, as this system allows profits to run. Total profit to worst loss was 99.20 to 17.46 or 5.68 to 1.

On the whole, the 29-week Price Channel (range) breakout rule has performed suprisingly well given its extreme simplicity of analysis and interpretation. Despite its simplicity, Price Channel obviously can be reasonably effective.

PRICE/DIVIDEND RATIO

The Price/Dividend Ratio is the inverse of dividend yield. It expresses stock prices as multiplies of dividends. It is calculated by dividing a market index by the amount of dividends paid per share of stock during the preceding 12 months. For example, if the market index is $100 and the dividends per share paid during the prior 12 months is $4, the price/dividend ratio is 25 ($100 divided by $4).

Very low readings indicate undervaluation and the potential for stock prices to rise, whereas very high readings imply overvaluation and the potential for stock prices to decline.

The Price/Dividend Ratio often is used as a fundamental valuation of a company, as well as a means of comparing various companies, industries, and the market as a whole. It can also be viewed in a technical fashion.

Exhibit P-9 shows a 72-year history of the Price/Dividend Ratio for the Dow Jones Industrial Average stocks in aggregate. As indicated on the chart, the norm for the 72-year period is 22.2 times dividends.

Early analysis of the Price/Dividend Ratio was conducted by Edison Gould and Arthur Merrill. More recently Ned Davis (Ned Davis Research, Inc., P.O. Box 2089, Venice, FL 34284) has performed extensive research on the Price/Dividend Ratio.* He notes that when the ratio goes above 30, the market is "expensive" or overvalued. On the other hand, when the ratio goes below 16, the market is offering "bargains" or is undervalued. These

---

*Reprinted with permission.

EXHIBIT P-9:
Price/Dividend Ratio (bottom) Versus Dow Jones Industrial Average (top) from 1915 to 1987

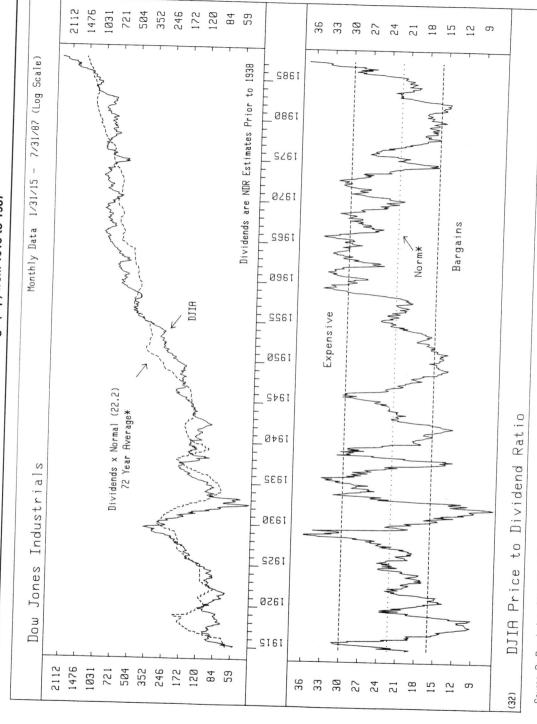

Source: By Permission of Ned Davis Research, Inc.

guidelines are not adequate for precise timing since extreme readings can be reached and maintained for lengthy periods of time. However, the ratio can be used as a warning sign that valuations are deviating from the norm.

Refer to the section on Dividend Yields for further examination of these concepts.

PRICE/EARNINGS RATIO

The Price/Earnings Ratio normally is calculated on an individual company basis by dividing the market price of a company's stock by the current annual earnings per share of stock for that company. For example, if the market price of a company's stock is $100 and the company's earnings per share is $5, the Price/Earnings Ratio is 20 ($100 divided by $5).

The Price/Earnings Ratio also can be calculated for a group of stocks or for the stock market as a whole. This is accomplished simply by adding up the market prices for the stocks and dividing the sum by the total of the earnings per share for that same group of stocks. In general, low readings are considered to indicate undervaluation (and the potential for the stock's or group of stocks' price to rise) and high readings imply overvaluation (and potential for the stock's or group of stocks' price to fall).

The Price/Earnings Ratio often is used as a fundamental valuation of a company, as well as a means of comparing various companies, industries, and the market as a whole. It also can be used in a technical fashion when viewed in its market aggregate form.

Exhibit P-10 shows an 82-year history of the Price/Earnings Ratio for the Dow Jones Industrial Average stocks in aggregate. As indicated on the chart, the norm for the 82-year period is a Price/Earnings Ratio equal to 13.6.

Ned Davis (Ned Davis Research, Inc., P.O. Box 2089, Venice, FL 34284) has performed extensive research on the Price/Earnings Ratio.* He noted that when this ratio goes above 18, the market is considered overvalued and therefore vulnerable to unfavorable surprises. On the other hand, when the ratio goes below 10.5, the market is considered undervalued and potentially attractive. Unfortunately, the Price/Earnings Ratio cannot be used as a precise indicator because extreme readings can be reached and maintained for

---

*Reprinted with permission.

EXHIBIT P-10:
Price/Earnings Ratio (bottom) Versus Dow Jones Industrial Average (top) from 1905 to 1987

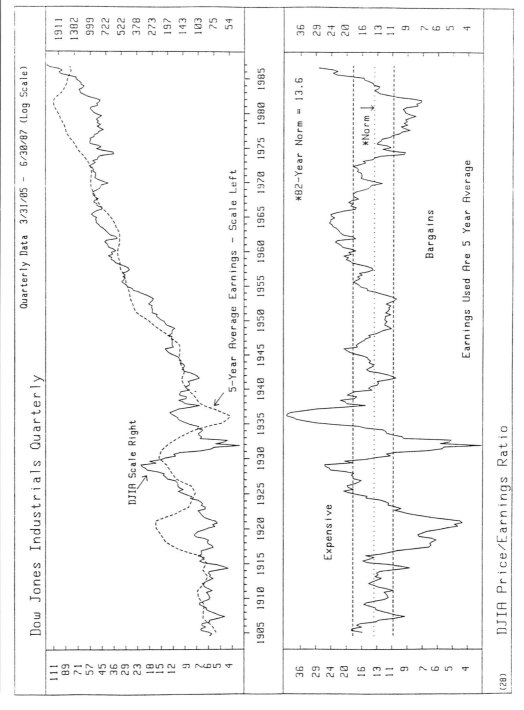

Source: By Permission of Ned Davis Research, Inc.

lengthy periods of time. However, the ratio can be used as a warning sign that market price valuations are deviating from the norm and thus may be vulnerable to a correction or return to the norm.

PRIME RATE INDICATOR

The Prime Rate Indicator is a long-term monetary indicator developed by Martin Zweig (The Zweig Forecast, P.O. Box 5345, New York, NY 10150).* The prime rate is the interest rate that banks charge their best customers. Prime rate changes occur on average less than once per month and normally only after there is a change in other interest rates, such as the federal funds rate.

Zweig contends that the lag in prime rate changes behind other interest rate changes is advantageous for investors. Changes in interest rates often precede changes in the stock market. Accordingly, prime rate changes, by lagging behind other interest rates, often can signal the point at which stocks will begin responding to a change in overall interest rates.

Zweig determined that 8% is a key prime rate level. The Prime Rate Indicator produces two buy signals and two sell signals, one each for above 8%, which is considered a relatively high prime rate level, and one each for below 8%, which is viewed as a relatively low prime rate level.

The first buy signal occurs on any initial reduction in the prime rate from a peak of less than 8%. For example, if the prime rate rises from 4% to 6 1/2% in several steps and subsequently is cut to 6%, an immediate buy signal is given.

Above the 8% level, a more significant prime rate change is required to invoke a buy signal. The second buy signal is given on the second of two cuts or a full 1% reduction, a rare occurrence, in the prime rate from a peak of 8% or greater. For example, if the prime rate rises in several steps to 12 1/2% and then is cut to 12%, a signal is not yet given. An additional cut from the 12% level is required for the buy signal.

The first sell signal occurs on any initial rise in the prime rate from a low of 8% or greater. For example, if the prime rate drops from 12% to 9% in several steps and subsequently is increased to 9 1/2%, an immediate sell signal is given.

---

*Reprinted with permission.

The second sell signal is given on the second of two increases or a full 1% rise, a rare occurrence, in the prime rate from a low of less than 8%. For example, if the prime rate is cut from 9% to 6% in several steps and subsequently is increased to 6 1/2%, followed by another increase to 7%, conditions for the sell signal are met.

Zweig tested the Prime Rate Indicator for the period of 1954 to 1984. His results indicated that 83% of the 18 buy signals were correct. Overall buy signals produced an average annualized return of 17.2% (as measured by the Standard & Poor's 500 Index), significantly higher than a buy-and-hold return of 6.2% per year for the same time period.

Sell signals were not as accurate as buy signals, being correct only 59% of 18 signals. An average annualized loss of 4.9% occurred in the S&P 500 subsequent to Prime Rate Indicator sell signals.

Further discussion of the Prime Rate Indicator appears in Zweig's 1986 book entitled *Winning On Wall Street* (Warner Books, New York, NY).

PUBLIC SHORT RATIO

Investors sell short stock when they anticipate its price going lower. At a later date, they must cover their short sales and buy the stock back. A profit is made if the stock is bought back at a lower price than when it was sold short.

On a weekly basis, the New York Stock Exchange releases information on short sales, including those made by stock exchange members and those made by nonmembers. The Public Short Ratio is computed by dividing total nonmember short sales by total short sales.

Since the public (nonmembers) normally is wrong about stock price trends, low public short ratio readings are viewed as bearish and high readings as bullish.

We tested the Public Short Ratio for the period of January 1946 to March 1987 on a weekly basis. In addition, we applied a 10-period simple moving average to the weekly readings to smooth out any erratic movements. The results are shown in Exhibits P-11 and P-12 (pages 400–401).

The test process was as follows. The indicator readings for the test period were divided into 20 ranges with approximately the same number of occurrences in each range. For each reading in a range, the gain or loss in four subsequent time periods (1 month later, 3 months later, 6 months later, and 12 months later) was calculated. The combined results for readings within each

EXHIBIT P-11:
Interpretation of Public Short Ratio's Weekly Readings

```
=====================================================================================
PUBLIC SHORT RATIO - WEEKLY DATA
PERIOD ANALYZED: JANUARY 1946 TO MARCH 1987
=====================================================================================

  INDICATOR RANGE              INTERPRETATION GIVEN INVESTOR'S TIME FRAME
-----------------    -----------------------------------------------------------------

          LESS
GREATER  THAN OR
  THAN   EQUAL TO    1 MONTH           3 MONTHS          6 MONTHS          12 MONTHS
-------  --------    ----------------  ----------------  ----------------  ----------------

 0.000    0.132      VERY BEARISH      VERY BEARISH      BEARISH           VERY BEARISH
 0.132    0.148      BEARISH           VERY BEARISH      SLIGHTLY BEARISH  SLIGHTLY BEARISH
 0.148    0.159      NEUTRAL           VERY BEARISH      BEARISH           VERY BEARISH
 0.159    0.168      NEUTRAL           VERY BEARISH      NEUTRAL           NEUTRAL
 0.168    0.177      NEUTRAL           NEUTRAL           NEUTRAL           NEUTRAL
 0.177    0.184      NEUTRAL           NEUTRAL           NEUTRAL           NEUTRAL
 0.184    0.192      NEUTRAL           NEUTRAL           NEUTRAL           BEARISH
 0.192    0.200      NEUTRAL           NEUTRAL           NEUTRAL           NEUTRAL
 0.200    0.208      NEUTRAL           NEUTRAL           NEUTRAL           NEUTRAL
 0.208    0.217      NEUTRAL           NEUTRAL           NEUTRAL           NEUTRAL
 0.217    0.227      NEUTRAL           NEUTRAL           NEUTRAL           NEUTRAL
 0.227    0.239      NEUTRAL           NEUTRAL           NEUTRAL           NEUTRAL
 0.239    0.252      NEUTRAL           NEUTRAL           NEUTRAL           NEUTRAL
 0.252    0.265      NEUTRAL           SLIGHTLY BULLISH  NEUTRAL           SLIGHTLY BULLISH
 0.265    0.282      NEUTRAL           NEUTRAL           NEUTRAL           NEUTRAL
 0.282    0.300      NEUTRAL           NEUTRAL           NEUTRAL           NEUTRAL
 0.300    0.323      SLIGHTLY BULLISH  NEUTRAL           NEUTRAL           BULLISH
 0.323    0.353      NEUTRAL           VERY BULLISH      VERY BULLISH      VERY BULLISH
 0.353    0.407      NEUTRAL           SLIGHTLY BULLISH  BULLISH           VERY BULLISH
 0.407    0.611      BULLISH           VERY BULLISH      VERY BULLISH      VERY BULLISH

=====================================================================================
```

Definitions of Very Bullish, Bullish, Slightly Bullish, Neutral, Slightly Bearish, Bearish, and Very Bearish are provided in Appendix A.

range were statistically compared, using chi-squared tests, to the performance of the overall market (as measured by the S&P 500). Varying degrees of bullishness and bearishness were noted on the basis of that comparison.

Our research results confirm that high indicator readings are very bullish and low readings are very bearish. In particular, during the past 40 years, when the 10-week moving average of the Public Short Ratio has been 0.35 or higher, an average gain has occurred in the overall market (as measured by the

EXHIBIT P-12:

Interpretation of Public Short Ratio's 10-Week Simple Moving Average Readings

```
=====================================================================================
PUBLIC SHORT RATIO - 10 WEEK MOVING AVERAGE
PERIOD ANALYZED: JANUARY 1946 TO MARCH 1987
=====================================================================================
```

INDICATOR RANGE		INTERPRETATION GIVEN INVESTOR'S TIME FRAME			
GREATER THAN	LESS THAN OR EQUAL TO	1 MONTH	3 MONTHS	6 MONTHS	12 MONTHS
0.000	0.150	VERY BEARISH	VERY BEARISH	VERY BEARISH	VERY BEARISH
0.150	0.162	NEUTRAL	VERY BEARISH	NEUTRAL	VERY BEARISH
0.162	0.170	NEUTRAL	VERY BEARISH	NEUTRAL	VERY BEARISH
0.170	0.176	BEARISH	NEUTRAL	NEUTRAL	NEUTRAL
0.176	0.183	NEUTRAL	BEARISH	SLIGHTLY BEARISH	NEUTRAL
0.183	0.190	NEUTRAL	NEUTRAL	NEUTRAL	NEUTRAL
0.190	0.198	NEUTRAL	BEARISH	NEUTRAL	NEUTRAL
0.198	0.204	NEUTRAL	NEUTRAL	NEUTRAL	NEUTRAL
0.204	0.211	NEUTRAL	NEUTRAL	BEARISH	BEARISH
0.211	0.220	NEUTRAL	NEUTRAL	NEUTRAL	NEUTRAL
0.220	0.231	NEUTRAL	NEUTRAL	NEUTRAL	NEUTRAL
0.231	0.242	SLIGHTLY BEARISH	NEUTRAL	NEUTRAL	SLIGHTLY BEARISH
0.242	0.252	NEUTRAL	NEUTRAL	NEUTRAL	NEUTRAL
0.252	0.262	NEUTRAL	NEUTRAL	NEUTRAL	NEUTRAL
0.262	0.273	BULLISH	VERY BULLISH	NEUTRAL	SLIGHTLY BULLISH
0.273	0.287	NEUTRAL	NEUTRAL	NEUTRAL	SLIGHTLY BULLISH
0.287	0.307	NEUTRAL	NEUTRAL	NEUTRAL	SLIGHTLY BULLISH
0.307	0.336	BULLISH	SLIGHTLY BULLISH	SLIGHTLY BULLISH	NEUTRAL
0.336	0.386	BULLISH	VERY BULLISH	VERY BULLISH	VERY BULLISH
0.386	0.511	VERY BULLISH	VERY BULLISH	VERY BULLISH	VERY BULLISH

```
=====================================================================================
```

Definitions of Very Bullish, Bullish, Slightly Bullish, Neutral, Slightly Bearish, Bearish, and Very Bearish are provided in Appendix A.

Standard & Poor's 500 Index) of 2.34% 1 month later, 6.13% 3 months later, 13.31% 6 months later, and 25.28% 12 months later. Exhibit P-13 (page 402) shows the results in greater detail. You should note that all signals generated within 3 months after an initial reading of 0.35 or higher were considered repeat signals and are not included in the results. It should also be noted that no readings of 0.35 or higher have occurred since 1974, suggesting that the value of this indicator may be diminishing.

EXHIBIT P-13:

Public Short Ratio's 10-Week Simple Moving Average Readings Equal to or Greater than 0.35 from 1947 to 1986

```
================================================================
PUBLIC SHORT RATIO - 10 WEEK MOVING AVERAGE
================================================================
```

		PERCENTAGE CHANGE IN S&P 500			
DATE	INDICATOR VALUE	1 MONTH LATER	3 MONTHS LATER	6 MONTHS LATER	12 MONTHS LATER
APR 19 1947	0.37	-4.39	11.23	8.37	7.81
AUG 1 1947	0.38	-4.43	-2.91	-7.47	0.63
FEB 11 1949	0.35	3.50	2.20	5.01	17.17
JUN 3 1949	0.45	3.27	11.96	18.43	32.38
OCT 1 1949	0.45	3.35	8.18	12.50	26.68
JAN 7 1950	0.35	1.52	2.57	3.22	23.58
SEP 11 1953	0.36	1.86	6.78	15.04	35.18
JAN 8 1954	0.35	5.21	9.83	20.90	40.55
NOV 22 1957	0.35	-3.30	-0.54	7.34	30.19
JAN 24 1958	0.35	-2.54	3.43	11.84	34.26
MAY 2 1958	0.42	1.76	8.70	17.35	31.95
JUN 29 1962	0.37	6.36	2.78	15.25	26.70
OCT 5 1962	0.36	2.24	13.44	20.06	27.65
OCT 14 1966	0.35	6.64	11.28	19.92	25.33
MAR 29 1968	0.36	8.61	13.02	15.52	16.52
MAY 8 1970	0.37	-3.97	-2.97	6.23	30.64
SEP 4 1970	0.39	4.85	8.00	19.98	19.87
SEP 13 1974	0.36	11.56	3.45	30.00	27.99
AVERAGE CHANGE		2.34	6.13	13.31	25.28

```
================================================================
```

PUBLIC/SPECIALIST SHORT RATIO

Investors sell short stock when they anticipate that its price will go lower. At a later date, they must cover their short sales and buy the stock back. A profit is made if the stock is bought back at a lower price than when it was sold short.

On a weekly basis, the New York Stock Exchange releases information on short sales, including those made by stock exchange specialists and those made by the public (nonmembers). Specialists are responsible for balancing incoming buy and sell orders to maintain orderly markets in the stocks in which they specialize. They normally are right about the trend of stock prices, while the public typically is wrong.

The Public/Specialist Short Ratio is computed by dividing the total public (nonmember) short sales by the total specialist short sales.

Since the public normally is wrong and specialists usually are right about the direction of stock prices, high Public/Specialist Short Ratio readings are considered bullish and low readings are considered bearish.

We tested the Public/Specialist Short Ratio for the period of January 1946 to March 1987 on a weekly basis. In addition, we applied a 10-period simple moving average to the weekly readings to smooth out any erratic movements. The results are shown in Exhibits P-14 and P-15 (pages 404–405).

The test process was as follows. The indicator readings for the test period were divided into 20 ranges with approximately the same number of occurrences in each range. For each reading in a range, the gain or loss in four subsequent time periods (1 month later, 3 months later, 6 months later, and 12 months later) was calculated. The combined results for readings within each range were statistically compared, using chi-squared tests, to the performance of the overall market (as measured by the Standard & Poor's 500 Index). Varying degrees of bullishness and bearishness were noted on the basis of that comparison.

Our research results confirm that low indicator readings are very bearish and high readings are very bullish. In particular, during the past 40 years, when the 10-week moving average of the Public/Specialist Short Ratio has been 0.75 or higher, an average gain has occurred in the overall market (as measured by the S&P 500) of 1.78% 1 month later, 6.04% 3 months later, 11.42% 6 months later, and 22.92% 12 months later. Exhibit P-16 (page 406) shows the results in greater detail. You should note that all signals generated within 3 months after an initial reading of 0.75 or higher were considered repeat signals and are not included in the results. It also should be noted that no readings of 0.75 or higher have occurred since 1974, suggesting that the value of this indicator may be diminishing.

EXHIBIT P-14:
Interpretation of Public/Specialist Short Ratio's Weekly Readings

```
=====================================================================================
PUBLIC/SPECIALIST SHORT RATIO - WEEKLY DATA
PERIOD ANALYZED:  JANUARY 1946 TO MARCH 1987
=====================================================================================

INDICATOR RANGE              INTERPRETATION GIVEN INVESTOR'S TIME FRAME
---------------    ------------------------------------------------------------------
          LESS
GREATER  THAN OR
  THAN   EQUAL TO   1 MONTH          3 MONTHS          6 MONTHS          12 MONTHS
-------  --------  ----------------  ----------------  ----------------  ----------------

0.000    0.221   BEARISH           VERY BEARISH      NEUTRAL           VERY BEARISH
0.221    0.266   NEUTRAL           SLIGHTLY BEARISH  NEUTRAL           VERY BEARISH
0.266    0.290   NEUTRAL           VERY BEARISH      VERY BEARISH      VERY BEARISH
0.290    0.315   NEUTRAL           BEARISH           VERY BEARISH      VERY BEARISH
0.315    0.337   NEUTRAL           BEARISH           SLIGHTLY BEARISH  BEARISH
0.337    0.361   NEUTRAL           NEUTRAL           NEUTRAL           NEUTRAL
0.361    0.382   NEUTRAL           NEUTRAL           SLIGHTLY BEARISH  NEUTRAL
0.382    0.401   NEUTRAL           NEUTRAL           NEUTRAL           NEUTRAL
0.401    0.424   NEUTRAL           BEARISH           NEUTRAL           NEUTRAL
0.424    0.448   NEUTRAL           NEUTRAL           NEUTRAL           NEUTRAL
0.448    0.474   NEUTRAL           NEUTRAL           NEUTRAL           BULLISH
0.474    0.504   NEUTRAL           NEUTRAL           NEUTRAL           NEUTRAL
0.504    0.535   NEUTRAL           NEUTRAL           NEUTRAL           BULLISH
0.535    0.564   NEUTRAL           NEUTRAL           NEUTRAL           NEUTRAL
0.564    0.607   NEUTRAL           NEUTRAL           NEUTRAL           NEUTRAL
0.607    0.654   NEUTRAL           NEUTRAL           NEUTRAL           NEUTRAL
0.654    0.712   SLIGHTLY BULLISH  SLIGHTLY BULLISH  VERY BULLISH      VERY BULLISH
0.712    0.804   SLIGHTLY BULLISH  SLIGHTLY BULLISH  NEUTRAL           VERY BULLISH
0.804    1.000   NEUTRAL           BULLISH           VERY BULLISH      VERY BULLISH
1.000    2.223   BULLISH           VERY BULLISH      VERY BULLISH      VERY BULLISH

=====================================================================================
```

Definitions of Very Bullish, Bullish, Slightly Bullish, Neutral, Slightly Bearish, Bearish, and Very Bearish are provided in Appendix A.

EXHIBIT P-15:

Interpretation of Public/Specialist Short Ratio's 10-Week Simple Moving Average Readings

```
============================================================================================
PUBLIC/SPECIALIST SHORT RATIO - 10 WEEK MOVING AVERAGE
PERIOD ANALYZED: JANUARY 1946 TO MARCH 1987
============================================================================================
```

INDICATOR RANGE		INTERPRETATION GIVEN INVESTOR'S TIME FRAME			
GREATER THAN	LESS THAN OR EQUAL TO	1 MONTH	3 MONTHS	6 MONTHS	12 MONTHS
0.000	0.267	BEARISH	VERY BEARISH	NEUTRAL	VERY BEARISH
0.267	0.304	VERY BEARISH	VERY BEARISH	NEUTRAL	BEARISH
0.304	0.329	SLIGHTLY BEARISH	VERY BEARISH	VERY BEARISH	VERY BEARISH
0.329	0.347	NEUTRAL	VERY BEARISH	VERY BEARISH	VERY BEARISH
0.347	0.364	NEUTRAL	NEUTRAL	NEUTRAL	VERY BEARISH
0.364	0.383	NEUTRAL	NEUTRAL	NEUTRAL	VERY BEARISH
0.383	0.401	NEUTRAL	NEUTRAL	NEUTRAL	NEUTRAL
0.401	0.422	NEUTRAL	SLIGHTLY BEARISH	VERY BEARISH	NEUTRAL
0.422	0.445	NEUTRAL	NEUTRAL	NEUTRAL	NEUTRAL
0.445	0.467	NEUTRAL	NEUTRAL	NEUTRAL	NEUTRAL
0.467	0.489	NEUTRAL	NEUTRAL	NEUTRAL	BULLISH
0.489	0.508	NEUTRAL	NEUTRAL	NEUTRAL	NEUTRAL
0.508	0.528	NEUTRAL	NEUTRAL	NEUTRAL	NEUTRAL
0.528	0.552	NEUTRAL	NEUTRAL	NEUTRAL	VERY BULLISH
0.552	0.582	NEUTRAL	BULLISH	BULLISH	SLIGHTLY BULLISH
0.582	0.622	NEUTRAL	NEUTRAL	NEUTRAL	NEUTRAL
0.622	0.666	NEUTRAL	NEUTRAL	SLIGHTLY BULLISH	BULLISH
0.666	0.742	VERY BULLISH	BULLISH	VERY BULLISH	VERY BULLISH
0.742	0.943	NEUTRAL	VERY BULLISH	VERY BULLISH	VERY BULLISH
0.943	1.549	VERY BULLISH	VERY BULLISH	VERY BULLISH	VERY BULLISH

```
============================================================================================
```

Definitions of Very Bullish, Bullish, Slightly Bullish, Neutral, Slightly Bearish, Bearish, and Very Bearish are provided in Appendix A.

EXHIBIT P-16:

Public/Specialist Short Ratio's 10-Week Simple Moving Average Readings Equal to or Greater than 0.75 from 1947 to 1986

```
==================================================================
PUBLIC/SPECIALIST SHORT RATIO - 10 WEEK MOVING AVERAGE
==================================================================
```

| | | PERCENTAGE CHANGE IN S&P 500 | | | |
DATE	INDICATOR VALUE	1 MONTH LATER	3 MONTHS LATER	6 MONTHS LATER	12 MONTHS LATER
APR 12 1947	0.78	0.69	9.41	8.24	5.08
AUG 1 1947	0.85	-4.43	-2.91	-7.47	0.63
FEB 11 1949	0.80	3.50	2.20	5.01	17.17
JUN 3 1949	1.23	3.27	11.96	18.43	32.38
OCT 1 1949	1.20	3.35	8.18	12.50	26.68
JAN 7 1950	0.79	1.52	2.57	3.22	23.58
JUL 31 1953	0.75	-5.78	-0.85	5.09	24.97
NOV 6 1953	1.14	0.93	6.34	15.77	34.17
FEB 26 1954	0.76	1.95	11.09	16.90	40.04
MAR 15 1957	0.76	2.04	9.31	1.70	-3.61
NOV 1 1957	0.75	2.72	5.00	8.28	26.78
JAN 3 1958	0.77	2.86	1.79	10.89	35.65
MAY 2 1958	1.11	1.76	8.70	17.35	31.95
JUN 22 1962	0.78	6.99	9.51	18.91	33.35
OCT 5 1962	0.89	2.24	13.44	20.06	27.65
NOV 29 1963	0.76	2.44	6.47	9.40	16.29
OCT 14 1966	0.77	6.64	11.28	19.92	25.33
MAR 29 1968	0.76	8.61	13.02	15.52	16.52
MAY 8 1970	0.81	-3.97	-2.97	6.23	30.64
SEP 4 1970	0.99	4.85	8.00	19.98	19.87
AUG 23 1974	0.76	-4.93	-4.71	13.82	16.10
AVERAGE CHANGE		1.78	6.04	11.42	22.92

```
==================================================================
```

PUT/CALL PREMIUM RATIO

The Put/Call Premium Ratio is a short-term sentiment indicator. It is calculated on a weekly basis using options-related information. You divide the average premium on all listed put options by the average premium on all listed call options. Data used in the calculation is available from the Options Clearing Corporation (141 West Jackson Boulevard, Chicago, IL 60604).

As with most sentiment indicators, the Put/Call Premium Ratio is a contrary indicator. The theory is that most investors are wrong about the direction of stock prices at extremes in the market. When investors are overly pessimistic, they bid put prices up excessively, thereby expanding put premiums and causing the Put/Call Premium Ratio to be high. This is considered bullish for stock prices. On the other hand, when investors are overly optimistic, they bid call prices up excessively, thereby expanding call premiums and causing the Put/Call Premium Ratio to be low—a bearish sign.

The Put/Call Premium Ratio for a 4-year period is charted in Exhibit P-17 (page 408). According to Ned Davis (Ned Davis Research, Inc., P.O. Box 2089, Venice, FL 34284) readings above 95% are considered bullish and readings below 42% are viewed as bearish for stock prices.

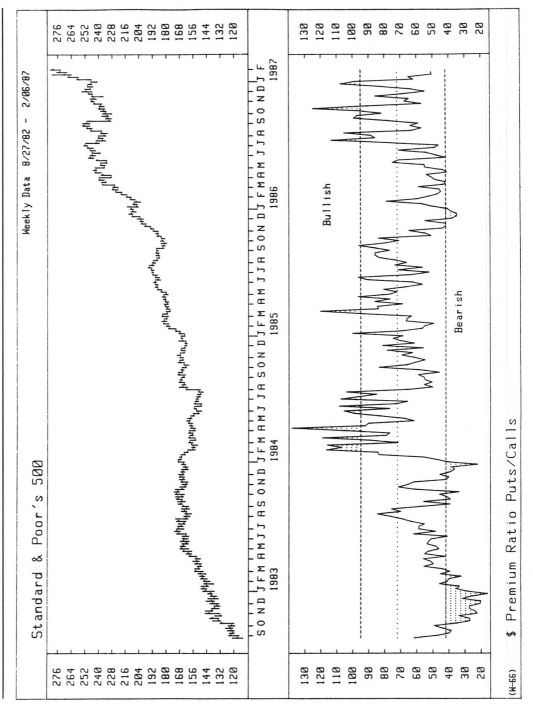

Weekly Data 8/27/82 - 2/06/87

Standard & Poor's 500

276
264
252
240
228
216
204
192
180
168
156
144
132
120

Bullish

Bearish

130
120
110
100
90
80
70
60
50
40
30
20

S O N D J F M A M J J A S O N D J F M A M J J A S O N D J F M A M J J A S O N D J F M A M J J A S O N D J F
1983   1984   1985   1986   1987

$ Premium Ratio Puts/Calls

(W-66)

Source: By permission of Ned Davis Research, Inc.

408

PUT/CALL RATIO

The Put/Call Ratio is a market sentiment indicator. It is calculated by dividing the volume of put options by the volume of call options. Daily Chicago Board Options Exchange (CBOE) data normally is used in the calculation.

As with many sentiment indicators, the Put/Call Ratio is interpreted in a contrary fashion. Since the public normally is wrong at extremes in the market, high indicator readings signifying that investors believe stocks prices are going lower are viewed as bullish. On the other hand, low indicator readings resulting from the anticipation of higher stock prices are considered bearish.

We tested the Put/Call Ratio for the period of December 1978 to March 1987 on a daily basis. In addition, we applied a 10-period simple moving average to the daily readings to smooth out any erratic movements. The results are shown in Exhibits P-18 and P-19 (pages 410–411).

The test process was as follows. The indicator readings for the test period were divided into 20 ranges with approximately the same number of occurrences in each range. For each readings in a range, the gain or loss in four subsequent time periods (1 month later, 3 months later, 6 months later, and 12 months later) was calculated. The combined results for readings within each range were statistically compared, using chi-squared tests, to the performance of the overall market (as measured by the Standard & Poor's 500 Index). Varying degrees of bullishness and bearishness were noted on the basis of that comparison.

Note that options, particularly put options, are relatively new instruments. Therefore, a final conclusion on the value of any option-related indicator is subject to question. However, some preliminary conclusions are justifiable based on our research results.

In particular, we discovered that extreme high indicator readings are very bullish. During the past 9 years, when the 10-day moving average of the Put/Call Ratio has been .70 or greater, an average gain has occurred in the overall market (as measured by the S&P 500) of 4.46% 1 month later, 10.89% 3 months later, 16.99% 6 months later, and 33.16% 12 months later. Exhibit P-20 (page 412) shows the results in greater detail. You should note that all signals generated within 3 months after an initial reading of .70 or higher were considered repeat signals and are not included in the results.

EXHIBIT P-18:
Interpretation of Put/Call Ratio's Daily Readings

```
================================================================================
PUT/CALL RATIO - DAILY DATA
PERIOD ANALYZED: DECEMBER 1978 TO MARCH 1987
================================================================================

INDICATOR RANGE                 INTERPRETATION GIVEN INVESTOR'S TIME FRAME
-----------------    ------------------------------------------------------------

          LESS
GREATER   THAN OR
THAN      EQUAL TO   1 MONTH           3 MONTHS          6 MONTHS          12 MONTHS
-------   --------   ----------------  ----------------  ----------------  ----------------

0.000     0.136      SLIGHTLY BEARISH  BEARISH           BULLISH           VERY BULLISH
0.136     0.170      SLIGHTLY BULLISH  NEUTRAL           VERY BULLISH      VERY BULLISH
0.170     0.217      NEUTRAL           NEUTRAL           NEUTRAL           NEUTRAL
0.217     0.260      NEUTRAL           NEUTRAL           NEUTRAL           VERY BEARISH
0.260     0.304      NEUTRAL           NEUTRAL           NEUTRAL           VERY BEARISH
0.304     0.338      BEARISH           NEUTRAL           VERY BEARISH      VERY BEARISH
0.338     0.367      SLIGHTLY BEARISH  SLIGHTLY BEARISH  VERY BEARISH      VERY BEARISH
0.367     0.393      NEUTRAL           NEUTRAL           BEARISH           BEARISH
0.393     0.413      NEUTRAL           SLIGHTLY BEARISH  VERY BEARISH      SLIGHTLY BEARISH
0.413     0.431      SLIGHTLY BEARISH  NEUTRAL           SLIGHTLY BEARISH  SLIGHTLY BEARISH
0.431     0.451      NEUTRAL           NEUTRAL           NEUTRAL           NEUTRAL
0.451     0.473      NEUTRAL           BEARISH           BEARISH           NEUTRAL
0.473     0.493      NEUTRAL           NEUTRAL           NEUTRAL           NEUTRAL
0.493     0.513      NEUTRAL           NEUTRAL           NEUTRAL           SLIGHTLY BULLISH
0.513     0.540      NEUTRAL           NEUTRAL           NEUTRAL           NEUTRAL
0.540     0.570      NEUTRAL           NEUTRAL           NEUTRAL           BULLISH
0.570     0.606      NEUTRAL           NEUTRAL           BULLISH           VERY BULLISH
0.606     0.659      NEUTRAL           NEUTRAL           VERY BULLISH      VERY BULLISH
0.659     0.749      NEUTRAL           SLIGHTLY BULLISH  VERY BULLISH      VERY BULLISH
0.749     2.403      SLIGHTLY BULLISH  VERY BULLISH      VERY BULLISH      VERY BULLISH

================================================================================
```

Definitions of Very Bullish, Bullish, Slightly Bullish, Neutral, Slightly Bearish, Bearish, and Very Bearish are provided in Appendix A.

EXHIBIT P-19:
Interpretation of Put/Call Ratio's 10-Day Simple Moving Average Readings

```
========================================================================================
PUT/CALL RATIO - 10 DAY MOVING AVERAGE
PERIOD ANALYZED: DECEMBER 1978 TO MARCH 1987
========================================================================================
```

INDICATOR RANGE		INTERPRETATION GIVEN INVESTOR'S TIME FRAME			
GREATER THAN	LESS THAN OR EQUAL TO	1 MONTH	3 MONTHS	6 MONTHS	12 MONTHS
0.000	0.143	VERY BEARISH	VERY BEARISH	NEUTRAL	VERY BULLISH
0.143	0.194	SLIGHTLY BULLISH	NEUTRAL	VERY BULLISH	VERY BULLISH
0.194	0.223	NEUTRAL	VERY BULLISH	SLIGHTLY BULLISH	NEUTRAL
0.223	0.258	VERY BULLISH	BULLISH	SLIGHTLY BULLISH	VERY BEARISH
0.258	0.321	NEUTRAL	NEUTRAL	NEUTRAL	VERY BEARISH
0.321	0.359	VERY BEARISH	VERY BEARISH	VERY BEARISH	VERY BEARISH
0.359	0.382	BEARISH	NEUTRAL	VERY BEARISH	BEARISH
0.382	0.402	BEARISH	NEUTRAL	VERY BEARISH	NEUTRAL
0.402	0.426	NEUTRAL	VERY BEARISH	VERY BEARISH	BEARISH
0.426	0.445	NEUTRAL	BEARISH	VERY BEARISH	VERY BEARISH
0.445	0.462	.NEUTRAL	NEUTRAL	SLIGHTLY BEARISH	NEUTRAL
0.462	0.481	NEUTRAL	SLIGHTLY BEARISH	NEUTRAL	NEUTRAL
0.481	0.499	NEUTRAL	NEUTRAL	NEUTRAL	VERY BULLISH
0.499	0.520	NEUTRAL	NEUTRAL	NEUTRAL	BULLISH
0.520	0.547	NEUTRAL	NEUTRAL	BULLISH	VERY BULLISH
0.547	0.576	NEUTRAL	NEUTRAL	NEUTRAL	VERY BULLISH
0.576	0.610	SLIGHTLY BULLISH	NEUTRAL	BULLISH	SLIGHTLY BULLISH
0.610	0.654	NEUTRAL	SLIGHTLY BULLISH	VERY BULLISH	NEUTRAL
0.654	0.707	NEUTRAL	VERY BULLISH	VERY BULLISH	BULLISH
0.707	0.864	BULLISH	VERY BULLISH	VERY BULLISH	VERY BULLISH

```
========================================================================================
```

Definitions of Very Bullish, Bullish, Slightly Bullish, Neutral, Slightly Bearish, Bearish, and Very Bearish are provided in Appendix A.

EXHIBIT P-20:
Put/Call Ratio's 10-Day Simple Moving Average Readings Equal to or Greater than 0.70 from 1979 to 1986

```
================================================================
PUT/CALL RATIO - 10 DAY MOVING AVERAGE
================================================================
```

		PERCENTAGE CHANGE IN S&P 500			
DATE	INDICATOR VALUE	1 MONTH LATER	3 MONTHS LATER	6 MONTHS LATER	12 MONTHS LATER
MAR 15 1982	0.70	5.83	0.47	11.69	38.69
AUG 9 1982	0.73	18.55	37.91	41.77	56.51
FEB 14 1984	0.72	0.51	0.89	4.99	15.26
JUN 1 1984	0.77	-0.03	8.72	6.96	22.52
AUG 16 1985	0.71	-2.55	6.45	19.53	32.80
AVERAGE CHANGE		4.46	10.89	16.99	33.16

```
================================================================
```

RANDOM WALK HYPOTHESIS

According to Ian S. Notley,* in 1900 Louis Bachelier wrote a provocative and scholarly paper, "Theory of Speculation," that became the basis for the Random Walk Hypothesis. It denies the validity of both technical and fundamental analysis. It holds that stock price variations are haphazard, and that the future cannot be predicted by any known method. It implies that stock price changes have no memory and that the past history of any data series cannot be used to predict the future in any meaningful way. This means that superior analysts who can consistently and reliably project economic events have no chance of earning extraordinary profits in the market and that the technical analysts using past price data could not succeed in determining future price trends. This hypothesis has few friends among investment professionals but enjoys popularity among academicians. No one in the latter group has improved on Bachelier's original ideas. They seem satisfied to endlessly discourage any hope of using creative intelligence to capitalize on market price fluctuations. The fact that some investors have succeeded greatly is always attributed to mere chance—despite any and all protests to the contrary.

In his 1976 book *Stock Market Logic* (Institute for Econometric Research, 3471 North Federal Highway, Fort Lauderdale, FL 33306), Norman G. Fosback noted that there have been a number of challenges to the Random Walk Hypothesis, although academic advocates may refuse to acknowledge them. Initially, the hard line random walkers were forced to admit that there has been a long-term uptrend in stock prices in line with the 200-year growth trend in earnings and dividends. Next, even allowing for long-term growth, they had to (grudgingly) admit to "other nonrandom discrepancies." Furthermore, they had to deny their earlier charges that technical strategies cannot make money, and now they reluctantly admit that technical methods very often do make profits.

Still, unbiased and thorough academic testing of optimized technical decision rules simply has not occurred. Instead, some "straw man" examples were set up and criticized as "adding little value" compared to a fully invested buy-and-hold long-term strategy. Although the latter has been quite profitable over the past two centuries, what remains generally unrecognized is that the buy-and-hold decision is an inconsistent and aggressive high risk strategy that has produced disastrous results in many time periods. A market historian can never forget that the buy-and-hold strategy lost 89% of invested capital

---

Trend and Cycle Analysis. Toronto, Ontario, Canada: Dominion Securities Limited, May 1977.

from 1929 to 1932, and it lost 20% to 50% of capital in many other "bear markets" in the past. Conservative investors reject such a risky strategy as totally unacceptable. Finally, there can be no guarantee that the long-term trend of economic growth will continue to propel stock prices upward. We have found many simple investment timing models that beat a passive buy-and-hold strategy and add weight to the argument that stock prices do not move randomly.

RATE OF CHANGE

Rate of change is a price momentum or velocity indicator. You simply divide the current price by the price *n* weeks ago and plot the result. For example, if the current price is 100 and the price *n* weeks ago was 80, then the *n*-week rate of change is simply 100 ÷ 80 or 1.25.

The only parameter to optimize is the time interval, *n*. We tested this indicator using Compu Trac software and two 9.75-year test periods of weekly data (consisting of high, low, close, and volume for each week) for the broad-based NYSE Composite Index. The first period ran from January 5, 1968 through September 30, 1977, and the second period ran from April 8, 1977 through December 31, 1986. The overlap in data was necessary to facilitate testing throughout the full time period. (Note that the Compu Trac software program multiplies the rate of change ratio by 100 for easier visual inspection and for better decimal processing. Therefore, all rate of change exhibits reflect the multiplication by 100.)

When the rate of change indicator value crossed over or below 100, a trend change and thus a trade position change was signaled in the direction of the crossing. The number of observations, *n*, that should be included in the calculation depends on the length of the cyclical movements in the time series. Optimal values were determined by a systematic trial-and-error procedure on the computer. We tested for *n* equal to 1 through 78, or rates of change ranging in length from 1 week up to 78 weeks (1.5 years). The results of optimization runs for each *n*-week time period are shown in Exhibits R-1 through R-4 (pages 415–420). "Equity" signifies total profits or losses accumulated for each pass.

The highest profit for combined optimization runs for 1968–1977 and 1977–1986 was produced by the 31-week rate of change. Total profit was 111.31, as shown in Exhibits R-8 (page 423) and R-12 (page 426). There were fairly good results for periods from 23 to 38 weeks, but very poor

EXHIBIT R-1:

Profitability Chart for Rate of Change (Period Lengths of 1 to 78 Weeks from 1977 to 1986)

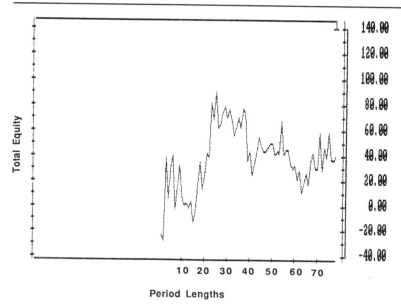

Period Lengths

results for the short periods. Note that the optimization graphs take on a relatively erratic shape, implying instability. Overall, average annual profitability of 10.88% exceeded that of our 40-week simple moving average crossover rule standard of comparison, but the 31-week rate of change suffered a larger maximum drawdown at 48.91%.

Overall, rate of change must be judged as too erratic relative to some other indicators, such as moving averages. The reason for this seems to be due to overdependence of rate of change on the oldest data. For example, for a 31-week rate of change, if price for this week was up moderately, but the price 31 weeks ago was rising steeply, then the rate of change calculation would fall sharply this week. Obviously, such a severe rate of change plunge would have nothing to do with the market's current trend. Despite that, a sell signal could be given, assuming that the previous week's rate of change calculation was only slightly positive. Thus, this dependence on old data may explain the more erratic behavior of the optimization curve for the rate of change indicator.

EXHIBIT R-2:
Profit Table for Rate of Change (Period Lengths of 1 to 78 Weeks from 1977 to 1986)

Pass	Short Equity	Long Equity	Max. Equity	Min. Equity	Total Equity	P/L	Best Trade	Worst Trade	Max. Open P/L	Min. Open P/L
1	-23.20	-53.42	30.22	0.00	-41.20	-23.20	14.67	-5.79	15.36	0.00
2	-27.55	-56.22	28.67	6.93	-34.83	-30.50	14.67	-9.41	18.37	-3.93
3	38.92	-23.00	61.92	48.69	-7.86	36.40	13.49	-6.15	17.18	-1.91
4	6.45	-38.91	45.36	29.06	-16.53	3.89	13.80	-9.41	17.74	-4.44
5	30.05	-27.20	57.25	64.80	-1.49	30.05	14.62	-9.41	17.74	-4.44
6	39.94	-22.12	62.06	63.79	-3.45	39.94	14.99	-11.07	17.79	-4.67
7	-2.90	-44.40	41.50	38.77	-6.18	-5.46	24.84	-12.51	29.32	-7.53
8	13.74	-35.74	49.48	53.03	-2.31	13.74	23.89	-9.41	29.32	-7.61
9	32.26	-26.26	58.52	43.71	-8.69	32.26	29.62	-4.44	34.17	-2.78
10	8.06	-37.94	46.00	45.23	-8.75	10.42	30.63	-9.41	36.31	-4.22
11	1.68	-40.74	42.42	26.77	-14.85	5.67	29.62	-9.41	34.17	-3.99
12	2.38	-40.64	43.02	22.44	-12.29	7.49	29.62	-7.02	34.17	-5.34
13	-1.15	-42.46	41.31	33.92	-16.48	1.80	26.37	-9.41	32.73	-3.09
14	3.77	-39.91	43.68	19.77	-36.52	6.29	26.47	-6.06	32.73	-4.67
15	-12.99	-47.93	34.94	17.08	-33.58	-10.43	23.58	-9.41	32.73	-5.24
16	-5.06	-44.76	39.70	28.33	-23.87	-5.06	23.54	-9.41	30.31	-6.43
17	18.08	-33.23	51.31	36.30	-14.02	15.13	26.57	-8.69	31.59	-7.89
18	34.49	-25.24	59.73	53.60	-10.27	31.97	25.48	-8.75	32.73	-8.69
19	13.64	-35.78	49.42	42.49	-19.47	11.08	25.86	-9.41	34.12	-8.69
20	25.46	-30.26	55.72	51.53	-18.00	25.46	27.05	-6.87	34.12	-5.80
21	41.63	-21.81	63.44	68.13	-12.00	46.74	29.63	-4.60	34.77	-5.11
22	39.20	-23.32	62.52	65.34	-8.64	42.15	29.63	-4.67	34.77	-5.62
23	81.09	-2.35	83.44	93.53	-4.35	83.61	29.12	-3.82	34.77	-3.77
24	68.99	-8.76	77.75	87.09	-8.67	71.55	39.58	-3.98	52.09	-2.56
25	89.99	2.11	87.88	101.29	-1.45	87.04	39.58	-3.15	52.09	-2.67
26	62.55	-11.72	74.27	77.69	-6.37	60.03	39.58	-4.72	52.09	-2.25
27	65.36	-10.99	76.35	77.68	-8.80	62.80	38.41	-3.98	50.24	-3.85
28	73.45	-7.26	80.71	84.63	-9.39	73.45	28.55	-4.61	39.93	-3.85
29	78.75	-4.53	83.28	86.95	-11.31	78.75	29.99	-5.03	40.50	-3.17
30	70.53	-8.89	79.42	81.99	-12.05	67.97	29.75	-4.37	39.37	-3.16
31	75.94	-4.97	80.91	82.68	-10.91	75.94	32.02	-2.53	38.76	-3.16
32	69.23	-8.42	77.65	75.97	-11.66	69.23	32.63	-4.81	39.37	-3.67
33	56.79	-14.23	71.02	63.53	-9.19	24.16	23.60	-5.20	39.37	-4.81
34	62.72	-11.76	74.48	69.46	-2.41	21.19	23.91	-5.72	48.27	-3.53
35	70.20	-8.33	78.53	76.94	-10.41	27.39	25.36	-6.23	49.55	-4.41
36	62.91	-12.03	74.94	69.65	-7.32	62.91	43.79	-6.23	50.53	-4.41
37	76.58	-4.87	81.45	83.32	-7.33	76.58	43.79	-5.84	50.53	-4.02
38	73.68	-6.20	79.88	80.42	-7.41	31.96	24.76	-3.00	48.46	-3.34
39	36.86	-25.54	62.40	43.60	-21.09	-4.86	17.98	-4.21	48.46	-3.34
40	43.21	-22.90	66.11	49.95	-15.70	1.14	17.98	-5.28	48.81	-4.40
41	25.57	-31.64	57.21	32.31	-22.08	-16.50	15.07	-5.12	48.81	-4.24
42	33.76	-27.88	61.64	40.50	-15.71	-8.72	15.07	-5.89	49.22	-5.79
43	42.90	-22.98	65.88	49.64	-7.59	0.42	15.07	-6.17	49.22	-5.23
44	55.43	-16.57	72.00	62.17	-11.86	10.37	14.87	-6.65	51.80	-5.49
45	48.88	-20.40	69.28	55.62	-13.15	4.22	15.49	-6.05	51.40	-5.95
46	43.15	-23.12	66.27	49.89	-12.31	0.13	13.94	-8.11	49.76	-7.30
47	43.63	-23.14	66.77	50.37	-6.81	0.61	13.94	-8.11	49.76	-7.30
48	47.50	-20.80	68.30	54.24	-11.01	4.81	15.35	-5.42	49.43	-6.70
49	49.91	-19.21	69.12	56.65	-9.09	8.31	20.09	-5.89	48.34	-4.73
50	49.84	-19.44	69.28	56.58	-9.10	8.24	19.22	-5.60	48.34	-4.11

EXHIBIT R-2: (continued)

Pass	Short Equity	Long Equity	Max. Equity	Min. Equity	Total Equity	P/L	Best Trade	Worst Trade	Max. Open P/L	Min. Open P/L
51	41.07	-23.83	64.90	47.81	-12.22	-0.53	14.48	-5.60	48.34	-4.12
52	44.15	-22.01	66.16	50.89	-11.19	2.55	20.17	-4.57	48.34	-3.69
53	43.06	-21.79	64.85	49.80	-10.51	3.52	20.55	-4.44	46.28	-3.66
54	67.01	-9.46	76.47	73.75	-5.27	23.99	21.41	-3.33	49.76	-2.39
55	41.38	-21.65	63.03	48.12	-11.88	-1.31	16.23	-4.99	49.43	-3.85
56	44.47	-20.07	64.54	51.21	-9.09	2.87	19.55	-6.68	48.34	-5.52
57	45.47	-19.13	64.60	52.21	-4.81	3.87	14.56	-6.30	48.34	-6.68
58	33.57	-25.03	58.60	40.31	-8.03	-8.03	12.12	-9.12	48.34	-7.96
59	29.38	-27.53	56.91	36.12	-12.22	-12.22	11.81	-9.47	48.34	-9.12
60	31.91	-25.82	57.73	38.65	-9.69	-9.69	10.38	-9.47	48.34	-7.73
61	21.54	-30.48	52.02	28.28	-22.44	-21.15	9.32	-8.91	49.43	-7.06
62	28.38	-27.70	56.08	35.12	-15.60	-14.31	9.43	-10.88	49.43	-10.07
63	10.64	-37.02	47.66	17.38	-30.96	-30.96	7.01	-7.86	48.34	-6.70
64	18.40	-33.26	51.66	25.14	-23.20	-23.20	10.38	-7.18	48.34	-5.33
65	26.76	-29.24	56.00	33.50	-12.78	-12.78	11.42	-8.00	46.28	-6.15
66	17.08	-33.34	50.42	23.82	-22.46	-22.46	11.17	-8.34	46.28	-7.18
67	35.81	-23.93	59.74	42.55	-5.79	-5.79	11.19	-6.15	48.34	-3.13
68	42.00	-20.20	62.20	48.74	-1.42	2.46	18.66	-8.57	46.28	-5.63
69	29.98	-25.13	55.11	36.72	-11.62	-11.62	18.10	-8.57	48.34	-5.63
70	29.55	-25.25	54.80	36.29	-13.80	-12.05	18.10	-10.32	48.34	-7.38
71	59.20	-10.16	69.36	65.94	-8.08	14.54	17.34	-6.54	51.40	-4.30
72	29.22	-25.07	54.29	35.96	-12.38	-12.38	17.49	-8.57	48.34	-5.63
73	46.00	-17.02	63.02	52.74	-9.95	2.98	13.95	-7.38	49.76	-5.64
74	38.18	-20.08	58.26	44.92	-13.94	-4.51	13.95	-7.72	49.43	-5.64
75	58.25	-10.76	69.01	64.99	-11.76	14.27	17.15	-7.38	50.72	-5.64
76	37.37	-21.92	59.29	44.11	-13.52	-4.23	15.02	-12.27	48.34	-9.33
77	36.06	-22.37	58.43	42.80	-10.95	-3.48	15.66	-10.32	46.28	-7.38
78	39.94	-20.15	60.09	46.68	-16.33	-1.66	14.62	-12.27	48.34	-9.33

Pass indicates period length.

Equity indicates the total number of points gained or lost.

Short equity indicates the number of points gained or lost on short positions.

Long equity indicates the number of points gained or lost on long positions.

Max. equity indicates the highest total profit recorded over the tested period.

Min. equity indicates the lowest total profit recorded over the tested period.

P/L indicates total number of points gained or lost in closed positions.

Best trade indicates the highest number of points gained in any closed trade.

Worst trade indicates the highest number of points lost in any closed trade.

Max. open P/L indicates the highest gain in a position which remains open at the end of the test run.

Min. open P/L indicates the highest loss in a position which remains open at the end of the test run.

EXHIBIT R-3:
Profitability Chart for Rate of Change (Period Lengths of 1 to 78 Weeks from 1968 to 1977)

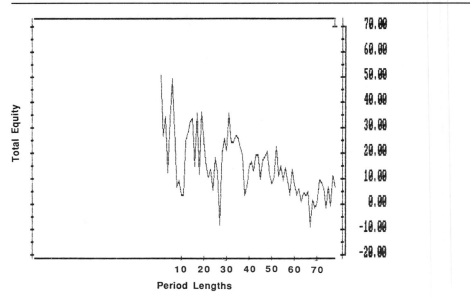

EXHIBIT R-4:

Profit Table for Rate of Change (Period Lengths of 1 to 78 Weeks from 1968 to 1977)

Pass	Short Equity	Long Equity	Max. Equity	Min. Equity	Total Equity	P/L	Best Trade	Worst Trade	Max. Open P/L	Min. Open P/L
1	50.52	25.94	24.58	72.18	-0.67	50.52	9.51	-3.24	10.26	0.00
2	26.69	13.69	13.00	40.35	0.00	26.69	8.95	-4.59	10.28	-2.00
3	34.14	16.89	17.25	50.34	0.00	34.14	9.10	-2.84	12.97	-1.91
4	12.44	5.65	6.79	20.56	-0.33	11.13	9.71	-2.84	12.97	-2.03
5	33.17	15.29	17.88	45.78	-1.57	33.17	10.49	-2.90	15.08	-2.03
6	49.16	23.28	25.88	55.34	-1.58	47.85	9.90	-3.55	15.08	-1.94
7	29.43	13.65	15.78	42.92	-1.11	28.20	8.32	-2.52	12.97	-2.35
8	6.57	1.67	4.90	18.84	-6.53	5.77	11.01	-4.49	16.19	-2.90
9	9.50	3.06	6.44	22.07	-4.92	8.70	13.44	-3.45	15.17	-3.18
10	3.74	0.20	3.54	17.22	-11.84	3.17	12.07	-4.13	14.94	-4.49
11	3.70	-0.03	3.73	15.43	-12.76	3.91	11.78	-4.55	16.65	-2.74
12	24.72	10.98	13.74	34.72	-10.71	24.93	13.86	-3.76	17.31	-1.83
13	28.42	13.70	14.72	40.09	-12.88	27.19	14.82	-5.11	17.31	-3.76
14	32.79	16.79	16.00	42.98	-9.45	32.86	14.32	-3.79	16.65	-3.31
15	34.06	17.32	16.74	41.72	-8.85	34.08	14.19	-3.69	16.65	-2.97
16	14.75	8.10	6.65	30.09	-5.72	15.49	12.86	-3.31	17.31	-2.72
17	35.51	18.88	16.63	49.59	-0.88	34.71	10.49	-3.87	14.94	-3.31
18	11.77	7.05	4.72	27.03	-8.02	11.77	9.71	-4.64	14.94	-2.60
19	36.53	19.05	17.48	46.24	-3.00	35.73	14.52	-4.64	20.19	-2.68
20	24.88	13.35	11.53	33.19	-1.17	23.57	14.52	-5.42	20.19	-3.03
21	15.31	9.00	6.31	24.95	-3.22	14.00	15.23	-6.25	20.19	-3.98
22	10.82	7.56	3.26	29.50	-3.65	9.59	14.25	-5.42	20.19	-3.98
23	14.01	9.11	4.90	29.73	-3.56	12.70	14.57	-3.86	22.58	-2.85
24	5.56	4.76	0.80	23.78	-3.31	4.25	12.18	-4.45	20.19	-2.85
25	17.97	10.62	7.35	29.15	-4.86	16.66	13.68	-4.77	22.58	-3.97
26	12.51	8.29	4.22	29.18	-5.91	10.92	13.52	-4.03	20.19	-2.91
27	-8.10	-1.63	-6.47	17.79	-11.00	-7.97	14.71	-5.57	23.61	-4.45
28	19.91	11.82	8.09	29.64	-6.79	20.04	14.40	-5.57	24.71	-4.45
29	25.33	13.84	11.49	36.12	-2.79	23.22	14.40	-4.45	24.71	-2.20
30	21.53	11.45	10.08	36.26	-2.90	19.42	13.91	-4.45	24.71	-3.39
31	35.37	18.51	16.86	48.56	0.00	33.26	13.06	-4.45	24.71	-2.20
32	24.66	13.60	11.06	38.63	0.00	22.66	15.79	-4.45	26.59	-2.20
33	24.12	13.35	10.77	38.45	0.00	22.81	14.45	-3.61	25.25	-2.80
34	27.01	14.82	12.19	34.74	-0.93	25.70	13.60	-4.39	25.25	-3.61
35	26.04	14.93	11.11	33.51	-1.35	24.73	13.68	-3.15	25.33	-2.37
36	22.31	13.00	9.31	30.36	-1.22	21.00	13.36	-4.40	25.33	-4.39
37	19.68	11.95	7.73	25.51	-3.26	18.45	15.33	-4.57	26.69	-4.40
38	3.50	4.08	-0.58	21.05	-6.30	2.70	12.40	-3.25	23.96	-3.39
39	6.98	6.20	0.78	16.49	-11.56	6.41	12.25	-3.55	23.96	-3.39
40	15.15	10.16	4.99	21.46	-7.45	15.36	12.25	-2.87	23.96	-3.39
41	16.58	11.34	5.24	27.35	-11.12	15.78	13.83	-3.98	26.69	-3.72
42	12.92	9.37	3.55	23.33	-6.44	12.99	11.10	-3.17	23.96	-3.70
43	19.20	12.17	7.03	26.87	-4.12	17.09	12.20	-2.66	25.25	-3.02
44	19.34	12.50	6.84	26.81	-8.30	17.34	13.64	-3.54	26.69	-3.28
45	10.22	8.53	1.69	16.05	-12.66	8.04	9.68	-4.72	23.96	-4.46
46	17.24	12.26	4.98	29.43	-7.96	15.93	11.76	-3.25	25.33	-5.16
47	18.88	13.67	5.21	29.37	-6.50	17.57	12.28	-4.19	25.33	-6.34
48	20.66	14.44	6.22	33.21	-10.42	19.35	12.41	-6.03	26.69	-6.10
49	11.77	9.96	1.81	27.28	-10.35	10.46	10.52	-5.96	23.96	-6.03
50	8.33	7.91	0.42	26.72	-5.51	7.02	9.68	-5.30	23.96	-5.37

EXHIBIT R-4: (continued)

Pass	Short Equity	Long Equity	Max. Equity	Min. Equity	Total Equity	P/L	Best Trade	Worst Trade	Max. Open P/L	Min. Open P/L
51	10.65	8.63	2.02	30.26	-4.63	9.34	11.51	-4.42	26.59	-4.93
52	22.36	14.25	8.11	34.77	-4.02	21.05	11.53	-2.10	26.59	-4.02
53	11.21	7.77	3.44	26.76	-2.35	9.10	9.56	-2.64	24.71	-5.13
54	14.97	9.96	5.01	26.84	-2.97	12.86	9.63	-2.76	24.71	-4.20
55	9.29	7.29	2.00	26.86	-6.01	7.98	11.53	-4.45	26.59	-4.20
56	14.59	10.08	4.51	28.48	-6.29	13.28	11.44	-4.73	26.59	-3.79
57	9.33	7.58	1.75	25.16	-3.85	8.02	9.15	-3.64	24.71	-5.13
58	3.65	4.74	-1.09	18.94	-8.03	2.34	8.42	-3.64	24.71	-3.71
59	13.44	8.47	4.97	23.03	-8.40	12.21	11.40	-2.66	26.69	-2.02
60	7.50	4.94	2.56	20.49	-7.28	6.70	8.11	-2.79	23.96	-3.39
61	3.96	3.24	0.72	20.81	-6.96	3.16	7.40	-4.70	23.96	-3.52
62	6.44	4.28	2.16	27.09	-5.08	5.87	10.86	-3.37	27.35	-3.47
63	1.54	2.30	-0.76	21.07	-6.90	1.75	8.87	-2.82	26.59	-2.89
64	4.32	4.18	0.14	19.31	-9.48	4.53	9.28	-3.80	27.00	-3.69
65	3.45	3.50	-0.05	15.96	-8.75	3.52	8.70	-3.52	24.71	-2.75
66	4.81	4.41	0.40	15.16	-9.55	4.88	7.19	-4.24	24.71	-3.77
67	-8.95	-2.60	-6.35	5.94	-18.77	-8.21	6.90	-5.74	24.71	-4.25
68	1.79	2.91	-1.12	10.86	-16.55	0.99	13.23	-6.02	27.00	-4.38
69	-1.02	2.17	-3.19	7.45	-17.26	-1.02	10.55	-6.55	24.71	-7.35
70	0.89	3.42	-2.53	6.58	-18.13	0.32	8.22	-6.78	24.71	-7.94
71	9.41	7.88	1.53	14.90	-13.27	8.18	9.28	-6.05	27.00	-8.34
72	8.71	7.19	1.52	13.90	-10.81	7.91	6.99	-5.54	24.71	-7.66
73	6.08	5.57	0.51	15.09	-13.17	5.28	9.80	-6.07	27.35	-7.05
74	-1.51	1.38	-2.89	12.82	-14.18	-2.31	8.78	-4.89	26.59	-6.26
75	7.11	4.65	2.46	19.80	-7.61	6.54	9.83	-5.39	27.00	-4.48
76	-0.62	0.11	-0.73	10.23	-14.48	-0.41	7.78	-3.46	24.71	-4.39
77	11.05	6.06	4.99	16.08	-9.41	11.26	7.35	-3.30	24.71	-3.46
78	7.06	4.73	2.33	20.95	-6.40	7.13	6.56	-3.80	23.89	-3.46

Pass indicates period length.

Equity indicates the total number of points gained or lost.

Short equity indicates the number of points gained or lost on short positions.

Long equity indicates the number of points gained or lost on long positions.

Max. equity indicates the highest total profit recorded over the tested period.

Min. equity indicates the lowest total profit recorded over the tested period.

P/L indicates total number of points gained or lost in closed positions.

Best trade indicates the highest number of points gained in any closed trade.

Worst trade indicates the highest number of points lost in any closed trade.

Max. open P/L indicates the highest gain in a position which remains open at the end of the test run.

Min. open P/L indicates the highest loss in a position which remains open at the end of the test run.

EXHIBIT R-5:
Simple Moving Average, 31 Weeks, 1977 to 1986

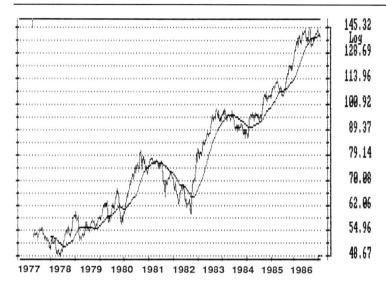

EXHIBIT R-6:
Rate of Change, 31 Weeks, 1977 to 1986

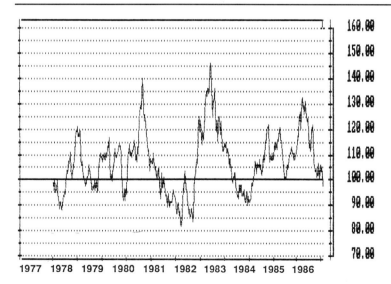

EXHIBIT R-7:
Total Equity for Rate of Change, 31 Weeks, 1977 to 1986

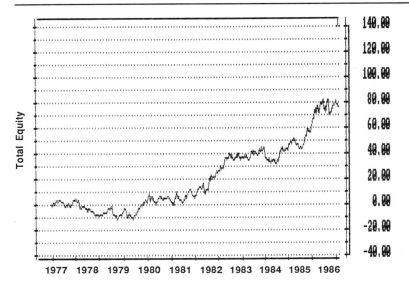

EXHIBIT R-8:

Profit Summary for Rate of Change, 31 Weeks, 1977 to 1986

Item		Long	Short	Net
Per Trade Ranges		*—— Per Trade Ranges ——*		
Best Trade	(Closed position yielding maximum P/L)	32.02	6.85	32.02
..Date		861231	820423	861231
Worst Trade	(Closed position yielding minimum P/L)	-1.90	-2.53	-2.53
..Date		810821	840106	840106
Max Open P/L	(Maximum P/L occurring in an open position)	38.76	12.58	38.76
..Date		860829	820312	860829
Min Open P/L	(Minimum P/L occurring in an open position)	-2.72	-3.16	-3.16
..Date		841207	790406	790406
Overall Ranges		*—— Overall Ranges ——*		
Max P/L	(Maximum P/L from all closed positions during the run)	75.94	43.92	75.94
..Date		861231	851011	861231
Min P/L	(Minimum P/L from all closed positions during the run)	-9.75	-10.91	-10.91
..Date		800314	800516	800516
Max Equity	(Maximum P/L from all closed and open positions)	82.68	75.94	82.68
..Date		860829	861231	860829
Min Equity	(Minimum P/L from all closed and open positions)	-10.91	-10.91	-10.91
..Date		800516	800516	800516
Statistics		*—— Statistics ——*		
Periods	(The number of periods in each position and entire run)	364	145	509
Trades	(The number of trades in each position and entire run)	16	16	32
# Profitable	(The number of profitable trades...)	8	5	13
# Losing	(The number of unprofitable trades...)	8	11	19
% Profitable	(The percent of profitable trades to total trades)	50.00	31.25	40.63
% Losing	(The percent of unprofitable trades to total trades)	50.00	68.75	59.38
Results		*—— Results ——*		
Commission	(Total commission deducted from closed trades)	0.00	0.00	0.00
Slippage	(Total slippage deducted from closed trades)	0.00	0.00	0.00
Gross P/L	(Total points gained in closed positions)	80.91	-4.97	75.94
Open P/L	(P/L in a position which remains open at the end)	0.00	0.00	0.00
P/L	(Net P/L: Gross P/L less Commission and Slippage)	80.91	-4.97	75.94
Equity	(Net P/L plus Open P/L at the end of the run)	80.91	-4.97	75.94

There are columns for Long trades, Short trades and Net. In the Long column, results are reported only for Long positions. In the Short column, results are reported for Short positions only. In the Net column for the "Per Trade Ranges" and "Overall Ranges," entries will be the extreme from either the Long or Short column. Net column entries for the "Statistics" and "Results" categories are the combined results of entries in the Long and Short columns.

423

EXHIBIT R-9:
Simple Moving Average, 31 Weeks, 1968 to 1977

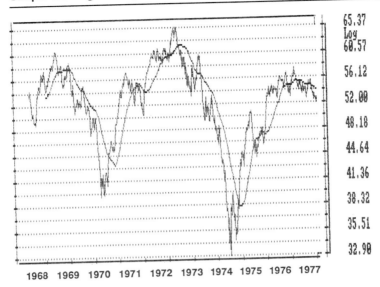

EXHIBIT R-10:
Rate of Change, 31 Weeks, 1968 to 1977

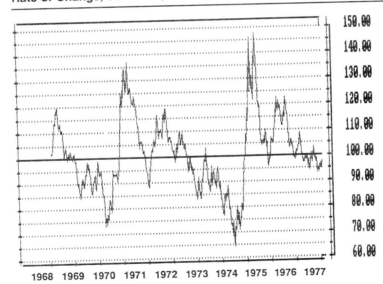

EXHIBIT R-11:
Total Equity for Rate of Change, 31 Weeks, 1968 to 1977

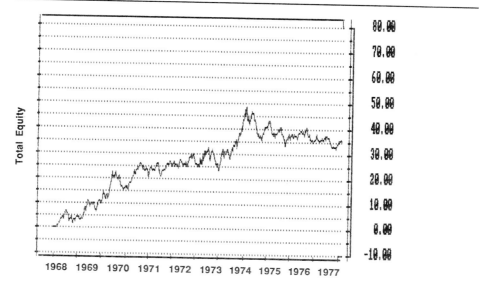

EXHIBIT R-12:

Profit Summary for Rate of Change, 31 Weeks, 1968 to 1977

Item		Long	Short	Net
		--- Per Trade Ranges ---		
Per Trade Ranges				
Best Trade	(Closed position yielding maximum P/L)	7.42	13.06	13.06
.. Date		711015	750307	750307
Worst Trade	(Closed position yielding minimum P/L)	-2.29	-4.45	-4.45
.. Date		731102	760109	760109
Max Open P/L	(Maximum P/L occurring in an open position)	10.68	24.71	24.71
.. Date		710423	741004	741004
Min Open P/L	(Minimum P/L occurring in an open position)	-1.57	-2.20	-2.20
.. Date		750404	760102	760102
		--- Overall Ranges ---		
Overall Ranges				
Max P/L	(Maximum P/L from all closed positions during the run)	38.20	36.91	38.20
.. Date		751205	750307	751205
Min P/L	(Minimum P/L from all closed positions during the run)	1.85	2.97	1.85
.. Date		690221	690228	690221
Max Equity	(Maximum P/L from all closed and open positions)	43.07	48.56	48.56
.. Date		750711	741004	741004
Min Equity	(Minimum P/L from all closed and open positions)	0.00	1.85	0.00
.. Date		680105	690221	680105
		--- Statistics ---		
Statistics				
Periods	(The number of periods in each position and entire run)	272	237	509
Trades	(The number of trades in each position and entire run)	13	12	25
# Profitable	(The number of profitable trades. . .)	10	5	15
# Losing	(The number of unprofitable trades. . .)	3	7	10
% Profitable	(The percent of profitable trades to total trades)	76.92	41.67	60.00
% Losing	(The percent of unprofitable trades to total trades)	23.08	58.33	40.00
		--- Results ---		
Results				
Commission	(Total commission deducted from closed trades)	0.00	0.00	0.00
Slippage	(Total slippage deducted from closed trades)	0.00	0.00	0.00
Gross P/L	(Total points gained in closed positions)	16.86	16.40	33.26
Open P/L	(P/L in a position which remains open at the end)	0.00	2.11	2.11
P/L	(Net P/L: Gross P/L less Commission and Slippage)	16.86	16.40	33.26
Equity	(Net P/L plus Open P/L at the end of the run)	16.86	18.51	35.37

There are columns for Long trades, Short trades and Net. In the Long column, results
are reported only for Long positions. In the Short column, results are reported for
Short positions only. In the Net column for the "Per Trade Ranges" and "Overall
Ranges," entries will be the extreme from either the Long or Short column. Net column
entries for the "Statistics" and "Results" categories are the combined results of entries
in the Long and Short columns.

RECESSION FORECASTS

Joel Levy of Smith Barney suggested that our "perfect" earnings forecasts model failed to produce worthwhile results because it did not distinguish between minor downticks in earnings and more significant general economic recessions.

Using more sensitive monthly (rather than quarterly) data, we developed a test that bought long 6 months before the economic upturn from a recession and sold our long position and sold short 6 months before the economic downturn into a recession.

We tested this decision rule against the Standard & Poor's 500 Index month-end closing price data from 1944 through 1986. This model's high profits were as surprising as the "perfect" earnings forecasts' low profits. This model filtered out 87% of the losing trades. Exhibit R-16 (page 430) demonstrates steady growth in cumulative profits with no serious or prolonged equity drawdowns. Exhibit R-15 (page 429) shows total profit of 381.49 S&P points and a Best Trade/Worst Trade (Reward/Risk) ratio of 42.62 to 10.35, or 4.12 to 1. Accuracy was high, with 88.24% of the 17 total transactions profitable. Now if only we could actually forecast recessions with accuracy. . . .

EXHIBIT R-13:
Standard & Poor's 500 Index Month-End Close, 1946 to 1986

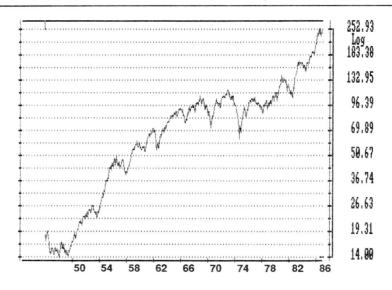

EXHIBIT R-14:
Total Equity for Perfect Recession Forecasts Model, Using Standard & Poor's 500 Index Month-End Closing Data, 1944 to 1986

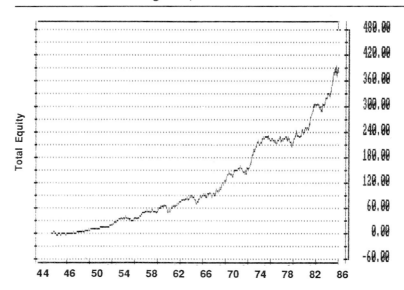

EXHIBIT R-15:

Perfect Recession Forecasts Model, Using Standard & Poor's 500 Index Month-End Closing Data, 1944 to 1986

Item		Long	Short	Net
Per Trade Ranges		---- Per Trade Ranges ----		
Best Trade	(Closed position yielding maximum P/L)	42.62	41.41	42.62
.. Date		680630	740930	680630
Worst Trade	(Closed position yielding minimum P/L)	1.85	-10.35	-10.35
.. Date		480531	800131	800131
Max Open P/L	(Maximum P/L occurring in an open position)	141.05	32.80	141.05
.. Date		860831	740831	860831
Min Open P/L	(Minimum P/L occurring in an open position)	-12.07	-8.79	-12.07
.. Date		800331	681130	800331
Overall Ranges		---- Overall Ranges ----		
Max P/L	(Maximum P/L from all closed positions during the run)	233.53	251.20	251.20
.. Date		810131	820531	820531
Min P/L	(Minimum P/L from all closed positions during the run)	-0.17	-2.02	-2.02
.. Date		480531	450430	450430
Max Equity	(Maximum P/L from all closed and open positions)	392.25	251.20	392.25
.. Date		860831	820531	860831
Min Equity	(Minimum P/L from all closed and open positions)	-2.86	-2.02	-2.86
.. Date		480229	450430	480229
Statistics		---- Statistics ----		
Periods	(The number of periods in each position and entire run)	401	108	509
Trades	(The number of trades in each position and entire run)	8	9	17
# Profitable	(The number of profitable trades. . .)	8	7	15
# Losing	(The number of unprofitable trades. . .)	0	2	2
% Profitable	(The percent of profitable trades to total trades)	100.00	77.78	88.24
% Losing	(The percent of unprofitable trades to total trades)	0.00	22.22	11.76
Results		---- Results ----		
Commission	(Total commission deducted from closed trades)	0.00	0.00	0.00
Slippage	(Total slippage deducted from closed trades)	0.00	0.00	0.00
Gross P/L	(Total points gained in closed positions)	175.13	76.07	251.20
Open P/L	(P/L in a position which remains open at the end)	130.29	0.00	130.29
P/L	(Net P/L: Gross P/L less Commission and Slippage)	175.13	76.07	251.20
Equity	(Net P/L plus Open P/L at the end of the run)	305.42	76.07	381.49

There are columns for Long trades, Short trades and Net. In the Long column, results are reported only for Long positions. In the Short column, results are reported for Short positions only. In the Net column for the "Per Trade Ranges" and "Overall Ranges," entries will be the extreme from either the Long or Short column. Net column entries for the "Statistics" and "Results" categories are the combined results of entries in the Long and Short columns.

EXHIBIT R-16:

Transaction Dates and Prices for Perfect Recession Forecasts Model, 1944 to 1986, Using Standard & Poor's 500 Index Month-End Closing Data

Exit Date	Short or Long*	Entry Date	Entry Price	Exit Price	Maximum P/L	Minimum P/L	Gross P/L	Net P/L	Maximum Equity	Minimum Equity	Cumulative Profit or Equity
450430	Sc	440831	12.82	14.84	0.04	-2.02	-2.02	-2.02	0.04	-2.02	-2.02
480531	Lc	450430	14.84	16.69	4.34	-0.84	1.85	1.85	2.32	-2.86	-0.17
490430	Sc	480531	16.69	14.74	2.07	-0.05	1.95	1.95	2.32	-2.86	1.78
530131	Lc	490430	14.74	26.38	11.83	-0.58	11.64	11.64	13.61	-2.86	13.42
531130	Sc	530131	26.38	24.76	3.06	0.00	1.62	1.62	16.48	-2.86	15.04
570228	Lc	531130	24.76	43.26	24.63	0.00	18.50	18.50	39.67	-2.86	33.54
571031	Sc	570228	43.26	41.06	2.20	-4.65	2.20	2.20	39.67	-2.86	35.74
591031	Lc	571031	41.06	57.52	19.45	-1.08	16.46	16.46	55.19	-2.86	52.20
600831	Sc	591031	57.52	56.96	3.15	-2.28	0.56	0.56	55.35	-2.86	52.76
680630	Lc	600831	56.96	99.58	42.62	-3.57	42.62	42.62	95.38	-2.86	95.38
700531	Sc	680630	99.58	76.55	23.03	-8.79	23.03	23.03	118.41	-2.86	118.41
730531	Lc	700531	76.55	104.95	41.50	-3.83	28.40	28.40	159.91	-2.86	146.81
740930	Sc	730531	104.95	63.54	41.41	-3.48	41.41	41.41	188.22	-2.86	188.22
790731	Lc	740930	63.54	103.81	43.92	0.00	40.27	40.27	232.14	-2.86	228.49
800131	Sc	790731	103.81	114.16	1.99	-10.35	-10.35	-10.35	232.14	-2.86	218.14
810131	Lc	800131	114.16	129.55	26.36	-12.07	15.39	15.39	244.50	-2.86	233.53
820531	Sc	810131	129.55	111.88	17.67	-6.45	17.67	17.67	251.20	-2.86	251.20
861231	oL	820531	111.88	242.17	141.05	-4.79	130.29	130.29	392.25	-2.86	381.49

*Lc indicates a long position that has been closed. oL indicates a long position that remains open. Sc indicates a short position that has been closed.

Exit Date indicates the date a trade is closed out.

Entry Date indicates the date a trade is opened or begun.

P/L indicates profit or loss on the trade.

Equity is the total cumulative P/L.

RELATIVE STRENGTH

Mathematically, the Relative Strength indicator is simply the ratio of one data series divided by another. Generally, a stock price or industry group index is divided by a broad general market index (such as the Standard & Poor's 500 Index) to demonstrate the trend of performance of the stock or group relative to the market as a whole. The ratio can be drawn as a line chart. Then trendline analysis, moving averages, and other analytical techniques can be applied to the line. Exhibit R-17 (page 432) shows the long-term price line of S&P capital goods stock groups on the upper half of the chart and the relative strength ratio of the capital goods group divided by the S&P 500 Index on the lower half of the chart.

According to Alan R. Shaw of Smith Barney, who for three decades has been a leading advocate of relative strength analysis on Wall Street, relative strength often runs in strong secular trends that can persist for many years. Groups in strong technical relative strength uptrends are likely to continue to outperform the market until relative strength loses momentum and changes direction on a major trend basis. That generally takes many months to develop. Conversely, groups in major negative relative strength trends can underperform the broad market for a very long time. Shaw plots relative strength ratios on both a weekly and monthly basis, and he analyzes them in conjunction with the raw price data, constantly watching for tandem confirmation (suggesting the continuation of an existing trend) or divergence (suggesting a significant trend change).

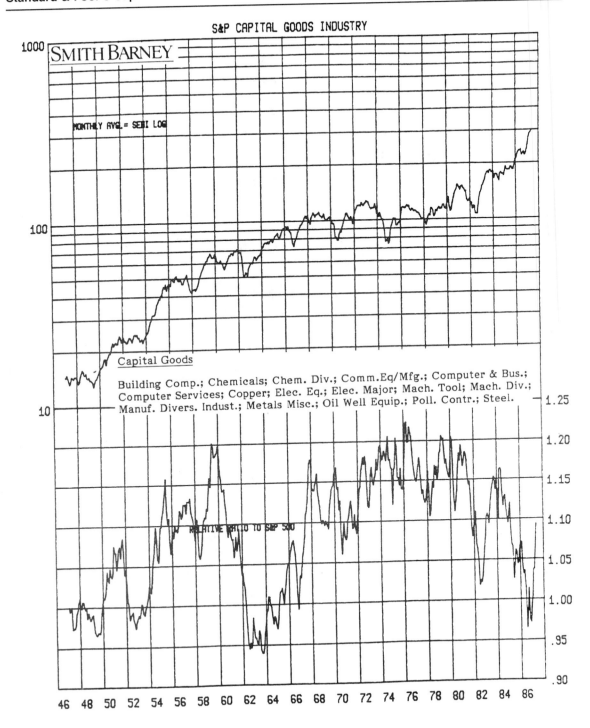

S&P CAPITAL GOODS INDUSTRY

SMITH BARNEY

MONTHLY AVG. = SEMI LOG

Capital Goods

Building Comp.; Chemicals; Chem. Div.; Comm.Eq/Mfg.; Computer & Bus.;
Computer Services; Copper; Elec. Eq.; Elec. Major; Mach. Tool; Mach. Div.;
Manuf. Divers. Indust.; Metals Misc.; Oil Well Equip.; Poll. Contr.; Steel.

RELATIVE RATIO TO S&P 500

RELATIVE STRENGTH INDEX

Relative Strength Index (RSI) is a price momentum indicator described by J. Welles Wilder, Jr., in his 1978 book *New Concepts in Technical Trading Systems* (PO Box 128, McLeansville, NC 27301).* Mathematically, RSI is represented as:

$$RSI = 100 - \frac{100}{1 + RS}$$

where

> RS is the ratio of the exponentially smoothed moving average of *n*-period gains divided by the absolute value (i.e., ignoring sign) of the exponentially smoothed moving average of *n*-period losses.

An example of calculating RSI follows on pages 434–435.

RSI quantifies price momentum. It depends solely on the changes in closing prices. Despite its name, it has absolutely nothing in common with the traditional relative strength concept, whereby the price of a stock is divided by a broad market index (such as the Standard & Poor's 500 Index) to arrive at a ratio that shows the trend of a stock's performance relative to the general market. Instead, Wilder's RSI is actually a front-weighted price velocity ratio for only one item (a stock, a futures contract, or an index).

RSI's method of calculation avoids the problem of erratic movement caused by dropping off the old data, the "take away" number that weakens the Rate of Change and Stochastics indicators. It also tames the indicators y-axis range to limits of 0 to 100, and it eliminates the need to work with long columns of historical data each day. Due to its use of ratios, however, RSI is subject to greater volatility, distortions, and erratic movement than smoothed indicators that are not dependent on ratios. This results in higher numbers of signals (and thus higher transaction costs) compared with smoothed momentum indicators that are not dependent on ratios.

The smaller *n* is, the shorter the period measured and the greater the noise (erratic movements and false signals) will be. Conversely, the larger *n* is, the longer the period measured and the more stable and less distorted the RSI will be. Short-term RSIs produce relatively high noise to signal ratios, as well as a large number of transactions. Long-term RSIs produce fewer and more reliable signals, but not as few or as reliable as moving average oscillators.

---

*Reprinted with permission.

Example of Welles Wilder's RSI over Four Periods

Year End Date	Price on the Close	Positive Change (Close Minus Previous Close)	Negative Change (Previous Close Minus Close)	P Previous	Multi-plied by $n-1=$	$Pp \times 3$	Add PC	Positive Sum	Divide by n for P
----	----	------	------	-----	-----	------	-----	-----	------
	C	PC	NC	Pp	$\times\ 3$	Product	$+\ PC$	PS	$\div\ 4 = P$
----	-----	------	------	-----		------	-----	-----	------ P
1968	58.90	N/A	N/A						
1969	51.53	0.00	7.37						
1970	50.23	0.00	1.30						
1971	56.43	6.20	0.00						
1972	64.48	8.05	0.00	N/A	$\times\ 3$	N/A	‡	‡	$\div\ 4 =$ 3.56‡
1973	51.82	0.00	12.66	3.56	$\times\ 3$	= 10.68	+ 0.00	= 10.68	$\div\ 4 =$ 2.67
1974	36.13	0.00	15.69	2.67	$\times\ 3$	= 8.01	+ 0.00	= 8.01	$\div\ 4 =$ 2.00
1975	47.64	11.51	0.00	2.00	$\times\ 3$	= 6.00	+ 11.51	= 17.51	$\div\ 4 =$ 4.38
1976	57.88	10.24	0.00	4.38	$\times\ 3$	= 13.14	+ 10.24	= 23.38	$\div\ 4 =$ 5.85
1977	52.50	0.00	5.38	5.85	$\times\ 3$	= 17.55	+ 0.00	= 17.55	$\div\ 4 =$ 4.39
1978	53.62	1.12	0.00	4.39	$\times\ 3$	= 13.17	+ 1.12	= 14.29	$\div\ 4 =$ 3.57
1979	61.95	8.33	0.00	3.57	$\times\ 3$	= 10.71	+ 8.33	= 19.04	$\div\ 4 =$ 4.76
1980	77.86	15.91	0.00	4.76	$\times\ 3$	= 14.28	+ 15.91	= 30.19	$\div\ 4 =$ 7.55
1981	71.11	0.00	6.75	7.55	$\times\ 3$	= 22.65	+ 0.00	= 22.65	$\div\ 4 =$ 5.66
1982	81.03	9.92	0.00	5.66	$\times\ 3$	= 16.98	+ 9.92	= 26.90	$\div\ 4 =$ 6.73
1983	95.18	14.15	0.00	6.73	$\times\ 3$	= 20.19	+ 14.15	= 34.34	$\div\ 4 =$ 8.59
1984	96.38	1.20	0.00	8.59	$\times\ 3$	= 25.77	+ 1.20	= 26.97	$\div\ 4 =$ 6.74
1985	121.58	25.20	0.00	6.74	$\times\ 3$	= 20.22	+ 25.20	= 45.42	$\div\ 4 =$ 11.36
1986	138.58	17.00	0.00	11.35	$\times\ 3$	= 34.05	+ 17.00	= 51.05	$\div\ 4 =$ 12.76

‡ Wilder uses an n-period simple moving average for the nth period. In this example, he would use a four-period simple moving average. Thereafter, Wilder smooths by multiplying the previous smoothed value by $n-1$ (in this case, 3), adding the current period's PC or NC, then dividing that sum by n (in this case, 4). This procedure is equivalent to exponential smoothing. Some computer software uses other variations of exponential smoothing which change RSI only insignificantly.

RSI is said to indicate an "overbought" condition when it is above 70 and an "oversold" condition below 30. Our computer testing, however, uncovered no significance to these arbitrary levels. Also, RSI momentum divergences, although frequently accurate, produced no significant advantages over simpler moving average oscillator divergence signals.

We tested RSI using Compu Trac software and two 9.75-year test periods of weekly data (consisting of high, low, close, and volume for each week) for the broad-based NYSE Composite Index. The first period ran from January

xample of Welles Wilder's RSI over Four Periods (continued)

N Previous / Np	Multiplied by n − 1 = / × 3 (× 3)	Np × 3 / Product	Add NC / + NC	Negative Sum / NS	Divide by n for N / ÷ 4 = N / N	Ratio of P ÷ N / RS	1 Plus RS / 1 + RS	100 ÷ (1 + RS) / RR	100 Minus RR / RSI
N/A	× 3	N/A	‡	‡	÷ 4 = 2.17‡	1.64	2.64	37.88	62.12
2.17	× 3 =	6.51	+ 12.66	= 19.17	÷ 4 = 4.79	0.56	1.56	64.10	35.90
4.79	× 3 =	14.37	+ 15.69	= 30.06	÷ 4 = 7.52	0.27	1.27	78.74	21.26
7.52	× 3 =	22.56	+ 0	= 22.56	÷ 4 = 5.64	0.78	1.78	56.18	43.82
5.64	× 3 =	16.92	+ 0	= 16.92	÷ 4 = 4.23	1.38	2.38	42.02	57.98
4.23	× 3 =	12.69	+ 5.38	= 18.07	÷ 4 = 4.52	0.97	1.97	50.76	49.24
4.52	× 3 =	13.56	+ 0	= 13.56	÷ 4 = 3.39	1.05	2.05	48.78	51.22
3.39	× 3 =	10.17	+ 0	= 10.17	÷ 4 = 2.54	1.87	2.87	34.84	65.16
2.54	× 3 =	9.62	+ 0	= 7.62	÷ 4 = 1.91	3.95	4.95	20.20	79.80
1.91	× 3 =	5.73	+ 6.75	= 12.48	÷ 4 = 3.12	1.81	2.81	35.59	64.41
3.12	× 3 =	9.36	+ 0	= 9.36	÷ 4 = 2.34	2.88	3.88	25.77	74.23
2.34	× 3 =	7.02	+ 0	= 7.02	÷ 4 = 1.76	4.88	5.88	17.01	82.99
1.76	× 3 =	5.28	+ 0	= 5.28	÷ 4 = 1.32	5.11	6.11	16.37	83.63
1.32	× 3 =	3.96	+ 0	= 3.96	÷ 4 = 0.99	11.64	12.64	7.91	92.09
0.99	× 3 =	2.97	+ 0	= 2.97	÷ 4 = 0.74	17.24	18.24	5.48	94.52

5, 1968 through September 30, 1977, and the second period ran from April 8, 1977 through December 31, 1986. The overlap in data was necessary to facilitate testing throughout the full time period.

In numerous trial runs of various combinations, the best and least ambiguous decision rule for interpreting RSI we found was to buy when RSI rises above 50, and sell and sell short when RSI falls below 50. The optimization runs shown in Exhibits R-18 to R-21 (pages 436–439) illustrate that the 21-week RSI produced peak profit of 110.72 NYSE points over the past 19 years.

Exhibits R-25 to R-29 (pages 442–445) show a total of 75 trades, about four per year, with 21 trades or 28% producing a profit and 54 or 72% producing losses. Average profit per trade came to 1.48 points. Worst drawdown at 14.90 was better than our standard. So the ratio of total profits to worst case drawdown was 110.76 to 14.90, or 7.43 to 1, which was relatively good. Overall, these RSI results were better than our standard of comparison, the 40-week simple moving average crossover rule, except for 32% greater trading frequency.

EXHIBIT R-18:
Profitability Chart for Relative Strength Index (Period Lengths of 1 to 30 Weeks from 1977 to 1986)

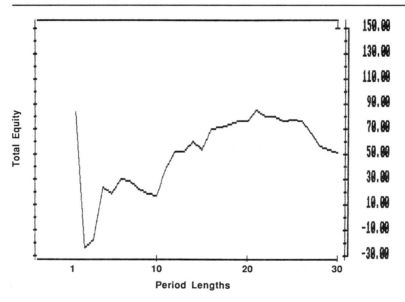

EXHIBIT R-19:

Profit Table for Relative Strength Index (Period Lengths of 1 to 30 Weeks from 1977 to 1986)

Pass	Total Equity	Short Equity	Long Equity	Max. Equity	Min. Equity	P/L	Best Trade	Worst Trade	Max. Open P/L	Min. Open P/L
1	83.64	0.00	83.64	90.38	-6.27	0.00	N/A	N/A	90.38	-6.27
2	-23.51	-54.20	30.69	13.94	-32.29	-26.46	12.87	-9.41	15.56	-2.00
3	-17.14	-51.03	33.89	29.71	-24.34	-20.09	13.49	-9.41	17.18	-2.89
4	24.21	-30.03	54.24	53.24	-6.36	21.69	30.63	-9.41	34.17	-2.89
5	19.11	-32.67	52.88	44.04	-6.83	19.11	30.63	-9.41	34.17	-2.89
6	29.88	-27.15	58.13	54.81	-10.10	29.88	30.63	-9.41	34.17	-2.89
7	29.10	-28.40	55.66	62.55	-9.58	29.10	29.62	-9.41	36.52	-2.89
8	22.12	-31.55	51.83	61.81	-6.30	22.12	29.62	-9.41	36.52	-2.89
9	18.54	-33.12	49.82	58.23	-2.60	18.54	28.95	-9.41	36.52	-2.89
10	17.06	-33.44	48.66	56.75	-2.74	17.06	28.95	-9.41	36.52	-2.89
11	38.22	-22.47	61.79	71.63	-8.22	38.22	29.63	-9.41	36.52	-2.89
12	52.74	-15.46	69.30	70.41	-7.88	52.74	29.63	-4.67	36.52	-2.89
13	52.99	-15.39	69.48	69.07	-8.63	52.99	29.63	-4.67	37.17	-2.89
14	60.01	-11.79	72.90	76.09	-5.09	60.01	29.63	-4.67	37.17	-2.89
15	53.67	-14.60	69.37	69.75	-5.81	53.67	26.54	-4.67	37.17	-2.89
16	69.66	-7.40	77.06	82.18	-2.45	66.78	26.63	-2.89	37.17	-2.00
17	70.76	-6.89	77.65	83.28	-3.21	67.88	26.63	-2.89	38.76	-2.00
18	73.97	-5.50	79.47	84.71	-2.40	70.20	26.25	-2.33	38.76	-1.13
19	76.22	-4.49	80.71	86.96	-2.17	72.45	26.86	-2.33	39.37	-1.13
20	76.86	-4.56	81.42	85.86	-2.95	72.22	26.86	-2.68	39.37	-0.73
21	85.47	0.11	85.36	93.57	-2.22	80.38	26.86	-1.49	39.37	-0.57
22	79.84	-3.00	82.84	86.58	-1.81	47.21	25.75	-3.98	39.37	-0.85
23	79.71	-3.04	82.75	86.45	-2.78	47.08	25.75	-3.98	39.37	-0.85
24	75.97	-5.27	81.24	82.71	-3.60	30.62	22.84	-1.87	52.09	-1.66
25	77.37	-4.20	81.57	84.11	-2.20	32.02	22.84	-1.87	52.09	-1.66
26	76.11	-4.94	81.05	82.85	-2.42	30.76	22.84	-2.00	52.09	-1.66
27	67.10	-10.12	77.22	73.84	-4.29	21.75	22.84	-2.46	52.09	-1.60
28	56.53	-15.72	72.25	63.27	-9.40	11.18	22.84	-2.89	52.09	-2.09
29	53.35	-17.23	70.58	60.09	-9.24	8.00	22.84	-3.67	52.09	-1.93
30	51.73	-18.29	70.02	58.47	-9.74	6.38	22.84	-3.67	52.09	-2.43

Pass indicates period length.

Equity indicates the total number of points gained or lost.

Short equity indicates the number of points gained or lost on short positions.

Long equity indicates the number of points gained or lost on long positions.

Max. equity indicates the highest total profit recorded over the tested period.

Min. equity indicates the lowest total profit recorded over the tested period.

P/L indicates total number of points gained or lost in closed positions.

Best trade indicates the highest number of points gained in any closed trade.

Worst trade indicates the highest number of points lost in any closed trade.

Max. open P/L indicates the highest gain in a position which remains open at the end of the test run.

Min. open P/L indicates the highest loss in a position which remains open at the end of the test run.

EXHIBIT R-20:

Profitability Chart for Relative Strength Index (Period Lengths of 1 to 30 Weeks from 1968 to 1977)

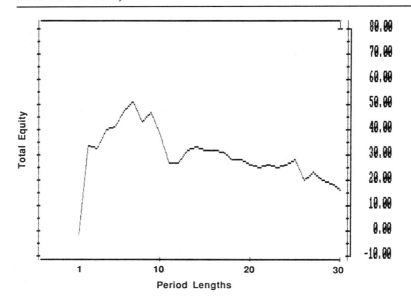

EXHIBIT R-21:

Profit Table for Relative Strength Index (Period Lengths of 1 to 30 Weeks from 1968 to 1977)

Pass	Total Equity	Short Equity	Long Equity	Max. Equity	Min. Equity	P/L	Best Trade	Worst Trade	Max. Open P/L	Min. Open P/L
1	-1.36	0.00	-1.36	11.20	-21.27	0.00	N/A	N/A	11.20	-21.27
2	33.77	17.23	16.54	42.55	0.00	33.77	7.08	-3.24	9.42	-0.73
3	32.74	16.19	16.55	41.24	0.00	32.74	10.03	-2.84	12.97	-1.04
4	39.80	19.33	20.47	47.06	0.00	38.49	9.71	-2.84	12.97	-1.04
5	41.09	19.25	21.84	50.03	-1.57	39.78	10.49	-2.76	15.08	-1.54
6	47.56	22.48	25.08	57.13	-1.58	46.25	12.74	-2.35	15.08	-1.12
7	51.11	24.49	26.62	60.68	-1.11	49.80	12.07	-2.17	15.08	-1.12
8	43.23	20.00	23.23	50.38	-2.21	41.92	12.07	-2.33	17.31	-0.98
9	46.84	21.73	25.11	54.70	-4.17	45.53	12.40	-2.36	19.13	-1.24
10	38.42	17.54	20.88	47.24	-7.75	37.11	12.40	-4.13	19.13	-2.32
11	26.76	11.50	15.26	37.48	-8.17	25.45	13.46	-4.55	19.13	-2.74
12	27.12	12.18	14.94	35.69	-8.61	25.81	13.46	-3.55	19.13	-1.74
13	31.90	15.44	16.46	40.55	-6.87	30.59	13.46	-2.07	19.13	-0.96
14	33.07	16.93	16.14	43.50	-6.26	31.76	13.19	-2.21	19.13	-0.71
15	31.58	16.08	15.50	42.01	-6.05	30.27	16.70	-2.21	24.71	-0.71
16	31.77	16.61	15.16	42.20	-5.18	30.46	16.70	-2.21	24.71	-0.71
17	31.49	16.87	14.62	42.87	-5.30	30.18	16.70	-2.21	24.71	-0.71
18	28.13	15.23	12.90	40.25	-5.36	26.82	16.70	-1.86	24.71	-0.76
19	28.39	14.98	13.41	39.39	-4.60	27.08	16.70	-1.86	24.71	-0.71
20	26.30	14.06	12.24	39.94	-4.85	24.99	16.70	-1.86	24.71	-0.95
21	25.25	13.97	11.28	38.84	-5.72	23.94	16.70	-1.86	24.71	-0.95
22	26.06	15.18	10.88	39.55	-7.33	24.75	15.81	-2.93	24.71	-1.95
23	24.81	14.51	10.30	38.08	-6.00	23.50	15.81	-2.84	24.71	-1.86
24	26.34	15.15	11.19	40.11	-3.97	25.03	15.81	-2.59	24.71	-1.61
25	28.19	15.73	12.46	41.96	-2.36	26.88	15.81	-2.03	24.71	-1.12
26	20.07	12.07	8.00	36.96	-6.13	18.76	14.40	-2.03	24.71	-2.70
27	23.38	14.11	9.27	37.25	-6.90	22.07	14.40	-2.03	24.71	-3.47
28	20.07	11.90	8.17	32.16	-5.79	18.76	14.40	-2.87	24.71	-2.36
29	18.53	10.44	8.09	30.08	-3.85	17.22	14.40	-2.87	24.71	-1.50
30	16.25	8.81	7.44	31.06	-2.87	14.94	14.40	-2.87	24.71	-1.50

Pass indicates period length.

Equity indicates the total number of points gained or lost.

Short equity indicates the number of points gained or lost on short positions.

Long equity indicates the number of points gained or lost on long positions.

Max. equity indicates the highest total profit recorded over the tested period.

Min. equity indicates the lowest total profit recorded over the tested period.

P/L indicates total number of points gained or lost in closed positions.

Best trade indicates the highest number of points gained in any closed trade.

Worst trade indicates the highest number of points lost in any closed trade.

Max. open P/L indicates the highest gain in a position which remains open at the end of the test run.

Min. open P/L indicates the highest loss in a position which remains open at the end of the test run.

EXHIBIT R-22:
New York Stock Exchange Composite Price Index Weekly High and Low from April 8, 1977 to December 31, 1986

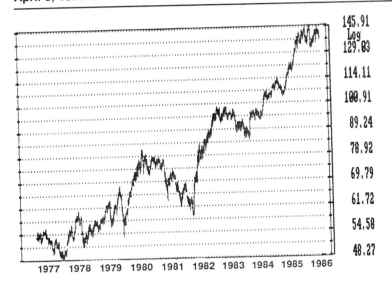

EXHIBIT R-23:
Relative Strength Index, 21 Weeks, 1977 to 1986

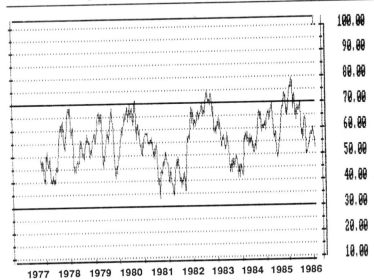

EXHIBIT R-24:
Total Equity for Relative Strength Index, 21 Weeks, 1977 to 1986

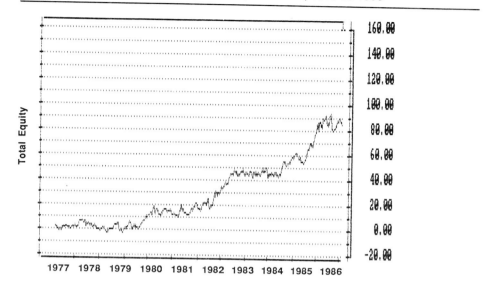

EXHIBIT R-25:

Profit Summary for Relative Strength Index, 21 Weeks, 1977 to 1986

Item		Long	Short	Net
		— Per Trade Ranges —		
Per Trade Ranges				
Best Trade	(Closed position yielding maximum P/L)	26.86	5.20	26.86
.. Date		860912	820827	860912
Worst Trade	(Closed position yielding minimum P/L)	-0.99	-1.49	-1.49
.. Date		771202	791116	791116
Max Open P/L	(Maximum P/L occurring in an open position)	39.37	12.89	39.37
.. Date		860829	820813	860829
Min Open P/L	(Minimum P/L occurring in an open position)	-0.23	-0.57	-0.57
.. Date		790601	791102	791102
		— Overall Ranges —		
Overall Ranges				
Max P/L	(Maximum P/L from all closed positions during the run)	81.06	80.38	81.06
.. Date		860912	860919	860912
Min P/L	(Minimum P/L from all closed positions during the run)	-1.21	-2.12	-2.12
.. Date		790511	791116	791116
Max Equity	(Maximum P/L from all closed and open positions)	93.57	81.06	93.57
.. Date		860829	860912	860829
Min Equity	(Minimum P/L from all closed and open positions)	-2.22	-2.12	-2.22
.. Date		790601	791116	790601
		— Statistics —		
Statistics				
Periods	(The number of periods in each position and entire run)	367	142	509
Trades	(The number of trades in each position and entire run)	14	14	28
# Profitable	(The number of profitable trades. . .)	7	3	10
# Losing	(The number of unprofitable trades. . .)	7	11	18
% Profitable	(The percent of profitable trades to total trades)	50.00	21.43	35.71
% Losing	(The percent of unprofitable trades to total trades)	50.00	78.57	64.29
		— Results —		
Results				
Commission	(Total commission deducted from closed trades)	0.00	0.00	0.00
Slippage	(Total slippage deducted from closed trades)	0.00	0.00	0.00
Gross P/L	(Total points gained in closed positions)	80.27	0.11	80.38
Open P/L	(P/L in a position which remains open at the end)	5.09	0.00	5.09
P/L	(Net P/L: Gross P/L less Commission and Slippage)	80.27	0.11	80.38
Equity	(Net P/L plus Open P/L at the end of the run)	85.36	0.11	85.47

There are columns for Long trades, Short trades and Net. In the Long column, results
are reported only for Long positions. In the Short column, results are reported for
Short positions only. In the Net column for the "Per Trade Ranges" and "Overall
Ranges," entries will be the extreme from either the Long or Short column. Net column
entries for the "Statistics" and "Results" categories are the combined results of entries
in the Long and Short columns.

EXHIBIT R-26:

New York Stock Exchange Composite Price Index Weekly High and Low from January 5, 1968 to September 30, 1977

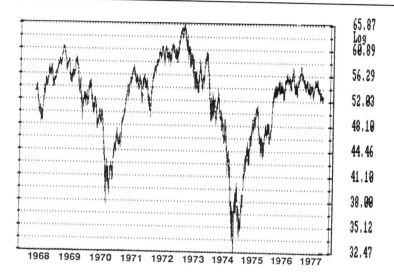

EXHIBIT R-27:

Relative Strength Index, 21 Weeks, 1968 to 1977

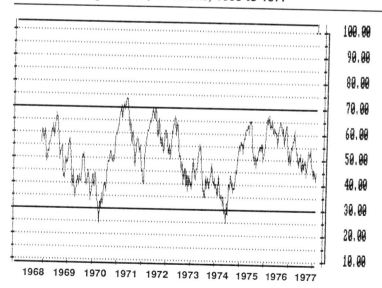

EXHIBIT R-28:
Total Equity for Relative Strength Index, 21 Weeks, 1968 to 1977

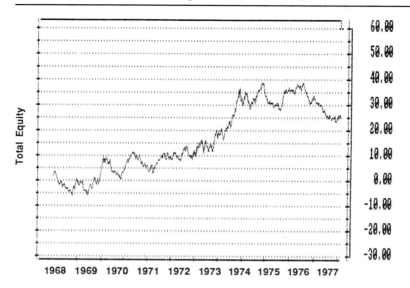

EXHIBIT R-29:

Profit Summary for Relative Strength Index, 21 Weeks, 1968 to 1977

Item		Long	Short	Net
Per Trade Ranges		*— Per Trade Ranges —*		
Best Trade	(Closed position yielding maximum P/L)	7.16	16.70	16.70
..Date		761022	750131	750131
Worst Trade	(Closed position yielding minimum P/L)	-1.79	-1.86	-1.86
..Date		761112	690502	690502
Max Open P/L	(Maximum P/L occurring in an open position)	10.76	24.71	24.71
..Date		760924	741004	741004
Min Open P/L	(Minimum P/L occurring in an open position)	-0.95	-0.71	-0.95
..Date		761105	770520	761105
Overall Ranges		*— Overall Ranges —*		
Max P/L	(Maximum P/L from all closed positions during the run)	35.24	33.77	35.24
..Date		761022	761029	761022
Min P/L	(Minimum P/L from all closed positions during the run)	-5.72	-4.63	-5.72
..Date		690606	690502	690606
Max Equity	(Maximum P/L from all closed and open positions)	38.84	36.76	38.84
..Date		760924	741004	760924
Min Equity	(Minimum P/L from all closed and open positions)	-4.93	-5.72	-5.72
..Date		690530	690606	690606
Statistics		*— Statistics —*		
Periods	(The number of periods in each position and entire run)	289	220	509
Trades	(The number of trades in each position and entire run)	24	23	47
# Profitable	(The number of profitable trades. . .)	6	5	11
# Losing	(The number of unprofitable trades. . .)	18	18	36
% Profitable	(The percent of profitable trades to total trades)	25.00	21.74	23.40
% Losing	(The percent of unprofitable trades to total trades)	75.00	78.26	76.60
Results		*— Results —*		
Commission	(Total commission deducted from closed trades)	0.00	0.00	0.00
Slippage	(Total slippage deducted from closed trades)	0.00	0.00	0.00
Gross P/L	(Total points gained in closed positions)	11.28	12.66	23.94
Open P/L	(P/L in a position which remains open at the end)	0.00	1.31	1.31
P/L	(Net P/L: Gross P/L less Commission and Slippage)	11.28	12.66	23.94
Equity	(Net P/L plus Open P/L at the end of the run)	11.28	13.97	25.25

There are columns for Long trades, Short trades and Net. In the Long column, results are reported only for Long positions. In the Short column, results are reported for Short positions only. In the Net column for the "Per Trade Ranges" and "Overall Ranges," entries will be the extreme from either the Long or Short column. Net column entries for the "Statistics" and "Results" categories are the combined results of entries in the Long and Short columns.

445

RESERVE REQUIREMENT

The reserve requirement is the minimum level of cash that all members of the Federal Reserve System must carry. The reserve requirement varies depending on the size of the bank and the type of deposits. In general, the larger the bank, the greater the reserve requirement.

For analysis purposes, technicians use the reserve requirement that applies to the largest city banks. That requirement has been as high as 26% in 1948. It has been set at 16.5% since 1975.

Changes in the reserve requirement occur infrequently—only 26 times since 1936. However, the historical change in stock prices has been so significant after such changes that investors are well advised to be prepared in the event of a future change.

Norman Fosback (The Institute for Econometric Research, 3471 North Federal Highway, Fort Lauderdale, FL 33306) has researched all reserve requirement increases and decreases since 1936.* His results are astonishing.

Reserve requirement increases are considered bearish since they reduce the money supply and reflect a tightening of monetary conditions. Since 1936, 11 increases have occurred. Fosback discovered that, following increases, the stock market (as measured by the Standard & Poor's 500 Index) declined on average 0.3%, 1.7%, 5.3%, 8.5%, and 13.3% after 20 days, 3 months, 6 months, 12 months, and 15 months, respectively.

Reserve requirement decreases are viewed as bullish because they increase the money supply and signal a loosening of monetary conditions. Since 1936, 15 cuts in reserve requirements have been made. Fosback noted that, following decreases, stock prices (as measured by the S&P 500) rose on average 1.7%, 8.2%, 19.9%, 29.0%, and 37.2% after 20 days, 3 months, 6 months, 12 months, and 18 months, respectively. Even more impressive is the fact that stock prices have been higher in every instance of a reserve requirement reduction after 6, 12, and 18 months. In addition, the market rose more than 20% in the 18 months after each reserve requirement decrease.

Fosback concludes that a cut in the reserve requirement for large city banks is "the single most bullish event in the world of stock price behavior." We agree with him.

---

*Reprinted with permission.

SCHULTZ ADVANCES/TOTAL ISSUES TRADED

Schultz Advances/Total Issues Traded (A/T) is a market breadth indicator. It is calculated by dividing the number of advancing issues by the total number of issues traded. Daily NYSE data normally is used in the calculation.

We tested the Schultz A/T for the period of January 1928 to March 1987 on a daily basis. In addition, we applied a 10-period simple moving average to the daily readings to smooth out any erratic movements. The results are shown in Exhibits S-1 and S-2 (pages 448–449).

The test process was as follows. The indicator readings for the test period were divided into 20 ranges with approximately the same number of occurrences in each range. For each reading in a range, the gain or loss in four subsequent time periods (1 month later, 3 months later, 6 months later, and 12 months later) was calculated. The combined results for readings within each range were statistically compared, using chi-squared tests, to the performance of the overall market (as measured by the Standard & Poor's 500 Index). Varying degrees of bullishness and bearishness were noted on the basis of that comparison.

Our results revealed a slight bullish tendency at relatively high indicator readings and a bearish tendency at extremely low indicator readings. However, the bullish and bearish patterns are not strong enough to warrant strong dependence on Schultz A/T for market timing purposes.

EXHIBIT S-1:
Interpretation of Schultz A/T's Daily Readings

```
==========================================================================================
SCHULTZ A/T - DAILY DATA
PERIOD ANALYZED:  JANUARY 1928 TO MARCH 1987
==========================================================================================
```

INDICATOR RANGE		INTERPRETATION GIVEN INVESTOR'S TIME FRAME			
GREATER THAN	LESS THAN OR EQUAL TO	1 MONTH	3 MONTHS	6 MONTHS	12 MONTHS
0.000	0.151	SLIGHTLY BEARISH	NEUTRAL	SLIGHTLY BEARISH	BEARISH
0.151	0.205	NEUTRAL	NEUTRAL	BEARISH	NEUTRAL
0.205	0.244	BEARISH	BEARISH	SLIGHTLY BEARISH	NEUTRAL
0.244	0.300	VERY BEARISH	NEUTRAL	NEUTRAL	NEUTRAL
0.300	0.323	NEUTRAL	NEUTRAL	NEUTRAL	SLIGHTLY BULLISH
0.323	0.344	NEUTRAL	NEUTRAL	NEUTRAL	NEUTRAL
0.344	0.361	NEUTRAL	NEUTRAL	NEUTRAL	SLIGHTLY BULLISH
0.361	0.379	NEUTRAL	NEUTRAL	NEUTRAL	NEUTRAL
0.379	0.396	NEUTRAL	NEUTRAL	NEUTRAL	NEUTRAL
0.396	0.414	NEUTRAL	NEUTRAL	NEUTRAL	NEUTRAL
0.414	0.430	NEUTRAL	NEUTRAL	NEUTRAL	NEUTRAL
0.430	0.448	NEUTRAL	NEUTRAL	NEUTRAL	NEUTRAL
0.448	0.467	NEUTRAL	NEUTRAL	NEUTRAL	NEUTRAL
0.467	0.488	NEUTRAL	NEUTRAL	NEUTRAL	NEUTRAL
0.488	0.510	SLIGHTLY BULLISH	NEUTRAL	NEUTRAL	NEUTRAL
0.510	0.538	NEUTRAL	NEUTRAL	NEUTRAL	NEUTRAL
0.538	0.576	BULLISH	SLIGHTLY BULLISH	SLIGHTLY BULLISH	NEUTRAL
0.576	0.637	NEUTRAL	SLIGHTLY BULLISH	SLIGHTLY BULLISH	NEUTRAL
0.637	0.923	NEUTRAL	NEUTRAL	NEUTRAL	NEUTRAL
0.637	0.923	NEUTRAL	NEUTRAL	NEUTRAL	NEUTRAL

```
==========================================================================================
```

Definitions of Very Bullish, Bullish, Slightly Bullish, Neutral, Slightly Bearish, Bearish, and Very Bearish are provided in Appendix A.

EXHIBIT S-2:

Interpretation of Schultz A/T's 10-Day Simple Moving Average Readings

```
===========================================================================================
SCHULTZ A/T - 10 DAY MOVING AVERAGE
PERIOD ANALYZED: JANUARY 1928 TO MARCH 1987
===========================================================================================
```

INDICATOR RANGE		INTERPRETATION GIVEN INVESTOR'S TIME FRAME			
GREATER THAN	LESS THAN OR EQUAL TO	1 MONTH	3 MONTHS	6 MONTHS	12 MONTHS
0.000	0.287	VERY BEARISH	BEARISH	BEARISH	NEUTRAL
0.287	0.313	NEUTRAL	BEARISH	SLIGHTLY BEARISH	NEUTRAL
0.313	0.330	NEUTRAL	SLIGHTLY BEARISH	VERY BEARISH	NEUTRAL
0.330	0.344	NEUTRAL	NEUTRAL	NEUTRAL	NEUTRAL
0.344	0.355	NEUTRAL	NEUTRAL	BEARISH	NEUTRAL
0.355	0.365	BEARISH	BEARISH	NEUTRAL	NEUTRAL
0.365	0.374	VERY BEARISH	NEUTRAL	NEUTRAL	NEUTRAL
0.374	0.383	NEUTRAL	NEUTRAL	NEUTRAL	NEUTRAL
0.383	0.390	NEUTRAL	NEUTRAL	NEUTRAL	NEUTRAL
0.390	0.398	NEUTRAL	NEUTRAL	NEUTRAL	NEUTRAL
0.398	0.406	NEUTRAL	NEUTRAL	NEUTRAL	NEUTRAL
0.406	0.413	NEUTRAL	NEUTRAL	NEUTRAL	NEUTRAL
0.413	0.421	NEUTRAL	NEUTRAL	NEUTRAL	NEUTRAL
0.421	0.429	SLIGHTLY BULLISH	NEUTRAL	NEUTRAL	NEUTRAL
0.429	0.437	NEUTRAL	NEUTRAL	SLIGHTLY BULLISH	BULLISH
0.437	0.447	NEUTRAL	SLIGHTLY BULLISH	NEUTRAL	NEUTRAL
0.447	0.458	NEUTRAL	NEUTRAL	NEUTRAL	NEUTRAL
0.458	0.471	BULLISH	NEUTRAL	BULLISH	NEUTRAL
0.471	0.492	BULLISH	BULLISH	SLIGHTLY BULLISH	NEUTRAL
0.492	0.668	SLIGHTLY BULLISH	VERY BULLISH	NEUTRAL	NEUTRAL

```
===========================================================================================
```

Definitions of Very Bullish, Bullish, Slightly Bullish, Neutral, Slightly Bearish, Bearish, and Very Bearish are provided in Appendix A.

SHORT INTEREST RATIO

The Short Interest Ratio is a long-term contrary opinion sentiment indicator. It is calculated by dividing the monthly short interest figure released by the New York Stock Exchange by the average volume of trading per day.

When a relatively large amount of short selling activity is occurring, investors obviously believe stock prices are going lower. The Short Interest Ratio is high at these times and is interpreted as bullish, contrary to the investors' thoughts. Eventually, bearish-minded investors will have to cover their shorts (buy the stock they previously sold short) at some time in the future, thus adding fuel to any upward move in stock prices.

Relatively low levels of short selling produce low Short Interest Ratio readings and are viewed as bearish since less short covering will be required in the future.

A 25-year chart of the Short Interest Ratio is provided in Exhibit S-3.* According to Ned Davis (Ned Davis Research, Inc., P.O. Box 2089, Venice, FL 34284), readings above 1.65 are considered bullish and readings below 1.25 are viewed as bearish.

The value of the Short Interest Ratio as a market indicator recently has been questioned as a result of the proliferation of complex arbitrage strategies. In June 1982, only 20% of the NYSE issues reporting short interest were affected by arbitrage transactions. This compares to June 1985 when 50% of the NYSE issues reporting short interest were influenced by arbitrage transactions. Suggestions have been made to modify the Short Interest Ratio to reflect such activity, but it may be too early to determine the value of doing this, given the dynamic nature of the newer derivative markets for options and futures.

---

*Reprinted with permission.

EXHIBIT S-3:
Short Interest Ratio (bottom) Versus The Standard & Poor's 500 Index (top) from 1962 to 1986

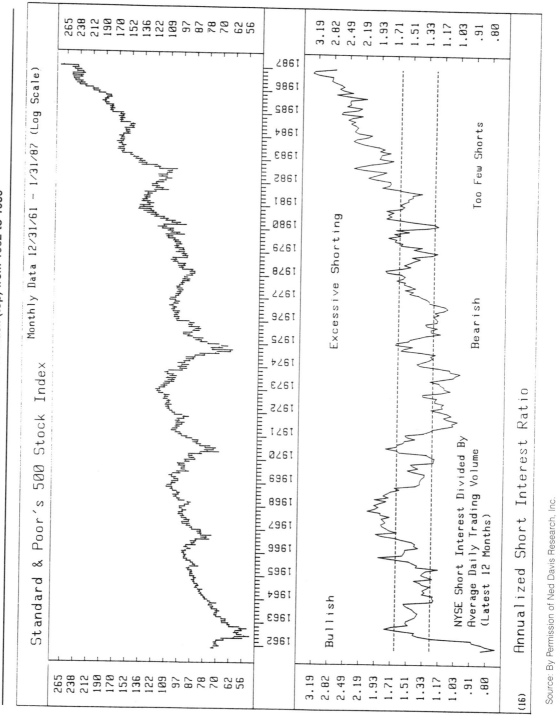

Source: By Permission of Ned Davis Research, Inc.

SIMPLE MOVING AVERAGE: MOVING ARITHMETIC MEAN

Mathematically, a simple arithmetic mean formula is represented as:

$$M_k = \frac{1}{n} \sum_{i=k-n+1}^{k} C_i = (C_{k-n+1} + C_{k-n+2} + C_{k-n+3} + \ldots + C_k) \div n$$

where

M_k is the simple moving average arithmetic mean at period k.

C_i is the closing price for period i.

n is the total number of periods to be included in the moving mean calculation.

k is the number of the position of the period being studied within the total number of periods in the database (see example, page 453).

This is perhaps the simplest, oldest and most widely used statistical method applied to stock price data. For example, the 200-day simple moving average has been a popular and moderately effective guide to stock market transaction timing for many decades. In this case, you simply add together the closing prices for the past 200 trading days and then divide the sum by 200. Many technicians make a further shortcut of adding up the weekly closing prices over 40 weeks, then dividing by 40.

Since only two prices affect the most recent simple moving average (M), updating the calculation can be accomplished quickly. The oldest data 40 weeks ago is deleted from the moving total, the newest data is added to the moving total, and the new moving total is divided by the number of periods averaged, which in this example is 40.

We tested this indicator using Compu Trac software and two 9.75-year test periods of weekly data (consisting of high, low, close, and volume for each week) for the broad-based NYSE Composite Index. The first period ran from January 5, 1968 through September 30, 1977, and the second period ran from April 8, 1977 through December 31, 1986. The overlap in data was necessary to facilitate testing of various moving averages throughout the full time period.

The simple moving average crossover rule for univariate analysis of time series data isolates the trend. When the NYSE weekly closing price crossed its own n-period simple moving average, a trend change and thus a trade position change was signaled in the direction of the crossing. The number of observations, n, that should be included in a simple moving average depends

Example of Simple Moving Average of Four Periods

Year End	Price NYSE Close	Four-Period Moving Total (T)	Four-Period Simple Moving Average (T ÷ 4)
1968	58.90		
1969	51.53		
1970	50.23		
1971	56.43	217.09	54.27
1972	64.48	222.67	55.67
1973	51.82	222.96	55.74
1974	36.13	208.86	52.22
1975	47.64	200.07	50.02
1976	57.88	193.47	48.37
1977	52.50	194.15	48.54
1978	53.62	211.64	52.91
1979	61.95	225.95	56.49
1980	77.86	245.93	61.48
1981	71.11	264.54	66.14
1982	81.03	291.95	72.99
1983	95.18	325.18	81.30
1984	96.38	343.70	85.93
1985	121.58	394.17	98.54
1986	138.58	451.72	112.93

on the length of the cyclical movements in the time series. Optimal values were determined by systematic trial-and-error procedure on the computer. We tested for n equal to 1 through 75 or simple moving averages ranging in length from 1 week (which is the indicator data itself) up to 75 weeks. The results of optimization runs for each n-week time length are shown in Exhibits S-4 to S-7 (pages 454–459). "Equity" signifies total profits or losses accumulated for each pass (length of n).

The highest combined profit for both optimization runs 1968–1977 and 1977–1986 was produced by the 45-week moving average crossover rule. There were fairly good results for periods from 38 to 62 weeks, but relatively poor results for periods under 14 weeks. note in Exhibit S-4 that the results take on the reassuring shape of a non-random bell-shaped curve and that 45 weeks is near the midpoint of the relatively successful range. As shown in Exhibits S-8 to S-15 (pages 460–465), combined profit of 111.79 NYSE points exceeded our 40-week simple moving average crossover rule standard of comparison. Exhibits S-10 and S-14 illustrate that equity drawdowns were not severe. Trading activity at 50 total transactions in 19 years was less active than standard, but accuracy at only 30% profitable trades was below standard. Overall, this simple trend-following indicator appears worthy of consideration.

DIRECTION OF A SIMPLE MOVING AVERAGE

The change of direction (from falling to rising or vice versa) of an n-period simple moving average produces exactly the same signals as an n-period rate of change crossing zero. This is because only two numbers affect both indicators: (1) the new data being added into the moving database of time length n used for indicator calculation, and (2) the oldest data being discarded from the moving database of time length n used for indicator calculation. Therefore, the optimal period for the direction of a simple moving average indicator is 31 weeks, the same as the optimal period for rate of change.

EXHIBIT S-4:
Profitability Chart for Simple Moving Average Period Lengths of 1 to 75 Weeks from 1977 to 1986

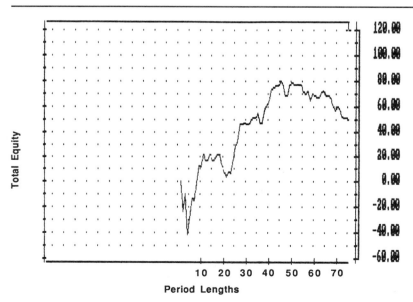

EXHIBIT S-5:
Profit Table for Simple Moving Average Period Lengths of 1 to 75 Weeks from 1977 to 1986

Pass	Total Equity	Short Equity	Long Equity	Max. Equity	Min. Equity	P/L	Best Trade	Worst Trade	Max. Open P/L	Min. Open P/L
1	0.00	0.00	0.00	0.00	0.00	0.00	N/A	N/A	0.00	0.00
2	-23.20	-53.42	27.66	0.00	-41.20	-23.20	14.67	-5.79	15.36	0.00
3	-9.97	-47.43	37.46	11.14	-28.73	-12.92	14.67	-6.93	15.56	-1.73
4	-41.54	-63.23	21.69	8.69	-51.21	-44.49	12.87	-9.41	15.56	-1.73
5	-28.93	-56.60	27.67	20.80	-37.71	-31.88	12.26	-9.41	15.56	-2.00
6	-13.37	-48.91	35.54	28.84	-20.57	-16.32	13.49	-9.41	17.18	-2.89
7	-15.60	-49.89	34.29	32.73	-22.80	-18.55	14.06	-9.41	17.18	-2.89
8	-1.80	-43.85	42.05	37.54	-8.42	-4.32	14.89	-9.41	18.43	-2.89
9	12.30	-36.46	48.76	35.17	-4.56	9.74	14.89	-9.41	18.43	-4.67
10	11.22	-36.78	46.16	42.03	-3.14	11.22	26.29	-9.41	31.72	-4.67
11	22.04	-30.95	51.15	52.85	-4.10	22.04	30.63	-9.41	34.17	-4.67
12	16.70	-33.23	48.09	47.51	-6.76	16.70	30.63	-9.41	34.17	-4.67
13	16.92	-33.37	48.45	47.73	-4.32	16.92	30.63	-9.41	34.17	-4.67
14	22.87	-30.45	51.48	49.60	-7.01	22.87	31.15	-9.41	36.31	-4.67
15	16.71	-33.44	48.31	49.76	-8.31	16.71	29.62	-9.41	36.31	-4.67
16	19.05	-31.91	49.12	52.10	-6.68	19.05	29.62	-9.41	34.17	-4.67
17	20.94	-31.76	50.86	53.99	-6.77	20.94	29.62	-9.41	34.17	-4.67
18	22.82	-30.86	51.84	55.87	-6.43	22.82	29.62	-9.41	34.17	-4.67
19	14.03	-35.47	47.66	47.08	-11.55	14.03	28.95	-9.41	34.17	-4.67
20	7.44	-38.88	44.48	40.49	-17.14	7.44	28.95	-9.41	34.17	-4.67
21	4.12	-40.93	43.21	43.41	-15.18	4.12	28.95	-9.41	34.17	-4.67
22	7.41	-38.92	44.49	46.70	-11.72	7.41	29.15	-9.41	34.17	-4.67
23	6.20	-39.82	44.18	45.49	-12.31	6.20	29.15	-9.41	34.17	-4.67
24	16.09	-34.85	49.10	55.38	-9.84	16.09	29.15	-9.41	34.17	-4.67
25	29.29	-28.61	56.06	64.46	-9.28	29.29	31.09	-9.41	34.17	-4.67
26	32.51	-26.63	57.30	67.68	-6.44	32.51	31.09	-9.41	34.17	-4.67
27	46.59	-19.70	64.45	70.14	-5.10	46.59	31.09	-7.61	34.17	-4.67
28	46.64	-20.35	65.15	68.60	-6.45	46.64	29.63	-7.61	34.77	-4.67
29	47.29	-20.34	65.79	69.25	-8.07	47.29	29.63	-7.61	37.17	-4.67
30	46.87	-20.47	65.50	68.83	-3.95	46.87	27.05	-7.61	37.17	-4.67
31	46.01	-21.15	65.32	67.97	-5.93	46.01	27.05	-7.61	37.17	-4.67
32	50.06	-17.91	66.13	72.02	-3.50	50.06	27.05	-7.61	37.17	-4.67
33	50.63	-17.72	66.51	72.59	-4.56	50.63	27.05	-7.61	37.17	-4.67
34	50.93	-17.16	66.25	72.89	-3.74	50.93	27.05	-7.61	37.17	-4.67
35	54.92	-15.66	68.74	76.88	-4.73	54.92	26.54	-7.61	37.17	-4.67
36	47.82	-19.52	65.50	70.18	-8.35	47.82	26.54	-4.67	37.17	-2.89
37	47.71	-19.63	65.50	70.07	-8.46	47.71	26.54	-4.67	37.17	-2.89
38	58.74	-13.79	73.63	74.82	-7.81	58.74	26.63	-4.67	37.17	-2.89
39	61.58	-12.25	76.71	74.10	-4.71	61.58	26.63	-3.85	37.17	-2.00
40	64.78	-11.58	79.24	77.30	-6.57	64.78	26.63	-2.89	37.17	-2.00
41	73.13	-7.94	84.84	83.87	-8.54	73.13	26.63	-2.89	38.76	-1.54
42	75.09	-6.88	87.06	83.19	-11.12	75.09	26.86	-2.89	39.37	-1.54
43	75.78	-6.87	115.28	82.52	-11.79	75.78	32.63	-2.89	39.37	-1.54
44	76.44	-6.21	115.28	83.18	-11.13	76.44	32.63	-2.89	39.37	-1.54
45	80.21	-4.18	84.39	86.95	-12.26	34.86	27.54	-2.89	52.09	-1.93
46	78.12	-5.78	83.90	84.86	-14.35	32.77	27.54	-3.75	52.09	-3.04
47	69.29	-10.05	79.34	76.03	-16.88	23.94	25.75	-3.46	52.09	-2.75
48	68.77	-10.57	79.34	75.51	-17.40	23.42	25.75	-3.98	52.09	-3.27
49	77.36	-5.87	83.23	84.10	-11.24	32.01	25.75	-3.17	52.09	-2.46
50	78.71	-4.81	83.52	85.45	-9.89	33.36	25.75	-2.40	52.09	-1.69

EXHIBIT S-5: (continued)

Pass	Total Equity	Short Equity	Long Equity	Max. Equity	Min. Equity	P/L	Best Trade	Worst Trade	Max. Open P/L	Min. Open P/L
51	77.30	-5.71	83.01	84.04	-11.30	31.95	25.75	-2.79	52.09	-2.08
52	77.29	-5.72	83.01	84.03	-11.31	31.94	25.75	-2.80	52.09	-2.09
53	77.55	-5.31	82.86	84.29	-11.05	32.20	25.75	-2.24	52.09	-1.53
54	77.04	-4.80	81.84	83.78	-12.01	31.69	25.75	-2.99	52.09	-1.81
55	70.99	-7.47	78.46	77.73	-12.84	25.64	22.72	-2.99	52.09	-1.81
56	69.74	-7.47	77.21	76.48	-14.09	24.39	22.72	-2.99	52.09	-1.81
57	72.55	-6.03	78.58	79.29	-11.28	27.20	22.72	-2.99	52.09	-1.81
58	65.33	-9.20	74.53	72.07	-12.68	19.98	19.81	-3.16	52.09	-1.87
59	70.15	-6.74	76.89	76.89	-10.56	24.80	19.81	-3.16	52.09	-1.87
60	68.28	-8.08	76.36	75.02	-6.17	22.93	19.81	-3.16	52.09	-1.87
61	67.39	-8.08	75.47	74.13	-7.06	22.04	19.81	-3.16	52.09	-1.87
62	66.98	-7.76	74.74	73.72	-7.47	21.63	19.81	-3.56	52.09	-2.74
63	71.14	-6.32	77.46	77.88	-5.48	25.79	19.81	-3.16	52.09	-1.87
64	72.04	-6.32	78.36	78.78	-4.58	26.69	19.81	-3.16	52.09	-1.87
65	68.58	-8.17	76.75	75.32	-4.34	25.08	19.81	-5.01	50.24	-3.16
66	68.90	-8.17	77.07	75.64	-4.02	25.40	19.81	-5.01	50.24	-3.16
67	67.42	-8.17	75.59	74.16	-5.50	23.92	19.81	-5.01	50.24	-3.16
68	61.87	-10.90	72.77	68.61	-5.59	18.37	19.81	-6.14	50.24	-4.29
69	57.84	-12.28	70.12	64.58	-6.86	14.34	19.81	-4.73	50.24	-2.88
70	59.38	-10.43	69.81	66.12	-9.02	14.03	19.81	-5.82	52.09	-3.58
71	59.19	-10.43	69.62	65.93	-9.21	13.84	19.81	-6.01	52.09	-3.77
72	52.24	-13.64	65.88	58.98	-11.11	6.89	19.81	-6.54	52.09	-4.30
73	51.12	-14.12	65.24	57.86	-11.27	5.77	19.33	-6.70	52.09	-4.46
74	51.26	-14.39	65.65	58.00	-11.25	5.91	19.25	-6.02	52.09	-3.78
75	49.56	-14.39	63.95	56.30	-12.95	4.21	19.25	-7.72	52.09	-5.48

Pass indicates period length.

Equity indicates the total number of points gained or lost.

Short equity indicates the number of points gained or lost on short positions.

Long equity indicates the number of points gained or lost on long positions.

Max. equity indicates the highest total profit recorded over the tested period.

Min. equity indicates the lowest total profit recorded over the tested period.

P/L indicates total number of points gained or lost in closed positions.

Best trade indicates the highest number of points gained in any closed trade.

Worst trade indicates the highest number of points lost in any closed trade.

Max. open P/L indicates the highest gain in a position which remains open at the end of the test run.

Min. open P/L indicates the highest loss in a position which remains open at the end of the test run.

EXHIBIT S-6:
Profitability Chart for Simple Moving Average Period Lengths of 1 to 75 Weeks from 1968 to 1977

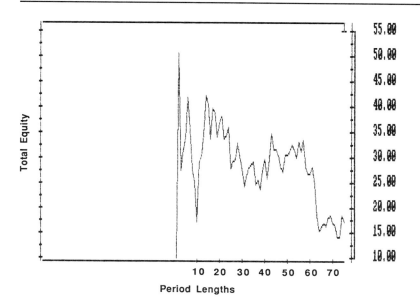

It would be redundant to optimize and follow both indicators. Since we believe that the data is more easily assimilated in the rate of change form, we refer the reader to the section on rate of change and Exhibits R-5, R-6, R-9 and R-10 (pages 421 and 424) for good examples. When the simple moving average changes direction, the rate of change crosses zero.

EXHIBIT S-7:
Profit Table for Simple Moving Average Period Lengths of 1 to 75 Weeks from 1968 to 1977

Pass	Total Equity	Short Equity	Long Equity	Max. Equity	Min. Equity	P/L	Best Trade	Worst Trade	Max. Open P/L	Min. Open P/L
1	0.00	0.00	0.00	0.00	0.00	0.00	N/A	N/A	0.00	0.00
2	50.52	25.94	24.58	72.18	-0.67	50.52	9.51	-3.24	10.26	0.00
3	27.47	14.08	13.39	44.71	0.00	27.47	7.08	-3.24	9.42	-1.04
4	31.50	15.57	15.93	40.44	0.00	31.50	9.13	-3.24	11.76	-1.43
5	33.78	18.32	17.46	40.66	0.00	33.78	9.13	-3.24	11.76	-0.98
6	41.95	19.68	22.27	49.19	-0.46	41.95	10.03	-2.84	12.97	-1.91
7	35.60	16.50	19.10	48.26	-0.47	34.29	9.71	-2.84	12.97	-1.08
8	27.73	12.80	14.93	39.49	0.00	26.42	9.71	-2.84	12.97	-1.25
9	25.03	10.90	14.13	36.69	-0.47	23.72	9.71	-2.84	12.97	-1.25
10	17.04	6.83	10.21	31.46	-2.36	15.73	8.95	-2.90	12.97	-1.25
11	29.08	12.87	16.21	43.58	-2.32	27.77	10.52	-2.90	15.08	-1.25
12	30.28	13.26	17.02	41.67	-2.74	28.97	10.52	-2.90	15.08	-1.25
13	34.38	15.81	18.57	47.09	-1.74	33.07	12.13	-2.90	17.31	-1.25
14	42.34	20.66	21.68	51.77	0.00	41.03	12.74	-2.90	17.31	-1.12
15	40.75	20.77	19.98	48.77	-0.21	39.44	12.07	-2.90	17.31	-1.12
16	33.62	17.10	16.52	41.64	0.00	32.31	12.07	-3.17	17.31	-1.13
17	39.55	20.50	19.05	45.91	-0.85	38.24	12.07	-3.17	17.31	-1.13
18	38.77	20.51	18.26	45.13	-4.94	37.46	12.07	-2.45	17.31	-1.50
19	34.09	18.21	15.88	41.41	-5.02	32.78	12.07	-2.45	17.31	-1.50
20	36.85	19.21	17.64	44.11	-4.18	35.54	11.78	-2.17	17.31	-1.50
21	38.14	19.98	18.16	40.87	-1.95	36.83	10.58	-2.97	17.31	-1.50
22	33.73	18.21	15.52	41.01	-2.82	32.42	14.68	-2.32	19.13	-1.50
23	34.40	19.35	15.05	41.74	-2.93	33.09	14.68	-2.32	19.13	-2.93
24	35.91	20.06	15.85	45.61	-2.84	34.60	17.94	-2.32	23.61	-2.84
25	27.96	15.96	12.00	40.66	-5.91	26.65	17.94	-2.32	23.61	-2.59
26	29.27	16.27	13.00	41.91	-4.66	27.96	17.94	-2.40	23.61	-1.90
27	29.75	16.91	12.84	42.39	-4.65	28.44	17.94	-2.40	23.61	-2.70
28	32.94	18.89	14.05	44.48	-5.42	31.63	17.94	-2.40	23.61	-3.47
29	30.29	17.01	13.28	43.73	-4.31	28.98	17.94	-2.71	23.61	-2.36
30	27.71	15.03	12.68	41.33	-2.25	26.40	17.67	-2.71	23.61	-1.57
31	24.51	12.94	11.57	42.37	-1.27	23.20	17.67	-2.71	23.61	-1.82
32	26.41	14.03	12.38	41.79	-1.55	25.10	17.67	-2.71	23.61	-1.57
33	28.18	15.36	12.82	40.00	-2.44	26.87	15.60	-2.71	23.61	-1.57
34	28.72	15.65	13.07	40.54	-2.48	27.41	15.60	-2.71	23.61	-1.57
35	29.01	15.82	13.19	42.61	-2.53	27.70	15.60	-1.86	23.61	-1.02
36	24.68	14.25	10.43	38.00	-3.72	23.37	15.60	-2.41	23.61	-1.44
37	25.63	14.66	10.97	36.07	-3.59	24.32	15.60	-2.41	23.61	-1.44
38	23.62	13.92	9.70	33.78	-4.12	22.31	15.60	-2.00	23.61	-0.98
39	27.50	16.08	11.42	37.66	-3.32	26.19	16.70	-1.86	24.71	-0.98
40	29.66	17.54	12.12	37.71	-4.08	28.35	16.70	-1.92	24.71	-1.09
41	25.93	15.55	10.38	35.42	-4.62	24.62	16.70	-2.31	24.71	-1.02
42	29.64	17.87	11.77	39.49	-5.55	28.33	16.70	-2.60	24.71	-1.77
43	34.82	20.32	14.50	44.67	-5.27	33.51	16.70	-2.32	24.71	-1.49
44	31.60	18.37	13.23	42.19	-4.59	30.29	15.81	-1.86	24.71	-1.02
45	31.58	18.62	12.96	42.39	-5.11	30.27	15.81	-2.16	24.71	-1.33
46	30.22	18.53	11.69	41.03	-6.29	28.91	15.81	-3.34	24.71	-2.51
47	28.26	17.77	10.49	40.53	-6.73	26.95	15.81	-3.78	24.71	-2.95
48	27.08	17.77	9.31	39.35	-7.91	25.77	15.81	-4.96	24.71	-4.13
49	30.58	19.40	11.18	39.91	-7.67	29.27	14.40	-4.72	24.71	-3.89
50	30.65	19.40	11.25	39.98	-7.60	29.34	14.40	-4.65	24.71	-3.82

EXHIBIT S-7: (continued)

Pass	Total Equity	Short Equity	Long Equity	Max. Equity	Min. Equity	P/L	Best Trade	Worst Trade	Max. Open P/L	Min. Open P/L
51	31.31	19.40	11.91	40.64	-6.94	30.00	14.40	-3.99	24.71	-3.16
52	32.61	19.61	13.00	41.94	-8.30	31.30	14.40	-4.23	24.71	-3.11
53	31.58	18.86	12.72	41.43	-8.81	30.27	14.40	-3.76	24.71	-2.64
54	30.13	17.23	12.90	41.42	-7.00	28.82	14.40	-2.64	24.71	-1.02
55	32.97	18.96	14.01	42.10	-8.14	31.66	14.40	-2.64	24.71	-1.45
56	31.13	18.21	12.92	40.26	-8.48	29.82	14.40	-2.91	24.71	-1.79
57	33.51	19.54	13.97	42.64	-6.34	32.20	14.40	-3.19	24.71	-2.07
58	28.21	17.02	11.19	39.84	-5.60	26.90	14.40	-3.45	24.71	-2.33
59	26.95	16.39	10.56	38.32	-5.60	25.64	13.91	-3.45	24.71	-2.33
60	26.98	15.24	11.74	38.35	-1.80	25.67	13.91	-2.64	24.71	-1.57
61	28.10	15.24	12.86	39.47	-0.68	26.79	13.91	-2.64	24.71	-1.57
62	24.54	13.53	11.01	34.63	-1.62	23.23	13.91	-2.29	24.71	-1.57
63	18.44	10.28	8.16	31.37	-2.02	17.13	13.91	-2.66	24.71	-0.95
64	15.44	9.25	6.19	27.11	-1.08	14.13	13.06	-2.87	24.71	-1.50
65	16.24	10.14	6.10	26.13	-2.06	14.93	13.06	-2.87	24.71	-1.50
66	16.73	10.14	6.59	26.62	-1.57	15.42	13.06	-2.87	24.71	-1.50
67	16.27	10.14	6.13	26.16	-2.03	14.96	13.06	-2.87	24.71	-1.50
68	18.23	10.99	7.24	28.12	-1.77	16.92	13.06	-2.66	24.71	-1.50
69	18.31	11.17	7.14	27.84	-2.05	17.00	13.06	-2.66	24.71	-1.50
70	16.98	11.17	5.81	26.51	-3.38	15.67	13.06	-3.17	24.71	-1.50
71	16.39	11.17	5.22	25.92	-3.97	15.08	13.06	-3.76	24.71	-1.68
72	14.03	10.19	3.84	25.52	-4.37	12.72	12.74	-4.16	24.71	-2.08
73	13.95	9.81	4.14	25.44	-3.69	12.64	12.74	-3.48	24.71	-1.50
74	18.38	11.72	6.66	27.61	-3.08	17.07	13.00	-3.04	24.71	-1.50
75	17.29	10.78	6.51	28.40	-2.29	15.98	13.00	-3.04	24.71	-1.50

Pass indicates period length.

Equity indicates the total number of points gained or lost.

Short equity indicates the number of points gained or lost on short positions.

Long equity indicates the number of points gained or lost on long positions.

Max. equity indicates the highest total profit recorded over the tested period.

Min. equity indicates the lowest total profit recorded over the tested period.

P/L indicates total number of points gained or lost in closed positions.

Best trade indicates the highest number of points gained in any closed trade.

Worst trade indicates the highest number of points lost in any closed trade.

Max. open P/L indicates the highest gain in a position which remains open at the end of the test run.

Min. open P/L indicates the highest loss in a position which remains open at the end of the test run.

EXHIBIT S-8:

Simple Moving Average: 45 Weeks of New York Stock Exchange Composite Weekly Data, 1977 to 1986

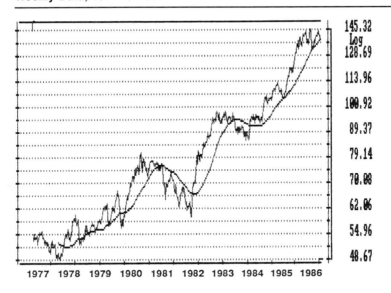

EXHIBIT S-9:

1/45 Ratio Oscillator of Close Versus Simple Moving Average: 45 Weeks, 1977 to 1986

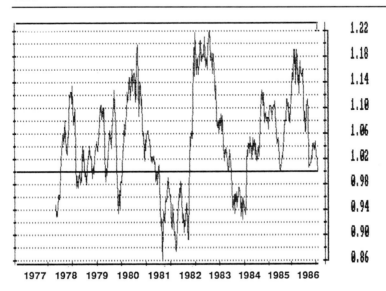

EXHIBIT S-10:
Total Equity for Simple Moving Average: 45 Weeks, 1977 to 1986

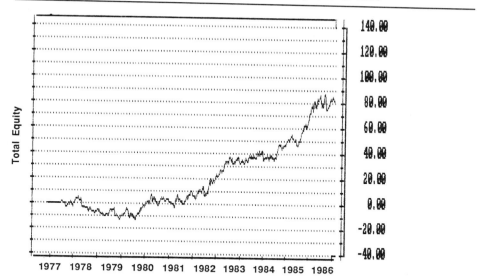

EXHIBIT S-11:
Profit Summary for Simple Moving Average: 45 Weeks, 1977 to 1986

Item		Long	Short	Net
		-- Per Trade Ranges --		
Per Trade Ranges				
Best Trade	(Closed position yielding maximum P/L)	27.54	7.87	27.54
.. Date		840127	820827	840127
Worst Trade	(Closed position yielding minimum P/L)	-1.48	-2.89	-2.89
.. Date		810821	790105	790105
Max Open P/L	(Maximum P/L occurring in an open position)	52.09	15.56	52.09
.. Date		860829	820813	860829
Min Open P/L	(Minimum P/L occurring in an open position)	0.00	-1.93	-1.93
.. Date		770408	780414	780414
		--- Overall Ranges ---		
Overall Ranges				
Max P/L	(Maximum P/L from all closed positions during the run)	33.32	34.86	34.86
.. Date		840127	840803	840803
Min P/L	(Minimum P/L from all closed positions during the run)	-11.10	-12.26	-12.26
.. Date		800314	800516	800516
Max Equity	(Maximum P/L from all closed and open positions)	86.95	41.92	86.95
.. Date		860829	840615	860829
Min Equity	(Minimum P/L from all closed and open positions)	-12.26	-12.26	-12.26
.. Date		800516	800516	800516
		------ Statistics ------		
Statistics				
Periods	(The number of periods in each position and entire run)	386	123	509
Trades	(The number of trades in each position and entire run)	10	11	21
# Profitable	(The number of profitable trades. . .)	4	2	6
# Losing	(The number of unprofitable trades. . .)	6	9	15
% Profitable	(The percent of profitable trades to total trades)	40.00	18.18	28.57
% Losing	(The percent of unprofitable trades to total trades)	60.00	81.82	71.43
		------ Results ------		
Results				
Commission	(Total commission deducted from closed trades)	0.00	0.00	0.00
Slippage	(Total slippage deducted from closed trades)	0.00	0.00	0.00
Gross P/L	(Total points gained in closed positions)	39.04	-4.18	34.86
Open P/L	(P/L in a position which remains open at the end)	45.35	0.00	45.35
P/L	(Net P/L: Gross P/L less Commission and Slippage)	39.04	-4.18	34.86
Equity	(Net P/L plus Open P/L at the end of the run)	84.39	-4.18	80.21

There are columns for Long trades, Short trades and Net. In the Long column, results are reported only for Long positions. In the Short column, results are reported for Short positions only. In the Net column for the "Per Trade Ranges" and "Overall Ranges," entries will be the extreme from either the Long or Short column. Net column entries for the "Statistics" and "Results" categories are the combined results of entries in the Long and Short columns.

EXHIBIT S-12:
Simple Moving Average: 45 Weeks, 1968 to 1977

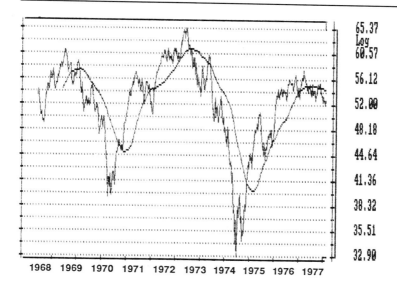

EXHIBIT S-13:
1/45 Week Simple Moving Average Ratio Oscillator, 1968 to 1977

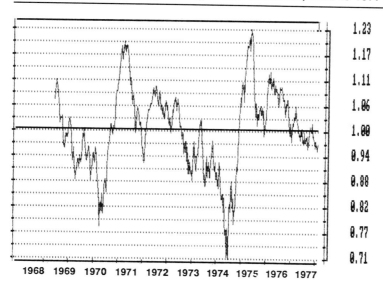

EXHIBIT S-14:
Total Equity for Simple Moving Average: 45 Weeks, 1968 to 1977

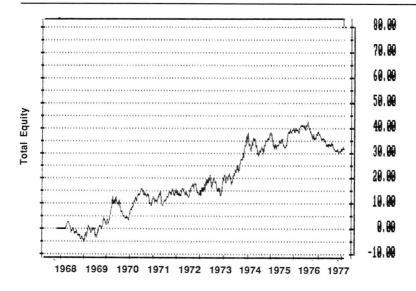

EXHIBIT S-15:

Profit Summary for Simple Moving Average: 45 Weeks, 1968 to 1977

Item		Long	Short	Net
Per Trade Ranges		— Per Trade Ranges —		
Best Trade	(Closed position yielding maximum P/L)	6.60	15.81	15.81
..Date		761022	750207	750207
Worst Trade	(Closed position yielding minimum P/L)	-2.16	-1.86	-2.16
..Date		690221	690502	690221
Max Open P/L	(Maximum P/L occurring in an open position)	11.47	24.71	24.71
..Date		710423	741004	741004
Min Open P/L	(Minimum P/L occurring in an open position)	-1.33	-1.02	-1.33
..Date		690110	770415	690110
Overall Ranges		— Overall Ranges —		
Max P/L	(Maximum P/L from all closed positions during the run)	38.79	37.32	38.79
..Date		761022	761029	761022
Min P/L	(Minimum P/L from all closed positions during the run)	-5.11	-4.02	-5.11
..Date		690606	690502	690606
Max Equity	(Maximum P/L from all closed and open positions)	42.39	38.79	42.39
..Date		760924	761022	760924
Min Equity	(Minimum P/L from all closed and open positions)	-5.11	-5.11	-5.11
..Date		690606	690606	690606
Statistics		— Statistics —		
Periods	(The number of periods in each position and entire run)	285	224	509
Trades	(The number of trades in each position and entire run)	15	14	29
# Profitable	(The number of profitable trades...)	6	3	9
# Losing	(The number of unprofitable trades...)	9	11	20
% Profitable	(The percent of profitable trades to total trades)	40.00	21.43	31.03
% Losing	(The percent of unprofitable trades to total trades)	60.00	78.57	68.97
Results		— Results —		
Commission	(Total commission deducted from closed trades)	0.00	0.00	0.00
Slippage	(Total slippage deducted from closed trades)	0.00	0.00	0.00
Gross P/L	(Total points gained in closed positions)	12.96	17.31	30.27
Open P/L	(P/L in a position which remains open at the end)	0.00	1.31	1.31
P/L	(Net P/L: Gross P/L less Commission and Slippage)	12.96	17.31	30.27
Equity	(Net P/L plus Open P/L at the end of the run)	12.96	18.62	31.58

There are columns for Long trades, Short trades and Net. In the Long column, results are reported only for Long positions. In the Short column, results are reported for Short positions only. In the Net column for the "Per Trade Ranges" and "Overall Ranges," entries will be the extreme from either the Long or Short column. Net column entries for the "Statistics" and "Results" categories are the combined results of entries in the Long and Short columns.

465

SPECIALIST SHORT RATIO

Investors sell short stock when they anticipate its price going lower. At a later date, they must cover their short sales and buy the stock back. A profit is made if the stock is bought back at a lower price than when it was sold short.

On a weekly basis, the New York Stock Exchange releases information on short sales, including those made by stock exchange specialists. Specialists are responsible for balancing incoming buy and sell orders to maintain orderly markets in the stocks in which they specialize. Specialists are considered by many to be particularly astute traders.

The Specialist Short Ratio is computed by dividing the total specialist short sales by total short sales. A 4-week moving average of the indicator is graphically displayed in Exhibit S-16.

Since specialists normally are right about the trend of stock prices, low Specialist Short Ratio readings are viewed as bullish and high readings are considered bearish.

We tested the Specialist Short Ratio for the period of January 1946 to March 1987 on a weekly basis. In addition, we applied a 10-period simple moving average to the weekly readings to smooth out any erratic movements. The results are shown in Exhibit S-17 and S-18 (pages 468–469).

The test process was as follows. The indicator readings for the test period were divided into 20 ranges with approximately the same number of occurrences in each range. For each reading in a range, the gain or loss in four subsequent time periods (1 month later, 3 months later, 6 months later, and 12 months later) was calculated. The combined results for readings within each range were statistically compared, using chi-squared tests, to the performance of the overall market (as measured by the Standard & Poor's 500 Index). Varying degrees of bullishness and bearishness were noted on the basis of that comparison.

Our research results confirm that low indicator readings are bullish, especially for 6 and 12 months in the future. In addition, high readings imply a bearish condition.

During the last 40 years, when the 10-week moving average of the Specialist Short Ratio was 0.38 or lower, an average gain occurred in the overall market (as measured by the S&P 500) of 9.87% 6 months later and 21.17% 12 months later. Exhibit S-19 (page 470) shows the results in greater detail. You should note that all signals generated within 3 months after an initial reading of 0.38 or lower were considered repeat signals and are not included in the results.

EXHIBIT S-16:
Specialist Short Ratio (bottom) Versus The Dow Jones Industrial Average (top) from 1979 to 1986

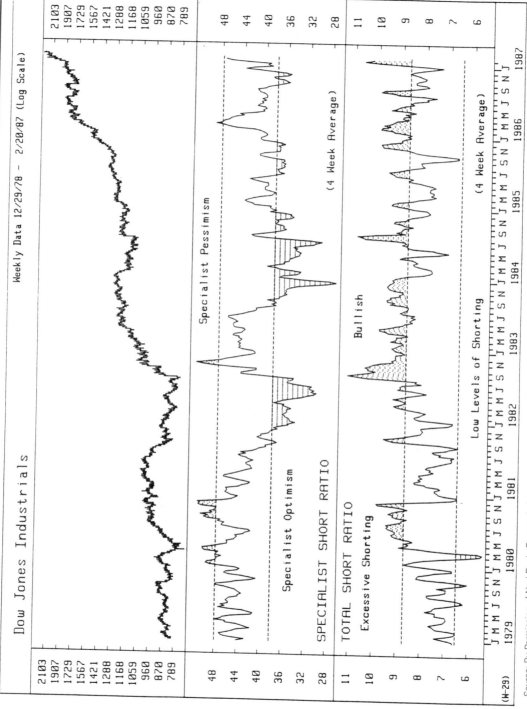

Source: By Permission of Ned Davis Research, Inc.

467

EXHIBIT S-17: Interpretation of Specialist Short Ratio's Weekly Readings

```
==============================================================================
SPECIALIST SHORTS - WEEKLY DATA
PERIOD ANALYZED: JANUARY 1946 TO MARCH 1987
==============================================================================
```

		INTERPRETATION GIVEN INVESTOR'S TIME FRAME			
INDICATOR RANGE					
GREATER THAN	LESS THAN OR EQUAL TO	1 MONTH	3 MONTHS	6 MONTHS	12 MONTHS
0.000	0.352	NEUTRAL	VERY BULLISH	VERY BULLISH	VERY BULLISH
0.352	0.377	NEUTRAL	NEUTRAL	SLIGHTLY BULLISH	VERY BULLISH
0.377	0.397	NEUTRAL	SLIGHTLY BULLISH	NEUTRAL	BULLISH
0.397	0.415	NEUTRAL	NEUTRAL	NEUTRAL	SLIGHTLY BULLISH
0.415	0.431	NEUTRAL	NEUTRAL	NEUTRAL	BULLISH
0.431	0.445	NEUTRAL	NEUTRAL	NEUTRAL	NEUTRAL
0.445	0.456	NEUTRAL	NEUTRAL	NEUTRAL	NEUTRAL
0.456	0.470	NEUTRAL	NEUTRAL	NEUTRAL	NEUTRAL
0.470	0.482	NEUTRAL	NEUTRAL	NEUTRAL	NEUTRAL
0.482	0.497	NEUTRAL	NEUTRAL	NEUTRAL	NEUTRAL
0.497	0.509	NEUTRAL	NEUTRAL	NEUTRAL	NEUTRAL
0.509	0.526	NEUTRAL	NEUTRAL	NEUTRAL	NEUTRAL
0.526	0.540	NEUTRAL	NEUTRAL	NEUTRAL	NEUTRAL
0.540	0.557	NEUTRAL	NEUTRAL	NEUTRAL	NEUTRAL
0.557	0.570	SLIGHTLY BEARISH	NEUTRAL	NEUTRAL	NEUTRAL
0.570	0.584	NEUTRAL	NEUTRAL	NEUTRAL	NEUTRAL
0.584	0.598	NEUTRAL	NEUTRAL	NEUTRAL	SLIGHTLY BEARISH
0.598	0.621	NEUTRAL	NEUTRAL	NEUTRAL	VERY BEARISH
0.621	0.648	NEUTRAL	BEARISH	BEARISH	VERY BEARISH
0.648	0.777	SLIGHTLY BEARISH	SLIGHTLY BEARISH	NEUTRAL	VERY BEARISH

```
==============================================================================
```

Definitions of Very Bullish, Bullish, Slightly Bullish, Neutral, Slightly Bearish, Bearish, and Very Bearish are provided in Appendix A.

EXHIBIT S-18:

Interpretation of Specialist Short Ratio's 10-Week Simple Moving Average Readings

```
==================================================================================================
SPECIALIST SHORTS - 10 WEEK MOVING AVERAGE
PERIOD ANALYZED:  JANUARY 1946 TO MARCH 1987
==================================================================================================

   INDICATOR RANGE                INTERPRETATION GIVEN INVESTOR'S TIME FRAME
-------------------   --------------------------------------------------------------------------

           LESS
GREATER   THAN OR
 THAN    EQUAL TO     1 MONTH            3 MONTHS           6 MONTHS           12 MONTHS
-------   --------    ---------------    ---------------    ---------------    ---------------

 0.000     0.366      NEUTRAL            NEUTRAL            VERY BULLISH       VERY BULLISH
 0.366     0.387      SLIGHTLY BULLISH   VERY BULLISH       BULLISH            VERY BULLISH
 0.387     0.407      BULLISH            NEUTRAL            BULLISH            VERY BULLISH
 0.407     0.425      NEUTRAL            NEUTRAL            NEUTRAL            NEUTRAL
 0.425     0.441      NEUTRAL            NEUTRAL            NEUTRAL            NEUTRAL
 0.441     0.450      BULLISH            NEUTRAL            NEUTRAL            NEUTRAL
 0.450     0.462      NEUTRAL            NEUTRAL            NEUTRAL            NEUTRAL
 0.462     0.474      NEUTRAL            NEUTRAL            NEUTRAL            SLIGHTLY BULLISH
 0.474     0.485      NEUTRAL            VERY BULLISH       BULLISH            NEUTRAL
 0.485     0.499      NEUTRAL            NEUTRAL            NEUTRAL            NEUTRAL
 0.499     0.511      BULLISH            NEUTRAL            NEUTRAL            NEUTRAL
 0.511     0.528      NEUTRAL            NEUTRAL            NEUTRAL            NEUTRAL
 0.528     0.539      NEUTRAL            NEUTRAL            NEUTRAL            NEUTRAL
 0.539     0.550      NEUTRAL            NEUTRAL            NEUTRAL            NEUTRAL
 0.550     0.563      NEUTRAL            NEUTRAL            NEUTRAL            NEUTRAL
 0.563     0.575      NEUTRAL            NEUTRAL            SLIGHTLY BEARISH   NEUTRAL
 0.575     0.588      SLIGHTLY BEARISH   NEUTRAL            NEUTRAL            SLIGHTLY BEARISH
 0.588     0.606      VERY BEARISH       VERY BEARISH       VERY BEARISH       VERY BEARISH
 0.606     0.625      NEUTRAL            VERY BEARISH       VERY BEARISH       VERY BEARISH
 0.625     0.692      SLIGHTLY BEARISH   NEUTRAL            NEUTRAL            VERY BEARISH

==================================================================================================
```

Definitions of Very Bullish, Bullish, Slightly Bullish, Neutral, Slightly Bearish, Bearish, and Very Bearish are provided in Appendix A.

EXHIBIT S-19:

Specialist Short Ratio's 10-Week Simple Moving Average Readings Less than or Equal to 0.38 from 1947 to 1986

```
===================================================================
SPECIALIST SHORTS - 10 WEEK MOVING AVERAGE
===================================================================
```

		PERCENTAGE CHANGE IN S&P 500			
DATE	INDICATOR VALUE	1 MONTH LATER	3 MONTHS LATER	6 MONTHS LATER	12 MONTHS LATER
MAY 17 1947	0.36	10.43	11.09	9.26	19.55
MAY 27 1949	0.38	-1.72	6.20	13.23	29.01
SEP 2 1949	0.38	3.60	7.33	13.08	22.17
SEP 25 1953	0.38	4.12	6.27	15.62	40.30
FEB 28 1958	0.37	3.09	7.96	16.70	36.46
NOV 2 1962	0.38	8.03	14.48	20.24	27.84
FEB 3 1978	0.37	-2.52	7.71	15.96	11.54
OCT 30 1981	0.38	3.45	-3.37	-4.17	9.60
JAN 8 1982	0.37	-4.12	-2.79	-8.97	18.75
MAY 7 1982	0.35	-8.24	-13.19	18.73	36.70
SEP 3 1982	0.37	-0.57	13.05	25.26	34.01
OCT 7 1983	0.38	-5.20	-1.11	-8.97	-4.61
JAN 6 1984	0.33	-6.62	-8.41	-10.07	-2.79
MAY 4 1984	0.36	-3.43	2.04	5.27	12.51
SEP 7 1984	0.37	-1.36	-0.98	8.96	13.93
JAN 4 1985	0.37	10.18	9.38	17.62	28.84
AUG 2 1985	0.38	-1.86	0.03	11.74	22.68
DEC 6 1985	0.37	2.45	11.62	18.21	24.66
AVERAGE CHANGE		0.54	3.74	9.87	21.17

```
===================================================================
```

STIX

STIX is an exponentially smoothed short-term market breadth indicator. It is calculated on a daily basis in two steps, using NYSE advance/decline data. First, you compute a ratio by dividing the number of advancing issues by the number of advancing issues plus the number of declining issues. That ratio is multiplied by 0.09 and added to the product of the previous day's STIX value multiplied by 0.91. This smoothing approximates a 21-day simple moving average.

It can be noted by close examination of the chart shown in Exhibit S-20 (page 472) that low STIX readings are bearish and high STIX readings are bullish for stock prices. This is consistent with our findings for other breadth indicators.

EXHIBIT S-20:
STIX (top) Versus The Standard & Poor's 500 Index (bottom) from 1984 to 1986

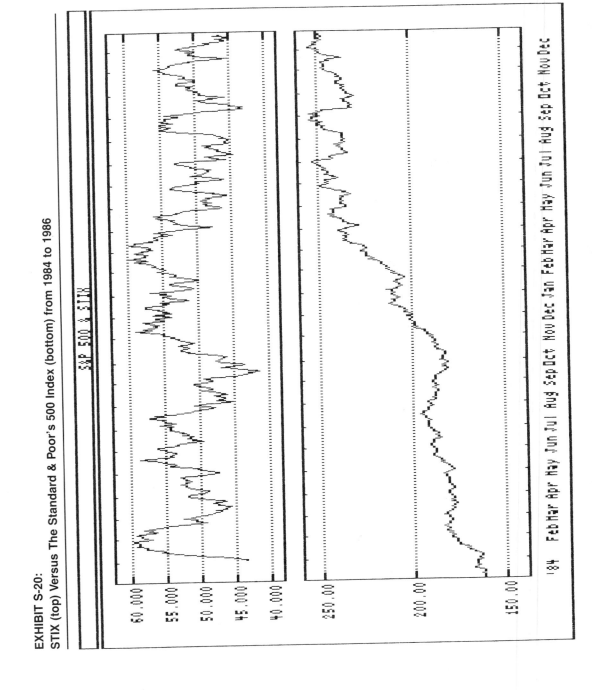

STOCHASTICS

Stochastics is a momentum or price velocity indicator developed by George C. Lane (Investment Educators, P.O. Box 2354, Des Plaines, IL). Like rate of change, it is a fixed period-to-period moving calculation that can jump around erratically due solely to data for the oldest period being dropped off. Thus, it suffers from a conceptual weakness that makes it theoretically vulnerable to instability and false signals. This probably accounts for many of its performance problems and the large number of trades.

Lane's Stochastics is easy to calculate:

$$K = \frac{(C - L)}{(H - L)} * 100$$

where

K is Lane's Stochastics.
C is the latest closing price of the stock or contract.
L is the n-period low price of the stock or contract.
H is the n-period high price of the stock or contract.
n can be any number (Lane suggests 5 to 21).

Furthermore, Lane has clearly stated that he recommends that K be smoothed twice with three-period simple moving averages: SK is the three-period simple moving average of K, and SD is the three-period simple moving average of SK.

Lane's interpretation of Stochastics can be complicated. First, look for a price trend reversal when SK diverges from price. (Unfortunately, the determination of divergence is not mechanical and thus cannot readily be incorporated into a computerized simulation.) That is, when price moves up to a new high but SK does not make a new high (for a negative divergence), look for a downturn in the price trend. Conversely, when price moves down to a new low but SK does not make a new low (for a positive divergence), look for an upturn in the price trend.

The actual signal to act on such a divergence comes when SK moves above SD for a buy signal, or when SK moves below SD for a sell signal. Lane says that it is more reliable when SD has already made a turn in the direction of the new trend when SK crosses SD. Also, it is better when signals are in the direction of the major trend. Finally, reliability is enhanced when buy signals are given in the 10% to 15% range and when sell signals are given in the 85% to 90% zone.

Various trials of these rules provided below average results in our test runs for the NYSE Composite Index for 1968–1986 monthly periods 1 through 24. The basic rule—buy when SK crosses above SD; sell and sell short when SK crosses under SD—produced consistent losses, as shown in Exhibit S-21. Requiring that SD be moving in the direction of the crossing of SD by SK improved results somewhat, as shown in Exhibit S-22. Adding a further requirement that both SK and SD be moving in the direction of the crossing of SD by SK added somewhat greater consistency but did not improve peak equity (cumulative profit). Requiring divergencies, right side crosses of SD and SK, and SK or SD signals within specified zones (such as 10% to 15% for buy and 85% to 90% for sell) added considerably to its complexity but did not improve performance up to our 40-week simple moving average crossover rule standard of comparison.

Next, we tested these same rules using Compu Trac software and two 9.75-year test periods of weekly data (consisting of high, low, close, and volume for each week) for the broad-based NYSE Composite Index. The first period ran from January 5, 1968 through September 30, 1977, and the second period ran from April 8, 1977 through December 31, 1986. The overlap in data was necessary to facilitate testing throughout the full time period. Using this weekly data, total profits were much lower and the number of trades

EXHIBIT S-21:
Profitability Chart for Stochastics: SK Crossing SD, Period Lengths 1 to 24 Months, 1968 to 1986

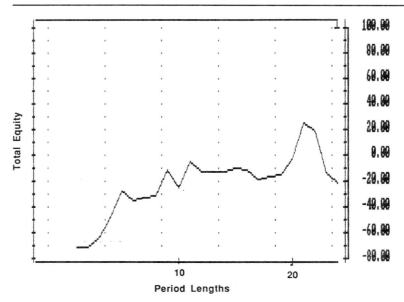

was much higher compared to our monthly data tests. For example, compare the weekly optimization run shown in Exhibit S-23 (page 476) with the same formula monthly run in Exhibit S-22 (page 475).

Other analysts have recommended that smoothed Stochastics be filtered by requiring that both SK and SD be rising for a buy signal and that both SK and SD be falling for a sell signal. Furthermore, SD must be "overbought" (at SD greater than 80%) for a sell signal, and SD must be "oversold" (at SD less than 20%) for a buy signal. These rules produced consistent losses in our tests over time frames from 1 to 90 weeks, as shown in Exhibit S-24 (page 476). Apparently, overbought/oversold filters degrade unfiltered results by precluding full participation in persistent major trends.

Schwager and Strahm* tried a wide range of parameter sets, including different moving average periods, in addition to the standard three-period simple moving average, a variety of periods for the basic K line, and daily and weekly data. They tested 25 different futures markets and concluded that

---

*Jack D. Schwager and Norman Strahm, *Technical Analysis of Stocks & Commodities* (P.O. Box 46518, Seattle, WA 98146), July 1986, p. 12.

EXHIBIT S-22:

Profitability for Stochastics: SK Crossing SD and SD Confirming by Moving in the Direction of the Crossing, Period Lengths 1 to 24 Months, 1968 to 1986

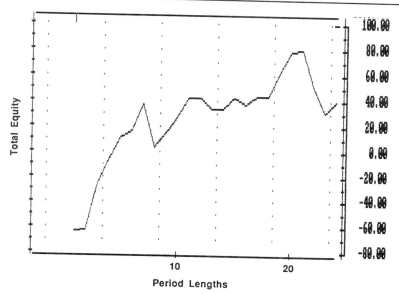

EXHIBIT S-23:
Profitability Chart for Stochastics: SK Crossing SD and SD Moving in the Direction of the Crossing (Period Lengths of 1 to 100 Weeks from 1977 to 1986)

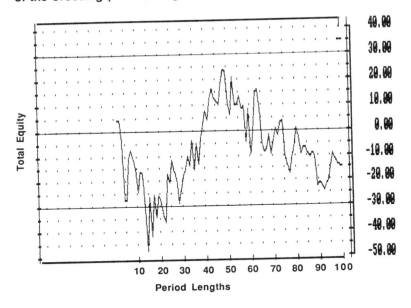

EXHIBIT S-24:
Profitability Chart for Stochastics with Overbought/Oversold Filters (Period Lengths of 1 to 100 Weeks from 1977 to 1986)

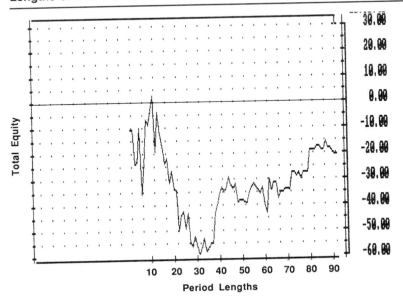

476

the value of stochastics as a technical indicator may be generally overstated. Rather, the parameters tested provided poor to mediocre results. Our tests confirmed this general conclusion.

K39W STOCHASTICS PROVES OPTIMAL

Using the two 9.75 weekly data periods for the NYSE Composite Index. brute force computer number crunching of thousands of combinations did uncover one profitable decision rule: For the 39-week unsmoothed K line(n = 39 with no moving averages), buy when K crosses above 50%, provided that both K and the closing price are above their previous week's levels. Sell and sell short when the 39-week K line crosses below 50%, provided that both K and the closing price are below their previous week's levels.

This rule produced fairly consistent profits using periods ranging between 38 and 66 weeks, but profits dropped off using shorter or longer periods. Periods shorter than 25 weeks produced most unsatisfactory results, including six losses for periods of less than 20 weeks. The 100-week optimization chart and table for the 1977–1986 period are shown in Exhibits S-25 and S-26 (pages 477–479). Note the peak profit at 39 to 41 weeks.

EXHIBIT S-25:

Profitability Chart for Stochastics: K Crossing 50% (Period Lengths of 1 to 100 Weeks from 1977 to 1986)

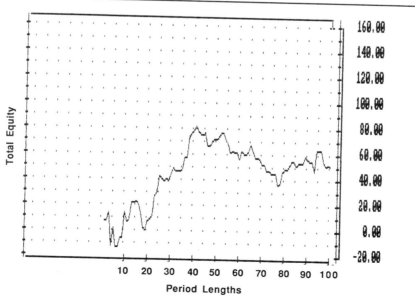

Profit Table for Stochastics: K Crossing 50% (Period Lengths of 1 to 100 Weeks from 1977 to 1986)

Pass	Total Equity	Short Equity	Long Equity	Max. Equity	Min. Equity	P/L	Best Trade	Worst Trade	Max. Open P/L	Min. Open P/L
1	7.13	-38.88	46.01	13.66	-26.31	4.18	14.67	-4.99	15.56	-1.73
2	7.75	-38.26	46.01	14.28	-25.69	4.80	14.67	-4.99	15.56	-1.73
3	14.15	-35.06	49.21	23.14	-9.70	11.20	12.87	-4.99	15.56	-1.73
4	-12.66	-48.42	35.76	24.80	-20.58	-15.18	12.58	-9.41	15.56	-2.00
5	0.86	-41.66	43.62	44.48	-5.74	0.86	14.67	-9.41	17.18	-2.89
6	-13.66	-49.78	34.28	35.00	-13.66	-13.66	14.89	-9.41	18.43	-4.67
7	-13.44	-49.11	33.83	34.64	-13.44	-13.44	14.89	-9.41	18.43	-4.67
8	-5.86	-45.32	37.62	29.72	-9.58	-5.86	14.89	-9.41	18.43	-4.67
9	-5.64	-44.79	37.31	25.17	-12.98	-5.64	14.89	-9.41	18.43	-4.67
10	14.34	-34.41	46.91	45.15	-9.94	14.34	30.63	-9.41	34.17	-4.67
11	6.47	-38.56	43.19	37.28	-11.59	6.47	30.63	-9.41	34.17	-4.67
12	8.69	-37.45	44.30	39.50	-10.81	8.69	29.62	-9.41	34.17	-4.67
13	20.65	-31.47	50.28	47.38	-5.97	20.65	31.15	-9.41	36.31	-4.67
14	21.19	-30.84	50.19	54.24	-2.23	21.19	29.62	-9.41	34.17	-4.67
15	22.98	-30.74	51.88	56.03	-1.94	22.98	29.62	-9.41	34.17	-4.67
16	19.46	-32.54	52.00	58.75	-2.02	21.30	28.95	-9.41	34.17	-4.67
17	13.49	-35.74	49.23	52.78	-5.00	15.33	29.15	-9.41	34.17	-4.67
18	1.58	-41.81	41.55	40.87	-8.91	1.58	29.15	-9.41	34.17	-4.67
19	-0.54	-43.26	40.88	38.75	-17.63	-0.54	29.15	-9.41	34.17	-4.67
20	7.80	-39.02	44.98	47.09	-15.66	7.80	29.63	-9.41	34.17	-4.67
21	9.02	-38.41	45.59	48.31	-14.44	9.02	29.63	-9.41	34.17	-4.67
22	11.69	-37.41	47.26	46.86	-15.89	11.69	29.63	-9.41	34.17	-4.67
23	26.99	-29.76	54.91	62.16	-5.35	26.99	29.63	-9.41	34.17	-4.67
24	29.53	-28.23	55.92	64.70	-4.41	29.53	29.63	-9.41	34.17	-4.67
25	42.49	-21.75	62.40	64.45	-4.41	42.49	29.63	-7.61	34.77	-4.67
26	39.66	-23.84	61.66	61.62	-7.24	39.66	29.63	-7.61	34.77	-4.67
27	38.69	-24.81	61.66	60.65	-8.21	38.69	29.63	-7.61	34.77	-4.67
28	39.89	-24.21	62.26	61.85	-8.21	39.89	29.63	-7.61	34.77	-4.67
29	38.87	-24.72	61.75	60.83	-8.21	38.87	29.12	-7.61	34.77	-4.67
30	44.27	-20.90	63.33	66.23	-5.97	44.27	31.01	-7.61	34.77	-4.67
31	49.07	-18.50	65.73	71.03	-5.97	49.07	31.01	-7.61	37.17	-4.67
32	46.03	-19.61	63.80	67.99	-8.15	46.03	30.75	-7.61	37.17	-4.67
33	46.36	-19.94	64.46	59.38	-9.49	46.36	29.13	-4.39	37.17	-2.89
34	46.04	-20.41	64.61	59.06	-9.81	46.04	29.13	-4.39	37.17	-2.89
35	49.29	-18.84	98.56	56.03	-11.92	49.29	30.43	-4.39	37.17	-2.89
36	57.22	-15.36	103.01	63.96	-11.80	57.22	30.43	-4.39	37.17	-2.89
37	57.14	-15.40	102.97	63.88	-11.80	57.14	30.43	-4.39	37.17	-2.89
38	73.84	-7.05	126.24	80.58	-12.77	73.84	45.35	-4.39	52.09	-2.89
39	76.27	-6.37	82.64	83.01	-13.84	30.92	27.54	-4.39	52.09	-2.89
40	78.76	-5.38	84.14	85.50	-11.35	33.41	27.54	-3.59	52.09	-2.88
41	81.04	-4.24	85.28	87.78	-9.07	35.69	27.54	-3.59	52.09	-2.88
42	77.30	-6.19	83.49	84.04	-9.23	31.95	25.75	-3.75	52.09	-3.04
43	75.46	-7.11	82.57	82.20	-11.07	30.11	25.75	-3.75	52.09	-3.04
44	75.46	-7.11	82.57	82.20	-11.07	30.11	25.75	-3.75	52.09	-3.04
45	76.07	-6.92	82.99	82.81	-11.30	30.72	25.75	-3.98	52.09	-3.27
46	65.65	-12.13	77.78	72.39	-13.08	20.30	22.84	-3.98	52.09	-3.27
47	66.84	-10.94	77.78	73.58	-11.89	21.49	22.84	-3.16	52.09	-2.08
48	69.58	-9.57	79.15	76.32	-10.41	24.23	22.84	-3.16	52.09	-2.08
49	70.88	-8.92	79.80	77.62	-10.73	25.53	22.84	-3.16	52.09	-2.08
50	70.87	-8.93	79.80	77.61	-10.74	25.52	22.84	-3.16	52.09	-2.09
51	73.49	-6.22	79.71	80.23	-8.96	28.14	22.84	-3.16	52.09	-1.87
52	76.23	-4.85	81.08	82.97	-7.59	30.88	22.84	-3.16	52.09	-1.87
53	76.23	-4.85	81.08	82.97	-7.59	30.88	22.84	-3.16	52.09	-1.87
54	71.62	-6.53	78.15	78.36	-8.84	26.27	19.81	-3.16	52.09	-1.87
55	66.97	-8.82	75.79	73.71	-8.91	21.62	19.33	-3.64	52.09	-2.35

Pass	Total Equity	Short Equity	Long Equity	Max. Equity	Min. Equity	P/L	Best Trade	Worst Trade	Max. Open P/L	Min. Open P/L
56	60.63	-11.55	72.18	67.37	-9.79	15.28	19.33	-4.29	52.09	-3.00
57	62.89	-10.37	73.26	69.63	-9.89	17.54	19.33	-4.29	52.09	-3.00
58	61.61	-10.97	72.58	68.35	-8.41	16.26	19.33	-2.89	52.09	-1.69
59	61.61	-10.97	72.58	68.35	-8.41	16.26	19.33	-2.89	52.09	-1.69
60	56.18	-13.16	69.34	62.92	-9.46	10.83	19.33	-3.75	52.09	-2.74
61	61.88	-10.94	72.82	68.62	-8.20	16.53	18.68	-3.75	52.09	-2.46
62	59.72	-12.02	71.74	66.46	-8.20	14.37	18.68	-2.89	52.09	-1.54
63	59.72	-12.02	71.74	66.46	-8.20	14.37	18.68	-2.89	52.09	-1.54
64	62.58	-10.59	73.17	69.32	-8.20	17.23	18.68	-2.89	52.09	-1.54
65	67.12	-8.32	75.44	73.86	-8.20	21.77	19.22	-2.89	52.09	-1.54
66	62.19	-10.74	72.93	68.93	-8.29	16.84	19.22	-3.16	52.09	-1.78
67	57.58	-12.41	69.99	64.32	-9.56	12.23	19.22	-3.67	52.09	-1.78
68	57.48	-11.38	68.86	64.22	-11.72	12.13	19.30	-5.82	52.09	-3.58
69	56.76	-11.38	68.14	63.50	-12.44	11.41	19.30	-6.54	52.09	-4.30
70	53.10	-13.21	66.31	59.84	-14.93	7.75	19.30	-6.54	52.09	-4.30
71	52.94	-13.21	66.15	59.68	-15.09	7.59	19.30	-6.70	52.09	-4.46
72	47.36	-15.49	62.85	54.10	-16.11	2.01	19.30	-7.72	52.09	-5.48
73	47.36	-15.49	62.85	54.10	-16.11	2.01	19.30	-7.72	52.09	-5.48
74	44.94	-17.93	62.87	51.68	-13.65	-0.41	16.86	-6.11	52.09	-4.06
75	44.94	-17.93	62.87	51.68	-13.65	-0.41	16.86	-6.11	52.09	-4.06
76	45.06	-17.87	62.93	51.80	-13.53	-0.29	16.86	-6.11	52.09	-4.06
77	36.20	-22.02	58.22	42.94	-15.75	-9.15	16.86	-7.06	52.09	-3.58
78	37.89	-20.88	58.77	44.63	-14.06	-7.46	16.86	-7.06	52.09	-4.17
79	46.66	-19.70	66.36	53.40	-6.89	1.31	16.86	-4.85	52.09	-1.59
80	48.48	-18.79	67.27	55.22	-6.89	3.13	16.86	-4.85	52.09	-1.54
81	48.68	-18.59	67.27	55.42	-6.69	3.33	16.86	-4.85	52.09	-1.34
82	51.14	-17.36	68.50	57.88	-5.50	5.79	16.86	-4.85	52.09	-1.34
83	55.40	-15.32	70.72	62.14	-5.68	10.05	16.86	-4.85	52.09	-1.52
84	55.21	-15.03	70.24	61.95	-4.91	9.86	16.86	-5.33	52.09	-0.85
85	51.71	-16.78	68.49	58.45	-4.91	6.36	16.86	-5.33	52.09	-0.85
86	53.79	-15.74	69.53	60.53	-4.91	8.44	15.91	-5.33	52.09	-0.85
87	53.79	-15.74	69.53	60.53	-4.91	8.44	15.91	-5.33	52.09	-0.85
88	54.10	-15.43	69.53	60.84	-4.60	8.75	15.91	-5.33	52.09	-0.85
89	58.24	-13.36	71.60	64.98	-4.60	12.89	16.82	-6.15	52.09	-0.85
90	56.13	-13.52	69.65	62.87	-2.81	10.78	16.82	-6.15	52.09	-1.98
91	54.63	-13.52	68.15	61.37	-4.31	9.28	16.82	-6.15	52.09	-2.04
92	54.55	-13.52	68.07	61.29	-4.39	9.20	16.82	-6.15	52.09	-2.12
93	47.75	-16.92	64.67	54.49	-6.78	2.40	15.87	-7.02	52.09	-2.12
94	63.41	-9.90	73.31	70.15	-5.16	-4.83	7.54	-2.47	74.98	-0.97
95	63.41	-9.90	73.31	70.15	-5.16	-4.83	7.54	-2.47	74.98	-0.97
96	63.41	-9.90	73.31	70.15	-5.16	-4.83	7.54	-2.47	74.98	-0.97
97	54.43	-14.89	69.32	61.17	-9.15	-9.15	7.54	-4.99	70.32	-0.97
98	51.03	-16.59	67.62	57.77	-12.55	-12.55	7.54	-4.99	70.32	-2.67
99	52.47	-15.15	67.62	59.21	-11.11	-11.11	7.54	-4.99	70.32	-2.67
100	51.73	-15.15	66.88	58.47	-11.85	-11.85	7.54	-4.99	70.32	-2.67

Pass indicates period length.
Equity indicates the total number of points gained or lost.
Short equity indicates the number of points gained or lost on short positions.
Long equity indicates the number of points gained or lost on long positions.
Max. equity indicates the highest total profit recorded over the tested period.
Min. equity indicates the lowest total profit recorded over the tested period.
P/L indicates total number of points gained or lost in closed positions.
Best trade indicates the highest number of points gained in any closed trade.
Worst trade indicates the highest number of points lost in any closed trade.
Max. open P/L indicates the highest gain in a position which remains open at the end of the test run.
Min. open P/L indicates the highest gain in a position which remains open at the end of the test run.

479

EXHIBIT S-27:
Profitability Chart for Stochastics: K Crossing 50% (Period Lengths of 1 to 100 Weeks from 1968 to 1977)

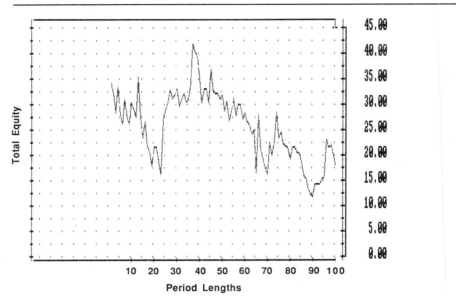

As shown in Exhibits S-32 (page 485) and S-34 (page 486), using 39 weeks, the K39W stochastics' 1968–1986 total profit was above our 40-week simple moving average crossover rule standard of comparison at 115.79 NYSE points. It took 44 trades (nearly 2.6 per year) for a profit of 2.63 per trade. Also, only 39% of the trades produced a profit. Finally, there was a somewhat larger than standard equity drawdown of 18.35 points (or 30.46%) from September 8, 1978 to June 1, 1979. Thus, the total profits to worst loss ratio was 6.31 to 1. In conclusion, using the simplified Stochastics like an ordinary trend-following indicator, the K39W rule appears to be effective, producing above standard results in our optimized tests.

Profit Table for Stochastics: K Crossing 50% (Period Lengths of 1 to 100 Weeks from 1968 to 1977)

Pass	Total Equity	Short Equity	Long Equity	Max. Equity	Min. Equity	P/L	Best Trade	Worst Trade	Max. Open P/L	Min. Open P/L
1	33.95	17.32	16.63	59.31	0.00	33.95	9.51	-3.24	9.82	-0.94
2	32.12	15.49	16.63	57.48	-1.42	32.12	9.51	-3.24	9.82	-0.94
3	28.30	13.58	14.72	39.06	0.00	28.30	8.90	-3.24	9.51	-1.43
4	33.47	15.44	18.03	43.55	-0.46	33.47	9.13	-3.24	11.76	-1.24
5	27.69	12.23	15.46	38.17	-0.47	27.69	10.03	-2.84	12.97	-1.43
6	26.11	11.44	14.67	35.81	-0.47	26.11	9.71	-2.84	12.97	-1.43
7	31.07	13.92	17.15	39.47	-0.47	29.76	9.71	-2.84	12.97	-1.31
8	27.36	11.80	15.56	36.34	-2.74	26.05	8.95	-3.04	12.97	-1.31
9	26.20	11.22	14.98	37.40	-2.74	24.89	8.95	-3.04	12.97	-1.38
10	30.44	13.34	17.10	40.58	-2.74	29.13	10.52	-3.63	13.36	-1.49
11	29.00	13.99	15.01	42.42	0.00	27.69	12.13	-4.49	17.31	-2.35
12	27.42	13.20	14.22	42.62	0.00	26.11	12.13	-4.49	17.31	-2.35
13	35.37	18.08	17.29	48.52	-0.21	34.06	12.64	-4.49	17.31	-2.35
14	27.55	14.50	13.05	37.84	-0.70	26.24	12.49	-4.49	17.31	-2.35
15	23.45	12.45	11.00	33.74	-0.70	22.14	12.07	-2.90	17.31	-1.13
16	26.53	14.43	12.10	36.82	-3.54	25.22	12.07	-2.70	17.31	-1.46
17	21.75	12.04	9.71	33.53	-4.75	20.44	12.07	-3.17	17.31	-1.50
18	20.54	11.18	9.36	32.32	-6.17	19.23	11.78	-3.17	17.31	-1.50
19	17.86	9.84	8.02	31.36	-3.83	16.55	12.40	-3.17	19.13	-1.57
20	21.51	12.10	9.41	36.07	-4.70	20.20	16.88	-3.17	23.61	-1.50
21	21.62	12.96	8.66	34.20	-6.31	20.31	17.94	-3.17	23.61	-2.93
22	18.79	11.43	7.36	31.03	-8.42	17.48	17.94	-3.69	23.61	-2.70
23	16.13	10.10	6.03	29.93	-12.84	14.82	17.94	-3.69	23.61	-2.70
24	27.15	15.61	11.54	40.95	-5.46	25.84	17.94	-2.40	23.61	-2.70
25	29.11	16.59	12.52	42.91	-3.97	27.80	17.94	-2.40	23.61	-2.70
26	30.46	17.65	12.81	42.14	-4.74	29.15	17.94	-2.40	23.61	-3.47
27	32.87	17.26	15.61	44.55	-1.55	31.56	17.94	-2.71	23.61	-1.57
28	31.37	16.51	14.86	45.61	-1.55	30.06	17.67	-2.71	23.61	-1.82
29	31.95	16.80	15.15	46.19	-1.55	30.64	17.67	-2.71	23.61	-1.82
30	33.27	17.46	15.81	46.75	-1.55	31.96	17.67	-2.71	23.61	-1.57
31	29.56	16.05	13.51	40.16	-2.44	28.25	15.60	-2.71	23.61	-1.57
32	31.08	16.83	14.25	41.44	-2.48	29.77	15.60	-2.80	23.61	-2.41
33	32.27	17.45	14.82	40.13	-2.53	30.96	15.60	-2.41	23.61	-1.44
34	30.50	17.16	13.34	38.44	-3.72	29.19	15.60	-2.21	23.61	-0.98
35	30.80	17.51	13.29	38.74	-4.12	29.49	15.60	-2.31	23.61	-0.98
36	34.04	19.13	14.91	39.87	-4.12	32.73	15.60	-2.83	23.61	-1.73
37	41.78	23.22	18.56	47.61	-4.56	40.47	16.70	-2.21	24.71	-0.98
38	40.36	22.89	17.47	48.09	-4.08	39.05	16.70	-2.21	24.71	-1.09
39	39.52	22.81	16.71	47.25	-4.76	38.21	16.70	-2.64	24.71	-1.77
40	35.26	20.68	14.58	42.99	-4.76	33.95	15.81	-2.64	24.71	-1.77
41	30.18	17.92	12.26	43.65	-4.32	28.87	15.81	-2.29	24.71	-1.33
42	33.26	19.46	13.80	43.79	-4.32	31.95	15.81	-2.29	24.71	-1.33
43	33.24	19.45	13.79	43.77	-5.13	31.93	15.81	-2.29	24.71	-1.33
44	30.26	18.55	11.71	41.03	-6.31	28.95	15.81	-3.34	24.71	-2.51
45	36.77	20.86	15.91	45.38	-4.78	35.46	15.81	-2.39	24.71	-1.02
46	32.57	18.76	13.81	41.18	-4.78	31.26	14.40	-2.39	24.71	-1.38
47	32.13	18.54	13.59	40.74	-6.64	30.82	14.40	-2.98	24.71	-1.66
48	32.13	18.54	13.59	40.74	-6.64	30.82	14.40	-2.98	24.71	-1.66
49	30.91	17.93	12.98	39.52	-7.16	29.60	14.40	-3.24	24.71	-2.66
50	31.87	18.41	13.46	40.48	-7.16	30.56	14.40	-3.24	24.71	-2.57
51	28.69	16.82	11.87	37.30	-8.14	27.38	14.40	-2.83	24.71	-2.57
52	30.65	17.80	12.85	39.26	-6.18	29.34	14.40	-2.83	24.71	-2.57
53	26.77	15.86	10.91	35.38	-5.78	25.46	14.40	-2.83	24.71	-2.57
54	28.31	16.80	11.51	36.92	-4.24	27.00	14.40	-2.66	24.71	-3.17
55	31.25	18.41	12.84	39.86	-3.45	29.94	14.40	-2.66	24.71	-3.45

Pass	Total Equity	Short Equity	Long Equity	Max. Equity	Min. Equity	P/L	Best Trade	Worst Trade	Max. Open P/L	Min. Open P/L
56	27.73	16.78	10.95	38.20	-3.71	26.42	14.40	-2.66	24.71	-3.71
57	30.08	16.30	13.78	41.51	-0.40	28.77	14.40	-2.66	24.71	-1.02
58	30.08	16.30	13.78	41.51	-0.40	28.77	14.40	-2.66	24.71	-1.02
59	27.18	14.85	12.33	37.35	-0.54	25.87	14.40	-2.66	24.71	-1.02
60	28.46	15.49	12.97	37.35	-0.54	27.15	14.40	-2.66	24.71	-1.02
61	26.62	14.84	11.78	35.51	-1.08	25.31	14.40	-2.66	24.71	-1.02
62	26.08	14.57	11.51	34.97	-1.08	24.77	14.40	-2.66	24.71	-1.02
63	24.34	14.19	10.15	33.23	-2.06	23.03	14.40	-3.04	24.71	-1.02
64	25.15	14.58	10.57	34.96	-2.03	23.84	14.40	-3.04	24.71	-1.48
65	16.47	10.24	6.23	29.76	-2.03	15.16	13.91	-3.04	24.71	-1.50
66	27.81	15.92	11.89	36.88	-2.05	26.50	13.06	-2.29	24.71	-1.50
67	20.79	12.41	8.38	29.86	-8.93	19.48	13.06	-3.19	24.71	-2.02
68	19.40	12.38	7.02	28.53	-10.26	18.09	13.06	-4.52	24.71	-3.17
69	17.35	11.65	5.70	25.54	-10.85	16.04	13.06	-5.11	24.71	-3.76
70	16.27	11.31	4.96	28.00	-11.25	14.96	12.74	-5.51	24.71	-4.16
71	22.48	11.66	10.82	33.39	-5.74	21.17	13.15	-2.74	24.71	-2.02
72	19.86	10.35	9.51	30.77	-5.74	18.55	13.15	-3.39	24.71	-2.48
73	22.82	11.83	10.99	32.33	-5.74	21.51	13.00	-3.39	24.71	-2.48
74	28.30	14.57	13.73	32.33	-5.74	26.99	13.00	-3.39	24.71	-2.48
75	23.32	12.08	11.24	28.09	-5.74	22.01	11.85	-2.82	24.71	-2.02
76	24.66	13.53	11.13	29.65	-4.18	23.35	11.85	-2.82	24.71	-2.02
77	22.06	12.23	9.83	25.63	-4.18	20.75	11.66	-2.82	24.71	-2.02
78	21.76	11.00	10.76	27.79	-2.02	20.45	10.43	-2.82	24.71	-2.92
79	21.29	10.53	10.76	27.32	-2.49	19.98	10.43	-2.82	24.71	-2.92
80	19.53	8.77	10.76	25.56	-4.25	18.22	10.43	-2.82	24.71	-4.25
81	21.49	10.81	10.68	27.68	-2.13	20.26	10.43	-2.82	24.71	-2.92
82	21.49	10.81	10.68	27.68	-2.13	20.26	10.43	-2.82	24.71	-2.92
83	20.63	10.38	10.25	27.68	-2.13	19.83	10.43	-2.82	24.71	-2.92
84	20.17	10.15	10.02	27.68	-2.13	19.60	10.43	-2.82	24.71	-2.92
85	18.61	9.37	9.24	27.68	-2.13	18.82	10.43	-2.82	24.71	-2.92
86	15.99	7.49	8.50	25.06	-4.01	16.20	10.43	-3.27	24.71	-3.09
87	15.24	7.33	7.91	25.49	-3.58	15.31	10.43	-2.84	24.71	-2.92
88	13.56	6.49	7.07	22.35	-3.58	13.63	10.43	-3.46	24.71	-2.92
89	12.22	5.82	6.40	22.35	-3.58	12.96	10.43	-3.46	24.71	-2.92
90	11.76	5.36	6.40	21.89	-4.04	12.50	10.43	-3.46	24.71	-3.12
91	14.44	8.04	6.40	24.57	-1.36	15.18	10.43	-3.46	24.71	-2.92
92	14.44	8.04	6.40	24.57	-1.36	14.44	10.43	-3.46	24.71	-2.92
93	14.24	7.94	6.30	24.57	-1.36	14.24	10.43	-3.46	24.71	-2.55
94	15.18	8.41	6.77	24.57	-1.36	8.66	10.43	-3.46	24.71	-2.55
95	15.80	9.03	6.77	25.19	-0.74	9.28	10.43	-3.46	24.71	-2.55
96	23.10	12.31	10.79	30.97	0.00	15.82	10.43	-2.29	24.71	-0.37
97	21.45	10.66	10.79	29.32	0.00	14.17	10.43	-2.29	24.71	-0.37
98	22.08	10.88	11.20	29.95	0.00	14.80	10.43	-1.91	24.71	-0.37
99	20.45	9.42	11.03	28.66	-0.90	13.34	10.43	-1.91	24.71	-0.90
100	17.97	7.91	10.06	28.12	-1.44	11.83	10.43	-1.91	24.71	-1.44

Pass indicates period length.
Equity indicates the total number of points gained or lost.
Short equity indicates the number of points gained or lost on short positions.
Long equity indicates the number of points gained or lost on long positions.
Max. equity indicates the highest total profit recorded over the tested period.
Min. equity indicates the lowest total profit recorded over the tested period.
P/L indicates total number of points gained or lost in closed positions.
Best trade indicates the highest number of points gained in any closed trade.
Worst trade indicates the highest number of points lost in any closed trade.
Max. open P/L indicates the highest gain in a position which remains open at the end of the test run.
Min. open P/L indicates the highest gain in a position which remains open at the end of the test run.

EXHIBIT S-29:
New York Stock Exchange Composite Price Index Weekly High and Low from
April 8, 1977 to December 31, 1986

EXHIBIT S-30:
K39W Stochastics, 1977 to 1986

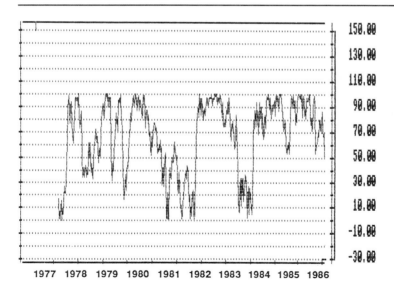

EXHIBIT S-31:
Total Equity for K39W Stochastics, 1977 to 1986

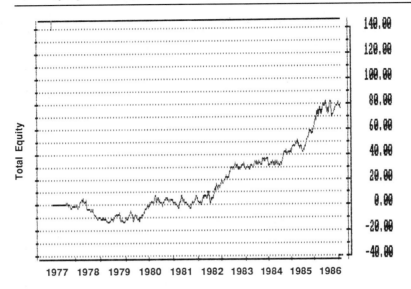

EXHIBIT S-32:
Profit Summary for K39W Stochastics, 1977 to 1986

Item		Long	Short	Net
		--- Per Trade Ranges ---		
Per Trade Ranges				
Best Trade	(Closed position yielding maximum P/L)	27.54	3.88	27.54
. . Date		840127	820827	840127
Worst Trade	(Closed position yielding minimum P/L)	-1.90	-4.39	-4.39
. . Date		810821	790112	790112
Max Open P/L	(Maximum P/L occurring in an open position)	52.09	11.57	52.09
. . Date		860829	820813	860829
Min Open P/L	(Minimum P/L occurring in an open position)	-0.84	-2.89	-2.89
. . Date		811218	790105	790105
		--- Overall Ranges ---		
Overall Ranges				
Max P/L	(Maximum P/L from all closed positions during the run)	29.38	30.92	30.92
. . Date		840127	840803	840803
Min P/L	(Minimum P/L from all closed positions during the run)	-12.83	-13.74	-13.74
. . Date		790511	791116	791116
Max Equity	(Maximum P/L from all closed and open positions)	83.01	37.98	83.01
. . Date		860829	840615	860829
Min Equity	(Minimum P/L from all closed and open positions)	-13.84	-13.74	-13.84
. . Date		790601	791116	790601
		--- Statistics ---		
Statistics				
Periods	(The number of periods in each position and entire run)	380	129	509
Trades	(The number of trades in each position and entire run)	10	11	21
# Profitable	(The number of profitable trades. . .)	4	3	7
# Losing	(The number of unprofitable trades. . .)	6	8	14
% Profitable	(The percent of profitable trades to total trades)	40.00	27.27	33.33
% Losing	(The percent of unprofitable trades to total trades)	60.00	72.73	66.67
		--- Results ---		
Results				
Commission	(Total commission deducted from closed trades)	0.00	0.00	0.00
Slippage	(Total slippage deducted from closed trades)	0.00	0.00	0.00
Gross P/L	(Total points gained in closed positions)	37.29	-6.37	30.92
Open P/L	(P/L in a position which remains open at the end)	45.35	0.00	45.35
P/L	(Net P/L: Gross P/L less Commission and Slippage)	37.29	-6.37	30.92
Equity	(Net P/L plus Open P/L at the end of the run)	82.64	-6.37	76.27

There are columns for Long trades, Short trades and Net. In the Long column, results are reported only for Long positions. In the Short column, results are reported for Short positions only. In the Net column for the "Per Trade Ranges" and "Overall Ranges," entries will be the extreme from either the Long or Short column. Net column entries for the "Statistics" and "Results" categories are the combined results of entries in the Long and Short columns.

EXHIBIT S-33:
New York Stock Exchange Composite Price Index Weekly High and Low from January 5, 1968 to September 30, 1977

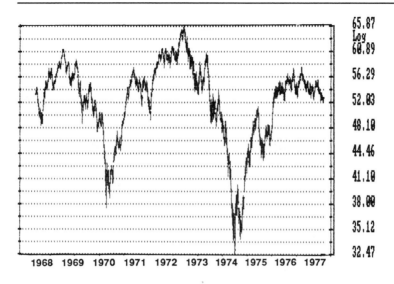

EXHIBIT S-34:
K39W Stochastics, 1968 to 1977

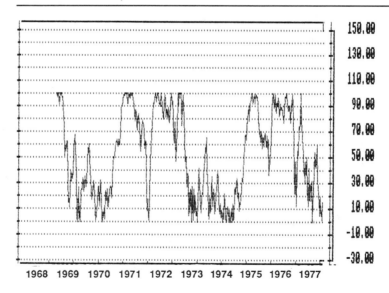

EXHIBIT S-35:
Total Equity for K39W Stochastics, 1968 to 1977

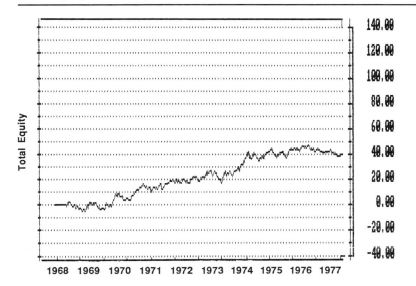

EXHIBIT S-36:
Profit Summary for K39W Stochastics, 1968 to 1977

Item		Long	Short	Net
Per Trade Ranges				
Best Trade	(Closed position yielding maximum P/L)	8.95	16.70	16.70
.. Date		711015	750131	750131
Worst Trade	(Closed position yielding minimum P/L)	-2.64	-1.86	-2.64
.. Date		731102	690502	731102
Max Open P/L	(Maximum P/L occurring in an open position)	12.21	24.71	24.71
.. Date		710423	741004	741004
Min Open P/L	(Minimum P/L occurring in an open position)	-1.77	-0.99	-1.77
.. Date		690110	761029	690110
Overall Ranges				
Max P/L	(Maximum P/L from all closed positions during the run)	44.13	42.70	44.13
.. Date		761015	761126	761015
Min P/L	(Minimum P/L from all closed positions during the run)	-4.76	-4.46	-4.76
.. Date		690530	690502	690530
Max Equity	(Maximum P/L from all closed and open positions)	47.25	44.93	47.25
.. Date		760924	761112	760924
Min Equity	(Minimum P/L from all closed and open positions)	-4.76	-4.76	-4.76
.. Date		690530	690530	690530
Statistics				
Periods	(The number of periods in each position and entire run)	286	223	509
Trades	(The number of trades in each position and entire run)	12	11	23
# Profitable	(The number of profitable trades...)	5	5	10
# Losing	(The number of unprofitable trades)	7	6	13
% Profitable	(The percent of profitable trades to total trades)	41.67	45.45	43.48
% Losing	(The percent of unprofitable trades to total trades)	58.33	54.55	56.52
Results				
Commission	(Total commission deducted from closed trades)	0.00	0.00	0.00
Slippage	(Total slippage deducted from closed trades)	0.00	0.00	0.00
Gross P/L	(Total points gained in closed positions)	16.71	21.50	38.21
Open P/L	(P/L in a position which remains open at the end)	0.00	1.31	1.31
P/L	(Net P/L: Gross P/L less Commission and Slippage)	16.71	21.50	38.21
Equity	(Net P/L plus Open P/L at the end of the run)	16.71	22.81	39.52

There are columns for Long trades, Short trades and Net. In the Long column, results are reported only for Long positions. In the Short column, results are reported for Short positions only. In the Net column for the "Per Trade Ranges" and "Overall Ranges," entries will be the extreme from either the Long or Short column. Net column entries for the "Statistics" and "Results" categories are the combined results of entries in the Long and Short columns.

STOCK MARKET PRICE INDEXES

Price indexes are important for judging market trends and measuring performance. The most popular are those published by Dow Jones in *The Wall Street Journal*. But a sample of only 30 stocks in the Dow Jones Industrial Average is hardly representative of the whole stock market, even if those 30 stocks are the most important ones. Moreover, according to Arthur Merrill, a professional statistician and market analyst, "Statisticians wince when they learn the weighting method" of the Dow Jones averages. The averages are price weighted, so a $100 stock has 10 times the influence of a $10 stock on the averages. Worse, if a stock splits two-for-one, its weight immediately drops in half. Finally, substitutions of stocks in the averages also have detracted from comparability of the averages to themselves over time. Still, the Dow averages generally reflect the trends of the market fairly well. We have observed over the years, however, more false signals (misleading breakouts and breakdowns) with the Dow than with better constructed indexes such as the Standard & Poor's or New York Stock Exchange composites. In fact, when the Dow Jones Industrial Average diverges from the S&P 500, the Dow is usually the one that proves to be wrong.

The Dow Jones transportation and utility averages suffer from the same weaknesses as the industrial average—price weighting, splits, substitutions, and small sample size (only 20 transportation stocks and 15 utilities). Takeover speculation in only one or two transportation equities can have a significant effect on the average. In 1980, when energy stocks were dominating the market, most of the utility average's movements were directly attributable to four natural gas stocks, rather than the staid electric utility equities most people think of when they consider the utility average.

Contrary to popular opinion, we've found that the Dow Jones Transportation Average is not a reliable leading indicator for the general market. The Dow Jones Utility Average is a fairly reliable leading indicator more often than not, although the lead may be long and variable.

The broad-based, capitalization-weighted S&P indexes and NYSE price indexes are measures of total market value. The most recent price of the hundreds of component stocks are multiplied by the number of shares outstanding. This product is then divided by a base date index number to make the index comparable over time. Splits have no impact, and substitutions of stocks are properly handled by adjusting the base date index number. Thus, valid and comparable market price data are available all the way back to 1873.

The NYSE Composite is composed of every common stock listed on the exchange, numbering more than 1500. The S&P Composite is a subset of the NYSE Composite, comprising the stocks of the 500 largest companies. The S&P 100 (OEX) index, used as the market index for the popular Chicago Board Options Exchange contract, is a subset of the S&P 500, listing the 100 largest stocks. As one might guess, there is a near perfect correlation between these capitalization-weighted indexes, all of which have the bulk of their weight in the 100 largest stocks.

The American Stock Exchange (AMEX) Market Value Index is also properly capitalization weighted. According to Alan R. Shaw of Smith Barney, its entire capitalization does not match that of only one stock, IBM, so its significance isn't great. Moreover, only 10 stocks account for about one third of the total weight, so distortions are possible. We have not found the AMEX index useful for technical analysis.

The Value Line Averages are unweighted geometric averages of 1665 stocks. The smallest stock has the same impact as the largest. According to Norman G. Fosback, in his 1976 book *Stock Market Logic* (Institute for Econometric Research, 3471 North Federal Highway, Fort Lauderdale, FL 33306), the geometric averaging method (based on logarithms) results in a negative, downward bias, so that the geometric average is always below the simple arithmetic average or mean. We have not found the Value Line composite useful in our technical work.

Fosback is also critical of the advance-decline line as a market barometer. Firstly, no consideration is given to the extent of price or market value change, but only to the direction of price change, up or down. Academic studies have proven that average price advances are larger than average price declines, so the advance-decline line's failure to take into account the size of any price change means that the advance-decline must underperform the stock market price indexes, which it does. Secondly, the number of listed stocks has increased over the years, thus destroying the comparability of the advance-decline line over time. (This can be adjusted for by dividing advances minus declines by advances plus declines or by total issues traded.) Thirdly, inclusion of preferred stocks, which fluctuate more with bond prices than with common stock prices, produces distortions, particularly when bond prices and common stock prices are trending in opposite directions, as they often have in the past. Given these substantial shortcomings in the advance-decline line, the failure of this breadth data to produce better results in our various tests becomes more understandable.

Fosback holds unweighted total return indexes in high regard. These are based on Quotron's "QCHA," which is the average percentage price change for each common stock listed on the NYSE. Including dividend return as well as percentage price change gives a more realistic overall representation, according to Fosback, because more than half of the long-term total return of all common stocks through history has been from dividends.

Although Fosback has made a good case for unweighted total return indexes, they still do not enjoy wide popularity. For one thing, the big institutions have difficulty trading large dollar amounts of small capitalization stocks, so they mostly stay with the big, high-capitalization stocks that dominate the S&P 500. Thus, they focus on that index. For another thing, unweighted total return indexes are not widely published in the popular press, and few people choose to spend the time necessary to make their own calculations.

In conclusion, like most researchers, we prefer the broad-based, capitalization-weighted indexes for our technical studies, specifically the S&P 500 or NYSE Composite, which for practical purposes are nearly the same.

THREE STEPS AND A STUMBLE

We first learned about the Three Steps and a Stumble rule in the early 1970s from the noted technician Edson Gould. More recently, it has been studied thoroughly by Norman Fosback (The Institute for Econometric Research, 3471 North Federal Highway, Fort Lauderdale, FL 33306).* It is a monetary indicator with a moderately successful record in predicting decreases in stock prices.

The Three Steps and a Stumble rule states that when the Federal Reserve increases any one of three items (the discount rate, margin requirement, or reserve requirement) three times in a row, stock prices will "stumble" and fall.

Fosback's research shows that between 1914 and 1983, 12 sell signals were given by the Three Steps and a Stumble rule. The results are summarized in the following table:

Time Period	Average Percent Change In S & P 500	Number of Times Market Declined
20 days later	−1.4%	5 out of 12
3 months later	−0.3%	6 out of 12
6 months later	−1.1%	6 out of 12
1 year later	−5.0%	8 out of 12

In addition, Fosback discovered that all sell signals eventually resulted in substantial decreases in stock prices (about 30% on average). However, the lead time before such decline was highly variable.

Rather than using the Three Steps and a Stumble rule as a precise indicator, it is best used as a warning signal that significant declines in market prices are likely. Other indicators should be used for more precise timing of market tops.

Refer to the section on Two Tumbles and a Jump for a related buy signal rule.

---

*Reprinted with permission.

TICK

TICK is a short-term indicator that measures market strength. It is calculated on an ongoing basis throughout the trading day as the net difference between all NYSE stocks with last sales occurring on an uptick (higher price than previous sale) and all NYSE stocks with last sales occurring on a downtick (lower price than previous sale). In essence, it is a moment-to-moment representation of net advancing issues.

Interpretation of TICK readings throughout the day is far from an exact science. In general, the object is to look for positive or negative trends. For example, if the TICK reading went from a negative reading, such as -200, to a positive reading, such as $+300$, it would be considered a short-term bullish sign.

In addition, some observers contend that extreme readings can be interpreted in a contrary manner. Extremely high TICK readings supposedly signify a short-term overbought condition and signal a reversal to the downside. On the other hand, extremely low TICK readings supposedly indicate a short-term oversold condition and are viewed as bullish in the near term.

Technicians frequently apply a 10-day moving average to closing TICK values in an attempt to smooth our erratic movements in the TICK readings. The 10-day moving average is then plotted relative to a market index. Divergencies between the trend of the 10-day moving average of TICK and the market index are interpreted in the normal way.

We performed no significant research with regard to TICK because, by its nature, its value is limited to extremely short-term traders. In addition, on a conceptual basis, using the closing TICK readings as a representation of a whole day's activity is questionable since, in reality, it only reflects a brief moment of activity.

TOTAL SHORT RATIO

The Total Short Ratio is a long-term contrary sentiment indicator. As with many other contrary indicators, it is designed to determine in which direction the majority of investors think stock prices are going and interpreted in an opposite fashion: bullish when investors believe stock prices will fall and bearish when stock prices are expected to increase.

The Total Short Ratio is calculated by dividing total short sales by total volume. Monthly NYSE data is appropriate for calculating the indicator.

Typically, the Total Short Ratio ranges between 5% and 10%. High readings reflect excessive shorting and are viewed as bullish. Low readings signify low levels of shorting and are considered bearish.

Ned Davis (Ned Davis Research, Inc., P.O. Box 2089, Venice, FL 34284) has thoroughly tested the Total Short Ratio.* He noted that a 4-month moving average, as illustrated in Exhibit T-1, can be used to smooth Total Short Ratio readings and produce profitable buy and sell signals. A buy signal is given when the 4-month average of the ratio rises above 8.4%. Sell signals occur when the 4-month moving average crosses from above to below 6.25%. Buy and sell signals are identified on the Dow Jones Industrial Average at the top of the chart by the letters B and S, respectively.

---

*Reprinted with permission.

EXHIBIT T-1:
Total Short Ratio (top) Versus Dow Jones Industrial Average (bottom) from 1966 to 1986

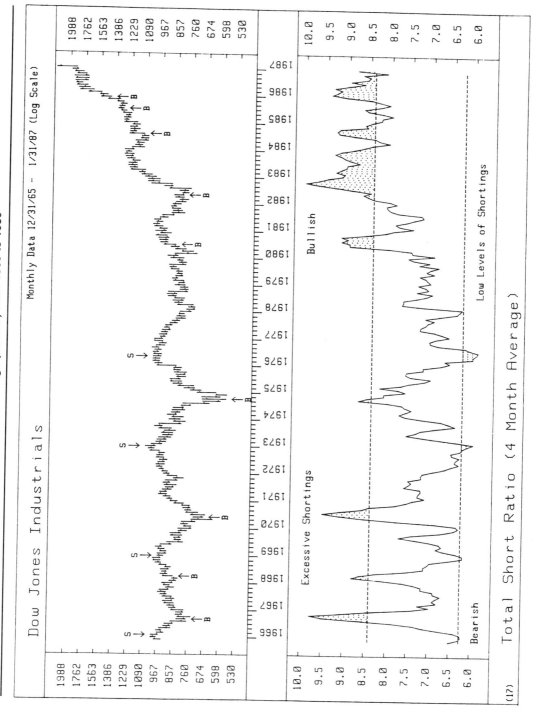

Total Short Ratio (4 Month Average)

Source: By Permission of Ned Davis Research, Inc.

25-DAY PLURALITY INDEX

The 25-Day Plurality Index is a market breadth indicator. It is calculated in two steps. First, you compute the absolute difference between the number of advancing issues and the number of declining issues for each of the last 25 days. Second, you add the absolute differences for the last 25 days together. NYSE data is typically used in the calculation.

The 25-Day Plurality Index is commonly interpreted as bullish for stock prices when it rises above the 12,000 level. On the other hand, readings under 6,000 are viewed as bearish.

We tested the 25-Day Plurality Index for the period of January 1928 to March 1987. The results are shown in Exhibit T-2 (page 497).

The test process was as follows. The indicator readings for the test period were divided into 20 ranges with approximately the same number of occurrences in each range. For each reading in a range, the gain or loss in four subsequent time periods (1 month later, 3 months later, 6 months later, and 12 months later) was calculated. The combined results for readings within each range were statistically compared, using chi-squared tests, to the performance of the overall market (as measured by the Standard & Poor's 500 Index). Varying degrees of bullishness and bearishness were noted on the basis of that comparison.

Our research results confirm that extremely high readings are very bullish for the stock market. However, low readings gave mixed signals. Readings below 3301 were very bullish for time periods of 1 and 3 months later. Other low ranges and time periods were very bearish.

In addition to the common method of calculating the 25-Day Plurality Index, we tested a slight variation that takes into consideration the increase over the years in the number of issues traded on the New York Stock Exchange. For each of the last 25 days, we calculated the absolute difference between the number of advancing issues and the number of declining issues and divided that difference by the total number of issues traded. We then added up the ratio values for the last 25 days. Our test procedures were similar to those performed for the 25-Day Plurality Index as it is customarily calculated. Our results, shown in Exhibit T-3 (page 498), indicate that relatively high readings and extremely low readings were very bearish during the 60-year test period. Midrange indicator readings showed a bullish tendency.

EXHIBIT T-2:

Interpretation of 25-Day Plurality Index's Daily Readings

```
=================================================================================
25 DAY PLURALITY INDEX
PERIOD ANALYZED:  JANUARY 1928 TO MARCH 1987
=================================================================================
```

INDICATOR RANGE		INTERPRETATION GIVEN INVESTOR'S TIME FRAME			
GREATER THAN	LESS THAN OR EQUAL TO	1 MONTH	3 MONTHS	6 MONTHS	12 MONTHS
0	3301	VERY BULLISH	VERY BULLISH	NEUTRAL	BEARISH
3301	3780	VERY BEARISH	BEARISH	NEUTRAL	VERY BEARISH
3780	4146	VERY BEARISH	NEUTRAL	NEUTRAL	VERY BEARISH
4146	4467	NEUTRAL	NEUTRAL	NEUTRAL	NEUTRAL
4467	4746	NEUTRAL	NEUTRAL	NEUTRAL	SLIGHTLY BEARISH
4746	5002	SLIGHTLY BEARISH	NEUTRAL	SLIGHTLY BEARISH	NEUTRAL
5002	5260	NEUTRAL	NEUTRAL	NEUTRAL	NEUTRAL
5260	5520	NEUTRAL	NEUTRAL	NEUTRAL	NEUTRAL
5520	5810	NEUTRAL	NEUTRAL	NEUTRAL	NEUTRAL
5810	6132	NEUTRAL	NEUTRAL	NEUTRAL	NEUTRAL
6132	6488	SLIGHTLY BULLISH	NEUTRAL	SLIGHTLY BEARISH	NEUTRAL
6488	6848	NEUTRAL	NEUTRAL	NEUTRAL	NEUTRAL
6848	7248	NEUTRAL	NEUTRAL	NEUTRAL	SLIGHTLY BEARISH
7248	7670	NEUTRAL	NEUTRAL	BULLISH	BULLISH
7670	8125	NEUTRAL	NEUTRAL	NEUTRAL	VERY BULLISH
8125	8586	SLIGHTLY BULLISH	BEARISH	NEUTRAL	VERY BULLISH
8586	9162	NEUTRAL	NEUTRAL	BEARISH	SLIGHTLY BULLISH
9162	9947	NEUTRAL	NEUTRAL	SLIGHTLY BEARISH	NEUTRAL
9947	11241	NEUTRAL	NEUTRAL	NEUTRAL	SLIGHTLY BULLISH
11241	18530	VERY BULLISH	VERY BULLISH	VERY BULLISH	VERY BULLISH

```
=================================================================================
```

Definitions of Very Bullish, Bullish, Slightly Bullish, Neutral, Slightly Bearish, Bearish, and Very Bearish are provided in Appendix A.

EXHIBIT T-3:
Interpretation of Modified 25-Day Plurality Index's Daily Readings

```
================================================================================
25 DAY PLURALITY INDEX
PERIOD ANALYZED:  JANUARY 1928 TO MARCH 1987
================================================================================

INDICATOR RANGE                INTERPRETATION GIVEN INVESTOR'S TIME FRAME
----------------     --------------------------------------------------------------
         LESS
GREATER  THAN OR
 THAN    EQUAL TO   1 MONTH            3 MONTHS          6 MONTHS          12 MONTHS
-------  --------   ----------------   ----------------  ----------------  ----------------

0.000    3.081      VERY BEARISH       VERY BEARISH      VERY BEARISH      VERY BEARISH
3.081    3.488      BEARISH            NEUTRAL           NEUTRAL           VERY BEARISH
3.488    3.814      NEUTRAL            NEUTRAL           SLIGHTLY BULLISH  NEUTRAL
3.814    4.086      NEUTRAL            BULLISH           SLIGHTLY BULLISH  NEUTRAL
4.086    4.304      NEUTRAL            NEUTRAL           SLIGHTLY BULLISH  SLIGHTLY BULLISH
4.304    4.500      BULLISH            NEUTRAL           NEUTRAL           SLIGHTLY BULLISH
4.500    4.699      VERY BULLISH       SLIGHTLY BULLISH  SLIGHTLY BULLISH  VERY BULLISH
4.699    4.887      NEUTRAL            BULLISH           VERY BULLISH      BULLISH
4.887    5.093      NEUTRAL            NEUTRAL           SLIGHTLY BULLISH  VERY BULLISH
5.093    5.324      NEUTRAL            NEUTRAL           BULLISH           VERY BULLISH
5.324    5.567      SLIGHTLY BULLISH   NEUTRAL           BULLISH           BULLISH
5.567    5.829      NEUTRAL            NEUTRAL           NEUTRAL           BULLISH
5.829    6.107      NEUTRAL            NEUTRAL           NEUTRAL           NEUTRAL
6.107    6.411      VERY BULLISH       SLIGHTLY BULLISH  VERY BULLISH      VERY BULLISH
6.411    6.739      SLIGHTLY BULLISH   NEUTRAL           NEUTRAL           NEUTRAL
6.739    7.127      NEUTRAL            NEUTRAL           NEUTRAL           NEUTRAL
7.127    7.612      NEUTRAL            NEUTRAL           VERY BEARISH      VERY BEARISH
7.612    8.289      NEUTRAL            NEUTRAL           VERY BEARISH      VERY BEARISH
8.289    9.147      VERY BEARISH       VERY BEARISH      VERY BEARISH      VERY BEARISH
9.147    14.196     NEUTRAL            VERY BEARISH      VERY BEARISH      VERY BEARISH
================================================================================
```

Definitions of Very Bullish, Bullish, Slightly Bullish, Neutral, Slightly Bearish, Bearish, and Very Bearish are provided in Appendix A.

TWO TUMBLES AND A JUMP

The Two Tumbles and a Jump rule was developed in 1973 by Norman Fosback (The Institute for Econometric Research, 3471 North Federal Highway, Fort Lauderdale, FL 33306).* It is a monetary indicator with a very successful record predicting increases in stock prices.

The Two Tumbles and a Jump rule states that when the Federal Reserve decreases any one of three items (the discount rate, margin requirement, or reserve requirement) two times in a row, stock prices will "jump."

Fosback's research shows that between 1914 and 1983, 17 buy signals were given by the Two Tumbles and a Jump rule. The results are summarized in the following table:

Time Period	Average Percent Change In S & P 500	Number of Times Market Advanced
20 days later	+ 3.6%	13 out of 17
3 months later	+ 11.3%	14 out of 17
6 months later	+ 16.1%	16 out of 17
1 year later	+ 30.5%	16 out of 17

On average, signals are given by this rule less than once every 4 years. However, its track record suggests that it is well worth watching for.

Refer to the section on Three Steps and a Stumble for a related sell signal rule.

---

*Reprinted with permission.

UNCHANGED ISSUES INDEX

The Unchanged Issues Index is calculated by dividing the number of unchanged issues by the total number of issues traded. Daily or weekly NYSE data normally is used in the calculation.

The popular assumption behind the indicator is that stock prices tend to bottom out very quickly, but form tops over long periods of time. Therefore, the ratio seems likely to be relatively low prior to a bottom and relatively high preceding a market peak.

Our findings are contrary to this common interpretation. We tested the Unchanged Issues Index for the period of January 1928 to March 1987 on a daily and weekly basis. In addition, we applied a 10-period simple moving average to both the daily and weekly readings to smooth out any erratic movements. The results are shown in Exhibits U-1 through U-4 (pages 501–504).

The test process was as follows. The readings for the test period were divided into 20 ranges with approximately the same number of occurrences in each range. For each reading in a range, the gain or loss in four subsequent time periods (1 month later, 3 months later, 6 months later, and 12 months later) was calculated. The combined results for readings within each range were statistically compared, using chi-squared tests, to the performance of the overall market (as measured by the Standard & Poor's 500 Index). Various degrees of bullishness and bearishness were noted on the basis of that comparison.

Our results show that the Unchanged Issues Index has, in fact, tended to be bearish at low readings and bullish at high readings, which is the exact opposite of popular expectations. The best signals were produced by using a 10-day moving average of the indicator and for time periods of 6 and 12 months after the signal.

EXHIBIT U-1:
Interpretation of Unchanged Issues Index's Daily Readings

```
=================================================================================
UNCHANGED ISSUES INDEX - DAILY DATA
PERIOD ANALYZED:  JANUARY 1928 TO MARCH 1987
=================================================================================

INDICATOR RANGE              INTERPRETATION GIVEN INVESTOR'S TIME FRAME
-----------------  --------------------------------------------------------------

          LESS
GREATER   THAN OR
 THAN     EQUAL TO   1 MONTH          3 MONTHS          6 MONTHS          12 MONTHS
-------   --------   ---------------  ----------------  ----------------  ----------------

0.000     0.139    NEUTRAL          NEUTRAL           BEARISH           VERY BEARISH
0.139     0.154    NEUTRAL          VERY BEARISH      VERY BEARISH      VERY BEARISH
0.154     0.164    NEUTRAL          NEUTRAL           BEARISH           VERY BEARISH
0.164     0.172    NEUTRAL          SLIGHTLY BEARISH  VERY BEARISH      VERY BEARISH
0.172     0.179    NEUTRAL          NEUTRAL           BEARISH           VERY BEARISH
0.179     0.186    NEUTRAL          NEUTRAL           VERY BEARISH      VERY BEARISH
0.186     0.191    NEUTRAL          NEUTRAL           NEUTRAL           BEARISH
0.191     0.197    NEUTRAL          NEUTRAL           SLIGHTLY BULLISH  NEUTRAL
0.197     0.202    NEUTRAL          NEUTRAL           NEUTRAL           VERY BEARISH
0.202     0.208    NEUTRAL          NEUTRAL           NEUTRAL           NEUTRAL
0.208     0.213    NEUTRAL          NEUTRAL           NEUTRAL           SLIGHTLY BULLISH
0.213     0.219    NEUTRAL          NEUTRAL           NEUTRAL           SLIGHTLY BULLISH
0.219     0.225    NEUTRAL          NEUTRAL           NEUTRAL           VERY BULLISH
0.225     0.232    NEUTRAL          NEUTRAL           BULLISH           VERY BULLISH
0.232     0.240    NEUTRAL          NEUTRAL           NEUTRAL           VERY BULLISH
0.240     0.248    NEUTRAL          SLIGHTLY BULLISH  BULLISH           VERY BULLISH
0.248     0.258    NEUTRAL          NEUTRAL           NEUTRAL           VERY BULLISH
0.258     0.271    SLIGHTLY BULLISH NEUTRAL           SLIGHTLY BULLISH  VERY BULLISH
0.271     0.292    NEUTRAL          NEUTRAL           BULLISH           BULLISH
0.292     0.493    NEUTRAL          NEUTRAL           VERY BULLISH      BULLISH

=================================================================================
```

Definitions of Very Bullish, Bullish, Slightly Bullish, Neutral, Slightly Bearish, Bearish, and Very Bearish are provided in Appendix A.

EXHIBIT U-2:
Interpretation of Unchanged Issues Index's 10-Day Simple Moving Average Readings

```
UNCHANGED ISSUES INDEX - 10 DAY MOVING AVERAGE
PERIOD ANALYZED: JANUARY 1928 TO MARCH 1987
```

INDICATOR RANGE		INTERPRETATION GIVEN INVESTOR'S TIME FRAME			
GREATER THAN	LESS THAN OR EQUAL TO	1 MONTH	3 MONTHS	6 MONTHS	12 MONTHS
0.000	0.155	NEUTRAL	NEUTRAL	VERY BEARISH	VERY BEARISH
0.155	0.165	NEUTRAL	NEUTRAL	VERY BEARISH	VERY BEARISH
0.165	0.172	NEUTRAL	SLIGHTLY BEARISH	VERY BEARISH	VERY BEARISH
0.172	0.178	NEUTRAL	NEUTRAL	BEARISH	VERY BEARISH
0.178	0.184	BULLISH	NEUTRAL	NEUTRAL	VERY BEARISH
0.184	0.189	NEUTRAL	VERY BEARISH	VERY BEARISH	VERY BEARISH
0.189	0.194	SLIGHTLY BEARISH	BEARISH	BEARISH	VERY BEARISH
0.194	0.198	NEUTRAL	NEUTRAL	NEUTRAL	VERY BEARISH
0.198	0.203	NEUTRAL	BULLISH	VERY BULLISH	NEUTRAL
0.203	0.207	BEARISH	SLIGHTLY BULLISH	NEUTRAL	NEUTRAL
0.207	0.212	NEUTRAL	NEUTRAL	NEUTRAL	NEUTRAL
0.212	0.218	NEUTRAL	NEUTRAL	NEUTRAL	BULLISH
0.218	0.223	NEUTRAL	NEUTRAL	NEUTRAL	VERY BULLISH
0.223	0.229	NEUTRAL	NEUTRAL	NEUTRAL	VERY BULLISH
0.229	0.235	SLIGHTLY BULLISH	VERY BULLISH	VERY BULLISH	VERY BULLISH
0.235	0.242	VERY BULLISH	NEUTRAL	VERY BULLISH	VERY BULLISH
0.242	0.250	SLIGHTLY BULLISH	SLIGHTLY BULLISH	VERY BULLISH	VERY BULLISH
0.250	0.260	NEUTRAL	NEUTRAL	VERY BULLISH	VERY BULLISH
0.260	0.274	SLIGHTLY BEARISH	NEUTRAL	VERY BULLISH	BULLISH
0.274	0.334	NEUTRAL	BULLISH	SLIGHTLY BULLISH	NEUTRAL

Definitions of Very Bullish, Bullish, Slightly Bullish, Neutral, Slightly Bearish, Bearish, and Very Bearish are provided in Appendix A.

EXHIBIT U-3:

Interpretation of Unchanged Issues Index's Weekly Readings

```
=================================================================================
UNCHANGED ISSUES INDEX - WEEKLY DATA
PERIOD ANALYZED:  JANUARY 1928 TO MARCH 1987
=================================================================================
```

INDICATOR RANGE		INTERPRETATION GIVEN INVESTOR'S TIME FRAME			
GREATER THAN	LESS THAN OR EQUAL TO	1 MONTH	3 MONTHS	6 MONTHS	12 MONTHS
0.000	0.069	NEUTRAL	NEUTRAL	NEUTRAL	NEUTRAL
0.069	0.078	NEUTRAL	NEUTRAL	NEUTRAL	NEUTRAL
0.078	0.085	NEUTRAL	NEUTRAL	NEUTRAL	NEUTRAL
0.085	0.090	NEUTRAL	NEUTRAL	SLIGHTLY BEARISH	NEUTRAL
0.090	0.094	NEUTRAL	NEUTRAL	NEUTRAL	NEUTRAL
0.094	0.098	NEUTRAL	NEUTRAL	NEUTRAL	NEUTRAL
0.098	0.102	NEUTRAL	NEUTRAL	NEUTRAL	SLIGHTLY BEARISH
0.102	0.105	NEUTRAL	NEUTRAL	SLIGHTLY BEARISH	NEUTRAL
0.105	0.108	NEUTRAL	NEUTRAL	NEUTRAL	NEUTRAL
0.108	0.112	NEUTRAL	NEUTRAL	SLIGHTLY BULLISH	NEUTRAL
0.112	0.115	NEUTRAL	NEUTRAL	NEUTRAL	NEUTRAL
0.115	0.119	NEUTRAL	BULLISH	NEUTRAL	SLIGHTLY BULLISH
0.119	0.122	NEUTRAL	NEUTRAL	NEUTRAL	NEUTRAL
0.122	0.126	NEUTRAL	NEUTRAL	NEUTRAL	SLIGHTLY BULLISH
0.126	0.130	NEUTRAL	NEUTRAL	NEUTRAL	BULLISH
0.130	0.135	NEUTRAL	NEUTRAL	NEUTRAL	NEUTRAL
0.135	0.143	NEUTRAL	NEUTRAL	NEUTRAL	SLIGHTLY BULLISH
0.143	0.152	SLIGHTLY BULLISH	NEUTRAL	NEUTRAL	SLIGHTLY BULLISH
0.152	0.167	NEUTRAL	NEUTRAL	NEUTRAL	NEUTRAL
0.167	0.259	SLIGHTLY BEARISH	NEUTRAL	NEUTRAL	NEUTRAL

```
=================================================================================
```

Definitions of Very Bullish, Bullish, Slightly Bullish, Neutral, Slightly Bearish, Bearish, and Very Bearish are provided In Appendix A.

EXHIBIT U-4:

Interpretation of Unchanged Issues Index's 10-Week Simple Moving Average Readings

```
============================================================================================
UNCHANGED ISSUES INDEX - 10 WEEK MOVING AVERAGE
PERIOD ANALYZED: JANUARY 1928 TO MARCH 1987
============================================================================================
```

INDICATOR RANGE		INTERPRETATION GIVEN INVESTOR'S TIME FRAME			
GREATER THAN	LESS THAN OR EQUAL TO	1 MONTH	3 MONTHS	6 MONTHS	12 MONTHS
0.000	0.079	NEUTRAL	SLIGHTLY BEARISH	VERY BEARISH	BEARISH
0.079	0.086	NEUTRAL	NEUTRAL	NEUTRAL	SLIGHTLY BULLISH
0.086	0.092	NEUTRAL	NEUTRAL	NEUTRAL	VERY BEARISH
0.092	0.096	NEUTRAL	NEUTRAL	NEUTRAL	VERY BEARISH
0.096	0.100	NEUTRAL	SLIGHTLY BEARISH	NEUTRAL	VERY BEARISH
0.100	0.103	NEUTRAL	VERY BEARISH	VERY BEARISH	VERY BEARISH
0.103	0.105	NEUTRAL	SLIGHTLY BEARISH	BEARISH	VERY BEARISH
0.105	0.107	BEARISH	NEUTRAL	NEUTRAL	NEUTRAL
0.107	0.110	NEUTRAL	NEUTRAL	NEUTRAL	NEUTRAL
0.110	0.112	NEUTRAL	NEUTRAL	VERY BULLISH	SLIGHTLY BULLISH
0.112	0.114	NEUTRAL	BULLISH	VERY BULLISH	VERY BULLISH
0.114	0.117	NEUTRAL	SLIGHTLY BULLISH	BULLISH	BULLISH
0.117	0.119	SLIGHTLY BULLISH	NEUTRAL	NEUTRAL	BULLISH
0.119	0.123	NEUTRAL	NEUTRAL	NEUTRAL	SLIGHTLY BULLISH
0.123	0.127	NEUTRAL	NEUTRAL	NEUTRAL	SLIGHTLY BULLISH
0.127	0.130	NEUTRAL	NEUTRAL	NEUTRAL	NEUTRAL
0.130	0.135	SLIGHTLY BULLISH	NEUTRAL	NEUTRAL	NEUTRAL
0.135	0.142	NEUTRAL	NEUTRAL	SLIGHTLY BULLISH	VERY BULLISH
0.142	0.154	NEUTRAL	NEUTRAL	SLIGHTLY BULLISH	SLIGHTLY BULLISH
0.154	0.194	NEUTRAL	NEUTRAL	NEUTRAL	BEARISH

```
============================================================================================
```

Definitions of Very Bullish, Bullish, Slightly Bullish, Neutral, Slightly Bearish, Bearish, and Very Bearish are provided in Appendix A.

UPSIDE/DOWNSIDE RATIO

The Upside/Downside Ratio is simply the volume of advancing issues divided by the volume of declining issues. Daily NYSE data normally is used in the calculation.

The Upside/Downside Ratio measures buying and selling pressure. High readings indicate buying pressure and are considered as bullish; low readings reflect selling pressure and are viewed as bearish.

We tested the Upside/Downside Ratio for the period of May 1964 to March 1987 on a daily basis. In addition, we applied a 10-period simple moving average to the daily readings to smooth out any erratic movements. The results are shown in Exhibits U-5 and U-6 (pages 506–507).

The test process was as follows. The readings for the test period were divided into 20 ranges with approximately the same number of occurrences in each range. For each reading in a range, the gain or loss in four subsequent time periods (1 month later, 3 months later, 6 months later, and 12 months later) was calculated. The combined results for readings within each range were statistically compared, using chi-squared tests, to the performance of the overall market (as measured by the Standard & Poor's 500 Index). Varying degrees of bullishness and bearishness were noted on the basis of that comparison.

Our research results confirm that common interpretation of the Upside/-Downside Ratio is correct. Relatively high readings are very bullish for stock prices, while relatively low readings (using a 10-day moving average) are very bearish in the short term.

Additional studies on the Upside/Downside Ratio have been performed. Martin Zweig (The Zweig Forecast, PO Box 5345, New York, NY 10150) has concluded that a daily Upside/Downside Ratio of greater than 9 to 1 is extremely bullish.* Although not infallible, Zweig noted that every bull market, and many strong intermediate up moves, have begun with a greater than 9 to 1 reading of the Upside/Downside Ratio. Furthermore, Zweig discovered that in cases where two readings greater than 9 to 1 occurred within a relatively short time period, average gains in stock prices were significant. During a test period of January 1960 to May 1985, 12 buy signals were given by two days having readings of greater than 9 to 1 within a 3-month period. In all cases, Zweig found that stock prices were up 6 and 12 months later. The average gain after 6 and 12 months was 14% and 20.7%, respectively.

---

*Reprinted with permission.

EXHIBIT U-5:
Interpretation of Upside/Downside Ratio's Daily Readings

```
=======================================================================================
UPSIDE/DOWNSIDE RATIO - DAILY DATA
PERIOD ANALYZED:  MAY 1964 TO MARCH 1987
=======================================================================================

   INDICATOR RANGE                  INTERPRETATION GIVEN INVESTOR'S TIME FRAME
-------------------     -----------------------------------------------------------------
            LESS
         THAN OR
GREATER  THAN OR
   THAN  EQUAL TO     1 MONTH          3 MONTHS          6 MONTHS          12 MONTHS
-------  --------     ---------------  ---------------   ---------------   ---------------

  0.000    0.205      NEUTRAL          NEUTRAL           NEUTRAL           NEUTRAL
  0.205    0.313      NEUTRAL          NEUTRAL           NEUTRAL           NEUTRAL
  0.313    0.410      SLIGHTLY BEARISH NEUTRAL           NEUTRAL           NEUTRAL
  0.410    0.513      NEUTRAL          NEUTRAL           NEUTRAL           NEUTRAL
  0.513    0.608      NEUTRAL          NEUTRAL           NEUTRAL           BULLISH
  0.608    0.722      NEUTRAL          NEUTRAL           NEUTRAL           NEUTRAL
  0.722    0.818      NEUTRAL          NEUTRAL           NEUTRAL           NEUTRAL
  0.818    0.918      NEUTRAL          NEUTRAL           NEUTRAL           NEUTRAL
  0.918    1.038      NEUTRAL          NEUTRAL           NEUTRAL           NEUTRAL
  1.038    1.158      NEUTRAL          NEUTRAL           NEUTRAL           NEUTRAL
  1.158    1.283      NEUTRAL          NEUTRAL           NEUTRAL           NEUTRAL
  1.283    1.428      NEUTRAL          NEUTRAL           NEUTRAL           NEUTRAL
  1.428    1.566      NEUTRAL          NEUTRAL           NEUTRAL           NEUTRAL
  1.566    1.742      NEUTRAL          NEUTRAL           NEUTRAL           NEUTRAL
  1.742    1.978      NEUTRAL          NEUTRAL           NEUTRAL           NEUTRAL
  1.978    2.265      NEUTRAL          NEUTRAL           NEUTRAL           SLIGHTLY BEARISH
  2.265    2.647      NEUTRAL          NEUTRAL           NEUTRAL           NEUTRAL
  2.647    3.216      NEUTRAL          NEUTRAL           NEUTRAL           NEUTRAL
  3.216    4.440      NEUTRAL          NEUTRAL           NEUTRAL           NEUTRAL
  4.440   41.939      BULLISH          BULLISH           VERY BULLISH      VERY BULLISH

=======================================================================================
```

Definitions of Very Bullish, Bullish, Slightly Bullish, Neutral, Slightly Bearish, Bearish, and Very Bearish are provided in Appendix A.

Further discussion of the Upside/Downside Ratio appears in Zweig's 1986 book entitled *Winning on Wall Street* (Warner Books, New York, NY).

EXHIBIT U-6:

Interpretation of Upside/Downside Ratio's 10-Day Simple Moving Average Readings

```
==================================================================================
UPSIDE/DOWNSIDE RATIO - 10 DAY MOVING AVERAGE
PERIOD ANALYZED: MAY 1964 TO MARCH 1987
==================================================================================
```

INDICATOR RANGE		INTERPRETATION GIVEN INVESTOR'S TIME FRAME			
GREATER THAN	LESS THAN OR EQUAL TO	1 MONTH	3 MONTHS	6 MONTHS	12 MONTHS
0.000	0.737	VERY BEARISH	VERY BEARISH	VERY BEARISH	NEUTRAL
0.737	0.872	NEUTRAL	NEUTRAL	NEUTRAL	NEUTRAL
0.872	0.985	NEUTRAL	NEUTRAL	NEUTRAL	NEUTRAL
0.985	1.077	NEUTRAL	NEUTRAL	NEUTRAL	NEUTRAL
1.077	1.158	NEUTRAL	NEUTRAL	NEUTRAL	NEUTRAL
1.158	1.230	NEUTRAL	NEUTRAL	NEUTRAL	NEUTRAL
1.230	1.303	SLIGHTLY BEARISH	SLIGHTLY BEARISH	SLIGHTLY BEARISH	NEUTRAL
1.303	1.375	NEUTRAL	NEUTRAL	SLIGHTLY BEARISH	SLIGHTLY BEARISH
1.375	1.452	NEUTRAL	NEUTRAL	SLIGHTLY BEARISH	BEARISH
1.452	1.519	NEUTRAL	NEUTRAL	NEUTRAL	NEUTRAL
1.519	1.592	NEUTRAL	NEUTRAL	NEUTRAL	NEUTRAL
1.592	1.671	NEUTRAL	NEUTRAL	NEUTRAL	NEUTRAL
1.671	1.741	NEUTRAL	NEUTRAL	NEUTRAL	NEUTRAL
1.741	1.815	NEUTRAL	NEUTRAL	NEUTRAL	NEUTRAL
1.815	1.906	NEUTRAL	NEUTRAL	SLIGHTLY BULLISH	SLIGHTLY BULLISH
1.906	2.009	NEUTRAL	NEUTRAL	NEUTRAL	NEUTRAL
2.009	2.147	NEUTRAL	NEUTRAL	NEUTRAL	NEUTRAL
2.147	2.353	NEUTRAL	NEUTRAL	NEUTRAL	SLIGHTLY BULLISH
2.353	2.714	VERY BULLISH	NEUTRAL	BULLISH	NEUTRAL
2.714	10.031	VERY BULLISH	VERY BULLISH	VERY BULLISH	VERY BULLISH

```
==================================================================================
```

Definitions of Very Bullish, Bullish, Slightly Bullish, Neutral, Slightly Bearish, Bearish, and Very Bearish are provided in Appendix A.

VOLATILITY RATIOS

To simplify what can be complex, volatility may be defined as the percentage price change or fluctuation over a given period of time, say, a week. One can divide the high by the low for a simple but useful measure (using NYSE data). To obtain the correct perspective, it is important to look at ratios or percentage changes rather than at point changes, which are influenced too much by the level of prices. For example, weekly high minus low differential point spreads have reached into unprecedented levels as high as 6 and 12 NYSE points in recent years of stock market strength, as shown in Exhibits V-2 and V-5 (page 512). However, weekly high/low ratios have stayed well within historical ranges, as shown in Exhibits V-3 (page 510) and V-6 (page 511). The mean ratio for 1968–1977 was 1.0247, or 2.47% per week. The range was 1.12250 to 1.00205, or 12.25% to 0.205%. In contrast, the mean ratio for 1977–1986 was 1.02565, or 2.565%, not significantly different from the previous 1968–1977 period. The range for 1977–1986 was 1.09274 to 1.00640, or 9.274% to 0.64%.

Although volatility is an interesting concept, we were not able to discover a symmetrical long and short decision rule that offered consistent profitability. For example, testing a rule that trades long when volatility is rising and short when volatility is falling produced profits for 86 of the 100 weekly rate of change lengths we tested. But the distribution of profits over the time lengths assumed the kind of erratic pattern that suggests random behavior, as Exhibits V-7 and V-8 illustrate (pages 512 and 513). This unreliability was confirmed by our tests of the 1968–1977 data (not shown), which produced losses for most rate of change periods. So, although it may well be interesting to observe volatility, it doesn't appear particularly fruitful to pay much attention to it for long-term investing.

EXHIBIT V-1:

New York Stock Exchange Composite Price Index Weekly High and Low from April 8, 1977 to December 31, 1986

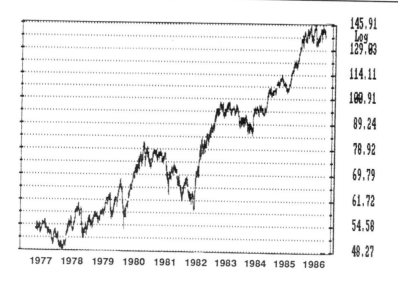

EXHIBIT V-2:

NYSE High-Low Differential Point Spread, 1977 to 1986

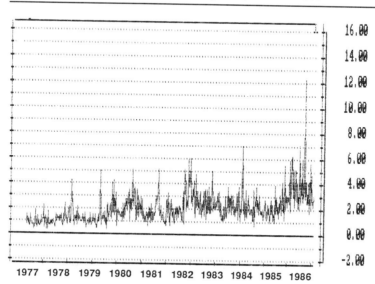

EXHIBIT V-3:
High/Low Ratio, 1977 to 1986

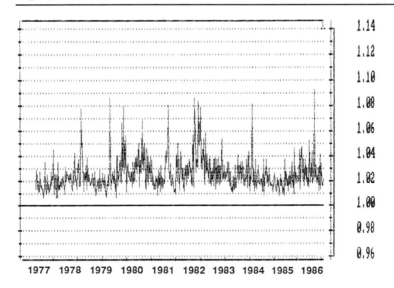

EXHIBIT V-4:

New York Stock Exchange Composite Price Index Weekly High and Low from January 5, 1968 to September 30, 1977

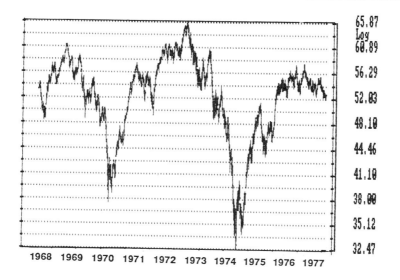

EXHIBIT V-5:

NYSE High-Low Differential Point Spread, 1968 to 1977

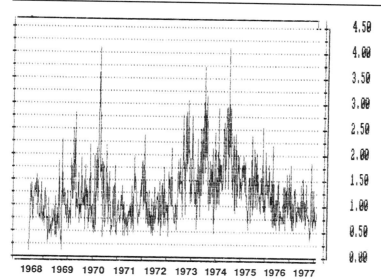

EXHIBIT V-6:
High/Low Ratio, 1968 to 1977

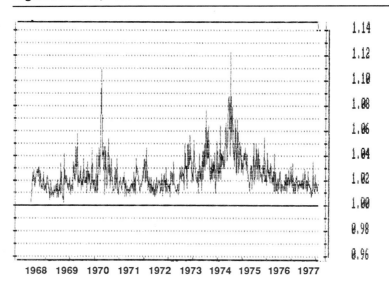

EXHIBIT V-7:
Profitability Chart for High/Low Volatility Ratio Rate of Change (Period Lengths of 1 to 100 Weeks from 1977 to 1986)

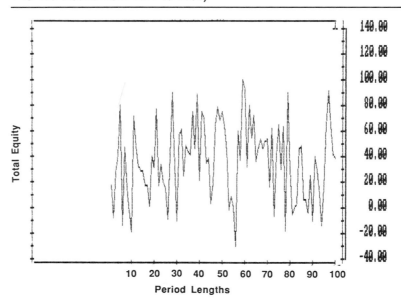

EXHIBIT V-8:
Profit Table for High/Low Volatility Ratio (Period Lengths of 1 to 100 Weeks from 1977 to 1986)

Pass	Total Equity	Short Equity	Long Equity	Max. Equity	Min. Equity	P/L	Best Trade	Worst Trade	Max. Open P/L	Min. Open P/L
1	17.60	-33.02	50.62	36.43	-33.44	17.60	8.07	-11.83	6.22	-12.51
2	-7.41	-46.15	38.74	3.77	-39.42	-7.41	7.58	-10.40	8.00	-11.08
3	27.56	-28.68	56.24	29.07	-17.33	27.56	11.07	-6.93	9.67	-10.14
4	41.27	-21.50	62.77	50.73	-8.66	41.27	12.51	-6.25	8.07	-11.62
5	80.15	-2.15	82.30	82.35	-0.27	80.15	11.08	-7.02	8.41	-12.04
6	-14.06	-49.12	35.06	6.83	-46.46	-16.62	9.65	-10.40	10.03	-11.08
7	47.36	-19.27	66.63	58.17	-19.81	49.92	12.51	-6.56	8.59	-7.62
8	15.26	-34.98	50.24	17.36	-31.03	15.26	11.08	-6.29	10.79	-10.14
9	-2.76	-43.77	41.01	10.40	-28.72	-5.28	8.63	-6.84	10.03	-7.01
10	-18.70	-51.32	32.62	6.48	-28.12	-18.70	9.23	-11.83	8.07	-12.51
11	71.42	-5.87	77.29	94.89	-4.53	68.47	9.34	-9.98	8.87	-11.08
12	48.08	-17.79	65.87	48.08	-25.85	48.08	11.08	-7.87	9.34	-12.04
13	32.89	-25.44	58.33	38.75	-13.31	29.94	8.57	-8.19	11.08	-11.08
14	28.77	-27.41	56.18	32.23	-15.17	25.82	11.07	-5.92	8.07	-10.14
15	28.19	-27.34	55.53	32.53	-27.06	25.24	12.51	-8.32	10.09	-10.14
16	17.78	-33.34	51.12	17.78	-17.81	15.26	11.08	-6.43	11.49	-9.64
17	17.56	-33.49	51.05	35.77	-24.78	15.00	16.63	-10.40	20.32	-11.62
18	0.97	-42.00	42.97	15.66	-17.39	-1.98	11.08	-8.91	8.07	-11.62
19	39.76	-22.72	62.48	62.21	-2.24	39.76	15.84	-11.18	17.18	-12.04
20	31.38	-27.30	58.68	31.86	-23.55	28.86	16.05	-6.89	17.18	-10.14
21	77.61	-3.82	81.43	77.61	-4.78	75.05	11.07	-6.84	9.49	-7.01
22	18.02	-33.91	51.93	18.35	-36.18	15.07	13.49	-5.43	17.18	-10.14
23	33.93	-25.93	59.86	39.12	-16.09	33.93	11.08	-8.18	11.49	-7.01
24	20.49	-33.01	53.50	26.75	-29.37	17.93	16.05	-10.40	17.18	-11.08
25	15.37	-35.20	50.57	25.74	-42.21	15.37	19.19	-9.62	20.32	-10.75
26	-8.41	-47.20	38.79	18.53	-23.58	-8.41	9.35	-11.38	11.49	-12.51
27	39.66	-23.84	63.50	66.59	-3.46	42.22	15.98	-11.65	17.35	-11.08
28	90.47	1.25	89.22	90.47	-18.78	90.47	12.51	-7.74	11.08	-8.13
29	32.57	-27.62	60.19	34.93	-33.78	29.62	11.08	-6.43	10.46	-6.41
30	-9.89	-49.10	39.21	7.70	-40.41	-9.89	10.59	-10.40	10.07	-11.08
31	57.70	-14.09	71.79	57.70	-16.69	55.18	12.51	-8.32	10.09	-5.77
32	61.73	-12.17	73.90	67.09	-21.59	59.17	11.08	-6.24	11.49	-7.01
33	25.37	-29.94	55.31	41.66	-23.75	22.42	15.98	-10.40	17.35	-11.08
34	48.58	-18.83	67.41	48.58	-12.96	48.58	11.08	-7.52	11.82	-10.75
35	43.98	-21.44	65.42	52.91	-18.42	39.99	15.48	-8.28	16.85	-9.41
36	41.09	-22.94	64.03	58.05	-3.28	38.14	21.66	-11.83	22.74	-12.51
37	75.24	-5.54	80.78	80.68	-19.42	72.29	19.93	-9.95	17.74	-11.08
38	46.44	-19.82	66.26	46.44	-22.28	43.92	12.51	-8.41	9.23	-5.99
39	88.84	0.45	88.39	90.94	-10.14	86.28	13.49	-5.85	17.18	-6.84
40	21.87	-33.57	55.44	39.41	-22.70	21.87	15.84	-11.83	17.18	-12.51
41	74.83	-7.01	81.84	87.84	-6.46	74.83	16.05	-10.40	17.18	-11.08
42	70.40	-9.56	79.96	70.73	-6.46	67.45	14.67	-7.88	17.18	-9.26
43	35.02	-26.92	61.94	44.95	-25.88	35.02	16.05	-9.62	17.18	-11.08
44	38.67	-24.95	63.62	56.89	-15.13	36.15	16.05	-11.83	17.18	-12.51
45	4.36	-42.66	47.02	19.39	-29.03	1.80	15.48	-8.28	16.85	-9.41
46	19.15	-35.12	54.27	41.47	-16.21	16.20	13.49	-11.83	17.18	-12.51
47	64.49	-12.71	77.20	69.70	-9.32	64.49	12.67	-8.19	14.04	-11.08
48	78.62	-5.24	83.86	78.87	-2.09	76.06	15.00	-5.69	15.41	-8.45
49	69.17	-9.58	78.75	72.21	-1.33	66.65	11.08	-5.22	11.49	-8.45
50	75.16	-6.78	81.94	75.67	-4.97	75.16	10.03	-10.40	11.09	-11.08
51	64.29	-12.22	76.51	68.13	-12.95	64.29	11.08	-5.26	11.82	-7.89
52	45.35	-21.41	66.76	48.97	-8.54	45.35	9.67	-5.59	10.03	-7.01
53	-1.26	-43.95	42.69	23.14	-24.19	-1.26	9.67	-8.61	8.67	-7.28
54	8.23	-38.85	47.08	24.64	-20.28	8.23	8.87	-11.38	7.07	-12.51
55	1.16	-41.76	42.92	10.26	-21.18	-1.40	7.41	-7.28	8.41	-9.26
56	-29.79	-57.20	27.41	3.41	-35.06	-29.79	8.69	-9.62	9.77	-12.51

EXHIBIT V-8: (continued)

Pass	Total Equity	Short Equity	Long Equity	Max. Equity	Min. Equity	P/L	Best Trade	Worst Trade	Max. Open P/L	Min. Open P/L
57	59.57	-12.08	71.65	59.64	-9.36	59.57	10.79	-6.67	8.63	-11.08
58	37.11	-23.26	60.37	37.43	-9.94	34.55	16.05	-6.76	17.18	-10.14
59	100.62	8.09	92.53	105.60	-2.42	98.10	19.19	-6.43	20.32	-7.01
60	94.35	5.40	88.95	98.13	-16.25	94.35	16.05	-11.83	17.18	-12.51
61	32.84	-24.83	57.67	47.64	-24.03	32.84	16.05	-5.79	17.18	-10.14
62	80.08	-1.85	81.93	82.96	-11.79	80.08	10.36	-5.99	11.49	-12.51
63	54.38	-15.15	69.53	65.96	-10.88	54.38	16.05	-5.79	17.18	-7.01
64	71.92	-6.50	78.42	71.92	-19.50	71.92	16.63	-9.68	20.32	-7.80
65	36.14	-24.55	60.69	47.43	-12.35	33.58	15.48	-7.80	16.85	-9.41
66	46.72	-18.52	65.24	51.88	-21.36	44.20	10.15	-11.83	11.49	-12.51
67	53.25	-15.21	68.46	58.31	-11.28	53.25	15.74	-9.62	17.18	-12.51
68	46.20	-18.10	64.30	59.86	-13.50	46.20	18.88	-8.63	20.32	-11.08
69	51.98	-14.13	66.11	61.18	-29.12	57.09	15.74	-5.73	17.18	-7.01
70	54.21	-12.92	67.13	62.33	-19.45	56.73	19.52	-7.03	20.32	-6.70
71	15.94	-31.79	47.73	30.62	-23.71	18.50	16.05	-6.43	17.18	-6.70
72	62.40	-8.48	70.88	63.34	-11.67	62.40	16.38	-7.80	17.18	-6.24
73	-6.30	-43.17	36.87	0.00	-35.49	-6.30	13.49	-7.02	17.18	-6.24
74	40.72	-18.81	59.53	47.02	-24.66	40.72	19.64	-6.71	20.02	-6.70
75	64.43	-7.67	72.10	80.44	-2.38	61.87	16.38	-8.41	17.18	-9.41
76	29.41	-25.90	55.31	43.69	-18.50	31.93	20.53	-8.04	20.02	-12.51
77	64.28	-8.26	72.54	79.10	-0.03	66.84	15.74	-8.68	17.18	-12.51
78	-18.04	-49.14	31.10	14.03	-42.65	-18.04	10.69	-7.50	11.49	-11.08
79	89.47	4.91	84.56	89.54	-10.30	89.47	22.64	-7.28	23.98	-8.32
80	29.84	-26.99	56.83	35.77	-9.72	29.84	10.69	-10.40	11.49	-11.08
81	-4.38	-45.22	40.84	1.85	-49.22	-4.38	12.51	-10.14	9.49	-7.83
82	0.51	-42.29	42.80	15.42	-23.40	3.03	11.08	-9.10	11.82	-7.90
83	3.58	-41.14	44.72	13.26	-22.53	6.14	8.61	-10.40	7.28	-11.08
84	46.18	-19.93	66.11	46.18	-12.93	46.18	24.98	-7.33	23.98	-7.44
85	49.30	-17.92	67.22	50.49	-2.14	46.78	11.07	-7.80	8.07	-5.38
86	5.79	-39.51	45.30	8.31	-39.28	3.23	11.08	-8.41	10.03	-10.75
87	6.72	-38.90	45.62	21.38	-20.13	11.83	10.69	-11.83	11.82	-12.51
88	-4.07	-44.67	40.60	22.89	-12.47	1.04	12.29	-10.43	13.63	-11.08
89	25.01	-29.90	54.91	33.09	-14.51	30.12	11.08	-10.80	11.82	-9.67
90	-10.34	-47.65	37.31	19.35	-24.27	-10.34	9.15	-9.62	10.49	-12.51
91	40.51	-21.33	61.84	60.15	-0.70	45.62	9.95	-11.83	11.08	-12.51
92	29.37	-26.15	55.52	46.03	-16.51	29.37	11.42	-11.38	11.82	-12.51
93	10.73	-36.00	46.73	20.31	-9.41	10.73	7.23	-5.97	8.91	-10.14
94	-13.45	-47.52	34.07	17.89	-16.01	-13.45	8.63	-8.17	7.82	-12.04
95	14.73	-34.03	48.76	28.57	-2.65	12.17	7.58	-7.84	7.60	-12.51
96	64.91	-9.40	74.31	88.31	-9.90	64.91	9.95	-8.32	11.08	-12.51
97	91.29	4.04	87.25	95.21	-1.42	91.29	8.59	-8.19	8.07	-11.08
98	65.54	-9.08	74.62	65.79	-6.07	62.98	11.07	-10.04	8.07	-10.40
99	41.75	-21.23	62.98	47.36	-1.95	38.80	11.08	-6.76	6.83	-5.40
100	38.83	-21.97	60.80	50.97	-4.22	38.83	12.09	-7.62	10.35	-5.77

Pass indicates period length.
Equity indicates the total number of points gained or lost.
Short equity indicates the number of points gained or lost on short positions.
Long equity indicates the number of points gained or lost on long positions.
Max. equity indicates the highest total profit recorded over the tested period.
Min. equity indicates the lowest total profit recorded over the tested period.
P/L indicates total number of points gained or lost in closed positions.
Best trade indicates the highest number of points gained in any closed trade.
Worst trade indicates the highest number of points lost in any closed trade.
Max. open P/L indicates the highest gain in a position which remains open at the end of the test run.
Min. open P/L indicates the highest loss in a position which remains open at the end of the test run.

VOLUME

Volume of transactions, or turnover, is the number of shares changing hands in a given period (hour, day, week, month, year, etc.). For purposes of this discussion, volume is defined as the number of shares traded each week on the New York Stock Exchange.

As a technical indicator, volume is subject to a number of distortions that might boost or depress the total for reasons other than the true demand and supply for stocks. These distortions include holidays, seasonal patterns, buy and sell programs, arbitrage, dynamic hedging, block trades, and index fund position adjustments. High and rising volume is said to confirm a trend, but often it is seen at turning points as crowd psychology reaches a climax.

Volume at times can be an erratic, unreliable barometer of the market. In general, indicators weighted significantly by volume appear to suffer from the instability of the volume data itself.

VOLUME ACCUMULATION OSCILLATOR

The Volume Accumulation Oscillator is a volume momentum indicator developed by Mark Chaikin (177 E. 77th Street, New York, NY 10021). Mathematically, the formula for Volume Accumulation (A) is expressed as follows:

$$A = \left[C - \left(\frac{H + L}{2} \right) \right] V$$

where

A is the Volume Accumulation for a period.
C is the closing price for a period.
H is the highest price for a period.
L is the lowest price for a period.
V is the total volume of trading activity for a period.

For example, if the current period's highest price is 180, the lowest price is 160, the close is 165, and the volume 2000, then:

$$A = \left[165 - \left(\frac{180 + 160}{2} \right) \right] *2000 = -10,000$$

This $-10,000$ is then subtracted from a running total.

The indicator weighs volume by where the price closed relative to the midpoint of its extreme range. The results for each period can be cumulated as a line against which to compare the price trend. For specific signals, the authors also suggest a moving average differential oscillator of that cumulative line. (Refer to section on oscillators.)

We tested this indicator using Compu Trac software and two 9.75-year test periods of weekly data (consisting of high, low, close, and volume for each week) for the broad-based NYSE Composite Index. The first period ran from January 5, 1968 through September 30, 1977, and the second period ran from April 8, 1977 through December 31, 1986. The overlap in data was necessary to facilitate testing throughout the full time period.

We tested many different oscillators. Exhibits V-9 to V-12 (pages 516–519) show the results of the best and simplest oscillator, comparing each period's raw A to an n-period moving average of A, with n ranging from

EXHIBIT V-9:

Profitability Chart for Volume Accumulation Oscillator (Period Lengths of 1 to 30 Weeks from 1977 to 1986)

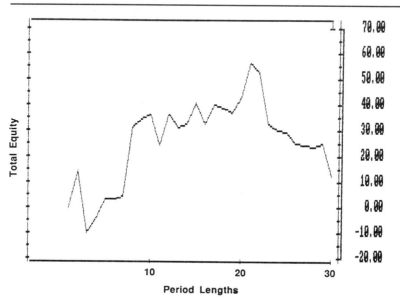

EXHIBIT V-10:

Profit Table for Volume Accumulation Oscillator (Period Lengths of 1 to 30 Weeks from 1977 to 1986)

Pass	Total Equity	Short Equity	Long Equity	Max. Equity	Min. Equity	P/L	Best Trade	Worst Trade	Max. Open P/L	Min. Open P/L
1	0.00	0.00	0.00	0.00	0.00	0.00	N/A	N/A	0.00	0.00
2	14.49	-35.20	49.69	31.81	-8.64	11.54	14.46	-5.59	15.83	-1.60
3	-10.00	-47.46	37.46	35.74	-19.23	-12.95	14.46	-5.59	15.83	-1.60
4	-4.25	-44.26	40.01	28.79	-13.92	-7.20	11.95	-5.59	17.35	-1.65
5	2.99	-40.73	43.72	32.34	-5.79	0.04	12.26	-5.33	17.35	-2.46
6	3.02	-40.58	43.60	40.28	-3.32	0.50	12.26	-5.33	17.35	-3.62
7	4.14	-40.88	45.02	41.12	-3.00	1.62	25.73	-6.15	31.13	-3.62
8	31.06	-27.08	58.14	46.73	-2.48	28.54	28.83	-6.15	33.31	-6.07
9	34.40	-25.19	59.59	49.99	-2.90	31.84	24.84	-6.15	29.32	-6.07
10	36.14	-23.90	60.04	49.95	-5.93	33.58	24.84	-5.83	29.32	-6.07
11	24.14	-29.51	53.65	43.07	-5.47	24.14	24.84	-5.10	29.32	-6.07
12	36.56	-23.55	60.11	46.73	-4.59	36.56	23.89	-5.10	29.32	-6.07
13	31.21	-26.28	57.49	41.38	-4.48	31.21	23.89	-5.10	29.32	-6.07
14	32.21	-25.69	57.90	38.95	-8.66	32.21	28.03	-5.10	34.77	-4.25
15	40.61	-21.13	61.74	47.35	-8.28	40.61	28.03	-5.10	34.77	-4.25
16	32.76	-25.85	58.61	39.50	-17.31	4.73	15.84	-5.10	34.77	-4.25
17	40.02	-22.26	62.28	46.76	-10.88	11.99	15.84	-5.10	34.77	-4.25
18	38.83	-23.07	61.90	45.57	-16.27	10.80	13.26	-6.12	34.77	-5.27
19	36.94	-24.13	61.07	43.68	-14.40	8.91	13.26	-6.12	34.77	-5.27
20	43.26	-21.36	64.62	50.00	-12.64	15.23	15.35	-6.12	34.77	-5.27
21	56.13	-14.56	70.69	62.87	-13.71	24.11	12.39	-6.12	38.76	-5.27
22	52.70	-16.57	69.27	59.44	-16.50	20.68	15.35	-5.27	38.76	-4.06
23	32.55	-26.62	59.17	39.29	-18.91	-2.38	15.35	-5.69	41.67	-4.06
24	29.97	-28.27	58.24	36.71	-23.87	-6.19	15.35	-6.64	42.90	-5.43
25	29.39	-28.19	57.58	36.13	-21.63	-5.54	15.35	-6.64	41.67	-5.43
26	25.19	-30.40	55.59	31.93	-18.19	-9.74	13.89	-6.64	41.67	-5.43
27	24.20	-31.57	55.77	30.94	-15.48	-10.73	13.89	-5.69	41.67	-3.43
28	23.91	-32.03	55.94	30.65	-15.77	-11.02	13.89	-5.69	41.67	-3.43
29	25.21	-31.30	56.51	31.95	-18.17	-9.72	13.89	-5.69	41.67	-3.43
30	12.81	-37.75	50.56	19.55	-24.51	-22.12	13.89	-5.69	41.67	-3.43

Pass indicates period length.

Equity indicates the total number of points gained or lost.

Short equity indicates the number of points gained or lost on short positions.

Long equity indicates the number of points gained or lost on long positions.

Max. equity indicates the highest total profit recorded over the tested period.

Min. equity indicates the lowest total profit recorded over the tested period.

P/L indicates total number of points gained or lost in closed positions.

Best trade indicates the highest number of points gained in any closed trade.

Worst trade indicates the highest number of points lost in any closed trade.

Max. open P/L indicates the highest gain in a position which remains open at the end of the test run.

Min. open P/L indicates the highest loss in a position which remains open at the end of the test run.

EXHIBIT V-11:

Profitability Chart for Volume Accumulation Oscillator (Period Lengths of 1 to 30 Weeks from 1968 to 1977)

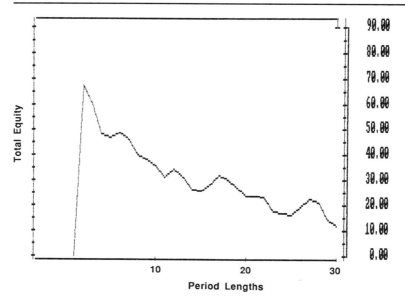

1 to 30. Note that the curves are not smooth; they jump sharply as the period length is changed. This implies some unreliability. Longer periods from 30 to 100 produced poor results. Even optimized results were below standard, with combined profits of 80.16 NYSE points over the 1968–1986 weekly data, as detailed in Exhibits V-16 and V-20 (pages 522 and 525). Using two moving averages rather than one did not improve profitability. In sum, we see limited value to this indicator.

EXHIBIT V-12:

Profit Table for Volume Accumulation Oscillator (Period Lengths of 1 to 30 Weeks from 1968 to 1977)

Pass	Total Equity	Short Equity	Long Equity	Max. Equity	Min. Equity	P/L	Best Trade	Worst Trade	Max. Open P/L	Min. Open P/L
1	0.00	0.00	0.00	0.00	0.00	0.00	N/A	N/A	0.00	0.00
2	67.53	34.11	33.42	70.47	-2.18	67.53	8.26	-3.24	10.60	-2.56
3	60.22	29.93	30.29	65.78	-7.00	60.29	8.26	-3.05	11.59	-2.56
4	48.32	23.59	24.73	51.60	-6.30	47.01	9.90	-3.05	15.08	-2.56
5	46.61	22.01	24.60	47.93	-9.91	45.30	10.63	-4.20	15.08	-2.97
6	48.62	23.01	25.61	49.36	-9.92	47.31	13.46	-4.20	19.13	-2.97
7	45.97	21.92	24.05	46.71	-7.57	44.66	13.46	-4.20	19.13	-2.97
8	39.93	18.35	21.58	40.67	-8.25	38.70	13.46	-7.53	19.13	-5.92
9	38.38	17.50	20.88	39.68	-8.56	37.58	13.46	-7.68	19.13	-6.07
10	35.34	16.00	19.34	37.22	-8.52	34.54	15.60	-7.64	23.61	-6.03
11	31.26	13.75	17.51	33.56	-9.82	30.46	15.60	-8.06	23.61	-6.45
12	34.48	15.86	18.62	38.96	-10.34	33.68	15.60	-7.06	23.61	-5.45
13	31.50	15.24	16.26	36.91	-8.60	30.70	15.60	-5.32	23.61	-3.71
14	26.11	13.45	12.66	32.14	-8.65	25.31	14.71	-3.51	23.61	-3.97
15	25.66	13.12	12.54	34.83	-7.32	24.86	13.30	-4.84	23.61	-4.26
16	28.01	14.73	13.28	35.50	-5.95	27.21	13.30	-4.83	23.61	-3.97
17	31.75	17.00	14.75	37.52	-5.15	30.95	13.30	-3.97	23.61	-3.17
18	29.97	16.15	13.82	36.04	-5.07	29.17	13.30	-4.12	23.61	-3.26
19	26.77	14.17	12.60	32.62	-5.71	25.97	12.81	-5.71	23.61	-5.27
20	24.06	12.94	11.12	29.91	-6.13	23.26	12.81	-5.46	23.61	-5.02
21	24.03	13.36	10.67	29.26	-5.26	23.23	12.81	-4.59	23.61	-4.15
22	22.90	13.60	9.30	28.13	-2.98	22.10	12.81	-3.36	23.61	-4.12
23	17.33	10.77	6.56	23.98	-3.07	16.53	12.81	-4.48	23.61	-4.83
24	17.00	10.48	6.52	24.01	-3.32	16.20	12.81	-4.48	23.61	-4.83
25	16.55	9.91	6.64	21.62	-6.16	15.75	13.44	-5.19	23.61	-4.03
26	19.29	11.68	7.61	23.66	-5.36	18.49	13.44	-5.15	23.61	-4.12
27	22.42	13.63	8.79	29.03	-4.45	21.62	14.54	-4.27	24.71	-4.12
28	21.53	12.63	8.90	28.14	-4.97	20.73	14.54	-5.44	24.71	-4.32
29	14.17	8.26	5.91	24.20	-6.35	13.37	13.06	-6.11	24.71	-4.93
30	12.03	6.70	5.33	22.64	-7.33	10.72	13.06	-7.09	24.71	-5.91

Pass indicates period length.

Equity indicates the total number of points gained or lost.

Short equity indicates the number of points gained or lost on short positions.

Long equity indicates the number of points gained or lost on long positions.

Max. equity indicates the highest total profit recorded over the tested period.

Min. equity indicates the lowest total profit recorded over the tested period.

P/L indicates total number of points gained or lost in closed positions.

Best trade indicates the highest number of points gained in any closed trade.

Worst trade indicates the highest number of points lost in any closed trade.

Max. open P/L indicates the highest gain in a position which remains open at the end of the test run.

Min. open P/L indicates the highest loss in a position which remains open at the end of the test run.

EXHIBIT V-13:

New York Stock Exchange Composite Price Index Weekly High and Low from April 8, 1977 to December 31, 1986

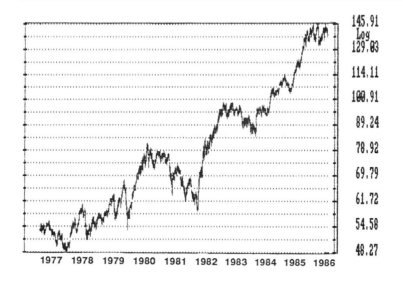

EXHIBIT V-14:

Volume Accumulation Oscillator, 1—21 Week Simple Moving Average, 1977 to 1986

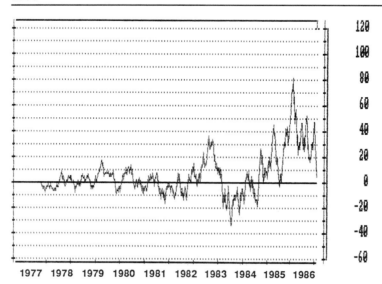

EXHIBIT V-15:

Total Equity for Volume Accumulation Oscillator, 1–21 Week Simple Moving Average, 1977 to 1986

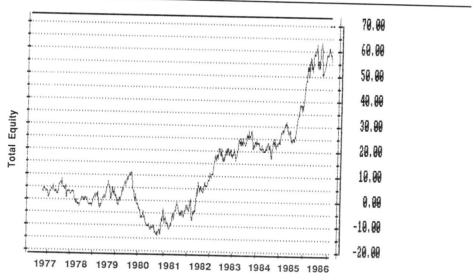

EXHIBIT V-16:

Profit Summary for Volume Accumulation Oscillator, 1–21 Week Simple Moving Average, 1977 to 1986

Item		Long	Short	Net
		Per Trade Ranges		
Per Trade Ranges				
Best Trade	(Closed position yielding maximum P/L)	12.39	7.84	12.39
.. Date		831021	820416	831021
Worst Trade	(Closed position yielding minimum P/L)	-3.86	-6.12	-6.12
.. Date		801205	801128	801128
Max Open P/L	(Maximum P/L occurring in an open position)	38.76	12.58	38.76
.. Date		860829	820312	860829
Min Open P/L	(Minimum P/L occurring in an open position)	-2.54	-5.27	-5.27
.. Date		790302	801121	801121
		Overall Ranges		
Overall Ranges				
Max P/L	(Maximum P/L from all closed positions during the run)	24.72	24.11	24.72
.. Date		851004	851011	851004
Min P/L	(Minimum P/L from all closed positions during the run)	-13.21	-13.16	-13.21
.. Date		810821	810710	810821
Max Equity	(Maximum P/L from all closed and open positions)	62.87	28.02	62.87
.. Date		860829	840615	860829
Min Equity	(Minimum P/L from all closed and open positions)	-13.71	-13.21	-13.71
.. Date		810724	810821	810724
		Statistics		
Statistics				
Periods	(The number of periods in each position and entire run)	315	194	509
Trades	(The number of trades in each position and entire run)	21	22	43
# Profitable	(The number of profitable trades. . .)	12	4	16
# Losing	(The number of unprofitable trades. . .)	9	18	27
% Profitable	(The percent of profitable trades to total trades)	57.14	18.18	37.21
% Losing	(The percent of unprofitable trades to total trades)	42.86	81.82	62.79
		Results		
Results				
Commission	(Total commission deducted from closed trades)	0.00	0.00	0.00
Slippage	(Total slippage deducted from closed trades)	0.00	0.00	0.00
Gross P/L	(Total points gained in closed positions)	38.67	-14.56	24.11
Open P/L	(P/L in a position which remains open at the end)	32.02	0.00	32.02
P/L	(Net P/L: Gross P/L less Commission and Slippage)	38.67	-14.56	24.11
Equity	(Net P/L plus Open P/L at the end of the run)	70.69	-14.56	56.13

There are columns for Long trades, Short trades and Net. In the Long column, results are reported only for Long positions. In the Short column, results are reported for Short positions only. In the Net column for the "Per Trade Ranges" and "Overall Ranges," entries will be the extreme from either the Long or Short column. Net column entries for the "Statistics" and "Results" categories are the combined results of entries in the Long and Short columns.

EXHIBIT V-17:

New York Stock Exchange Composite Price Index Weekly High and Low from January 5, 1968 to September 30, 1977

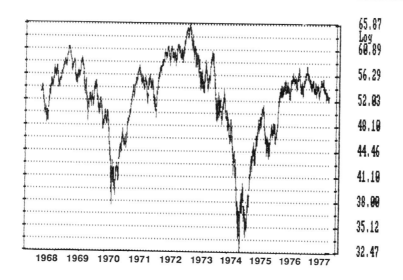

EXHIBIT V-18:

Volume Accumulation Oscillator, 1—21 Week Simple Moving Average, 1968 to 1977

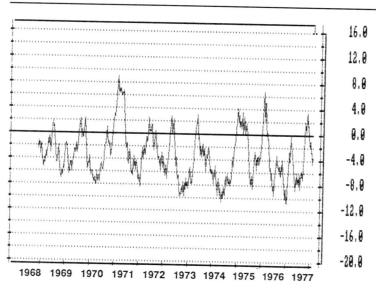

EXHIBIT V-19:

Total Equity for Volume Accumulation Oscillator, 1—21 Week Simple Moving Average, 1968 to 1977

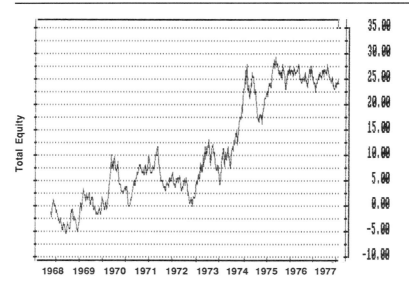

EXHIBIT V-20:

Profit Summary for Volume Accumulation Oscillator, 1 — 21 Week Simple Moving Average, 1968 to 1977

Item	Long	Short	Net
	— Per Trade Ranges —		
Per Trade Ranges			
Best Trade (Closed position yielding maximum P/L)	6.51	12.81	12.81
.. Date	710521	750221	750221
Worst Trade (Closed position yielding minimum P/L)	-2.83	-4.59	-4.59
.. Date	731109	681122	681122
Max Open P/L (Maximum P/L occurring in an open position)	8.24	23.61	23.61
.. Date	710423	741004	741004
Min Open P/L (Minimum P/L occurring in an open position)	-1.73	-4.15	-4.15
.. Date	731102	681115	681115
	— Overall Ranges —		
Overall Ranges			
Max P/L (Maximum P/L from all closed positions during the run)	26.70	25.04	26.70
.. Date	760319	770624	760319
Min P/L (Minimum P/L from all closed positions during the run)	-5.26	-4.59	-5.26
.. Date	681227	681122	681227
Max Equity (Maximum P/L from all closed and open positions)	27.55	29.26	29.26
.. Date	760220	750912	750912
Min Equity (Minimum P/L from all closed and open positions)	-5.26	-5.26	-5.26
.. Date	681227	681227	681227
	— Statistics —		
Statistics			
Periods (The number of periods in each position and entire run)	119	390	509
Trades (The number of trades in each position and entire run)	13	13	26
# Profitable (The number of profitable trades. . .)	5	6	11
# Losing (The number of unprofitable trades. . .)	8	7	15
% Profitable (The percent of profitable trades to total trades)	38.46	46.15	42.31
% Losing (The percent of unprofitable trades to total trades)	61.54	53.85	57.69
	— Results —		
Results			
Commission (Total commission deducted from closed trades)	0.00	0.00	0.00
Slippage (Total slippage deducted from closed trades)	0.00	0.00	0.00
Gross P/L (Total points gained in closed positions)	10.67	12.56	23.23
Open P/L (P/L in a position which remains open at the end)	0.00	0.80	0.80
P/L (Net P/L: Gross P/L less Commission and Slippage)	10.67	12.56	23.23
Equity (Net P/L plus Open P/L at the end of the run)	10.67	13.36	24.03

There are columns for Long trades, Short trades and Net. In the Long column, results are reported only for Long positions. In the Short column, results are reported for Short positions only. In the Net column for the "Per Trade Ranges" and "Overall Ranges," entries will be the extreme from either the Long or Short column. Net column entries for the "Statistics" and "Results" categories are the combined results of entries in the Long and Short columns.

VOLUME OF ADVANCING ISSUES

The volume of advancing issues is the total volume of those stocks that end the current day at a higher price than their previous closing price. It is generally viewed as an indication of buying pressure by noting that when advancing volume (or a moving average of advancing volume) expands, it is bullish, and when it contracts, it is bearish. Advancing volume is most often used as a component of another indicator. Refer to the following indicators for their use of advancing volume: Cumulative Volume Index, the Arms' Short-Term Trading Index, and the Upside/Downside Ratio.

VOLUME OF DECLINING ISSUES

The volume of declining issues is the total volume of those stocks that end the current day at a lower price than their previous closing price. It is generally viewed as an indication of selling pressure by noting that when declining volume (or a moving average of declining volume) expands, it is bearish, and when it contracts, it is bullish. Declining volume is most often used as a component of another indicator. Refer to the following indicators for their use of declining volume: Cumulative Volume Index, the Arms' Short-Term Trading Index, and the Upside/Downside Ratio.

VOLUME OSCILLATOR

Oscillators are quite effective in taming raw price data into a complete investment timing model. For price data, we found that the 1-week versus the 45-week simple moving average percentage differential oscillator produced the highest total profit of any oscillator we tested. (Refer to section on oscillators.)

We applied the same testing method to raw volume data. We tested 1-week versus n-week simple moving average percentage oscillators of total weekly volume traded on the New York Stock Exchange using Compu Trac software and two 9.75-year test periods of weekly data (consisting of high, low, close, and volume for each week) for the broad-based NYSE Composite Index. The first period ran from January 5, 1968 through September 30, 1977, and the second period ran from April 8, 1977 through December 31, 1986.

The overlap in data was necessary to facilitate testing of various oscillators throughout the full time period.

Our basic statistical testing technique was the simple moving average crossover rule for univariate analysis of time series data to isolate the trend. When the total volume for 1 week crossed its own n-week simple average, a trend change and thus a trade position change was signaled in the direction of the crossing. The number of observations, n, that should be included in a moving average designed to isolate a trend depends on the length of the cyclical movements in the time series. Optimal values were determined by a systematic trial-and-error procedure on the computer. We tested for n equal to 1 through 208, or simple moving averages ranging in length from 1 week (the indicator data itself) up to 208 weeks. The results of optimization runs for each n-week time length are shown in Exhibits V-21 through V-24 (pages 527–537). "Equity" signifies total profits or losses accumulated for each length of n.

The highest combined profit of 108.61 NYSE points for both periods, 1968–1977 and 1977–1986, was produced by the 105-week simple moving

Text continued on page 537.

EXHIBIT V-21:

Profitability Chart for Volume Oscillator (Simple Moving Average Period Lengths of 1 to 208 Weeks from 1977 to 1986)

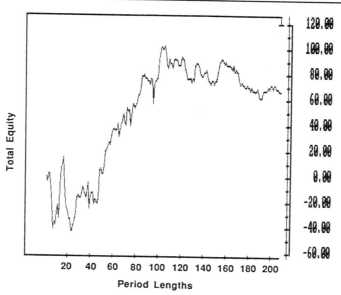

EXHIBIT V-22:
Profit Table for Volume Oscillator (Simple Moving Average Period Lengths of 1 to 208 Weeks from 1977 to 1986)

Pass	Total Equity	Short Equity	Long Equity	Max. Equity	Min. Equity	P/L	Best Trade	Worst Trade	Max. Open P/L	Min. Open P/L
1	0.00	0.00	0.00	0.00	0.00	0.00	N/A	N/A	0.00	0.00
2	-3.14	-43.39	40.25	25.81	-10.61	-5.70	8.63	-11.83	8.07	-12.51
3	2.13	-41.38	43.51	56.48	-4.56	-0.82	8.09	-11.83	8.00	-12.51
4	0.82	-42.05	42.87	47.25	-6.30	-1.74	8.41	-11.83	8.87	-12.51
5	-9.29	-46.78	37.49	40.50	-15.33	-12.24	15.98	-11.83	17.35	-12.51
6	-22.95	-53.70	30.75	28.32	-31.26	-25.90	12.67	-11.83	14.04	-12.51
7	-41.68	-62.93	21.25	16.77	-45.00	-44.63	12.67	-10.40	14.04	-11.08
8	-36.64	-61.27	24.63	22.99	-39.59	-39.59	12.67	-9.95	14.04	-11.08
9	-37.50	-61.36	23.86	10.85	-51.70	-40.06	15.56	-9.95	14.04	-11.08
10	-29.30	-57.04	27.74	21.01	-32.33	-31.86	11.73	-9.95	15.56	-11.08
11	-22.88	-53.41	30.53	28.11	-25.91	-25.44	10.16	-9.95	15.56	-11.08
12	-32.12	-57.64	25.52	25.09	-35.15	-34.68	10.16	-10.89	15.56	-11.08
13	-8.62	-46.14	37.52	24.69	-11.65	-11.18	12.47	-11.38	15.56	-12.51
14	6.11	-38.83	44.94	36.31	-11.12	3.55	17.74	-9.95	15.56	-11.08
15	8.59	-37.50	46.09	41.65	-11.88	6.03	17.74	-11.38	15.56	-12.51
16	15.05	-33.91	48.96	40.77	-8.98	12.49	17.74	-11.38	15.56	-12.51
17	-4.64	-44.55	39.91	22.13	-14.89	-7.20	17.39	-11.38	17.74	-12.51
18	-19.52	-52.03	32.51	19.55	-24.51	-22.08	21.05	-11.38	18.87	-12.51
19	-25.05	-55.01	29.96	9.44	-32.90	-27.61	21.05	-9.95	18.87	-11.08
20	-27.98	-56.59	28.61	7.97	-35.83	-30.54	21.05	-9.95	18.87	-11.08
21	-34.06	-60.02	25.96	4.35	-41.21	-36.62	16.57	-9.95	21.05	-11.08
22	-33.25	-59.25	26.00	5.02	-40.40	-35.81	16.57	-9.95	21.05	-11.08
23	-42.28	-64.06	21.78	2.13	-47.27	-44.84	16.57	-9.95	21.05	-11.08
24	-42.07	-63.93	21.86	2.64	-47.06	-44.63	16.57	-9.95	21.05	-11.08
25	-38.09	-62.30	24.21	1.71	-45.29	-40.65	16.57	-9.95	21.05	-11.08
26	-34.49	-60.13	25.64	7.46	-40.31	-37.05	16.57	-9.95	21.05	-11.08
27	-29.05	-57.52	28.47	10.52	-38.45	-31.61	16.57	-9.95	21.05	-11.08
28	-16.20	-51.77	35.57	16.81	-30.10	-18.76	16.57	-9.95	21.05	-11.08
29	-15.11	-51.54	36.43	16.18	-32.47	-17.67	18.30	-9.95	21.05	-11.08
30	-16.51	-52.16	35.65	14.78	-33.87	-19.07	18.30	-9.95	21.05	-11.08
31	-16.85	-52.58	35.73	12.06	-36.59	-19.41	18.30	-9.95	21.05	-11.08
32	-15.36	-50.62	35.26	16.55	-30.32	-17.92	18.30	-9.95	21.05	-11.08
33	-9.29	-47.68	38.39	17.74	-30.35	-11.85	18.30	-9.95	21.05	-11.08
34	-9.41	-47.33	37.92	19.34	-26.89	-11.97	18.30	-9.95	21.05	-11.08
35	-13.84	-50.04	36.20	15.85	-29.94	-16.40	18.30	-9.95	21.05	-11.08
36	-16.20	-51.53	35.33	16.71	-35.28	-18.76	18.30	-9.95	21.05	-11.08
37	-12.79	-49.88	37.09	13.92	-31.87	-15.35	18.30	-9.95	21.05	-11.08
38	-5.00	-45.66	40.66	20.43	-26.46	-7.56	18.30	-9.95	21.05	-11.08
39	-24.80	-55.44	30.64	12.23	-33.56	-27.36	18.30	-9.95	21.05	-11.08
40	-14.56	-51.25	36.69	21.19	-25.70	-17.12	18.30	-9.95	21.05	-11.08
41	-12.53	-50.77	38.24	23.22	-23.67	-15.09	18.30	-9.95	21.05	-11.08
42	-12.55	-50.70	38.15	23.46	-22.77	-15.11	18.30	-9.95	21.05	-11.08
43	-21.00	-55.26	34.26	16.01	-31.22	-23.56	18.30	-9.95	21.05	-11.08
44	-17.00	-52.93	35.93	20.01	-27.22	-19.56	18.30	-9.95	21.05	-11.08
45	-20.11	-54.34	34.23	22.26	-24.97	-22.67	15.62	-9.95	21.05	-11.08
46	-21.84	-55.76	33.92	20.29	-26.70	-24.40	15.62	-9.95	21.05	-11.08
47	-17.81	-53.60	35.79	23.96	-23.03	-20.37	15.62	-9.95	21.05	-11.08
48	4.89	-42.51	47.40	36.42	-13.91	2.33	21.34	-9.95	22.14	-11.08
49	5.76	-41.67	47.43	34.59	-15.74	3.20	21.34	-9.95	22.14	-11.08
50	2.07	-43.13	45.20	35.84	-14.49	-0.49	21.34	-9.95	22.14	-11.08

EXHIBIT V-22: (continued)

Pass	Total Equity	Short Equity	Long Equity	Max. Equity	Min. Equity	P/L	Best Trade	Worst Trade	Max. Open P/L	Min. Open P/L
51	2.14	-43.29	45.43	35.29	-15.04	-0.42	21.34	-9.95	22.14	-11.08
52	6.91	-40.91	47.82	37.70	-15.03	4.35	21.34	-9.95	22.14	-11.08
53	19.93	-34.12	54.05	41.96	-13.03	17.37	21.34	-11.38	22.14	-12.51
54	21.28	-32.68	53.96	43.31	-11.68	18.72	21.34	-11.38	22.14	-12.51
55	23.93	-31.00	54.93	45.96	-10.71	21.37	21.34	-11.38	22.14	-12.51
56	26.76	-28.96	55.72	48.79	-11.96	24.20	21.34	-11.38	22.14	-12.51
57	25.51	-29.55	55.06	47.54	-12.03	22.95	21.34	-11.38	22.14	-12.51
58	31.15	-26.29	57.44	50.94	-9.97	28.59	21.34	-11.38	22.14	-12.51
59	35.11	-24.26	59.37	54.90	-9.29	32.55	21.34	-11.38	22.14	-12.51
60	37.84	-23.30	61.14	57.63	-8.48	35.28	21.34	-11.38	22.14	-12.51
61	36.57	-23.49	60.06	54.34	-10.87	34.01	21.34	-8.12	22.14	-7.64
62	36.02	-23.24	59.26	53.79	-14.16	33.46	21.34	-8.12	22.14	-7.64
63	37.94	-22.92	60.86	55.71	-12.24	35.38	21.34	-8.12	22.14	-7.64
64	41.84	-21.42	63.26	59.61	-8.34	39.28	21.34	-8.12	22.14	-7.64
65	31.38	-26.77	58.15	49.11	-8.10	28.82	21.34	-8.12	22.14	-7.64
66	37.26	-23.99	61.25	52.13	-6.70	34.70	21.34	-8.12	22.14	-8.19
67	41.76	-21.00	62.76	54.85	-2.47	39.20	21.34	-8.12	22.14	-8.19
68	43.65	-20.01	63.66	55.66	-4.68	41.09	21.34	-8.12	22.14	-8.19
69	48.58	-16.91	65.49	60.59	-5.95	46.02	21.34	-8.12	22.14	-8.19
70	42.62	-18.81	61.43	54.63	-8.11	40.06	21.34	-8.12	22.14	-8.19
71	39.99	-20.03	60.02	52.00	-8.30	37.43	21.34	-8.12	22.14	-8.19
72	54.20	-12.66	66.86	66.21	-7.63	51.64	21.34	-8.12	22.14	-8.19
73	51.64	-13.86	65.50	63.65	-7.95	49.08	21.34	-8.12	22.14	-8.19
74	53.12	-13.46	66.58	65.13	-7.27	50.56	21.34	-8.12	22.14	-8.19
75	40.00	-19.17	59.17	52.01	-8.97	37.44	21.34	-8.12	22.14	-8.19
76	47.77	-16.00	63.77	59.78	-7.54	45.21	21.34	-8.12	22.14	-8.19
77	55.73	-12.74	68.47	67.74	-4.54	53.17	21.34	-8.12	22.14	-8.19
78	55.32	-12.74	68.06	67.33	-4.95	52.76	21.34	-8.12	22.14	-8.19
79	54.26	-12.99	67.25	66.27	-4.39	51.70	21.34	-8.12	22.14	-8.19
80	56.13	-11.76	67.89	68.14	-4.96	53.57	21.34	-8.12	22.14	-8.19
81	58.24	-12.79	71.03	63.97	-9.13	55.68	21.34	-8.12	22.14	-8.19
82	63.34	-11.36	74.70	68.12	-6.89	60.78	21.34	-8.12	22.14	-8.19
83	65.51	-9.79	75.30	70.29	-7.86	62.95	21.34	-8.12	22.14	-8.19
84	68.26	-8.80	77.06	73.04	-4.95	65.70	21.34	-8.12	22.14	-8.19
85	78.24	-3.90	82.14	79.46	-6.51	75.68	21.34	-8.77	22.14	-8.19
86	79.14	-3.00	82.14	80.36	-5.61	76.58	21.34	-8.77	22.14	-8.19
87	80.21	-2.30	82.51	81.43	-5.28	77.65	21.34	-8.77	22.14	-8.19
88	77.86	-3.33	81.19	79.08	-4.99	75.30	21.34	-8.77	22.14	-8.19
89	77.91	-3.68	81.59	79.13	-5.74	75.35	21.34	-8.77	22.14	-8.19
90	75.13	-4.84	79.97	79.91	-5.28	72.57	21.34	-8.77	22.14	-8.19
91	74.56	-5.20	79.76	79.34	-5.13	72.00	21.34	-8.77	22.14	-8.19
92	72.17	-5.50	77.67	76.95	-2.64	69.61	21.34	-8.77	22.14	-8.19
93	76.61	-2.53	79.14	77.83	-4.14	74.05	21.34	-8.77	23.82	-8.12
94	75.33	-3.70	79.03	76.55	-3.08	72.77	21.34	-8.77	23.82	-8.12
95	56.91	-12.34	69.25	58.13	-4.22	54.35	21.34	-8.77	23.82	-8.12
96	72.89	-4.95	77.84	74.11	-3.02	70.33	21.34	-8.77	23.82	-8.12
97	75.27	-4.22	79.49	76.49	-2.10	72.71	21.34	-8.77	23.82	-8.12
98	76.31	-3.45	79.76	77.53	-1.60	73.75	21.34	-7.60	23.82	-6.95
99	77.92	-2.89	80.81	79.14	-2.09	75.36	21.34	-7.60	23.82	-6.95
100	91.55	3.67	87.88	92.77	-2.60	88.99	21.34	-7.60	23.82	-6.95

EXHIBIT V-22: (continued)

Pass	Total Equity	Short Equity	Long Equity	Max. Equity	Min. Equity	P/L	Best Trade	Worst Trade	Max. Open P/L	Min. Open P/L
101	96.17	6.70	89.47	97.39	-0.33	93.61	21.34	-7.60	23.82	-6.95
102	101.29	9.63	91.66	102.91	-1.07	98.73	21.34	-7.60	23.82	-6.95
103	99.64	9.07	90.57	101.26	-1.60	97.08	21.34	-7.60	23.82	-6.95
104	99.59	9.07	90.52	101.21	-1.65	97.03	21.34	-7.60	23.82	-6.95
105	102.56	11.01	91.55	104.18	-2.56	100.00	21.34	-4.87	23.82	-7.60
106	97.75	8.35	89.40	99.37	-2.05	95.19	21.34	-7.21	23.82	-9.42
107	87.87	3.19	84.68	89.49	-1.61	85.31	21.34	-10.37	23.82	-9.42
108	85.22	2.02	83.20	86.84	-1.92	82.66	21.34	-10.37	23.82	-9.42
109	93.06	5.62	87.44	94.68	-1.28	90.50	21.34	-10.37	23.82	-9.42
110	89.22	3.06	86.16	95.96	0.00	89.22	21.34	-10.37	23.82	-9.42
111	88.44	3.06	85.38	95.18	-0.51	88.44	21.34	-10.37	23.82	-9.42
112	85.37	1.70	83.67	92.11	-0.86	85.37	21.34	-10.37	23.82	-9.42
113	91.23	4.34	86.89	97.97	-0.28	91.23	35.59	-10.37	39.13	-9.42
114	91.94	5.39	86.55	98.68	-1.02	74.86	35.59	-10.37	39.13	-9.42
115	91.73	5.50	86.23	98.47	-1.45	74.65	26.48	-4.22	39.13	-4.89
116	91.37	5.50	85.87	98.11	-1.81	74.29	26.48	-4.22	39.13	-4.89
117	87.44	3.62	83.82	94.18	-1.98	70.36	26.48	-4.22	39.13	-4.89
118	87.00	3.62	83.38	93.74	-2.42	69.92	26.48	-4.22	39.13	-4.89
119	87.65	3.62	84.03	94.39	-1.77	70.57	26.48	-4.22	39.13	-4.89
120	93.87	6.59	87.28	100.61	-1.49	76.79	26.48	-3.64	39.13	-4.89
121	92.07	6.11	85.96	98.81	-2.33	74.99	26.48	-3.64	39.13	-4.89
122	91.47	6.11	85.36	98.21	-2.93	74.39	26.48	-3.64	39.13	-4.89
123	83.96	3.01	80.95	90.70	-4.24	66.88	26.48	-4.82	39.13	-6.84
124	82.90	3.01	79.89	89.64	-5.30	65.82	26.48	-4.82	39.13	-6.84
125	76.30	-0.17	76.47	83.04	-5.54	59.22	26.48	-4.82	39.13	-6.84
126	75.84	-0.17	76.01	82.58	-6.00	58.76	26.48	-4.82	39.13	-6.84
127	76.85	-0.17	77.02	83.59	-4.99	59.77	26.48	-4.82	39.13	-6.84
128	77.76	0.63	77.13	84.50	-5.68	60.68	26.48	-4.82	39.13	-6.84
129	74.30	-0.70	75.00	81.04	-8.61	57.22	26.48	-4.82	39.13	-6.84
130	76.74	0.20	76.54	83.48	-7.97	59.66	26.48	-4.82	39.13	-6.84
131	75.59	0.20	75.39	82.33	-9.12	58.51	26.48	-5.20	39.13	-6.84
132	87.01	3.86	83.15	93.75	-5.02	69.93	28.21	-4.82	39.13	-7.01
133	88.68	3.86	84.82	95.42	-3.35	71.60	28.21	-4.82	39.13	-7.01
134	89.34	3.86	85.48	96.08	-2.69	72.26	28.21	-4.82	39.13	-7.01
135	88.11	3.86	84.25	94.85	-3.92	71.03	28.21	-4.82	39.13	-7.01
136	85.06	2.11	82.95	91.80	-4.37	67.98	28.21	-4.82	39.13	-7.01
137	80.17	0.35	79.82	86.91	-3.00	63.09	28.21	-7.45	39.13	-11.62
138	78.92	-0.00	78.92	85.66	-3.55	61.84	28.21	-7.45	39.13	-11.62
139	79.13	0.63	78.50	85.87	-4.60	62.05	28.21	-4.82	39.13	-6.84
140	81.56	2.27	79.29	88.30	-5.45	64.48	28.21	-4.82	39.13	-6.84
141	80.77	2.27	78.50	87.51	-6.24	63.69	28.21	-4.82	39.13	-6.84
142	83.47	3.31	80.16	90.21	-5.62	66.39	28.21	-7.31	39.13	-11.48
143	79.68	1.49	78.19	86.42	-5.77	62.60	24.48	-7.31	35.40	-11.48
144	75.33	-1.04	76.37	82.07	-6.48	58.25	24.48	-4.82	35.40	-6.84
145	73.35	-1.04	74.39	80.09	-8.46	56.27	24.48	-5.94	35.40	-6.84
146	72.56	-1.04	73.60	79.30	-9.25	55.48	24.48	-6.73	35.40	-7.12
147	75.37	1.03	74.34	82.11	-10.58	58.29	24.48	-8.06	35.40	-8.45
148	74.56	1.03	73.53	81.30	-11.39	57.48	24.48	-8.87	35.40	-9.26
149	73.07	1.03	72.04	79.81	-12.88	55.99	24.48	-10.36	35.40	-10.75
150	74.50	1.03	73.47	81.24	-11.45	57.42	24.48	-8.93	35.40	-9.32

EXHIBIT V-22: (continued)

Pass	Total Equity	Short Equity	Long Equity	Max. Equity	Min. Equity	P/L	Best Trade	Worst Trade	Max. Open P/L	Min. Open P/L
151	74.84	1.03	73.81	81.58	-11.11	57.76	24.48	-8.59	35.40	-8.98
152	80.41	3.39	77.02	87.15	-10.26	63.33	24.48	-7.74	35.40	-8.13
153	84.40	3.39	81.01	91.14	-6.27	67.32	24.48	-4.82	35.40	-6.84
154	89.81	5.65	84.16	96.55	-3.25	72.73	24.48	-4.82	35.40	-6.84
155	91.64	5.65	85.99	98.38	-1.42	74.56	24.48	-4.82	35.40	-6.84
156	93.06	5.65	87.41	99.80	0.00	75.98	24.48	-4.82	35.40	-6.84
157	89.69	4.53	85.16	96.43	-0.74	72.61	18.54	-1.09	29.46	-9.82
158	88.64	4.53	84.11	95.38	-1.79	71.56	18.54	-1.09	29.46	-9.82
159	90.43	4.53	85.90	97.17	0.00	73.35	18.54	-1.09	29.46	-9.82
160	87.91	4.53	83.38	94.65	0.00	70.83	18.54	-1.09	29.46	-9.82
161	87.59	4.53	83.06	94.33	-0.26	70.51	18.54	-1.09	29.46	-9.82
162	87.85	4.53	83.32	94.59	0.00	70.77	18.54	-1.09	29.46	-9.82
163	86.41	4.53	81.88	93.15	0.00	69.33	18.54	-1.09	29.46	-9.82
164	84.59	4.53	80.06	91.33	0.00	67.51	18.54	-1.09	29.46	-9.82
165	84.20	4.53	79.67	90.94	0.00	67.12	18.54	-1.09	29.46	-9.82
166	87.73	6.91	80.82	94.47	-1.03	70.65	18.54	-0.88	29.46	-9.82
167	82.67	5.11	77.56	89.41	-2.49	65.59	18.54	-1.40	29.46	-9.82
168	83.60	5.11	78.49	90.34	-1.56	66.52	18.54	-1.40	29.46	-9.82
169	82.46	5.11	77.35	89.20	-2.70	65.38	18.54	-1.40	29.46	-9.82
170	81.73	5.11	76.62	88.47	-3.43	64.65	18.54	-1.40	29.46	-9.82
171	74.96	1.91	73.05	81.70	-3.80	57.88	18.54	-1.40	29.46	-9.82
172	72.56	1.91	70.65	79.30	-6.20	55.48	18.54	-1.40	29.46	-9.82
173	73.30	1.91	71.39	80.04	-5.46	56.22	18.54	-1.40	29.46	-9.82
174	72.96	1.91	71.05	79.70	-5.80	55.88	18.54	-1.40	29.46	-9.82
175	71.59	1.91	69.68	78.33	-7.17	54.51	18.54	-1.68	29.46	-9.82
176	70.33	1.91	68.42	77.07	-8.43	53.25	18.54	-2.94	29.46	-9.82
177	69.93	1.91	68.02	76.67	-8.83	52.85	18.54	-3.34	29.46	-9.82
178	71.87	1.91	69.96	78.61	-6.89	54.79	18.54	-1.40	29.46	-9.82
179	70.27	1.91	68.36	77.01	-8.49	53.19	18.54	-3.00	29.46	-9.82
180	69.75	1.91	67.84	76.49	-9.01	52.67	18.54	-3.52	29.46	-9.82
181	67.59	1.91	65.68	74.33	-11.17	50.51	18.54	-5.68	29.46	-9.85
182	69.41	1.91	67.50	76.15	-9.35	52.33	18.54	-3.86	29.46	-9.82
183	67.66	1.91	65.75	74.40	-11.10	50.58	18.54	-5.61	29.46	-9.82
184	67.06	1.91	65.15	73.80	-11.70	49.98	18.54	-6.21	29.46	-10.38
185	65.88	1.61	64.27	72.62	-12.88	48.80	18.54	-4.81	29.46	-10.96
186	66.90	1.61	65.29	73.64	-11.86	49.82	18.54	-3.79	29.46	-9.94
187	68.27	1.61	66.66	75.01	-10.49	51.19	18.54	-2.42	29.46	-9.82
188	67.45	1.61	65.84	74.19	-11.31	50.37	18.54	-3.24	29.46	-9.82
189	62.84	1.61	61.23	69.58	-15.92	45.76	18.54	-7.85	29.46	-14.00
190	61.63	1.61	60.02	68.37	-17.13	44.55	18.54	-9.06	29.46	-15.21
191	60.78	1.61	59.17	67.52	-17.98	43.70	18.54	-9.91	29.46	-16.06
192	64.64	1.61	63.03	71.38	-14.12	47.56	18.54	-6.05	29.46	-12.20
193	67.64	1.61	66.03	74.38	-11.12	50.56	18.54	-3.05	29.46	-9.82
194	67.74	3.01	64.73	74.48	-13.82	50.66	18.54	-5.75	29.46	-11.90
195	68.12	3.91	64.21	74.86	-15.24	51.04	18.54	-7.17	29.46	-13.32
196	68.14	3.91	64.23	74.88	-15.22	51.06	18.54	-7.15	29.46	-13.30
197	69.48	3.67	65.81	76.22	-13.40	52.40	26.50	-5.33	29.46	-11.48
198	68.59	3.67	64.92	75.33	-14.29	51.51	26.50	-6.22	29.46	-12.37
199	71.20	3.67	67.53	77.94	-11.68	54.12	26.50	-3.61	29.46	-9.82
200	71.65	3.67	67.98	78.39	-11.23	54.57	26.50	-3.16	29.46	-9.82

EXHIBIT V-22: (continued)

Pass	Total Equity	Short Equity	Long Equity	Max. Equity	Min. Equity	P/L	Best Trade	Worst Trade	Max. Open P/L	Min. Open P/L
201	68.75	2.50	66.25	75.49	-11.79	51.67	26.53	-3.72	29.46	-9.87
202	70.78	2.50	68.28	77.52	-9.76	53.70	26.53	-1.69	29.46	-9.82
203	71.13	2.50	68.63	77.87	-9.41	54.05	26.53	-1.34	29.46	-9.82
204	68.45	2.50	65.95	75.19	-12.09	51.37	26.53	-4.02	29.46	-10.17
205	69.12	2.50	66.62	75.86	-11.42	52.04	26.53	-3.35	29.46	-9.82
206	67.26	2.50	64.76	74.00	-13.28	50.18	26.53	-5.21	29.46	-11.36
207	66.49	2.50	63.99	73.23	-14.05	49.41	26.53	-5.98	29.46	-12.13
208	65.99	2.50	63.49	72.73	-14.55	48.91	26.53	-6.48	29.46	-12.63

Pass indicates period length.
Equity indicates the total number of points gained or lost.
Short equity indicates the number of points gained or lost on short positions.
Long equity indicates the number of points gained or lost on long positions.
Max. equity indicates the highest total profit recorded over the tested period.
Min. equity indicates the lowest total profit recorded over the tested period.
P/L indicates total number of points gained or lost in closed positions.
Best trade indicates the highest number of points gained in any closed trade.
Worst trade indicates the highest number of points lost in any closed trade.
Max. open P/L indicates the highest gain in a position which remains open at the end of the test run.
Min. open P/L indicates the highest loss in a position which remains open at the end of the test run.

EXHIBIT V-23:

Profitability Chart for Volume Oscillator (Simple Moving Average Period Lengths of 1 to 208 Weeks from 1968 to 1977)

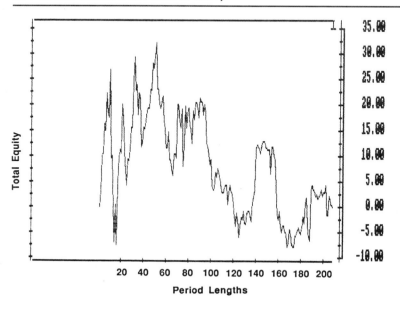

EXHIBIT V-24:

Profit Table for Volume Oscillator (Simple Moving Average Period Lengths of 1 to 208 Weeks from 1968 to 1977)

Pass	Total Equity	Short Equity	Long Equity	Max. Equity	Min. Equity	P/L	Best Trade	Worst Trade	Max. Open P/L	Min. Open P/L
1	0.00	0.00	0.00	0.00	0.00	0.00	N/A	N/A	0.00	0.00
2	3.04	2.20	0.84	22.07	-0.67	2.30	5.18	-4.52	5.51	-2.70
3	10.15	5.42	4.73	35.32	-1.69	9.41	5.86	-4.52	5.05	-2.70
4	10.58	5.11	5.47	39.58	-2.51	9.84	5.86	-6.75	5.18	-7.85
5	16.30	7.58	8.72	38.17	-2.73	15.56	6.35	-4.30	5.86	-5.31
6	15.09	6.25	8.84	28.78	-2.33	14.35	5.72	-6.75	6.35	-7.85
7	22.24	9.82	12.42	37.69	-3.73	21.50	6.86	-6.75	7.66	-7.85
8	18.35	8.11	10.24	35.80	-3.34	17.61	6.86	-5.80	7.66	-5.86
9	17.63	7.20	10.43	30.46	-8.72	17.63	6.55	-5.80	7.52	-5.86
10	26.86	11.74	15.12	37.43	-7.68	26.86	5.86	-4.21	6.73	-5.31
11	9.74	3.20	6.54	35.67	-2.32	8.51	5.86	-6.55	6.73	-5.31
12	9.94	3.09	6.85	37.89	-2.74	8.71	5.86	-8.11	7.65	-6.55
13	-0.28	-1.52	1.24	28.53	-2.98	-1.51	5.86	-8.11	6.73	-6.55
14	-6.92	-3.97	-2.95	16.15	-8.61	-8.15	7.11	-8.05	7.52	-8.11
15	0.19	0.49	-0.30	21.30	-4.01	-1.04	7.11	-8.05	7.52	-8.11
16	-7.64	-3.53	-4.11	15.65	-9.33	-8.87	7.11	-8.05	7.52	-8.11
17	4.59	3.02	1.57	27.78	-2.61	3.36	8.55	-8.05	9.05	-8.11
18	9.73	5.99	3.74	30.78	-3.31	8.50	8.55	-7.61	9.05	-8.11
19	11.21	6.77	4.44	32.26	-1.85	9.98	8.55	-7.61	9.05	-8.11
20	10.53	6.05	4.48	31.34	-3.05	9.30	8.55	-7.61	9.05	-8.11
21	19.94	10.88	9.06	31.09	-3.30	18.71	8.55	-7.61	9.05	-8.11
22	17.45	10.07	7.38	29.34	-4.17	16.22	8.55	-7.61	9.05	-8.11
23	11.04	7.67	3.37	25.81	-5.78	9.81	8.94	-6.57	9.05	-8.11
24	7.11	5.66	1.45	25.34	-5.69	5.88	8.94	-6.57	9.05	-8.11
25	4.48	4.22	0.26	22.71	-5.44	3.25	8.94	-6.57	9.05	-8.11
26	9.31	6.29	3.02	27.60	-4.75	8.08	8.94	-6.57	9.05	-8.11
27	9.05	6.56	2.49	26.27	-5.55	7.82	8.94	-6.57	9.05	-8.11
28	11.40	8.12	3.28	27.66	-6.32	10.17	8.94	-6.57	9.05	-8.11
29	15.51	9.62	5.89	33.57	-4.81	14.28	8.94	-6.57	9.05	-8.11
30	15.71	9.03	6.68	34.33	-3.43	14.48	8.94	-6.57	9.05	-8.11
31	24.51	12.94	11.57	42.05	-2.45	23.28	8.94	-6.57	9.05	-8.11
32	29.41	15.53	13.88	48.51	-2.17	28.18	8.94	-6.57	9.05	-8.11
33	22.72	12.63	10.09	41.82	-1.28	21.49	8.94	-6.57	9.05	-8.11
34	23.86	13.22	10.64	42.96	-1.24	22.63	9.71	-6.57	10.68	-8.11
35	18.19	10.41	7.78	37.29	-1.19	16.96	8.95	-6.57	10.68	-8.11
36	22.12	12.97	9.15	39.54	0.00	20.89	8.95	-6.57	10.68	-8.11
37	21.17	12.43	8.74	38.59	0.00	19.94	8.95	-6.57	10.68	-8.11
38	11.92	8.07	3.85	30.74	0.00	10.69	8.95	-6.57	10.68	-8.11
39	12.44	8.55	3.89	30.48	-0.41	11.21	8.95	-6.73	10.68	-8.11
40	15.56	10.49	5.07	30.24	-1.17	14.33	8.95	-6.73	10.68	-8.11
41	15.33	10.25	5.08	30.01	-0.92	14.10	8.95	-6.73	10.68	-8.11
42	16.82	11.46	5.36	29.94	-1.85	15.59	14.33	-6.73	14.48	-8.11
43	18.76	12.29	6.47	33.33	-1.57	17.53	14.33	-6.73	14.48	-8.11
44	19.44	12.29	7.15	34.01	-0.89	18.21	14.33	-6.73	14.48	-8.11
45	19.32	12.49	6.83	33.89	-1.41	18.09	14.33	-6.73	14.48	-8.11
46	22.66	14.75	7.91	37.03	-0.23	21.43	14.33	-6.73	14.48	-8.11
47	22.96	15.12	7.84	38.61	-0.67	21.73	8.95	-6.73	14.48	-8.11
48	28.28	18.37	9.91	43.93	-1.85	27.05	8.95	-6.73	10.68	-8.11
49	27.16	17.69	9.47	42.81	-1.61	25.93	8.95	-6.73	10.68	-8.11
50	29.27	18.71	10.56	45.69	-1.54	28.04	8.95	-6.73	10.68	-8.11

EXHIBIT V-24: (continued)

Pass	Total Equity	Short Equity	Long Equity	Max. Equity	Min. Equity	P/L	Best Trade	Worst Trade	Max. Open P/L	Min. Open P/L
51	32.19	19.84	12.35	46.35	-0.88	30.96	8.95	-6.73	10.68	-8.11
52	23.21	14.91	8.30	37.37	0.00	21.98	8.95	-6.73	10.68	-8.11
53	22.74	14.44	8.30	35.72	0.00	21.51	8.95	-6.73	10.68	-8.11
54	19.93	12.13	7.80	32.91	-0.26	18.70	8.95	-6.57	10.68	-8.11
55	19.31	12.13	7.18	32.29	-0.88	18.08	8.95	-6.57	10.68	-8.11
56	20.37	12.83	7.54	33.35	-0.54	19.14	8.67	-6.57	10.68	-8.11
57	21.51	13.54	7.97	34.21	-0.26	20.28	8.67	-6.57	10.68	-8.11
58	16.73	11.28	5.45	34.45	0.00	15.50	8.67	-6.57	10.68	-8.11
59	15.35	10.59	4.76	33.51	0.00	14.12	8.67	-6.57	10.68	-8.11
60	11.56	7.53	4.03	29.72	-1.86	10.33	8.67	-6.57	10.68	-8.11
61	11.82	7.10	4.72	27.24	-2.98	10.59	8.67	-6.57	10.68	-8.11
62	14.84	8.68	6.16	27.38	-2.84	13.61	8.67	-6.57	10.68	-8.11
63	9.40	5.76	3.64	26.91	-3.24	8.17	8.67	-6.57	10.68	-8.11
64	8.92	5.99	2.93	26.65	-2.30	7.69	8.67	-6.57	10.68	-8.11
65	7.46	5.75	1.71	27.85	-1.32	6.23	8.67	-6.57	10.68	-8.11
66	6.17	4.86	1.31	26.78	-1.81	4.94	8.67	-6.57	10.68	-8.11
67	10.29	7.15	3.14	30.12	-1.35	9.06	8.67	-6.57	10.68	-8.11
68	10.39	7.07	3.32	29.86	-1.61	9.16	8.67	-6.57	10.68	-8.11
69	9.57	6.80	2.77	30.14	-1.33	8.34	8.67	-6.57	10.68	-8.11
70	20.08	12.72	7.36	36.46	0.00	18.85	8.67	-6.57	10.68	-8.11
71	19.65	12.80	6.85	35.87	0.00	18.42	8.67	-6.57	10.68	-8.11
72	16.41	11.38	5.03	34.97	0.00	15.18	8.67	-6.57	10.68	-8.11
73	15.73	10.70	5.03	34.29	0.00	14.50	8.67	-6.57	10.68	-8.11
74	19.12	12.09	7.03	35.96	0.00	17.89	8.67	-6.57	10.68	-8.11
75	7.97	6.12	1.85	30.18	0.00	6.74	8.67	-6.57	10.68	-8.11
76	12.13	7.16	4.97	33.50	-0.21	10.90	10.60	-6.57	10.68	-8.11
77	19.60	10.22	9.38	37.14	-1.56	18.37	10.60	-6.57	10.68	-8.11
78	15.75	8.41	7.34	33.29	-1.33	14.52	10.60	-6.57	10.68	-8.11
79	18.18	10.29	7.89	35.72	0.00	16.95	10.60	-6.57	10.68	-8.11
80	19.34	9.79	9.55	35.56	-0.11	18.11	10.60	-6.57	10.68	-8.11
81	16.03	7.90	8.13	32.25	-0.58	14.80	10.60	-6.57	10.68	-8.11
82	15.27	6.64	8.63	31.49	-2.34	14.04	10.60	-6.73	10.68	-8.11
83	12.65	5.73	6.92	28.31	-1.54	11.42	10.60	-6.73	10.68	-8.11
84	18.87	8.98	9.89	33.55	-1.82	17.64	10.60	-6.73	10.68	-8.11
85	17.27	8.22	9.05	30.27	-1.74	16.04	15.29	-6.73	17.92	-8.11
86	20.46	10.38	10.08	33.46	-0.61	19.23	15.29	-6.73	17.92	-8.11
87	20.29	10.21	10.08	33.29	-0.78	19.06	15.29	-6.73	17.92	-8.11
88	19.27	9.13	10.14	32.27	-1.92	18.04	15.29	-6.73	17.92	-8.11
89	17.50	8.44	9.06	30.50	-1.53	16.27	15.29	-6.73	17.92	-8.11
90	21.33	10.68	10.65	34.33	-0.88	20.10	15.29	-6.73	17.92	-8.11
91	20.72	10.07	10.65	33.72	-1.49	19.49	15.29	-6.73	17.92	-8.11
92	20.26	9.61	10.65	33.26	-1.95	19.03	15.29	-6.73	17.92	-8.11
93	18.13	8.65	9.48	32.45	-1.74	16.90	15.29	-6.73	17.92	-8.11
94	19.87	10.39	9.48	34.19	0.00	18.64	15.29	-6.73	17.92	-8.11
95	18.70	10.39	8.31	33.02	-0.44	17.47	15.29	-6.73	17.92	-8.11
96	12.56	7.10	5.46	29.90	0.00	11.33	15.29	-6.73	17.92	-8.11
97	11.94	7.10	4.84	29.28	0.00	10.71	15.29	-6.73	17.92	-8.11
98	10.20	5.86	4.34	28.54	0.00	8.97	15.29	-6.57	17.92	-8.11
99	8.55	4.21	4.34	26.89	0.00	7.32	15.29	-6.57	17.92	-8.11
100	9.46	4.57	4.89	26.82	0.00	8.23	15.29	-6.57	17.92	-8.11

EXHIBIT V-24: (continued)

Pass	Total Equity	Short Equity	Long Equity	Max. Equity	Min. Equity	P/L	Best Trade	Worst Trade	Max. Open P/L	Min. Open P/L
101	4.07	1.23	2.84	21.43	-0.60	2.84	15.29	-6.57	17.92	-8.11
102	3.53	0.69	2.84	20.89	-1.14	2.30	15.29	-6.57	17.92	-8.11
103	3.87	1.03	2.84	21.23	-0.80	2.64	15.29	-6.57	17.92	-8.11
104	6.82	2.65	4.17	24.18	-1.09	5.59	15.29	-6.57	17.92	-8.11
105	6.05	2.67	3.38	23.41	-0.28	4.82	15.29	-6.57	17.92	-8.11
106	7.63	3.32	4.31	24.45	0.00	6.40	10.04	-6.57	12.38	-8.11
107	6.75	2.44	4.31	23.57	0.00	5.52	9.16	-6.57	11.50	-8.11
108	5.74	1.43	4.31	22.56	-0.17	4.51	8.67	-6.57	10.68	-8.11
109	3.89	-0.69	4.58	20.71	-2.56	2.66	8.67	-6.57	10.68	-8.11
110	2.73	-0.92	3.65	19.55	-1.86	1.50	8.67	-6.57	10.68	-8.11
111	2.94	-0.69	3.63	19.76	-1.61	1.71	8.67	-6.57	10.68	-8.11
112	3.65	0.02	3.63	20.47	-0.90	2.42	8.67	-6.57	10.68	-8.11
113	4.33	0.81	3.52	21.15	0.00	3.10	8.67	-6.57	10.68	-8.11
114	4.27	0.75	3.52	21.09	0.00	3.04	8.67	-6.57	10.68	-8.11
115	0.63	-1.58	2.21	17.45	-1.23	-0.60	8.67	-6.57	10.68	-8.11
116	2.78	-0.78	3.56	19.60	-1.56	1.55	8.67	-6.57	10.68	-8.11
117	4.34	0.78	3.56	21.16	0.00	3.11	8.67	-6.57	10.68	-8.11
118	3.25	0.07	3.18	20.07	0.00	2.02	15.29	-6.57	17.92	-8.11
119	2.41	-0.77	3.18	19.23	0.00	1.18	15.29	-6.57	17.92	-8.11
120	0.58	-2.47	3.05	17.66	-1.11	-0.65	15.29	-6.57	17.92	-8.11
121	-1.72	-4.50	2.78	15.36	-3.41	-2.95	15.29	-6.57	17.92	-8.11
122	-3.82	-5.94	2.12	13.26	-5.51	-5.05	15.29	-6.57	17.92	-8.11
123	-1.16	-5.18	4.02	15.92	-3.35	-2.39	15.29	-6.73	17.92	-8.11
124	-2.63	-6.65	4.02	14.45	-4.82	-3.86	15.29	-6.73	17.92	-8.11
125	-6.01	-9.69	3.68	11.75	-7.70	-7.24	15.29	-6.73	17.92	-8.11
126	-3.67	-7.35	3.68	14.09	-5.36	-4.90	15.29	-6.73	17.92	-8.11
127	-2.17	-6.66	4.49	15.59	-5.06	-3.40	15.29	-6.73	17.92	-8.11
128	-2.53	-7.40	4.87	15.23	-4.22	-3.76	15.29	-6.73	17.92	-8.11
129	-1.01	-5.88	4.87	16.75	-2.70	-2.24	15.29	-6.73	17.92	-8.11
130	-3.05	-7.92	4.87	14.71	-4.74	-4.28	15.29	-6.73	17.92	-8.11
131	-3.43	-8.30	4.87	14.33	-5.12	-4.66	15.29	-6.73	17.92	-8.11
132	-1.37	-6.82	5.45	16.39	-3.94	-2.60	15.29	-6.73	17.92	-8.11
133	-0.92	-5.79	4.87	16.84	-2.61	-2.15	15.29	-6.73	17.92	-8.11
134	-0.79	-5.66	4.87	16.97	-2.48	-2.02	15.29	-6.73	17.92	-8.11
135	-1.60	-5.99	4.39	17.12	-3.29	-2.83	15.29	-6.73	17.92	-8.11
136	-2.66	-6.75	4.09	16.66	-4.35	-3.89	15.29	-6.73	17.92	-8.11
137	0.90	-5.57	6.47	18.30	-3.71	-0.33	14.54	-6.73	19.13	-8.11
138	1.76	-4.10	5.86	19.16	-1.63	0.53	14.54	-6.73	19.13	-8.11
139	3.39	-2.47	5.86	20.79	0.00	2.16	14.54	-6.73	19.13	-8.11
140	11.50	1.90	9.60	28.90	-0.07	10.27	14.54	-6.73	19.13	-8.11
141	12.11	2.17	9.94	28.97	0.00	10.88	14.54	-6.73	19.13	-8.11
142	11.96	2.17	9.79	28.82	0.00	10.73	14.54	-6.73	19.13	-8.11
143	11.18	2.17	9.01	28.04	-0.47	9.95	14.54	-6.73	19.13	-8.11
144	10.49	2.17	8.32	27.35	-1.16	9.26	14.54	-6.73	19.13	-8.11
145	12.30	3.00	9.30	29.16	-1.01	11.07	14.54	-6.73	19.13	-8.11
146	12.83	3.00	9.83	29.69	-0.48	11.60	14.54	-6.73	19.13	-8.11
147	12.75	2.79	9.96	28.33	-0.82	11.52	14.54	-6.73	19.13	-8.11
148	12.39	2.43	9.96	27.97	-1.18	11.16	14.54	-6.73	19.13	-8.11
149	11.68	2.36	9.32	27.26	-0.61	10.45	14.54	-6.73	19.13	-8.11
150	11.21	1.89	9.32	26.79	-1.08	9.98	14.54	-6.73	19.13	-8.11

EXHIBIT V-24: (continued)

Pass	Total Equity	Short Equity	Long Equity	Max. Equity	Min. Equity	P/L	Best Trade	Worst Trade	Max. Open P/L	Min. Open P/L
151	11.12	1.89	9.23	26.70	-1.17	9.89	14.54	-6.73	19.13	-8.11
152	11.23	2.53	8.70	27.87	0.00	10.00	14.54	-6.73	19.13	-8.11
153	6.60	1.22	5.38	23.24	0.00	5.37	14.54	-6.73	19.13	-8.11
154	11.95	4.11	7.84	26.81	-0.02	10.72	14.54	-6.73	19.13	-8.11
155	12.01	4.13	7.88	26.83	0.00	10.78	14.54	-6.73	19.13	-8.11
156	10.14	3.35	6.79	26.52	0.00	10.35	14.54	-6.73	19.13	-8.11
157	9.28	3.35	5.93	25.66	0.00	9.49	14.54	-6.73	19.13	-8.11
158	4.07	0.86	3.21	23.61	0.00	4.28	15.29	-6.73	17.92	-8.11
159	-1.63	-1.64	0.01	17.03	-2.15	-1.42	15.29	-6.73	17.92	-8.11
160	-2.58	-1.64	-0.94	16.08	-3.10	-2.37	15.29	-6.73	17.92	-8.11
161	-0.99	-0.58	-0.41	16.31	-2.37	-0.78	8.67	-6.73	9.63	-8.11
162	-4.15	-1.80	-2.35	13.15	-5.53	-3.94	8.67	-6.73	9.63	-8.11
163	-4.95	-1.80	-3.15	12.35	-6.33	-4.95	8.67	-6.73	9.63	-8.11
164	-3.83	-1.72	-2.11	13.31	-5.37	-3.83	8.67	-6.73	9.63	-8.11
165	-3.82	-1.72	-2.10	13.32	-5.36	-3.82	8.67	-6.73	9.63	-8.11
166	-5.10	-1.72	-3.38	12.04	-6.64	-5.10	8.67	-6.73	9.63	-8.11
167	-5.46	-1.72	-3.74	11.68	-7.00	-5.46	8.67	-6.73	9.63	-8.11
168	-7.82	-2.47	-5.35	10.06	-8.34	-7.82	15.29	-6.73	17.92	-8.11
169	-7.32	-2.47	-4.85	10.56	-7.84	-7.32	15.29	-6.73	17.92	-8.11
170	-4.47	-0.85	-3.62	11.75	-6.17	-4.47	15.29	-6.73	17.92	-8.11
171	-5.22	-0.85	-4.37	11.00	-6.92	-5.22	15.29	-6.73	17.92	-8.11
172	-7.53	-1.64	-5.89	8.69	-9.23	-7.53	15.29	-6.73	17.92	-8.11
173	-7.79	-1.64	-6.15	8.43	-9.49	-7.79	15.29	-6.73	17.92	-8.11
174	-7.74	-1.64	-6.10	8.48	-9.44	-7.74	15.29	-6.73	17.92	-8.11
175	-5.68	-0.91	-4.77	9.08	-8.84	-5.68	15.29	-6.73	17.92	-8.11
176	-5.36	-0.91	-4.45	9.40	-8.52	-5.36	15.29	-6.73	17.92	-8.11
177	-4.60	-0.91	-3.69	10.16	-7.76	-4.60	15.29	-6.73	17.92	-8.11
178	-3.93	-0.91	-3.02	10.83	-7.09	-3.93	15.29	-6.73	17.92	-8.11
179	-4.96	-0.91	-4.05	9.80	-8.12	-4.96	15.29	-6.73	17.92	-8.11
180	-5.21	-1.11	-4.10	9.55	-8.37	-5.21	15.29	-6.73	17.92	-8.11
181	-4.04	-1.11	-2.93	10.72	-7.20	-4.04	15.29	-6.73	17.92	-8.11
182	-2.03	-0.37	-1.66	11.25	-6.67	-2.77	15.29	-6.73	17.92	-8.11
183	-3.11	-0.37	-2.74	10.17	-7.75	-3.85	15.29	-6.73	17.92	-8.11
184	0.95	1.95	-1.00	14.69	-3.59	0.21	15.29	-6.73	17.92	-8.11
185	1.74	1.95	-0.21	15.48	-2.80	1.00	15.29	-6.73	17.92	-8.11
186	-3.31	-0.65	-2.66	10.43	-7.49	-4.05	15.29	-6.73	17.92	-8.11
187	-5.84	-2.92	-2.92	8.42	-9.50	-6.58	15.29	-6.73	17.92	-8.11
188	-6.58	-3.66	-2.92	7.68	-10.24	-7.32	15.29	-6.73	17.92	-8.11
189	3.03	1.55	1.48	15.15	-5.61	2.29	14.54	-6.73	19.13	-8.11
190	4.53	3.05	1.48	16.65	-4.11	3.79	14.54	-6.73	19.13	-8.11
191	3.39	3.05	0.34	15.51	-5.25	2.65	14.54	-6.73	19.13	-8.11
192	3.25	3.05	0.20	15.37	-5.39	2.51	14.54	-6.73	19.13	-8.11
193	2.13	2.44	-0.31	14.25	-5.49	1.39	14.54	-6.73	19.13	-8.11
194	2.45	2.44	0.01	14.57	-5.17	1.71	14.54	-6.73	19.13	-8.11
195	1.47	1.46	0.01	13.59	-6.15	0.73	14.54	-6.73	19.13	-8.11
196	2.17	2.01	0.16	13.99	-5.75	1.43	14.54	-6.73	19.13	-8.11
197	2.45	2.29	0.16	14.27	-5.47	1.71	14.54	-6.73	19.13	-8.11
198	3.33	2.29	1.04	15.15	-4.59	2.59	14.54	-6.73	19.13	-8.11
199	2.09	1.05	1.04	13.91	-5.83	1.35	14.54	-6.73	19.13	-8.11
200	2.84	1.05	1.79	14.66	-5.08	2.10	14.54	-6.73	19.13	-8.11

EXHIBIT V-24: (continued)

Pass	Total Equity	Short Equity	Long Equity	Max. Equity	Min. Equity	P/L	Best Trade	Worst Trade	Max. Open P/L	Min. Open P/L
201	2.93	1.14	1.79	14.75	-4.99	2.19	14.54	-6.73	19.13	-8.11
202	4.24	1.14	3.10	16.06	-3.68	3.50	14.54	-6.73	19.13	-8.11
203	-1.62	-1.98	0.36	13.86	-4.35	-2.36	15.29	-6.73	17.92	-8.11
204	-1.52	-1.88	0.36	13.96	-4.25	-2.26	15.29	-6.73	17.92	-8.11
205	2.18	1.44	0.74	17.66	-1.02	1.44	8.67	-6.73	9.63	-8.11
206	1.70	1.44	0.26	17.18	-1.50	0.96	8.67	-6.73	9.63	-8.11
207	0.37	1.44	-1.07	15.85	-2.83	-0.37	8.67	-6.73	9.63	-8.11
208	0.07	1.44	-1.37	15.55	-3.13	-0.67	8.67	-6.73	9.63	-8.11

Pass indicates period length.
Equity indicates the total number of points gained or lost.
Short equity indicates the number of points gained or lost on short positions.
Long equity indicates the number of points gained or lost on long positions.
Max. equity indicates the highest total profit recorded over the tested period.
Min. equity indicates the lowest total profit recorded over the tested period.
P/L indicates total number of points gained or lost in closed positions.
Best trade indicates the highest number of points gained in any closed trade.
Worst trade indicates the highest number of points lost in any closed trade.
Max. open P/L indicates the highest gain in a position which remains open at the end of the test run.
Min. open P/L indicates the highest gain in a position which remains open at the end of the test run.

average crossover rule, as shown in Exhibits V-29 and V-34 (pages 540 and 543). Stated another way, the 1/105 percentage differential oscillator gave the best results. Note, however, that although the distribution of profitability over the smoothing periods takes on the reassuring non-random appearance of a bell-shaped curve for the more recent 1977–1986 period, as shown in Exhibits V-21 and V-22 (pages 527 and 528), the similar distribution for the earlier 9.75-year period of 1968–1977 appears much more erratic and much less profitable, as shown in Exhibits V-23 and V-24 (pages 532 and 533). Moreover, the distributions for the two 9.75-year periods do not match well in their high profit zones. This suggests some question as to future reliability of the 1/105 week optimized parameters for this volume oscillator.

EXHIBIT V-25:

New York Stock Exchange Composite Price Index Weekly High and Low from April 8, 1977 to December 31, 1986

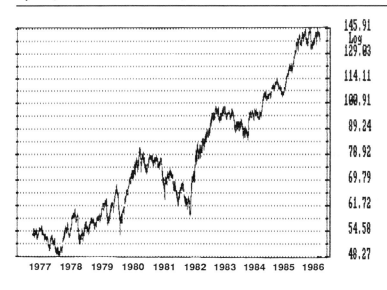

EXHIBIT V-26:

105-Week Simple Moving Average of Volume (solid line), Total Weekly New York Stock Exchange Composite Index Volume (dashes), 1977 to 1986

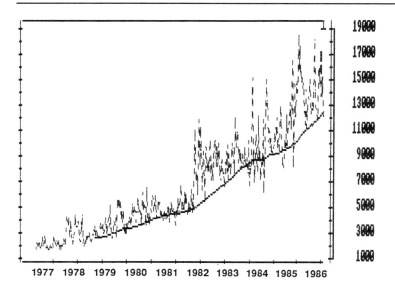

EXHIBIT V-27:

Volume Oscillator, 1/105 Week Simple Moving Average Percentage Differential, 1977 to 1986

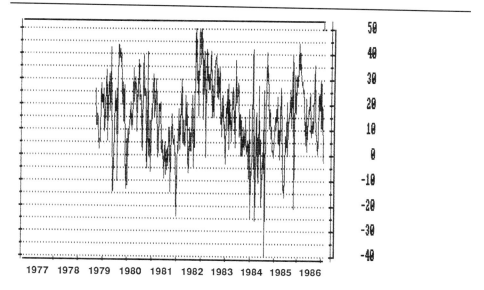

EXHIBIT V-28:

Total Equity for Volume Oscillator, 1/105 Weeks, 1977 to 1986

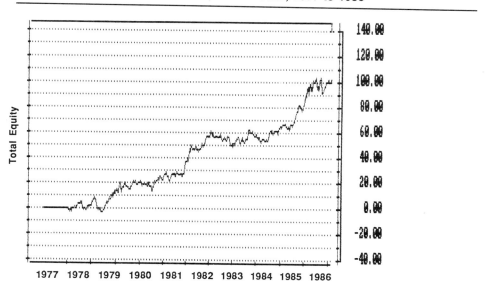

EXHIBIT V-29:

Profit Summary for Volume Oscillator, 1/105 Weeks Percentage Differential, 1977 to 1986

Item	Long	Short	Net
Per Trade Ranges	— Per Trade Ranges —		
Best Trade (Closed position yielding maximum P/L)	21.34	3.70	21.34
.. Date	821231	820115	821231
Worst Trade (Closed position yielding minimum P/L)	-4.87	-2.64	-4.87
.. Date	840330	830107	840330
Max Open P/L (Maximum P/L occurring in an open position)	23.82	3.16	23.82
.. Date	860829	840615	860829
Min Open P/L (Minimum P/L occurring in an open position)	-7.60	-1.40	-7.60
.. Date	840309	841123	840309
Overall Ranges	— Overall Ranges —		
Max P/L (Maximum P/L from all closed positions during the run)	100.00	80.36	100.00
.. Date	861226	860103	861226
Min P/L (Minimum P/L from all closed positions during the run)	-1.97	-2.29	-2.29
.. Date	800502	800425	800425
Max Equity (Maximum P/L from all closed and open positions)	104.18	102.56	104.18
.. Date	860829	861231	860829
Min Equity (Minimum P/L from all closed and open positions)	-2.56	-2.29	-2.56
.. Date	790511	800425	790511
Statistics	— Statistics —		
Periods (The number of periods in each position and entire run)	451	58	509
Trades (The number of trades in each position and entire run)	32	31	63
# Profitable (The number of profitable trades...)	16	16	32
# Losing (The number of unprofitable trades...)	16	15	31
% Profitable (The percent of profitable trades to total trades)	50.00	51.61	50.79
% Losing (The percent of unprofitable trades to total trades)	50.00	48.39	49.21
Results	— Results —		
Commission (Total commission deducted from closed trades)	0.00	0.00	0.00
Slippage (Total slippage deducted from closed trades)	0.00	0.00	0.00
Gross P/L (Total points gained in closed positions)	91.55	8.45	100.00
Open P/L (P/L in a position which remains open at the end)	0.00	2.56	2.56
P/L (Net P/L: Gross P/L less Commission and Slippage)	91.55	8.45	100.00
Equity (Net P/L plus Open P/L at the end of the run)	91.55	11.01	102.56

There are columns for Long trades, Short trades and Net. In the Long column, results are reported only for Long positions. In the Short column, results are reported for Short positions only. In the Net column for the "Per Trade Ranges" and "Overall Ranges," entries will be the extreme from either the Long or Short column. Net column entries for the "Statistics" and "Results" categories are the combined results of entries in the Long and Short columns.

EXHIBIT V-30:

New York Stock Exchange Composite Price Index Weekly High and Low from January 5, 1968 to September 30, 1977

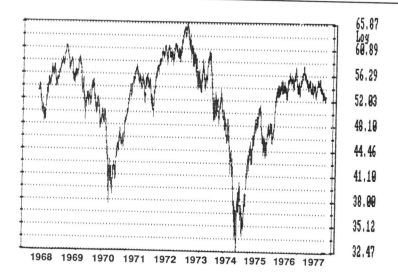

65.87	
Log	
60.89	
56.29	
52.03	
48.10	
44.46	
41.10	
38.00	
35.12	
32.47	

1968 1969 1970 1971 1972 1973 1974 1975 1976 1977

EXHIBIT V-31:

105-Week Simple Moving Average of Volume (solid line), Total Weekly New York Stock Exchange Composite Index Volume (dashes), 1968 to 1977

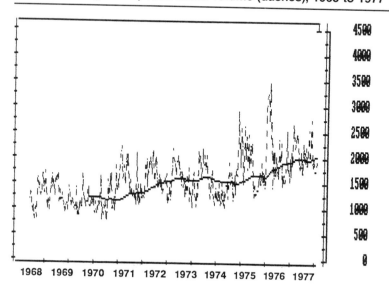

4500
4000
3500
3000
2500
2000
1500
1000
500
0

1968 1969 1970 1971 1972 1973 1974 1975 1976 1977

EXHIBIT V-32:
Volume Oscillator, 1/105 Weeks Percentage Differential, 1968 to 1977

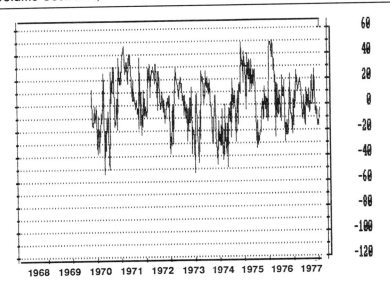

EXHIBIT V-33:
Total Equity for Volume Oscillator, 1/105 Weeks Percentage Differential Oscillator, 1968 to 1977

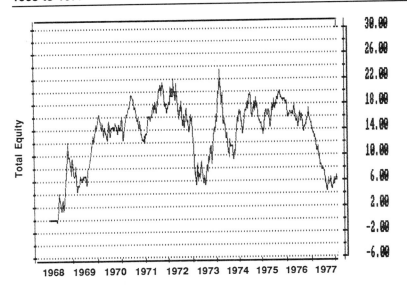

EXHIBIT V-34:

Profit Summary for Volume Oscillator, 1/105 Weeks Percentage Differential, 1968 to 1977

Item		Long	Short	Net
		— Per Trade Ranges —		
Per Trade Ranges				
Best Trade	(Closed position yielding maximum P/L)	8.54	15.29	15.29
.. Date		710702	740920	740920
Worst Trade	(Closed position yielding minimum P/L)	-6.57	-3.94	-6.57
.. Date		740118	700828	740118
Max Open P/L	(Maximum P/L occurring in an open position)	10.68	17.92	17.92
.. Date		710423	740913	740913
Min Open P/L	(Minimum P/L occurring in an open position)	-8.11	-2.31	-8.11
.. Date		731214	700821	731214
Overall Ranges		— Overall Ranges —		
Max P/L	(Maximum P/L from all closed positions during the run)	19.93	20.78	20.78
.. Date		760416	740920	740920
Min P/L	(Minimum P/L from all closed positions during the run)	-0.28	4.58	-0.28
.. Date		700109	700828	700109
Max Equity	(Maximum P/L from all closed and open positions)	21.41	23.41	23.41
.. Date		730105	740913	740913
Min Equity	(Minimum P/L from all closed and open positions)	-0.28	-0.28	-0.28
.. Date		700109	700109	700109
Statistics		— Statistics —		
Periods	(The number of periods in each position and entire run)	317	192	509
Trades	(The number of trades in each position and entire run)	47	46	93
# Profitable	(The number of profitable trades...)	18	19	37
# Losing	(The number of unprofitable trades...)	29	27	56
% Profitable	(The percent of profitable trades to total trades)	38.30	41.30	39.78
% Losing	(The percent of unprofitable trades to total trades)	61.70	58.70	60.22
Results		— Results —		
Commission	(Total commission deducted from closed trades)	0.00	0.00	0.00
Slippage	(Total slippage deducted from closed trades)	0.00	0.00	0.00
Gross P/L	(Total points gained in closed positions)	3.38	1.44	4.82
Open P/L	(P/L in a position which remains open at the end)	0.00	1.23	1.23
P/L	(Net P/L: Gross P/L less Commission and Slippage)	3.38	1.44	4.82
Equity	(Net P/L plus Open P/L at the end of the run)	3.38	2.67	6.05

There are columns for Long trades, Short trades and Net. In the Long column, results are reported only for Long positions. In the Short column, results are reported for Short positions only. In the Net column for the "Per Trade Ranges" and "Overall Ranges," entries will be the extreme from either the Long or Short column. Net column entries for the "Statistics" and "Results" categories are the combined results of entries in the Long and Short columns.

VOLUME PRICE TREND

Volume Price Trend (VPT) is a volume-weighted price momentum indicator. According to Steven L. Kille, in his *Back Trak Software Manual* (Micro Vest, P.O. Box 272, Macomb, IL 61455), the Volume Price Trend formula is represented as:

$$VPT = \sum_{i=1}^{n} (C_i - C_p) * V$$

where

C$_i$ is the close for the time period.
C$_p$ is the previous period's close.
V is the volume for the period.

For example, if a period's price change is a decline of 4 points and the volume is 200, the period's VPT is -800. Summing over the past *n*-periods creates a moving total and a price times volume momentum indicator. If the *n*-period moving total is positive, buy long. When the *n*-period moving total is negative, sell long positions and sell short.

We tested this indicator using Back Trak software and a 19-year test period of weekly data (consisting of high, low, close, and volume for each week) for the broad-based NYSE Composite Index. The period ran from January 5, 1968 through December 31, 1986.

The time length, *n*, of the Volume Price Trend indicator is the only parameter to be optimized. We tested weekly periods from 1 to 120 weeks

EXHIBIT V-35:
Volume Price Trend Moving Total: 51 Weeks, 1968 to 1986

Number Of Trades Made	> 35	Commissions Paid	> 0
Number Of Weeks In Market	> 939	Frequency Of Trades	> 1.00
Number Of Winning Trades	> 16	Largest Winning Trade	> 4791
Total Of Winning Trades	> 14492	Average Winning Trade	> 905
Number Of Losing Trades	> 19	Largest Losing Trade	> −442
Total Of Losing Trades	> −2852	Average Losing Trade	> −150
Largest Winning Streak	> 4	Largest Losing Streak	> 4
Win/Loss Ratio	> 0.84	Profit/Margin Ratio	> 5.82
Number Of Stops Hit	> 0	Stops Frequency	> 0.00
Largest Drawdown	> −1597	Largest Unrealized Loss	> −449
Largest Obtained Equity	> 12058	Number Of Tradeable Weeks	> 939
Short Profit Or Loss	> 1734	Long Profit Or Loss	> 9906
Total Profit Or Loss	> 11640	Average Weekly Gain/Loss	> 12.40

and found 51 weeks produced the highest total profit of 116.40 NYSE points, as shown in Exhibit V-35. This profit was above our 40-week simple moving average crossover rule standard of comparison.

VOLUME REVERSAL

The Volume Reversal technique was implemented and refined by Mark Lei-bovit, editor of *The Volume Reversal Survey* market newsletter (P.O. Box 1546, Chicago, IL 60690).* It is based on the concept that volume precedes price and, therefore, changes in the trend of prices often can be signaled by the expansion and contraction of volume. The Volume Reversal technique can be used to project stock, commodity, or index future prices.

In order to understand the Volume Reversal technique, you first must understand the following definitions:

Rally Day   A day when the intra-day high is higher than the previous day's high and the intra-day low is the same or higher than the previous day's low.

Reaction Day   A day when the intra-day low is lower than the previous day's low and the intra-day high is the same or lower than the previous day's high.

Inside Day   A day when the intra-day high is the same or lower than the previous day's high and the intra-day low is the same or higher than the previous day's low.

Outside Day   A day when the intra-day high is higher than the previous day's high and the intra-day low is lower than the previous day's low.

A Volume Reversal occurs when a change from a rally day to a reaction day, or vice versa, is accompanied by an increase in volume. Thus, if volume increases and the criteria for a reaction day are met, it is considered a negative Volume Reversal and time to sell. If, on the other hand, volume increases and the criteria for a rally day are met, it is considered a positive Volume Reversal and time to buy. Inside and outside days are ignored in the Volume Reversal technique.

Volume Reversal is a registered trademark of Almarco Trading Corporation, the publisher of Mark Leibovit's *The Volume Reversal Survey*, a semi-monthly market newsletter focusing on volume trends. A 32-page booklet, *Using the Volume Reversal Survey in Market Analysis*, is available for a fee from Almarco Trading Corporation, P.O. Box 1546, Chicago, IL 60690.

Let's look at two examples, one illustrating a negative Volume Reversal and one showing a positive Volume Reversal.

Note that January 9 was a rally day (higher high and higher low) followed by an outside day (higher high and lower low) on January 10. On January 11, a reaction day (lower high and lower low) occurred accompanied by an increase in volume signaling a negative Volume Reversal and time to sell.

Example 1
Dow Jones Industrial Average January 6–11, 1984

1984		High	Low	Close	Dow 30 Industrial Volume
Jan	6	1293.66	1271.78	1286.75	15,403
	9	1295.32	1275.85	1286.22	15,076
	10	1295.44	1273.97	1278.48	12,479
	11	1284.13	1267.59	1277.32	17,253

In Example 2, a positive Volume Reversal signaled that it was time to buy. February 23 was a reaction day (lower high and lower low) immediately followed on February 24 by a rally day (higher high and higher low) accompanied by greater volume.

Example 2
Dow Jones Industrial Average February 22–24, 1984

1984		High	Low	Close	Dow 30 Industrial Volume
Feb	22	1145.83	1128.66	1134.21	8,925
	23	1142.38	1114.95	1134.63	9,042
	24	1167.09	1137.04	1165.10	10,005

One final point: The closing price is not used in the Volume Reversal technique. The technique assumes that the range between the low and the high of a day gives a better indication of what actually is happening than the price at the end of the day.

VOLUME UP DAYS/DOWN DAYS

The Volume Up Days/Down Days indicator was developed by Arthur Merrill (Merrill Analysis, Inc., Box 228, Chappaqua, NY 10514).* It is calculated by dividing the total volume on the last 5 trading days the stock market rose by the total volume on the last 5 trading days the stock market declined.

For example, assume the following situation:

Day	Volume (Millions of Shares)	Stock Market Up or Down
1	183	Up
2	165	Down
3	177	Down
4	242	Up
5	234	Up
6	212	Down
7	195	Up
8	152	Down
9	145	Down
10	163	Down
11	159	Down
12	180	Up

The indicator is calculated as follows:

$$\text{Volume Up Days/Down Days} = \frac{(183 + 242 + 234 + 195 + 180)}{(212 + 152 + 145 + 163 + 159)} = 1.24$$

(bullish)

According to Merrill's research, readings above 1.05 are considered bullish, whereas readings below 0.95 are viewed as bearish.

---

*Reprinted with permission.

WALL $TREET WEEK TECHNICAL MARKET INDEX

The *Wall $treet Week (W$W)* Technical Market Index is one of the most widely followed technical market indicators. It is a consensus index of 10 different stock market indicators created by Robert J. Nurock, President/Market Strategist of Investor's Analysis, Inc. (P.O. Box 988, Paoli, PA 19301) and a regular panelist on *Wall $treet Week* with Louis Rukeyser since its inception in 1970.*

Introduced to the *Wall $treet Week* audience on October 6, 1972, the *W$W* Index is updated weekly. It is composed entirely of 10 technical indicators, so it ignores fundamental data on the economy, corporate earnings, and dividends. These 10 indicators are compiled into one number to facilitate the perception of changes in investor psychology, market action, speculation, and monetary conditions that are usually present at key market turning points. The Index attempts to identify intermediate to long-term market moves (3–6 months or longer), rather than short-term swings. It is of value in confirming the continuation of a current trend (when the majority of its components are neutral) and in providing early warning of a change in a prevailing trend (when five or more of its components are positive or negative).

PERFORMANCE RECORD

The *W$W* Index's ability to forecast the Dow Jones Industrial Average (DJIA) was statistically tested by Arthur Merrill (Merrill Analysis, Inc., Box 228, Chappaqua, NY 10514). Merrill examined all index readings of +5 or greater to determine whether or not the Dow Jones Industrial Average (DJIA) was higher 1, 5, 13, 26 and 52 weeks later. He also checked whether or not the DJIA was lower over the same time frames after the *W$W* Index rendered sell warnings at net index readings of −5 or lower.

For the 12 1/4-year period from October 18, 1974 (the date of *W$W* Index's first revision) through December 31, 1986, the *W$W* Index correctly forecasted the DJIA 58.5% of the time 1 week in advance; 62.6% of the time 5 weeks in advance; 70.4% of the time 13 weeks in advance; 79.5% of the time 26 weeks in advance; and 81.6% of the time 52 weeks in advance. All are highly significant statistical readings. Over the most recent 5-year period, from January 1, 1982 through December 31, 1986, the comparable

---

*Reprinted with permission.

percentages of correct readings were: 1 week, 60.6%; 5 weeks, 64.4%; 13 weeks, 74.0%; 26 weeks, 88.5%; and 52 weeks, 79.2%. Once again, these readings were highly significant in a statistical sense.

HOW THE INDEX IS CONSTRUCTED

In computing the *W$W* Index, Nurock monitors 10 well-known technical indicators (summarized in Exhibit W-1, page 550). They are:

1. Dow Jones Momentum Ratio—This indicator measures the percentage difference between the DJIA and its 30-day simple moving average. It is calculated by adding up the closing DJIA for the past 30 days, dividing that total by 30 to obtain an average, and then dividing the DJIA's latest close by its most recent 30-day average. This indicator flashes overbought/oversold warnings when the DJIA deviates more than 3% from its 30-day average.

2. NYSE Hi-Lo Index—This indicator compares the total number of stocks attaining new highs versus the number dropping to new lows over the past 10 trading days. Ten-day moving totals of both new highs and new lows are computed and compared. At significant market bottoms, few new highs are attained. At market tops, few new lows are registered. A reversal from either extreme confirms a change in market direction.

3. Market Breadth Indicator—This indicator is a moving total of the net difference between advances and declines over the past 10 trading days. It measures the underlying strength of market moves by indicating whether or not the majority of stocks are moving in the same direction as the market averages, confirming market strength or weakness.

4. Arms' Short-Term Trading Index—This indicator is a 10-day moving average of the ratio of volume going into advancing stocks versus the volume going into declining stocks on the New York Stock Exchange. It is computed by dividing the number of issues advancing by the number of issues declining and dividing the resulting quotient by the ratio of the volume of advancing stocks to the volume of declining stocks. Next, calculate a 10-day moving average. Readings above 1.20 are positive; readings below .80 are negative. These indicate extreme peaks in pessimism and enthusiasm on a short-term basis.

5. Prices of NYSE Stocks Versus Their Moving Averages—This data, compiled by Investor's Intelligence (30 Church Street, New Rochelle, NY 10801), is considered positive when less than 30% of NYSE stocks are trading above their own 10-week moving averages and less than 40% of NYSE stocks are trading above their own 30-week moving averages. It is negative when

EXHIBIT W-1:
Summary of Wall Street Week Technical Market Index Components

WALL $TREET WEEK TECHNICAL MARKET INDEX

INDICATOR	INTERMEDIATE BOTTOM INDICATION (Positive Reading)	INTERMEDIATE TOP INDICATION (Negative Reading)
1. DOW JONES MOMENTUM RATIO (DJIA vs. 30 day moving average)	DJIA more than 3% below its moving average	DJIA more than 3% above its moving average
2. NYSE HI-LOW INDEX (10 day total of new highs compared to 10 day total of new lows)	An expansion of the 10 day average of new highs from less than 10 until it exceeds the average number of new lows is positive.	An expansion of the 10 day average of new lows from less than 10 until it exceeds the average number of new highs is negative.
3. MARKET BREADTH INDICATOR (10 day moving total of net advances or declines)	An expansion of this index from below +1000 to the point where it peaks out and declines 1000 points from this peak is positive. Readings between +1000 and -1000 are neutral.	A contraction of this index from above -1000 to the point where it bottoms out and rises 1000 points from this trough is negative. Readings between -1000 and +1000 are neutral.
4. ARMS (TRADING) INDEX (10 day moving average of volume in advancing stocks/volume in declining stocks)	10 day average above 1.20	10 day average below 0.80
5. % OVER MOVING AVERAGES (percent NYSE stocks selling above their 10 and 30 week moving averages)	A 10 week reading below 30% and a 30 week reading below 40%	A 10 week reading above 70% and a 30 week reading above 60%
6. PREMIUM RATIO ON OPTIONS (Weekly average premium puts/calls)	Ratio above 95.5%	Ratio below 42.0%
7. ADVISORY SERVICE SENTIMENT (percent services bearish plus 1/2 those looking for correction)	Above 51.5%	Below 35.3%
8. LOW-PRICED ACTIVITY RATIO (Weekly ratio of volume in Barron's Low-Priced Stock Index to Volume in DJIA stocks)	Below 2.82%	Above 7.59%
9. INSIDER ACTIVITY RATIO (Weekly ratio of insider sell transactions/buy transactions)	Below 1.42	Above 3.61
10. FED POLICY (Weekly ratio of Fed Funds rate/Discount rate)	Below 103%	Above 125%

Exact criteria will be updated annually to reflect most recent five years' actual experience.

Source: By Permission of Investor's Analysis, Inc.

more than 70% of NYSE stocks are above their own 10-week averages and more than 60% are above their own 30-week moving averages. Thus, this indicator warns of overbought and oversold extremes.

6. Premium Ratio on Options—This indicator divides the average premium on all listed put options by the average premium on all listed call options on a weekly basis. The raw data is from the Options Clearing Corporation (142 W. Jackson Blvd., Chicago, IL 60604). When the premium ratio is above 95.5%, it indicates investors are overly pessimistic and bidding put prices up excessively, which is positive. When the ratio is below 42%, it indicates investors are overly optimistic and bidding call prices up excessively, which is negative.

7. Advisory Service Sentiment—This indicator categorizes the forecasts of about 100 stock market newsletters as bullish, bearish, or expecting a market correction. The data is compiled by Investor's Intelligence. In the aggregate, advisory service sentiment tends to follow the market's trend rather than anticipate a change in it. Therefore, when sentiment as measured by this indicator becomes distinctly one-sided, a contrary move in the market may be anticipated. When the percentage of bears plus half of the percentage expecting a correction rises above 51.5%, it is positive. When the same calculation results in a reading below 35.5%, it is negative.

8. Low-Priced Activity Ratio—This indicator relates the level of trading volume in more speculative low-priced stocks to volume in the blue chip Dow Jones Industrials. The data is available weekly on the Market Laboratory page in *Barron's*. Speculative trading activity is usually high (7.59%) at market tops and low (below 2.82%) at market bottoms.

9. Insider Activity Ratio—This indicator is a ratio of insider sell transactions relative to buy transactions on a weekly basis, as computed by Vickers Stock Research Corporation (Box 59, Brookside, NJ 07926). A ratio of more than 3.61 sellers to buyers indicates that key corporate insiders believe their stocks are overvalued and that a downward price reaction is likely. A ratio below 1.42 implies that insiders believe their stocks are undervalued and that an upward move is likely. Insiders are usually right.

10. Fed Policy—This indicator provides a guide to the direction of Federal Reserve Board policy, as reflected by the level of the Federal Funds rate relative to the Discount rate. It is compiled by taking the ratio of the closing bid price for Fed Funds to the Discount rate on a daily basis, and computing a 4-day average of the ratios for Friday, Monday, Tuesday, and Thursday each week. Wednesday readings are omitted as they are unusually volatile due to end of the bank week transactions when individual banks even up reserve positions. It is negative above 125%, since a high Fed Funds rate relative to the Discount rate signifies that money is "tight" and borrowing is being discouraged. The effect of this is to slow down the growth of business and choke the stock market. It is positive below 103%, since a low Fed Funds rate relative to the Discount rate indicates that money is "easy" and borrowing is being encouraged. Under such conditions the expansion of business is encouraged and the stock market gets a lift.

HOW THE INDEX IS CALCULATED

The *W$W* Index is based on an evaluation of weekly trends in the foregoing 10 indicators in accordance with the criteria outlined in Exhibit W-2. It is calculated every Friday using readings of the most current data available at the market's close the previous Thursday.

- When an indicator reaches an extreme usually registered at market bottoms, it is assigned a plus (+).
- When an indicator reaches an extreme usually registered at market tops, it is assigned a minus (−).
- Indicator readings between extremes are designated neutral (0).
- The first time an indicator moves directly from one extreme to another (from positive to negative, or vice versa), it is assigned a neutral (0) reading that is maintained until a plus or minus reading is reached again.

Once this evaluation is completed, the net total of the number of positive (+) and negative (−) indicators is the *W$W* Index reading for the week.

HOW THE INDEX IS INTERPRETED

The Technical Market Index readings are interpreted as follows:

+ 5 or higher	Extremely bullish. Buy now.
+ 4	Strongly bullish. Get ready to buy.
+ 3	Bullish
+ 2	Mildly bullish
+ 1	Neutral
0	Neutral
− 1	Neutral

EXHIBIT W-2:

Wall $treet Week Technical Market Index Versus The New York Stock Exchange Composite Index (posted through May 8, 1987)

WALL $TREET WEEK TECHNICAL MARKET INDEX vs. NYSE COMPOSITE INDEX
(posted through May 8, 1987)

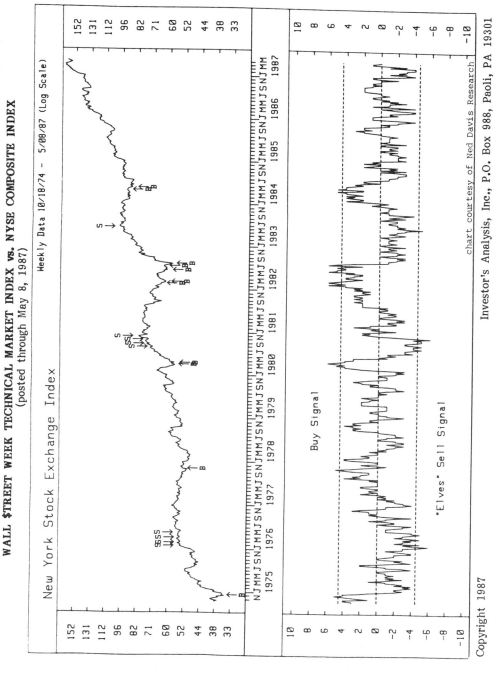

Weekly Data 10/18/74 — 5/08/87 (Log Scale)

Copyright 1987

Investor's Analysis, Inc., P.O. Box 988, Paoli, PA 19301

chart courtesy of Ned Davis Research

Source: By Permission of Investor's Analysis, Inc. and Ned Davis Research, Inc.

-2	Mildly bearish
-3	Bearish
-4	Strongly bearish. Get ready to sell.
-5 or lower	Extremely bearish. Sell now.

As an example, the Index reading for August 27, 1982, was:

4 indicators positive	=	$+4$
5 indicators neutral	=	0
1 indicator negative	=	-1
Index Reading:		$+3$
Interpretation		Bullish

WEIGHTED MOVING AVERAGE: MOVING POSITION WEIGHTED ARITHMETIC MEAN

Mathematically, a single-weighted arithmetic mean formula is represented as:

$$W_k = \frac{\sum\limits_{i=1}^{n} iC_{k-n+i}}{\sum\limits_{i=1}^{n} i} = \frac{1C_{k-n+1} + 2C_{k-n+2} + 3C_{k-n+3} + \ldots + nC_k}{1 + 2 + 3 + \ldots + n}$$

where

W_k is the weighted arithmetic mean at period k.

C_i is the closing price for period i.

n is the total number of periods to be included in the weighted mean calculation.

k is the number of the position of the period being studied within the total number of periods in the database (see example, page 555).

W simply weights each data point in the average by its position. The first data point is multiplied by 1, the second data point is multiplied by 2, the third data point is multiplied by 3. . .and the n data pont is multiplied by

Three Examples of Front-Weighted Moving Average Over Four Periods

Number of the Position = K	Year End	Price of NYSE Close	Times Weight	Price Times Weight	Four Period Totals of Price Times Weight	Divide by Four Period Total Weights 1+2+3+4=10	Current Front-Weighted Moving Average
1	1968	58.90	× 1 =	58.90			
2	1969	51.53	× 2 =	103.06			
3	1970	50.23	× 3 =	150.69			
4	1971	56.43	× 4 =	225.72	538.37	÷ 10 =	53.84
5	1972	64.48	blank	538.37 total			57.92
6	1973	51.82	blank				56.38
7	1974	36.13	blank				48.54
8	1975	47.64	blank				46.71
9	1976	57.88	blank				49.85
10	1977	52.50	× 1 =	52.50			51.50
11	1978	53.62	× 2 =	107.24			53.54
12	1979	61.95	× 3 =	185.85			57.15
13	1980	77.86	× 4 =	311.44	657.03	÷ 10 =	65.70
14	1981	71.11	blank	657.03 total			69.55
15	1982	81.03	blank				75.51
16	1983	95.18	× 1 =	95.18			84.39
17	1984	96.38	× 2 =	192.76			90.42
18	1985	121.58	× 3 =	364.74			104.69
19	1986	138.58	× 4 =	554.32	1207.00	÷ 10 =	120.70
				1207.00 total			

n. Then the sum of these products is divided by the sum of $1 + 2 + 3 + \ldots + n$. A mathematical shortcut to arrive at this divisor is represented as:

$$\sum_{i=1}^{n} i = .5 * n * (n + 1) = 1 + 2 + 3 + \ldots + n$$

We tested the weighted moving average using Compu Trac software and two 9.75-year test periods of weekly data (consisting of high, low, close, and volume for each week) for the broad-based NYSE Composite Index. The first period ran from January 5, 1968 through September 30, 1977, and the second period ran from April 8, 1977 through December 31, 1986. The overlap in

EXHIBIT W-3:
Profitability Chart for Weighted Moving Average Period Lengths of 1 to 75 Weeks
from 1977 to 1986

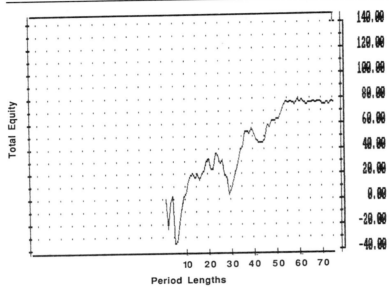

data was necessary to facilitate testing of various moving averages throughout the full time period.

When the weekly closing price crossed above its own n-period weighted moving average, we interpreted it as a signal that the trend had turned up, so we bought the NYSE. We held a long position until the NYSE weekly closing price crossed below its own n-period weighted moving average, then we sold our long position and also sold short. Exhibits W-3 to W-6 (pages 556–561) show our trial runs for n equal to 1 through 75. "Equity" is cumulative profits. Note that for both 9.75-year periods, profit was high and consistent for weighted moving average period lengths greater than 54 weeks. This increases our confidence in the stability and reliability of this indicator. For period lengths from 9 through 53 weeks, results were profitable but relatively erratic.

Exhibits W-7 and W-11 (pages 562 and 565) show the raw NYSE price data with the combined optimal 69-week weighted moving average. Exhibits W-8 and W-12 (pages 562 and 565) show the ratio oscillator of raw NYSE price divided by the 69-week weighted moving average. Thus, the latter shows the price/weighted moving average crossovers as a price velocity (or

EXHIBIT W-4:

Profit Table for Weighted Moving Average Period Lengths of 1 to 75 Weeks from 1977 to 1986

Pass	Total Equity	Short Equity	Long Equity	Max. Equity	Min. Equity	P/L	Best Trade	Worst Trade	Max. Open P/L	Min. Open P/L
1	0.00	0.00	0.00	0.00	0.00	0.00	N/A	N/A	0.00	0.00
2	-23.20	-53.42	27.66	0.00	-41.20	-23.20	14.67	-5.79	15.36	0.00
3	-2.95	-43.92	40.97	6.33	-34.33	-5.90	14.67	-4.99	15.56	0.00
4	2.90	-41.01	43.91	18.39	-22.06	-0.05	12.87	-4.99	15.56	-1.13
5	-34.55	-59.41	24.86	15.18	-44.22	-37.50	12.87	-9.41	15.56	-1.73
6	-33.13	-58.79	25.66	20.04	-41.91	-36.08	12.26	-9.41	15.56	-1.73
7	-18.50	-51.34	32.84	27.01	-29.26	-21.45	14.67	-9.41	17.18	-2.00
8	-6.08	-45.99	39.91	31.71	-13.28	-9.03	13.49	-9.41	17.18	-2.00
9	2.48	-41.37	43.85	37.53	-4.72	-0.47	14.06	-9.41	17.18	-2.89
10	5.62	-39.58	45.20	44.16	-1.40	3.10	14.89	-9.41	18.43	-2.89
11	13.32	-35.31	48.63	44.00	-2.24	10.80	14.89	-9.41	18.43	-2.89
12	19.24	-31.96	51.20	44.90	-3.74	16.68	14.89	-9.41	18.43	-2.89
13	20.14	-31.76	53.00	48.53	-5.69	20.14	30.63	-9.41	34.17	-2.89
14	15.77	-34.00	50.87	40.70	-5.07	15.77	30.63	-9.41	34.17	-2.89
15	20.13	-31.73	50.02	51.34	-6.85	20.13	30.63	-9.41	34.17	-2.89
16	15.61	-33.63	47.40	46.42	-8.41	15.61	30.63	-9.41	34.17	-4.67
17	20.12	-32.17	50.45	50.93	-6.50	20.12	30.63	-9.41	34.17	-4.67
18	22.50	-31.02	51.68	53.31	-5.56	22.50	30.63	-9.41	34.17	-4.67
19	30.25	-27.36	55.77	56.98	-9.43	30.25	31.36	-9.41	36.52	-4.67
20	32.02	-26.59	56.77	58.75	-9.66	32.02	31.36	-9.41	36.52	-4.67
21	23.92	-31.03	53.11	56.97	-11.44	23.92	29.62	-9.41	36.52	-4.67
22	24.37	-30.44	52.97	57.42	-10.27	24.37	29.62	-9.41	36.31	-4.67
23	35.86	-24.99	59.01	68.91	-4.10	35.86	29.62	-9.41	36.31	-4.67
24	34.49	-25.65	58.30	67.54	-5.04	34.49	29.62	-9.41	36.31	-4.67
25	28.85	-28.83	55.84	61.90	-7.40	28.85	29.62	-9.41	36.31	-4.67
26	31.01	-27.38	56.55	64.06	-5.45	31.01	29.62	-9.41	36.31	-4.67
27	18.83	-33.58	50.57	58.12	-5.67	18.83	28.95	-9.41	34.17	-4.67
28	17.86	-34.74	50.76	57.15	-6.64	17.86	28.95	-9.41	34.17	-4.67
29	3.93	-42.02	44.11	43.22	-8.97	3.93	28.95	-9.41	34.17	-4.67
30	8.47	-39.67	46.30	47.76	-8.81	8.47	28.95	-9.41	36.31	-4.67
31	15.53	-36.39	50.08	54.82	-7.33	15.53	28.95	-9.41	36.31	-4.67
32	22.50	-31.69	52.35	61.79	-6.98	22.50	29.15	-9.41	36.31	-4.67
33	29.35	-28.36	55.87	68.64	-3.45	29.35	29.15	-9.41	36.31	-4.67
34	40.39	-22.43	60.98	75.56	-1.24	40.39	29.63	-9.41	36.31	-4.67
35	41.80	-22.22	62.18	76.97	-0.25	41.80	29.63	-9.41	36.52	-4.67
36	53.96	-16.45	68.57	77.51	-0.87	53.96	29.63	-7.61	36.52	-4.67
37	53.85	-16.56	68.57	77.40	-0.98	53.85	29.63	-7.61	36.52	-4.67
38	52.26	-17.03	67.45	75.81	-0.33	52.26	29.63	-7.61	36.52	-4.67
39	56.08	-15.00	69.24	79.63	-0.09	56.08	29.63	-7.61	36.52	-4.67
40	52.40	-17.77	68.33	74.36	-1.95	52.40	29.63	-7.61	37.17	-4.67
41	46.93	-21.04	66.13	68.89	-4.17	46.93	29.63	-7.61	37.17	-4.67
42	45.33	-21.76	65.25	67.29	-3.31	45.33	27.05	-7.61	37.17	-4.67
43	44.66	-22.43	65.25	66.62	-3.98	44.66	27.05	-7.61	37.17	-4.67
44	45.28	-21.79	65.23	67.64	-2.87	45.28	27.05	-4.67	37.17	-2.89
45	49.29	-19.64	67.09	71.65	-2.58	49.29	27.05	-4.67	37.17	-2.89
46	58.16	-15.76	75.02	74.24	-3.69	58.16	27.05	-4.67	37.17	-2.89
47	57.43	-15.98	74.51	73.51	-3.40	57.43	26.54	-4.67	37.17	-2.89
48	61.97	-13.97	77.04	78.05	-3.92	61.97	26.54	-4.67	37.17	-2.89
49	62.78	-13.16	77.04	78.86	-3.11	62.78	26.54	-4.67	37.17	-2.89
50	63.55	-12.39	77.04	79.63	-2.34	63.55	26.54	-4.67	37.17	-2.89

EXHIBIT W-4: (continued)

Pass	Total Equity	Short Equity	Long Equity	Max. Equity	Min. Equity	P/L	Best Trade	Worst Trade	Max. Open P/L	Min. Open P/L
51	63.16	-12.78	77.04	79.24	-2.73	63.16	26.54	-4.67	37.17	-2.89
52	68.87	-9.93	79.90	84.95	-2.74	68.87	26.63	-4.67	37.17	-2.89
53	73.31	-7.43	83.62	85.83	-3.16	73.31	26.63	-2.89	37.17	-2.00
54	77.32	-4.66	84.86	89.84	-1.63	77.32	26.63	-2.89	38.76	-2.00
55	76.61	-4.66	84.15	89.13	-2.34	76.61	26.63	-2.89	38.76	-2.00
56	77.14	-3.77	80.91	87.88	-3.59	73.37	26.63	-2.68	38.76	-1.23
57	76.15	-4.23	80.38	86.89	-3.66	72.38	26.63	-2.68	38.76	-1.23
58	74.65	-4.54	79.19	85.39	-9.02	70.88	26.86	-2.89	39.37	-1.54
59	79.21	-2.21	81.42	87.31	-9.12	74.12	26.86	-2.89	39.37	-1.61
60	77.70	-3.37	81.07	85.80	-8.31	72.61	26.86	-2.89	39.37	-1.54
61	78.79	-2.38	81.17	85.53	-9.20	46.16	25.75	-2.89	39.37	-1.69
62	76.60	-2.95	79.55	83.34	-10.25	43.97	25.75	-3.56	39.37	-2.74
63	75.20	-4.29	79.49	81.94	-9.97	42.57	25.75	-2.89	39.37	-1.54
64	76.10	-4.29	80.39	82.84	-9.07	43.47	25.75	-2.89	39.37	-1.54
65	76.34	-4.29	80.63	83.08	-8.83	43.71	25.75	-2.89	39.37	-1.54
66	77.66	-3.79	81.45	84.40	-7.51	45.03	25.75	-2.89	39.37	-1.54
67	76.18	-3.79	79.97	82.92	-8.99	43.55	25.75	-2.89	39.37	-1.54
68	77.33	-3.17	80.50	84.07	-10.10	31.98	25.75	-2.89	52.09	-1.54
69	77.68	-2.36	80.04	84.42	-11.37	32.33	25.75	-3.66	52.09	-1.54
70	75.52	-2.36	77.88	82.26	-13.53	30.17	25.75	-5.82	52.09	-3.58
71	75.33	-2.36	77.69	82.07	-13.72	29.98	25.75	-6.01	52.09	-3.77
72	75.64	-1.94	77.58	82.38	-14.25	30.29	25.75	-6.54	52.09	-4.30
73	75.48	-1.94	77.42	82.22	-14.41	30.13	25.75	-6.70	52.09	-4.46
74	77.72	-1.16	78.88	84.46	-12.17	32.37	25.75	-6.02	52.09	-3.78
75	76.02	-1.16	77.18	82.76	-13.87	30.67	25.75	-7.72	52.09	-5.48

Pass indicates period length.
Equity indicates the total number of points gained or lost.
Short equity indicates the number of points gained or lost on short positions.
Long equity indicates the number of points gained or lost on long positions.
Max. equity indicates the highest total profit recorded over the tested period.
Min. equity indicates the lowest total profit recorded over the tested period.
P/L indicates total number of points gained or lost in closed positions.
Best trade indicates the highest number of points gained in any closed trade.
Worst trade indicates the highest number of points lost in any closed trade.
Max. open P/L indicates the highest gain in a position which remains open at the end of the test run.
Min. open P/L indicates the highest loss in a position which remains open at the end of the test run.

momentum) indicator crossing 1. Momentum divergencies can also be subjectively interpreted from the chart.

From Exhibits W-9, W-10, W-13, and W-14 (pages 563–567), you can note combined total profits of 118.21 NYSE points over both 9.75-year periods. This not only beat our 40-week simple moving average crossover rule standard of comparison, but it was one of the very best results we encountered. Trading activity (at 40 transactions) was relatively low, so profit

EXHIBIT W-5:

Profitability Chart for Weighted Moving Average Period Lengths of 1 to 75 Weeks from 1968 to 1977

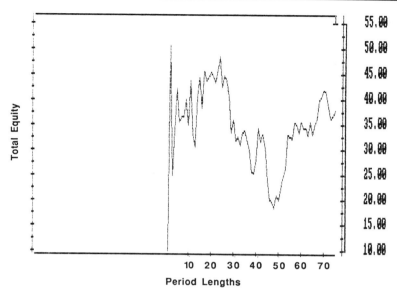

per trade was quite high at 2.96 NYSE points. Equity drawdowns (loss strings) were about standard at 15.43 NYSE points, while the total profit to maximum drawdown ratio at 7.66 to 1 ranked quite high and above our standard of 6.13 to 1. Overall, the 69-week weighted moving average crossover rule and ratio oscillator are considered to be tools worth using.

DIRECTION OF WEIGHTED MOVING AVERAGE

When an *n*-period weighted moving average changes direction, from falling to rising or vice versa, it produces exactly the same signal and result as when the raw data crosses a simple moving average calculated over $n - 1$ periods, for *n* greater than 6. A full mathematical proof is beyond the scope of this book, but compare Exhibits W-15 and W-16 (pages 568–570) to Exhibits S-4 and S-5 (pages 454–455) for a typical example. Therefore, it would be redundant to optimize and follow both the direction of a weighted moving average and a simple moving average crossover. Both for simplicity of calculation and ease of assimilation, we prefer the latter.

EXHIBIT W-6:
Profit Table for Weighted Moving Average Period Lengths of 1 to 75 Weeks from 1968 to 1977

Pass	Total Equity	Short Equity	Long Equity	Max. Equity	Min. Equity	P/L	Best Trade	Worst Trade	Max. Open P/L	Min. Open P/L
1	0.00	0.00	0.00	0.00	0.00	0.00	N/A	N/A	0.00	0.00
2	50.52	25.94	24.58	72.18	-0.67	50.52	9.51	-3.24	10.26	0.00
3	24.89	12.79	12.10	51.47	0.00	24.89	7.08	-3.24	9.42	-0.73
4	33.64	16.64	17.00	41.14	0.00	33.64	7.71	-3.24	9.42	-1.04
5	42.24	20.55	21.69	49.74	0.00	42.24	9.13	-3.24	11.76	-1.04
6	35.77	16.59	19.18	42.91	-0.46	35.77	9.13	-3.24	11.76	-0.73
7	36.44	16.92	19.52	44.06	-0.47	36.44	10.03	-2.84	12.97	-0.98
8	36.45	17.16	19.29	45.41	0.00	36.45	10.03	-2.84	12.97	-0.98
9	39.99	18.38	21.61	46.71	-0.47	39.99	9.71	-2.84	12.97	-1.91
10	34.94	15.78	19.16	41.66	-0.62	33.63	9.71	-2.84	12.97	-1.91
11	43.62	20.14	23.48	50.34	-0.58	42.31	9.71	-2.84	12.97	-1.04
12	32.76	14.50	18.26	41.04	-2.74	31.45	9.71	-2.84	12.97	-1.04
13	30.56	13.90	16.66	40.52	-1.74	29.25	8.95	-2.84	12.97	-1.12
14	40.50	19.74	20.76	51.78	0.00	39.19	10.49	-2.08	15.08	-1.12
15	44.27	22.53	21.74	56.99	-0.21	42.96	10.52	-2.08	15.08	-1.12
16	38.50	19.54	18.96	51.30	0.00	37.19	10.52	-2.35	15.08	-1.12
17	45.51	23.48	22.03	53.24	-0.70	44.20	12.74	-2.35	15.08	-1.12
18	43.69	22.97	20.72	53.12	-1.50	42.38	12.74	-2.35	15.08	-1.12
19	44.29	23.31	20.98	54.75	-1.58	42.98	12.74	-2.35	17.31	-1.12
20	45.39	23.48	21.91	55.85	-0.82	44.08	12.74	-2.35	17.31	-1.12
21	44.74	23.28	21.46	49.26	-1.07	43.43	12.07	-2.35	17.31	-0.80
22	43.45	23.07	20.38	47.97	-1.94	42.14	12.07	-2.35	17.31	-0.80
23	45.60	24.95	20.65	50.12	-3.55	44.29	12.07	-2.17	17.31	-1.03
24	48.35	26.28	22.07	50.12	-3.38	47.04	12.07	-2.17	17.31	-0.94
25	42.62	23.29	19.33	47.27	-4.09	41.31	12.07	-2.59	17.31	-1.61
26	44.63	23.95	20.68	49.28	-3.40	43.32	12.07	-2.17	17.31	-1.50
27	43.75	23.91	19.84	48.40	-4.20	42.44	12.40	-2.70	19.13	-1.72
28	40.76	22.80	17.96	46.12	-4.97	39.45	12.40	-3.47	19.13	-2.49
29	33.31	18.52	14.79	38.67	-3.86	32.00	12.40	-2.36	19.13	-1.50
30	35.85	19.10	16.75	41.21	-2.48	34.54	12.40	-1.76	19.13	-1.24
31	31.75	16.56	15.19	38.07	-6.16	30.44	13.46	-2.33	19.13	-1.24
32	32.45	17.05	15.40	38.77	-5.88	31.14	13.46	-2.33	19.13	-1.24
33	30.98	16.76	14.22	38.94	-4.99	29.67	13.46	-2.33	19.13	-1.24
34	33.54	18.06	15.48	39.60	-5.03	32.23	13.46	-2.33	19.13	-1.24
35	33.71	18.17	15.54	39.77	-4.56	32.40	13.46	-2.07	19.13	-1.02
36	31.86	17.84	14.02	37.92	-5.77	30.55	13.46	-2.21	19.13	-1.02
37	30.03	16.86	13.17	36.09	-5.64	28.72	13.46	-2.21	19.13	-1.02
38	25.48	14.85	10.63	31.54	-6.17	24.17	13.46	-2.71	19.13	-1.57
39	25.44	15.05	10.39	31.50	-6.61	24.13	13.46	-2.71	19.13	-1.57
40	28.26	16.84	11.42	33.93	-6.81	26.95	17.94	-2.71	23.61	-1.57
41	34.49	19.83	14.66	38.28	-6.56	33.18	17.94	-2.71	23.61	-1.57
42	31.46	18.78	12.68	37.15	-7.49	30.15	17.67	-2.71	23.61	-1.57
43	33.14	19.48	13.66	42.92	-7.21	31.83	17.67	-2.21	23.61	-1.02
44	30.66	17.90	12.76	42.34	-6.53	29.35	17.67	-2.21	23.61	-1.02
45	24.06	14.86	9.20	37.30	-7.05	22.75	17.67	-2.21	23.61	-1.02
46	20.00	13.42	6.58	33.24	-7.55	18.69	15.60	-2.51	23.61	-1.02
47	19.62	13.45	6.17	32.86	-7.99	18.31	15.60	-2.95	23.61	-1.14
48	18.44	13.45	4.99	31.68	-9.17	17.13	15.60	-4.13	23.61	-2.32
49	20.88	14.55	6.33	34.12	-8.93	19.57	16.70	-3.89	24.71	-2.08
50	19.99	14.07	5.92	36.25	-8.84	18.68	16.70	-3.82	24.71	-2.01

EXHIBIT W-6: (continued)

Pass	Total Equity	Short Equity	Long Equity	Max. Equity	Min. Equity	P/L	Best Trade	Worst Trade	Max. Open P/L	Min. Open P/L
51	22.27	14.88	7.39	35.19	-8.18	20.96	16.70	-3.16	24.71	-1.35
52	24.83	15.72	9.11	37.75	-7.30	23.52	16.70	-2.28	24.71	-1.02
53	26.10	16.12	9.98	39.02	-6.83	24.79	16.70	-2.03	24.71	-1.02
54	32.83	18.58	14.25	42.32	-3.78	31.52	16.70	-1.86	24.71	-1.02
55	32.43	18.69	13.74	41.92	-4.40	31.12	16.70	-1.86	24.71	-1.02
56	32.09	18.69	13.40	41.58	-4.74	30.78	16.70	-1.86	24.71	-1.02
57	35.35	20.46	14.89	44.84	-5.02	34.04	16.70	-2.07	24.71	-1.02
58	35.09	20.46	14.63	44.58	-5.28	33.78	16.70	-2.33	24.71	-1.02
59	33.59	19.71	13.88	43.08	-5.28	32.28	16.70	-2.33	24.71	-1.02
60	35.48	19.49	15.99	45.93	-2.95	34.17	16.70	-1.86	24.71	-1.02
61	34.36	18.37	15.99	44.81	-4.07	33.05	16.70	-2.98	24.71	-1.66
62	34.32	18.42	15.90	44.77	-3.93	33.01	16.70	-2.84	24.71	-1.52
63	32.96	17.54	15.42	45.09	-4.33	31.65	16.70	-3.24	24.71	-1.92
64	35.78	19.42	16.36	47.91	-3.39	34.47	15.81	-2.30	24.71	-1.02
65	33.04	18.54	14.50	45.17	-2.41	31.73	15.81	-1.79	24.71	-1.02
66	35.09	19.32	15.77	47.22	-2.90	33.78	15.81	-1.81	24.71	-1.02
67	36.23	20.12	16.11	48.36	-2.44	34.92	15.81	-1.79	24.71	-1.02
68	40.01	21.88	18.13	49.72	-2.70	38.70	15.81	-1.61	24.71	-1.02
69	40.53	22.28	18.25	50.24	-2.42	39.22	15.81	-1.73	24.71	-1.02
70	41.86	23.61	18.25	51.57	-1.09	40.55	15.81	-1.73	24.71	-1.02
71	41.27	23.61	17.66	50.98	-1.68	39.96	15.81	-1.73	24.71	-1.02
72	38.37	22.36	16.01	50.58	-2.08	37.06	15.81	-2.08	24.71	-1.29
73	36.23	20.95	15.28	48.44	-1.40	34.92	14.40	-1.73	24.71	-0.95
74	36.72	20.89	15.83	50.11	-0.79	35.41	14.40	-1.73	24.71	-0.95
75	37.81	21.04	16.77	51.20	0.00	36.50	14.40	-1.73	24.71	-0.95

Pass indicates period length.

Equity indicates the total number of points gained or lost.

Short equity indicates the number of points gained or lost on short positions.

Long equity indicates the number of points gained or lost on long positions.

Max. equity indicates the highest total profit recorded over the tested period.

Min. equity indicates the lowest total profit recorded over the tested period.

P/L indicates total number of points gained or lost in closed positions.

Best trade indicates the highest number of points gained in any closed trade.

Worst trade indicates the highest number of points lost in any closed trade.

Max. open P/L indicates the highest gain in a position which remains open at the end of the test run.

Min. open P/L indicates the highest loss in a position which remains open at the end of the test run.

EXHIBIT W-7:
NYSE Composite and Its Weighted Moving Average: 69 Weeks, 1977 to 1986

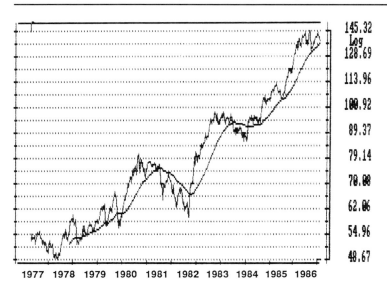

1977 1978 1979 1980 1981 1982 1983 1984 1985 1986

EXHIBIT W-8:
1/69 Weighted Moving Average Ratio Oscillator, 1977 to 1986

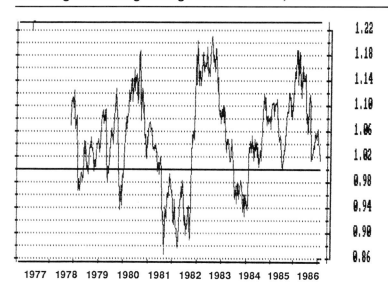

1977 1978 1979 1980 1981 1982 1983 1984 1985 1986

EXHIBIT W-9:
Total Equity For Weighted Moving Average: 69 Weeks, 1977 to 1986

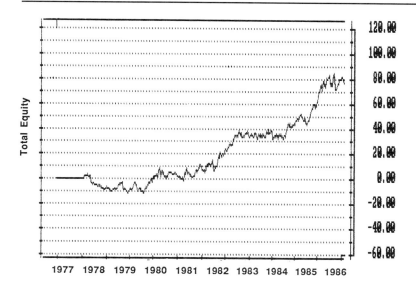

EXHIBIT W-10:
Profit Summary for Weighted Moving Average: 69 Weeks, 1977 to 1986

Item		Long	Short	Net
		--- Per Trade Ranges ---		
Per Trade Ranges				
Best Trade	(Closed position yielding maximum P/L)	25.75	7.87	25.75
..Date		840203	820827	840203
Worst Trade	(Closed position yielding minimum P/L)	-3.66	-2.89	-3.66
..Date		781027	790105	781027
Max Open P/L	(Maximum P/L occurring in an open position)	52.09	15.56	52.09
..Date		860829	820813	860829
Min Open P/L	(Minimum P/L occurring in an open position)	-1.42	-1.54	-1.54
..Date		781020	781208	781208
		--- Overall Ranges ---		
Overall Ranges				
Max P/L	(Maximum P/L from all closed positions during the run)	32.58	32.33	32.58
..Date		840203	840803	840203
Min P/L	(Minimum P/L from all closed positions during the run)	-10.21	-11.37	-11.37
..Date		800314	800516	800516
Max Equity	(Maximum P/L from all closed and open positions)	84.42	39.39	84.42
..Date		860829	840615	860829
Min Equity	(Minimum P/L from all closed and open positions)	-11.37	-11.37	-11.37
..Date		800516	800516	800516
		--- Statistics ---		
Statistics				
Periods	(The number of periods in each position and entire run)	404	105	509
Trades	(The number of trades in each position and entire run)	10	10	20
# Profitable	(The number of profitable trades...)	4	1	5
# Losing	(The number of unprofitable trades...)	6	9	15
% Profitable	(The percent of profitable trades to total trades)	40.00	10.00	25.00
% Losing	(The percent of unprofitable trades to total trades)	60.00	90.00	75.00
		--- Results ---		
Results				
Commission	(Total commission deducted from closed trades)	0.00	0.00	0.00
Slippage	(Total slippage deducted from closed trades)	0.00	0.00	0.00
Gross P/L	(Total points gained in closed positions)	34.69	-2.36	32.33
Open P/L	(P/L in a position which remains open at the end)	45.35	0.00	45.35
P/L	(Net P/L: Gross P/L less Commission and Slippage)	34.69	-2.36	32.33
Equity	(Net P/L plus Open P/L at the end of the run)	80.04	-2.36	77.68

There are columns for Long trades, Short trades and Net. In the Long column, results
are reported only for Long positions. In the Short column, results are reported for
Short positions only. In the Net column for the "Per Trade Ranges" and "Overall
Ranges," entries will be the extreme from either the Long or Short column. Net column
entries for the "Statistics" and "Results" categories are the combined results of entries
in the Long and Short columns.

EXHIBIT W-11:
NYSE Composite and Its Weighted Moving Average: 69 Weeks, 1968 to 1977

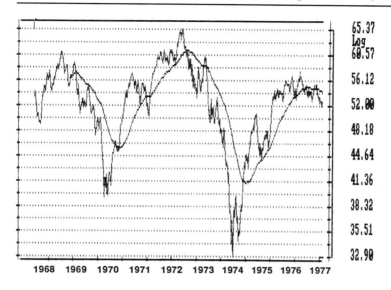

EXHIBIT W-12:
1/69 Weighted Moving Average Ratio Oscillator, 1968 to 1977

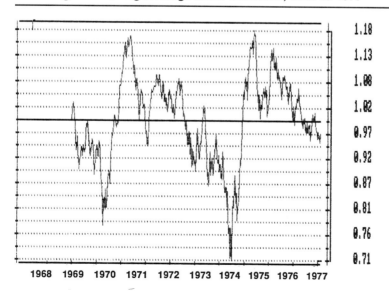

EXHIBIT W-13:
Total Equity for Weighted Moving Average: 69 Weeks, 1968 to 1977

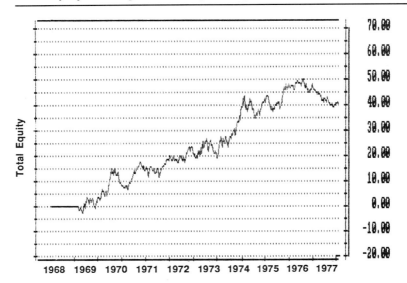

EXHIBIT W-14:
Profit Summary for Weighted Moving Average: 69 Weeks, 1968 to 1977

Item		Long	Short	Net
		--- Per Trade Ranges ---		
Per Trade Ranges				
Best Trade	(Closed position yielding maximum P/L)	11.30	15.81	15.81
.. Date		761112	750207	750207
Worst Trade	(Closed position yielding minimum P/L)	-1.73	-1.51	-1.73
.. Date		731102	761119	731102
Max Open P/L	(Maximum P/L occurring in an open position)	15.22	24.71	24.71
.. Date		760924	741004	741004
Min Open P/L	(Minimum P/L occurring in an open position)	-0.61	-1.02	-1.02
.. Date		770708	770415	770415
		--- Overall Ranges ---		
Overall Ranges				
Max P/L	(Maximum P/L from all closed positions during the run)	46.32	44.81	46.32
.. Date		761119	761119	761112
Min P/L	(Minimum P/L from all closed positions during the run)	-2.42	-1.33	-2.42
.. Date		690606	690502	690606
Max Equity	(Maximum P/L from all closed and open positions)	50.24	46.32	50.24
.. Date		760924	761112	760924
Min Equity	(Minimum P/L from all closed and open positions)	-2.42	-2.42	-2.42
.. Date		690606	690606	690606
		--- Statistics ---		
Statistics				
Periods	(The number of periods in each position and entire run)	301	208	509
Trades	(The number of trades in each position and entire run)	10	10	20
# Profitable	(The number of profitable trades...)	3	3	6
# Losing	(The number of unprofitable trades...)	7	7	14
% Profitable	(The percent of profitable trades to total trades)	30.00	30.00	30.00
% Losing	(The percent of unprofitable trades to total trades)	70.00	70.00	70.00
		--- Results ---		
Results				
Commission	(Total commission deducted from closed trades)	0.00	0.00	0.00
Slippage	(Total slippage deducted from closed trades)	0.00	0.00	0.00
Gross P/L	(Total points gained in closed positions)	18.25	20.97	39.22
Open P/L	(P/L in a position which remains open at the end)	0.00	1.31	1.31
P/L	(Net P/L: Gross P/L less Commission and Slippage)	18.25	20.97	39.22
Equity	(Net P/L plus Open P/L at the end of the run)	18.25	22.28	40.53

There are columns for Long trades, Short trades and Net. In the Long column, results are reported only for Long positions. In the Short column, results are reported for Short positions only. In the Net column for the "Per Trade Ranges" and "Overall Ranges," entries will be the extreme from either the Long or Short column. Net column entries for the "Statistics" and "Results" categories are the combined results of entries in the Long and Short columns.

EXHIBIT W-15:

Profitability Chart for Directional Weighted Moving Average Period Lengths of 1 to 75 Weeks from 1977 to 1986

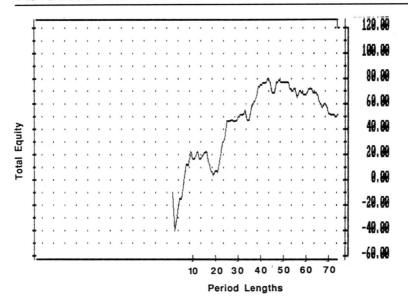

EXHIBIT W-16:

Profit Table for Directional Weighted Moving Average Period Lengths of 2 to 75 Weeks from 1977 to 1986

Pass	Total Equity	Short Equity	Long Equity	Max. Equity	Min. Equity	P/L	Best Trade	Worst Trade	Max. Open P/L	Min. Open P/L
2	-9.97	-47.43	37.46	11.14	-28.73	-12.92	14.67	-6.93	15.56	-1.73
3	-40.12	-62.52	22.40	10.11	-49.79	-43.07	12.87	-9.41	15.56	-1.73
4	-28.93	-56.60	27.67	20.80	-37.71	-31.88	12.26	-9.41	15.56	-2.00
5	-15.07	-49.76	34.69	27.14	-22.27	-18.02	13.49	-9.41	17.18	-2.89
6	-15.60	-49.89	34.29	32.73	-22.80	-18.55	14.06	-9.41	17.18	-2.89
7	-1.80	-43.85	42.05	37.54	-8.42	-4.32	14.89	-9.41	18.43	-2.89
8	12.30	-36.46	48.76	35.17	-4.56	9.74	14.89	-9.41	18.43	-4.67
9	11.22	-36.78	46.16	42.03	-3.14	11.22	26.29	-9.41	31.72	-4.67
10	22.04	-30.95	51.15	52.85	-4.10	22.04	30.63	-9.41	34.17	-4.67
11	16.70	-33.23	48.09	47.51	-6.76	16.70	30.63	-9.41	34.17	-4.67
12	16.92	-33.37	48.45	47.73	-4.32	16.92	30.63	-9.41	34.17	-4.67
13	22.87	-30.45	51.48	49.60	-7.01	22.87	31.15	-9.41	36.31	-4.67
14	16.71	-33.44	48.31	49.76	-8.31	16.71	29.62	-9.41	36.31	-4.67
15	19.05	-31.91	49.12	52.10	-6.68	19.05	29.62	-9.41	34.17	-4.67
16	20.94	-31.76	50.86	53.99	-6.77	20.94	29.62	-9.41	34.17	-4.67
17	22.82	-30.86	51.84	55.87	-6.43	22.82	29.62	-9.41	34.17	-4.67
18	14.03	-35.47	47.66	47.08	-11.55	14.03	28.95	-9.41	34.17	-4.67
19	7.44	-38.88	44.48	40.49	-17.14	7.44	28.95	-9.41	34.17	-4.67
20	4.12	-40.93	43.21	43.41	-15.18	4.12	28.95	-9.41	34.17	-4.67
21	7.41	-38.92	44.49	46.70	-11.72	7.41	29.15	-9.41	34.17	-4.67
22	6.20	-39.82	44.18	45.49	-12.31	6.20	29.15	-9.41	34.17	-4.67
23	16.09	-34.85	49.10	55.38	-9.84	16.09	29.15	-9.41	34.17	-4.67
24	29.29	-28.61	56.06	64.46	-9.28	29.29	31.09	-9.41	34.17	-4.67
25	32.51	-26.63	57.30	67.68	-6.44	32.51	31.09	-9.41	34.17	-4.67
26	46.59	-19.70	64.45	70.14	-5.10	46.59	31.09	-7.61	34.17	-4.67
27	46.64	-20.35	65.15	68.60	-6.45	46.64	29.63	-7.61	34.77	-4.67
28	47.29	-20.34	65.79	69.25	-8.07	47.29	29.63	-7.61	37.17	-4.67
29	46.87	-20.47	65.50	68.83	-3.95	46.87	27.05	-7.61	37.17	-4.67
30	46.01	-21.15	65.32	67.97	-5.93	46.01	27.05	-7.61	37.17	-4.67
31	50.06	-17.91	66.13	72.02	-3.50	50.06	27.05	-7.61	37.17	-4.67
32	50.63	-17.72	66.51	72.59	-4.56	50.63	27.05	-7.61	37.17	-4.67
33	50.93	-17.16	66.25	72.89	-3.74	50.93	27.05	-7.61	37.17	-4.67
34	54.92	-15.66	68.74	76.88	-4.73	54.92	26.54	-7.61	37.17	-4.67
35	47.82	-19.52	65.50	70.18	-8.35	47.82	26.54	-4.67	37.17	-2.89
36	47.71	-19.63	65.50	70.07	-8.46	47.71	26.54	-4.67	37.17	-2.89
37	58.74	-13.79	73.63	74.82	-7.81	58.74	26.63	-4.67	37.17	-2.89
38	61.58	-12.25	76.71	74.10	-4.71	61.58	26.63	-3.85	37.17	-2.00
39	64.78	-11.58	79.24	77.30	-6.57	64.78	26.63	-2.89	37.17	-2.00
40	73.13	-7.94	84.84	83.87	-8.54	73.13	26.63	-2.89	38.76	-1.54
41	75.09	-6.88	87.06	83.19	-11.12	75.09	26.86	-2.89	39.37	-1.54
42	75.78	-6.87	115.28	82.52	-11.79	75.78	32.63	-2.89	39.37	-1.54
43	76.44	-6.21	115.28	83.18	-11.13	76.44	32.63	-2.89	39.37	-1.54
44	80.21	-4.18	84.39	86.95	-12.26	34.86	27.54	-2.89	52.09	-1.93
45	78.12	-5.78	83.90	84.86	-14.35	32.77	27.54	-3.75	52.09	-3.04
46	69.29	-10.05	79.34	76.03	-16.88	23.94	25.75	-3.46	52.09	-2.75
47	68.77	-10.57	79.34	75.51	-17.40	23.42	25.75	-3.98	52.09	-3.27
48	77.36	-5.87	83.23	84.10	-11.24	32.01	25.75	-3.17	52.09	-2.46
49	78.71	-4.81	83.52	85.45	-9.89	33.36	25.75	-2.40	52.09	-1.69
50	77.30	-5.71	83.01	84.04	-11.30	31.95	25.75	-2.79	52.09	-2.08
51	77.29	-5.72	83.01	84.03	-11.31	31.94	25.75	-2.80	52.09	-2.09

EXHIBIT W-16: (continued)

Pass	Total Equity	Short Equity	Long Equity	Max. Equity	Min. Equity	P/L	Best Trade	Worst Trade	Max. Open P/L	Min. Open P/L
52	77.55	-5.31	82.86	84.29	-11.05	32.20	25.75	-2.24	52.09	-1.53
53	77.04	-4.80	81.84	83.78	-12.01	31.69	25.75	-2.99	52.09	-1.81
54	70.99	-7.47	78.46	77.73	-12.84	25.64	22.72	-2.99	52.09	-1.81
55	69.74	-7.47	77.21	76.48	-14.09	24.39	22.72	-2.99	52.09	-1.81
56	72.55	-6.03	78.58	79.29	-11.28	27.20	22.72	-2.99	52.09	-1.81
57	65.33	-9.20	74.53	72.07	-12.68	19.98	19.81	-3.16	52.09	-1.87
58	70.15	-6.74	76.89	76.89	-10.56	24.80	19.81	-3.16	52.09	-1.87
59	68.28	-8.08	76.36	75.02	-6.17	22.93	19.81	-3.16	52.09	-1.87
60	67.39	-8.08	75.47	74.13	-7.06	22.04	19.81	-3.16	52.09	-1.87
61	66.98	-7.76	74.74	73.72	-7.47	21.63	19.81	-3.56	52.09	-2.74
62	71.14	-6.32	77.46	77.88	-5.48	25.79	19.81	-3.16	52.09	-1.87
63	72.04	-6.32	78.36	78.78	-4.58	26.69	19.81	-3.16	52.09	-1.87
64	68.58	-8.17	76.75	75.32	-4.34	25.08	19.81	-5.01	50.24	-3.16
65	68.90	-8.17	77.07	75.64	-4.02	25.40	19.81	-5.01	50.24	-3.16
66	67.42	-8.17	75.59	74.16	-5.50	23.92	19.81	-5.01	50.24	-3.16
67	61.87	-10.90	72.77	68.61	-5.59	18.37	19.81	-6.14	50.24	-4.29
68	57.84	-12.28	70.12	64.58	-6.86	14.34	19.81	-4.73	50.24	-2.88
69	59.38	-10.43	69.81	66.12	-9.02	14.03	19.81	-5.82	52.09	-3.58
70	59.19	-10.43	69.62	65.93	-9.21	13.84	19.81	-6.01	52.09	-3.77
71	52.24	-13.64	65.88	58.98	-11.11	6.89	19.81	-6.54	52.09	-4.30
72	51.12	-14.12	65.24	57.86	-11.27	5.77	19.33	-6.70	52.09	-4.46
73	51.26	-14.39	65.65	58.00	-11.25	5.91	19.25	-6.02	52.09	-3.78
74	49.56	-14.39	63.95	56.30	-12.95	4.21	19.25	-7.72	52.09	-5.48
75	50.95	-14.41	65.36	57.69	-11.52	6.29	18.60	-6.29	51.40	-4.05

Pass indicates period length.

Equity indicates the total number of points gained or lost.

Short equity indicates the number of points gained or lost on short positions.

Long equity indicates the number of points gained or lost on long positions.

Max. equity indicates the highest total profit recorded over the tested period.

Min. equity indicates the lowest total profit recorded over the tested period.

P/L indicates total number of points gained or lost in closed positions.

Best trade indicates the highest number of points gained in any closed trade.

Worst trade indicates the highest number of points lost in any closed trade.

Max. open P/L indicates the highest gain in a position which remains open at the end of the test run.

Min. open P/L indicates the highest loss in a position which remains open at the end of the test run.

WILLIAMS' PERCENT RANGE (%R)

This indicator, attributed to Larry Williams (P.O. Box 8162, Rancho Santa fe, CA 92067), is the exact inverse of Lane's Stochastics. Refer to section on Stochastics.

WILLIAMS' VARIABLE ACCUMULATION DISTRIBUTION

Williams' Variable Accumulation Distribution (WVAD) is a volume-weighted price momentum indicator. Mathematically, the WVAD formula is represented as:

$$WVAD = \sum_{i=1}^{n} \left(\frac{C - O}{H - L} * V \right)$$

where

C is the current period's closing price.
O is the current period's opening price.
H is the current period's high price.
L is the current period's low price.
V is the current period's volume.

For a one-period WVAD, for example, if the current period's opening price was 175, the high was 180, the low was 160, the close was 165, and the volume was 2000 shares, then:

$$WVAD = \frac{165 - 175}{180 - 160} * 2000 = -1000$$

For an n-period WVAD, -1000 would become part of an n-day moving total.

This indicator, developed by Larry Williams (P.O. Box 8162, Rancho Santa fe, CA 92067), measures buying and selling pressure by calculating the relationship between the number of points that the market has moved from open to close relative to the period's entire range. Specifically, it is calculated by subtracting the opening price from the closing price and dividing this value by the high minus the low. The result is then multiplied by the volume. This product is summed over n periods of time for a moving total. If the sum is negative, net selling pressure is evident and a short position is taken. If the sum is positive, net buying pressure is dominant and a long position is initiated.

We tested this indicator using Back Trak software and a 19-year test period of weekly data (consisting of high, low, close, and volume for each week) for the broad-based NYSE Composite Index. The period ran from January 5, 1968 through December 31, 1986.

The time length, n, of this indicator is the only parameter to be optimized. We tested weekly periods of 4 to 105 weeks, using the 19-year NYSE weekly data. The optimal time length was 24 weeks. As shown in Exhibit W-17, total profit was 89.15 NYSE points from 1968 through 1986. This profit was slightly below our 40-week simple moving average crossover rule standard of comparison.

EXHIBIT W-17:

Profit Summary for William's Variable Accumulation Distribution Rate of Change: 24 Weeks, 1968 to 1986

Number Of Trades Made	> 79	Commissions Paid	> 0
Number Of Weeks In Market	> 966	Frequency Of Trades	> 1.00
Number Of Winning Trades	> 30	Largest Winning Trade	> 4722
Total Of Winning Trades	> 15963	Average Winning Trade	> 532
Number Of Losing Trades	> 49	Largest Losing Trade	> −811
Total Of Losing Trades	> −7048	Average Losing Trade	> −143
Largest Winning Streak	> 2	Largest Losing Streak	> 6
Win/Loss Ratio	> 0.61	Profit/Margin Ratio	> 4.46
Number Of Stops Hit	> 0	Stops Frequency	> 0.00
Largest Drawdown	> −2073	Largest Unrealized Loss	> −811
Largest Obtained Equity	> 9333	Number Of Tradeable Weeks	> 966
Short Profit Or Loss	> 239	Long Profit Or Loss	> 8676
Total Profit Or Loss	> 8915	Average Weekly Gain/Loss	> 9.23

APPENDIX A

INDICATOR INTERPRETATION DEFINITIONS

The terms *very bullish*, *bullish*, *slightly bullish*, *neutral*, *slightly bearish*, *bearish*, and *very bearish* are used in exhibits throughout this book to interpret various indicator ranges and time horizons (1, 3, 6, and 12 months in the future). The use of these terms relates to the statistical significance of the values in the various indicator ranges versus the direction, up or down, of stock prices. Chi-squared testing (with Yates correction and one degree of freedom) was used used to determine such significance.

The chi-squared test is a frequently used statistical test that enables you to determine the odds of events occurring by chance or fluke. By comparing actual (or observed) results to expected results, the probability of something occurring by sheer random luck can be determined.

In this case, we compared the actual number of times that the stock market went up or down after a specified time period (1, 3, 6, or 12 months) for indicator readings in a given range to the number of times you would expect the stock market to go up or down, based on an analysis of the Standard & Poor's 500 Index during the same time period. The less likely it is that the stock market went up or down by chance, the more reliance can be placed on indicator readings and, therefore, the more bullish or bearish is its interpretation.

The following definitions were used for interpretational purposes:

Very Bullish   Probability less than 1 in 1000 that the stock market rose by random chance alone after an indicator reading in this range of values for the specified time frame. Therefore, we can be 99.9% confident that the indicator is significant.

Bullish   Probability less than 1 in 100 (but not less than 1 in 1000) that the stock market rose by random chance alone after an indicator reading in this range of values for the specified time frame. Therefore, we can be 99% confident that the indicator is significant.

Slightly Bullish   Probability less than 1 in 20 (but not less than 1 in 100) that the stock market rose by random chance alone after an indicator reading in this range of values for the specified time frame. Therefore, we can be 95% confident that the indicator is significant.

Neutral   Probability greater than 1 in 20 that the stock market went up or down by random chance alone after an indicator reading in this range of values for the specified time frame. Therefore, we can not be confident that the indicator is significant.

Slightly Bearish   Probability less than 1 in 20 (but not less than 1 in 100) that the stock market went down by random chance alone after an indicator reading in this range of values for the specified time frame. Therefore, we can be 95% confident that the indicator is significant.

Bearish   Probability less than 1 in 100 (but not less than 1 in 1000) that the stock market went down by random chance alone after an indicator reading in this range of values for the specified time frame. Therefore, we can be 99% confident that the indicator is significant.

Very Bearish   Probability less than 1 in 1000 that the stock market went down by random chance alone after an indicator reading in this range of values for the specified time frame. Therefore, we can be 99.9% confident that the indicator is significant.

INDEX